Online Computation and Competitive Analysis

In online computation a computer algorithm must decide how to act on incoming items of information without any knowledge of future inputs. For example, how should the next phone call be routed? Which cache block should be removed when the cache is full? Given the history of currency rates, should any U.S. dollars be converted to Japanese yen? This book provides an in-depth presentation of competitive analysis, an attractive framework within which such problems can be analyzed. In this framework, the quality of an online algorithm is measured relative to the best possible performance of an algorithm that has complete knowledge of the future. This methodology for the analysis of online decision making has become a standard approach in computer science.

Beginning with the basic definitions of the competitive analysis model, the authors present the essential techniques through various examples, some of which are central to the field, such as list accessing, paging in a virtual memory system, routing in a communication network, metrical task systems, k-server systems, load balancing, and financial portfolio selection. The book also relates competitive analysis to more classical subjects such as game theory and decision theory.

This is a comprehensive text and an invaluable reference for researchers and graduate students in computer science and in operations research.

T0213359

Online Computation and Competitive Analysis

Allan Borodin

University of Toronto

Ran El-Yaniv

Technion – Israel Institute of Technology

CAMBRIDGE
UNIVERSITY PRESS

PUBLISHED BY THE PRESS SYNDICATE OF THE UNIVERSITY OF CAMBRIDGE
The Pitt Building, Trumpington Street, Cambridge, United Kingdom

CAMBRIDGE UNIVERSITY PRESS
The Edinburgh Building, Cambridge CB2 2RU, UK
40 West 20th Street, New York NY 10011–4211, USA
477 Williamstown Road, Port Melbourne, VIC 3207, Australia
Ruiz de Alarcón 13, 28014 Madrid, Spain
Dock House, The Waterfront, Cape Town 8001, South Africa

http://www.cambridge.org

First published 1998
First paperback edition 2005

Typeset in Times Roman 10.5/13 pt, in LaTeX 2$_\varepsilon$

A catalogue record for this book is available from the British Library

Library of Congress Cataloguing in Publication Data

Borodin, Allan, 1941–
Online computation and competitive analysis / Allan Borodin, Ran El-Yaniv.
    p. cm.
ISBN 0 521 56392 5 (hardback)
1. Computer algorithms. 2. Computational complexity.
3. Mathematical optimization. I. El-Yaniv, Ran, 1962– II. Title.
QA76.9.A43B67 1998
005.1–DC21   97-38652
                                                         CIP

ISBN 0 521 56392 5 hardback
ISBN 0 521 61946 7 paperback

To our families
   Even though we cannot predict the future,
   we do know that we can depend on you.

Contents

Preface

Why competitive analysis?

In *online computation*, an algorithm must produce a sequence of decisions that will have an impact on the final quality of its overall performance. Each of these decisions must be made based of past events without secure information about the future. Such an algorithm is called an *online algorithm*. Online algorithms are a natural topic of interest in many disciplines such as computer science, economics, and operations research. Many computational problems are intrinsically online in that they require immediate decisions to be made in real time. Paging in a virtual memory system is perhaps the most studied of such computational problems. Routing in communications networks is another obvious application. Our main concern in this text is these and other applications related to traditional computing issues. We will also discuss some applications in algorithmic decision making in the field of finance, another obvious area of interest.

The traditional approach to studying online algorithms falls within the framework of *distributional* (or *average-case*) complexity, whereby one hypothesizes a distribution on events (event sequences) and studies the expected total cost (payoff) or expected cost (payoff) per event. During the past 10 years the interest in this subject has been renewed largely as a result of the approach of *competitive analysis*, whereby the quality of an online algorithm on each input sequence is measured by comparing its performance to that of an *optimal offline algorithm*, which is (for an online problem) an unrealizable algorithm that has full knowledge of the future. Competitive analysis thus falls within the framework of worst-case complexity.

Online algorithms have been implicitly and explicitly studied for approximately 30 years in the context of scheduling, optimization, data structures, and other computational topics. The roots of competitive analysis can be found in classical combinatorial optimization theory (see Chapter 12 in this text and, in particular, Graham's analysis of the online greedy algorithm for scheduling jobs on identical processors [175]) and in the analysis of data structures (see Chapter 1 in this text and the history of the list accessing problem in the context of self- adjusting data structures). Although many fundamental combinatorial optimization problems (e.g., bin packing, machine scheduling, and load balancing) do not always have to be solved online (i.e., they are traditionally considered offline problems), for such problems online algorithms constitute an interesting restricted class of algorithms that may sometimes yield surprisingly good approximate solutions.

Approximation algorithms for NP-hard combinatorial problems are of particular importance. Here the classic and perhaps most studied problem is (one-dimensional) bin packing,
where simple online algorithms such as first-fit or best-fit provide reasonable approximations (always within a factor of 1.7) of the optimal (and necessarily offline) solution that
(if P $\neq$ NP) require nonpolynomial time to compute in the worst case. Perhaps the first
explicit application of competitive analysis (although not so named) in the computer science literature was by Yao [341], who studied how well online bin packing algorithms
could perform (see Chapter 12 in this text). At approximately the same time (but using the
terminology of "recursive combinatorics" rather than "online algorithms"), Kierstead and
Trotter [224] exhibited an optimal 3-competitive algorithm for online coloring of interval
graphs (see Chapter 13 in this text). There are many more such "classical" results relat-
ing to problems in combinatorial optimization that at least implicitly concern competitive
analysis. Moreover, this type of analysis can also be found in the literature of decision
theory (see Chapter 15 in this text) as well as in the area of finance (see Chapter 14 in
this text).

We have chosen to focus on the competitive analysis of online algorithms. A more
general study of online algorithms is a much more ambitious topic, and is itself only
one aspect of "decision making in the absence of complete information." In emphasizing
competitive analysis, we make no definitive claims on its ultimate "practical value" either
in itself or relative to the more traditional distributional studies. We believe competitive
analysis stands on its own merits as an interesting framework for mathematical algorithmic analysis. More important, competitive analysis leads to the derivation and study of
particular algorithms that would not naturally be contemplated using a conceptually different model. The question is whether or not algorithms suggested by competitive analysis
can be used as the starting point for algorithms whose performance is really "competitive" with or superior to algorithms based on other approaches. It is probably too early to
understand the ultimate value of competitive analysis. We should not expect competitive
analysis to be uniformly worthwhile over all possible application areas; however, it is becoming apparent that in some application areas such as communication network routing,
it has practical relevance. Further, in some applications such as financial planning there
may be situations in which (worst-case) guarantees on performance are necessary; here,
competitive analysis (or very similar methods) are essential.

Any conceptual model has limitations as well as benefits. Competitive analysis has
the disadvantage of being too pessimistic, assuming a malicious adversary that chooses
the worst input by which to measure an algorithm's performance. (This is, of course, the
limitation in any worst-case analysis.) The disadvantage of distributional complexity is that
the distribution is rarely known precisely, and often the distributional assumptions must be
unrealistically crude to allow for mathematical tractability. However, again, the conceptual
assumptions need to reflect reality only closely enough to suggest algorithmic approaches.
It is taste and experience that leads different people to advocate particular viewpoints. The
consummate analyst considers and often combines all plausible approaches.

A large number of online problems in a diverse set of application areas have been
studied using the competitive analysis approach. These are more than a collection of
well-motivated yet possibly unrelated problems. Perhaps the main accomplishment of
(classical) complexity theory thus far has been to give structure to classes of problems,
models, and algorithms. In the same way, competitive analysis thus far has provided some
structure to the study of online computation. Abstract models of online computation have

provided a framework in which a number of general techniques and solutions and other fundamental issues have been identified and studied.

The text is organized as follows. Chapter 1 begins with a short introduction to competitive analysis. This introduction includes a few basic concepts and definitions that are used throughout the text. We then initiate our study of competitive analysis with the well-known problem of list accessing. The chapter includes a proof of the competitiveness of the move-to-front heuristic using a potential function argument; this proof technique plays a significant role in competitive analysis. This chapter also includes analyses of several other list accessing algorithms. In Chapter 2 we introduce randomized online algorithms and continue to investigate the list accessing problem. In Chapter 3, we begin our study of the paging problem, a problem to which we frequently refer throughout the text. The chapter covers only deterministic paging algorithms. Chapter 4 continues the study of paging, introducing different types of adversaries in the context of randomized paging algorithms. In Chapter 5, we again study paging, this time looking at some variants and alternatives to pure competitive analysis. In particular, we discuss the models of competitive paging using access graphs and Markov paging.

Having introduced two specific problems (list accessing and paging), we are now prepared to consider online algorithms and their analysis in a more general context. One can view competitive analysis as a two-person game between an online algorithm and an adversary. This leads us in Chapters 6, 7, and 8 to study game theory and its relation to online problems. We first consider, in Chapter 6, different forms of randomization in two-person games. In Chapter 7 we provide a very general definition of online problems and algorithms and, in this abstract framework called request–answer systems, establish a basic relationship concerning the different types of adversaries that can be used against randomized algorithms. Chapter 8 discusses the classical minimax theorem for zero-sum games and its application (Yao's principle) in proving lower bounds for randomized algorithms. Chapter 9 discusses another abstract model (a subcase of request–answer systems), that of metrical task systems. Several general analysis techniques (e.g., cruel adversaries and nearly oblivious and traversal algorithms) are formulated in this chapter. We introduce a work function algorithm that provides a simple proof of the optimal bound for metrical task systems. Chapter 10 follows with yet another abstract model, that of k-server systems. The intriguing k-server problem and k-server conjecture provided an initial focal point for the subject of competitive analysis. Because of the interest generated by the k-server conjecture, Chapter 10 is quite extensive, covering both general concepts and approaches and specific server systems. In particular, we present a work function algorithm that provides an almost complete resolution to the k-server conjecture. Chapter 11 continues with k-server systems and focuses on randomized server algorithms. In particular, we study k-server algorithms and their connection to random walks in a graph. We turn to some traditional optimization topics in Chapter 12, where we consider the classic problems of load balancing and bin packing. This leads us to Chapter 13, where we study online call admission/circuit routing and path coloring. In Chapter 14 we change direction somewhat and study some traditional problems in the area of finance: search, trading, and portfolio selection. This naturally leads to Chapter 15, which provides a wider perspective on competitive analysis by looking at the competitive ratio within the context of classical decision theory.

We have necessarily included only a small sample of applications and results in the hope that these applications reflect a good overview of the history, techniques, and issues.

Space limitations force us to omit many interesting applications of competitive analysis to problems such as (distributed) file allocation and migration, online graph algorithms, online scheduling, exploration and navigation, and online learning.

Usage of This Text

We presume familiarity with an elementary knowledge of mathematics and some concepts from computer science. For those majoring in computer science, the first and second years of a four-year undergraduate program will most likely suffice; however, we recommend a third-year algorithms course and a text such as Cormen, Leiserson, and Rivest [116] or Aho, Hopcroft, and Ullman [2]. In particular, we assume the reader has some basic knowledge of combinatorics and probability theory, graph theory and algorithms, and data structures. Although some familiarity with NP-completeness (e.g., Garey and Johnson [168], or Cormen, Leiserson, and Rivest [116], chap. 36) is assumed, NP-completeness issues may be skipped over with no severe loss. Other occasional uses of material not covered by the above reference list are provided in the text or the appendices.

The book can be used as the basis for a one-semester course (for example, 45 lectures) for advanced undergraduates or graduate students. One of our goals in developing the book was to provide sufficient breadth and depth so that a researcher or student new to the area would be able to begin research on online algorithms and competitive analysis upon completion of the text. In addition to presenting the more essential ideas under a unified notation, we have tried to provide an accurate contextual background and to list a number of open questions that we find interesting. We have suggested a value for each open problem. This value is composed of the following two components. The first component (denoted by I) is our assessment of the relative interest/importance of the problem. The interest/importance of a problem is based on a combination of historical, conceptual, and practical significance. Obviously, any "interest rating" is very subjective. The second component (denoted by a T) is our assessment of the difficulty of the problem. Rating the difficulty of a problem is, of course, very much of a conjecture in that there is no way to judge ultimate difficulty until the problem has been solved (and even then, the difficulty of a problem may decrease over time). Our assessment of difficulty is based on a combination of the (conjectured) need for technical depth and for substantially new insights and techniques. Both the interest and difficulty components are rated on a scale of 1 to 5, with 5 representing the most interesting (respectively, the most difficult) rating. Although our ratings do reflect comments from colleagues, they should be considered as imprecise and error-prone suggestions from the authors; by no means do they represent a consensus.

Acknowledgments

This text was initiated in the graduate course *6.892 Complexity Theory for Fun and Profit*, which was taught in the fall of 1993 at the MIT Laboratory for Computer Science. Some of the chapters are based on scribe notes taken by the participants of the course. We thank, in particular, Rosario Gennaro, Shai Halevi, Esther Jesurum, Yuan Ma, and Stephen Ponzio.

A preliminary version of this text was used in the graduate course *CSC 2421 Algebraic and Combinatorial Techniques in Complexity Theory*, which was taught in the fall of 1995 at the University of Toronto Department of Computer Science. This text has benefited greatly from all the corrections and suggestions that arose during that class. In particular, we thank Demetrios Achlioptas, Chi-Lok Chan, Theodoulos Garefalakis, Rod Hynes, James Sedgwick, Panagiotis Tsaparas, and Hai Wang.

We are indebted to a number of friends and colleagues for their explanations, comments, and criticisms. In particular, we thank Susanne Albers, Sabah al-Binali, Israel Aumann, Yossi Azar, Yair Bartal, Avrim Blum, Andrew Chou, Josep Diaz, Vincent Feltkamp, Amos Fiat, Vincent Gogan, Sergiu Hart, Sandy Irani, Alexander Ivrii, David Johnson, Adam Kalai, Jon Kleinberg, Elias Koutsoupias, Michael Molloy, Erik Ordentlich, Christos Papadimitriou, Erez Petrank, Serge Plotkin, Kirk Pruhs, Yuval Rabani, Yuri Rabinovich, Prabhakar Raghavan, Yiftach Ravid, Charles Rackoff, Adi Rosén, Jiří Sgall, Gabor Tardos, Jeffrey Westbrook, Neal Young, and Shmuel Zamir.

During the final stages of preparing this text, we relied on the help and detailed comments of Yossi Azar, Yair Bartal, Amos Fiat, Adam Kalai, Adi Rosén, and Jiří Sgall.

In addition, we thank William Burley, Marek Chrobak, Tom Cover, Yoav Freund, Tzachi Gilboa, Yoram Halevy, Nati Linial, Todd Mowry, Ian Munro, Moty Ricklin, Michael Saks, Ken Sevcik, Bernhard von Stengel, Michael Stumm, and Tali Tishby for helping us with the collection of bibliographic material and/or for sending preprints.

Special thanks to our colleagues who provided figures and allowed us to reprint or modify these figures. Specifically, we thank Tom Cover for Figure 14.2; Amos Fiat and Zvi Rosen for Figures 5.2 and 5.3; Serge Plotkin for Figure 13.1; and Neal Young for Figure 3.1. Also, special thanks to Martin Osborn for providing us with his LATEX game macros, to Ronny Wells for his help and advice on generating figures, and to Dan Astoorian, John DiMarco, and Lloyd Smith for their advice and excellent computing environment.

More generally, we have been extremely fortunate to have excellent colleagues and friends at the Hebrew University and the University of Toronto whose advice and support made this text possible. Specifically, many, many thanks to Rutie Cohen, Stephen Cook, Faith Fich, Sergiu Hart, Pam Linnemann, Nati Linial, Charles Rackoff, Hana Shemesh, Tali Tishby, and Avi Wigderson.

We sincerely thank Brenda Brown, who carefully read and critiqued many versions of this text. And we are grateful to Vicki Shum, not only for all her help on this text but, moreover, for taking care of all secretarial and administrative matters for 25 years. We are extremely pleased with our choice of the publisher, in particular, we appreciate the expert help provided by Nancy Brochin, Lauren Cowles, and Rena Wells. Last, but certainly not least, we are indebted to Judy Borodin and Brenda Brown for their patience and support throughout the writing of this text.

About the Cover

The idea for the cover originated over a lunchtime discussion at the IBM Resarch Center in Yorktown Heights, New York. The vague idea was to have an adversary and an online player who was walking on a line. This vague idea was creatively and artistically transformed by our cover designer John Lown into what we believe is an excellent symbolic rendering of the major theme of this text: the contest between an all powerful adversary who knows or, rather, generates the future and a skillful online player (i.e., algorithm). The explicit concept of a malicious adversary is perhaps unique to the field of computer science, playing an essential role in areas such as complexity theory, cryptography, distributed systems, and scheduling. Our acrobatic online player has to walk a tightrope balancing the competing demands of different requests, depicted by the puzzle pieces. We had a healthy debate with our publisher and many colleagues over how menacing the adversary should appear and about the relative sizes of the adversary and the online player. But whether or not the adversary is menacing or just impersonally challenging the acrobat, the ultimate advantage is that the adversary sees the whole picture.

CHAPTER 1

Introduction to Competitive Analysis: The List Accessing Problem

We begin this text by introducing the competitive analysis approach in the context of the list accessing problem, a problem of significant historical, theoretical, and practical interest. Before defining the list accessing problem, we introduce the basic concepts and definitions that will be used throughout our study.

1.1 Basic Ideas and Terminology

A few basic definitions and notations will be used throughout the text. In this section, we provide the basic background, with additional concepts being accumulated along the way. In order to avoid introducing a large amount of notation, we will keep the discussion rather informal and rely on some examples from which the basic concepts will emerge. In particular, we will postpone the definitions of an online problem and an online algorithm. We provide a formal framework in Chapter 7, where we introduce a general model for online algorithms called request–answer games.

1.1.1 Offline and Online Optimization Problems

We begin with a discussion of the concept of an **optimization problem**, which may be one of either cost minimization or profit maximization. An optimization problem $\mathcal{P}$ of cost minimization consists of a set $\mathcal{I}$ of inputs and a cost function C. Associated with every input I is a set of feasible outputs (or solutions) $F(I)$, and associated with each feasible solution O in $F(I)$ is a positive real, $C(I, O)$, representing the cost of the output O with respect to the input I.[1] The kind of optimization problems we are typically concerned with are of cost minimization; therefore, the discussion here is primarily in terms of cost problems. It is not difficult to develop the analogous concepts for profit maximization problems.[2]

---

[1] For the purpose of (Boolean) complexity theory, it is usual to assume that costs are positive integers. Here we need a more general formulation where costs are positive reals.

[2] However, as shown later in this text (e.g., in Chapter 8), cost minimization and profit maximization problems can differ in some meaningful ways.

For example, consider the bin packing problem (see Section 12.5). This problem presents an unbounded number of uniform bins, each having some fixed size or capacity, say 1. An input is a sequence of items $x_1, x_2, \ldots, x_n$ where x_i represents the size of the ith item. All item sizes satisfy $0 < x_i \leq 1$. The goal is to "pack" all items into bins in the most compact way. Given an input, a feasible solution is any assignment of all the input items x_i such that the sum of the item sizes assigned to any bin does not exceed the bin capacity (which is 1). The cost of a (feasible) solution is the number of bins used to pack all the items. Originally, this bin packing problem was studied as an "offline problem." That is, an algorithm is allowed to consider the entire list of items in order to compute the best solution. In order to view bin packing as an "online problem," each item x_i must be assigned without knowledge of items $x_{i+1}, \ldots, x_n$ and, of course, the assignment of items $x_1, \ldots, x_i$ must be a feasible solution for each i; furthermore, when we pack x_i, we are not allowed to alter the bin assignment of previously packed items. Thus, an online feasible solution is a sequence of assignments. Exactly as in the offline problem, the total cost of an online solution is the total number of bins used. Equivalently, we can consider the cost of each online assignment of one item to be either 0 or 1, depending on whether or not the item assignment opened a new bin (during the online assignment) and the total cost becomes the sum of the individual item assignment costs.

Given any legal input I, an algorithm ALG for an optimization problem $\mathcal{P}$ computes a feasible output (solution) $\text{ALG}[I] \in F(I)$. The cost associated with this feasible output is denoted by $\text{ALG}(I) = C(I, \text{ALG}[I])$. An **optimal algorithm** OPT is such that for all legal inputs,

$$\text{OPT}(I) = \min_{O \in F(I)} C(I, O).$$

An algorithm ALG is a **c-approximation algorithm** for a minimization problem $\mathcal{P}$ if there is a constant $\alpha \geq 0$ such that for all legal inputs

$$\text{ALG}(I) - c \cdot \text{OPT}(I) \leq \alpha.$$

More precisely, such an algorithm is called an **asymptotic c-approximation algorithm**; we reserve the term *c-approximation algorithm* to mean $\alpha = 0$.

In the analogous definition of a maximization problem, we require that $\text{OPT}(I) - c \cdot \text{ALG}(I) \leq \alpha$, where $\text{ALG}(I)$ denotes the profit of ALG. In both cases, the approximation factor is greater than or equal 1; the closer it is to 1, the better the approximation.

Optimization problems in which the input is received in an online manner and in which the output must be produced online are called **online problems**. The complication inherent in online algorithms is that each online output influences the cost of the overall solution. This suggests a "natural" partition of optimization problems into online and offline problems (and their respective algorithms). Many problems are intrinsically offline. For example, in most instances of linear programming, it is natural to assume that the input is given offline.[3] In other optimization problems, such as job scheduling and bin packing, both the online and offline versions of the problem are naturally meaningful. Last, many problems such as paging, telephone circuit switching, and investment planning are intrinsically online. For these problems, offline algorithms are not acceptable. Nevertheless,

---

[3] It also makes sense to view linear programming as an "online" problem without full information or with the information distributed between several players (e.g., see Papadimitriou and Yannakakis [272]).

even for intrinsically online problems, we could hypothesize an offline algorithm (that must then have clairvoyant abilities).

1.1.2   The Competitive Ratio and Competitiveness

An online algorithm ALG is c-**competitive** if there is a constant α such that for all finite input sequences I,

$$\text{ALG}(I) \leq c \cdot \text{OPT}(I) + \alpha.$$

When the **additive constant** α is less than or equal to zero (i.e., $\text{ALG}(I) \leq c \cdot \text{OPT}(I)$), we may say for emphasis that ALG is **strictly c-competitive**. Allowing a positive constant α reflects the view that for intrinsic online problems such as paging, list accessing, and so on, we have an arbitrarily long input sequence with unbounded cost. The constant α becomes insignificant as we consider longer and longer (and more costly) initial subsequences. Moreover, even for finite input sequences, the use of the additive constant α allows for an intrinsic performance ratio that does not depend on initial conditions. However, for "bounded cost" optimization problems such as (offline or online) graph coloring where at most N colors are needed, it is clearly more significant if and how α depends on N, the "size" of the problem.

A (strictly) c-competitive online algorithm ALG is a c-approximation algorithm with the restriction that ALG must compute online. Thus, for each input I, a c-competitive algorithm is guaranteed to incur a cost within a factor c of the optimal offline cost (up to the additive constant α). We note again that the competitive ratio is always at least 1, and the smaller it is, the better ALG performs with respect to OPT. If ALG is c-competitive, we sometimes say that ALG attains a **competitive ratio** c. An algorithm is called **competitive** if it attains a "constant" competitive ratio c. Although c may be a function of the problem parameters, it must be independent of the input I. For example, in a scheduling problem concerning N machines, we might have a competitive ratio c that depends on N, but c must be independent of the number and type of jobs being scheduled. The infimum over the set of all values c such that ALG is c-competitive is called **the competitive ratio** of ALG and is denoted by $\mathcal{R}(\text{ALG})$.

We make no requirements or assumptions concerning the computational efficiency of a competitive online algorithm. In the more traditional offline complexity studies, we are primarily concerned with approximation algorithms that compute within polynomial time. Thus, strictly speaking, c-competitive online algorithms and polynomial time c-approximation algorithms are not comparable. However, in practice, we usually seek "efficient" competitive online algorithms and, in particular, algorithms that do compute within polynomial (in the relevant parameters) time.

1.1.3   Games and Adversaries

There are several meaningful ways to view the problem of analyzing online algorithms. One way, which we use throughout the text, is to view the problem as a game between an **online player** and a malicious **adversary**. The online player runs an online algorithm on an input that is created by the adversary. The adversary, based on the knowledge of the algorithm used by the online player, constructs the worst possible input so as to maximize the competitive ratio. That is, the adversary tries to make the task costly to the online player but, at the same time, inexpensive for the optimal offline algorithm. We sometimes identify the adversary and the optimal offline algorithm as one entity: the **offline player**. For deterministic online algorithms, the adversary knows exactly what the online player's response will be to each input element; in other words, the offline player determines the malicious input sequence in advance. For randomized online algorithms, the nature of the offline player is a more subtle issue. We defer the discussion on randomized competitiveness to Chapters 2, 4, 6, 7, and 8.

1.2   The List Accessing Problem

Suppose we have a filing cabinet containing ℓ labeled but unsorted files. We receive a sequence of requests to access certain files. Each request is a label of a file. After a request to access a file "x" is given, we must locate the file and remove it from the cabinet (for example, in order to get some information from this file). Suppose that the only way this can be done is by flipping through the files from the beginning until the file is located. In accessing the ith file in the cabinet, we incur a cost (search time) of i; and if the file is not in the cabinet, we incur a cost of ℓ (since we must scan the whole file cabinet). After taking out the file, we must return it to the cabinet before the next request for another file is made known; however, we may reorganize the cabinet, for instance, by reinserting the accessed file closer to the front of the cabinet. The incentive for such a reorganization is that it may save us some search time in the future; for example, if a certain file is requested frequently, it is wise to insert it closer to the front. Our goal is to find a reorganization rule that minimizes the search time.

This example illustrates a fascinating problem that has been extensively studied in the literature. The problem is called the **list accessing** or **list update** problem. From a more general standpoint, the list accessing problem revolves around the management of a particular data structure for the implementation of an abstract data type (ADT) called a **dictionary**.[4] The data structure must support a sequence of requests, where each request is one of the following three types: ACCESS(x), INSERT(x), or DELETE(x), where x is the name (or "key") of an item stored in the dictionary. In the list accessing problem, we associate certain costs with each of these operations as follows: the cost of servicing each request for an item x is 1 plus the number of items preceding x on the list (one plus the length of the list if the item is not on the list). That is, accessing or deleting the ith item on the list costs i. Inserting a new item costs $\ell + 1$, where ℓ is the number of items currently on the list before the insertion.

Any algorithm for maintaining the list may reorganize the list at any time. The work associated with a reorganization is measured in terms of the minimum number of transpositions of consecutive items needed for this reorganization. However, immediately after accessing or inserting an item, we allow this item to be moved free of charge to any location closer to the front of the list. The transpositions (or exchanges) used to perform this move are called **free**, whereas all other transpositions are called **paid** and cost 1 each. The motivation for this formulation in terms of free and paid transpositions is clear when we consider the filing cabinet mentioned above (or an unsorted linked list). As we scan a filing cabinet while searching for a particular file, we can keep a pointer at any location

---

[4] For a discussion of dictionaries and ADTs, see, for example, Aho, Hopcroft, and Ullman [2], p. 117, or Cormen, Leiserson, and Rivest [116], p. 197.

along the way and then insert the accessed file in that location almost free of additional search or reorganization costs.

The list accessing problem is of course a cost minimization optimization problem, and the goal is to devise an algorithm for reorganizing the list (by performing free and/or paid transpositions) that minimizes search and reorganization costs.

A **linked list** of unsorted items is probably the most appropriate data structure for implementing the dictionary data type when constrained by the costs prescribed by the above list accessing cost model.[5] The search costs are related to the time it takes to scan the list for the requested item: we pay 1 for traversing a link on the list and making one comparison (for the requested item). However, justifying the cost of 1 attributed to a paid exchange is problematic. For example, to exchange the ith item with the item following it, we must first access this item and then perform the exchange. If our starting point is the front of the list, this costs $O(i)$.[6] In addition, we can argue that there is no such thing as a free exchange and/or that the exchange cost differs from the link traversal (plus comparison) cost. Of course, different cost formulations lead to different models for the list accessing problem; indeed, several cost models are mentioned in this chapter.

The relevancy of the list accessing problem stems from the fact that the linked-list data structure is very often used in practice, mainly because of its great simplicity and the fact that memory need not be preallocated. Furthermore, online algorithms for the list accessing problem can be directly exploited to produce simple and efficient data compression schemes (see Section 1.7). However, for many applications the linked list is not the most efficient data structure; there are various other more efficient data structures that induce different sets of costs for maintaining a dictionary. Some other frequently used data structures are: unordered arrays, ordered arrays, search trees, and hash tables (see also Section 1.7.1).

1.2.1 Models

We will call the list accessing model described in Section 1.2 the **dynamic list accessing model**. Much of the work on list accessing is concerned with a simplified version of the dynamic model called the **static list accessing model**. In the static list accessing model, there are no insertions or deletions, only a fixed set of ℓ items on the list so that the only requests are to access items on the list. Although the static list model is simpler than the dynamic model, it does address the intrinsic issue of how to reorganize the list so that future searches can be made more quickly.

1.2.2 Three List Accessing Algorithms

Many of the algorithms that have been proposed for managing the list are variants of the following three algorithms:

- MTF (MOVE-TO-FRONT): After accessing or inserting an item, move it to the front of the list, without changing the relative order of the other items.

---

[5] See Aho, Hopcroft, and Ullman [2].

[6] Nevertheless, since most of the online list accessing algorithms that have been studied do not use paid exchanges, allowing the optimal offline to use paid exchanges only increases its power. Arguably, this cost model is simply more "protective" against unexpected behavior of an optimal offline algorithm.

- **TRANS** (TRANSPOSE): After accessing or inserting an item, transpose it with the immediately preceding item.
- **FC** (FREQUENCY-COUNT): Maintain a frequency counter for each item. Upon inserting an item, initialize its counter to 0. After accessing or inserting an item, increment its counter by 1. Immediately after updating a frequency counter, reorganize the list so that items on the list are ordered in nonincreasing order of their frequencies.

MTF and TRANS appear much more attractive than FC. First, MTF and TRANS require no memory other than that required for the list itself. In contrast, FC requires an arbitrarily large additional memory for "bookkeeping" – namely, one counter per item, where each counter may be incremented an arbitrarily large number of times. Also, the transpositions performed by MTF and TRANS are easier to implement than those performed by FC.

1.2.3   On Free and Paid Transpositions

The three online list accessing algorithms of Section 1.2.2 use only free transpositions to arrange their lists. Does there exist an optimal offline list accessing algorithm using only free transpositions?

The following exercise shows that paid exchanges are in general essential.

Exercise 1.1 (paid exchanges necessary) Consider the three-element list with the following initial configuration: $\langle x_1, x_2, x_3 \rangle$ (i.e., x_1 is at the front). Prove that the optimal offline cost to serve the request sequence x_3, x_2, x_3, x_2 is 8. Now consider an optimal offline algorithm without paid exchanges and prove that it pays 9 to serve the same sequence.

The following exercise shows that any list accessing algorithm (offline or online) can be transformed to an algorithm that uses only paid transpositions without increasing the cost.

Exercise 1.2 Let ALG be any list accessing algorithm and let σ be any request sequence. Prove that there is an algorithm ALG$'$ that uses only paid transpositions (before the access) such that ALG$'(\sigma)$ = ALG(σ). Consider a variant of the list accessing problem in which the algorithm is charged $f(i)$ for accessing the ith item (assume the static model). Prove that the above result holds whenever the cost of transposing the ith and $(i + 1)$st items is $f(i + 1) - f(i)$.

1.3   The Sleator–Tarjan Result

Sleator and Tarjan examined MTF against the optimal offline strategy and found that MTF obtains a competitive ratio of 2. For an algorithm ALG, let ALG$_P(\sigma)$ be the number of paid transpositions made by ALG when processing the request sequence σ. Similarly, let ALG$_F(\sigma)$ be the number of free transpositions, and let ALG$_C(\sigma)$ be the cost of all operations other than paid transpositions. Notice that ALG(σ) = ALG$_C(\sigma)$ if ALG is MTF, TRANS, or FC, since these algorithms use only free transpositions. The proof of the following theorem, which bounds the cost ratio between MTF and OPT, does not require any knowledge of what the algorithm OPT actually does. The proof uses a "potential function" argument, which will be developed further in Section 1.4.

Theorem 1.1 *Let σ be a request sequence consisting of n requests. Suppose that* MTF *and* OPT *start with the same list configuration. Then,*

$$\text{MTF}(\sigma) \leq 2 \cdot \text{OPT}_C(\sigma) + \text{OPT}_P(\sigma) - \text{OPT}_F(\sigma) - n. \tag{1.1}$$

PROOF. Imagine that both MTF and OPT process the requests in σ, while each algorithm works on its own list starting from the empty list. Let $a_i = t_i + \Phi_i - \Phi_{i-1}$, where t_i is the actual cost that MTF incurs for processing this request, and Φ_i is a "potential function"; this potential function maps the list configurations of MTF and OPT into the nonnegative reals just after both algorithms have finished processing the ith request. We call a_i the "amortized cost" for MTF to process the ith request. Specifically, Φ_i is defined to be the number of **inversions** in MTF's list with respect to OPT's list, where an inversion is defined to be an ordered pair of items x_j and x_k, where x_j precedes x_k on MTF's list but x_k precedes x_j in OPT's list. For example, the list $\langle x_1, x_2, x_3 \rangle$ has three inversions with respect to $\langle x_3, x_2, x_1 \rangle$. Notice that Φ_i is always nonnegative and that the initial potential function Φ_0 is a constant whose value depends only on the initial configurations of MTF's and OPT's lists. Since we assume that the lists are initially the same, $\Phi_0 = 0$.

It is easy to see that

$$\text{MTF}(\sigma) = \sum_{i=1}^{n} t_i = \Phi_0 - \Phi_n + \sum_{i=1}^{n} a_i.$$

Hence, by bounding the total amortized cost of processing all n requests, we can bound the total actual cost incurred by MTF. Recall that Φ_n is nonnegative and that $\Phi_0 = 0$.

For all $1 \leq j \leq \ell$, let x_j denote the item that is positioned at location j in OPT's list just after processing request $i - 1$. Using the above potential function, we show that the amortized cost to process request i, whether it is an ACCESS(x_j), an INSERT(x_j), or a DELETE(x_j), is at most $(2s - 1) + P - F$, where s is the search cost (not including transpositions) incurred by OPT for this request, and P and F are, respectively, the number of paid and free transpositions performed by OPT for processing the request. Once this is established, the theorem is proven, since the -1s, one per operation, sum to $-n$.

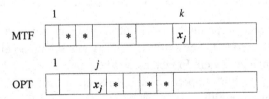

Figure 1.1: The configurations of MTF and OPT.

It remains to prove this claim. Consider OPT's list and that of MTF as illustrated in Figure 1.1. Item x_j is positioned at location j in OPT's list and at position k in MTF's list. The asterisks indicate items located before x_j in MTF's list but after x_j in OPT's list; that is, each asterisk represents an inversion involving x_j. There may be other inversions involving x_j that are not indicated by asterisks (namely, items that appear in front of x_j in OPT's list but after x_j in MTF's list). Suppose there are ν such inversions. Then $k - 1 - \nu$ items precede x_j in both lists (*at least* this number of items precedes x_j in OPT's list). This implies that

$k - 1 - \nu \leq j - 1$, since x_j is in the jth position in OPT's list. Hence, $k - \nu \leq j$. When MTF then moves x_j to the front of its list, it creates $k - 1 - \nu$ new inversions with respect to OPT's list before OPT processes the request. Also, MTF's action eliminates ν inversions. Hence, the contribution to the amortized cost is

$$k + (k - 1 - \nu) - \nu = 2(k - \nu) - 1 \leq 2j - 1 = 2s - 1.$$

The search cost s incurred by OPT for this request is exactly j. When the request is an INSERT(x_j) or an ACCESS(x_j) when x_j is not on the list, exactly the same argument holds, with $j = \ell + 1$. In the case of deletion, the situation is even better; no new inversions are being created and the contribution to the amortized cost is

$$k - \nu \leq j = s \leq 2s - 1.$$

Clearly, the search cost of OPT does not contribute to the change in the potential; however, each paid transposition contributes at most 1 to the amortized cost and each free transposition contributes -1. Thus, the proof of the claim is complete, since OPT performs P paid transpositions and F free ones.   ∎

Remark 1.1 We can obtain a similar result for the case when MTF and OPT do not start with the same list configuration. All we need is to add an additive constant of Φ_0 to the right-hand side of equation (1.1).

A simple corollary of Theorem 1.1 is that $\mathcal{R}(\text{MTF}) \leq 2 - \frac{1}{\ell}$ in the static list model. According to Theorem 1.1, for any σ, $\text{MTF}(\sigma) \leq 2\text{OPT}(\sigma) - n$, with $n = |\sigma|$. Clearly, $\text{OPT}(\sigma) \leq n\ell$. Hence,

$$2\text{OPT}(\sigma) - n \leq \left(2 - \frac{1}{\ell}\right)\text{OPT}(\sigma),$$

which proves this corollary.

In general, upper bounds for the static list model usually extend to the dynamic list model, as in the following exercise.

Exercise 1.3 Show that the above $2 - \frac{1}{\ell}$ upper bound holds for the dynamic list accessing problem where ℓ is the maximum number of items present in the list at any point in time.

Theorem 1.1 is fairly surprising. At the outset, it seems that MTF is "over-reacting." However, when compared to the best offline strategy (for which no efficient algorithm is known), MTF performs quite well. In fact, as we show in Theorem 2.1 and Exercise 1.11, MTF attains the best possible competitive ratio. In Section 1.5, we also prove that neither TRANS nor FC is at all competitive.

Theorem 1.1 generalizes in several ways, which we present as exercises.

Exercise 1.4 (fractional MTF) Let MTF_d ($d \geq 1$) be a variant of MTF that moves an accessed or inserted item at position i at least $i/d - 1$ positions closer to the front of the list. Show that

$$\text{MTF}_d(\sigma) \leq d\left(2 \cdot \text{OPT}_C(\sigma) + \text{OPT}_P(\sigma) - \text{OPT}_F(\sigma) - n\right).$$

Exercise 1.5 (MTF every-other-access) Prove that the algorithm "MTF every other access" (i.e., move the item to the front on every even request for that item) is strictly 2-competitive.

1.4 The Potential Function Method

The potential function argument just described plays an essential role in the competitive analysis of online algorithms. We now summarize this technique in terms of an online algorithm ALG, attempting to minimize the cost of servicing a request sequence σ, and present two styles for its usage. As usual, let OPT be an optimal offline algorithm for the same problem as ALG. To formulate the potential function method, we need to introduce two terms: the event sequence and configuration of an algorithm.

Suppose that both ALG and OPT are processing a request sequence σ. In order to process a request in σ, each of these algorithms performs a sequence of computational operations. For example, in the list accessing problem these operations consist of link traversals between two consecutive items on the list, item comparisons, and transpositions. Not all operations (e.g., free transpositions) add to the cost function.[7]

With any request sequence and an algorithm, we can associate a unique sequence of operations. If we have two such sequences, one for ALG and one for OPT, we can now combine the two sequences into one compound sequence that specifies the actions of both algorithms. We may combine the sequences in any desirable order of operations, provided that we keep some chronological order of operations. That is, in the grand sequence we may interleave actions of ALG and OPT in any order, provided that ALG's actions involved in processing request $j + 1$ do not appear before actions of OPT that process request j, and vice versa.

Any partition of this grand list of operations into segments is called an **event sequence**, and each segment is called an **event**. In many cases, an event will simply be all the operations associated with ALG's response to a request or the operations associated with OPT's response to a request. In the analysis of MTF in Section 1.3, three types of events for each request are shown: one type of event corresponds to the free transpositions of OPT, a second type corresponds to the paid transpositions by OPT, and the third type corresponds to all other operations performed by first MTF and then OPT to serve a request.

Next, we need to define an algorithm's **configuration**. In essence, this is the algorithm's state with respect to the outside world. In the list accessing problem, a configuration of an algorithm is the current order of the list maintained by the algorithm. This should not be confused with the algorithm's internal state, which consists of its control and internal memory. In the FC algorithm, the internal memory records the frequency count for each item in the current list. We avoid a formal definition here, assuming that the concept is clear.

Let S_{ALG} and S_{OPT} be the sets of possible configurations for ALG and OPT, respectively. Let Φ be any mapping, $\Phi : S_{ALG} \times S_{OPT} \to \mathbb{R}$. That is, Φ maps configurations of ALG and OPT to a real number. Any such function Φ is called a **potential function.** The idea is to define a useful potential function that satisfies certain conditions with respect to event sequences.

Specifically, let $e_1, e_2, \ldots, e_n$ be any event sequence corresponding to some request sequence. For each $i = 1, 2, \ldots, n$, let Φ_i be the value of Φ just after the ith event. Let Φ_0 be the value of Φ just before the start of the game. Notice that Φ_0 is a constant that depends only on the initial configurations of ALG and OPT. Suppose we want to prove that ALG is

---

[7] Of course, even operations that are free of any "optimization cost" do have an "algorithmic cost" such as time or space complexity, but we do not count these algorithmic costs in competitive analysis.

c-competitive by using a potential function argument. Several proof styles can achieve this. Here we present two popular styles that are used frequently (the first of which we used for the proof of Theorem 1.1).

First Style: Amortized Costs

Denote by ALG_i (OPT_i) the cost incurred by ALG (respectively, OPT) during the ith event. ALG_i (OPT_i) is called the ALG's (OPT's) **actual cost** for the ith event. Let Φ be a potential function. For each event e_i ($i = 1, 2, \ldots, n$), define a_i, the **amortized cost** of ALG for the ith event,

$$a_i = \text{ALG}_i + \Phi_i - \Phi_{i-1}.$$

To prove that ALG is c-competitive, it is sufficient to prove that the following conditions hold with respect to any possible event sequence:

1. For each event e_i, $a_i \leq c \cdot \text{OPT}_i$.
2. There exists a constant b independent of the request sequence such that for all i, $\Phi_i \geq b$.

We can refine this method and prove a separate inequality for each type of event and then add these events separately. This is precisely what we did in the proof of Theorem 1.1.

Second Style: Interleaving Moves

To prove that ALG is c-competitive, it is sufficient to find a potential function Φ satisfying the following conditions with respect to any possible event sequence:

1. If only the adversary (OPT) moves (i.e., is active) during event e_i and pays x for this move, then $\Delta\Phi = \Phi_i - \Phi_{i-1} \leq cx$; that is, Φ increases by at most cx.
2. If only ALG moves during event e_i and pays x for this move, then $\Delta\Phi = \Phi_i - \Phi_{i-1} \leq -x$; that is, Φ decreases by at least x.
3. There exists a constant b independent of the request sequence such that for all i, $\Phi_i \geq b$.

An example of this proof style can be found in the proof of Theorem 10.2.

Exercise 1.6 Prove that both styles of the potential function proof technique yield the appropriate competitive ratio bound.

Remark 1.2 The potential function method generalizes in a straightforward manner to randomized algorithms. An example is given in the proof of Theorem 2.1.

1.5 Some Lower Bounds

The proof of the following lower bound will make use of an averaging technique that will be utilized a number of times throughout the text. In this technique we make use of a "cruel" adversary that causes the online player to pay the maximum for every request.

Theorem 1.2 *For the static list accessing problem with a list of ℓ items, any deterministic online algorithm has a competitive ratio of at least $2 - \frac{2}{\ell+1}$.*

PROOF. Given an initial list of size ℓ, the cruel strategy (or adversary) repeatedly makes requests to the last item on the list. That is, the cruel adversary selects an arbitrarily long request sequence (say, of length n). Each request is an access to the last item on the online algorithm's list. The total cost incurred by the online algorithm is clearly ℓn.

Consider $\ell!$ static offline algorithms that correspond to the $\ell!$ permutations of the initial ordering of the list as follows. Each of these algorithms initially orders the list according to a distinct permutation, at a cost of at most b, where b is a constant that depends only on ℓ (i.e., it is easy to see that $b = O(\ell^2)$), and then processes the requests with no additional reorganizations.

For any ACCESS(x) request, look at the sum of costs over all $\ell!$ static algorithms to process that single request for x. Since for each of the ℓ possible positions of x there are $(\ell - 1)!$ different permutations of the remaining items, this sum of costs is exactly

$$\sum_{i=1}^{\ell} i(\ell - 1)! = (\ell - 1)! \frac{\ell(\ell + 1)}{2}.$$

Hence the total cost for the entire cruel sequence, for all these $\ell!$ strategies, is at most

$$n(\ell - 1)! \frac{\ell(\ell + 1)}{2} + \ell! b.$$

It follows that the average cost over all static algorithms is at most $\frac{1}{2}n(\ell + 1) + b$ and at least one of the static algorithms has a total cost of, at most, the average. This bounds from above the cost of the best optimal offline algorithm. Hence, the ratio of the online algorithm's cost to the optimal algorithm's cost is at least ℓn divided by $\frac{1}{2}n(\ell + 1) + b$. As n grows relative to b, this ratio approaches $\frac{2\ell}{\ell+1}$. ∎

Exercise 1.7 Instead of using a bound on the average (over all initial configurations) static optimal to derive the $\frac{2\ell}{\ell+1}$ lower bound, show that we can use the static offline algorithm that first rearranges the list according to the frequency count of items in the request sequence. Note that this does not contradict the fact that online algorithm FC is not competitive (see below).

Notice that the lower bound of Theorem 1.2 does not match exactly the $2 - \frac{1}{\ell}$ upper bound for algorithm MTF. According to Exercise 1.11, MTF is strictly $\left(2 - \frac{2}{\ell+1}\right)$-competitive in the static list model, thus matching the lower bound of Theorem 1.2.

Lower Bound for TRANS

Cruel adversary strategies are often useful for proving lower bounds. In the following example we use the cruel strategy to prove that TRANS is not competitive for the dynamic list model. We first consider the static list case.

For the algorithm TRANS, the cruel strategy is extremely simple and involves requests to only two items. Since the cruel sequence always requests the last item on TRANS's list, TRANS will keep transposing the last two elements on the list. For each pair of requests, TRANS incurs a cost of 2ℓ, where ℓ is the length of its list. Algorithm OPT, on the other hand, moves these two items to the first and second positions on its list (using free or paid exchanges) and then incurs a cost of 3 for each pair of requests. For a request sequence of length n (assume that n is even), the cost ratio, online to offline, is $\frac{n\ell}{(n/2-1)3+2\ell}$. As n grows, this ratio approaches $\frac{2\ell}{3}$. Formally speaking, algorithm TRANS, like any algorithm that does not perform paid transpositions, is competitive for the static list problem; obviously, it achieves a ratio no worse than ℓ, and our definition of competitiveness allows "constants" that depend on the problem parameters. However, it should be clear that for a problem such as static list accessing, such "constants" are meaningless. For the dynamic list accessing problem, there is no a priori bound on the length of the list; thus the previous argument (coupled with a sufficiently long sequence of initial insertions) establishes the noncompetitiveness of TRANS.

The above cruel sequence, which is a worst case for algorithm TRANS, may not be typical in "real life." However, for many applications in computer systems (e.g., memory pages requested by a computer program) the sequence of requests often consists of clusters of repeated requests from some set called a locality.[8] Although the exact sequence that failed TRANS is not necessarily typical in the presence of such "locality of reference," algorithm TRANS may encounter request sequences that will cause an effect similar to that caused by the above cruel sequence.

Lower Bound for FC

It is not difficult to prove that algorithm FC is also not competitive. Again, first consider the static list accessing problem. Let k be any integer greater than ℓ. Let $x_1, x_2, \ldots, x_\ell$ be the items on the list. We construct the following request sequence, σ. The first segment of σ consists of k requests for x_1; the second segment, of $k-1$ requests for x_2. In general, the ith segment, where $i = 1, 2, \ldots, \ell$, consists of $k+1-i$ requests for x_i.

Now consider how FC processes this request sequence. Since the x_i are requested in decreasing order of relative frequencies, upon requesting x_i for the first time, FC will move x_i to the ith position from the front and will never change its position thereafter. It is now easy to give a lower bound on FC(σ). If the x_i's are initially ordered by decreasing frequencies (i.e., x_i is in the ith position) then

$$\text{FC}(\sigma) = \sum_{i=1}^{\ell} i \cdot (k+1-i)$$

$$= \frac{k\ell(\ell+1)}{2} + \frac{\ell(1-\ell^2)}{3}.$$

To prove a lower bound, we must find some upper bound on OPT(σ). For this purpose we can make use of any other (online or offline) algorithm for which we can calculate an upper bound on its cost to serve σ. Obviously, the more "competitive" the algorithm is, the tighter our upper bound on OPT(σ) will be. Because MTF is simple, chances are that we can easily derive an upper bound on its cost to serve σ. In addition, MTF is the "most competitive" algorithm we know so far. If we use MTF for the upper bound, we are guaranteed to bound OPT(σ) within a factor of 2.

Assume that the list is initially organized in the worst possible order for MTF. Item x_1 is initially at the far end of the list and is brought to the front after it is requested for the first time. Then, x_2, which is now at the far end of the list, is brought to the front, and so

[8] See Denning [130] and Denning and Schwartz [131].

on. In general, x_i is located at the last position when it is first requested, incurring a cost of ℓ, and then it is brought to the front, where it remains for the $k - i$ subsequent requests. Thus,

$$\text{MTF}(\sigma) \leq \sum_{i=1}^{\ell} [\ell + (k - i)] = \ell(\ell + k) - \frac{\ell(\ell + 1)}{2}.$$

This implies that

$$\frac{\text{FC}(\sigma)}{\text{OPT}(\sigma)} \geq \frac{k\ell(\ell + 1)/2 + \ell(1 - \ell^2)/3}{\ell(\ell + k) - \ell(\ell + 1)/2}.$$

It is not hard to see that as k grows, this ratio approaches $\frac{\ell+1}{2}$.

We can conclude that both TRANS and FC are not competitive for the dynamic list accessing problem and that both algorithms perform poorly (in the competitive sense) for the static list accessing problem. (Recall that in the static list model every algorithm is at worst ℓ-competitive.)

1.6 The List Factoring Technique

We now introduce another technique for analyzing list accessing algorithms. This technique enables a reduction of the competitive analysis of list accessing algorithms to lists of size 2. The benefit is substantial and quite obvious, as even complicated list accessing algorithms are surprisingly simple when they are restricted to lists of size 2. In particular, an optimal offline algorithm can be easily described for lists of size 2.

Exercise 1.8 Let L be a list of two elements x and y. Prove that there is an optimal offline algorithm OPT for L that satisfies the following properties: (i) OPT does not use paid exchanges; and (ii) whenever there is a run of two or more consecutive requests for x (y), OPT moves x (y) to the front (if it is not already there) after the first request (of this run) using free exchanges.

The main idea underlying the factoring technique is to count the cost of accesses in the following way. To motivate this access cost counting method consider an algorithm ALG that processes a certain list L in the static model. When ALG accesses an item x located i positions from the front, it pays i. This cost counts the number of comparisons ALG makes while searching for x. Among these i comparisons, $i - 1$ are with items different from x. We call such comparisons **negative comparisons**. The last comparison (with x) is called a **positive comparison**. The number of positive comparisons is the same for all algorithms and equals the length of the request sequence. It makes sense then to ignore the number of positive comparisons (see also Chapter 3). We call the model variant in which we do not count positive comparisons the **partial cost model**. The usual model in which we do count positive comparisons is called the **full cost model**. Here, we proceed with the partial cost (static list) model.

In the partial cost model the total cost of an algorithm that does not use paid exchanges is ascribed only to negative comparisons. It is natural to "attribute" the entire access cost of $i - 1$ to the accessed item. Instead, we now attribute the access cost for the ith item, x, to all items appearing in front of x. Since each of these items caused a negative comparison, we divide this total access cost of $i - 1$ between all of them equally so that each one of them "pays" 1; a "penalty" for blocking access to x.

Formally, we proceed as follows. Let ALG be a list accessing algorithm that does not use any paid exchanges, and let $\sigma = r_1, r_2, \ldots, r_n$ be any request sequence. For each item x, and integer $1 \le j \le n$, we use ALG(x, j) to denote the penalty attributed to item x for being in the way while ALG accesses r_j (the jth request). That is,

$$\mathrm{ALG}(x, j) = \begin{cases} 1 & \text{if } x \text{ is in front of } r_j; \\ 0 & \text{otherwise (including the case } x = r_j). \end{cases} \tag{1.2}$$

Use ALG$^*(\sigma)$ to denote the cost incurred by ALG for serving σ within the partial cost model. We can now write

$$\mathrm{ALG}^*(\sigma) = \sum_{1 \le j \le n} \sum_{x \in L} \mathrm{ALG}(x, j)$$

$$= \sum_{x \in L} \sum_{1 \le j \le n} \mathrm{ALG}(x, j)$$

$$= \sum_{x \in L} \sum_{y \in L} \sum_{j: r_j = y} \mathrm{ALG}(x, j)$$

$$= \sum_{\substack{x, y \in L \\ x \ne y}} \sum_{j: r_j = y} \mathrm{ALG}(x, j)$$

$$= \sum_{\substack{\{x, y\} \subseteq L \\ x \ne y}} \sum_{j: r_j \in \{x, y\}} [\mathrm{ALG}(x, j) + \mathrm{ALG}(y, j)]. \tag{1.3}$$

For every x and y in L, and request sequence σ, we denote the internal summation of the expression in equation (1.3) by $\mathrm{ALG}^*_{xy}(\sigma)$. That is,

$$\mathrm{ALG}^*_{xy}(\sigma) = \sum_{j: r_j \in \{x, y\}} [\mathrm{ALG}(x, j) + \mathrm{ALG}(y, j)].$$

We can now write equation (1.3) as

$$\mathrm{ALG}^*(\sigma) = \sum_{\substack{\{x, y\} \subseteq L \\ x \ne y}} \mathrm{ALG}^*_{xy}(\sigma). \tag{1.4}$$

Use σ_{xy} to denote the projection of σ over x and y, defined to be σ after deletion of all the requests for items other than x or y. It is assumed that $x, y \in L$ with $x \ne y$. Similarly, we define L_{xy} as the projection of the list L over x and y (i.e., L_{xy} is the two-element list holding x and y). Using these symbols, we define $\mathrm{ALG}^*(\sigma_{xy})$ as the total cost that ALG pays for serving the projected request sequence σ_{xy} while operating on the projected list

L_{xy}. Notice that the initial relative positions of x and y are preserved in L_{xy}. We say that the algorithm ALG satisfies the **pairwise property** if

$$\text{ALG}^*(\sigma_{xy}) = \text{ALG}^*_{xy}(\sigma). \tag{1.5}$$

We emphasize again that in equation (1.5) the costs are measured in the partial cost model.

What online algorithms satisfy the pairwise property? The following easy lemma gives a useful characterization.

Lemma 1.1 (Pairwise property lemma) *An algorithm satisfies the pairwise property if and only if for every request sequence σ, when ALG serves σ, the relative order of every two elements x and y in L is the same as their relative order in L_{xy} when ALG serves σ_{xy}.*

The proof of the this lemma is simple and is left as an exercise.

Exercise 1.9 Prove Lemma 1.1.

Example 1.1 Algorithm MTF satisfies the pairwise property. To see that, consider two elements x and y on the list L. Element x appears in front of y if and only if x was requested more recently, if and only if x appears in front of y in L_{xy}.

Algorithm FC also satisfies the pairwise property. The relative order of x and y depends only on the number of times they have been requested so far. Note that if this number is equal for both of them, their relative ordering depends on the initial ordering, or on which one of them had a larger frequency count more recently.

In contrast, TRANS does not satisfy the pairwise property. Notice that TRANS is equivalent to MTF when they both maintain lists of size 2. Nevertheless, these two algorithms are different on larger lists; therefore, by Lemma 1.1 it is impossible that TRANS satisfies the pairwise property.

We are now in a position to describe the **list factoring technique**. Suppose that the on-line algorithm ALG (that does not uses paid exchanges) satisfies the pairwise property (1.5). Assume for the moment that OPT also satisfies this property and equation (1.4) as well. Now suppose we have a proof that ALG is strictly c-competitive for all projected lists of size 2. That is, we assume that for all pairs $\{x, y\} \subseteq L$, and for every σ,

$$\text{ALG}^*(\sigma_{xy}) \le c \cdot \text{OPT}^*(\sigma_{xy}). \tag{1.6}$$

By the pairwise property (of ALG and OPT), we obtain

$$\text{ALG}^*_{xy}(\sigma) \le c \cdot \text{OPT}^*_{xy}(\sigma).$$

Using equation (1.4), we can conclude that ALG is strictly c-competitive.

Exercise 1.10 Show that the above derivation holds without strict competitiveness. That is, if in equation (1.6) there is some additive constant α, then ALG is c-competitive up to an additive constant of $\frac{\alpha \ell(\ell-1)}{2}$.

One caveat: in general, OPT cannot avoid paid exchanges (see Exercise 1.1), and the development leading to equation (1.3) (and (1.4)) does not apply to OPT. Moreover, it can be shown that OPT does not in general satisfy the pairwise property. Nevertheless, we can show that OPT does satisfy the following inequality for every pair of items, x and y

$$\text{OPT}^*(\sigma_{xy}) \le \text{OPT}^*_{xy}(\sigma) + \text{OPT}^*_{P;xy}(\sigma), \tag{1.7}$$

where $\text{OPT}^*_{P;xy}(\sigma)$ is the total cost incurred by OPT for paid exchanges between x and y while serving σ. To prove this inequality, notice that the right-hand side of equation (1.7) gives the total cost of some offline (not necessarily optimal) algorithm that is a "projection" of OPT over x and y. Namely, this projected algorithm operates on L_{xy} and serves the request sequence σ_{xy} according to the relative order of x and y in L as maintained by OPT while serving σ. The *optimal* offline algorithm for the two-item list, whose total cost in serving σ_{xy} is the left-hand side of equation (1.7), surely pays no more than any other offline algorithm; therefore, the inequality must hold. The following is another identity that is easy to prove:

$$\text{OPT}^*(\sigma) = \sum_{\substack{\{x,y\} \subseteq L \\ x \ne y}} \left[\text{OPT}^*_{xy}(\sigma) + \text{OPT}^*_{P;xy}(\sigma) \right]. \tag{1.8}$$

This identity is obtained using a development similar to the one leading to identity (1.3), with the inclusion of the costs incurred by OPT for paid exchanges.

Therefore, if inequality (1.6) holds for all pairs $\{x, y\} \subseteq L$, by the pairwise property of ALG, and by inequality (1.7), we have

$$\text{ALG}^*_{xy}(\sigma) \le c \cdot \left[\text{OPT}^*_{xy}(\sigma) + \text{OPT}^*_{P;xy}(\sigma) \right],$$

and we can conclude, from equations (1.4) and (1.8), that ALG is strictly c-competitive. Thus we have the following lemma.

Lemma 1.2 (Factoring lemma) *Let ALG be an online list accessing algorithm that does not use paid exchanges and that satisfies the pairwise property, and let L be a list. Suppose that for every pair $\{x, y\} \subseteq L$, and for every request sequence σ, $\text{ALG}^*(\sigma_{xy}) \le c \cdot \text{OPT}^*(\sigma_{xy})$. Then ALG is strictly c-competitive for L in the partial cost model.*

The factoring lemma applies only to the partial cost model. What about the full cost model? Under another assumption on ALG, the lemma can be used to derive upper bounds in the full cost model.

An algorithm is called **cost independent** if the decisions it makes are independent of the costs it pays, that is, if the algorithm operates in the same way under all cost models. All the online algorithms we have introduced so far are cost-independent.

Lemma 1.3 *Let ALG be a cost-independent, (strictly) c-competitive online algorithm in the partial cost model. Then ALG is (strictly) c-competitive in the full cost model.*

PROOF. Denote by OPT* and OPT the optimal offline algorithm for the partial cost and full cost models, respectively. Let σ be any request sequence. Recall that $\text{ALG}^*(\sigma)$ and $\text{ALG}(\sigma)$ denote the cost paid by ALG in the two models, respectively. Since the number of positive comparisons made by every algorithm is exactly $|\sigma|$, we can write $\text{OPT}(\sigma) = B + |\sigma|$, where B is the total optimal offline cost attributed for negative comparisons and paid exchanges. Clearly, $\text{OPT}^*(\sigma) \leq B$. Note that without further knowledge of the nature of OPT^* (OPT), we may infer that OPT^* pays less than B (if OPT^* is cost dependent). Since ALG is (strictly) c-competitive in the partial cost model, we conclude:

$$\begin{aligned}
\text{ALG}(\sigma) &= \text{ALG}^*(\sigma) + |\sigma| \\
&\leq c \cdot \text{OPT}^*(\sigma) + |\sigma| + \alpha \\
&\leq c \cdot B + |\sigma| + \alpha \\
&\leq c \cdot \text{OPT}(\sigma) + \alpha.
\end{aligned}$$
∎

Lemma 1.3 implies that the factoring lemma can derive *upper bounds* for the full cost model.

It has taken considerable effort to formulate the factoring technique. It is now time to realize some benefits. We begin with an alternative, simple proof that MTF is 2-competitive in the static model.

Corollary 1.3 MTF *is (strictly) 2-competitive for the static list accessing model.*

PROOF. Let L be the list and fix any request sequence σ. By the factoring lemma, and Lemma 1.3, it is sufficient to prove, within the partial cost model, that for every $\{x, y\} \subseteq L$, $\text{MTF}^*(\sigma_{xy}) \leq 2 \cdot \text{OPT}^*(\sigma_{xy})$. Let i and j, $i < j$, be two indices of requests in σ_{xy} for which MTF pays 1 (while operating on the two-element list). Without loss of generality, assume that immediately before serving the ith request, x appears in front of y in the list maintained by MTF. The ith request is for y because MTF pays 1 to serve it. It must then be that one of the requests between the ith and the jth (or maybe the jth itself) is for x. It follows that for at least one of the requests between the ith and the jth (or for one of them), OPT pays 1. This observation entails a cost ratio, online to offline, of at most 2 for the entire request sequence. Hence, MTF is 2-competitive in the partial cost model. Since MTF is cost independent, the result holds, by Lemma 1.3, in the full cost model. ∎

Exercise 1.11 (tight bound for MTF) Refine the factoring lemma (Lemma 1.2) so that its conclusion holds in the full cost model. Then prove that MTF is strictly $\left(2 - \frac{2}{\ell+1}\right)$-competitive where ℓ is the size of a static list or an upper bound on the size of a dynamic list at any point in time.

1.6.1 Phase Partitioning Technique

The next application of the factoring method is used in conjunction with a phase partition technique that we introduce in this section. We use the factoring with partitioning technique to show that the following algorithm is 2-competitive.

> **Algorithm TIMESTAMP:** Upon a request for an item x, insert x in front of the first (from the front of the list) item y that precedes x on the list and was requested at most once since the last request for x. Do nothing if there is no such item y or if x has been requested for the first time.

Exercise 1.12 Prove that TIMESTAMP satisfies the pairwise property.

Theorem 1.4 $\mathcal{R}(\text{TIMESTAMP}) \leq 2$ *in the static model.*

PROOF. Let L be the list maintained by TIMESTAMP and fix any request sequence σ. According to Exercise 1.12, TIMESTAMP satisfies the pairwise property; consequently, by the factoring lemma, it remains to prove that for any pair $\{x, y\} \subseteq L$,

$$\text{TIMESTAMP}^*(\sigma_{xy}) \leq 2 \cdot \text{OPT}^*(\sigma_{xy}). \tag{1.9}$$

Fix any pair $\{x, y\} \subseteq L$. We partition σ_{xy} into phases, each of which terminates with two consecutive requests for the same item. A phase can be one of two types. Phases of the first type have one of the following three forms:

   (a) $x^i yy$,
   (b) $x^i (yx)^k yy$,
   (c) $x^i (yx)^k x$,

where i and k are integers satisfying $i \geq 0$ and $k \geq 1$. Phases of the second type are defined exactly the same, with x and y interchanged. The parsing of the request sequence σ_{xy} into phases is defined in terms of the configuration of the list L_{xy} maintained by TIMESTAMP. Phases of the first type always start when x is at the front of L_{xy}; phases of the second type always start when y is at the front. For example, suppose that initially x is at the front of L_{xy}. Then the first phase is of the first type. If the first phase terminates with xx (form (c)), then the second phase is again of the first type. Otherwise, the first phase terminated with yy (forms (a) or (b)) and the second phase is of the second type, and so on. Thus, we obtain a unique partition of σ_{xy} into such phases. Note that the last phase in σ_{xy} may be incomplete. That is, it may be a proper prefix of one of the forms. Hence, we must also consider any proper prefix of any of the above forms. However, we can pad each incomplete phase of the first (respectively, second) type with the sequence yy (respectively, xx) and make it complete. This results in an additive constant of at most 2 for each projected list σ_{xy} and hence in an additive constant of at most $2\binom{\ell}{2}$ for the full request sequence. Therefore, for the analysis here, we ignore incomplete phases.

Table 1.1: Costs and cost ratios obtained by TIMESTAMP and OPT for serving phases of the first type.

	TIMESTAMP*	OPT*	max ratio, TIMESTAMP*/OPT*
(a) $x^i yy$	2	1	2
(b) $x^i (yx)^k yy$	$2k$	$k+1$	2
(c) $x^i (yx)^k x$	$2k-1$	k	2

   Table 1.1 specifies the costs incurred by TIMESTAMP and OPT, and the maximum cost ratios (online to offline) for the three possible phases of the first type. We now verify that the numbers in Table 1.1 are correct. Recall that TIMESTAMP* and OPT* are the partial costs incurred by TIMESTAMP and OPT, respectively. For example, let us calculate the costs incurred by TIMESTAMP. Assume that x is at the front of L_{xy}. Clearly, form (a) phases, $x^i yy$, cost exactly 2 because all the requests for x cost TIMESTAMP nothing; the first request for y costs 1, and y is left in its place. Form (b) phases, $x^i (yx)^k yy$, cost TIMESTAMP exactly $2k$. Again, serving the prefix x^i costs nothing. The first request for y costs 1, and y is left in the back. Then the second request for y costs 1, and y moves to the front. Each subsequent

request for y or x in $(yx)^k y$ costs 1, and the last request for y costs nothing. This gives a total of $2k$. Similar calculation gives a total of $2k - 1$ for form (c) phases. Exactly the same analysis (with x and y interchanged) yields the same costs for phases of the second type with y initially at the front.

To conclude the proof, we must verify that the maximum cost ratios are 2 in all three cases. This can be easily done. For sequences of form (a), 2 is actually obtained; for sequences of form (b) or (c), the maximum cost ratio approaches 2 from below. ∎

Exercise 1.13 Prove that $\mathcal{R}(\text{TIMESTAMP}) \leq 2$ also in the dynamic list model. Hint: Prove first that the additive constants of 2 used for incomplete phases in the proof of Theorem 1.4 are not necessary.

1.7 Historical Notes and Open Questions

We refer the reader to a recent survey of competitive analysis of list accessing (and other self-organizing data structures) by Albers and Westbrook [9]. It is somewhat surprising that competitive analysis as an approach to solving problems that are *intrinsically* online, such as list accessing and paging, was not explicitly advocated until Sleator and Tarjan [318] did so. The Sleator and Tarjan paper was motivated by, and indeed is part of, the important topic of self-adjusting data structures and amortized analysis (see Tarjan [325] and Bentley and McGeoch [58]). Inspired by the Bentley and McGeoch paper, Sleator and Tarjan pioneered the new approach by giving two explicit examples of competitive analysis for the related online problems of list accessing and paging.[9] The competitive analysis approach presented in their paper was sufficiently appealing that it attracted the attention of many theoretical computer scientists and gained much recognition as an approach for the study of online problems. In particular, Karlin, Manasse, Rudolph, and Sleator [212] soon followed this approach in their study of "snoopy caching." Indeed, they introduced the term "competitive algorithm" in that paper.

In addition to its inherent computational significance, the list accessing problem (also referred to as "self-organizing sequential search") provides an important example in which many of the early distributional analysis results are not consistent with empirical evidence, and in which the findings of competitive analysis better match and explain the empirical results. In spite of the stochastic analysis support in favor of TRANS (see Appendix B), it was found empirically that MTF performs much better in practice (see Bentley and McGeoch [58] and also McGeoch [261]).[10] A circumstantial conclusion is that "real-life" sequences do not adhere to simple static probability distributions. The stochastic assumption (that each item has a probability of being requested that is independent of previous accesses) failed to accommodate a property of "real-life" request sequences called locality where certain accesses are strongly (but perhaps very intricately) correlated

[9] As discussed in Sleator and Tarjan [318], list accessing and paging are examples of a general memory accessing problem using different cost functions. In addition, as observed by Rivest [294], every list accessing algorithm can be interpreted as a paging algorithm (see Chapter 3 in this text for further details).

[10] In contrast, Rivest [294] reported on extensive simulation results that consistently favor TRANS over MTF for lists of length $3 \leq \ell \leq 12$ when requests are independent observations of Zipf's distribution. See, for example, Knuth [228], p. 397, for some practical aspects of Zipf's distribution.

to immediately preceding accesses (in an a priori unknown manner). In addition, in many "real" applications the underlying distribution of requests is evolving (or even completely changing) throughout the lifetime of the data structure. It is, of course, quite possible that more sophisticated stochastic modeling (e.g., high-order Markov models) can provide a proper understanding of empirical results.

Brief History. From an historical perspective, the disparity between early stochastic and empirical results for the list accessing problem was the motivation for Bentley and Mc-Geoch [58] to study the list accessing problem. They used a new approach that combined worst-case assumptions, cost amortization, and comparison with an offline benchmark algorithm. The results of their work offered a persuasive argument for a new approach beyond the prevailing use of stochastic analysis. Specifically, Bentley and McGeoch studied the static list accessing problem and compared MTF, TRANS, and FC to S-OPT (the static optimal offline algorithm). They showed that MTF is "2-competitive" with respect to S-OPT. They also showed that FC shares this property as well. Surprisingly, TRANS is not competitive in this respect and therefore not competitive at all (see also Section 1.5).

Bentley and McGeoch's results motivated Sleator and Tarjan to propose competitive analysis as a general approach. In their seminal paper [318], Sleator and Tarjan showed that $\text{MTF}(\sigma) \leq 2 \cdot \text{OPT}(\sigma)$ for the dynamic list model (see Section 1.2.1). Karp and Raghavan (reported in Irani [195]) proved a lower bound of $2 - \frac{2}{\ell+1}$ on the competitive ratio of any deterministic algorithm for the static model. Irani [195] gave a matching upper bound for MTF, showing that MTF is the optimal online algorithm judged from the competitive analysis perspective. For several years, MTF was the only algorithm known to be 2-competitive, until Albers [4] introduced the $\left(2 - \frac{1}{\ell}\right)$-competitive algorithm TIMESTAMP. Recently, El-Yaniv [139] presented an infinite family of algorithms, all of which are $\left(2 - \frac{1}{\ell}\right)$-competitive. This family contains TIMESTAMP, and the limit member of this family is MTF.

Proof Techniques. The potential function technique of Section 1.4 was first suggested by D. Sleator (see Tarjan [325]) and explicitly used in competitive analysis by Sleator and Tarjan [318] (see also Sleator and Tarjan [319] and Cormen, Leiserson, and Rivest [116], Chap. 18). The factoring technique of Section 1.6 was first used by Bentley and McGeoch [58]. It was then extended and improved first by Irani [194] and Teia [326] and then by Albers [4] and Albers, von Stengel, and Werchner [8], who also introduced the phase partitioning technique of Section 1.6.1.

Other Problem Variants. In addition to the static, dynamic, and partial and full cost variants of the list accessing problem studied in this chapter, there are other variants. In the **paid exchange model** (defined in Sleator and Tarjan [318]), there are no free exchanges (all exchanges cost 1). The **Δ-paid exchange model** is the paid exchange model, but exchanges cost Δ each (with Δ typically greater than 1, the link traversal cost).

Several results concerning the Δ-paid exchange model are given in Reingold, Westbrook, and Sleator [291] and in Irani, Reingold, Westbrook, and Sleator [199]. In particular, a deterministic algorithm that is 5-competitive and a lower bound of 3 is given for deterministic and randomized algorithms (against adaptive adversaries). Recently, Westbrook presented a deterministic online algorithm for the Δ-paid exchange model that achieves a competitive ratio of $\frac{5+\sqrt{17}}{2} \approx 4.56$ (reported in Albers and Westbrook [9]).

A parallel computation version of the (static) list update problem is studied in Luccio and Pedrotti [250]. They analyze the competitive ratio for accessing N lists by an N-processor EREW–PRAM parallel computer.

The Optimal Offline Algorithm. Quite a few of the competitive analyses of the list accessing problem were carried out without any specific knowledge of the nature of the optimal offline algorithm (e.g., Theorem 1.1). To date there is no known polynomial (in ℓ, the length of the list) time algorithm for OPT, and the best-known optimal offline algorithm, due to Reingold and Westbrook [290], requires $O(n2^\ell(\ell-1)!)$ time and $O(\ell!)$ space, where n is the number of requests and ℓ is an upper bound on the length of the list. This is an improvement over the $O(n(\ell!)^2)$ time (and $O(\ell!)$ space) bounds via an application of a straightforward dynamic programming algorithm for metrical task systems (see Chapter 9).

List Accessing and Compression. From a practical point of view, the list accessing problem and online algorithms for maintaining the list are of considerable importance. For the implementation of small-size dictionaries, linked lists are often the data structure of choice. An additional important application of online algorithms for list accessing is as an "engine" for data compression. The application, introduced in Bentley, Sleator, Tarjan, and Wei [59] is as follows: suppose that a transmitter wants to send a (compressed) message to a receiver. Each word of the message is an element of some set (dictionary). Both the transmitter and the receiver maintain a list containing all the words in the dictionary. Initially both lists are in the same order. Also, they both agree upon some (deterministic) list accessing algorithm. When the transmitter wants to send a word, he sends, instead of the word, the current position of the word in his list, which is encoded using some variable-length prefix-free binary encoding. The receiver can decode the word, since he maintains the same list. After each word is transmitted, both the transmitter and receiver use the list accessing algorithm to reorganize their lists. This basic compression scheme has many variations. For example, there is no need to have an initial list containing all possible words; the dynamic list model can be used. Both the transmitter and receiver start with empty lists, and whenever there is an insertion of a new word, the transmitter sends both the word and a symbol indicating that this is an insertion. Bentley et al. showed that if the words are independent observations of a probability distribution D and the engine of this compression scheme is MTF, then the expected number of bits needed to encode a word is linear in the entropy of D. According to Shannon's source coding theorem, this is optimal up to a constant factor. Compared to Huffman coding, it is empirically shown that this scheme is sometimes much better but never much worse. Recently, Albers and Mitzenmacher [6] studied the performance of this compression scheme using the algorithm TIMESTAMP, due to Albers [4]. They proved that TIMESTAMP is better than MTF with respect to a random source and showed empirically that it compresses better than MTF on standard corpus files. However, further empirical tests by Bachrach and El-Yaniv [36] showed that the compression achieved by straightforward applications of the scheme introduced by Bentley et al. is not competitive with some of the better compression tools (such as the Lempel–Ziv-based tool `gzip`). These tests considered most of the known list accessing algorithms and many variable-length binary encoding schemes.

Several other ideas implement the compression scheme of Bentley et al. in combination with other methods. The most impressive example is that of Burrows and Wheeler [87], who applied the MTF-based compression method not on the string itself but to a special transformation of this string (which results in a string that exhibits much higher locality of reference). Using this combined method, Burrows and Wheeler report an improvement of 6% over `gzip`. Another interesting variant of the basic scheme is offered by Grinberg, Rajagopalan, Venkatesan, and Wei [177].

Credit for Exercises. Exercise 1.4 is due to Sleator and Tarjan [318]. Exercise 1.5 is due to Westbrook (personal communication). Exercises 1.1 and 1.2 are due to Reingold and Westbrook [290]. Exercise 1.11 is due to Irani [195]. Exercise 1.12 is due to Albers, von Stengel, and Werchner [8]. Exercise 1.13 is due to Albers [4].

1.7.1   Open Questions

1.1 (*Value = l5/T3*) Consider data structures other than the linked list. An obvious one to study is a binary search tree. However, here the analogue to MTF, MOVE-TO-ROOT, is not uniquely defined (does it approach a linked list quickly?), and for any versions considered so far, none of the analogies seem to perform well. (See Bitner [68, 69] and Allen and Munro [11] for some stochastic results concerning MOVE-TO-ROOT.) Sleator and Tarjan [319] introduce the splay-tree heuristic and show that splay trees attain an optimal "competitive ratio" relative to a *static* optimal offline algorithm (such as S-OPT of page 358), but leave open the splay-tree conjecture: "Are splay trees within a constant factor of the best (dynamic) offline optimal?" Also, no lower bound is known for this problem.

1.2 (*Value = l4/T3*) Consider data structures for other ADTs, such as priority queues.

1.3 (*Value = l4/T4*) Given an ADT, does there exist an intrinsic competitive ratio ρ for the ADT? That is, for any implementation (i.e., data structure) of the ADT, the competitive ratio is at least ρ, and ρ can be realized (at least, in the limit) by some implementation.

1.4 (*Value = l2/T4*) Improve the bounds known for the Δ-paid exchange model (see page 20).

1.5 (*Value = l4/T4*) Is there an efficient (polynomial in n and ℓ) offline strategy for static list accessing? As mentioned on page 21, so far the best-known optimal offline algorithm requires $O(n2^{\ell}(\ell - 1)!)$ time (see Reingold and Westbrook [290]).

CHAPTER 2

Introduction to Randomized Algorithms: The List Accessing Problem

For the static list accessing problem, we know that the optimal deterministic competitive ratio is exactly $2 - \frac{2}{\ell+1}$, where ℓ is the length of the list (see Theorem 1.2 and Exercise 1.11). Can randomization be used to improve upon this bound?

We introduce the concept of randomized online algorithms and extend the definition of the competitive ratio appropriately. We begin our study of randomized algorithms in the context of list accessing.

2.1 The Competitive Ratio of Randomized Algorithms

If we allow the online player to use randomness, smaller competitive ratios are attainable for the list accessing problem. The introduction of randomness to our game is natural and well motivated, given the important role of randomization in game theory (see Chapter 6) and approximation algorithms. We now define the online game and the competitive ratio for randomized algorithms. The question of how much power the adversary has in terms of information about the online algorithm's random choices introduces some subtlety to the definitions. In this section we present only one type of randomized model corresponding to an "oblivious adversary." In Chapter 4 we introduce other types of adversaries, and in Chapter 7 we give an in-depth treatment of all these adversary models.

Let ALG be a randomized online algorithm. Based on the knowledge of ALG – in particular, the probability distribution(s) ALG uses – the oblivious adversary must choose a finite request sequence σ in advance. ALG is **c-competitive against an oblivious adversary** if for every such σ,

$$\mathbf{E}[\text{ALG}(\sigma)] \leq c \cdot \text{OPT}(\sigma) + \alpha,$$

where α is a constant independent of σ, and $\mathbf{E}[\cdot]$ is the mathematical expectation operator taken with respect to the random choices made by ALG.[1] Since the offline player does not have information about the outcomes of the random choices made by the online player,

---

[1] Intuitively, we have defined the randomized competitive ratio as a ratio of expectations. This has been considered the "standard" definition. It is also reasonable to consider defining the randomized competitive ratio as an expectation of the online to optimal offline ratio; further comments on this issue can be found in Chapters 6, 7, and 8.

OPT(σ) is not a random variable; consequently, there is no need to take its expectation. As is true for deterministic algorithms, the infimum c, such that ALG is c-competitive against an oblivious adversary, is called ALG's expected competitive ratio against an oblivious adversary. We write $\overline{\mathcal{R}}(\text{ALG}) = c$.

2.2   Algorithm BIT

Consider the following simple randomized algorithm for static list accessing called BIT, due to Reingold and Westbrook [289]. For each element x on the list, BIT maintains one mod-2 counter, $b(x)$.

> **Algorithm BIT:** For each element x on the list, randomly initialize its bit $b(x)$ independently and uniformly. When a request to access an element x is given, first complement its bit $b(x)$. Then, if $b(x) = 1$, move x to the front; otherwise ($b(x) = 0$) do nothing.

One striking feature of BIT is that it is **barely random**. That is, it uses a fixed (ℓ) number of random bits to serve request sequences of arbitrary length. Since algorithm BIT tosses coins only before its action, it can be viewed as a probability distribution over deterministic algorithms. Specifically, BIT randomly chooses one deterministic algorithm from a set of 2^ℓ algorithms. Borrowing from game theory terminology, we call such an algorithm a "mixed algorithm." This is in contrast to a "behavioral algorithm" that uses random coins throughout the course of its action.[2]

The proof of the following theorem, showing that $\overline{\mathcal{R}}(\text{BIT}) \leq \frac{7}{4}$, is similar to the proof of Theorem 1.1 and uses the potential function technique via the amortized cost style (see Section 1.4).

Theorem 2.1 *Let σ be a request sequence of n accesses. Then*

$$\mathbf{E}[\text{BIT}(\sigma)] \leq \frac{7}{4} \cdot \text{OPT}(\sigma) - \frac{3n}{4}.$$

PROOF. First notice that anytime during the game, each bit $b(x)$ is uniformly (and independently) distributed in $\{0, 1\}$. This is true, since the bit $b(x)$ is initially chosen independently and uniformly and the value of $b(x)$ at any stage of the game is simply the number (mod 2) of accesses to x so far. However, the initial random choice for $b(x)$ is kept secret from the adversary. This observation is used throughout the proof without explicit mention.

Fix a request sequence σ. Imagine that BIT and OPT are processing each request in σ in interleaving order (say, first BIT and then OPT). This order defines a sequence of events, defined in terms of the operations of both algorithms on their respective lists. As with the analysis in Theorem 1.1, we consider two simple kinds of events. One kind is an event in which OPT performs a paid exchange. The second kind is an event that includes all other operations performed by either BIT or OPT to serve an access request.

With respect to the partition into events, we denote by Φ_i the value of the potential function (yet to be defined) immediately after the ith event.

---

[2] See Chapter 6, where the relationship between mixed and behavioral algorithms is discussed.

Define the amortized cost for BIT with respect to the ith event as $a_i = \text{BIT}_i + \Phi_i - \Phi_{i-1}$, where BIT_i is the actual cost incurred by BIT during the ith event. Clearly,

$$\text{BIT}(\sigma) = \sum_i \text{BIT}_i = \Phi_0 - \Phi_{\text{last}} + \sum_i a_i,$$

where Φ_{last} is the value of Φ after the last event. Since BIT is randomized, a_i is a random variable. By linearity of expectation the proof will be complete once we prove that the following two conditions hold: (i) for each event i,

$$\mathbf{E}[a_i] \le \frac{7}{4} \cdot \text{OPT}_i, \tag{2.1}$$

where OPT_i is the cost incurred by OPT during the ith event; and (ii) Φ_{last} is bounded below.

Similar to the potential function used in the proof of Theorem 1.1, the potential function we use here counts the number of inversions between BIT and OPT's lists. We again define an inversion as an *ordered* pair of items $\langle x, y \rangle$ such that x precedes y on BIT's list and y precedes x on OPT's list. We define $w(x, y)$, the weight of the inversion $\langle x, y \rangle$, as the number of accesses to y before y passes x in BIT's list. Since y passes x by moving to the front, by the definition of $b(y)$, $w(x, y) = b(y) + 1$. Define the potential Φ as

$$\Phi = \sum_{\text{inversions } \langle x, y \rangle} w(x, y).$$

Clearly, Φ is nonnegative so Φ_{last} is bounded below. In the particular case in which BIT and OPT start with the same list organization, $\Phi_0 = 0$. Otherwise, we may need some positive additive constant.

First consider what happens when the ith event is a paid exchange by OPT. By definition, $\text{OPT}_i = 1$, and this action does not influence the BIT_i-component of the amortized cost a_i. In the worst case, this transposition creates a new inversion. The probability that the new inversion is of either weight (1 or 2) is $\frac{1}{2}$. Hence,

$$\mathbf{E}[a_i] = \frac{1}{2}(2 + 1) \le \frac{3}{2} \cdot \text{OPT}_i.$$

The more demanding part of the proof concerns the case in which the ith event is an access to y (by either BIT or OPT). Suppose that just before the access, y is located at position k in OPT's list; that is, $\text{OPT}_i = k$. (OPT may perform some additional paid exchanges, but those operations are not included in this event.) Let I be a random variable counting the number of inversions $\langle x, y \rangle$ of either weight. As in Theorem 1.1, we see that y is located in BIT's list at most at location $k + I$. In other words, $\text{BIT}_i \le k + I$.

The change in potential as a result of the ith event, $\Phi_i - \Phi_{i-1}$, is a random variable that depends on the free transpositions performed by BIT and OPT. To analyze the change, we express the change as $\Phi_i - \Phi_{i-1} = A + B + C$, where A, B, and C are random variables: A is the contribution of new inversions created, B is the (negative) contribution of old inversions removed, and C is the contribution of (old) inversions that remain but change weight.

We first consider B and C. If $b(y) = 1$ just before the access, y stays in place in BIT's list; however, since $b(y)$ is flipped to 0, each inversion $\langle x, y \rangle$ changes its weight from 2 to 1. Since y stays in place, BIT does not eliminate any old inversions. Furthermore, OPT's free transpositions will not eliminate any old inversions that are counted by I, but they may eliminate inversions of the form $\langle y, z \rangle$. Overall, in this case, $(b(y) = 1)$, $C = -I$ and $B \leq 0$.

If $b(y) = 0$ just before the access, then y is moved to the front in BIT's list. This move eliminates all inversions $\langle x, y \rangle$ that were of weight 1 prior to the access. Clearly, there are no old inversions that change weight. That is, $B = -I$ and $C = 0$. We learn that independent of the value of $b(y)$, $B + C \leq -I$. Therefore,

$$\mathbf{E}[a_i] = \mathbf{E}[\text{BIT}_i + A + B + C] \leq \mathbf{E}[k + I + A - I] = k + \mathbf{E}[A].$$

It remains to find the expected value of A, the contribution of new inversions created. Since either algorithm may move x forward using free transpositions, A depends on both BIT and OPT. Denote by $x_1, x_2, \ldots, x_{k-1}$ the items preceding x in OPT's list just before the access to y (recall that y is assumed to be in the kth location on OPT's list just before the access). A new inversion can be created only when, for some j, x_j also precedes y in BIT's list and one of either BIT or OPT (but not both) moves y in front of x_j. Suppose that OPT moves y forward to position k'. Let X_j ($j = 1, 2, \ldots, j-1$) be a random variable giving the contribution of the inversion $\langle y, x_j \rangle$ if it is created.

If $b(y) = 0$ just before the access, then $b(y)$ is flipped to 1 and y is moved to the front in BIT's list. In this case, a new inversion $\langle y, x_j \rangle$ of weight $b(x_j) + 1$ is created, where $j = 1, 2, \ldots, k'-1$. That is, for $1 \leq j < k'$, $X_j = b(x_j) + 1$, and for $k' \leq j \leq k-1$, $X_j = 0$.

On the other hand, if $b(y) = 1$ just before the move, then y is not moved and $b(y)$ is flipped to 0. This implies that $X_j = 0$ for $1 \leq j \leq k'-1$ and $X_j = 1$ for $k' < j \leq k-1$. To summarize,

$$\mathbf{E}[A] = \sum_{j=1}^{k-1} \mathbf{E}[X_j] \leq \sum_{j=1}^{k'-1} \frac{1}{2}\left(\frac{1}{2} \cdot 1 + \frac{1}{2} \cdot 2\right) + \sum_{j=k'}^{k-1} \frac{1}{2} \cdot 1 \leq \frac{3}{4}(k-1).$$

Therefore, the expected amortized cost of the ith event is no greater than $\frac{7k}{4} - \frac{3}{4}$. That is, $\mathbf{E}[a_i] \leq \frac{7}{4} \cdot \text{OPT}_i - \frac{3}{4}$.   ∎

Exercise 2.1 Consider the following modification to the BIT algorithm. Instead of always complementing $b(x)$ on every access of element x, complement $b(x)$ only if it is not at the front of the list. Show that this modified BIT algorithm is not $\frac{7}{4}$-competitive.

Exercise 2.2 Modify the BIT algorithm and the proof of Theorem 2.1 so that they also work for the dynamic list model.

Exercise 2.3 Use Theorem 2.1 to prove that $\overline{\mathcal{R}}(\text{BIT}) \leq \frac{7}{4} - \frac{3}{4\ell}$ for both the dynamic and static list models. As in Exercise 1.3, for dynamic lists ℓ is the maximum number of items present in the list at any point in time.

2.3 Algorithm RMTF: Barely Random Versus Random

Clearly, the reason algorithm BIT succeeds in obtaining a relatively low competitive ratio, and in particular, "breaking" the deterministic bound of 2, is because it uses randomness.

It is only more impressive that it achieves the 1.75 bound with a fixed number of random bits for arbitrarily long request sequences. Consider the following variation of BIT (and MTF), called RMTF (RANDOM-MTF).

> **Algorithm RMTF:** Upon a request for an item x, move x to the front with probability $\frac{1}{2}$.

Thus, algorithm RMTF is the behavioral analogue of the mixed algorithm BIT. At the outset, one may expect this algorithm to be at least as good as BIT. Indeed, algorithm BIT appears to be a "pseudo random" version of algorithm RMTF. Surprisingly, RMTF is no better than 2-competitive.

We now describe a nemesis request sequence showing that for any given ε, there exists sufficiently large list length ℓ such that $\overline{\mathcal{R}}(\text{RMTF}) > 2 - \varepsilon$. Let α and ε be given. Assume a list of $\ell = \ell(\varepsilon)$ elements initially organized as $\langle x_1, x_2, \ldots, x_\ell \rangle$ with x_1 at the front. Let k be some integer whose value will be determined, and consider the following request sequence σ:

$$\sigma = (x_\ell)^k, (x_{\ell-1})^k, \ldots, (x_1)^k.$$

For large k, with high probability, algorithm RMTF will move x_i to the front while RMTF services the segment $(x_i)^k$. On average, x_i is moved to the front at the second request. Hence, the expected cost for RMTF to serve σ is at least $2\ell^2 + 2\ell k - 2\ell$. On the other hand, $\text{MTF}(\sigma) = \ell(\ell + k - 1)$. Thus, for any $\delta > 0$, there exists sufficiently large k and $\ell \gg k$ so that

$$\Pr[\text{RMTF}(\sigma)/\text{MTF}(\sigma) > 2 - \varepsilon] > 1 - \delta.$$

To complete this lower bound, it remains to show how this procedure can be repeated sufficiently to outweigh any additive constant α (that may depend on ℓ). To be able to repeat the above procedure using the sequence σ, one must guarantee that RMTF returns to the initial configuration. For every k and ℓ, the probability that RMTF will not return to the initial configuration after serving σ is no larger than $p = \frac{\ell}{2^k}$, regardless of the particular starting configuration. It follows that the adversary can repeat the sequence σ so that the desired competitive ratio $2 - \varepsilon$ is obtained.

Exercise 2.4 Consider the following generalization of RMTF. For any real $p \in [0, 1]$, let RMTF$_p$ be the algorithm that, upon a request for an item x, moves x to the front with probability p. Generalize the above lower bound to RMTF$_p$ for each $p \in (0, 1)$.

Every competitive mixed (barely random) algorithm can be transformed into a behavioral algorithm with only a small increase in the competitive ratio. Specifically, we will restart the barely random algorithm periodically. If we restart the algorithm rarely enough, the competitive ratio of the resulting (behavioral) algorithm will not increase by much.

2.4 List Factoring–Phase Partitioning Revisited

We revisit the factoring and partitioning technique introduced in Section 1.6.1 for the analysis of randomized algorithms. We first use this approach to provide an alternative proof that $\overline{\mathcal{R}}(\text{BIT}) \leq \frac{7}{4}$. We then apply this approach in Section 2.5 to the analysis of an improved randomized algorithm called COMB. We first must explain what it means for a randomized list accessing algorithm to satisfy the pairwise property. Fix an input sequence σ and fix the random choices made by a randomized algorithm. We then obtain a deterministic execution of the algorithm. We say that a randomized algorithm satisfies the pairwise property if for every setting of the random choices, the pairwise property (1.5) holds.

Let L be BIT's list, and fix any request sequence σ. According to the factoring lemma (for the partial cost model), it is sufficient to prove that (i) BIT satisfies the pairwise property; and (ii) for any pair $\{x, y\} \subseteq L$,

$$\mathbf{E}[\text{BIT}^*(\sigma_{xy})] \leq \tfrac{7}{4} \cdot \text{OPT}^*(\sigma_{xy}). \tag{2.2}$$

Proving (i) is easy using the pairwise lemma. We can use an argument similar to the one used in Example 1.1 for MTF. It remains to prove (ii). Fix any pair $\{x, y\} \subseteq L$. We partition σ_{xy} into phases using the partitioning technique of Section 1.6.1, and prove that equation (2.2) holds with respect to each possible phase.

It is again sufficient to consider only phases of the first type. The calculation for phases of the second type can be done in exactly the same way, with x and y interchanged.

Table 2.1: Costs and cost ratios obtained by BIT and OPT for serving phases of the first type.

	BIT*	OPT*	max ratio, BIT*/OPT*
(a) $x^i yy$	$\tfrac{3}{2}$	1	$\tfrac{3}{2}$
(b) $x^i (yx)^k yy$	$\tfrac{3k}{2} + 1$	$k + 1$	$\tfrac{3}{2}$
(c) $x^i (yx)^k x$	$\tfrac{3k}{2} + \tfrac{1}{4}$	k	$\tfrac{7}{4}$

Table 2.1 specifies the costs and maximum cost ratios (online to offline) of BIT and OPT with respect to each of the three forms of phases of the first type. We now verify that the numbers in Table 2.1 are correct. We make use of the following two lemmas.

Lemma 2.1 *Suppose that x is initially in the front of BIT's list. Then after serving the sequence yx, with probability $\tfrac{3}{4}$, item x is at the front.*

Lemma 2.2 *Immediately after BIT serves the sequence yxy, with probability $\tfrac{3}{4}$, item y is at the front (independent of the initial order of x and y).*

Lemmas 2.1 and 2.2 can be easily verified (e.g., by using a simple case analysis). Their proofs are left as an exercise.

For BIT, the calculations of the costs specified in Table 2.1 are not difficult if Lemmas 2.1 and 2.2 are utilized. For example, we now calculate the expected cost incurred by BIT to serve form (c) phases. Serving the initial i requests of the sequence (c) costs BIT nothing (recall that we assume the partial cost model) because x is initially at the front (this is a phase of the first type). The first request for y costs 1, then, with probability $\tfrac{1}{2}$, BIT moves y to the front. Thus, the expected cost to serve the next request for x is $\tfrac{1}{2}$. According to Lemma 2.1 after serving this request, x is at the front with probability $\tfrac{3}{4}$. Hence, the next request for y costs on average $\frac{3}{4}$. As BIT has now finished serving yxy, we can apply Lemma 2.2. According to Lemma 2.2, y is in now at the front with probability $\frac{3}{4}$, and the following request for x costs $\frac{3}{4}$. We can continue applying Lemma 2.1 (or its "symmetric version," with x and y interchanged) and deduce that each pair of requests xy in the sequence $(yx)^k$ costs (on average) $\frac{3}{4} + \frac{3}{4} = \frac{3}{2}$. According to Lemma 2.2, after serving $x^i(yx)^k$, x is at the front with probability $\frac{3}{4}$; consequently, the last request for x costs on average $\frac{1}{4}$. Thus, the total expected cost for BIT to serve form (c) is $\frac{3k}{2} + \frac{1}{4}$. The expected costs corresponding to the rest of the forms can be calculated similarly.

We now verify the maximum cost ratios specified in Table 2.1. Phases of form (a) result in an expected cost ratio, online to offline, of $\frac{3}{2}$; phases of form (b), a ratio of $\frac{3k/2+1}{k+1}$, and phases of form (c), a ratio of $\frac{3k/2+1/4}{k}$. It is clear that the ratio corresponding to form (b) increases with k and that its limit, as k grows, approaches $\frac{3}{2}$. The ratio corresponding to form (c) decreases with k; for the minimum possible value of k, which is 1, it is exactly $\frac{7}{4}$.

Exercise 2.5 Prove Lemmas 2.1 and 2.2.

2.5   COMB: An 8/5-Competitive Algorithm

To date, the best-known randomized algorithm is COMB, a random combination of BIT and TIMESTAMP.[3] As such, COMB is also a barely random and mixed algorithm.

> **Algorithm COMB:** Given a request sequence σ, with probability $\frac{4}{5}$, use BIT to serve σ; with probability $\frac{1}{5}$, use TIMESTAMP.

Theorem 2.2 $\overline{\mathcal{R}}(\text{COMB}) = \frac{8}{5}$ in the static list accessing model.

PROOF. First, note that COMB satisfies the pairwise property. This follows from the fact that both BIT and TIMESTAMP satisfy this property. Hence, the factoring method can be applied. Using the analysis for BIT and TIMESTAMP and, in particular, Tables 1.1 and 2.1, we now use the phase partition technique and calculate the cost ratios, online to offline, for each of the three forms of phases of the first type. Here the online cost is a random variable, and in these ratios we use the expected cost incurred by COMB for each of the forms. Namely, for each form ϕ we take the mixture $\frac{4}{5} \cdot \text{BIT}^*(\phi) + \frac{1}{5} \cdot \text{TIMESTAMP}^*(\phi)$.

For phases of form (a), COMB pays on average $\frac{8}{5}$; for phases of form (b), $\frac{8}{5}k + \frac{4}{5}$; and for phases of form (c), $\frac{8}{5}k$. The respective costs for OPT are 1, $k+1$, and k. The ratios are all within a factor $\frac{8}{5}$ of the optimal offline cost. ∎

Exercise 2.6 Extend the result of Theorem 2.2 to the dynamic model.

2.6   Historical Notes and Open Questions

Although we chose to introduce randomized online algorithms in terms of the list accessing problem, we note that the first use of randomization and the demonstration of its advantage

---

[3] The deterministic algorithm TIMESTAMP is a particular instance of a general randomized algorithm called TIMESTAMP$_p$, which is randomized for all $p > 0$. TIMESTAMP$_{p'}$ is described in Section 2.6.

in the competitive analysis context was by Borodin, Linial, and Saks [82] with regard to *metrical task systems* (see also Chapter 9). The first example of a randomized list accessing algorithm (called SPLIT) attaining a competitive ratio smaller than the deterministic one for the static model was given by Irani⁴[195, 196] and Irani, Reingold, Westbrook, and Sleator [199]. The competitive ratio obtained is $\frac{15}{8} = 1.875$, independent of the length of the list. The elegant "BIT" algorithm of Reingold and Westbrook [289] (see also [199] and [291]) is shown to be $\frac{7}{4}$-competitive for the dynamic model (see Section 2.2). BIT is one member of the COUNTER family of randomized algorithms defined by Reingold, Westbrook, and Sleator [291]. Albers and Mitzenmacher [7] provide lower bounds for algorithms in this family and, in particular, provide a lower bound of 1.625 for BIT. They also show that there is a mixture of two COUNTER algorithms achieving a competitive ratio of $\frac{12}{7} \approx 1.714$, which is better than $\sqrt{3} \approx 1.732$, the best-known upper bound for a single COUNTER algorithm.

For several years the best-known randomized algorithm (against an oblivious adversary) was a member of the family of algorithms RANDOM-RESET$_{(s,D)}$ due to Reingold, Westbrook, and Sleator [291]. Let s be a positive integer and D, a probability distribution on the set $S = \{0, 1, \ldots, s-1\}$ such that for $i \in S$, $D(i)$ is the probability of i.

Algorithm RST$_{(s,D)}$**:** For each item x on the list, maintain a counter $c(x)$, initially set randomly to a number $i \in \{0, 1, \ldots, s-1\}$ with probability $D(i)$. Upon a request for an item x, decrement $c(x)$ by 1. If $c(x) = 0$, then move x to the front and randomly reset $c(x)$ using D.

The best RST$_{(s,D)}$ algorithm, in terms of competitive ratio, is obtained with $s = 3$ and D such that $D(2) = \frac{\sqrt{3}-1}{2}$ and $D(1) = \frac{3-\sqrt{3}}{2}$. The competitive ratio attained in this case is $\sqrt{3} \approx 1.732$. Garefalakis [166] defined and analyzed a general class of Markov chain algorithms that contains RMTF, all COUNTER algorithms including BIT, and all RST algorithms. Garefalakis derived upper and lower bounds for algorithms in this class in terms of hitting times of the corresponding Markov chains. Using this analysis, it follows that RMTF is 2-competitive, matching the lower bound in Section 2.3, which is due to Reingold and Westbrook (personal communication).

In 1995, Albers presented a new family of randomized algorithms. This family is called TIMESTAMP$_p$, with p being a real in [0, 1]. Albers proved that TIMESTAMP$_p$ is c-competitive where $c = \max\{2 - p, 1 + p(2 - p)\}$. It follows that with $p = \frac{3-\sqrt{5}}{2}$, TIMESTAMP$_p$ is ϕ-competitive where ϕ is the Golden Ratio, $\phi = \frac{1}{2}(1 + \sqrt{5}) \approx 1.618$.

Continuing Albers's work, Albers, von Stengel, and Werchner [8] invented the randomized algorithm COMB, and proved that it is 1.6-competitive. To date, COMB is the most competitive algorithm for the list accessing problem.

With regard to the history of lower bound results for randomized list accessing, Raghavan and Karp first proved a lower bound of $\frac{9}{8}$ for any algorithm against an oblivious adversary (reported in Irani [195]). Using a similar technique, Reingold and Westbrook [289], and independently Chrobak and Larmore (reported in Irani [195]), obtained a lower bound of approximately 1.27. Finally, Teia [326] proved a lower bound of $\frac{3}{2} - \frac{5}{\ell+5}$ for any randomized algorithms against oblivious adversaries for the static list accessing model.

Credit for Exercises. Exercise 2.2 is due to Reingold and Westbrook [289]. Exercises 2.1 and 2.4 are also due to Reingold and Westbrook (personal communication). Exercise 2.5 is due to Albers, von Stengel, and Wercher [8].

2.6.1 Open Questions

2.1 (*Value = I4/T3*) Close or diminish the gap of [1.5, 1.6] in the competitive ratio for randomized list accessing algorithms against an oblivious adversary.

2.2 (*Value = I3/T4*) Determine the competitive ratio of RMTF$_p$ for each $p \in (0, 1)$. Is any RMTF$_p$ better than 2-competitive for arbitrary-size lists?

2.3 (*Value = I3/T4*) Close or diminish the gap of [1.625, 1.75] in the competitive ratio for the BIT algorithm.

CHAPTER 3

Paging: Deterministic Algorithms

Consider the following two-level **virtual memory system**. Each level can store a number of fixed-size memory units (or "slots") called **pages**. The first level, called the **slow memory**, stores a fixed set $P = \{p_1, p_2, \ldots, p_N\}$ of N pages. The second level, called the **fast memory**, can store any k-subset of P where $k < N$. Given a request for a page p_i, the system must make page p_i available in the fast memory. If p_i is already in the fast memory (called a **hit**), the system need not do anything. Otherwise (on a **miss**), the system incurs one **page fault** and must copy the page p_i from the slow memory to one of the locations in the fast memory. In doing so, the system is faced with the problem of which page to evict from the fast memory to make space for p_i. In order to minimize the number of page faults, the choice of which page to evict must be made wisely.

Typically for paging, the random access memory (RAM) is the fast memory and the disk constitutes the slow memory. For **caching** (where a page is typically called a block), the cache is the fast memory and the RAM now becomes the slow memory. Caching algorithms often use a set associative organization where the placement algorithm (usually a simple mod function) maps a block to a set of blocks in the cache. If the size of a set is k, then the cache is said to be k-way associative. We disregard the direct mapping aspect of blocks to sets and view a cache as a disjoint collection of fully associative caches. For simplicity (but at the risk of mixing terminology), we will also refer to the fast memory in the paging problem as the cache, since our abstract model does not distinguish between caching and paging. However, we should note that there are many ways in which paging and caching differ. Some factors that distinguish between paging and caching are the typical size of a page versus that of a block, the absolute and relative number of slow and fast memory pages, and the degree of software versus hardware implementation. The abstract cost model presented above is called the **page fault model**; that is, we charge 1 to bring a page into the fast memory and 0 for reading from or writing to a page in the fast memory. This cost model does not address any of these factors. Moreover, the page fault model does not address the fact that access to a fast memory page is not completely free of charge. A more accurate model should make explicit the ratio between the time for a fast memory access and the time to fetch a page from the slow memory into the fast memory. In the **full access cost model,** we charge 1 for each access to the fast memory and s to move a page from slow to fast memory. Equivalently, a move from slow to fast memory can cost 1, and an access of fast memory then costs $1/s$; thus, it is clear that the page fault model is the limiting case as s approaches infinity. Thus, the full access cost model is parameterized by the ratio s as well as by k, the number of fast memory pages. Typically, the number of slow memory pages, N, is very large or even considered infinite; hence, N is usually not considered a relevant parameter. We naturally view paging as an online problem, which means that the decision of how to service the next request for a page can depend only on previous requests. For pure competitive analysis, we make no assumptions concerning the nature of future requests. In this chapter, we focus only on the competitive analysis of deterministic paging algorithms, leaving randomized algorithms and more recent work concerning refinements of competitive analysis to Chapters 4 and 5.

The paging problem is a well-understood online problem from the competitive analysis perspective in the sense that optimal deterministic and randomized algorithms are known. However, as we will see, competitive analysis results obtained for paging are not entirely satisfactory, since they do not provide adequate theoretical explanation for empirical findings. Thus, the results on paging indicate a fundamental weakness of pure competitive analysis. Nevertheless, as shown in Chapters 4 and 5, the competitive analysis of deterministic paging algorithms serves as a basis for stronger results on paging algorithms. In addition, techniques developed for competitive paging analysis are useful in the study of the more abstract (and much more general) k-server problem (see Chapter 10).

3.1 Some Paging Algorithms

Because of its important role in the performance of almost every computer system, the paging problem has been extensively studied since the 1960s. A large variety of page replacement algorithms and variations can be found in existing computer systems. Perhaps the most basic and well-known deterministic algorithms are the following:

- **LRU** (LEAST-RECENTLY-USED): When eviction is necessary, replace the page whose most recent request was earliest.
- **CLOCK** (CLOCK-REPLACEMENT): An approximation to LRU in which a single "use bit" replaces the implicit (time of last access) timestamp of LRU.[1]
- **FIFO** (FIRST-IN/FIRST-OUT): Replace the page that has been in the fast memory longest.
- **LIFO** (LAST-IN/FIRST-OUT): Replace the page most recently moved to the fast memory.
- **LFU** (LEAST-FREQUENTLY-USED): Replace the page that has been requested the least since entering the fast memory.
- **LFD** (LONGEST-FORWARD-DISTANCE): Replace the page whose next request is latest.

LFD is an offline algorithm; it requires full knowledge of future requests. All other algorithms are online. Also, all algorithms are **demand paging**, which means that unless there is a page fault, they never evict a page from the cache. In general, the following is true:

Exercise 3.1 Prove that any page replacement algorithm (online or offline) can be modified to be demand paging without increasing the overall cost on any request sequence.

---

[1] More specifically, CLOCK maintains the addresses of the fast memory pages in a circular queue. There is a counter that points to the last page brought into the fast memory. Whenever a page is accessed, its use bit is set to 1. Upon a page fault, the counter is incremented and the algorithm seeks a page whose use bit is unset; in doing so, it unsets the use bit for each page considered.

It is interesting to compare these page replacement algorithms in terms of their resource requirements (i.e., space and time). These different algorithms can require substantially different resource costs in order to maintain their "internal control." Assume that the fast memory (that is, the page "table") is implemented by an array A of k memory cells where $A[i]$ records the slow memory address of the page presently occupying the ith slot of the fast memory. It is reasonable to assume that when a page is placed in slot i of the fast memory, it stays there until it is evicted. We assume that this array (which corresponds to the configuration of the algorithm as discussed in Section 1.4) is not counted as part of the internal control memory (see further discussion of this issue in Section 6.4.1). In addition to its page table, LRU must maintain a sorted list of pages (sorted with respect to the implicit "timestamp" of the most recent access to each page), this requires at least $k \log k$ bits of additional memory to encode $k!$ states. If this sorted list is implemented by a doubly linked list, then this list can be reordered in constant time following each page request. Such an implementation is quite time consuming if only done in software and difficult to implement in hardware, so that existing paging systems often utilize approximations to LRU such as CLOCK. On the other hand, set associative cache systems usually have a very small degree of associativity, where typically $k = 2, 4$, or at most 8 (called a 2-way, 4-way, or 8-way cache, respectively). For such a small k, algorithm LRU becomes feasible. Algorithms CLOCK and FIFO can be implemented using a single mod k counter pointing to the page table when viewed as a circular queue. Therefore, FIFO uses only $\log k$ bits of additional memory and constant time to update the queue after each page fault. Algorithm CLOCK uses the same $\log k$ bits for the counter plus k use bits and, in the worst case, time proportional to k to find the page to evict.

Exercise 3.2 What are the space and time requirements of LIFO, LFU, and LFD?

3.2 The (h, k)-Paging Problem

A natural generalization of the paging problem is the following. Let k and h be positive integers satisfying $h \leq k$. In the (h, k)-**paging problem,** we measure the performance of an online paging algorithm with a cache of size k relative to an optimal offline paging algorithm with cache of size $h \leq k$. That is, if $h < k$, we provide the optimal offline algorithm with strictly less resources. In fact, some natural algorithms (such as algorithm FIFO, presented later) incur what is known as **Belady's anomaly**; namely, on some input sequences the algorithm may perform better when it has a smaller fast memory. It is easy to see that an optimal algorithm does not incur Belady's anomaly (since it does not need to use all its cache pages). It is also the case that LRU does not incur the anomaly, but the anomaly does warn us that paging results can be subtle.

Exercise 3.3 Show that LRU does not incur Belady's anomaly but that FIFO does incur the anomaly.

Why is this (h, k)-paging generalization interesting? Although at first glance it seems "unfair" to reduce the power of the offline player, we should keep in mind that in competitive analysis, we give the offline player unrealistic powers. By parameterizing the size of the optimal offline cache separately, we can measure the strength of online paging algorithms against weaker adversaries where the power of the adversary is quantitatively controlled.

3.3   List Accessing Algorithms as Paging Algorithms

Every list accessing algorithm also gives rise to a paging algorithm. Consider any list algorithm ALG maintaining a list of k elements in the following manner. In the case of an access for an item x, if x is in the list, then ALG updates the list as usual; otherwise, delete the last item in the list and insert x in the position prescribed by ALG. Viewing the list as a fast memory, we immediately obtain a paging algorithm. Note, however, that the cost models for list accessing and paging are different and it is not clear if there is a relationship between the competitive ratio of a list accessing algorithm and the competitive ratio of its derived paging algorithm.

Using this paradigm, it is clear that MTF becomes LRU and FC becomes LFU. FIFO is derived from the list accessing algorithm that inserts a new element in the front of the list but does no rearrangements at all for accesses of items already in the list.

There is no apparent converse to this observation. That is, it is not clear how to interpret any paging algorithm as a dynamic or even static list accessing algorithm.

3.4   LFD – An Optimal Offline Paging Algorithm

Here we prove that algorithm LFD is an optimal offline algorithm for paging. This means that for paging, OPT has a very concise description that is efficient to compute. One implementation of LFD requires $O(k \cdot |\sigma|)$ steps for a request sequence σ. This is in contrast to many other online problems for which either it is known that the offline OPT problem is NP-hard (for example, the bin packing problem of Section 12.5) or the only known algorithms for OPT are rather complicated and/or require high time complexity (for example, the list accessing problem of Chapter 1). Although we can in principle carry out competitive analysis without knowledge of a specific OPT algorithm, it is often the case that knowledge about the nature of OPT can simplify the analysis. This is, of course, precisely why the list factoring technique of Section 1.6 was so beneficial in the analysis of list accessing algorithms. Furthermore, it is often the case that we can develop competitive online algorithms by making online approximations to the offline optimal (or to an offline approximation algorithm). This is the case, for example, in the work function algorithms considered in Chapters 9 and 10 and, more to the point of LFD, in the the algorithm FAR considered in Chapter 5.

The optimality of LFD was proven by Belady [51]. Although Belady's result seems very intuitive (as the "natural" offline greedy algorithm), the proof does require some care (although it is similar to other greedy algorithm optimality results).

Theorem 3.1 LFD *is an optimal offline algorithm for paging.*

PROOF.   We show how any optimal offline paging algorithm can be modified to act like LFD without degrading its performance. The proof is based on the following claim.

Claim: Let ALG be any paging algorithm. Let σ be any request sequence. For any i, $i = 1, 2, \ldots, |\sigma|$, it is possible to construct an offline algorithm ALG_i that satisfies the following three properties: (i) ALG_i processes the first $i - 1$ requests exactly as ALG does; (ii) if the ith request results in a page fault, ALG_i

evicts from its fast memory the page with the "longest forward distance"; and
(iii) $\text{ALG}_i(\sigma) \le \text{ALG}(\sigma)$.

This claim, once established, proves the theorem by applying it $n = |\sigma|$ times, as
follows. Fix any request sequence σ. Starting with any optimal offline algorithm OPT, we
apply the claim with $i = 1$ to obtain OPT_1, then apply the claim to algorithm OPT_1 with
$i = 2$ to obtain OPT_2, and so on. Clearly, OPT_n acts identically to LFD with respect to σ.

It remains to prove the claim. Given ALG, we now construct algorithm ALG_i. For a set
of pages X and a page p, denote by $X + p$ the union of the set X with the singleton $\{p\}$.
Assume that immediately after processing the ith request the fast memories of ALG and
ALG_i contain the page sets $X + v$, $X + u$, respectively, where X is some set of $k - 1$
(common) pages and v and u are any pages. Without loss of generality, we assume that
$v \ne u$ (that is, the ith request resulted in a page fault). Until v is requested, in order to
serve the subsequent requests, ALG_i mimics ALG except for evicting u if ALG evicts v. This
is feasible, since after servicing any request in this fashion, the number of common pages
remains at least $k - 1$. Further, if at any time the number of common pages becomes k
(i.e., if ALG evicts v), ALG_i identifies with ALG from that point onward and the proof is
complete.

If v is eventually requested and ALG and ALG_i have not yet been identified, this will
incur a page fault to ALG_i but not to ALG. However, by the time v is requested, since it had
the longest forward distance when evicted, there must have been at least one request for
u after the ith page fault. The first such request incurs a page fault to ALG but not to ALG_i.
Thus, the total number of page faults for ALG_i after servicing v is equal to that for ALG.
Finally, in order to serve the request for v, ALG_i evicts u, and the two algorithms identify.
∎

3.5 Marking and Conservative Algorithms and the Competitiveness of LRU, CLOCK, FIFO, and FWF

In this section we show that LRU, CLOCK, and FIFO all attain the optimal competitive
ratio in the page fault model. Moreover, we show that a very naive algorithm called
FLUSH-WHEN-FULL, or FWF for short, also attains the optimal competitive ratio. FWF is
defined as follows:

Algorithm FWF: Whenever there is a page fault and there is no space left in the
cache, evict all pages currently in the cache (call this action a "flush").

Clearly, FWF is not a demand paging algorithm. It blatantly flushes its cache each time
the cache is full. However, FWF can be easily "upgraded" to be demand paging. Instead of
flushing the cache, it can simply mark all the flushed pages, and whenever there is new
page fault, it can accommodate the new page by evicting an arbitrary marked page. In fact,
any reasonable implementation of FWF must behave like that. Nevertheless, for the sequel
we use the definition of the naive (and wasteful) FWF as presented above.

We first define a general class of algorithms called "marking algorithms" and prove
that every marking algorithm attains a competitive ratio of $\frac{k}{k-h+1}$ for the (h, k)-paging
problem. In particular, this gives an upper bound of k for the basic paging problem (i.e.,

(k, k)-paging). With the exception of FIFO, it is easy to show that all the above algorithms are marking algorithms and, therefore, all these algorithms attain the $\frac{k}{k-h+1}$-competitive ratio. We then define "conservative algorithms", which provide a similar but different general class of algorithms (including FIFO) that achieve the same $\frac{k}{k-h+1}$-competitive ratio. This section concludes with a lower bound of k on the competitive ratio of any deterministic online paging algorithm. This lower bound can be generalized to the (h, k)-paging problem; therefore, all the above algorithms are optimal for (h, k)-paging. (The proof of the more general lower bound of $\frac{k}{k-h+1}$ is deferred to Chapter 10.)

3.5.1 Marking Algorithms

Consider a fast memory of size k. Fix any request sequence σ. We divide the request sequence into **phases** as follows: phase 0 is the empty sequence. For every $i \geq 1$, phase i is the maximal sequence following phase $i-1$ that contains at most k distinct page requests; that is, if it exists, phase $i+1$ begins on the request that constitutes the $(k+1)$st distinct page request since the start of the ith phase. Such a partition is called a k-**phase partition**. This partition is well defined and is independent of how any particular algorithm processes σ.

Let σ be any request sequence and consider its k-phase partition. Associate (implicitly in the analysis or explicitly in the algorithm) with each page of the slow memory a bit called its **mark**. For each page, when its mark bit is set we say that the page is **marked**; otherwise, it is **unmarked**. Suppose that at the beginning of each k-phase, we unmark all the pages currently in the fast memory. During a k-phase, we mark a page when it is first requested during the k-phase. A **marking algorithm** never evicts a marked page from its fast memory. We can consider FWF as the most elementary marking algorithm.

We now determine an upper bound on the competitiveness of any online marking algorithm. The proof of the theorem does not make use of any property of OPT (except that it is a paging algorithm with a cache of size h).

Theorem 3.2 *Let* ALG *be any marking algorithm with a cache of size k, and let* OPT *be any optimal offline algorithm with a cache of size $h \leq k$. Then* ALG *is $\frac{k}{k-h+1}$-competitive.*

PROOF. Fix any request sequence σ and consider its k-phase partition. We first claim that for any phase $i \geq 1$, a marking algorithm ALG incurs at most k page faults. This follows because there are k distinct page references in each phase (except for, possibly, the last phase, which may be incomplete and have less than k distinct page references). Once a page is accessed, it is marked and therefore cannot be evicted until the phase has been completed. Consequently, ALG cannot fault twice on the same page. For any $i \geq 1$, let q be the first request of phase i and consider the input sequence starting with the second request of phase i up to and including the first request of phase $i+1$ (assuming that phase $i+1$ exists). Algorithm OPT has $h-1$ pages not including q, and there are k requests in this sequence not counting q, so that OPT must incur at least $k-(h-1) = k-h+1$ faults to service this sequence of requests. If phase i is the last phase, then our argument shows only that OPT will pay at least $k'-h+1$, where k' is the number of distinct page requests during the last phase. We will ignore this cost to OPT.

During each phase, ALG faults at most k times, and for each phase except the last, we can charge OPT with at least $k - h + 1$ faults. Hence, we obtain that for every request sequence,

$$\text{ALG}(\sigma) \leq \frac{k}{k - h + 1} \cdot \text{OPT}(\sigma) + \alpha,$$

where $\alpha \leq k$ is the maximum number of page faults incurred by ALG during the last phase.

∎

Exercise 3.4 Let $h = k$ and assume that ALG and OPT initially have the same pages in their respective caches. Modify the proof of Theorem 3.2 to show that ALG is strictly k-competitive.

Lemma 3.1 LRU *is a marking algorithm.*

PROOF. Fix any request sequence σ and consider its k-phase partition. Suppose, by contradiction, that LRU is not a marking algorithm. Then LRU evicts a marked page x during some k-phase. Consider the first request for x during this k-phase. Immediately after this request for x is serviced, x is marked and is the *most* recently used page in the cache. At this time, LRU holds k distinct pages in its cache. In order for x to leave the cache, LRU must incur a page fault while x is the *least* recently used page. However, if this is the case, it must be that at least $k + 1$ different pages were requested during the k-phase. These are exactly the k pages including x after the first request to x, plus the page that swapped x out. Hence, this k-phase contains requests to at least $k + 1$ distinct pages, which contradicts the definition of a k-phase. Therefore, LRU must be a marking algorithm.

∎

Exercise 3.5 Prove that CLOCK and FWF are marking algorithms.

Note that CLOCK and FWF are explicit marking algorithms, whereas LRU is an implicit marking algorithm.

Using Theorem 3.2, Lemma 3.1, and Exercise 3.5, we obtain the following easy corollary.

Corollary 3.3 *Algorithms* LRU, CLOCK, *and* FWF *are* $\frac{k}{k-h+1}$*-competitive.*

Exercise 3.6 Let $h < k$ and assume that the initial cache of OPT is a subset of the initial cache of LRU. Show that LRU is not strictly $\frac{k}{k-h+1}$-competitive.[2] Hint: Consider $h = 2$ and $k = 3$.

Exercise 3.7 Show that algorithm FIFO is not a marking algorithm.

---

[2] Counting the number of page evictions is almost equivalent to counting the number of page faults. These are the same events for any demand paging algorithm once the cache is filled up. It is easy to show that for this "page eviction" cost model, the proof of Theorem 3.2 yields a strict $\frac{k}{k-h+1}$-competitive result if we assume that initially both ALG and OPT have empty caches.

3.5.2 Conservative Algorithms

We say that a paging algorithm ALG is **conservative** if it satisfies the following condition: *On any consecutive input subsequence containing k or fewer distinct page references,* ALG *will incur k or fewer page faults.*

The proof of the following result can be obtained by an easy modification of Theorem 3.2.

Theorem 3.4 *Let* ALG *be any online conservative paging algorithm with a cache of size k, and let* OPT *be any optimal offline algorithm with a cache of size $h \leq k$ that is initially a subset of the cache of* ALG. *Then* ALG *is $\frac{k}{k-h+1}$-competitive.*

Exercise 3.8 Prove that LRU, FIFO, and CLOCK are conservative algorithms.

Corollary 3.5 *Algorithm* FIFO *is $\frac{k}{k-h+1}$-competitive.*

Exercise 3.9 Show that FWF is not a conservative algorithm.

3.5.3 A Lower Bound

We now prove a lower bound of k on the competitive ratio of any deterministic paging algorithm. The proof relies on behavior of algorithm LFD but does not rely on its optimality.

Theorem 3.6 *Let* ALG *be any paging algorithm. Then $\mathcal{R}(\text{ALG}) \geq k$.*

For the proof of Theorem 3.6, we use the following simple lemma.

Lemma 3.2 *For any finite sequence σ of requests chosen from a set of $k + 1$ pages,* LFD$(\sigma) \leq \frac{|\sigma|}{k}$.

PROOF. Suppose that for servicing the ith request, r_i, LFD evicts the page p. By the definition of LFD, and since there are $k + 1$ pages in all, it must be that all the pages in the cache (except perhaps r_i) must be requested prior to the next request for p. Hence, LFD faults at most once every k requests. ∎

Proof of Theorem 3.6. Assume that there are $k+1$ pages, $p_1, \ldots, p_{k+1}$, in all. We prove that there is an arbitrarily long (and costly) request sequence σ for which $|\sigma| = \text{ALG}(\sigma) \geq k \cdot \text{OPT}(\sigma)$. Without loss of generality, assume that ALG initially holds $p_1, \ldots, p_k$ in its cache. We define a cruel request sequence σ inductively: $r_1 = p_{k+1}$, and r_{i+1} is defined to be the unique page not in ALG's cache just after servicing the request sequence $r_1, \ldots, r_i$. This sequence is well defined, since ALG is deterministic. Clearly, σ can be made arbitrarily long and ALG faults on each request. That is, on every finite sequence σ, ALG$(\sigma) = |\sigma|$. According to Lemma 3.2, the proof is complete. ∎

3.6 LIFO and LFU Are Not Competitive

It is not difficult to show that algorithms LIFO and LFU are not competitive (relative to an optimal offline algorithm with a fast memory of size k).

We consider LIFO first. Let $p_1, p_2, \ldots, p_{k+1}$ be the pages in the slow memory. Assume that LIFO initially holds the pages $p_1, \ldots, p_k$ in its cache. Consider the request sequence

$$\sigma = p_1, p_2, \ldots, p_k, p_{k+1}, p_k, p_{k+1}, p_k, p_{k+1}, \ldots.$$

Clearly, starting from the $(k + 1)$st request, LIFO will incur a page fault on every request whereas OPT will incur at most $k + 1$ faults in all.

We now prove that LFU is not competitive. Let ℓ be any positive integer, and consider the following request sequence:

$$\sigma = p_1^\ell, p_2^\ell, \ldots, p_{k-1}^\ell, (p_k, p_{k+1})^{\ell-1}.$$

Clearly, LFU will incur a page fault on every request just after the first $(k - 1)\ell$ requests. In contrast, OPT will incur only one page fault. Since ℓ can be made arbitrarily large, and this sequence can be repeated arbitrarily often, LFU is not competitive. For LIFO and LFU, we made use of only $k + 1$ pages in all.

3.7   The Full Access Cost Model

The page fault model we have been studying ignores the fact that accesses to fast memory pages are not completely free of cost. In the full access cost model, we charge 1 for an access to fast memory and $s \geq 1$ to move a page from slow to fast memory. The question is what is the most appropriate way to interpret and measure s. One simplistic interpretation is to define s in terms of the expected time to access one "word" of fast memory. For some paging environments (and this is highly dependent on many factors) $s = 10^5$ is a reasonable estimate. Another, perhaps more meaningful, interpretation is to measure s relative to the expected time a typical page is being accessed before an access to a different page is issued. That is, we replace a word access time by expected "page access" time. Of course, this concept of a page access is highly dependent on the application. In order to avoid this dependence, we might assume that the expected page access time is proportional to the page size. Using this interpretation it is reasonable to estimate $s \approx 10$. (See, e.g., Hennessy and Patterson [187].)

Does the full access cost model lead to significantly different results? Although the analysis is essentially the same, results for the full access cost model can differ significantly from results for the page fault model in two important ways. Unlike the page fault model, the full access model is capable of reflecting both the benefit of high "locality of reference" and the benefit of lookahead. The fact that lookahead cannot help in the page fault model follows simply because the adversary can repeat requests arbitrarily (see the discussion of this "deficiency" in Chapter 10). In the full access cost model, repeated consecutive requests clearly work in favor of the online algorithm.

In order to formalize and quantify the locality of reference in a request sequence, we introduce the following definition. Let σ be a request sequence and let $\sigma = \sigma_1, \sigma_2, \ldots, \sigma_p$ denote its k-phase partition; that is, σ has p phases. Define $L(\sigma) = \frac{|\sigma|}{p}$ to be the average length of a phase. Clearly, $L(\sigma) \geq k$, and "large" $L(\sigma)$ indicates that σ has high locality of reference. We have the following easy modification of Theorem 3.2.

Theorem 3.7 *Let* ALG *be any marking algorithm with a cache of size k and let σ be an arbitrary request sequence. Then $\frac{\text{ALG}(\sigma)}{\text{OPT}(\sigma)} \leq 1 + \frac{(k-1)s}{L(\sigma)+s}$ and $\mathcal{R}(\text{ALG}) \leq \frac{k(s+1)}{k+s}$.*

PROOF. Let $n = |\sigma|$ and let $p = \frac{n}{L(\sigma)} \le \frac{n}{k}$ denote the number of phases. Then $\text{ALG}(\sigma) \le n + kps$, since any marking algorithm faults at most k times per phase and every algorithm pays n for the cost of the cache accesses. Similarly, $\text{OPT}(\sigma) \ge n + ps$, since OPT faults at least once for every phase. Therefore,

$$\frac{\text{ALG}(\sigma)}{\text{OPT}(\sigma)} \le \frac{n + kps}{n + ps} = \frac{n + ksn/L(\sigma)}{n + sn/L(\sigma)} = \frac{L(\sigma) + ks}{L(\sigma) + s} = 1 + \frac{(k-1)s}{L(\sigma) + s}.$$

It follows that ALG is $\frac{k(s+1)}{k+s}$-competitive, since $L(\sigma) \ge k$, and the preceding ratio is then maximized when $L(\sigma) = k$.   ■

An easy modification of Theorem 3.6 yields a corresponding lower bound:

Theorem 3.8 $\mathcal{R}(\text{ALG}) \ge \frac{k(s+1)}{k+s}$.

Exercise 3.10 Prove Theorem 3.8.

Clearly, the smaller the value of s, the better the competitive ratio (e.g., for s = 1, the ratio is less than 2); however, as s increases, the ratio obviously approaches k – the ratio for the page fault model. Whatever the value of s, we can describe locality relative to s and then immediately see how high locality implies a small competitive ratio. The next observation is an immediate consequence of Theorem 3.7.

Corollary 3.9 *Let* $L(\sigma) = a \cdot s$ *for some parameter a. Then for any marking algorithm* ALG, $\frac{\text{ALG}(\sigma)}{\text{OPT}(\sigma)} \le 1 + \frac{k-1}{a+1}$.

3.8   Theory Versus Practice

In Section 3.5, we learned that all conservative and all marking algorithms are optimally competitive. Although this provides a nice unification of known results, it also exposes a serious question concerning the competitive analysis of paging algorithms.

Although at the outset FWF appears to be a poor algorithm, competitive analysis suggests that FWF is not inferior to LRU, FIFO and CLOCK. However, from a practical viewpoint, FWF is indeed inferior. It is well known among practitioners that LRU performs substantially better in practice than both FIFO and FWF. Moreover, there are experimental results suggesting that in practice, the "empirical competitive ratio" of LRU (and also that of FIFO) is a small constant independent of the cache size (for sufficiently large cache sizes). In contrast, the (theoretical) competitive ratio is an increasing function of the cache size. Consider Figure 3.1, which summarizes the results of such experimental evidence.[3] The figure graphs the "competitiveness" of various paging algorithms as a function of the cache size with respect to a particular input sequence consisting of 692,057 requests to 642 distinct pages of 1024 bytes each.[4] The sequence was generated by two "X windows" network processes, a "makefile" (program compilation), and a "disk copy" running concurrently. The requests include data reads and writes and instruction fetches. The algorithms presented in the graph are: LRU, FIFO, FWF, RAND (Section 4.2), MARK (Section 4.3), and OPT.

---

[3] The figure was reproduced by permission from Young [342].

[4] As attributed and described by Young [342], this input sequence was traced by Sites and Agarwal [317].

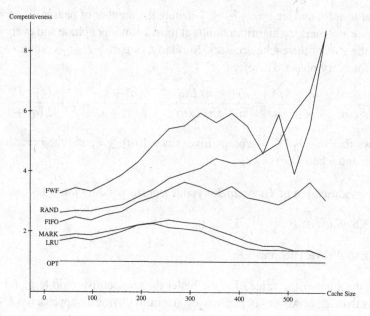

Figure 3.1: Empirical "competitiveness" of various paging algorithms.

These findings raise some critical questions: Why is there such discrepancy between the theoretical and empirical results? Is the competitive ratio an adequate performance measure for paging algorithms? What about other online problems? We are led to conclude that *pure* competitive analysis is too coarse to distinguish between some "good' and "not so good" deterministic paging algorithms and therefore that it is not an entirely satisfactory performance measure for paging. However, as suggested at the start of this chapter, there exist more refined versions of competitive analysis that do successfully distinguish between algorithms such as FIFO and LRU (see Chapter 5).

3.9   Historical Notes and Open Questions

The paging (or caching) problem models one important aspect (i.e., the page replacement strategy) of an optimization problem occurring in any hierarchy of memories constituting a virtual memory system.[5] Other essential aspects, such as page placement, page identification, write strategy (see [187]) and prefetching, have not been considered in this abstraction of the paging problem.

Prior to the publication of the Sleator–Tarjan paper [318], which was the first to analyze the competitive performance of paging algorithms, most of the work on paging algorithms was distributional.[6]

Sleator and Tarjan proved that LRU and FIFO are $\frac{k}{k-h+1}$-competitive for (h, k)-paging. They also proved a matching deterministic lower bound. The proof of the lower bound presented here (Theorem 3.6) is drawn from Goemans [172] and is different from the

---

[5] See, for example, Bic and Shaw [66], Denning [130], Hennessy and Patterson [187], and Peterson and Silberschatz [273].

[6] See, for example, Kuck and Lawrie [235], Shemer and Gupta [313], Coffman and Denning [112], Franaszek and Wagner [160], Spirn [321], and Denning [130].

original Sleator–Tarjan proof, which, in fact, gives a lower bound of $\frac{k}{k-h+1}$ for the more general (h, k)-paging problem. The proof here is simpler because it relies on a specific offline algorithm LFD. In Chapter 10 we prove the more general lower bound for (h, k)-paging in the context of the k-server problem. In addition, Sleator and Tarjan showed that LIFO and LFU are not competitive. Algorithm FWF, due to Karlin, Manasse, Rudolph, and Sleator [212], was proven by them to be optimal for deterministic (h, k)-paging. The definition of a conservative algorithm is due to Young [342], who observed that the $\frac{k}{k-h+1}$ upper bound applies to all conservative algorithms. Based on the definition of the (randomized) marking algorithm MARK by Fiat, Karp, Luby, McGeoch, Sleator, and Young (see Section 4.3), the general concept of a marking algorithm can be found in Borodin, Irani, Raghavan, and Schieber [80]. Following Young, Torng [328] explicitly observed that all marking algorithms are $\frac{k}{k-h+1}$-competitive. This fact is also implicit in the proof of optimality for FWF by Karlin et al. [212]. The results concerning the full cost model are due to Torng [328]. Motivated by applications such as paging in a multitasking environment, Web page caching, and so forth, other cost models for paging have been studied (e.g., see Feuerstein [149], Irani [197], and Young [346]).

The proof for LFU was suggested by an anonymous referee. The optimality of LFD is due to Belady [51]. The proof we use was provided by Achlioptas (personal communication). Belady's anomaly was first published in Belady, Nelson, and Shedler [52] (see also chap. 6 in Peterson and Silberschatz [273]).

The observation that every list accessing algorithm gives rise to a paging algorithm is due to Rivest [294].

3.9.1 Open Questions

3.1 (*Value = I2/T3*) Does there exist a ("natural") deterministic paging algorithm that is k-competitive for the standard (k, k)-paging problem but not $\frac{k}{k-h+1}$-competitive for the (h, k) problem with $h < k$?

3.2 (*Value = I2/T2*) All deterministic paging algorithms discussed in this chapter are either optimally competitive or not competitive at all. Is there a "natural" paging algorithm that is competitive but not optimal?

3.3 (*Value = I3/T2*) Does there exist a ("natural") deterministic paging algorithm that is k-competitive for $N = k + 1$ but not for larger N? (For randomized algorithms an analogous phenomenon does occur; see the discussion of algorithm MARK in Chapter 4.)

3.4 (*Value = I3/T2*) Consider a list accessing algorithm ALG and its derived paging algorithm ALG'. Is there a functional relation between $\mathcal{R}(\text{ALG})$ and $\mathcal{R}(\text{ALG}')$?

CHAPTER 4

Paging: Randomized Algorithms

The study of deterministic paging algorithms leads naturally to the question of whether (and how much) randomization can help in reducing the competitive ratio. As shown in Chapter 2, randomized list accessing algorithms proved to be somewhat superior to the optimal deterministic algorithms. In this chapter we present a more thorough study of competitive analysis of randomized online algorithms and define additional adversary models. In particular, we demonstrate how randomization can dramatically improve the competitive ratio for the paging problem. Also, we discuss concepts that are used in Chapter 7, where we introduce a general framework for online problems called request–answer games. Within the request-answer games framework, we will study the relative power of randomized online algorithms with respect to the various adversary models.

4.1 Randomized Competitive Analysis

When dealing with deterministic online algorithms, we have one "natural" model for the adversary. This adversary knows the online algorithm and chooses the worst input sequence in order to maximize the competitive ratio. This is no longer the case with randomized algorithms. The key issue that requires distinction between possible adversary models is the extent to which the adversary knows (and can exploit) the outcomes of the random choices made by the online player. Intuitively, it seems that by concealing such knowledge from the adversary, the online player can fool the adversary so that there is uncertainty as to what is the worst possible request sequence.

As in the deterministic case, we would like to measure the quality of a randomized online algorithm by a quantity similar to the competitive ratio. That is, we consider a game between an online player (algorithm) and an adversary that constructs the input sequence in order to maximize the ratio of the expected online cost to the "adversary cost." However, this adversary cost may have various forms depending on the exact nature of the adversary model.

4.1.1 Adversary Models

In Chapter 1 we introduced one type of adversary: the oblivious adversary. We now introduce two other types of adversaries. In all three types, we assume that the adversary knows the online algorithm (including, of course, the probability distributions used by the algorithm).

The first distinction is between **oblivious** and **adaptive** adversaries: at each time, an adaptive adversary knows all the actions taken by the online player for servicing the requests thus far. The adaptive adversary may choose the next request based on this knowledge. In contrast, an oblivious adversary must choose the entire request sequence in advance, without any knowledge of the actions taken by the online player. Oblivious adversaries are more "standard" in that they correspond to the adversaries that we use in the analysis of offline randomized algorithms. Adaptive adversaries can be motivated in several ways. First, we can envisage online problems where the actions of the online algorithm do influence future requests. For example, consider a paging algorithm being used by a real time application that reads the system clock to determine appropriate actions. A random choice by the paging algorithm will influence the timing and, consequently, the actions (including future page requests) of the real time application. Another motivation for studying adaptive adversaries is that in some cases it may be easy to design a randomized algorithm that is competitive against an adaptive adversary. Chapter 7 shows that such randomized algorithms can be used to derive competitive deterministic algorithms.

The oblivious "adversary cost" is measured exactly as in the deterministic case: via the optimal offline cost. Measuring the "adversary cost" of the adaptive adversary is a bit more subtle, and we make a further distinction between two types of adaptive adversaries. The first type is called **adaptive-offline**, and its "adversary cost" is, again, the optimal offline cost (on the request sequence that is created *online* by this adversary). There is also an intermediate type of adversary called **adaptive-online**, which is less powerful. This adversary must service each request it generates before the online player services the request; in a sense, then, the adaptive-online adversary is also performing in an online fashion except that it knows its own strategy for generating requests as well as the description of the online algorithm and all its actions taken thus far. To summarize, we consider the following three types of adversaries:

- OBL (oblivious): must construct the request sequence in advance and pays optimally.
- ADON (adaptive-online): serves the current request online and then chooses the next request based on the online algorithm's actions so far.
- ADOF (adaptive-offline): chooses the next request based on the online algorithm's actions thus far, but pays the optimal offline cost to service the resulting request sequence.

Having defined these three adversary types, we have yet to define the competitive ratio with respect to each adversary. In general, let ADV be any adversary (of type OBL, ADON, or ADOF). We say that the online algorithm ALG is c-competitive against ADV if there exists a constant α such that for all request sequences, σ,

$$\mathbf{E}\left[\mathrm{ALG}(\sigma) - c \cdot \mathrm{ADV}(\sigma)\right] \le \alpha. \tag{4.1}$$

Here the expectation is taken over the random choices made by ALG, and $\mathrm{ADV}(\sigma)$ is the adversary cost. As usual, α is referred to as the additive constant.

Both $\mathrm{OBL}(\sigma)$ and $\mathrm{ADOF}(\sigma)$ are exactly $\mathrm{OPT}(\sigma)$. That is, the "adversary cost" in the case of oblivious or adaptive-offline adversaries is exactly the optimal offline cost to serve σ. However, there is a fundamental difference between $\mathrm{OBL}(\sigma)$ and $\mathrm{ADOF}(\sigma)$. $\mathrm{OBL}(\sigma)$ is a fixed quantity, since the oblivious adversary constructs the request sequence independently of the random choices made by ALG. On the other hand, $\mathrm{ADOF}(\sigma)$ is a random variable, since the choice of σ depends on the random choices made by ALG. That is, σ is a random variable and, therefore, ADOF(σ) = OPT(σ) is a random variable as well.

In the case of an adaptive-online adversary, σ and therefore ADON(σ) are again, random variables. However, in this case, we do not have a concise characterization of the adversary cost (such as "the optimal offline cost").

To summarize, in the case of an oblivious adversary, the inequality defining the competitive ratio, equation (4.1), can be written as

$$\mathbf{E}\left[\text{ALG}(\sigma)\right] - c \cdot \text{OPT}(\sigma) \leq \alpha.$$

In the case of the adaptive-offline adversary, equation (4.1) can be written as

$$\mathbf{E}\left[\text{ALG}(\sigma) - c \cdot \text{OPT}(\sigma)\right] \leq \alpha.$$

Given any problem and a randomized online algorithm ALG for this problem, we define $\overline{\mathcal{R}}_{\text{ADV}}(\text{ALG})$, the competitiveness of ALG against an adversary of type ADV, as the infimum over all numbers c such that ALG is c-competitive against ADV. Whenever the type of the adversary ADV is clear, we may omit the subscript ADV from the functional $\overline{\mathcal{R}}$.

Exercise 4.1 Given a problem (such as list accessing or paging) and a randomized online algorithm ALG for this problem, informally prove[1] that

$$\overline{\mathcal{R}}_{\text{OBL}}(\text{ALG}) \leq \overline{\mathcal{R}}_{\text{ADON}}(\text{ALG}) \leq \overline{\mathcal{R}}_{\text{ADOF}}(\text{ALG}).$$

(This explains why the adversaries are sometimes referred to as the "weak," "medium," and "strong" adversaries, respectively.)

In light of Exercise 4.1, when we prove upper bounds on randomized competitive ratios, the stronger the adversary type, the stronger the result is. In contrast, when we prove lower bounds, the weaker the adversary, the stronger the result. For instance, a lower bound with respect to the oblivious adversary holds against adversaries of any type.

4.2   The Competitiveness of RANDOM

Having introduced the above adversary models, we return to the paging problem. In this section we analyze the performance of a very simple strategy called RANDOM (RAND, for short).

Algorithm RAND: Whenever a page fault occurs, evict a page chosen randomly and uniformly among all fast memory pages.

We shall prove a result, from Raghavan and Snir [284], stating that for the (h, k) paging problem,

$$\overline{\mathcal{R}}_{\text{ADON}}(\text{RAND}) = \frac{k}{k - h + 1}.$$

---

[1] Formally, we need a precise definition of an online problem, and relative to such a definition we need to define the various adversaries (see Chapter 7).

As we learned in Chapter 3, the (deterministic) competitiveness of algorithms LRU, FIFO and CLOCK is also $\frac{k}{k-h+1}$. What makes this result interesting is that algorithm RAND does not require any memory at all. In contrast, LRU requires $k \log k$ bits of memory, and FIFO, and CLOCK each require $\Omega (\log k)$ bits of memory. Instead of using memory, RAND uses $O(\log k)$ random bits per page fault. Thus, in some sense RAND trades memory for randomness.

From a practical point of view, the simplicity of algorithm RAND and the fact that it requires $O(1)$ time to serve each request and no memory at all make RAND an excellent candidate for practical implementations. From the competitive analysis viewpoint, RAND fairs well with the optimal deterministic paging algorithms.

Theorem 4.1 *Algorithm* RAND *is* $\frac{k}{k-h+1}$-*competitive against an adaptive-online adversary for the* (h, k)-*paging problem.*

PROOF. Set $c = \frac{k}{k-h+1}$ and let ADON be any adaptive-online adversary. The proof makes use of a potential function technique via the first style with amortized costs (see Section 1.4). The potential function we use measures the similarity between the caches maintained by algorithm RAND and the adversary. Define $\Phi_i = c(h - \phi_i)$, where ϕ_i, a function from cache configurations to the nonnegative integers, gives the number of pages RAND and the adversary have in common in their caches just after servicing the ith request (by both players).

As usual, the amortized cost of RAND for the ith request is

$$a_i = \text{RAND}_i + \Phi_i - \Phi_{i-1},$$

where RAND_i is the actual cost incurred by RAND to serve the ith request. Clearly, RAND_i and Φ_i (and therefore, a_i) are random variables. For all i, Φ_i is surely bounded below; consequently, to complete the proof, it is sufficient to prove that for each request i, $\mathbf{E}[a_i] \leq c\mathbf{E}[\text{ADON}_i]$ (where ADON_i is the actual cost incurred by ADON to serve the ith request). Equivalently, we prove that for each request r_i,

$$\mathbf{E}[\Phi_i - \Phi_{i-1}] \leq c \cdot \mathbf{E}[\text{ADON}_i] - \mathbf{E}[\text{RAND}_i]. \qquad (4.2)$$

Consider the game just after the $(i-1)$st request has been serviced ($i \geq 1$). Let P denote the set of all pages common to RAND's and ADON's caches at this stage (i.e., $|P| = \phi_{i-1}$). Using a simple case analysis, we examine the change in potential following the actions taken by both players to service the ith request for a page p. We assume, without loss of generality, that p is chosen (by ADON) such that p is not currently in RAND's cache (otherwise, RAND will not incur incur any cost for this request, and even if the adversary incurs a page fault, the potential will not increase).

- *Case 1: p is in the adversary's cache.* If RAND evicts a common page, there is no change in the potential (RAND must bring p into its cache). Otherwise, ϕ increases by 1, so the potential Φ decreases by $c(\phi + 1) - c\phi = c$. With probability $\frac{\phi_{i-1}}{k}$, RAND evicts a common page so the expected *decrease* in the potential is $c \cdot \frac{k - \phi_{i-1}}{k} = \frac{k}{k-h+1} \cdot \frac{k - \phi_{i-1}}{k}$. Just before this move, RAND does not hold p in its cache; consequently, it must be that $\phi_{i-1} \leq h - 1$, which means that the expected decrease in potential is at least 1. As RAND pays 1 for this move and the adversary does not move at all, inequality (4.2) clearly holds.

• *Case 2:* The adversary does not hold p and evicts a page not in P. In this case ϕ can only increase (it remains the same only if RAND evicts a common page). Hence, the potential can only decrease, that is, $\Phi_i - \Phi_{i-1} \leq 0$. Since $c \cdot \text{ADON}_i - \text{RAND}_i = c \cdot 1 - 1 \geq 0$, it follows that inequality (4.2) holds.

• *Case 3:* The adversary does not hold p but evicts a page $q \in P$. If RAND evicts q as well, then we are done, since there is no change in potential (ϕ remains the same). This is also the case if RAND evicts a page not in P. Otherwise, RAND evicts a page in P different from q. In this case, ϕ decreases by 1. Since this event happens with probability $\frac{\phi_{i-1}-1}{k}$, the expected increase in potential is

$$c \cdot \frac{\phi_{i-1} - 1}{k} \leq \frac{k}{k-h+1} \cdot \frac{h-1}{k} = \frac{h-1}{k-h+1}.$$

However,

$$c \cdot \text{ADON}_i - \text{RAND}_i = c \cdot 1 - 1 = \frac{k}{k-h+1} - 1 = \frac{h-1}{k-h+1};$$

consequently, inequality (4.2) holds.

These three cases are mutually exclusive and exhaustive; therefore, the proof is complete.   ∎

Exercise 4.2 Show that the above proof collapses if we assume that the adversary is adaptive-offline.

In Chapter 10, we show that against adaptive online adversaries, any randomized paging algorithm can be at best $\frac{k}{k-h+1}$-competitive. We now prove a lower bound for the competitive ratio of algorithm RAND against an oblivious adversary. We use the following basic lemma.

Lemma 4.1 *Let W be a random variable giving the "waiting time" for a success in a sequence of Bernoulli trials with a success probability p. For any positive integer j, define the "truncated" random variable, W_j,*

$$W_j = \begin{cases} W & \text{if } W \leq j; \\ j & \text{otherwise.} \end{cases}$$

Then $\mathbf{E}[W_j] = \frac{1}{p}\left(1 - (1-p)^j\right)$.

PROOF.

$$\mathbf{E}[W_j] = j \cdot \Pr[W > j] + \sum_{i=1}^{j} i \cdot \Pr[\text{success occurs at round } i]$$

$$= j \cdot (1-p)^j + p \sum_{i=0}^{j-1} (i+1)(1-p)^i$$

$$= j \cdot (1-p)^j + p \left[\frac{1 - jp(1-p)^j - (1-p)^j}{p^2} \right]$$

$$= \frac{1}{p}\left[1 - (1-p)^j \right].$$

∎

Theorem 4.2 *The competitive ratio of* RAND *against an oblivious adversary for the* (h, k)-*paging problem is at least* $\frac{k}{k-h+1}$.

PROOF. Let ε be given. Let $b_1, b_2, \ldots$ be pages that are not initially in RAND's cache. Consider the following request sequence:

$$\sigma = (b_1, a_2, \ldots, a_h)^\ell, (b_2, a_2, \ldots, a_h)^\ell, (b_3, a_2, \ldots, a_h)^\ell, \ldots,$$

where ℓ is an integer whose value will be determined later. In this sequence the a_i and b_i are all distinct page references. For each $i = 1, 2, \ldots$, the subsequence $(b_i, a_2, \ldots, a_h)^\ell$ of σ is called the ith block consisting of ℓ repetitions of the segment $b_i, a_2, \ldots, a_h$.

Clearly, the adversary can service σ while incurring exactly one page fault during the ith block, $i = 1, 2, \ldots$.

At the beginning of ith block, RAND holds in its cache at most $h - 1$ of the pages requested in that block (it cannot hold b_i). Consider the cache of RAND as it is about to process a segment $b_i, a_2, \ldots, a_h$ (during the ith block). Suppose the cache contains at most $h - 1$ of the pages requested in this segment. We say that RAND "succeeds" on this segment if on its last page fault (which must occur), RAND has exactly $h - 1$ of the pages $\{b_i, a_2, \ldots, a_h\}$ in its cache and it evicts a page different from $b_i, a_2, \ldots, a_h$. For each segment repetition until after a success, RAND incurs at least one page fault.

The probability of a success is at most $\frac{k-(h-1)}{k}$. It follows, by Lemma 4.1 (with $p = \frac{k-h+1}{k}$ and $j = \ell$), that the expected number of page faults incurred by RAND during the ith block is at least[2]

$$\frac{k}{k-h+1}\left(1 - \left(\frac{h-1}{k}\right)^\ell\right). \tag{4.3}$$

Since the right factor in equation (4.3) approaches 1 (from below), for any given $\varepsilon > 0$, there exists (sufficiently large) ℓ such that the cost ratio, online to offline, with respect to σ is greater than $\frac{k}{k-h+1} - \varepsilon$. Moreover, the adversary can choose σ with sufficiently many blocks to dominate any finite additive constant. ∎

This proof of Theorem 4.2 uses an unbounded number of slow memory pages. However, it is possible to modify the proof so that only $k + 1$ slow memory pages are used.

Exercise 4.3 Modify the proof of Theorem 4.2 to work with only $k + 1$ slow memory pages.

4.3 The MARK Algorithm

We now present an algorithm called MARK. This simple randomized algorithm is $2H_k$-competitive against an oblivious adversary. H_k is called the **kth harmonic number**. Harmonic numbers play an important role in the analysis of randomized algorithms. For any positive integer k, the kth harmonic number, H_k, is defined as

$$H_k = 1 + \frac{1}{2} + \frac{1}{3} + \cdots + \frac{1}{k}. \tag{4.4}$$

---

[2] In Lemma 4.1, it is clear that if the probability of success is at most p rather than equal to p, then the expected waiting time is at least as large as the stated bound.

Exercise 4.4 Prove that for any $k \geq 1$

$$\ln k < H_k \leq 1 + \ln k. \tag{4.5}$$

As its name suggests, algorithm MARK is a marking algorithm (see Section 3.5.1). In fact, algorithm MARK was the first explicit marking algorithm to be defined. Thus MARK associates a mark bit with each of its k fast memory slots.

> **Algorithm MARK:** Initially, all the pages are marked. If there is a request for a page p that is in the cache but unmarked, then p is marked. Otherwise, if p is not in the cache, then p is brought *marked* into the cache, replacing a randomly and uniformly chosen page from the set of all unmarked pages. If all pages in the cache are marked when p is about to be brought in, then they are all unmarked first.

Theorem 4.3 $\overline{\mathcal{R}}_{\mathrm{OBL}}(\mathrm{MARK}) \leq 2H_k$.

PROOF. We assume that algorithm MARK and the adversary start with the same set of initial pages in their caches (otherwise, it is possible to attribute the difference to an additive constant). Fix any request sequence σ and consider its k-phase partition.

For each phase i, we call the pages in the cache immediately prior to the start of the phase the **old** pages. A non-old page requested in the ith phase is called **new**. Notice that each request is either to an old or a new page and that repeated requests to either old or new pages do not contribute anything to the online cost, since each page requested during a phase is kept in the fast memory until the end of the phase.

Consider the ith phase. Let m_i be the number of new pages requested in this phase. It is clear that within the phase, the worst possible order to the online player is that first requests to new pages precede all requests to old pages. Ordered in this way, the first m_i requests to new pages incur m_i page faults. We now investigate the expected number of page faults that resulted from the $k - m_i$ (first) requests to old pages.

The key observation is that the jth old page (in the order they are requested for this phase) requested for the first time during the ith phase is in the cache with probability exactly $\frac{k-m_i-(j-1)}{k-(j-1)}$. To see this, note that the numerator represents the number of old unmarked pages in the cache and the denominator represents the number of old unmarked pages. The probability of a fault caused by this request is exactly $\frac{m_i}{k-j+1}$. Hence, the expected number of faults during the ith phase is

$$m_i + \sum_{j=1}^{k-m_i} \frac{m_i}{k-j+1} = m_i + m_i(H_k - H_{m_i}) = m_i(H_k - H_{m_i} + 1) \leq m_i H_k.$$

It is easy to bound $\mathrm{OPT}(\sigma)$ from below. By the definition of a phase and the definition of m_i, during the ith and $(i-1)$st phases, at least $k + m_i$ distinct pages have been requested. Thus, for each phase i (except the first phase), the number of page faults made by OPT during the ith and $(i-1)$st phases is at least m_i. The number of faults made by OPT during the first phase is at least m_1. Hence, the total optimal offline cost is at least $\frac{1}{2} \sum_i m_i$. Since the expected number of online faults is at most $H_k \sum_i m_i$, the proof is complete. $\blacksquare$

Exercise 4.5 Prove that MARK is H_k-competitive against an oblivious adversary when the total number N of pages in the slow memory is $k + 1$.

Exercise 4.6 Prove that in general, MARK is not H_k-competitive. (Hint: It is sufficient to consider the case $k = 2$, $N = 4$.)

In fact, it can be shown for all $k \geq 2$ that $\overline{\mathcal{R}}(\text{MARK}) = 2H_k - 1$ for $N \geq k + 2$. Finally, we note that for the (h, k)-paging problem with $h < k$,

$$\overline{\mathcal{R}}(\text{MARK}) \leq 2\left(\ln \frac{k}{k-h} - \ln \ln \frac{k}{k-h} + \frac{1}{2}\right)$$

if $\frac{k}{k-h} > e$. Otherwise, $\overline{\mathcal{R}}(\text{MARK}) \leq 2$.

4.4   A Lower Bound for Randomized Paging Algorithms

In this section we prove a lower bound of H_k for any randomized paging algorithms with a fast memory of size k. The proof of the following theorem is from Fiat, Karp, Luby, McGeoch, Sleator, and Young [153].

Theorem 4.4 *Let* ALG *be any randomized paging algorithm with a cache of size k, and let $N \geq k + 1$. Then $\overline{\mathcal{R}}(\text{ALG}) \geq H_k$.*

PROOF. Assume a slow memory of $N = k+1$ pages. We show how an oblivious adversary can construct a request sequence that will force a competitive ratio of H_k on ALG. For each $j = 1, 2, \ldots, N$, the adversary maintains the probability p_j that the jth slow memory page is not currently in ALG's cache. The calculation of the p_j is possible, since the adversary knows the probability distribution used by ALG. The N-tuple $(p_1, p_2, \ldots, p_N)$ is maintained such that after each request, $\sum_j p_j = 1$ (i.e., this N-tuple is a probability distribution). It follows that ALG's expected cost for a request to the ith page costs ALG p_i on average.

The "bad" sequence for ALG is composed of an arbitrarily large number of k-phases (see Section 3.5.1). For this purpose, the algorithm used by the adversary to construct the "bad" request sequence is a marking algorithm (see Section 3.5.1). That is, at all times the adversary stores the set of pages that are currently marked. We show how the adversary constructs one k-phase and prove that on each such k-phase, ALG's expected number of page faults is at least H_k . Clearly, OPT can serve any k-phase with at most one page fault.

Each k-phase is constructed of k subphases such that at the start of the ith subphase, the number of unmarked pages is exactly $k - i + 1$. At the end of the kth subphase, the last page requested remains marked, all other pages become unmarked, and a new k-phase begins. We show how to construct the ith subphase such that the expected cost for ALG is $\frac{1}{k-i+1}$. Once this is established, the proof is complete, since the total expected cost incurred by ALG for a k-phase is $\sum_{i=1}^{k} \frac{1}{k-i+1} = H_k$. It remains to show how to construct the subphases.

Each subphase consists of zero or more requests to marked pages followed by one request to an unmarked page (which then becomes marked). We now show how to construct the jth subphase. Let M be the set of marked pages at the start of the jth subphase. Thus, $|M| = j$, and the number of unmarked pages is $u = k + 1 - j$. Let $\gamma = \sum_{i \in M} p_i$. If $\gamma = 0$, there must be at least one unmarked page a with $p_a \geq \frac{1}{u}$. In this case, the adversary requests page a and the subphase ends. Otherwise, $\gamma > 0$ and there must be a page $m \in M$ such that $p_m > 0$. Let $\varepsilon = p_m$. The first request of this subphase is for page m. The remaining requests (to marked pages) of this subphase are generated by the adversary using the following loop:

> While the total expected cost to ALG for this subphase is less than $\frac{1}{u}$, and while $\gamma > \varepsilon$, request page $\ell \in M$ such that $\ell = \arg\max_{i \in M} p_i$:

First notice that this loop must terminate: $\gamma > \varepsilon$ at the start of any iteration that executes. Each iteration thus contributes at least $\frac{\gamma}{|M|} > \frac{\varepsilon}{|M|}$ to the total expected cost incurred by ALG for this subphase. When the loop terminates, if the total expected cost incurred by ALG thus far is at least $\frac{1}{u}$, then the subphase ends with a request to an arbitrary unmarked page. Otherwise, the loop terminates with $\gamma \leq \varepsilon$. In this case, the adversary requests the unmarked page b with the highest probability value. Clearly, $p_b \geq \frac{1-\gamma}{u}$. Hence, the total expected cost incurred by ALG is at least $\varepsilon + p_b$. However,

$$\varepsilon + p_b \geq \varepsilon + \frac{1-\gamma}{u} \geq \varepsilon + \frac{1-\varepsilon}{u} \geq \frac{1}{u}.$$

It follows that against an oblivious adversary, ALG cannot attain a competitive ratio smaller than H_k. Clearly, this bound must hold against the stronger adaptive adversaries. ∎

The PARTITION algorithm from McGeoch and Sleator [263] is H_k-competitive against an oblivious adversary. Hence, H_k is indeed the competitiveness of randomized paging against an oblivious adversary.

4.5 Historical Notes and Open Questions

The distinction between oblivious and adaptive adversaries was first made by Raghavan and Snir [284]. The distinction between adaptive-online and adaptive-offline adversaries was further made by Ben-David, Borodin, Karp, Tardos, and Wigderson [55], who also gave basic results on the relative powers of the three adversaries (as discussed in Chapter 7).

The first randomized paging algorithm, MARK, was discovered by Fiat, Karp, Luby, McGeoch, Sleator, and Young [152, 153]. They note that algorithm MARK can be viewed as an adaptation of the randomized algorithm for *uniform task systems* from Borodin, Linial, and Saks [82] (see Chapter 9). Fiat et al. proved that algorithm MARK is $2H_k$-competitive against an oblivious adversary. Also, they showed that MARK is H_k-competitive when $N = k+1$ (recall that N is the total number of pages in the slow memory) but, in general, that MARK is not H_k-competitive. An exact bound for algorithm MARK was provided by Achlioptas, Chrobak, and Noga [1], who showed that $\overline{\mathcal{R}}(\text{MARK}) = 2H_k - 1$ for $N \geq k+2$. Fiat et al. [153] also showed that H_k is a lower bound on the competitive ratio of any randomized online paging algorithm against an oblivious adversary. An alternative proof of this lower bound can be obtained by modifying the lower bound proof for *uniform task systems* from Borodin, Linial, and Saks [82]. This proof is less direct and appeals to "Yao's principle" (see Chapter 8).

McGeoch and Sleator [263] closed the $(H_k, 2H_k)$ gap for randomized paging against an oblivious adversary by introducing a new algorithm that attains the ratio H_k. Their algorithm, called the PARTITION algorithm, is substantially more complicated than MARK and uses $\Omega(N)$ memory. Later, Achlioptas, Chrobak, and Noga [1] gave a somewhat simpler (to state and analyze) H_k-competitive algorithm EQUITABLE that uses only $O(k^2 \log k)$ memory and $O(k^2)$ time per page request.

Young [342, 343, 344] generalized the randomized lower bound of $H_k \approx \ln k$ for paging to the (h, k)-paging problem. For $h < k$ and $\frac{k}{k-h} > e$ this bound is

$$\ln \frac{k}{k-h} - \ln \ln \frac{k}{k-h} + \frac{2}{k-h}.$$

Young also showed that for the (h, k)-paging problem with $h < k$ and $\frac{k}{k-h} > e$,

$$\overline{\mathcal{R}}(\text{MARK}) \leq 2 \left(\ln \frac{k}{k-h} - \ln \ln \frac{k}{k-h} + \frac{1}{2} \right)$$

and thus MARK is within a factor of 2 from the lower bound.

Raghavan and Snir [284] studied algorithm RAND and proved that $\overline{\mathcal{R}}_{\text{ADON}}(\text{RAND}) = \frac{k}{k-h+1}$. They also studied further issues concerning randomized online algorithms. Aside from studying adversary models and the relationships between them, they also investigated the tradeoff between memory and randomness. In particular, they showed a lower bound of k for any "memoryless" paging algorithm against an oblivious adversary. They defined as a "memoryless" algorithm one that does not make use of any information other than which pages are stored in the array that implements fast memory (see Chapter 6). Other important issues concerning the tradeoff of memory and randomness are discussed in [284].

Credits for Exercises. Exercises 4.5 and 4.6 are from Fiat et al. [153].

4.5.1 Open Questions

To conclude, most of the immediate questions regarding competitive analysis of randomized paging have already been answered. One question that remains open is as follows.

4.1 (*Value = I3/T5*) Determine the precise randomized competitiveness for (h, k)-paging against an oblivious adversary.

Although the competitiveness of (oblivious) randomized paging is already determined by the H_k-competitive PARTITION of McGeoch and Sleator [263] and the EQUITABLE algorithm of Achlioptas, Chrobak, and Noga [1], it is interesting to find other optimal randomized paging algorithms, and more generally to study the tradeoff between memory, competitiveness, and randomness as advocated in Raghavan and Snir [284].

4.2 (*Value = I4/T4*) Find other optimal randomized paging algorithms against an oblivious adversary. Does there exist an optimal H_k-competitive algorithm using only $O(k)$ memory? Does there exist a bounded memory randomized algorithm that is $O(\log k)$-competitive? (See also Chapter 6.)

CHAPTER 5

Alternative Paging Models:
Beyond Pure Competitive Analysis

Given the importance of memory hierarchies and the ever-changing "technological imperatives," it is not surprising that paging (and caching) continues to be an active research topic. It is also clear that a simple (or "elegant") one-parameter model (such as competitive analysis with the only important parameter being k, the number of main memory pages) can provide only limited insight into a very complex and varied problem. In particular, even in the full cost model (of Section 3.7), competitive analysis does not distinguish between the performance of, for example, FIFO and LRU. In this chapter we introduce a number of modifications/refinements to pure competitive analysis in the context of the paging problem. These alternatives motivate new algorithms as well as help to refine our understanding about the relative merits of known algorithms.

5.1 The Access Graph Model

In Chapter 3 we introduced the important concept of locality of reference. The full cost model of paging allowed for one possible definition of locality in terms of the average length of a phase in the k-phase partition of the input. We now consider what is perhaps a more natural way to study locality that is independent of the cache size k. The basic idea is to limit the adversaries' ability to create nemesis sequences. Our first approach is to specify deterministically the possible choices for the next page request as a function of the present page request. In Section 5.3.1 we refine the approach and require that the next page request be a probabilistic function of the current page request.

Let $G = (V, E)$ be an N-node graph, either undirected or directed. We call G an **access graph** when we use G to specify what page requests are allowed to follow the present page request. Specifically, the request sequence $\sigma = r_1, r_2, \ldots, r_n$ is **consistent** with the access graph G if $(r_i, r_{i+1}) \in E$ for all i ($1 \leq i < n$). That is, after requesting page r_i, the adversary must choose a page that is adjacent to r_i in its access graph.

The access graph model brings competitive analysis closer to the observed practice of paging. For example, page requests to a large data set normally satisfy an undirected graph structure corresponding to the data structure used to organize the data. In addition, page requests also follow the directed graph corresponding to the control flow of an algorithm. Moreover, within the access graph model, we can find a theoretical basis for the relative superiority of LRU over FIFO. We see that FIFO cannot significantly exploit the access graph directly, whereas on some important classes of access graphs, LRU performs much better than FIFO and, indeed (in competitive terms), performs as well as any online algorithm. Using this model, we can easily document a common pitfall of LRU, namely, its poor performance on cyclic sequences of page requests when the length of the cycle is slightly larger than the size of the cache. This leads us to ask if there is a "universal" online algorithm that works well for *every* access graph. Throughout this section, we restrict attention to *undirected* access graphs. Some results concerning directed access graphs are discussed in Section 5.4.

Let $G = (V, E)$ be an access graph and ALG a paging algorithm. Without loss of generality, we can assume that all access graphs are connected. Fix an arbitrary k (i.e., the number of cache pages). We say ALG is **c-competitive on G** if there exists a constant α such that $\text{ALG}(\sigma) \leq c \cdot \text{OPT}(\sigma) + \alpha$ for all σ consistent with G. The competitive ratio of ALG on G, denoted $\mathcal{R}(\text{ALG}, G)$, is the infimum of all c such that ALG is c-competitive on G.

We follow the notational convention of Chapters 3 and 4 and do not explicitly denote the parameter k (the size of the cache) or the parameter N (the size of the slow memory). The reason for this convention is that we expect paging algorithms to be "uniform" in the parameters k and N. That is, the algorithm will need to know k (and perhaps N), but we expect that the "general nature" of the algorithm will not depend on the particular choice of k or N.[1] We can, however, expect that a paging algorithm might be customized for a particular access graph; hence, we do explicitly denote the access graph as a parameter. We also need the concept and notation for the "best competitive ratio for access graph G"; we define $\mathcal{R}(G) = \min_{\text{ALG}} \mathcal{R}(\text{ALG}, G)$. We say ALG is optimal for a given G if (for any k) $\mathcal{R}(\text{ALG}, G) = \mathcal{R}(G)$. The following fact shows that this concept is well defined (i.e., it uses minimum rather than infimum); moreover, there always is a "computable" optimal online algorithm.[2] Here we say "computable algorithm" in the sense that each paging decision of the algorithm can be deterministically computed (albeit perhaps not in any practical sense) from the sequence of requests up to and including the present request.

We leave the following fact as a simple exercise.

Exercise 5.1 Let H be a subgraph of G. Then $\mathcal{R}(H) \leq \mathcal{R}(G)$. Show, however, that there is an algorithm ALG such that $\mathcal{R}(\text{ALG}, H) > \mathcal{R}(\text{ALG}, G)$.

Note that for $N \geq k + 1$, if the access graph is the complete graph on N nodes (denoted K_N), then for any deterministic online algorithm ALG, $\mathcal{R}(\text{ALG}, K_N) \geq k$. We seek algorithms that, for particular access graphs G, achieve competitive ratios on G that are significantly better than k.

---

[1] One way to make this concept of uniformity precise is to consider an instantiation of the algorithm for each value of k and N; then, for a uniform algorithm, we would say these instances could be "efficiently" generated (efficiently in terms of k). If for infinitely many values of k we were considering "really different" algorithms, then we could not hope to generate these algorithms efficiently. See chap. 9 of Wegener [335] for a discussion of uniform versus nonuniform models in the context of complexity theory.

[2] Consistent with previous terminology, "optimal online algorithm" refers to the optimality of the best attainable competitive ratio. It is less ambiguous but more cumbersome to say "optimally competitive online algorithm."

Theorem 5.1 *Let G be an arbitrary N-node access graph. There exists a (computable) deterministic online algorithm ALG such that $\mathcal{R}(\text{ALG}, G) = \mathcal{R}(G)$.*

PROOF. We only sketch the proof. The main observation is that once we have any upper bound on the optimal competitive ratio, as Exercise 5.2 shows, we can restrict attention to finite memory algorithms. In this case, since k is an upper bound for any access graph, we can restrict attention to algorithms with at most $(3k+2)^{N^k}$ memory states and at most $T = (3k+2)^{N^k} \times N^k$ memory state–cache configuration pairs. Therefore, every request sequence of length T causes a cycle in the state–configuration pair. An adversary must therefore extract the worst competitive ratio by using sequences of length $\leq T$. Thus, the desired ALG is one that minimizes the maximum ratio $\frac{\text{ALG}(\sigma)}{\text{OPT}(\sigma)}$, where the maximum is taken over all consistent request sequences of length $\leq T$. ∎

Exercise 5.2 Consider a paging problem with at most P possible cache configurations. For example, if there are k cache pages and N slow memory pages, then $P \leq \binom{N}{k}$. Suppose there exists a c-competitive algorithm for this problem. Prove that there is a finite state c-competitive algorithm ALG for this problem where ALG has at most $(3c+2)^P$ memory states. Hint: Consider an optimal offline algorithm using dynamic programming.

An algorithm ALG is called **uniformly competitive** if there exist constants b_1, b_2 such that for every access graph G (and for every cache size k) $\mathcal{R}(\text{ALG}, G) \leq b_1 \mathcal{R}(G) + b_2$; that is, for *any* access graph, ALG is within a constant factor of the best competitive ratio obtainable.[3] We seek a "natural" and "efficient" (in the sense that each online decision can be efficiently computed in terms of both time and memory requirements) uniformly competitive algorithm.

5.1.1 FIFO in the Access Graph Model

Although FIFO is k-competitive (and hence optimal) in the pure competitive analysis model for paging, we now see that (consistent with what is well understood in practice) FIFO does not adequately exploit locality of reference.

Theorem 5.2 *For any N-node connected graph G with $N \geq k+1$, $\mathcal{R}(\text{FIFO}, G) \geq \frac{(k+1)}{2}$.*

PROOF. According to Exercise 5.1, it is sufficient to choose a connected $(k+1)$-node subgraph H of G, restrict requests to H, and show $\mathcal{R}(\text{FIFO}, H) \geq \frac{(k+1)}{2}$. Any connected graph H must contain at least one node w that is not an "articulation point."[4] The adversary constructs the input sequence in stages. We refer to any node of H that is not presently in the cache as a **(cache) hole**. Since we have $k+1$ nodes in H and FIFO is a demand paging algorithm, we can assume that there is exactly one hole. At the start of each stage, we have w as the most recent page brought into the cache and the hole will be at a node v_1 that is adjacent to w. Let $v_1, v_2, \ldots$ be the sequence of nodes that the hole traverses during a stage. Suppose the hole is at node $v_i \neq w$. The adversary will request page v_i and, by the definition of this request sequence, FIFO will respond by evicting a node v_{i+1} (and will cause the hole to jump to v_{i+1}). If $i < k+1$, then by the definition of FIFO, $v_{i+1} \neq w$.

---

[3] In the literature, the term used is "strongly competitive" rather than "uniformly competitive."
[4] An articulation point of H is a node whose removal would disconnect H.

The adversary will then request the nodes on a path in H from v_i to v_{i+1} not including w (which is possible, since w is not an articulation point). Note that repeated requests to pages along this path do not change the order in which the current cache pages have been brought into the cache and hence does not affect the behavior of FIFO. When the hole reaches $v_k \neq w$ (and FIFO has incurred $k-1$ faults), it is the case that w is the page that was least recently brought into the cache. An adversary request for v_k then moves the hole from v_k to w and makes v_k the page least recently brought into the cache. A final fault at node w moves the hole back to node v_1, making w the page most recently brought into the cache. The stage is now complete. During such a stage, FIFO incurs exactly $k+1$ page faults. By evicting w to satisfy v_1 and evicting v_1 to satisfy w, OPT can serve all requests in a stage incurring only two page faults. Hence, $\mathcal{R}(\text{FIFO}, H) \geq \frac{k+1}{2}$. ∎

Exercise 5.3 Let L_N be an $(N = k+1)$-node line. Show that $\mathcal{R}(\text{FIFO}, L_N) = k$.

Exercise 5.4 Let S_N be an $(N = k+1)$-node star graph. Show that $\mathcal{R}(\text{LRU}, S_N) = \mathcal{R}(\text{FIFO}, S_N) = k-1$.

5.1.2 LRU in the Access Graph Model

Unlike FIFO, LRU can often exploit locality of reference as formalized in the access graph model. In particular, we see that LRU is an optimal online algorithm for any access graph that is a tree. Trees represent the underlying access graph for many data structures. Moreover, trees are often embedded within other data structures. We now derive a precise and easily stated characterization for $\mathcal{R}(G)$ when G is a tree. For any tree T, let $\ell(T)$ denote the number of leaves in T, and for any connected graph G, let

$$\mathcal{T}_l(G) = \{T \mid T \text{ is an } l\text{-node subtree of } G\}.$$

Theorem 5.3 *Let G be an arbitrary graph with $N \geq k+1$ nodes. Then*

$$\mathcal{R}(G) \geq \max_{T \in \mathcal{T}_{k+1}(G)} \{\ell(T) - 1\}.$$

PROOF. Let ALG be any deterministic algorithm. The adversary chooses an appropriate tree T and always keeps the OPT hole on a leaf of T so that all internal nodes of T are always in the cache of OPT. The adversary then acts as a cruel adversary subject to the access graph requirement. Since all internal nodes of T are in the optimal offline cache, the adversary can "walk" on T and continue to request the online hole. By using a longest forward distance strategy on the leaves of T, OPT has at most one page fault for every $\ell(T) - 1$ leaves that are requested, whereas ALG faults on every leaf requested (by the nature of the cruel adversary). ∎

Note, in particular, that when G is an $(N \geq k+1)$-node line, Theorem 5.3 leaves open the possibility that $\mathcal{R}(G) = 1$ in contrast to the performance of FIFO for the line access graph. Whenever G is a tree, we show that LRU achieves a matching upper bound to Theorem 5.3. We do so by using the following "amortized charging technique."[5] Here we briefly describe this method in the context of paging.

---

[5] This method, which is commonly used in data structure analysis, can be shown to be equivalent to the potential method (see Tarjan [325] and Section 1.4).

Lemma 5.1 (Amortized charging technique applied to paging) *Assume that whenever* OPT *faults, we distribute (conceptually for the analysis but not in the algorithm) at most c "tokens" among the nodes of G. Suppose further that on any online* ALG *fault we can pay for this fault by spending (i.e., destroying) one token. Then* ALG *is c-competitive on G.*

PROOF. The proof is quite straightforward; the use of the tokens clearly demonstrates that there are at most c online faults for each OPT fault. ∎

Theorem 5.4 *Let G be any tree. Then*

$$\mathcal{R}(\text{LRU}, G) = \max_{T \in \mathcal{T}_{k+1}(G)} \{\ell(T) - 1\}.$$

Thus, $\mathcal{R}(\text{LRU}, G) = \mathcal{R}(G)$.

PROOF. We recall from Theorem 3.1 that LFD is an optimal offline algorithm. For any time t, consider the set of nodes of G corresponding to the tth request r_t and the k pages presently in the cache of LRU (respectively, the cache of LFD) before the request is served.[6] Clearly (by a simple induction on t), this set is a subtree of G (i.e., it is not a forest), which we denote as $tree_t[\text{LRU}]$ (respectively, $tree_t[\text{LFD}]$). In particular, whenever LRU (or LFD) faults, it faults on a leaf of $tree_t[\text{LRU}]$ (respectively, $tree_t[\text{LFD}]$) and it serves this fault by evicting a page corresponding to a leaf.

Every time LFD faults, we will distribute at most $\max_{T \in \mathcal{T}_{k+1}(G)} \{\ell(T) - 1\}$ "tokens" on pages in the cache of LRU. Whenever there is an LRU fault, the evicted page will (as shown in Lemma 5.3) possess a token and will release this token in order to pay for the fault. Hence, according to Lemma 5.1, we obtain the desired bound on $\mathcal{R}(\text{LRU}, G)$. The specific charging scheme is as follows:

> **Charging scheme:** Consider an LFD fault on the tth request r_t. For every leaf $v \neq r_t$ in $tree_t[\text{LRU}]$, follow the path in $tree_t[\text{LRU}]$ from v to r_t and place a token on the first node (which is a page in the cache of LRU) that does not already possess a token.

The proof is complete when we establish the following two lemmas. ∎

Lemma 5.2 *Upon an* LFD *fault on* r_t, *at most* $\ell(tree_t[\text{LRU}]) - 1$ *tokens are distributed by the charging scheme. Note: The charging scheme guarantees that at most* $\ell(tree_t[\text{LRU}])$ *tokens are distributed.*

PROOF. If the requested node r_t is a leaf of $tree_t[\text{LRU}]$, then the lemma clearly holds. Consequently, we need consider only the case in which r_t is an interior node of $tree_t[\text{LRU}]$ and show there is some leaf v of $tree_t[\text{LRU}]$ such that every node on the path from v to r_t possesses a token.

If a node u is in the cache of LRU (respectively, LFD) but not in the cache of LFD (respectively, LRU), then u is called a **lonely LRU page** (respectively, lonely LFD page). If LFD faults (on one of the leaves $r_t \in tree_t[\text{LFD}]$), and if this is an interior node of $tree_t[\text{LRU}]$, then r_t

---

[6] We assume that initially the caches of LRU and LFD are identical and that there are exactly k pages in the cache. Moreover, for the base of the inductive proof we need to assume that these pages are a subtree of G. Alternatively, we can assume that initially the caches are empty and that the indicated subtrees have fewer than k nodes until the kth distinct page request has occurred.

is a lonely LRU page; moreover, there is a path from r_t to a leaf of $tree_t[\text{LRU}]$ such that all nodes on this path are lonely. It suffices, then, to show that every lonely LRU page possesses a token. We show this by induction on t.

Base case. By assumption, LFD and ALG initially have the same k pages in the cache; therefore, when $t = 1$ there are no lonely LRU pages.

Induction step. Assume the claim is true before the tth request r_t and show that it is true after the tth request. A page u in $tree_t[\text{LRU}]$ can become a lonely LRU page only if LFD faults on r_t and LFD evicts u to serve r_t. However, then there is a path from r_t to some leaf v in $tree_t[\text{LRU}]$ that passes through u. (Possibly u is a leaf and then $v = u$.) Every node $u' \neq u$ on the path from u to v must also correspond to a lonely LRU page and hence by the inductive assumption must possess a token. The charging scheme then places a token on u (unless it already possesses one). ∎

Lemma 5.3 *Whenever LRU evicts a page u (in $tree_t[\text{LRU}]$) to service a fault, u possesses a token.*

PROOF. Consider the time t_1 when u becomes the least recently used page (i.e., the last such time before its eviction). If u possesses a token at time t_1, we are done; therefore, assume that u does not possess a token at time t_1. If LFD faults on or before the next LRU fault, we are also done; the charging scheme first places a token on u, since (as already observed) u is a leaf in $tree_{t_1}[\text{LRU}]$. Hence, the next LRU fault might occur before the next LFD fault and at the location of a lonely LFD page.

Removal of the nodes in $tree_{t_1}[\text{LRU}]$ (except for u) disconnects G into components (i.e., subtrees). Let $T(u)$ denote the component (i.e., subtree) containing u. It suffices to show that at time t_1 all lonely LFD pages are located in $T(u)$, since this would ensure that u is requested before any lonely LFD request and, hence (at some time after t_1 but before the next request of a lonely LFD page), that u would no longer be the least recently used page (contradicting the assumption that t_1 is the last time that u becomes the least recently used page prior to its eviction). Let $t_0 < t_1$ be the last time that u was requested, and let I denote the time interval $(t_0, t_1]$. In order for u to become the least recently used node at time t_1, it must be that all nodes (other than u) in $tree_{t_1}[\text{LRU}]$ have been requested during I and no node in $T(u)$ has been requested. We now establish a sequence of inequalities that will ensure that all lonely LFD pages are located in $T(u)$.

$$
\begin{pmatrix} \text{No. of LFD} \\ \text{pages in } T(u) \\ \text{at time } t_0 \end{pmatrix} \geq \begin{pmatrix} \text{No. of LRU pages in} \\ T(u) \text{ without tokens} \\ \text{at time } t_0 \end{pmatrix} \quad \begin{matrix} \text{Because every lonely LRU page has} \\ \text{a token (see Lemma 5.2).} \end{matrix}
$$

$$
\geq \begin{pmatrix} \text{No. of tokens} \\ \text{placed on } T(u) \\ \text{during } I \end{pmatrix} \quad \begin{matrix} \text{No node in } T(u) \text{ is requested during } I, \text{ so no} \\ \text{node in } T(u) \text{ can receive a token more than} \\ \text{once.} \end{matrix}
$$

$$
\geq \begin{pmatrix} \text{No. of LFD} \\ \text{faults during } I \end{pmatrix} \quad \begin{matrix} \text{For any time } t \in I, tree_t[\text{LRU}] \text{ has a leaf } v \text{ in } T(u). \\ \text{Since } u \text{ does not receive a token, some node in } T(u) \\ \text{on the path from } v \text{ to } u \text{ receives a token.} \end{matrix}
$$

$$
\geq \begin{pmatrix} \text{No. of pages in } T(u) \\ \text{evicted by LFD during } I \end{pmatrix} + \begin{pmatrix} \text{No. of lonely LRU} \\ \text{pages at time } t_1 \end{pmatrix}.
$$

The last inequality is established as follows. At time t_1, there are no lonely LRU pages in $T(u)$, since there are no LRU pages in $T(u)$ except for u, and u cannot be lonely or else it would possess a token. Every lonely LRU page at time t_1 is in $tree_{t_1}[\text{LRU}]$ and has been requested during I. In order for such a page to be lonely, LFD must have evicted this page during I. That is,

$$(\text{No. of LFD faults}) \geq \begin{pmatrix} \text{No. of pages not in} \\ T(u) \text{ evicted by} \\ \text{LFD during } I \end{pmatrix} + \begin{pmatrix} \text{No. of pages in} \\ T(u) \text{ evicted by LFD} \\ \text{during } I \end{pmatrix}$$

$$\geq \begin{pmatrix} \text{No. of lonely} \\ \text{LRU pages} \end{pmatrix} + \begin{pmatrix} \text{No. of pages in} \\ T(u) \text{ evicted by} \\ \text{LFD during } I \end{pmatrix}.$$

Combining these inequalities, we have

$$\begin{pmatrix} \text{No. of LFD pages in} \\ T(u) \text{ at time } t_0 \end{pmatrix} \geq \begin{pmatrix} \text{No. of pages in } T(u) \\ \text{evicted by LFD during} \\ I \end{pmatrix} + \begin{pmatrix} \text{No. of lonely LRU} \\ \text{pages at time } t_1 \end{pmatrix}.$$

Thus,

$$\begin{pmatrix} \text{No. of LFD pages in} \\ T(u) \text{ at time } t_1 \end{pmatrix} = \begin{pmatrix} \text{No. of LFD pages in} \\ T(u) \text{ at time } t_0 \end{pmatrix} - \begin{pmatrix} \text{No. of pages in } T(u) \\ \text{evicted by LFD during} \\ I \end{pmatrix}$$

$$\geq \begin{pmatrix} \text{No. of lonely LRU} \\ \text{pages at time } t_1 \end{pmatrix}$$

$$= \begin{pmatrix} \text{No. of lonely LFD} \\ \text{pages at time } t_1 \end{pmatrix}$$

so that all lonely LFD pages must be in $T(u)$. ∎

The following corollary follows immediately and together with Exercise 5.3 provides an extreme example where LRU outperforms FIFO.

Corollary 5.5 *When G is a line, $\mathcal{R}(\text{LRU}, G) = \mathcal{R}(G) = 1$.*

Furthermore, LRU always performs at least as well as FIFO for *any* access graph. We state the following theorem without proof:[7]

Theorem 5.6 *For any access graph G, $\mathcal{R}(\text{LRU}, G) \leq \mathcal{R}(\text{FIFO}, G)$.*

Theorem 5.4 characterizes the competitive performance of LRU on trees, showing LRU to be optimal for trees. What happens when G is not a tree? In particular, Theorem 5.3 does not provide a useful lower bound when G is a cycle. (If G has $k + 1$ nodes, then $\mathcal{T}_{k+1} = \varnothing$, and if G has more than $k + 1$ nodes, then every $T \in \mathcal{T}_{k+1}(G)$ is a line with $\ell(T) = 2$.) However, as is well known in practice, LRU performs poorly on small cycles, as formalized in the following theorems.

---

[7] See Chrobak and Noga [108].

Theorem 5.7 *Let C_N be a cycle on $N = k + 1$ nodes. Then*

$$\mathcal{R}(\text{LRU}, C_N) = \mathcal{R}(\text{FIFO}, C_N) = k.$$

PROOF. The adversary requests the nodes of G in clockwise order, forcing both LRU and FIFO to fault on every request. LFD will fault only once for every k requests. ∎

Exercise 5.5 Let G be a $N = k + g$ node cycle for some $g \geq 1$. Extend the lower bound in Theorem 5.7 to show $\mathcal{R}(\text{LRU}, G) \geq \frac{k+g-1}{g}$. (Similarly, $\mathcal{R}(\text{FIFO}, G) \geq \frac{k+g-1}{g}$.)

In contrast, there is a relatively simple marking algorithm that is optimal for a small cycle. In fact, this algorithm is the uniformly competitive algorithm FAR that will be defined for arbitrary G in the next section. Here, we describe FAR only in terms of the $N = (k+1)$-node cycle C_N.

> **Algorithm FAR (on a $(k + 1)$-node cycle):** FAR is a marking algorithm. During a k-phase, the sets of marked and unmarked nodes are both paths (i.e., arcs) in C_N. On a fault, after marking the current request, FAR evicts an unmarked page that is at the midpoint on the path of unmarked nodes.[8]

Theorem 5.8 *Let C_N be an $(N = k + 1)$-node cycle. The marking algorithm* FAR *satisfies*

$$\mathcal{R}(\text{FAR}, C_N) = \mathcal{R}(C_N) = \lceil \log(k + 1) \rceil.$$

PROOF. FAR faults at most $1 + \lfloor \log k \rfloor = \lceil \log(k + 1) \rceil$ times in a phase; at the start of a phase, there are k unmarked nodes (after the requested node that starts a new phase is marked) and the adversary must request (and therefore mark) at least half of the unmarked nodes in order to request an unmarked node not presently in the cache. The algorithm iterates this process at most $\lfloor \log k \rfloor$ times before there is only one unmarked node, and this unmarked node will result in one additional fault with the start of a new phase. We recall from the proof of Theorem 3.2 (with $h = 1$) that any algorithm (including OPT) must fault at least once per phase. Therefore, $\mathcal{R}(\text{ALG}, G) \leq \lceil \log(k + 1) \rceil$.

The upper bound for FAR motivates the general lower bound $\mathcal{R}(G) \geq \lceil \log(k + 1) \rceil$. Let ALG be an arbitrary online algorithm. Recall that the k-phase partition of a request sequence is well defined independent of the algorithm. Whether or not ALG is a marking algorithm, for the purpose of the analysis we continue to say that a node is marked when it has been requested during a phase (and it is unmarked otherwise). We ensure that at the start of a phase, OPT and ALG have their hole in the same node and as always there is one marked (and k unmarked) nodes at the start of a phase. If ALG ever evicts a marked node, then the adversary will request that node via a path of marked nodes incurring no cost to itself. Hence, we can assume that ALG must also act as a marking algorithm. The adversary will then continue to request the hole of ALG by traversing a path in G that hits the fewest unmarked nodes (i.e., at most half of the remaining unmarked nodes) until it

---

[8] By restricting the definition of FAR here to a $(k + 1)$-node cycle, we have been able to simplify the definition in such a way as to motivate the lower bound. The algorithm is well defined even when all k pages in the cache are marked. When the next fault occurs (at the remaining node), all the existing cache pages become unmarked and a new phase begins (with one marked node).

requests only one unmarked node, which the adversary requests to begin a new phase. Clearly, ALG incurs at least $\lceil \log(k+1) \rceil$ faults per phase. ∎

The lower bounds of Theorems 5.3 and 5.7 and Exercise 5.5 inspire a reasonably good graph theoretic characterization for the performance of LRU on any access graph G. For any N-node connected graph G and $l \leq N$, we let $\mathcal{S}_l = \{H \mid H$ is a *node-induced* connected subgraph of G, and H has l nodes$\}$. Define

$$a(G) = \max_{1 \leq g \leq k} \max_{H \in \mathcal{S}_{k+g}(G)} \frac{k + g - \alpha(H) - 1}{g},$$

where $\alpha(H)$ is the number of articulation points in H. We state the following theorem without proof.[9]

Theorem 5.9 *Let G be any $(N \geq k+1)$-connected graph. Then $a(G) \leq \mathcal{R}(\text{LRU}, G) \leq 2a(G) + 2$.*

We observe that the lower bounds in Theorem 5.3 and Exercise 5.5 are indeed special cases of the lower bound in Theorem 5.9. If G is a tree, then every node-induced connected subgraph of G is a tree (i.e., $\mathcal{S}_{k+g} = \mathcal{T}_{k+g}$) and for any $H \in \mathcal{T}_{k+g}$, $\alpha(H) = |H| - \ell(H)$. Hence,

$$\frac{k + g - \alpha(H) - 1}{g} = \frac{\ell(H) - 1}{g}.$$

Furthermore, $\max_{H \in \mathcal{T}_{k+g}(G)} \frac{\ell(H)-1}{g}$ is clearly maximized when $g = 1$. When G is a $(k+g)$-node cycle, then every *proper* connected subgraph H is a path with $\alpha(H) = |H| - 2$, so that

$$\frac{k + g - \alpha(H) - 1}{g} = \frac{1}{g} \leq 1.$$

Hence, when G is a cycle, the only useful bound for $a(G)$ is obtained by choosing $H = G$; we conclude that

$$a(G) = \frac{k + g - \alpha(G) - 1}{g} = \frac{k + g - 1}{g},$$

since G is biconnected and hence $\alpha(G) = 0$.

Corollary 5.10 *Let G be a $\left(\sqrt{N} \times \sqrt{N}\right)$ array with $N \geq k+1$. Then $k = \mathcal{R}(\text{LRU}, G) \leq \left(\frac{3}{2} + o(1)\right)\mathcal{R}(G)$.*

PROOF. It is not difficult to show that for $k \geq 7$, G contains a $(k+1)$-node biconnected subgraph H. That is, $\alpha(H) = 0$, so that $a(G) = k$ and $\mathcal{R}(\text{LRU}, G) = k$. However, G also contains a subtree $T \in \mathcal{T}_{k+1}(G)$ with $\ell(T) > \frac{2}{3}(k+1) - 3\sqrt{(k+1)}$, so that $\mathcal{R}(G) \geq a(G) \geq \frac{2}{3}(k+1) - O(\sqrt{k})$. ∎

[9] See Borodin, Irani, Raghavan, and Schieber [80] for a proof.

5.1.3 FAR: A Uniformly Competitive Paging Algorithm

We have already introduced the online marking algorithm FAR specialized for a specific access graph, the $(k + 1)$-node cycle. For this access graph, it is easy to regard FAR as an online approximation of the optimal offline algorithm LFD in the following sense. By locality of reference, we can regard the marked nodes as being likely to be requested again in the near future. Among the unmarked nodes, we choose to evict a page that is *graph theoretically* farthest from the set of marked nodes. That is, we approximate "farthest in future" by "graph theoretically farthest."[10] The above motivation essentially defines the algorithm FAR for any access graph.

> **Algorithm FAR:** Let G be an arbitrary undirected access graph. Let M be the set of marked nodes (at any time during a k-phase) including the current request. If the current request is not in the cache, then evict an (unmarked) page u such that $\text{dist}_G(M, u)$ is maximized; that is, for every unmarked node v, $\text{dist}_G(M, v) \leq \text{dist}_G(M, u)$ where $\text{dist}_G(M, v) = \min\{\text{dist}_G(z, v) \mid z \in M\}$.

The remainder of this section is devoted to proving that FAR is uniformly competitive; that is, $\mathcal{R}(\text{FAR}, G) = O(\mathcal{R}(G))$ for every access graph G.

Let σ be a request sequence and consider its k-phase partition. From Section 4.3 we recall that a "new" page in a phase is a page not requested in the preceding phase, and from the analysis of Theorem 4.3 we recall $\text{OPT}(\sigma) \geq \frac{\Sigma m_i}{2}$, where m_i is the number of new pages in the ith phase. Our goal is to show that in an amortized sense, FAR is asymptotically optimal for each phase. More precisely, for some constant c, we need to show the following theorem.

Theorem 5.11 *Let $\sigma(i)$ denote the ith phase. Then* $\text{FAR}(\sigma(i)) \leq c \cdot \mathcal{R}(G) \cdot m_i \leq c \cdot \mathcal{R}(G) \cdot \text{OPT}(\sigma(i))$.

As an immediate consequence we obtain the desired result.

Corollary 5.12 *For every sequence σ consistent with G,*

$$\text{FAR}(\sigma) = O(\mathcal{R}(G) \cdot \text{OPT}(\sigma)).$$

We need to develop a graph theoretic property that we can apply to obtain a lower bound when G does not contain a small cycle. First, we have the following extension of the lower bound in Theorem 5.8, which we state as an exercise.

Exercise 5.6 Let G contain (as a subgraph) a cycle on $k + g$ nodes for $1 \leq g \leq k$. Prove that $\mathcal{R}(G) \geq \lfloor \log k - \log g \rfloor / 2$.

Next, we combine the logarithmic lower bound technique in Theorem 5.8 with the simple lower bound provided by the number of leaves in any embedded $(k + 1)$-node tree. This leads us to the definition of a "vine decomposition." A **vine decomposition** $\mathcal{V}(H) = (T, \mathcal{P})$ of a connected graph H consists of a tree T and a collection of simple

---

[10] Section 5.2 describes another natural way to use (a weighted) graph theoretical distance to approximate "farthest in future."

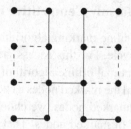

Figure 5.1: A vine decomposition $\mathcal{V}(H) = (T, \mathcal{P})$ of a (4×4) mesh H. Solid lines denote edges in the tree T, and dashed lines denote edges in the vines P_1 and P_2.

paths $\mathcal{P} = \{P_1, P_2, \ldots, P_q\}$ such that the nodes of H are partitioned between the nodes of the tree T and the interior nodes of the paths (called **vines**) P_i, with the endpoints (called **anchors**) of each vine P_i being nodes in T.

Let n_T be the number of leaves in T that are not anchors. We define the value of a vine P_i to be $val(P_i) = \lceil \log(\text{number of edges in } P_i) \rceil$ and the **value of the vine decomposition** $\mathcal{V}(H)$ as $val(\mathcal{V}(H)) = \sum_{i=1}^{q} val(P_i) + n_T - 1$.

Example 5.1 (Vine decomposition) Consider Figure 5.1, where we have a vine decomposition $\mathcal{V}(H) = (T, \mathcal{P})$ of a (4×4) mesh (array) H. Clearly,

$$val(\mathcal{V}(H)) = val(P_1) + val(P_2) + n_T - 1$$
$$= 2 + 2 + 4 - 1.$$

Theorem 5.13 (Vine decomposition lower bound) *Let G be a connected graph with $N \geq k+1$ and let H be a $(k+1)$-node connected subgraph of G with vine decomposition $\mathcal{V}(H)$. Then $\mathcal{R}(G) \geq val(\mathcal{V}(H))$.*

PROOF. Let ALG be an arbitrary online algorithm. The adversary restricts all page requests to H and hence will incur at most one fault per k-phase. It remains to show that the adversary can cause ALG to have at least $val(\mathcal{V}(H))$ faults per phase. Although ALG need not be a marking algorithm, as in Theorem 5.8, we say a node is marked when it has been requested during a phase. The adversary is essentially a cruel adversary that tries to request ALG's hole "as efficiently as possible," subject to the access graph restriction. If ALG's hole is on a tree node (of the decomposition), then the adversary walks to that node using only marked nodes or internal tree nodes. If ALG's hole is on the interior node of a vine P_i, then the adversary walks to that node using only marked nodes, internal tree nodes, anchors, and at most half the unmarked nodes of P_i. It is clear that during a phase, the hole will occur at each of the n_T nonanchor leaves and will also occur at least $val(P_i)$ times on each vine P_i. ∎

For notational convenience we let $val(H) = \lfloor \log k - \log g \rfloor / 2$ when H is a $(k+g)$-node cycle and define $val(H) = \max_{\mathcal{V}(H)} val(\mathcal{V}(H))$ when H is a $(k+1)$-node connected graph that is not a cycle.

Proof of Theorem 5.11. For the ith phase, $\sigma(i)$, with $m = m_i$ new nodes, we need to show that there is a subgraph H such that $val(H) \geq \frac{\delta}{m} \cdot \text{FAR}(\sigma_i)$ for some $\delta = \frac{1}{c} > 0$. That is, H either is a cycle or has an appropriate vine decomposition.

Consider the sequence of nodes (i.e., pages) that were vacated (i.e., evicted) during the phase, and partition this sequence into blocks of $m + 1$ consecutive nodes. Suppose there are R blocks.[11] We show that there is an H with $val(H) \geq \delta \cdot R$.

For each block, we select a "representative" node. Since there are m new nodes in the phase, the number of nodes vacated during a phase and currently outside the cache is at most m. Since there are $m + 1$ nodes in a block, at least one node of the block must be marked before any node in the next block is vacated. We choose one such node and call it a **rep**.

We partition the set of R reps into two types and use them to show the existence of a subgraph with $\Omega(R)$ value.

The definition of the "type" of a representative is somewhat technical. Consider the set V of nodes that are marked during a phase. The order in which these nodes are marked defines a k-node directed tree $T = (V, E)$, in which $\langle u, v \rangle$ is a directed edge (from u to v) if and only if the first request for v immediately follows a request for u. Note that the root of T is the first node marked in the phase (i.e., the node that begins the phase).

A **chain** in T is a directed path in T whose interior nodes (having in-degree = out-degree = 1 in T) all have degree 2 in G (such nodes are called **chain nodes**) and whose endpoints are not chain nodes. Note that a nonchain node is either the root of T or a leaf in T or has degree ≥ 3 in G. Intuitively, chains are good candidates for vines in the vine decomposition that we want to construct.

A rep is called **type 1** if it is not a chain node or if it is one of the first four reps or the last rep in a chain. Otherwise a rep is called **type 2**. To complete the proof, we establish the following two properties in Appendix D.

Lemma 5.4 *Let there be R_1 type 1 reps. Then there is a $(k + 1)$-node subtree T' in G with $\Omega(R_1)$ leaves; hence, by Theorem 5.13 (or by Theorem 5.3), $\mathcal{R}(G) = \Omega(R_1)$.*

Lemma 5.5 *Let there be R_2 type 2 reps. Then there is a subgraph H of G with $val(H) = \Omega(R_2)$; hence, by Theorem 5.13, $\mathcal{R}(G) = \Omega(R_2)$.*

∎

5.2 Dynamic Access Graphs and Experimental Studies

As presented, the access graph model assumes a priori knowledge of the underlying access graph. The most immediate application for algorithms suggested by this model (and the Markov chain model presented in Section 5.3.1) is user-specific customized paging. In order to apply "universal" algorithms such as FAR to the general (i.e., not user-specific) paging problem, we need to be able to dynamically evolve a good approximation of the access graph.

In this section we consider one way to dynamically evolve a weighted (undirected) access graph. The larger the weight on an edge (u, v), the less likely it is that page v (respectively, u) will be the next page requested after page u (respectively, v). This approach

---

[11] Without loss of generality, we can assume that $m < k$; otherwise, any algorithm must incur k faults for this phase. Thus, there is at least one complete block, and we ignore the last block if it contains fewer than $m + 1$ nodes.

uses these weights as distances and thus extends the underlying idea of the FAR algorithm by using a weighted graph theoretic distance to approximate LFD.

More specifically, we consider the following way to dynamically construct (or "learn") a weighted access graph G. As before, the nodes of G correspond to pages. When two nodes (i.e., pages) u, v are requested successively for the first time, an edge (u, v) with a weight of 1 is created. Every time such a pair $\{u, v\}$ is again requested successively, the weight w of the edge is reduced to $\min(\alpha w, 1)$ by some factor $\alpha < 1$. Periodically, say, every γk requests, the weight of every edge is increased by a factor $\beta > 1$. Thus, the access graph tends to reflect more current access patterns as it gradually tends to forget old patterns.

In conjunction with the above learning algorithm (and given a setting of the parameters α, β, and γ), we can run any access graph algorithm such as FAR to obtain a general algorithm for paging. One preliminary experimental study indicates that the following modification of the FAR algorithm is promising.

> **Algorithm FARL (FARTHEST-TO-LAST-REQUEST):** Let G be an access graph. (G can be an a priori known access graph or a dynamically evolving weighted graph.) Upon a page fault, FARL evicts that page u such that $\text{dist}_G(v, u)$ is maximized where v is the current page accessed just before the page fault.

FARL is also a reasonably natural approximation of LFD. FARL is not a marking algorithm; in fact, it can be shown that the competitive ratio (with respect to the optimal offline algorithm) of FARL is $\Theta(k \log k)$. However, one study indicates that FARL

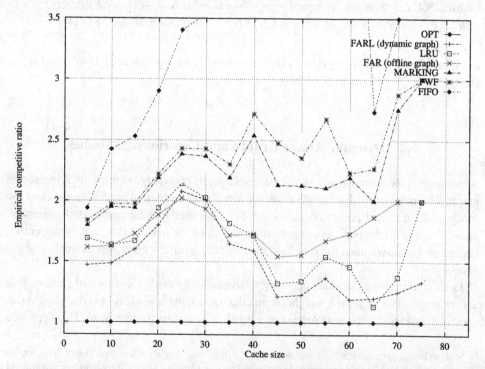

Figure 5.2: Simulation of paging strategies on page traces derived from execution of LaTeX program.

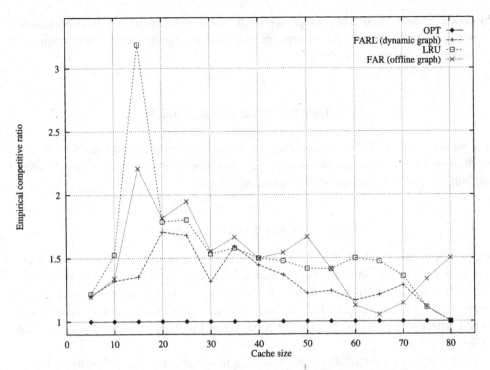

Figure 5.3: Simulation of paging strategies on page traces derived from execution of gnuplot program.

seems to outperform FAR, which in turn seems to be comparable in performance to LRU. One possible explanation is that marking algorithms guard against worst-case behavior; however, the set of marked pages is a crude (and sometimes poor) approximation for the set of pages most likely to be used in the near future. Figures 5.2 and 5.3 display simulations of the performance (i.e., "empirical competitive ratio") of various paging strategies based on page trace sequences obtained from the execution of LATEX (Figure 5.2) and gnuplot (Figure 5.3) programs.[12] The dynamic access graph curve refers to the performance of FARL using a dynamically constructed undirected access graph.[13] The performance of the same algorithm on a dynamically constructed directed access graph was not as good, even though these page traces correspond to the performance of programs that are naturally viewed as directed graphs. The FAR curve in the tables refers to the online performance of FAR on the actual access graph (which was computed offline).

Although the conclusions drawn from such initial studies are necessarily very tentative, it does seem clear that competitive analysis can offer new insights and lead to performance improvements in what is perhaps the most well-studied computational online problem.[14] We caution, however, that any gains in page fault performance must be evaluated in the context of complexity considerations (i.e., the time and space required for executing the algorithm). In this regard even LRU is considered "expensive" and is often approximated

---

[12] LATEX is a mathematical text processing utility, and gnuplot is a graph plotting utility.

[13] The parameters used for the dynamic construction of the access graph were $\alpha = 0.8$, $\beta = 1.5$, and $\gamma = 10$.

[14] In particular, in the context of a single user, the simulated cache sizes are significantly smaller than currently available cache sizes, and the page traces contain relatively few distinct page references.

by CLOCK. Clearly, the dynamic graph approach entails considerable computational costs. New paging applications (such as network access of files) might permit more computationally costly paging algorithms.

5.3   Distributional Paging Models

The access graph model for competitive paging analysis clearly resides within the framework of worst-case analysis. We now wish to consider a distributional approach while retaining the comparative aspect of competitive analysis.

5.3.1   The Markov Chain Model

We use the access graph model as the basis for a simple distributional approach. For example, we can weight the edge (u, v) in an access graph by the probability that v will be the next request following a request for u. Obviously, such a weighted graph represents a Markov chain. A Markov chain model provides perhaps the simplest probabilistic model reflecting locality of reference. A more general probabilistic model is considered in Section 5.3.2.

Once we adopt a distributional viewpoint, a reasonable measure of performance of a paging algorithm is the expected page fault rate. However, we retain one aspect of competitive analysis and compare the expected fault rate of an online algorithm with that of the expected fault rate of the optimal offline algorithm LFD. Throughout this section, we assume that the request sequence of pages is generated by a Markov chain known to the online player. Of course, if the Markov chain is not known, it could be (approximately) learned, for example, by using a frequency count based on a sufficiently large initial prefix of the request sequence.

Let the matrix M describe a Markov chain model (i.e., the (i, j)th entry of the matrix represents the probability that page j will be requested next after page i) and let ALG be a paging algorithm. Define

$$\text{ALG}(M) = \limsup_{n \to \infty} \frac{\mathbf{E}[\text{ALG}(\sigma)]}{n},$$

where σ is a length n sequence generated by the Markov chain M. Thus, ALG(M) measures an (upper bound) on the expected cost per request (i.e., the **fault rate**). As we do in the development of the access graph model, we can define the concept of an optimal online algorithm. Specifically, we want an online algorithm that minimizes the expected cost per request. This optimization can be formulated within the framework of the "Markov decision theory"; one can obtain the following result from a fundamental result in Markov decision theory.[15]

---

[15]   See, for example, Derman [132]. More generally, we can assume that the page requests are generated by an ℓ-stage Markov process whereby the next request is a probabilistic function of the last ℓ requests, in which case the underlying Markov process has $N^\ell \binom{N}{k}$ states instead of $N \binom{N}{k}$ states, as in the (one-stage) Markov chain model.

Theorem 5.14 *Consider a paging problem with N and k denoting the number of slow and fast memory pages, respectively. Let M be a Markov chain on N nodes. There exists a computable deterministic online algorithm* ON-OPT *such that* ON-OPT$(M) \leq$ ALG(M) *for all (deterministic or randomized) online algorithms* ALG *for this paging problem. Furthermore, each paging decision can be determined by solving a linear program in* $N\binom{N}{k}$ *variables.*

Theorem 5.14 shows that the algorithm ON-OPT is computable from the matrix M; however, this particular algorithm requires that a linear program in $N\binom{N}{k}$ variables be solved for each paging decision. Our goal, then, is to find a reasonably natural and efficient online algorithm that for all M is always within a constant factor of ON-OPT. That is, we want a result that is analogous to the existence of the uniformly competitive algorithm FAR (in the context of the access graph model).

It is surprising that many reasonable online algorithms do not perform well in the Markov chain model setting. In particular, no marking algorithm can, in general, perform better than MARK, and many natural (online) approximations of LFD perform rather poorly. To give examples of some Markov chains that cause problems for particular algorithms, we consider the Markov chain induced by a uniform random walk on a graph (see Appendix C). We define two problematic graphs: the **lollipop** and the **forked lollipop** (as depicted in Figure 5.4). The lollipop graph $L(m, n)$ is an $(n + m)$-node graph consisting of an n-clique including a connection node w and a length m path (called the handle) between the connection node w and the end node y of the handle. The forked lollipop graph $FL(m, n)$ is an $(n + m)$-node graph that is similar to the lollipop graph but has two nodes x and y adjacent to the end of a length $m - 1$ handle.

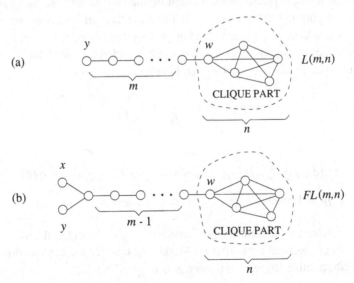

Figure 5.4: (a) Lollipop $L(m, n)$, and (b) forked lollipop $FL(m, n)$ graphs.

Exercise 5.7 Consider a random walk on the lollipop graph $G = L(m, n)$ starting at the connection node w. Let $f(m, n)$ denote the probability that y will be requested before all nodes in the clique part are requested. Show that $f(m, n) = \Theta\left(\frac{\log n}{mn}\right)$.

Theorem 5.15 *Let k be even. There is a $(k+1)$-state Markov chain M such that for any online (deterministic or randomized) marking algorithm* ALG, $\text{ALG}(M) \geq d_k \cdot H_{(k/2)} \cdot \text{ON-OPT}(M)$, *where* $\lim_{k \to \infty} d_k = \frac{1}{2}$ *and* H_m *is the mth harmonic number.*

PROOF. Let M be the Markov chain corresponding to a uniform random walk on the lollipop graph $G = L\left(\frac{k}{2}+1, \frac{k}{2}\right)$, with node y being the node at the end of the lollipop handle (see Figure 5.4 (a)). Consider the k-phase partition of an input sequence σ generated by M. Let $\text{ALG}(\phi_M)$ denote the expected cost of ALG to process a random phase ϕ_M in σ. Since the k-phase partition is independent of the algorithm, the ratio $\frac{\text{ALG}(M)}{\text{ON-OPT}(M)}$ is equal to the ratio $\frac{\text{ALG}(\phi_M)}{\text{ON-OPT}(\phi_M)}$. Suppose y is the node that begins a new k-phase. Then, clearly, the next phase will be started by a node z in the clique part of G. However, according to Theorem 4.4, the expected number of faults incurred by ALG is at least $H_{(k/2)}$. Consider a phase that starts at a node in the clique part of G and let $f_k = f\left(\frac{k}{2}+1, \frac{k}{2}\right)$ be a lower bound (see Exercise 5.7) on the probability that all nodes in the clique part will be requested before y is requested. That is, with probability at least f_k, y will be the node that begins the next phase. We thus have,

$$\text{ALG}(\phi_M) = \text{expected cost per phase}$$
$$\geq (\text{probability that phase starts at node } y) \cdot H_{(k/2)}$$
$$= \frac{f_k}{1 + f_k} H_{(k/2)}.$$

In contrast, consider an online algorithm **ALTR** that alternately evicts y and an arbitrary (fixed) node z in the clique of G. We define the number of faults in a phase by counting the fault that begins the next phase (but not counting the fault that began the present phase). When a phase begins at y, ALTR has one fault in this phase and starts the next phase with a hole at y. A phase beginning at a node v in the clique is called a "bad phase" if the next phase also begins at a node in the clique. On a bad phase, ALTR has two faults. The probability of a bad phase is $\frac{1}{1+f_k}(1 - f_k)$. Hence,

$$\text{ALTR}(\phi_M) \leq \frac{f_k}{1 + f_k} \cdot 1 + \frac{1 - f_k}{1 + f_k} \cdot 2.$$

Setting $d_k = \frac{f_k}{2 - f_k}$, we have

$$\text{ALG}(\phi_M) \geq d_k \cdot H_{(k/2)} \cdot \text{ALTR}(\phi_M) \geq d_k \cdot H_{(k/2)} \cdot \text{ON-OPT}(M).$$

Since $\lim_{k \to \infty} f_k = 1$, we have $\lim_{k \to \infty} d_k = \frac{1}{2}$, as desired. ∎

We now consider two natural approximations of LFD (the optimal offline algorithm), which are quite nonoptimal for particular Markov chains. (In the next section we present a uniformly competitive strategy in a more general setting.)

Algorithm MHT (MAXIMUM-HITTING-TIME): On a fault for page r, MHT evicts that page in cache whose expected time to be reached from r (i.e., the hitting time) is a maximum.

Algorithm LAST (HIGHEST-PROBABILITY-TO-BE-LAST): On a fault, evict the page that has the highest probability of being the last of the k pages in the cache to be requested.

Theorem 5.16 *There is a constant c such that for all k,*

1. *There is a $(k+1)$-state Markov chain M such that* MHT$(M) \geq c \cdot k \cdot$ ON-OPT(M).
2. *There is a $(k+1)$-state Markov chain M such that* LAST$(M) \geq c \cdot k \cdot$ ON-OPT(M).

PROOF.

1. Let M be the Markov chain induced by the random walk on a $(k+1)$-node forked lollipop graph $G = FL\left(\frac{k}{3}, \frac{2k}{3}\right)$, as shown in Figure 5.4 (b). Using the characterization of the commute time in terms of electrical networks (see Appendix C and Theorem 11.11), we have $h_{uv} + h_{vu} = 2 \cdot |E| \cdot R_{uv}$, where h_{uv} is the hitting time from u to v and R_{uv} is the effective resistance between u and v. For nodes x and y, the two nodes creating the fork at the end of the handle of G, we have $R_{xy} = 2$. Clearly, $|E| = \frac{4k^2}{9} + O(k)$. Since $h_{xy} = h_{yx}$ (according to the symmetry of this graph), we have

$$h_{xy} = h_{yx} = \frac{8k^2}{9} + O(k).$$

We now consider the hitting time from either x or y to any other node u in G. The hitting time to the connecting node w is approximately the hitting time for a random walk on a line of length $\frac{k}{3}$; that is,

$$h_{xw} = h_{yw} = \frac{k^2}{9} + O(k).$$

Clearly, any other node on the handle has a smaller hitting time. Moreover, upon reaching w, for any node u in the clique part, with probability $\frac{1}{2}$ the random walk will hit u before hitting the predecessor of w on the handle. It follows that the hitting time from either x or y to u is $\frac{2k^2}{9} + O(k)$. Thus, MHT will always alternate its hole between x and y with fault rate $\frac{1}{h_{xy}+h_{yx}} = \Omega\left(\frac{1}{k^2}\right)$. On the other hand, consider algorithm ALTR, which alternates its hole between, for example, x and some arbitrary node u in the clique part. ALTR will have fault rate $\frac{1}{h_{xu}+h_{ux}} = O\left(\frac{1}{k^3}\right)$, using the same analysis (from Theorem 11.11 and the easily observable fact that R_{xu} is approximately $\frac{k}{3}$) to calculate the commute cost $h_{xu} + h_{ux}$.

2. Consider the Markov chain induced by a random walk on a $(k+1)$-node undirected cycle. It is (at first) a surprising fact that starting at any node on the cycle, every other node is equally likely to be the node to be reached last. When the probabilities are slightly skewed (e.g., by some $\varepsilon > 0$ in the clockwise direction), it is the counter-clockwise neighbor that is most likely to be reached last. For the uniform random walk, the commute time characterization shows that the hitting time to a neighbor is $O(k)$, and this does not change with the ε-skewing. Hence, the expected fault rate of LAST is $\Theta\left(\frac{1}{k}\right)$. On the other hand, by alternating holes at two fixed antipolar nodes, the hitting time is $O(k^2)$ and hence the expected fault rate is $\Theta\left(\frac{1}{k^2}\right)$. ∎

5.3.2 A More General Distributional Model

The Markov chain paging model is a special case of a Markov process paging model. A Markov process model for paging would hypothesize a set of states (finite or infinite). For each pair of states s_i, s_j and page r, there is a probability $p(s_i, s_j, r)$ that when the process is in state s_i, the next page request will be r and the process will go into state s_j. Typically, we would restrict attention to a finite ℓ-stage Markov process paging model where the set of states

$$S = \{s \mid s \text{ corresponds to the vector of the last } \ell \text{ page requests}\},$$

and the next page request (and, hence, the next state) is a probabilistic function of the present state. Clearly, Markov chain paging is a one-stage Markov process paging model.

A finite state (for some small ℓ) Markov model obviously provides a better probabilistic model, but at what computational cost? That is, can we hope to derive a computationally efficient, uniformly competitive algorithm?[16] Perhaps surprisingly, the answer is yes and, indeed, this universal algorithm can be applied to a broader class (than finite state Markov processes) of input distributions.

Let D be a distribution generating the next page request. We say that D is **pairwise-predictive** if for all pairs of distinct pages q, r we can "efficiently" compute the probability $p(q, r)$ that page r will be requested before page q. To be more precise, we assume that for all distinct q, r we can compute $p(q, r)$ with complexity bounded by a polynomial in N.[17] Let $\mathcal{D}_{pp}$ be the class of all pairwise-predictive distributions.

Exercise 5.8 Let M denote an ℓ-stage Markov paging model. Show that $M \in \mathcal{D}_{pp}$. Specifically, for a fixed ℓ, show how to determine any $p(q, r)$ in time bounded by a polynomial in N, the total number of pages.

A pairwise-predictive distribution D and an online paging algorithm ALG naturally induce a weighted tournament on its set of states S. A **weighted tournament** $T(S, p)$ is a set of states S and a (probability) weight function $p : S \times S \to [0, 1]$ satisfying the property that $p(q, r) + p(r, q) = 1$ for all $r \neq q$ in S and $p(r, r) = 0$ for all $r \in S$. Given a pairwise-predictive distribution D and paging algorithm ALG, the weight function p is determined (by the definition of a pairwise-predictive distribution) by D (e.g., just before each new request), and S will be the set of ALG's cache pages. A **dominating distribution** $\tilde{p}$ for a tournament $T(S, p)$ is a probability function $\tilde{p} : S \to [0, 1]$ such that for every $q \in S$, if $u \in S$ is chosen with probability $\tilde{p}(u)$ then $\mathbf{E}[p(q, u)] \leq \frac{1}{2}$. This expectation is taken with respect to both the distribution D and the probability function $\tilde{p}$. Restated in terms of pairwise-predictive distributions and paging algorithms, for every q in the cache, if u in the cache is chosen with probability $\tilde{p}(u)$, then with probability $\geq \frac{1}{2}$, q's next request will occur no later than u's next request.

Theorem 5.17 *Every weighted tournament $T(S, w)$ has a dominating distribution.*

PROOF. We consider the computation of $\tilde{p}$ as the solution of a linear programming optimization. For example, we wish to minimize c subject to

$$\sum_{u \in S} p(q, u)\tilde{p}(u) \leq c \qquad \forall q \in S,$$

$$\sum_{u \in S} \tilde{p}(u) = 1,$$

$$\tilde{p}(u) \geq 0 \qquad \forall u \in S.$$

It suffices to show $c \leq \frac{1}{2}$, which we leave as an exercise.   ∎

---

[16] As in Markov chain paging, there is an exponential time algorithm.

[17] We can then assume that all $\{p(q, r)\}$ are precomputed or computed at most once if needed.

Exercise 5.9 Show that $c \leq \frac{1}{2}$, as stated in the proof of Theorem 5.17. Hint: Consider the dual linear program.

The proof of Theorem 5.17 shows that the dominating distribution is (polynomial time) computable.

Corollary 5.18 *The dominating distribution for any weighted tournament can be found by solving a linear programming problem in $|S|$ variables.*

We use these dominating distributions to construct a universally competitive algorithm for $\mathcal{D}_{pp}$.

> **Algorithm (DOMINATING-DISTRIBUTION):** Let $D \in \mathcal{D}_{pp}$ be the input distribution and let $\sigma = r_1, r_2, \ldots$ be a request sequence. On the tth request r_t, if r_t is in the cache, then do not evict any page (i.e., DOM is a demand paging algorithm); perhaps, however, one must change the "state" of the given distribution D. If r_t is a page fault, then (as determined by D) construct a weighted tournament $T_t(S, p)$ on the k pages presently in the cache. Evict page q with probability $\tilde{p}_t(q)$ where $\tilde{p}_t$ is the dominating distribution for the tournament $T_t(S, p)$.

Theorem 5.19 *For all request sequences σ, $\mathbf{E}[\mathrm{DOM}(\sigma)] \leq 4 \cdot \mathrm{ON\text{-}OPT}(\sigma)$. Note: The complexity per page fault is bounded by a polynomial in k, the cache size, assuming that for all distinct pairs of pages q, r, we have precomputed $p(q, r)$.*

PROOF. We define a charging scheme (only for the analysis) for each fault by DOM. When DOM evicts a page p, we charge the fault to a page $q = ch(p)$ in the cache of DOM before the fault but in the cache of ON-OPT after the fault. Moreover, no page has more than two "active charges" at any time.

Let $S^+_{\mathrm{ON\text{-}OPT}}$ be the set of pages in the cache of ON-OPT after serving r_t and let S^-_{DOM} be the set of pages in the cache of DOM before serving r_t. The charging scheme is as follows:

1. On an eviction of u by DOM, if $u \notin S^+_{\mathrm{ON\text{-}OPT}}$, then set $ch(u) = u$.
2. Otherwise, we claim that there is a page $q \in S^-_{\mathrm{DOM}} - S^+_{\mathrm{ON\text{-}OPT}}$ such that $ch(v) \neq q$ for all $v \in S^+_{\mathrm{ON\text{-}OPT}} - S^-_{\mathrm{DOM}}$. For such a q, set $ch(u) = q$.
3. If $ch(u) = q \neq u$ and u is later evicted by ON-OPT, then reset $ch(u) = u$.
4. Whenever u is requested, drop the charge by u; that is, $ch(u) = $ 'nil'.

Note that the requested page r_t (causing the eviction of u) is in $S^+_{\mathrm{ON\text{-}OPT}} - S^-_{\mathrm{DOM}}$, and according to rule 4, $ch(r_t) = $ 'nil'. Since

$$|S^+_{\mathrm{ON\text{-}OPT}} - S^-_{\mathrm{DOM}}| = |S^-_{\mathrm{DOM}} - S^+_{\mathrm{ON\text{-}OPT}}|,$$

there must be a $q \in S^-_{\mathrm{DOM}} - S^+_{\mathrm{ON\text{-}OPT}}$ that satisfies rule 3.

We next note that for any q and at any point in time, $|\{u \mid ch(u) = q\}| \leq 2$, since q can be charged at most once by a $u \neq q$ and at most once by q itself. Furthermore, we claim that with probability $\geq \frac{1}{2}$, $ch(u)$ will be requested no later than u: when we set $ch(u) \neq u$, it must be that $ch(u) \in S^-_{\mathrm{DOM}}$; hence, the construction of $\tilde{p}$ guarantees that $ch(u)$ will be requested before u with probability $\geq \frac{1}{2}$. Whenever $ch(u)$ is set or reset to u, this trivially ensures that $ch(u)$ will be requested no later than u.

We conclude the proof (somewhat informally) as follows. We charge at most two evictions (of, e.g., u_1 and u_2) by DOM to a given page q that is not in the cache of ON-OPT. The page q has probability $\geq \frac{1}{2}$ of being requested no later than the next request of either u_1 or u_2. Therefore, for every two evictions by DOM, with probability $\geq \frac{1}{2}$, ON-OPT will be charged a page fault. That is, the expected number of page faults by ON-OPT will be at least $\frac{1}{4}$ the number of evictions by DOM.   ∎

5.3.3   The Restricted Bayesian Compromise

One way to think about the results of the two previous subsections is to assume that the adversary announces in advance the class of distributions $\mathcal{D}$ from which one distribution $D \in \mathcal{D}$ will be used to generate the input sequence. For example, $\mathcal{D}$ can be the set of distributions generated by Markov chains. An online algorithm can attempt to dynamically learn or approximate the input distribution and then (if one exists) apply a uniformly competitive algorithm. More ambitiously, for some distribution classes $\mathcal{D}$, it might be possible to have a "fixed" algorithm (such as LRU) that performs well (i.e., as well as any online algorithm) for the entire class or we might have an algorithm that gradually learns a distribution while applying a uniformly competitive algorithm for the class. In any case, we want to extend the definition of competitiveness to the context in which the adversary is restricted to a class of distributions $\mathcal{D}$.

We can use a "restricted Bayesian" framework to formulate the concept of the competitive ratio in the context of restricted adversaries. Consider any online problem (for definiteness, say the paging problem). We assume that we know a class of distributions $\mathcal{D}$ such that the input sequence is generated by some distribution $D \in \mathcal{D}$. The online algorithm knows $\mathcal{D}$ and chooses an algorithm ALG that attempts to perform well for any $D \in \mathcal{D}$. The adversary seeing ALG then chooses $D \in \mathcal{D}$ in order to make the ratio of the expected performance of ALG to the expected performance of OPT as large as possible. That is, we define $\text{ALG}(D) = \mathbf{E}_\sigma[\text{ALG}(\sigma)|\sigma \text{ generated by } D]$, and we say that ALG is *c*-**competitive against the class** $\mathcal{D}$ if there exists a constant α such that for all $D \in \mathcal{D}$,

$$\text{ALG}(D) \leq c \cdot \text{OPT}(D) + \alpha.$$

The $\mathcal{D}$-**restricted competitive ratio** of ALG, denoted $\mathcal{R}(\text{ALG}, \mathcal{D})$, is then defined as $\inf\{c|\text{ALG is c-competitive against } \mathcal{D}\}$.

Clearly, this definition generalizes the pure competitive ratio (and, similarly, other nondistributional models such as the access graph model) by taking $\mathcal{D} = \{D_\sigma \mid \sigma \text{ is a fixed input sequence}\}$, where D_σ gives probability 1 to σ and probability 0 to all other input sequences. However, this approach is used primarily with respect to interesting classes of distributions, such as (for example) those generated by Markov processes.

We state without proof one interesting theorem showing for the paging problem that LRU is optimal against the following ε-**diffuse adversary**.[18] Let $\mathcal{D}_\varepsilon$ denote the class of all distributions D such that for every (page) request r and every sequence of requests σ,

$$0 \leq \Pr[r \text{ is the next page}|\sigma \text{ is the sequence of requests thus far}] \leq \varepsilon.$$

[18]   See Koutsoupias and Papadimitriou [231] and Young [345].

Theorem 5.20 *Let $\varepsilon > 0$ and let $N \geq \frac{k+1}{\varepsilon}$. Then* LRU *is an optimal online algorithm against the class* $\mathcal{D}_\varepsilon$. *That is, for all online* ALG, $\mathcal{R}(\text{LRU}, \mathcal{D}_\varepsilon) \leq \mathcal{R}(\text{ALG}, \mathcal{D}_\varepsilon)$. *Moreover, closed form bounds exist that are within a factor of 2 for the competitive ratio of* LRU, FIFO, *and* MARK. *For example, we have (approximately)*

- *For $\varepsilon \leq \frac{1}{k}$,*
    1.

$$\mathcal{R}(\text{LRU}, \mathcal{D}_\varepsilon) \leq 2 \left(1 + \ln \frac{1}{1 - \varepsilon k + \varepsilon} \right).$$

  And the same upper bound holds for FIFO *and* MARK.

    2. *For any deterministic or randomized online algorithm* ALG,

$$\ln \left(\frac{1}{1 - \varepsilon k + \varepsilon)} \right) \leq \mathcal{R}(\text{ALG}, \mathcal{D}_\varepsilon).$$

- *For $\varepsilon \geq \frac{1}{k}$,*
    1.

$$\mathcal{R}(\text{LRU}, \mathcal{D}_\varepsilon) \leq 2 \left(1 + k - \frac{1}{\varepsilon} + \ln \frac{1}{\varepsilon} \right)$$

  And the same upper bound holds for FIFO *and* MARK.

    2. *For any deterministic or randomized online algorithm* ALG

$$\left(1 + k - \frac{1}{\varepsilon} + \ln \frac{1}{\varepsilon} \right) \leq \mathcal{R}(\text{ALG}, \mathcal{D}_\varepsilon).$$

5.4 Historical Notes and Open Questions

The Access Graph Model. The access graph model was introduced in Borodin, Irani, Raghavan, and Schieber [80] and further developed in Irani, Karlin, and Phillips [198] and in Fiat and Karlin [151]. In particular, the results of Section 5.1.1 and 5.1.2 characterizing FIFO and LRU are due to Borodin et al. [80], and FAR is shown to be within a factor of $O(\log k)$ of the online optimal ratio. Chrobak and Noga [108] show that LRU is never worse than FIFO on any access graph. Irani, Karlin, and Phillips [198] prove Theorem 5.11, showing that FAR is uniformly competitive (i.e., within a constant factor of the online optimal). The study of *directed* access graphs was also initiated in Borodin et al. [80] and by Irani, Karlin, and Phillips [198]. More specifically, they study a class of directed graphs called "structured program graphs" that correspond to the control graph of a program that has been recursively constructed from composition statements, conditional statements, and loops (i.e., not allowing "go to" statements or exits from within a loop). Irani, Karlin, and Phillips [198] define an algorithm EVEN and show that EVEN is uniformly competitive for structured program graphs.

Fiat and Karlin [151] extend the access graph model to the "multifinger" access graph model in order to model multiprocess paging environments. They introduce a marking algorithm MP, which is uniformly competitive in the multifinger access graph model. Fiat and Karlin also define a randomized algorithm that is uniformly competitive with respect to oblivious adversaries.

Dynamic Access Graphs. Dynamic access graphs are defined and studied in Fiat and Rosen [156]. They define the FARL algorithm and experimentally study its performance in comparison with a number of other known paging algorithms.

Distributional Paging Models. Distributional (or average case) complexity is, of course, the more traditional analytic framework for studying paging. Franaszek and Wagner [160] compare the page fault rate for FIFO and LRU in a probabilistic input model when every page request is drawn independently from an arbitrary (but fixed) distribution. Shedler and Tung [312] were the first to suggest a Markov model for capturing locality of reference. The analysis of the Markov chain model in Section 5.3.1 is due to Karlin, Phillips, and Raghavan [211]. They analyze a number of plausible algorithms (beyond those discussed in Section 5.3.1) that are *not* uniformly competitive in the Markov chain paging model. They then define and analyze an algorithm COMMUTE, which they prove is uniformly competitive.

The more general problem of distributional paging is defined and considered in Lund, Phillips, and Reingold [252]. They show that the randomized algorithm DOM is uniformly competitive for the class $\mathcal{D}_{pp}$ of pairwise-predictive distributions; that is, those D for which we can compute (for each pair of pages u, v) at any point in time the probability $p(u, v)$ that page v will be referenced before page u.

The ε-diffuse adversary model is defined by Koutsoupias and Papadimitriou [232], who prove that LRU is optimal for the class $\mathcal{D}_\varepsilon$ of ε bounded distributions. For this ε-diffuse adversary model, Young [345] provides the closed form upper bound in Theorem 5.20 for the competitive ratio of LRU, FIFO and MARK that is within a factor of 2 of his lower bound for any deterministic or randomized algorithm. An ε-diffuse adversary is a particular example of the "restricted Bayesian" approach advocated in Koutsoupias and Papadimitriou [232]. This approach is well known in the general context of statistics and decision making under uncertainty. (See Chapter 15.)

Lookahead. In terms of pure competitive analysis, it is well understood that the standard (page fault) cost model for paging cannot address lookahead issues, since any fixed amount of lookahead can be negated if the adversary repeats each request sufficiently many times. See, for example, a short discussion of this issue in the context of the k-server problem in Ben-David and Borodin [54]. By introducing and considering the full cost, Torng [328] is able to relate the issues of lookahead and locality of reference. Another approach is suggested by Koutsoupias and Papadimitriou [231]. As part of a general framework they call comparative analysis, they compare the performance of an online algorithm with that of the best algorithm having limited lookahead. Of course, lookahead considerations can also be combined with other approaches, such as distributional paging.

Credit for Exercises. Exercise 5.2 is due to Manasse, McGeoch, and Sleator [256], where it is proved in the more general setting of task systems (see Chapter 9). Exercise 5.5 is due to Borodin et al. [80], and the related Exercise 5.6 is due to Irani, Karlin, and Phillips [198]. Exercise 5.7 is suggested in Irani, Karlin, and Phillips [198], and the exact bound stated here is due to Rabinovich [280]. Exercise 5.9 is due to Lund, Phillips, and Reingold [252].

Open Questions

5.1 (*Value = 12/T4*) Theorem 5.9 provides an asymptotic graph theoretic characterization for $\mathcal{R}(\text{LRU}, G)$. Does there exist an *exact* graph theoretic characterization?

5.2 (*Value = I4/T4*) Does there exist a "natural and reasonably efficient" *optimal* online algorithm for access graph paging? For what access graphs, if any, is FAR not optimal?

5.3 (*Value = I4/T4*) Does there exist a "natural and reasonably efficient" *optimal* online algorithm for Markov chain or Markov process paging?

5.4 (*Value = I4/T3*) For what other natural classes of distributions (considered as a "diffuse adversary") is LRU an optimal or asymptotically optimal online algorithm? Are there other "fixed" online algorithms that are optimal or near optimal for interesting classes of distributions?

CHAPTER 6

Game Theoretic Foundations

Competitive analysis (and, in general, any worst-case analysis) of an online problem can be viewed as the analysis of a two-person zero-sum game. In particular, determining the optimal competitive ratio of an online problem is equivalent to determining the "value" of the corresponding game.

In this chapter we review several basic game theoretic results that are relevant to the foundations of competitive analysis. We then focus on one particular issue: the representations of randomized algorithms and the relationships between them. In particular, we present a simple example (in the context of competitive analysis) in which different representations of randomized algorithms lead to different competitive ratios. The development here also lays the foundation for Chapter 8, where we study the minimax theorem and its relation to competitive analysis.

6.1 Games in Extensive and Strategic Forms

There are two primary mathematical abstractions of games: extensive and strategic. The extensive form representation of a game is what is commonly referred to as a "game tree." It specifies explicitly the rules of the game via the order of the moves for the various players, the information and choices available to a player whenever it is that player's turn to move, and the payoff obtained by all players in any possible play. Indeed, one possible way to depict or imagine a game in extensive form is via a tree.

A game in strategic form (also called "normal form") is commonly referred to as a "matrix game." As the name suggests, this representation abstracts away the individual moves and focuses only on strategies. As a more abstract representation of a game, it provides an important theoretical tool. The following example illustrates the extensive and strategic forms of a game.

Example 6.1 (Matching pennies) Consider Figure 6.1(a), in which an extensive form of a **matching pennies** game is given. In this game there are two players. Player 1 chooses "heads" (H) or "tails" (T). Then player 2 chooses H or T without knowledge of the first player's choice. If their choices are identical, player 1 pays one penny to player 2. Otherwise, player 2 pays one penny to player 1.

The root of the tree represents player 1's decision node (or choice set) consisting of the two possible moves: H and T. Similarly, the two nodes on the second level represent

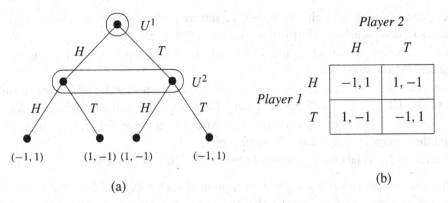

Figure 6.1: Matching pennies: in extensive form (a) and strategic form (b)

player 2's decision nodes with their possible move. Each one of the leaves is labeled with an ordered pair (h^1, h^2) that specifies the payoffs. Here, the first (respectively, second) coordinate h^1 (respectively, h^2) specifies the payoff for player 1 (respectively, 2). The oval shapes surrounding the root and the two nodes on the second level are called "information sets." Their purpose is to specify the information available to the players whenever they are called to make their move. For example, the information set U^2 (of player 2) includes two decision nodes. The interpretation is that player 2 cannot distinguish between the two nodes in this information set. This reflects the condition that player 2 does not know player 1's choice when it is his turn to move. The information set U^1 contains only one decision node and therefore reflects the fact that player 1, at this time, has no informational restrictions. (In any case, player 1 does not know anything relevant at this stage.)

The strategic form of the game is given in Figure 6.1(b). Here player 1 is the "row player" and player 2 is the "column player." Each row represents a strategy for player 1, and each column represents a strategy for player 2. The entries of the game matrix specify the payoffs for both players. Here again, the first (respectively, second) coordinate specifies the payoff for player 1 (respectively, 2).

We can now formally define the extensive and strategic forms of a game. For simplicity, the formulations that follow deal only with **finite games**, which have a finite set of players and a finite total number of decision alternatives for each player. The modeling of (competitive analysis of) online problems requires, in general, infinite games with two players: the online player and the adversary. In such games, the adversary has a "stop" alternative at each of its decision nodes, that is, an edge $e = (u, v)$ in the game tree with v being a leaf. All the basic game theoretic definitions and results presented in this chapter can be extended in a straightforward manner to countably infinite games having (at most) a countably infinite number of leaves.

6.1.1 Games in Extensive Form

An n-**person game in extensive form** consists of a set $N = \{1, 2, \ldots, n\}$ of **players** and a rooted tree T called the **game tree**. The game tree has the following structure:

1. The set of internal nodes of T is partitioned into $n + 1$ subsets P^i, $i = 0, 1, \ldots, n$, where for each $i \geq 1$ the members of P^i are called "the (decision) nodes of player i."

A node in P^0 is called a **chance node** (or a **nature node**); for each such node, there is an associated probability distribution over its outgoing edges.

2. All the outgoing edges of each internal node associated with a player are distinctly labeled by **action labels**.

3. For each $i = 1, 2, \ldots, n$, the set P^i of decision nodes is partitioned into k_i **information sets**, $U_1^i, U_2^i, \ldots, U_{k_i}^i$, such that for each information set U_j^i all the decision nodes in U_j^i are "isomorphic" in the sense that they have the same number of outgoing edges, and these outgoing edges have the same labels.

4. Each leaf of T is labeled by an n-tuple $(h^1, h^2, \ldots, h^n)$ of **payoffs**.

The above model gives a complete description of each "play" of the game under the following interpretation.[1] We define a **play** of the game Γ as any path from the root to a leaf, with the understanding that this path was obtained by the players (and chance) as follows. If, during a play of the game, a chance node v is reached, the probability distribution associated with v is "invoked" to choose one outgoing edge of v. The role of the players' decision nodes and payoffs is also self-explanatory. For a better understanding of the role of information sets, consider the following interpretation. Imagine that each player i is in command of k_i "agents" who play the game for her. For $j = 1, 2, \ldots, k_i$, the jth agent (of player i) is in charge of all decision nodes in the jth information set U_j^i. Before the start of the game, player i instructs the agents and gives each of them a strategy. After the game starts, the agents cannot communicate with each other (and with their boss). Now, suppose that the play of the game has progressed to a certain node $v \in U_j^i \subseteq P^i$; that is, the next move should be played by the jth agent of player i, who must choose one outgoing edge of node v. At this time the only information available to this agent is the description of the game Γ and instructions obtained from his "boss" (player i) before the start of the game. In particular, all nodes in U_j^i appear identical to this agent, since he is not told which path led to his information set. Since all nodes in the same information set are "isomorphic," the agent specifies one choice that is valid for any node in the information set.

The introduction of information sets allows for descriptions of complex games in which the players have incomplete information not only on the actions of the other players but also on their own previous actions. Formally, we say that a game is of **complete information** if and only if each information set is a singleton. Otherwise, we say that a game is of **incomplete information**. Examples of games of complete information include chess and tic-tac-toe. Examples of games of incomplete information include bridge and poker.

Example 6.2 Consider a specific online problem, such as paging with N slow memory pages and a fast memory of size k, and suppose that the online algorithm has unbounded memory (and therefore remembers all the requests thus far). Depending upon the type of adversary (oblivious, adaptive-online, or adaptive-offline), we can construct a two-person game in extensive form that defines a "game" between an online algorithm player and an adversary. In this example, we consider only the oblivious adversary and the adaptive-offline adversary. The root of the countably infinite game tree is an adversary decision

---

[1] In fact, as part of the definition, we must add the requirement that the extensive form description is "common knowledge" among the n players. This means that all players know it, each player knows that all the other players know it, each one knows that everyone else knows it, and so on (*ad infinitum*). For a discussion of why this requirement is necessary, see Myerson [265, sect. 2.7].

node. The next level consists of decision nodes of the online player. From then on, the levels alternate between the adversary and the online player. Each decision node for the adversary has $N + 1$ choices, one for each of the N possible requests and one leading to a leaf indicating that the adversary has stopped the game. Each decision node for the online player has k choices. If the most recent request is not in the cache, then the k choices correspond to each of the possible evictions. If the most recent request is in the cache, then there are $k - 1$ choices corresponding to the (nondemand) evictions and one choice corresponding to leaving the cache unchanged.

For an adaptive adversary, all the information sets are singletons, reflecting the fact that the adversary knows both the requests and the sequence of paging decisions that have been made thus far. For an oblivious adversary, all adversary decision nodes corresponding to the same request (sub)sequences are in the same information set.

The issue of a payoff function is somewhat problematic because of the way we have defined the competitive ratio of a randomized algorithm. Had we defined the competitive ratio as the expected ratio of the online cost to optimal offline cost, the payoff at each leaf would simply be this ratio. Instead, we have defined the concept of being c-competitive as, essentially (ignoring a possible additive constant), the ratio of expected online cost to (expected) optimal offline cost. To accommodate this definition, for each constant c (and for each additive constant α), we define the payoff value for the online player as follows.[2]

$$(\text{No. of online evictions}) - c \cdot (\text{No. of optimal offline evictions}) - \alpha.$$

Therefore, we have a countable collection $\{T(c, \alpha)\}$ of game trees. Clearly, a pure strategy (deterministic algorithm) for the online player is c-competitive if and only if there exists one tree $T' = T(c, \alpha)$ such that every leaf in T' has a nonpositive value. Namely, T' is the pruned game tree in which each decision node of the online player has outdegree 1 corresponding to the move determined by the algorithm given the entire sequence of requests thus far.

Exercise 6.1 Consider Example 6.2. Show how to construct the extensive form of the paging game for an adaptive-online adversary.

6.1.2   Games in Strategic Form

An n-**person game in strategic form** consists of a set $N = \{1, 2, \ldots, n\}$ of players; for each player i, $i = 1, 2, \ldots, n$, there is a set S^i of **pure strategies**. Also, there is a function $H : S^1 \times S^2 \times \cdots S^n \to \mathbb{R}^n$, called the **payoff function**. Each vector $\mathbf{s} \in S^1 \times S^2 \times \cdots S^n$ is called a pure strategy **profile**; for each strategy profile $\mathbf{s}$, the ith coordinate $H^i(\mathbf{s})$ of $H(\mathbf{s})$ specifies the payoff for the ith player for a play in which the players choose their respective strategies according to $\mathbf{s}$.

Example 6.3 Figure 6.1(b) illustrates a two-person game in strategic form in which the set of players is $N = \{1, 2\}$. Player 1 is the row player, and player 2 is the column player. The sets of pure strategies are $S^1 = S^2 = \{H, T\}$, and the payoff function is given by the matrix. For example, $H(T, T) = (-1, 1)$, so that $H^1(T, T) = -1$ and $H^2(T, T) = 1$.

---

[2] Since this is a zero-sum game (see Chapter 8), the payoff component for the adversary is minus the payoff value of the online player.

6.1.3   Transformations Between Strategic and Extensive Forms

In this section we deal with transformations between extensive and strategic forms. As may be expected, going from extensive form to strategic form abstracts away some information given in the extensive form (e.g., the order of the moves) so that some information is lost.[3] However, this transformation always preserves the sets of pure and mixed strategy sets and their (expected) payoffs.

Strategic $\mapsto$ Extensive

Given a game in strategic form, its corresponding extensive form is constructed as follows. The root of the game tree is player 1's decision node, which has $|S^1|$ outgoing edges labeled by the $|S^1|$ pure strategies in S^1. Each of these edges connects the root to the $|S^1|$ decision nodes of player 2. All these nodes are in the same information set, and each of them has $|S^2|$ outgoing edges that correspond to (and are labeled by) the $|S^2|$ pure strategies of player 2. Similarly, we construct the decision nodes (and information sets) for the rest of the players. In the final step, after constructing the $(|S^1| \cdot |S^2| \cdots |S^n|)$ decision nodes (and one information set) of player n, we construct $|S^n|$ outgoing edges from each of these decision nodes where each of these edges is connected to a leaf. The payoff vector at each leaf is $H(s^1, s^2, \ldots, s^n)$, where the pure strategy profile $(s^1, s^2, \ldots, s^n)$ represents the (unique) labeled path leading to this leaf.

Extensive $\mapsto$ Strategic

A key step in showing this transformation is to define the "pure strategies" in the extensive form game. Intuitively, in an extensive form game, a pure strategy for a player is a list of edge labels, one for each of his information sets. Formally, we proceed as follows. Let Γ be an n-person game in extensive form. Consider player i and let $U^i = \left\{ U_1^i, U_2^i, \ldots, U_{k_i}^i \right\}$ be the set of his k_i information sets. Each information set U_j^i contains decision nodes that have the same number of outgoing edges; we denote the set of choices (labels of outgoing edges) of each node in U_j^i by $D(U_j^i) = \{1, 2, \ldots, d_j^i\}$. Without loss of generality, we can assume that $\left| D(U_j^i) \right| > 1$. Each vector $(s_1, s_2, \ldots, s_{k_i})$ where $s_j \in D(U_j^i)$ is a pure strategy of player i. That is, player i has $\prod_{j=1}^{k_i} d_j^i$ pure strategies. Use S^i to denote the set of pure strategies of player i.

Now we calculate the payoff vector associated with a pure strategy profile $\mathbf{s} = (s^1, s^2, \ldots, s^n)$ of the n players. In general, if Γ includes chance moves, the payoff for each player is a random variable that depends on the chance moves. For each pure strategy profile $\mathbf{s}$ and for each leaf ℓ, use $p(\ell|\mathbf{s})$ to denote the probability that the leaf ℓ is reached given the profile $\mathbf{s}$. We calculate $p(\ell|\mathbf{s})$ as follows. If the unique path from the root to ℓ is not consistent with the path specified by $\mathbf{s}$, then $p(\ell|\mathbf{s}) = 0$. Otherwise, for each chance node along the path to ℓ, we multiply together the (chance) probabilities to choose the edge that falls on the path to ℓ.

---

[3] Whenever the extensive form has chance nodes, the payoffs are random variables; therefore, a transformation to strategic form results in a payoff matrix whose entries are *expected* payoffs (i.e., the first moment), so we also lose probabilistic information (i.e., the rest of the moments). (Of course, we could put a probability distribution in each entry.)

We can now define the payoff vector $H(\mathbf{s})$. For each leaf ℓ, use $H(\ell)$ to denote the vector of expected payoffs associated with ℓ (as defined by the extensive form). Then,

$$H(\mathbf{s}) = \sum_{\text{leaf } \ell} p(\ell | \mathbf{s}) H(\ell).$$

Thus, we have defined the strategic form corresponding to Γ.

Example 6.4 As shown above, each game in extensive form has a unique representation in strategic form. Nevertheless, two different extensive forms can give rise to the same strategic form. For example, consider Figure 6.2. Here the extensive forms (a) and (b) are "translated" into the same strategic form (c).

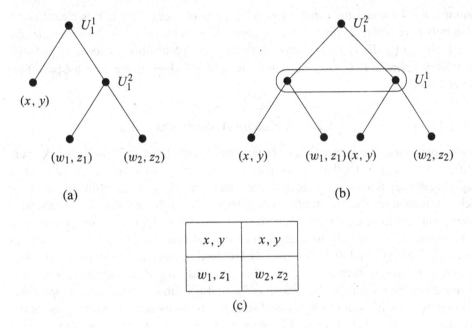

Figure 6.2: Two games (a,b) in extensive form having (c) the same strategic form.

Example 6.4 shows that the transformation from extensive to strategic is many to one. Nevertheless, it is easy to argue that all the possible representations (e.g., the two extensive representations and the strategic representation in Figure 6.2) do specify, in effect, the same game. Example 6.6 presents a situation in which the transformation from extensive to strategic does "lose structure" (i.e., in which pure paths occurring in the game tree are not represented in the game matrix).

6.2 Randomized Strategies: Mixed, Behavioral, and General

6.2.1 Mixed Strategies

A **mixed strategy** x^i for a player i (for games in either strategic form or extensive form) is a probability distribution over the set of his pure strategies S^i. For each pure strategy $s \in S^i$, we denote by $x^i(s)$ the probability that s will be chosen (i.e., $\sum_{s \in S^i} x^i(s) = 1$).

The interpretation is that the player uses some randomizing device before the start of the game and chooses one pure strategy according to this probability distribution. Given a mixed strategy profile $\mathbf{x} = (x^1, x^2, \ldots, x^n)$, where x^i is the mixed strategy of player i, the expected payoff vector $H(\mathbf{x})$ for the n players is given by

$$H(\mathbf{x}) = \sum_{\mathbf{s}} \mathbf{x}(\mathbf{s}) H(\mathbf{s}),$$

where $\mathbf{s} = (s^1, s^2, \ldots, s^n)$ is any pure strategy profile, and

$$\mathbf{x}(\mathbf{s}) = \prod_{i \in N} x^i(s^i).$$

Example 6.5 Consider the matching pennies game of Example 6.1. It is clear that by using only pure strategies the worst-case payoff of each player is -1. Now consider the mixed strategy $\left(\frac{1}{2}; H, \frac{1}{2}; T\right)$ for player 1; that is, with probability $\frac{1}{2}$ choose H and with probability $\frac{1}{2}$ choose T. Clearly, no matter what player 2 chooses, the expected payoff for player 1 is 0.

6.2.2   Behavioral Strategies

When a player uses a mixed strategy, she chooses, prior to the start of the game, one pure strategy at random. After that, her actions are completely deterministic. An alternative way to randomize is to make an independent random choice at each decision point (i.e., at each information set). Such a randomized strategy is called "behavioral." For complicated games, and also from an algorithmic viewpoint, behavioral strategies often appear to be more "natural." Nevertheless, for analysis it is often desirable to deal with mixed strategies (see, e.g., Chapters 7 and 8). In the context of (offline) complexity theory (under standard computational models such as Turing machines), it is easy to see the equivalence in terms of computational power between behavioral and mixed algorithms. Specifically, suppose that a Turing machine is running a behavioral strategy. In this case, the machine periodically (whenever it reaches a decision node), either generates random bits or refers to a tape of random bits and consumes enough bits to perform the randomized decision. There is no loss of generality by assuming that the random bits are chosen (and written on the tape) prior to the start of the computation; therefore, the random tape fixes, in effect, a pure strategy (a deterministic algorithm). All that is left for the machine to do is to read the random bits and copy them to its working tape. Hence, we can view this computation as an invocation of a mixed strategy. Thus, in worst-case analysis of offline problems, and whenever there are no memory restrictions on the machine, there is a complete equivalence between two types of randomized algorithms.[4]

With regard to games of incomplete information, the situation is similar, but perhaps more extreme. Here again, whenever there are no memory restrictions, the two types of randomizations are equivalent. However, under memory restrictions, the equivalence no longer holds. In fact, there is even a third type of randomization (that is typically

---

[4] It is well known that this equivalence need not hold in offline computational models when there are memory restrictions. See a negative example given for the "WAG" model by Beame, Borodin, Raghavan, Ruzzo, and Tompa [50] and a discussion in Poon [278].

neglected!). Therefore, we cannot simply assume that all representations of randomized algorithms are equivalent for (memory-bounded) online algorithms.

Example 6.6 (The absentminded driver) Consider a person sitting in a bar late at night after a long evening of drinking (he is currently sober but a little bit absentminded). In order to return home (payoff 1), he must take the highway and then get off using the second exit. Getting off at the first exit or continuing on the highway after the second exit leads to dangerous areas and a risk of being killed (payoff 0). The driver knows that he is absentminded and realizes, while still in the bar, that he would not be able to distinguish between the first and second exits because they look exactly the same. What is the optimal strategy for this person?

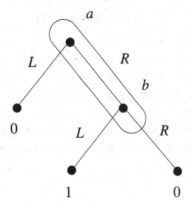

Figure 6.3: One-person game with incomplete information and imperfect recall.

The absentminded driver problem can be presented as a one-person game in extensive form (see Figure 6.3). Clearly, this is a game of incomplete information because the two decision nodes, a and b, are in the same information set. This means that the player cannot distinguish between them. Specifically, in any deterministic strategy the player chooses the same action at each of these nodes. Here, the set of pure strategies for the player is $\{L, R\}$ (L for "leave" the highway, and R for "remain"). Any probability mixture of them yields an expected payoff of 0, since once a pure strategy has been probabistically chosen, the player either leaves the highway immediately or never leaves the highway. In contrast, a behavioral strategy that chooses L or R with probability $\frac{1}{2}$ (independently at each decision node) has an expected payoff of $\frac{1}{4}$. Hence, if the absentminded driver uses a mixed strategy, he is surely going to endanger himself; if he uses a behavioral strategy, he has some chance to return home.

Example 6.6 demonstrates that in some games, behavioral strategies provide a distinct advantage over mixed strategies. Simply stated, in this example any (probabilistic) choice of a pure strategy eliminates more advantageous paths. Before we turn to another example that demonstrates the converse statement, we need (for the development that follows) to define behavioral strategies and their associated payoffs.

Clearly, when defining a behavioral strategy, we must take into consideration the constraints given by the information sets. Since a player cannot distinguish between any two nodes in the same information set, she must use the same randomizing device (i.e., probability distribution) for all nodes in the same information set. Formally, a behavioral strategy b^i for player i is a k_i-tuple $(b_1^i, b_2^i, \ldots, b_{k_i}^i)$ of probability distributions. The probability distribution b_j^i is over the set $D(U_j^i) = \{1, 2, \ldots, d_j^i\}$ of decision alternatives in each node in the jth information set U_j^i. Given a behavioral strategy profile $\mathbf{b} = (b^1, b^2, \ldots, b^n)$, where b^i is the behavioral strategy chosen by player i, we calculate the expected payoffs as follows. Use $\mathbf{b}(\mathbf{s})$ to denote the probability that the pure strategy profile $\mathbf{s}$ is chosen under $\mathbf{b}$ (defined similarly to $\mathbf{x}(\mathbf{s})$). Then, for each leaf ℓ use $p(\ell|\mathbf{b})$ to denote the probability that ℓ is reached given $\mathbf{b}$. That is,

$$p(\ell|\mathbf{b}) = \sum_{\mathbf{s}} \mathbf{b}(\mathbf{s}) p(\ell|\mathbf{s}).$$

Then, define the expected payoff vector

$$H(\mathbf{b}) = \sum_{\text{leaf}\,\ell} p(\ell|\mathbf{b}) H(\ell).$$

An n-person game (in extensive or strategic form) is **zero-sum** if each payoff vector $(h^1, h^2, \ldots, h^n)$ satisfies $\sum_{i=1}^{n} h^i = 0$. Two-person zero-sum games are of particular importance to us because they represent a strict antagonistic conflict between the two players such as the one between an online player and an adversary. When we describe two-person zero-sum games, we specify the payoffs only for the first player, with the understanding that the payoffs for the second player are the respective (additive) inverses.

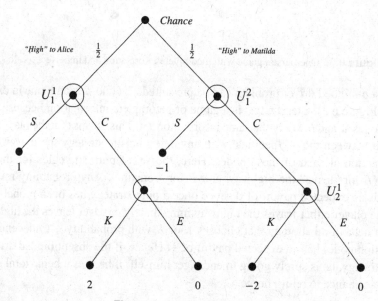

Figure 6.4: Kuhn's card game.

Example 6.7 (Kuhn) Consider the two-person zero-sum game depicted in Figure 6.4. As noted above, we specify the payoffs only for the first player, with the understanding that a payoff h for the first player at a leaf implies a payoff $-h$ for the second player in the same leaf. The extensive form given in this figure represents the following simple card game. The two players are a couple, Alice and Bob (the agents of the first player), and their guest, Matilda. The game starts with a chance move: two cards marked "high" and "low" are shuffled randomly and dealt; one card is given to Alice and the other to Matilda. The player who receives the low card pays \$1 to the player receiving the high card. Then the player who received the high card has the option to stop (labeled "S") or continue (labeled "C"). If the play continues, Bob, without knowing who received "high," instructs Alice and Matilda to exchange their cards or to keep them. After this move (and the exchange, if instructed by Bob), the holder of the low card pays $1 to the holder of the high card.

Let us now find optimal mixed and behavioral strategies for the players. We begin with mixed strategies. To this end, it is convenient to consider the strategic form of the game. A brief calculation gives the strategic form of the game:

Matilda

	S	C
(S, K)	0	$-\frac{1}{2}$
(S, E)	0	$\frac{1}{2}$
(C, K)	$\frac{1}{2}$	0
(C, E)	$-\frac{1}{2}$	0

Alice and Bob

Here again, since this is a zero-sum game, only the payoffs for the first player (Alice and Bob) are specified. Also, a pure strategy (x, y) for Alice and Bob means that Alice plays x and Bob plays y. The second row clearly "dominates" the first row (which means that under any choice by the second player, the second row gives a payoff that is either higher than or the same as the first row). Similarly, the third row dominates the forth row. In determining an optimal strategy, it is therefore sufficient to consider the "reduced" game in strategic form where the dominated strategies are eliminated.

Matilda

	S	C
(S, E)	0	$\frac{1}{2}$
(C, K)	$\frac{1}{2}$	0

Alice and Bob

Clearly, the optimal mixed strategy for both players is to randomize $\frac{1}{2} : \frac{1}{2}$ between their two pure strategies (in the reduced game). In particular, notice that this strategy guarantees the first player an expected payoff of $\frac{1}{4}$.

Now we calculate the optimal behavioral strategy for the first player. Suppose that Alice randomizes her decision in the information set U_1^1 using the probability distribution $(p : S, \ (1 - p) : C)$ (i.e., with probability p she chooses S, and with probability $(1 - p)$ she chooses C), and suppose that Bob randomizes in U_2^1 using the probability distribution $(q : K, \ (1 - q) : E)$. Then the expected payoff for player 1 is H^1, where

$$H^1 = \begin{cases} \frac{1}{2}(p + (1 - p)2q) - \frac{1}{2} = (1 - p)(q - \frac{1}{2}) & \text{if player 2 chooses } S; \\ \frac{1}{2}(p + (1 - p)2q) - q = p(\frac{1}{2} - q) & \text{if player 2 chooses } C. \end{cases}$$

Hence, player 1 cannot guarantee more than

$$\max_{p,q} \min \left\{ (1 - p)(q - \tfrac{1}{2}), \ p(\tfrac{1}{2} - q) \right\} \leq 0.$$

In Example 6.7, the behavioral strategies are inferior to the mixed ones because the first players (Alice and Bob) forgot what they already knew in the first information set. In contrast, mixed strategies allow the first player to make the random choices so that the decisions in the two information sets can be correlated.

6.2.3   General Strategies

Examples 6.6 and 6.7 show that there are games in which mixed strategies are superior to behavioral strategies and there are games in which behavioral strategies are superior to mixed strategies. However, yet another class of randomized strategies exists. Let Γ be a game in extensive form. A **general strategy** for a player i is a probability measure on the set of his behavioral strategies B^i. Given a general strategy g^i for player i, we denote by $g^i(b^i)$, with $b^i \in B^i$, the probability of b^i. Then, given a general strategy profile $\mathbf{g} = (g^1, g^2, \ldots, g^n)$, the definition of payoff vector $H(\mathbf{g})$ associated with $\mathbf{g}$ is straightforward. For each behavioral strategy profile $\mathbf{b}$, let $\mathbf{g(b)}$ be the joint probability $\mathbf{g(b)} = \prod_i g^i(b^i)$. Then,

$$H(\mathbf{g}) = \sum_{\mathbf{b}} \sum_{\text{leaf}\,\ell} \mathbf{g(b)} H(\ell).$$

Remark 6.1 Note that we can define the (expected) payoff vector even when the individual players use different types of (randomized) strategies.

In Example 6.8, we show how all three families of strategies can be different.

Example 6.8 (Isbell) Consider the two-person zero-sum game in extensive form shown in Figure 6.5. The first player has two information sets: U_1^1, with three decision alternatives x_1, x_2, x_3, and U_2^1, with two decision alternatives y_1 and y_2. The second player has one information set with two decision alternatives, L and R.

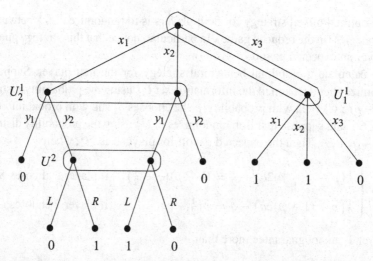

Figure 6.5: Two-person zero-sum game distinguishing between general, mixed, and behavioral strategies.

Consider the general strategy that chooses with probability $\frac{1}{2}$ the behavioral strategy

$$b_1 = \left(\tfrac{3}{4} : x_1, \; 0 : x_2, \; \tfrac{1}{4} : x_3, \; 0 : y_1, \; 1 : y_2\right),$$

and with probability $\frac{1}{2}$ the behavioral strategy

$$b_2 = \left(0 : x_1, \; \tfrac{3}{4} : x_2, \; \tfrac{1}{4} : x_3, \; 1 : y_1, \; 0 : y_2\right).$$

This general strategy guarantees the first player an expected payoff of $\frac{9}{16}$. Now we consider mixed strategies. When dominated strategies are eliminated, the following game results by transforming the extensive form into the strategic form.

Player 2

		L	R
Player 1	(x_1, y_2)	0	1
	(x_2, y_1)	1	0

Hence, using his optimal mixed strategy (with probability $\frac{1}{2}$ choose the first row), the first player obtains an expected payoff of $\frac{1}{2}$.

Finally, we calculate the optimal behavioral strategy for the first player. Using x_i and y_i to denote the probabilities of choosing the corresponding labels (i.e., $x_1 + x_2 + x_3 = 1$ and $y_1 + y_2 = 1$) and p to denote the probability that the second player chooses L, we find that the expected payoff for the first player is

$$H^1 = x_1 y_2 (1 - p) + x_2 y_1 p + x_3 (x_1 + x_2).$$

By symmetry, it follows that the first player must choose his probability distributions such that $x_1 = x_2$ and $y_1 = y_2 = \frac{1}{2}$. Substituting $x_3 = 1 - x_1 - x_2$ and the above identities, we find that, independent of the value of p,

$$H^1 = -4x_1^2 + \tfrac{5}{2}x_1.$$

This parabola attains its maximum at $x_1 = \frac{5}{16}$, and at this point it evaluates to $\frac{25}{64}$.

Hence, for the game in Example 6.8, general strategies are strictly better than mixed ones, and mixed strategies are better than behavioral strategies.

These examples generate several important questions. Perhaps the most important one is: Under what conditions are these three kinds of randomizations equivalent?

Exercise 6.2 Construct a game for which the optimal general strategy is better than the optimal behaviorial strategy, which, in turn, is better than the optimal mixed strategy.

6.3   Equivalence Theorems for Linear Games and Games of Perfect Recall

An n-person game in extensive form is called **linear** if for each player i no information set of player i is intersected twice by a path from the root to a leaf. For example, the absentminded driver game illustrated in Figure 6.3 and the game in Figure 6.5 are not linear. (All the other games presented thus far in this chapter are linear.)

The first equivalence theorem states that in a linear game every general strategy of any player is equivalent to some mixed strategy. The theorem follows from Lemma 6.1, which states that in a linear game, behavioral strategies are a special case of mixed strategies. Before we start, however, it is necessary to define the equivalence relation between strategies. Let Γ be a game. We say that two strategies of player i, x^i, and y^i are **equivalent** if for any strategy profile of the other players $\mathbf{s}^{\{-i\}}$,

$$H\left(x^i, \mathbf{s}^{\{-i\}}\right) = H\left(y^i, \mathbf{s}^{\{-i\}}\right).$$

That is, the resulting payoff vector (consisting of the payoffs for all players) is the same under x^i and y^i. In particular, x^i and y^i are equivalent if for each leaf ℓ the probability of reaching ℓ, given the strategy profile $(x^i, \mathbf{s}^{\{-i\}})$, equals the probability of reaching ℓ given the profile $(y^i, \mathbf{s}^{\{-i\}})$.

Lemma 6.1 *Let Γ be a linear game. Then for any behavioral strategy b^i for player i there is an equivalent mixed strategy x^i.*

PROOF. Let $b^i = \left(b_1^i, b_2^i, \ldots, b_{k_i}^i\right)$ be the behavioral strategy. Recall that for each $j = 1, 2, \ldots, k_i$, the probability distribution b_j^i is defined over the set of decision alternatives $D(U_j^i) = \{1, 2, \ldots, d_j^i\}$ of the jth information set U_j^i of player i. Use $b_j^i(d)$, where $d \in U_j^i$, to denote the probability of choosing d while in U_j^i. Let $s^i \in S^i$ be any pure strategy of player i. Thus, s^i specifies a path from the root to some leaf $\ell(s^i)$.

For each pure strategy $s^i \in S^i$ and for each information set U_j^i of player i, use $s^i(U_j^i)$ to denote the (unique) choice in $D(U_j^i)$ as specified by s^i. Define

$$x^i(s^i) = \prod_{j=1}^{k_i} b_j^i\left(s^i(U_j^i)\right),$$

which is the probability of choosing the pure strategy s^i. Since the game is linear, each information set of player i appears only once on the path from the root to $\ell(s^i)$; therefore, $x^i(s^i)$ is precisely the probability of reaching $\ell(s^i)$ under b^i. ∎

Hence, in a linear game the set of behavioral strategies B^i for player i is, in effect, a subset of the set of his mixed strategies X^i. In fact, B^i is a small subset of X^i. The number of independent probabilities (i.e., degrees of freedom) required to specify a behavioral strategy of player i is

$$\beta = \sum_{j=1}^{k_i}\left(\left|D(U_j^i)\right| - 1\right).$$

For a mixed strategy, this number is

$$\chi = \prod_{j=1}^{k_i}\left(\left|D(U_j^i)\right| - 1\right).$$

Thus, β is linear in the number $\sum_j |D(U_j^i)|$ of total choices of player i, whereas χ is exponential.[5]

In contrast, as shown in Example 6.6, Lemma 6.1 does not hold for nonlinear games.

The following theorem is a simple conclusion of Lemma 6.1.

Theorem 6.1 (Isbell 1957) *In a linear game, every general strategy g^i of player i is equivalent to a mixed strategy x^i.*

PROOF. The general strategy g^i is a probability measure over the set B^i of behavioral strategies. According to Lemma 6.1, every behavioral b^i strategy is equivalent to some mixed strategy x^i. Clearly, a probability measure over a set of mixed strategies is equivalent to some mixed strategy. ∎

We now turn to our second equivalence theorem. First we define games of "perfect recall." Intuitively, a player has perfect recall if at all times during a play he remembers what he knew as well as what he chose at all previous decision nodes.

We say that an edge e **precedes** a decision node v when there is a path on the game tree, starting with e and leading to v. **Player i has perfect recall** if for each edge e, outgoing from a node in an information set U_j^i, and each decision node $v \in U_k^i$, if e precedes v, then e precedes any other $x \in U_k^i$.

For example, in the game shown in Figure 6.4, player 1 does not have perfect recall, since the edge labeled C, outgoing from U_1^1, precedes the left decision node in the information set U_2^1 but not the right decision node of that set. Player 2, on the other hand, does have perfect recall (his only information set is a singleton). Note that in the definition of perfect recall, the information sets U_j^i and U_k^i need not be distinct. For example, consider the game shown in Figure 6.3. The player in this game does not have perfect recall, since the first (top) edge labeled R precedes the node b but does not precede the node a. This observation leads to the following lemma.

Lemma 6.2 *Any game in which every player has perfect recall is linear.*

Exercise 6.3 Prove Lemma 6.2.

We are now ready for the second equivalence theorem.

Theorem 6.2 (Kuhn 1953) *Let Γ be any game in extensive form. If player i has perfect recall, then every mixed strategy x^i of player i has an equivalent behavioral strategy b^i.*

PROOF. Let s^i be a pure strategy and let U_j^i be any information set of player i. We say that U_j^i is "reachable (under s^i)" if there exists a path from the root to a leaf, consistent with s^i, that intersects U_j^i.

Let x^i be any mixed strategy of player i. Recall that for each pure strategy s^i, $x^i(s^i)$ is the probability of choosing s^i. For each information set U_j^i of player i, $j = 1, 2, \ldots, k_i$,

---

[5] Recall that, without loss of generality, $|D(U_j^i)| > 1$. In algebraic terminology, we say that β (respectively, χ) is the dimension of the smallest vector space containing the set of behavioral (respectively, mixed) strategies.

define

$$p^i(U_j^i) = \Pr\left[U_j^i \text{ is reachable under } x^i\right]$$

$$= \sum_{s^i\,:\,U_j^i \text{ is reachable under } s^i} x^i(s^i).$$

Similarly, for each $d \in D(U_j^i)$, define

$$p^i(U_j^i; d) = \Pr\left[U_j^i \text{ is reachable under } x^i \text{ and the choice there is } d\ \right].$$

Now define the behavioral strategy $b^i = (b_1^i, b_2^i, \ldots, b_{k_i}^i)$. For each $j = 1, 2, \ldots, k_i$, and for each decision label $d \in D(U_j^i)$, set

$$b^i(d) = \frac{p^i(U_j^i; d)}{p^i(U_j^i)} \tag{6.1}$$

if $p^i(U_j^i)$ is positive. Otherwise, set $b^i(d)$ arbitrarily. (In the case where $p^i(d)$ vanishes, the value of $b^i(d)$ does not matter, since the information set U_j^i will not be reached when player i uses x^i.)

Let $\mathbf{x}^{\{-i\}}$ be a strategy profile of all players other than i. For each leaf ℓ, we prove that the probability of reaching ℓ under the profile $(x^i, \mathbf{x}^{\{-i\}})$ equals the probability of reaching ℓ under the profile $(b^i, \mathbf{x}^{\{-i\}})$. Fix any leaf ℓ and use π to denote the path from the root to ℓ. Let γ be the probability that all players other than i (and including chance moves) always choose edges of π while they are at decision nodes along π. Similarly, let χ and β be the probabilities that under x^i and b^i, respectively, player i chooses edges of π. It is then sufficient to prove that $\gamma\chi = \gamma\beta$, or that $\chi = \beta$ whenever $\gamma > 0$. Note that β is the product of all probabilities given by equation (6.1) of all the choices of player i along the path π.

Consider any edge e along π, outgoing from an information set U_j^i, and the consecutive decision node v of player i on the path π (i.e., there is no other decision node of player i in the path between e and v). Let U_k^i be the information set of v. Since e precedes v and since player i has perfect recall, e precedes all the nodes of U_k^i. Therefore, U_k^i is reachable under x^i if and only if U_j^i is reachable under x^i and the choice at U_j^i is e. Hence,

$$p^i(U_j^i; e) = p^i(U_k^i),$$

and it follows that the product β telescopes and reduces to $\beta = p^i(U_m^i; d_m)$, where U_m^i is the last information set along π, and d_m is the choice there (consistent with π). However, $p^i(U_m^i; d_m)$ is the probability that U_m^i is reachable under x^i and the choice there is d_m. It follows (by induction on m, and the perfect recall assumption) that $p^i(U_m^i; d_m)$ is the probability that under x^i all the choices are along π, which is precisely χ. ∎

Corollary 6.3 *In games of perfect recall, all three classes of randomized strategies (behavioral, mixed, and general) are equivalent.*

Every game of complete information is, in particular, a game of perfect recall; consequently, we derive the following corollary.

Corollary 6.4 *In games of complete information, all three classes of randomized strategies are equivalent.*

6.4 An Application to Paging and Competitive Analysis

Consider again Example 6.2, in which we formulate the competitive analysis of the paging problem as a game in extensive form. In the case of unbounded memory paging algorithms, the online player has perfect recall. Hence, by Corollary 6.3, all three classes of randomized algorithms are equivalent. However, when the online player has bounded memory, he clearly experiences imperfect recall. Therefore, in this case, we cannot assume any equivalence between the three types of randomizations.

Memory-bounded online algorithms are, of course, desired in any practical implementation. For example, all paging and list accessing algorithms presented in the previous chapters are bounded memory. However, presently we do not have general results concerning the relative power of the three types of (memory-bounded) randomized online algorithms. In the following subsections, we study a concrete example demonstrating the difference between mixed and behavioral algorithms with respect to competitive analysis. In particular, we distinguish between optimal (memoryless) mixed and behavioral paging algorithms.

6.4.1 Memoryless Behavioral Paging Algorithms

Consider a paging problem with a fast memory of size k and a slow memory of size $N > k$. A deterministic paging algorithm ALG can be defined as a function

$$\text{ALG} : \mathcal{S} \times \mathcal{C} \times \mathcal{R} \to \mathcal{S} \times \mathcal{C},$$

where $\mathcal{S}, \mathcal{C},$ and $\mathcal{R}$ are the state, configuration, and request sets, respectively. The configuration of a paging algorithm is simply the contents of its fast memory. We assume that the fast memory consists of k distinct pages. Based on the current state and configuration of the algorithm and the present request, ALG changes state and (if the request is not in the current configuration) changes configuration by evicting some node and then including the present request. A paging algorithm is called **bounded memory** if $\mathcal{S}$ is finite (i.e., independent of the length of the request sequence), and it is called **memoryless**[6] if $|\mathcal{S}| = 1$, that is, there is only one state, in which case

$$\text{ALG} : \mathcal{C} \times \mathcal{R} \to \mathcal{C}.$$

The same definitions can be applied to randomized algorithms. For behavioral algorithms we simply say that the function ALG is a probabilistic function; that is, ALG maps $\mathcal{S} \times \mathcal{C} \times \mathcal{R}$ to probability distributions over $\mathcal{S} \times \mathcal{C}$. For example, algorithm RAND of Section 4.2 is a behavioral memoryless paging algorithm, whereas algorithm MARK of Section 4.3 is a memory bounded (albeit not memoryless) behavioral algorithm.

---

[6] The appropriateness of this definition is arguable. Clearly, a more restrictive definition would permit only trivial (and noncompetitive) paging algorithms. On the other hand, a less restrictive definition might allow the algorithm to have access to an ordering of the fast memory pages. Under this definition, algorithms such as LRU and FIFO are memoryless.

Consider a deterministic or randomized memoryless online algorithm ALG. Since ALG is memoryless, a request for a node that is already in the current configuration is ignored. Therefore, in the case of a deterministic algorithm or a randomized algorithm against an adaptive adversary, we can assume that the adversary is "cruel," which means that it requests only those nodes not in the current cache of ALG. When $N = k + 1$, each (demand paging) algorithm exposes a single hole at all times and we can summarize the situation as follows: Wherever a randomized memoryless algorithm ALG has its hole (say, at node u), the adversary requests u, causing ALG to move the hole to some node v (and incur one page fault) according to some distribution that depends only on u.

We now point ahead to Chapter 11, where we prove the following result (see Corollary 11.10):

> For $N = k + 1$ the optimal competitive ratio of a memoryless behavioral demand paging algorithm against an oblivious adversary is at least k.

Of course, since algorithm RAND is k-competitive (for any N), the bound k is tight.

6.4.2 Memoryless Mixed Paging Algorithms

Using the definition of a deterministic memory-bounded (memoryless) algorithm, we immediately obtain the class of mixed randomized memory-bounded (respectively, memoryless) paging algorithms.

Let π be a cyclic permutation of $\{1, 2, \ldots, N\}$ (i.e., the set of slow memory pages). Let $\pi^{(m)}$ denote the m-fold composition of the (cyclic) permutation π. Consider the following deterministic "permutation" algorithm.

> **Algorithm PERM$_\pi$:** Upon a page fault on page i, evict page $\pi^{(m^*)}(i)$ such that m^* is the minimum m with $\pi^{(m)}(i)$ currently in the cache.

We first note that PERM$_\pi$ is memoryless (it does not store any information between successive requests). Also, when $N = k + 1$, algorithm PERM$_\pi$ always evicts page $\pi(i)$ for a fault on page i. Further, when $N = k + 1$, $\pi^{(m)}(i)$ is the configuration of PERM$_\pi$ after m faults starting in the configuration i.

Exercise 6.4 Show that algorithm PERM$_\pi$ is neither a marking algorithm (for $N \geq k + 1$) nor a conservative algorithm (for $N \geq k + 2$). Nevertheless, PERM$_\pi$ is k-competitive for all $N > k$.

When $N = k + 1$, we can denote any configuration of a permutation algorithm by an integer in $\{1, \ldots, N\}$. For all i and j, define

$$d_\pi(i, j) = \arg \min_m \pi^{(m)}(i) = j.$$

For example, if $k = 4$, then $d_{12354}(2, 1) = 4$ and $d_{12354}(1, 2) = 1$.

Clearly, the range of the function $d_\pi(i, j)$ is $\{1, \ldots, k\}$. Fix i and j with $i \neq j$. Each value in this range is obtained by exactly $(k - 1)!$ different permutations. Therefore, we obtain the following lemma.

Lemma 6.3 *For all $i, j \in \{1, \ldots, N\}$, $i \neq j$, $\sum_\pi d_\pi(i, j) = \frac{(k+1)!}{2}$.*

Consider any request sequence. We apply the standard k-phase partition technique.[7] Since $N = k+1$, during each k-phase the optimal offline algorithm incurs exactly one fault. It follows that the adversary can benefit by always prolonging each k-phase, thus forcing a particular configuration on the online algorithm. Therefore, we seek to characterize the behavior of MIXPERM with respect to such request sequences. Use $\phi_k(j)$ to denote the set of all k-phases that do not include a request to page j (that is, a sequence is in $\phi_k(j)$ if and only if it includes references to all pages $i \neq j$).

Lemma 6.4 *Let $\sigma \in \phi_k(j)$. Then* $\text{PERM}_\pi(\sigma)$, *the cost of* PERM_π *to process σ, is less than or equal $d_\pi(i, j)$ if it starts at configuration i.*

Proof of Lemma 6.4. We prove the lemma by induction on $n = |\sigma|$, where $\sigma = r_1, r_2, \ldots, r_n$ is any suffix of a k-phase in $\phi_k(j)$. The claim clearly holds for the empty suffix. Now, consider the first request r_1 of σ. If $r_1 \neq i$, PERM_π does not change its configuration and by the induction hypothesis, $Z_i = \text{PERM}_\pi(r_2, \ldots, r_n) \leq d_\pi(i, j)$, with Z_i denoting the cost of PERM_π for processing the suffix $r_2, \ldots, r_n$ starting at configuration i. Otherwise, $r_1 = i$ and by the induction hypothesis $Z_{\pi(i)} \leq d_\pi(\pi(i), j) = d_\pi(i, j) - 1$, so $\text{PERM}_\pi(\sigma) = 1 + Z_{\pi(i)} \leq d_\pi(i, j)$. ∎

Exercise 6.5 Show how the adversary can extend each k-phase so that in the worst case, the inequality in Lemma 6.4 is replaced with equality.

Clearly, there are $(N - 1)!$ different permutation algorithms. Define MIXPERM to be the uniform mixture of all the permutation algorithms, each with probability $\frac{1}{(N-1)!}$.

Theorem 6.5 *For $N = k+1$, MIXPERM is $\frac{k+1}{2}$-competitive against an oblivious adversary.*

PROOF. Now, suppose that all the permutation algorithms work concurrently and start at configuration i. Consider any k-phase $\sigma \in \phi_k(j)$. It is clear that upon processing σ, all permutation algorithms will end in configuration j. According to Lemmas 6.3 and 6.4 and Exercise 6.5, the total cost of all permutation algorithms to process σ is $\frac{(k+1)!}{2}$. Since there are $k!$ permutation algorithms, the expected cost of MIXPERM for this k-phase is $\frac{k+1}{2}$ and Theorem 6.5 follows. ∎

Exercise 6.6 Let $\pi_1 = (1, 2, \ldots, N)$ and $\pi_2 = (N, N - 1, \ldots, 1)$ be two permutations. Let MIX2PERM be the uniform mixture of PERM_{π_1} and PERM_{π_2}. For $N = k + 1$, show that MIX2PERM is also $\frac{k+1}{2}$-competitive.

6.5 Historical Notes and Open Questions

For a general study of game theory, see the texts by Myerson [265] and Luce and Raiffa [251].

It is difficult to trace the first use and formulation of games in extensive form and the notions of complete and incomplete information. A notable historical theorem (regarding games of complete information) is Zermelo's famous theorem regarding Chess (proving

---

[7] See Section 3.5.1.

that either White can force a win, or Black can force a win or else both can force a draw). The first in-depth study of the equivalence of behavioral and mixed strategies was by Kuhn [236], who stated and proved Theorem 6.2. Our version of this theorem, as well as the general game theoretic formulation used in this chapter, is based on the presentation by Hart [182]). Isbell [203] distinguishes between linear and nonlinear games and proved that behavioral strategies are a special case of mixed strategies in linear games. Isbell also gave a counter example that distinguishes between behavioral, mixed, and general strategies in nonlinear games. It is interesting to note that many game theory textbooks define extensive form as linear (i.e., they do not allow an information set to be intersected more than once by a path). Indeed, for the most part nonlinear games are ignored in game theory. Kuhn's theorem was proven only for finite games. Nevertheless, this theorem can be extended in a straightforward manner for infinite games, whenever the length of the game and the number of choices in each information set are at most countable. The theorem was extended by Aumann [21] to the case in which the number of choices in some information sets is uncountable. In general, games in which time is continuous do not fit in the model presented here.

Example 6.6 is known in the game theoretic folklore. Our particular interpretation is borrowed from Piccione and Rubinstein [275] (see also Aumann, Hart, and Perry [22]). Example 6.7 is from Kuhn [236]. The definition of a memory-bounded (behavioral) paging algorithm and, more generally, a memory-bounded behavioral k-server algorithm (see Chapter 11) is from Raghavan and Snir [284], and Corollary 11.10 is from Coppersmith, Doyle, Raghavan, and Snir [114]. Algorithm PERM$_\pi$ is from Chrobak, Karloff, Payne, and Vishwanathan [100], who showed that PERM$_\pi$ is k-competitive.[8] Algorithm MIXPERM and Theorem 6.5 are from Borodin and El-Yaniv [79].

Credit for Exercises. Exercise 6.2 and Exercise 6.3 are due to Chan (personal communication).

6.5.1   Open Questions

The issue of bounded recall, nonlinear games and, in general, of games involving bounded memory algorithms is not well studied in game theory. Nevertheless, it is of fundamental importance for the theory of computation. Therefore, we pose the following open questions.

6.1 (*Value = I4/T4*) Determine the relative power of general and mixed memoryless paging algorithms.

6.2 (*Value = I4/T4*) Determine the relative power of general, behavioral, and mixed memoryless list accessing algorithms.

6.3 (*Value = I5/T5*) Compare the relative power of general, behavioral, and mixed algorithms for bounded memory paging and list accessing algorithms.

6.4 (*Value = I4/T4*) The extensive form representation is not necessarily the most appropriate model for studying algorithmic problems such as the competitive analysis of (memory-bounded) online algorithms. (For example, it is instructive to try to model a few

---

[8]   Chrobak et al. called this algorithm ROTATE.

stages of the "competitive game" of a list accessing algorithm with three bits of memory against an adversary.) It would be of interest to devise a more suitable model for games involving bounded memory algorithms.

6.5 (*Value = 14/T5*) Characterize two-person zero-sum online games of imperfect recall (games involving bounded algorithms) for which Kuhn's theorem is still valid.

6.6 (*Value = 14/T3*) Find other examples of natural online games in which optimal (memory-bounded) behavioral, mixed (and general) algorithms attain different competitive ratios.

CHAPTER 7

Request–Answer Games

Thus far we have introduced a number of general online concepts (e.g., competitive-ness, adversaries, and so on) essentially within two specific online settings: list accessing and paging. If online algorithm analysis is to be more than an ad hoc collection of specific online problems, a more general framework is needed. Ben-David, Borodin, Karp, G. Tardos, and Wigderson [55] introduce a very general framework called request–answer games that can model most online settings studied in the literature. Within this framework we study randomized competitiveness, with respect to the various adversary models. It is possible to convert a randomized online algorithm against an adaptive-online adversary into a deterministic algorithm with at most a quadratic blow-up in the competitive ratio.

7.1 Request–Answer Games

A **request–answer system** consists of a **request set** R, a sequence of finite nonempty **answer sets** $A_1, A_2, \ldots$, and a sequence of cost functions, $cost_n : R^n \times A_1 \times A_2 \times \cdots \times A_n \to \mathbb{R}^+ \cup \{\infty\}$, $n = 1, 2, \ldots$.

A particular request–answer system is completely determined by the choice of R, the sequence $\{A_n\}$, and the cost function sequence $\{cost_n\}$. In many cases (such as the paging and static list accessing problems), it is natural to have one answer set A; that is, $A_i = A$, $i = 1, \ldots, n$.

Example 7.1 The paging problem with cache size k and slow memory size N is a request–answer system in which the request set is $P = \{1, 2, \ldots, N\}$ and the (single) answer set is $\{0, 1, \ldots, k\}$, where the answer "i" to a request "p" ($p \in P$) is interpreted as "replace the page currently stored in the ith cache slot with page p"; and the answer "0" is: "do nothing." The family of cost functions can be defined accordingly. We must ensure that the rules of paging are obeyed. This can be accomplished by assigning an infinite cost to invalid answers (e.g., an answer that does not result in the most recently requested page being in the cache).

Exercise 7.1 Verify that the static and dynamic list accessing problems can be modeled within the request–answer framework. Show that it is possible (but less natural) to model the dynamic problem using only a single (finite) answer set.

Remark 7.1 The requirement that each answer set A_i of a request–answer system is finite is an obvious limitation that excludes some known online problems from being request–answer systems. For instance, the trading game that is introduced in Chapter 14 assumes an infinite (and, in fact, continuous) answer set. Nevertheless, this finiteness requirement does not seem to be of great conceptual importance; we can usually "approximate" an infinite or even continuous answer set by a sufficiently large finite answer set. The restriction is introduced to facilitate the proof of Theorem 7.3.

We proceed by formally defining online algorithms. Next we define the various adversaries and the **request–answer game**, which is the interaction between the two players: the online algorithm and the adversary. Then we define the competitive ratio against these various adversaries.

7.1.1 Online Algorithms

A **deterministic online algorithm** ALG is a sequence of functions

$$g_i : R^i \to A_i, \qquad i = 1, 2, \dots.$$

Given an online algorithm ALG $= \{g_i\}$ and a request sequence $\sigma = \langle r_1, \dots, r_n \rangle \in R^n$, let ALG$[\sigma] = \langle a_1, \dots, a_n \rangle \in A_1 \times A_2 \cdots \times A_n$ with $a_j = g_j(r_1, \dots, r_j)$, $j = 1, 2, \dots, n$. The tuple ALG$[\sigma]$ is called the **answer sequence** of ALG with respect to σ. The cost incurred by ALG on σ, denoted by ALG(σ), is defined as

$$\text{ALG}(\sigma) = cost_n(\sigma, \text{ALG}[\sigma]).$$

A **randomized online algorithm** ALG is now defined as a mixed strategy, that is, as a probability distribution over the set of all deterministic online algorithms $\{\text{ALG}_x\}$. As discussed in Chapter 6, there are also behavioral and general randomized strategies. We recall that these three types of randomization are equivalent whenever there are no memory restrictions on the online algorithms involved. Throughout this chapter we assume unbounded memory algorithms; hence, there is no loss of generality in defining randomized algorithms as mixed strategies. Moreover, whenever it is convenient, we can use the behavioral representation of a randomized algorithm (see Theorem 7.3). It is important to realize that the results of this chapter have not been established for the case of bounded memory algorithms.

Given a request sequence σ, both the answer sequence ALG$[\sigma]$ and the cost ALG(σ) incurred by ALG are random variables.

7.1.2 Adversaries and Their Interaction with Algorithms

An adversary is viewed as a pair (Q, S), where Q is the **requesting component**, responsible for creating the request sequence, and S is the **servicing component**, which is an algorithm that is supposed to answer all the requests created by Q. The nature of these components determines the type of the adversary. As discussed in Chapter 4, we distinguish between **oblivious**, **adaptive-online**, and **adaptive-offline** adversaries.

The servicing component of an oblivious or adaptive-offline adversary is simply an optimal-offline answer sequence; that is, for a request sequence σ, it is the answer sequence

a that minimizes $cost_n(\sigma, a)$. This means that both these adversaries are completely determined by their requesting component, Q (and therefore can be uniquely identified by Q).

For the oblivious adversary, the requesting component Q is a fixed choice of a finite request sequence that may depend on the online algorithm against which the adversary is playing.

In contrast, for adaptive adversaries, the requesting component Q is a sequence of functions $q_i : A_1 \times A_2 \times \cdots \times A_{i-1} \to R \cup \{stop\}$, $i = 1, 2, \ldots, d_Q$. The index d_Q is a constant (chosen by the adversary) that may depend on the online algorithm, but not on the answer sequence generated by the algorithm. (That is, the adversary may produce only a bounded number of requests. In particular, the d_Qth request must be a *stop* request.)

This restriction on the adversary and the previous restriction on the finiteness of the answer sets are a simple way to guarantee (in Theorem 7.3) a finite expected value for the cost of the algorithm against the adversary and for the cost of the adversary against the algorithm (as long as an infinite cost answer is never chosen). Since this bound d_Q can be arbitrarily large, this restriction does not cause a significant problem for lower bound proofs (i.e., for constructing adversaries), and any restriction on the adversary can be viewed as a strengthening of the main result of this chapter, namely Corollary 7.4.

The game between an adaptive adversary (Q, S) and a randomized online algorithm ALG is an interaction between Q and ALG, resulting in request and answer sequences that will now be defined. To simplify the presentation, we assume at first that ALG is a deterministic algorithm. Then, to obtain the definitions for a randomized algorithm we treat the relevant variables as random variables, and take the expected values (with respect to the probability distribution induced by the randomized algorithm) of these variables.

We use $\sigma(\text{ALG}, Q)$ to denote the resulting request sequence, and $a(\text{ALG}, Q)$ to denote the resulting answer sequence. These sequences are of length n, and $n - 1$, respectively, where $n = n(\text{ALG}, Q)$ and n is determined by the interaction between Q and ALG with the restriction that $n \leq d_Q$. That is, $\sigma(\text{ALG}, Q) = \langle r_1, \ldots, r_n \rangle$ and $a(\text{ALG}, Q) = \langle a_1, \ldots, a_{n-1} \rangle$. The requests r_i are constructed by Q in response to the answers of ALG thus far. Formally, for $i = 0, 1, \ldots, n - 1$, $r_{i+1} = q_i(a_1, \ldots, a_i)$, and $r_n = stop$. We note that the answers of ALG are defined above (i.e., $a_i = g_i(r_1, \ldots, r_i)$). Since we are still considering a deterministic ALG, we have uniquely defined the **request–answer sequence**

$$r_1, a_1, r_2, a_2, \ldots, r_{n-1}, a_{n-1}, \; stop.$$

To complete the definitions of the adversaries, it remains only to define the online servicing component S of the adaptive-online adversary. S is defined as a sequence of functions

$$p_i : R^i \times A_1 \times A_2 \cdots \times A_{i-1} \to A_i,$$

for $i = 1, 2, \ldots$.[1] That is, S is a deterministic online algorithm that also has access to the previous answers of ALG, and answers the request sequence $\sigma(\text{ALG}, Q)$. With respect to an adaptive-online adversary ADV $= (Q, S)$, we denote the answer sequence of S by $b(\text{ALG}, Q) = \langle b_1, \ldots, b_{n-1} \rangle \in A_1 \times \cdots \times A_{n-1}$ where $n = n(\text{ALG}, Q)$.

---

[1] In fact, we can say $p_i : A_1 \times A_2 \times \cdots \times A_{i-1}, \to A_i$, since the servicing component S knows the requesting component Q and can therefore deduce the requests thus far from the answers of the online algorithm.

An alternative definition of the servicing component S gives this adversary less power by making S's answers independent of ALG's answer. In this case, S is simply an online algorithm. Therefore, we define a **blind adaptive-online adversary** to be one whose servicing component S is a sequence of functions $p_i : R^i \to A_i$, for $i = 1, 2, \ldots$.

7.1.3 The Competitive Ratio

We now formulate the previously introduced concepts of optimal offline cost and competitive ratio in terms of the above terminology. Given a request sequence $\sigma \in R^n$, the **optimal offline cost** on σ, denoted by OPT(σ), is defined as

$$\text{OPT}(\sigma) = \min\{cost_n(\sigma, a) : a \in A_1 \times \cdots \times A_n\}.$$

The optimal offline cost is our yardstick for measuring the competitiveness of deterministic algorithms and randomized algorithms against oblivious and adaptive-offline adversaries, but not against adaptive-online adversaries.

In this chapter γ and δ denote linear functions, $\gamma, \delta : \mathbb{R} \to \mathbb{R}$. For $\gamma(t)$ and $\delta(t)$, $(\gamma \circ \delta)(t)$ denotes the composition $\gamma(\delta(t))$. We use such linear functions to define the competitive ratio in a slightly more compact way (that encapsulates both the competitive ratio and the additive constant). In the following definitions, ALG$_x$ denotes a deterministic algorithm and ALG denotes a randomized algorithm, distributed over the set $\{\text{ALG}_x\}$ of all deterministic algorithms. Also, for all the following definitions, $\gamma(t) = c \cdot t + \alpha$ with $c \geq 1$.

- **Deterministic competitiveness:** ALG is γ-competitive (with a competitive ratio c) if for any request sequence σ,

$$\text{ALG}(\sigma) \leq \gamma\,(\text{OPT}(\sigma))\,.$$

- **Oblivious competitiveness:** ALG is γ-competitive against an oblivious adversary if for all σ,

$$\text{ALG}(\sigma) = \mathbf{E}_x\,[\text{ALG}_x(\sigma)] \leq \gamma\,(\text{OPT}(\sigma))\,,$$

where we abuse notation and use $\mathbf{E}_x$ to denote the expectation with respect to the distribution over the set $\{\text{ALG}_x\}$, which defines ALG.

- **Adaptive-online competitiveness:** Let ADV $= (Q, S)$ be an adaptive-online adversary and let ALG be a deterministic or randomized online algorithm. Abusing notation again, the cost of ALG against ADV will sometimes be denoted by ALG(ADV) or ALG(Q), where ALG(ADV) $=$ ALG$(Q) = cost_n(\sigma(\text{ALG}, Q), a(\text{ALG}, Q)) = \text{ALG}(\sigma)$, where $\sigma = \sigma(\text{ALG}, Q)$ (i.e., σ is constructed by Q via an interaction with ALG) and $n = n(\text{ALG}, Q)$. Similarly, we denote the adversary cost against ALG by ADV(ALG), defining it to be the quantity $cost_n(\sigma(\text{ALG}, Q), b(\text{ALG}, \text{ADV}))$. If ALG is randomized, then these costs, ALG(ADV) and ADV(ALG), will be random variables.

  We say that ALG is γ-competitive against an adaptive-online adversary if for all adaptive-online adversaries ADV $= (Q, S)$,

$$\mathbf{E}[\text{ALG}(\text{ADV})] = \mathbf{E}_x[\text{ALG}_x(\sigma(\text{ALG}_x, Q))]$$
$$\leq \gamma\,(\mathbf{E}_x[\text{ADV}(\text{ALG}_x)]) = \gamma\,(\mathbf{E}[\text{ADV}(\text{ALG})])\,.$$

- **Adaptive-offline competitiveness:** ALG is γ-competitive against an adaptive-offline adversary if for all adaptive-offline adversaries Q,

$$\mathbf{E}[\text{ALG}(Q)] = \mathbf{E}_x[\text{ALG}_x(\sigma(\text{ALG}_x, Q))]$$

$$\leq \gamma \mathbf{E}_x[(\text{OPT}(\sigma(\text{ALG}_x, Q)))] = \gamma(\mathbf{E}[\text{OPT}(\sigma(\text{ALG}, Q))]).$$

7.1.4   Request–Answer Games and Profit Maximization Problems

We briefly consider how to modify these definitions in order to develop a general model for profit maximization problems rather than a model for cost minimization problems. First we must reinterpret the $cost_n$ functions to stand for profit. Then for the definition of deterministic γ-competitiveness, we require the following inequality to hold for all σ:

$$\gamma(\text{ALG}_x(\sigma)) \geq \text{OPT}(\sigma).$$

Similarly, in all the other definitions of competitiveness, we simply move γ to the left side and reverse the inequality.

Exercise 7.2 Write the appropriate inequalities that define competitiveness for each of the adversaries in profit maximization games.

7.2   Randomized Adversaries

A **randomized adversary** is one whose requesting and/or servicing component is a randomized function. We now show that for request–answer games, randomization cannot help any of the three types of adversaries. The intuitive game theoretic reasoning for this statement is quite simple. Whenever the adversary is about to make a randomized decision, it can instead deterministically choose the decision that maximizes the intended ratio of expected costs. We now formally prove this assertion.

We recall (from Chapter 4) the notation $\overline{\mathcal{R}}_{\text{ADV}}(\text{ALG})$, which stands for the randomized competitive ratio of an algorithm ALG with respect to an adversary of type ADV.

Theorem 7.1 (Randomized adversaries) *Let G be any request–answer system and let* ALG *be any randomized online algorithm. Let* ADV *be any adversary and let* ADV' *be any randomized adversary of the same type as* ADV. *Then,* $\overline{\mathcal{R}}_{\text{ADV}}(\text{ALG}) \geq \overline{\mathcal{R}}_{\text{ADV'}}(\text{ALG})$.

PROOF.   Fix any request–answer system and let ALG be any mixed randomized algorithm. That is, ALG is a probability measure on the set of deterministic algorithms. For simplicity, we assume in this proof that the set of deterministic algorithms is enumerable. That is, we assume that ALG is a discrete probability distribution $\{z(i)\}$ where i is the index of the ith deterministic algorithm in some fixed enumeration.[2] We first establish the following simple result.

---

[2] The proof for the case in which the randomized algorithm is not a discrete probability distribution (e.g., when algorithms are parameterized by real numbers so that the set of deterministic algorithms is not enumerable) is only technically more complicated.

Claim: Let $a(i)$ and $b(i, j)$ be arbitrary functions from the nonnegative integers to the nonnegative reals. Let $\{p(i)\}$ and $\{q(j)\}$ be probability distributions. Let

$$\frac{a(i^*)}{b(i^*, j^*)} = \max_{i, j} \frac{a(i)}{b(i, j)}.$$

Then,

$$\frac{\sum_i a(i)p(i)}{\sum_{i,j} b(i, j)p(i)q(j)} \leq \frac{a(i^*)}{b(i^*, j^*)}.$$

The proof of the claim is easily established as follows. For all i, j,

$$\frac{a(i^*)}{b(i^*, j^*)} \geq \frac{a(i)}{b(i, j)};$$

therefore, clearly, $a(i^*)b(i, j) - b(i^*, j^*)a(i) \geq 0$. Since all the quantities involved are nonnegative, we retain the inequality after multiplying both sides by $p(i)q(j)$ and then summing over i and j. Hence,

$$0 \leq \sum_{i,j} p(i)q(j) \cdot \big(a(i^*)b(i, j) - b(i^*, j^*)a(i)\big)$$

$$= a(i^*) \sum_{i,j} b(i, j)p(i)q(j) - b(i^*, j^*) \sum_{i,j} p(i)q(j)a(i)$$

$$= a(i^*) \sum_{i,j} b(i, j)p(i)q(j) - b(i^*, j^*) \sum_i \left(p(i)a(i) \sum_j q(j) \right)$$

$$= a(i^*) \sum_{i,j} b(i, j)p(i)q(j) - b(i^*, j^*) \sum_i p(i)a(i).$$

Let $\{\text{ALG}_k\}$ be an enumeration of deterministic online algorithms and let $\{z(k)\}$ be a discrete probability distribution on deterministic algorithms defining a randomized online algorithm ALG. We illustrate the proof by considering the case of an adaptive (say, for definiteness, blind) online adversary.[3] Let $\text{ADV}' = (Q', S')$ be any randomized blind adaptive-online adversary where the requesting component $Q' = \{p(i)\}$ is a probability distribution over the set $\{Q_i\}$ of deterministic requesting components, and the servicing component $S' = \{q(j)\}$ is a probability distribution over the set $\{S_j\}$ of deterministic online algorithms.[4] Define

$$a(i) = \sum_k \big[z(k) \cdot \text{ALG}_k \left(\sigma(Q_i, \text{ALG}_k)\right)\big];$$

$$b(i, j) = \sum_k \big[z(k) \cdot S_j \left(\sigma(Q_i, \text{ALG}_k)\right)\big].$$

---

[3] The proof for adaptive-offline and oblivious adversaries is somewhat simpler in that these adversaries can only randomize their requesting components, whereas an adaptive-online adversary can also randomize its servicing component. The fact that randomization does not help an oblivious adversary can also be obtained as a direct consequence of Lemma 8.2.

[4] Here again, for simplicity we assume that this distribution is discrete.

Notice that

$$c(i, j) = \frac{a(i)}{b(i, j)}$$

is the cost ratio, online to adversary, obtained for the randomized algorithm ALG with respect to a (deterministic) blind adaptive-online adversary (Q_i, S_j). Thus the "optimal adversary" can force ALG to have a ratio of $\max_{i,j} c(i, j)$. According to the claim, this ratio is not smaller than any ratio obtained against any randomized adaptive-online adversary.

∎

7.3   Relating the Adversaries

In this section we state and prove two interesting theorems. The first theorem connects the three adversaries, and the second theorem states that the adaptive-offline adversary is so powerful that randomization cannot be of help against it.

Theorem 7.2 *Let* ALG *be a γ-competitive online algorithm against an adaptive-online adversary and suppose there exists a δ-competitive online algorithm* ALG' *against an oblivious adversary. Then,* ALG *is $(\gamma \circ \delta)$-competitive against an adaptive-offline adversary.*

PROOF. Fix any adaptive-offline adversary Q for ALG. ALG is γ-competitive against any (deterministic) adaptive-online adversary. According to Theorem 7.1, ALG performs at least as well against a randomized adaptive-online adversary as it performs against the best deterministic adaptive-online adversary. In particular, ALG is γ-competitive against the blind, randomized adaptive-online adversary $V = (Q, \text{ALG}')$, which uses as a requesting component the (adaptive-offline) requesting component Q and as a servicing component, the online algorithm ALG'. Denoting ALG = $\{\text{ALG}_x\}$ and ALG' = $\{\text{ALG}'_y\}$, we thus have

$$\mathbf{E}_x[\text{ALG}_x(\sigma(\text{ALG}_x, Q))] \le \gamma\big(\mathbf{E}_x\mathbf{E}_y[\text{ALG}'_y(\sigma(\text{ALG}_x, Q))]\big).$$

ALG' is δ-competitive relative to the optimal offline algorithm. Hence, for all x,

$$\mathbf{E}_y[\text{ALG}'_y(\sigma(\text{ALG}_x, Q))] \le \delta(\text{OPT}(\sigma(\text{ALG}_x, Q))).$$

Using the linearity of the expectation operator and combining these two inequalities, we have

$$\mathbf{E}_x[\text{ALG}_x(Q)] \le (\gamma \circ \delta)(\mathbf{E}_x[\text{OPT}(\sigma(\text{ALG}_x, Q))]).$$

∎

We now argue that given only the premises of Theorem 7.2, one cannot conclude that ALG is more competitive than $\gamma \circ \delta$ against an adaptive-offline algorithm.[5] To do so, we consider the paging problem and let ALG and ALG' be algorithms RAND and MARK, respectively, of Chapter 4. We assume a fast memory of size k and a slow memory of

---

[5] Irani and Karp (reported in [56]) show that Theorem 7.2 is optimal in a stronger sense than that suggested in Exercise 7.3. They show that for any γ and δ, there exist a request–answer system and algorithms ALG and ALG', as in the theorem, such that *no algorithm* is better than $\gamma \circ \delta$-competitive against an adaptive-offline adversary.

size $N = k + 1$. We know that against any adaptive-online adversary, the competitiveness of RAND is k. We also know that MARK is H_k-competitive against an oblivious adversary when $N = k + 1$. We need to derive a lower bound on the competitiveness of RAND against adaptive-offline adversaries. Since a lower bound is our goal, it is sufficient to obtain this result with respect to a particular adaptive-offline adversary. Consider the following adaptive-offline adversary ADV $= (Q, S)$ where the requesting component Q is a "cruel adversary" that always requests the page that is missing from RAND's fast memory. The servicing component S is algorithm LFD of Chapter 3. Clearly, RAND pays one for each request. The coupon collector problem (see Section 8.3) can now be used to obtain an upper bound on ADV(RAND). We present the following claim as an exercise:

Exercise 7.3 Consider the random request sequences generated by the interaction of the cruel adversary Q and RAND. With respect to such request sequences, let X_i be a family of random variables where X_i is the number of page requests following the $(i - 1)$st fault by LFD up to and including its ith fault. Prove that $\mathbf{E}[X_i] \geq (k + 1) H_k$. Conclude that the competitive ratio of RAND against ADV $= (Q, \text{LFD})$ is at least $(k + 1) H_k$.

The next theorem shows that there is no advantage to using randomization against adaptive-offline algorithms.

Theorem 7.3 *Let* ALG *be a γ-competitive randomized online algorithm against adaptive-offline adversaries. Then there exists a deterministic γ-competitive online algorithm.*

PROOF. Let Q be any adaptive-offline adversary. For this proof, it is convenient to view the request–answer game between Q and ALG in extensive form, where the game tree branches at nodes in odd layers represent choices that Q can make, and branches at nodes in even layers represent choices that ALG can make.

With respect to this game tree, the adversary Q is simply a function that maps each node in odd layers to a branch. As a behavioral algorithm, ALG specifies a probability distribution over the branches for each node in even layers. A "position" in the game is a node on the game tree. The game starts at the root, and the position is updated according to the choices made by Q and ALG. Thus, we can uniquely identify each position by a pair (σ, a), where σ and a are (respectively) request and answer sequences leading to this node.

An odd-layered node in the game tree is called an "instantly winning" position for the adversary if for the pair (σ, a) associated with this node, $cost(\sigma, a) > \gamma(\text{OPT}(\sigma))$.

An odd-layered node in the game tree is called "winning" for the adversary if there exists a bound B such that the adversary's strategy (that is, a sequence of choices for all odd-layered nodes in the subtree) is such that no matter what the online algorithm's choices are (for even-layered nodes in the subtree), each path resulting from their interaction reaches an instantly winning node within fewer than B steps. Any path from a winning node to an instantly winning node is called a "winning path."

If ALG is γ-competitive against an adaptive-offline adversary, then for every (adaptive-offline) requesting component Q, there exists some deterministic algorithm ALG_x such that $\text{ALG}_x(Q) \leq \gamma(\text{OPT}(\sigma(\text{ALG}_x, Q)))$. This must be true, since the expected cost of ALG, $\mathbf{E}_x[\text{ALG}(Q)]$, is a weighted average of the costs incurred by all deterministic algorithms and at least one of the deterministic algorithms must achieve the average. Thus we have

$$\forall Q \, \exists \text{ALG}_x : \text{ALG}_x(\sigma(\text{ALG}_x, Q)) \leq \gamma(\text{OPT}(\sigma(\text{ALG}_x, Q))).$$

Notice that we are not done yet. We need to prove the same statement with the opposite order of quantification; namely:

$$\exists \text{ALG}_x \ \forall Q : \text{ALG}_x(\sigma(\text{ALG}_x, Q)) \leq \gamma(\text{OP\.{T}}(\sigma(\text{ALG}_x, Q))).$$

That is, we need to prove that there exists a deterministic algorithm that cannot be defeated by *any* adversary.

Clearly, the root of the game tree is not a winning position for any adversary (otherwise, ALG is not γ-competitive). Fix the first request and consider all the choices for answers that a (deterministic) algorithm can make at this stage (we are now on a node in the second layer). If for each choice x there is an adversary $Q(x)$ such that the next position is winning, since there is only a finite number of answers, we can combine all the adversaries $Q(x)$ to form a single adversary that has a winning position already at the root of the game tree (clearly, this is a winning position because all the winning positions have bounded length winning paths and there are only finitely many of them). Hence, we conclude that there is at least one choice x that does not lead to a winning position. By induction, if we have already determined a sequence of answers $x_1, x_2, \ldots, x_{i-1}$, each of which does not lead to a winning position, we can repeat the same argument and prove that there exists a choice for the next level, x_i, which does not lead to a winning position. Hence, there exists a deterministic algorithm that is never defeated by any adaptive-offline adversary, and it follows that this algorithm is γ-competitive.   ∎

Exercise 7.4 Show that the proof of Theorem 7.3 collapses if we consider adaptive-online adversaries instead of adaptive-offline adversaries.

Exercise 7.5 The proof of Theorem 7.3 used a "behavioral" representation of the randomized algorithm ALG (i.e., the algorithm was represented by a collection of probability distributions each giving weights for branches of the outgoing edges of an even-layered node). Show that the theorem can be proven for a mixed randomized algorithm (i.e., ALG is a distribution over deterministic algorithms).

Theorems 7.2 and 7.3 yield two useful and easy corollaries.

Corollary 7.4 *Let* ALG *be a γ-competitive online algorithm against an adaptive-online adversary and suppose there exists a δ-competitive online algorithm against an oblivious adversary. Then there exists a $(\gamma \circ \delta)$-competitive deterministic online algorithm.*

Corollary 7.5 *Let* ALG *be a γ-competitive online algorithm against an adaptive-online adversary. Then there exists a $(\gamma \circ \gamma)$-competitive deterministic online algorithm.*

Notice that Theorem 7.3 (and the subsequent corollaries) is not constructive. It merely asserts that there exists a deterministic $(\gamma \circ \delta)$-competitive algorithm. There are two constructive versions of this theorem. We do not state these theorems here but note that one of them assumes that we know a proof for the γ-competitiveness of ALG that is based on a computable potential function.[6]

---

[6] All potential function arguments used in this text are based on computable potential functions; for example, consider the potential functions used in Theorems 4.1 and 11.17

The second constructive version of Theorem 7.3 requires that the particular instance of the request–answer system is such that past requests and answers cannot have too much of an effect on future costs.

We note that the constructive versions of Theorem 7.3 can be applied in several interesting cases (e.g., the derandomization of the HARMONIC k-server algorithm of Section 11.5). However, in general, Theorem 7.3 cannot be made constructive.

Exercise 7.6 Show that Theorems 7.2 and 7.3 hold for profit maximization problems.

7.4 Historical Notes and Open Questions

Raghavan and Snir [284] introduced the concept of an adaptive adversary. Theorems 7.2 and 7.3 were obtained by Ben-David, Borodin, Karp, Tardos, and Wigderson [56]. Raghavan and Snir [284] then obtained results similar to these theorems. The difference between these two sets of parallel results is that the Raghavan and Snir theorems are stated in terms of a different definition of the competitive ratio based on the limit of the ratio with respect to infinitely long request sequences. We note that in many cases of interest, their definition is provably equivalent to the more standard definition used here.

Ben-David et al. [56] provide two constructive versions of Theorem 7.3 and its corollaries. However, Deng and Mahajan [129] argue that, in general, Theorem 7.3 cannot be made constructive.

Credit for Exercises. Exercise 7.3 is from Karlin (reported in [56]).

7.4.1 Open questions

Regarding the power of the adversaries, we are not familiar with a single "natural" example (e.g., for any of the specific applications of this text) in which a randomized algorithm against an adaptive-online adversary beats the best deterministic algorithm. We also know that for the abstract k-server model (Chapter 10) the best-known deterministic upper bound $(2k - 1)$ is within a factor of 2 of the general lower bound (k) for randomized algorithms against an adaptive-online adversary. This leads to the following question.

7.1 (*Value = I4/T4*) Find a "natural" problem for which there is an algorithm against an adaptive-online adversary that attains a competitive ratio smaller than the deterministic one. Alternatively, prove that there is no such problem/algorithm for a wide class of problems.

7.2 (*Value = I2/T3*) The requirements that each answer set be finite and that the adversary must choose an upper bound d_Q on the length of the request sequence were introduced in order to guarantee (in the proof Theorem 7.3) a finite expected value for the cost of the algorithm against the adversary and for the cost of the adversary against the algorithm. Can these assumptions be eliminated, or what is the most general setting in which Theorem 7.3 still holds?

7.3 (*Value = I2/T3*) We defined adaptive-online adversaries in terms of a nonblind adversary. We do not know whether there is an equivalence between blind and nonblind adversaries. Nevertheless, all the known upper bounds hold with respect to nonblind adversaries, as do the lower bounds (and Theorem 7.2) with respect to blind adversaries. Therefore, in retrospect, all known results apply to both kinds of adversaries.

For bounded memory algorithms, the randomized competitive ratio is not well defined until we specify the class of randomized algorithms. Given the practical importance of bounded memory, it would be very interesting to consider request–answer games in the context of bounded memory algorithms. In particular, we ask the following.

7.4 (*Value* = l5/T4) Can Corollary 7.4 be extended to the case of bounded memory algorithms with respect to mixed, behavioral, and general randomized strategies?

Following the definition of the deterministic competitive ratio in terms of the inequality $\text{ALG}(\sigma) \leq \gamma(\text{OPT}(\sigma))$, we are naturally led to consider the inequality $\mathbf{E}[\text{ALG}(\sigma)] \leq \gamma(\mathbf{E}[\text{OPT}(\sigma)])$ for the randomized competitive ratio. That is, we study the ratio of expected costs. It is also possible to consider the ratio $\frac{\text{ALG}(\sigma)}{\text{OPT}(\sigma)}$ and then generalize this to $\mathbf{E}\left[\frac{\text{ALG}(\sigma)}{\text{OPT}(\sigma)}\right]$ in order to define the randomized competitive ratio. That is, we could study the expectation of the ratio of costs. One can reconsider this chapter in terms of this alternative definition.

7.5 (*Value* = l4/T3) Consider an adaptive adversary, and now let the randomized competitive ratio be defined as the expectation of the ratio of the online to adversary costs. Can an analogue of Corollary 7.4 be proven?

CHAPTER 8

Competitive Analysis and Zero-Sum Games

In this chapter we continue to study some game theoretic basic results that have applications and implications to competitive analysis. In particular, based on the formulations (in Chapter 6) of games in strategic form, and pure and mixed strategies, we study two-person zero-sum games, the minimax theorem, and some of its implications. One of the more useful applications of the minimax theorem is "Yao's principle," which we develop and explain in depth in Section 8.3.

8.1 Two-Person Zero-Sum Games

Recall from Chapter 6 the definition of a two-person zero-sum game. The competitive analysis of an online problem can be seen as a solution of a two-person zero-sum game. In particular, given any finite request–answer game (e.g., of profit maximization), one possible way to view it as a two-person zero-sum game is the following. The first player who is the online player seeks a strategy that maximizes the payoff, defined as the reciprocal of its competitive performance; that is, the payoff is the ratio of online profit to optimal offline profit.[1] The adversary seeks a strategy that minimizes the online player's payoff. Thus, the two players are in strict opposition and the game is zero-sum. In this section, and for the remainder of this chapter, we present a few results for two-person zero-sum games that have some implications for competitive analysis.

Unless otherwise is stated, we will be concerned with games of perfect recall in which we have an equivalence between general, mixed, and behavioral strategies (see Theorem 6.2). In general, the theorems stated here, such as the minimax theorem, do not apply with respect to behavioral strategies under games of imperfect recall (and nonlinear games). However, under perfect recall we can assume, without loss of generality, that all games are given in their strategic form.

We consider a finite game in strategic form in which the payoffs for the first player are specified by the matrix $G = (h_{ij})$. In what follows, the row index, i, enumerates the pure strategies for the first player. Similarly, the column index, j, enumerates the pure strategies of the second player. If the first player chooses i and the second player chooses j, the payoff for the first player is $h(i, j) = h_{ij}$. (In this case, we say that the pair (i, j) was chosen.)

---

[1] There is a reason for this particular definition: one cannot take the payoff function to be the optimal offline profit over the online profit (so that player 1 is the minimizer). See Section 8.3 for details.

A pair (i^*, j^*) of pure strategies is called a **saddle point** if for all i and j,

$$h(i, j^*) \le h(i^*, j^*) \le h(i^*, j). \tag{8.1}$$

In other words, the payoff $h(i^*, j^*)$ is a guaranteed gain or "security value" for player 1, which means that if player 1 plays i^*, he is guaranteed to receive a payoff $h(i^*, j^*)$ regardless of player 2's choice. In the same way, $h(i^*, j^*)$ is also a maximum loss for player 2. Equivalently, the "maximin strategy" guarantees to player 1 a payoff $h(i^*, j^*)$, and the "minimax strategy" guarantees to player 2 a negative payoff of no more than $h(i^*, j^*)$. (Clearly, when the minimax strategy for player 1 and the maximin strategy for player 2 yield the same payoff, these strategies form a saddle point.) Hence, a strategy (i^*, j^*) is a saddle point if and only if

$$\max_i \min_j h(i, j) = h(i^*, j^*) = \min_j \max_i h(i, j).$$

When a saddle point exists, we say that the game "has a value with pure strategies" (and the value is $h(i^*, j^*)$) or that the game has a "pure strategy equilibrium." In general, a saddle point need not be unique (however, it follows by definition that the values corresponding to all saddle points are identical). As shown in the following example, saddle points do not exist in general.

Figure 8.1: (a) The left game has two pure equilibrium pairs, and (b) the right game does not have a pure equilibrium.

Example 8.1 Consider the games shown in Figure 8.1. The game in (a) has two pure equilibriums (or saddle points), $(1, 1)$ and $(1, 3)$ (in both cases, the value is 3). To see this, notice that the pure strategy 1 is a "maximin" strategy with the maximin value, $\max_i \min_j h(i, j) = 3$. On the other hand, strategies 1 and 3 are both "minimax" strategies for player 2, giving values of $\min_j \max_i h(i, j) = 3$.

The game in Figure 8.1(b) does not have a saddle point, since $\max_i \min_j h(i, j) \ne \min_j \max_i h(i, j)$.

Let $G = (h_{ij})$ be a (two-person zero-sum) game. For mixed strategies $x = (x_1, x_2, \ldots, x_m)$ and $y = (y_1, y_2, \ldots, y_n)$, for players 1 and 2, respectively, we define

$$H(x, y) = H_G(x, y) = \sum_{i=1}^{m} \sum_{j=1}^{n} h(i, j) x_i y_j,$$

the expected payoff for player 1 under x and y. The game with players 1 and 2 using $H(x, y)$ as payoff function is called the **mixed extension of** G.

A saddle point of the mixed extension of G is any pair (x^*, y^*) of mixed strategies such that for any x and y,

$$H(x, y^*) \leq H(x^*, y^*) \leq H(x^*, y).$$

In this case, we say that $H(x^*, y^*)$ is the value of the mixed extension of G or that it is the **value of G under mixed strategies**. Also, we call the pair (x^*, y^*) a "mixed strategy equilibrium." Clearly, for any mixed strategy equilibrium (x^*, y^*),

$$H(x^*, y^*) = \max_x \min_y H(x, y) = \min_y \max_x H(x, y).$$

Example 8.2 Consider the game in Figure 8.1(b). Let $x_p = (p, 1 - p)$ denote the mixed strategy of player 1 in which p is the probability of choosing the first row. Analogously, use $y_q = (q, 1 - q)$ to denote the mixed strategy of player 2. The pair given by $p = \frac{1}{2}$ and $q = \frac{3}{4}$ is a mixed equilibrium of the game and the value is $\frac{5}{2}$. First, it is easy to see that under the mixed pair (x_p, y_q) the expected payoff for player 1 is

$$H(x_p, y_q) = 4pq - 3p - 2q + 4.$$

Now it is easy to verify that

$$\max_p \min_q H(x_p, y_q) = \min_q \max_p H(x_p, y_q) = \frac{5}{2}.$$

In their influential monograph *Theory of Games and Economic Behavior*, von Neumann and Morgenstern [333] proved their celebrated "minimax theorem," stating that any finite two-person zero-sum game in strategic form has a value (under mixed strategies).

Before we state and prove the minimax theorem, consider the following lemma, which summarizes what we have already used indirectly: the two alternative (and equivalent) conditions for the fact that a game has a value.

Lemma 8.1 *Let Γ be a two-person zero-sum game. The following conditions are equivalent:*

(a) Γ *has a value v;*
(b) $\max_x \min_y H(x, y) = \min_y \max_x H(x, y)$;
(c) *There is a real number v, and mixed strategies x and y such that*

$$H(x, j) = \sum_{i=1}^{m} h(i, j)x_i \geq v, \quad \text{for } j = 1, 2, \ldots, n,$$

$$H(i, y) = \sum_{j=1}^{n} h(i, j)y_j \leq v, \quad \text{for } i = 1, 2, \ldots, m.$$

Exercise 8.1 Prove Lemma 8.1.

We state and prove the minimax theorem based on Brouwer's fixed point theorem.[2]

---

[2] For a proof of Brouwer's fixed point theorem, consult Smart [320] or Hurewicz, Wallman, and Hurewicz [193].

Theorem 8.1 (Brouwer's fixed point theorem) *Any continuous map* $\phi : X \to X$ *of a compact convex set* X *in* $\mathbb{R}^n$ *has a fixed point. That is, there exists a point* $x \in X$ *with* $\phi(x) = x$.

Theorem 8.2 (von Neumann) *Every finite two-person zero-sum game has a value. That is,*

$$\max_x \min_y H(x, y) = \min_y \max_x H(x, y). \tag{8.2}$$

PROOF. Given any mixed strategies x and y, for players 1 and 2, we define for $i = 1, \ldots, m$ and $j = 1, \ldots, n$,

$$p_i = p_i(x, y) = H(i, y) - H(x, y),$$

$$q_j = q_j(x, y) = H(x, y) - H(x, j).$$

Thus, using condition (c) in Lemma 8.1, it is sufficient to prove that there exists a pair x, y with $p_i \leq 0$ and $q_j \leq 0$ for all i and j. Use X to denote the set of all m-ary probability vectors. Similarly, Y is the set of all n-ary probability vectors. We define the mapping $\phi : X \times Y \to X \times Y$ as follows. For each x and y, $\phi(x, y)$ is the pair (χ, η) of probability vectors given by

$$\chi_i = \frac{x_i + \max\{p_i, 0\}}{1 + \sum_{k=1}^m \max\{p_k, 0\}}, \quad i = 1, \ldots, m,$$

$$\eta_j = \frac{y_i + \max\{q_j, 0\}}{1 + \sum_{k=1}^n \max\{q_k, 0\}}, \quad j = 1, \ldots, n.$$

It is easy to verify that ϕ is continuous. Hence, by Brouwer's fixed point theorem, there exists a pair (x^*, y^*) such that $\phi(x^*, y^*) = (x^*, y^*)$. Hence, for each $1 \leq i \leq m$,

$$x_i^* \sum_{k=1}^m \max\{p_k, 0\} = \max\{p_i, 0\},$$

where $p_\ell = p_\ell(x^*, y^*)$ for all $1 \leq \ell \leq m$. We claim that for some i, $x_i^* > 0$ and $p_i \leq 0$, which implies that for all i, $\max\{p_i, 0\} = 0$. To prove this claim, consider any index i for which $x_i^* > 0$ (there must be such an i, since x^* is a probability vector). Assume by contradiction that $p_i > 0$. It must be that $x_i^* = 1$; however, by definition $p_i = 0$, which proves the claim. It follows that for all i, $p_i \leq 0$. Analogously, we prove that for all j, $q_j \leq 0$. ∎

Notice that Theorem 8.2 is existential. It does not tell us how to compute a pair of optimal (mixed) strategies. Nevertheless, there are various algorithms for computing optimal mixed strategies.[3]

One interpretation of the minimax theorem is that in any two-person zero-sum game any player does not lose anything by revealing his best mixed strategy before the start of the game. Further, a simple observation is that if player 1 (respectively, player 2) knows

---

[3] Perhaps the most well-known (and efficient) algorithms are based on the equivalence between minimax and the duality theorem of linear programming (see, e.g., Raghavan [286]).

that player 2 (respectively, player 1) uses (an optimal) mixed strategy, one of his optimal (mixed) strategies is deterministic. This is established in the following simple lemma (which is a corollary of the minimax theorem).

Lemma 8.2 (Loomis's lemma) *Let x^* and y^* be optimal mixed strategies for players 1 and 2. Then,*

$$\max_i H(i, y^*) = \min_j H(x^*, j) = H(x^*, y^*).$$

Alternatively,

$$\min_y \max_i H(i, y) = \max_x \min_j H(x, j) = H(x^*, y^*). \tag{8.3}$$

PROOF. Set $v = H(x^*, y^*)$, the value of the game. According to Theorem 8.2, v is well defined. Clearly, for all j, $v \le H(x^*, j)$. Hence $v \le \min_j H(x^*, j)$. Assume, by contradiction, that $v < \min_j H(x^*, j)$. Then for all j, $v < H(x^*, j)$. Setting $y^* = (y_1^*, y_2^*, \ldots, y_n^*)$, we have

$$v = \sum_{j=1}^{n} v y_j^* < \sum_{j=1}^{n} H(x^*, j) y_j^* = H(x^*, y^*).$$

However, this clearly contradicts the minimax theorem (Theorem 8.2). Hence,

$$v = \min_j H(x^*, j).$$

An analogous argument proves that

$$v = \min_i H(i, y^*).$$

∎

Lemma 8.2 entails a simple but very useful conclusion: Yao's principle. Specifically, from equality (8.3), it follows that for any mixed strategy y for player 2,

$$\max_i H(i, y) \ge \max_x \min_j H(x, j). \tag{8.4}$$

This means that we can obtain a bound on player 1's best (randomized) payoff by calculating his best deterministic payoff with respect to any mixed strategy for player 2. Since in this game player 1 is a (profit) maximizer, this bound is an upper bound (i.e., a negative result concerning player 1's performance). We refer to inequality (8.4) as **Yao's inequality**. When player 1 is a (cost) minimizer, Yao's inequality is

$$\min_i H(i, y) \le \min_x \max_j H(x, j) \tag{8.5}$$

for any mixed strategy y. The application of Yao's inequality (as a tool for obtaining bounds) is straightforward in standard complexity theory. Nevertheless, for the purpose of competitive analysis it is somewhat delicate. Before we discuss Yao's principle and its application to competitive analysis in Section 8.3, we conclude our study of the minimax theorem with a discussion of the applicability and generality of the minimax theorem.

8.2   On Generalizations of the Minimax Theorem for Infinite Games

As presented and proven here, the minimax theorem (Theorem 8.2) applies only to finite matrix games. There are numerous generalizations of this theorem for special classes of infinite games. In the general case, we consider spaces I and J of pure strategies for players 1 and 2 and denote the payoff by an arbitrary function h. Typically, h is a real-valued function; however, it can map $I \times J$ to other sets such as $\mathbb{R}^n$ (such games are called games with "vector payoffs"). For the rest of this discussion, we consider a real-valued function h. For general games we will be satisfied in many cases with ε-equilibrium, which means that we will be willing to replace the min and max operators in the minimax theorem with inf and sup, respectively.

One quick observation is that the "easy direction" of the minimax theorems is always true. Specifically, we have the following lemma.

Lemma 8.3 *Let $h(i, j)$ be any real-valued function defined on $I \times J$. Then,*

$$\inf_j \sup_i h(i, j) \geq \sup_i \inf_j h(i, j).$$

Further, when I and J are compact and h is continuous (or when I and J are finite), the sup *and* inf *can be replaced by* max *and* min, *respectively.*

PROOF.   Clearly, for any i and j, $\sup_{i'} h(i', j) \geq h(i, j)$. Therefore, for all i,

$$\inf_{j'} \sup_{i'} h(i', j') \geq \inf_{j'} h(i, j'),$$

and the lemma follows.   ■

Before we state various generalizations of the minimax theorem, it is important to note that the theorem does not hold for many games in which the sets of pure strategies are infinite.

Example 8.3 (A game with no value) Consider the following game. The sets of pure strategies are $I = J = \mathbb{N}$. Players 1 and 2 each choose a positive integer, i and j, respectively. The payoff function is

$$h(i, j) = \begin{cases} 1 & \text{if } i > j; \\ 0 & \text{if } i = j; \\ -1 & \text{if } i < j \end{cases}$$

(i.e., $h(i, j) = \text{sgn}(i - j)$). The objective is to choose the largest number.

A mixed strategy for player 1 is a probability distribution $x = \{x_i\}_{i \geq 1}$ over the natural numbers, with x_i denoting the probability to choose i.

Let x be an arbitrary mixed strategy for player 1. Since $\sum_i x_i = 1$, the summation $\sum_{i=n}^{\infty} x_i$ is arbitrarily small for sufficiently large n. Hence, player 2, while knowing x, can limit player 1 to a payoff that is arbitrarily close to -1. In other words, $\inf_j h(x, i) = -1$, where $h(x, i)$ stands for $\sum_i x_i h(i, j)$. Therefore, $\sup_x \inf_j h(x, i) = -1$. A symmetric argument implies that $\inf_y \sup_i h(i, y) = 1$. Hence, the game has no value.

The following list specifies selected extensions of the minimax theorem.[4] In particular, in each of these cases, the minimax ("infsup") theorem applies under the specified conditions on h.

- **Continuous games**: h is continuous.
- **Concave-convex games**: I and J are real line segments, and $h(i, j)$ is concave in i (for each j) and convex in j (for each i). (In this case, the game clearly has a saddle point in pure strategies.)
- **Games of timing**: I and J are both (the same) real line segment, and h is

$$h(i, j) = \begin{cases} A(i, j) & \text{if } i < j; \\ \varphi(i) & \text{if } i = j; \\ B(i, j) & \text{if } i > j, \end{cases}$$

where A is defined and continuous whenever $i \leq j$, B is continuous whenever $j \leq i$, and φ is continuous over I.

8.3 Yao's Principle: A Technique for Obtaining Lower Bounds

In this section we study Yao's inequality, which was established in Section 8.1 (inequality 8.4). In general this technique can be used for proving lower bounds on the competitive ratio of randomized online algorithms against an oblivious adversary (and thus against all adversary types). For a profit maximization problem the method is essentially the following: to obtain a lower bound of c on the competitive ratio of the best randomized algorithms, it is sufficient to choose any probability distribution y over inputs (request sequences) and to bound from below, by some constant c, the ratio of average optimal offline profit to average online profit of any *deterministic* online algorithm (where the expectations are taken with respect to y). In this case, c is a lower bound on the competitive ratio of the best randomized online algorithm. There are several variations of this method, depending on whether the online problem is finite or not and whether the profit is bounded or not.

Unfortunately, the technique applied for profit maximization problems differs somewhat from its counterpart for cost minimization problems. We first develop the technique for profit maximization problems and then develop it for cost minimization problems.

8.3.1 Yao's Principle for Profit Maximization Problems

A profit maximization request–answer game is called **finite** if both the set of deterministic online algorithms and the set of request sequences are finite.[5] Denote the finite set of deterministic algorithms by

$$\mathcal{A} = \{\text{ALG}_1, \text{ALG}_2, \ldots, \text{ALG}_m\}.$$

---

[4] The list is by no means exhaustive. For other types of games in which the minimax theorem applies, the reader is referred to Owen [271] and Raghavan [286].

[5] Here we use the terminology finite request–answer "game" rather than "system" to indicate that the definition of finiteness implies an a priori bound on the length of any request sequence generated during the game.

Similarly, let the finite set of possible request sequences be

$$\Sigma = \{\sigma_1, \sigma_2, \ldots, \sigma_n\}.$$

We now define the following two-person zero-sum game G. Player 1 is the online player, and $\mathcal{A}$ is the set of his pure strategies. Player 2 is the adversary, and Σ is the set of his pure strategies. It remains to define the payoff function. Here we have several possibilities. Perhaps the most natural choice for the payoff function is

$$h_1(i, j) = \frac{\mathrm{OPT}(\sigma_j)}{\mathrm{ALG}_i(\sigma_j)}.$$

At the outset, this choice for the payoff function seems to be a natural one, since it explicitly gives the competitive ratio. Nevertheless, this is not quite the case. Consider the right-hand side of Yao's inequality (8.5) as specified by h_1:

$$\min_{x(i)} \max_j \mathbf{E}_{x(i)} \left[\frac{\mathrm{OPT}(\sigma_j)}{\mathrm{ALG}_i(\sigma_j)} \right], \tag{8.6}$$

where $x = x(i)$ and $\mathbf{E}_{x(i)}[\cdot]$ denote a mixed strategy for player 1 and the expectation with respect to x, respectively. Similarly, we use the same notation for $y = y(j)$ and $\mathbf{E}_{y(j)}[\cdot]$. Notice that this expression, which is supposed to specify the optimal randomized competitive ratio, is not quite compatible with our definition of the competitive ratio. Specifically, according to our "standard" definition, the optimal randomized competitive ratio is

$$\min_{x(i)} \max_j \frac{\mathrm{OPT}(\sigma_j)}{\mathbf{E}_{x(i)} \left[\mathrm{ALG}_i(\sigma_j) \right]}.$$

However, in general for a random variable X, $\mathbf{E}\left[\frac{1}{X}\right] \neq \frac{1}{\mathbf{E}[X]}$. Hence, we cannot prove lower bounds on the standard randomized competitive ratio using this definition.[6] As seen in the following result, this confusion may lead to erroneous conclusions.

Example 8.4 (Wrong usage of Yao's principle) Consider the following online problem, given by the following matrix.

	σ_1	σ_2	$\cdots$	σ_i	$\cdots$	σ_k	σ_{k+1}
ALG_1	$\frac{k}{1}$	$\frac{k}{2}$	$\cdots$	$\frac{k}{i}$	$\cdots$	$\frac{k}{k}$	$\frac{2k}{2k}$
ALG_2	$\frac{k}{k}$	$\frac{k}{k}$	$\cdots$	$\frac{k}{k}$	$\cdots$	$\frac{k}{k}$	$\frac{2k}{k}$

The (i, j) entry of this matrix is a fraction of the form $\frac{\mathrm{OPT}(\sigma_j)}{\mathrm{ALG}_i(\sigma_j)}$ that corresponds to the payoff function h_1. Consider the following mixed strategy for the adversary:

$$y = \left(\frac{1}{k H_k}, \ldots, \frac{1}{k H_k}, 1 - \frac{1}{H_k} \right).$$

---

[6] Of course, it is certainly legitimate to *define* the randomized competitive ratio for a profit maximization problem by using the form (8.6).

It is easy to verify that, for $i = 1, 2$,

$$\mathbf{E}_{y(j)} \left[\frac{\text{OPT}(\sigma_j)}{\text{ALG}_i(\sigma_j)} \right] \geq 2 - o(1).$$

Hence, according to Yao's principle, we have that

$$\min_{x(i)} \max_{j} \mathbf{E}_{x(i)} \left[\frac{\text{OPT}(\sigma_j)}{\text{ALG}_i(\sigma_j)} \right] \geq 2 - o(1).$$

Nevertheless, it is easy to verify that mixing ALG_1 and ALG_2 with probabilities $\frac{1}{3}$ and $\frac{2}{3}$ is 1.5-competitive.

A slight modification of the payoff function (i.e., taking $\frac{1}{h_1}$ instead of h_1 and letting player 1 be the maximizer) yields a correct "Yao's principle." Moreover, we can formulate Yao's principle using a different game. This is established in the following theorem.

Theorem 8.3 (Yao's principle: finite game, profit problems) *Let G be any finite request–answer game.[7] Let ALG be any online randomized algorithm for G. Let $y(j)$ be any probability distribution over request sequences. Then,*

$$\overline{\mathcal{R}}_{\text{OBL}}(\text{ALG}) \geq \max \left\{ \min_{i} \frac{\mathbf{E}_{y(j)}[\text{OPT}(\sigma_j)]}{\mathbf{E}_{y(j)}[\text{ALG}_i(\sigma_j)]}, \; \min_{i} \frac{1}{\mathbf{E}_{y(j)} \left[\frac{\text{ALG}_i(\sigma_j)}{\text{OPT}(\sigma_j)} \right]} \right\}.$$

PROOF. We first show that $\overline{\mathcal{R}}_{\text{OBL}}(\text{ALG})$ is at least

$$\frac{1}{\max_i \mathbf{E}_{y(j)} \left[\frac{\text{ALG}_i(\sigma_j)}{\text{OPT}(\sigma_j)} \right]}.$$

Formulate the request–answer game as a two-person zero-sum game using the payoff function

$$h_2(i, j) = \frac{1}{h_1(i, j)} = \frac{\text{ALG}_i(\sigma_j)}{\text{OPT}(\sigma_j)}$$

(i.e., using h_2, the online player is the maximizer). Suppose that for some c and some mixed strategy $y(j)$ for the adversary we have

$$\frac{1}{c} \geq \max_{i} \mathbf{E}_{y(j)} \left[\frac{\text{ALG}_i(\sigma_j)}{\text{OPT}(\sigma_j)} \right].$$

According to Yao's inequality (8.4), we have

$$\frac{1}{c} \geq \max_{x(i)} \min_{j} \mathbf{E}_{x(i)} \left[\frac{\text{ALG}_i(\sigma_j)}{\text{OPT}(\sigma_j)} \right]$$

$$= \max_{x(i)} \min_{j} \frac{\mathbf{E}_{x(i)}[\text{ALG}_i(\sigma_j)]}{\text{OPT}(\sigma_j)}$$

$$\geq \frac{1}{\overline{\mathcal{R}}_{\text{OBL}}(\text{ALG})}.$$

---

[7] The finiteness requirement ensures that the von Neumann minimax theorem holds. It can be relaxed whenever the request–answer game can be appropriately formulated as a two-person zero-sum game with a payoff function that guarantees minimax.

We now prove that

$$\min_i \frac{\mathbf{E}_{y(j)}[\text{OPT}(\sigma_j)]}{\mathbf{E}_{y(j)}[\text{ALG}_i(\sigma_j)]}$$

is also a lower bound on the (best) randomized competitive ratio. For each constant c, consider a two-person zero-sum game $G(c)$ between the online player (player 1) against the adversary (player 2). For each pure strategy pair i and j, the payoff to the online player is

$$h_3(i,j) = c \cdot \text{ALG}_i(\sigma_j) - \text{OPT}(\sigma_j).$$

Again, the online player is the maximizer. According to the minimax theorem, the game $G(c)$ has a value $V(c)$, and by Loomis's lemma (Lemma 8.2),

$$V(c) = \max_{x(i)} \min_j \mathbf{E}_{x(i)} h_3(i,j).$$

Clearly, $V(c) \geq 0$ if and only if the best randomized algorithm for the online player is c-competitive. Notice that for any mixed strategy $y(j)$ for the adversary,

$$0 > \max_i \mathbf{E}_{y(j)}[h_3(i,j)]$$

if and only if

$$\min_{i^{\lambda}} \frac{\mathbf{E}_{y(j)}[\text{OPT}(\sigma_j)]}{\mathbf{E}_{y(j)}[\text{ALG}_i(\sigma_j)]} > c. \tag{8.7}$$

Suppose that the inequality (8.7) holds. Then, based on Yao's inequality (8.4),

$$0 > \max_{x(i)} \min_j \mathbf{E}_{x(i)}[h_3(i,j)] = V(c),$$

and therefore the best randomized algorithm for the online player is not c-competitive. ∎

Example 8.5 Continuing Example 8.4, we now show how to use Theorem 8.3 to obtain a correct (and tight) lower bound to the problem of Example 8.4. Consider the following mixed strategy y for the adversary with y_i, the ith component of y being

$$y_i = \begin{cases} \frac{1}{2^{i+1}} & i = 1, 2, \ldots, k-1; \\ \frac{1}{2^k} & i = k; \\ \frac{1}{2} & i = k+1. \end{cases}$$

Clearly, $\sum_i y_i = 1$, and a lower bound of $\frac{3}{2} - o(1)$ can be proved, using this distribution, via Theorem 8.3 (with the ratio of expectations).

Theorem 8.3 can be applied only when the von Neumann minimax theorem applies. As we already know, the theorem always holds with respect to finite games. For infinite games the minimax theorem holds only for special classes of games, but it does not hold in general (see Section 8.2). Fortunately, for unbounded (and therefore infinite) games we have the following version of Yao's principle, which is somewhat more complicated to state but does not rely at all on the minimax theorem.

Theorem 8.4 (Yao's principle: unbounded profit problems) *Let G be any unbounded profit request–answer system. Let* ALG *be any randomized online algorithm for G. Let $y(j)$ be any probability distribution over the set of all finite request sequences, $\{\sigma_j\}$. For each positive integer n, let $y^n(j)$ be the marginal distribution over the set $\{\sigma_j^n\}$ of all request sequences of length n.[8] Suppose that the following two conditions are satisfied:*

$$\limsup_{n \to \infty} \frac{\mathbf{E}_{y(j)}\left[\mathrm{OPT}_x\left(\sigma_j^n\right)\right]}{\sup_i \mathbf{E}_{y(j)}\left[\mathrm{ALG}_i\left(\sigma_j^n\right)\right]} \geq c, \tag{8.8}$$

$$\limsup_{n \to \infty} \mathbf{E}_{y(j)}\left[\mathrm{OPT}\left(\sigma_j^n\right)\right] = \infty. \tag{8.9}$$

Then, $\overline{\mathcal{R}}_{\mathrm{OBL}}(\mathrm{ALG}) \geq c$.

PROOF. Suppose that (8.8) and (8.9) hold with respect to some probability distribution $y(j)$. Assume, by way of contradiction, that the competitive ratio of the (randomized) algorithm ALG (represented by the distribution $x(i)$) is $c' < c$. By definition, there exists a constant α such that

$$c' \cdot \mathbf{E}_{x(i)}\left[\mathrm{ALG}_i\left(\sigma_j^n\right)\right] \geq \mathrm{OPT}\left(\sigma_j^n\right) + \alpha,$$

for each of the sequences in $\{\sigma_j^n\}$. Taking the expectation of both sides with respect to $y(j)$, we obtain

$$c' \cdot \mathbf{E}_{y(j)}\mathbf{E}_{x(i)}\left[\mathrm{ALG}_i\left(\sigma_j^n\right)\right] \geq \mathbf{E}_{y(j)}\left[\mathrm{OPT}\left(\sigma_j^n\right)\right] + \alpha.$$

Since the profits ALG($\cdot$) are nonnegative, we can exchange the order of the expectations (whether they are defined by sums, or integrals) in the left-hand side,

$$c' \cdot \mathbf{E}_{x(i)}\mathbf{E}_{y(j)}\left[\mathrm{ALG}_i\left(\sigma_j^n\right)\right] \geq \mathbf{E}_{y(j)}\left[\mathrm{OPT}\left(\sigma_j^n\right)\right] + \alpha.$$

Set

$$A_n^* = \sup_i \mathbf{E}_{y(j)}\left[\mathrm{ALG}_i\left(\sigma_j^n\right)\right].$$

Clearly,

$$c' \cdot A_n^* \geq c' \cdot \mathbf{E}_{x(i)}\mathbf{E}_{y(j)}\left[\mathrm{ALG}_i\left(\sigma_j^n\right)\right].$$

Hence, for all sufficiently large n (for which $A_n^* > 0$),

$$\frac{\mathbf{E}_{y(j)}\left[\mathrm{OPT}\left(\sigma_j^n\right)\right]}{A_n^*} + \frac{\alpha}{A_n^*} \leq c' < c.$$

According to assumption (8.9) and since ALG is c'-competitive, it must be that $\frac{\alpha}{A_n^*} \to 0$. However, this contradicts assumption (8.8). It follows that $\overline{\mathcal{R}}_{\mathrm{OBL}}(\mathrm{ALG}) \geq c$. ∎

---

[8] The marginal distribution $y^n(j)$ is obtained by normalizing probabilities of sequences of length n with respect to the sum of these probabilities.

8.3.2 Yao's Principle for Cost Minimization Problems

For cost minimization problems, we have two theorems analogous to Theorems 8.3 and 8.4 (i.e., for finite games and unbounded request–answer systems). The theorems for cost minimization and their proofs are almost analogous to the profit maximization theorems. The main difference is with the finite request–answer game, in which, in the case of cost minimization, we do not resort to the inversion of the "natural" payoff function (h_1 in the case of profit maximization).

Theorem 8.5 (Yao's principle: finite game, cost problems) *Let G be any finite cost minimization request—answer game.[9] Let* ALG *be any online randomized algorithm for G. Let* $y(j)$ *be any probability distribution over request sequences. Then,*

$$\overline{\mathcal{R}}_{\mathrm{OBL}}(\mathrm{ALG}) \geq \max\left\{ \min_i \frac{\mathbf{E}_{y(j)}[\mathrm{ALG}_i(\sigma_j)]}{\mathbf{E}_{y(j)}[\mathrm{OPT}(\sigma_j)]}, \ \min_i \mathbf{E}_{y(j)}\left[\frac{\mathrm{ALG}_i(\sigma_j)}{\mathrm{OPT}(\sigma_j)}\right] \right\}.$$

Theorem 8.6 (Yao's principle: unbounded cost problems) *Let G be any unbounded cost request–answer system. Let* ALG *be any randomized online algorithm for G. Let* $y(j)$ *be a probability distribution over the set of all finite request sequences,* $\{\sigma_j\}$. *For each positive integer n, let* $y^n(j)$ *be the marginal distribution over the set of all request sequences of length n* $\{\sigma_j^n\}$. *Suppose that the following two conditions hold:*

$$\liminf_{n\to\infty} \frac{\inf_i \mathbf{E}_{y(j)}\left[\mathrm{ALG}_i(\sigma_j^n)\right]}{\mathbf{E}_{y(j)}\left[\mathrm{OPT}(\sigma_j^n)\right]} \geq c, \tag{8.10}$$

$$\limsup_{n\to\infty} \mathbf{E}_{y(j)}\left[\mathrm{OPT}(\sigma_j^n)\right] = \infty. \tag{8.11}$$

Then, $\overline{\mathcal{R}}_{\mathrm{OBL}}(\mathrm{ALG}) \geq c.$

Exercise 8.2 Prove Theorems 8.5 and 8.6.

8.4 Paging Revisited

We now apply Yao's principle (Theorem 8.6) to obtain an alternative proof for the lower bound of H_k on the competitive ratio of any online randomized paging algorithm against an oblivious adversary.

Theorem 8.7 *Let* ALG *be any (randomized) paging algorithm with a cache of size k. If* $N \geq k + 1$, *then* $\overline{\mathcal{R}}_{\mathrm{OBL}} \geq H_k$.

PROOF. Suppose that the slow memory contains a set P of exactly $k + 1$ pages. Let D be a probability distribution over the set of all finite request sequences $\{\sigma_y\}$ such that the ith request is chosen from P uniformly and independently of all previous requests.

---

[9] Here again the finiteness requirement ensures that the von Neumann minimax theorem holds and can be relaxed whenever the request–answer game can be formulated as a two-person zero-sum game with a payoff function that guarantees minimax.

Clearly, every deterministic paging algorithm ALG_x with a fast memory of size k, faults on any given request with probability $\frac{1}{k+1}$. Hence, the expected number of page faults incurred by ALG_x on a sequence of n requests, σ_y^n, is exactly $\frac{n}{k+1}$ no matter what the initial configuration of ALG_x is. This also applies to the best online algorithm. That is, $\min_x \mathbf{E}_y \text{ALG}_x(\sigma_y^n) = \frac{n}{k+1}$.

Hence, to prove a lower bound of H_k, it is sufficient, according to Theorem 8.6, to prove that

$$\lim_{n \to \infty} \frac{n}{(k+1)\mathbf{E}_y\big[\text{OPT}(\sigma_y^n)\big]} \geq H_k, \tag{8.12}$$

$$\lim_{n \to \infty} \mathbf{E}_y\big[\text{OPT}(\sigma_y^n)\big] = \infty. \tag{8.13}$$

We now prove that equations (8.12) and (8.13) hold. Let σ_y^n be a random request sequence chosen according to D. We divide σ_y^n into (stochastic) phases in the usual way. Each phase begins after the previous phase ends and terminates immediately before, for the first time, every page in P is requested at least once. The first phase begins on the first request (and, of course, the last phase may not be "complete"). Since OPT has exactly k pages in its cache and $|P| = k + 1$, it must be that OPT faults at least once on every (complete) phase. On the other hand, if for the first fault at the start of a phase, OPT evicts the page requested in the beginning of the next phase, it can service each phase incurring exactly one fault.

Let X_i, $i = 1, 2, \ldots$, be a sequence of random variables where X_i is the number of requests during the ith (complete) phase. The properties of D make it clear that the X_i's are independent and identically distributed. Let $S_j = \sum_{i=1}^j X_i$. That is, $S_{j-1} + 1$ is the index of the first request of the jth phase (set $S_0 = 0$). Define

$$N(n) = \max\{j : S_j \leq n\}.$$

Thus, $N(n)$ is the number of complete phases in the sequence σ_y^n. According to the preceding discussion, $N(n) + 1$ bounds from above the total cost $\text{OPT}(\sigma_y^n)$ incurred by the adversary (the extra 1 accounts for the last incomplete phase, if there is one).

The family of random variables $\{N(n), n \geq 1\}$ is a stochastic process called a **renewal process**. We now make use of a basic result from renewal theory. (See Appendix E, where a self-contained presentation of the relevant material is given.)

According to the elementary renewal theorem (Theorem E.3),

$$\lim_{n \to \infty} \frac{n}{\mathbf{E}[N(n)]} = \mathbf{E}[X_i]. \tag{8.14}$$

From equation (8.14) it follows that to prove equation (8.12), it is sufficient to prove that

$$\mathbf{E}[X_i] = (k+1)H_k.$$

Also, from equation (8.14) it follows that equation (8.13) holds, since $\mathbf{E}[X_i] < \infty$.

We now show that $\mathbf{E}[X_i] = (k + 1)H_k$, from which the theorem readily follows. We prove this claim by introducing and solving the following well-known "coupon collector problem."

The coupon collector problem: There are N different kinds of coupons (with an unlimited supply of each kind). At each round a player obtains a coupon chosen randomly, independently, and uniformly from the N possible types. What is the expected number of rounds to collect all N coupon types?

The coupon collector problem is easy to solve. Suppose that the player has already accumulated i types of coupons. The coupon drawn in the next round is of a new type, with probability $\frac{N-i}{N}$. Therefore, the expected number of rounds to obtain a new type is $\frac{N}{N-i}$. Define $Z_i, i = 0, \ldots, N-1$, to be a random variable giving the number of rounds to obtain a new coupon having collected i different coupons. The expected number of rounds to collect all N coupons is

$$\mathbf{E}\left[\sum_{i=0}^{N-1} Z_i\right] = \sum_{i=0}^{N-1} \mathbf{E}[Z_i] = \sum_{i=0}^{N-1} \frac{N}{N-i} = NH_N.$$

The expected number of requests for "collecting" requests to k distinct pages following the first fault in a phase is clearly equivalent to the expected number of rounds for collecting $N = k + 1$ coupons in the coupon collector problem minus the first round. Hence, the expected number of requests per phase is $\mathbf{E}[X_i] = (k+1)H_{k+1} - 1 = (k+1)H_k$. ∎

8.5　Historical Notes

The minimax theorem was published in 1928 by von Neumann [332]. It was not until 1944, after the publication of *Theory of Games and Economic Behavior* by von Neumann and Morgenstern [333], that the theorem caught the attention of mathematicians and social scientists and triggered extensive work in game theory. Many proofs of the fundamental minimax theorem have been established since then. The proof presented in this chapter (based on Brouwer's fixed point theorem) is due to Nash [267]. Yao's principle follows from Loomis's lemma [247]. The first application of Yao's principle in the context of randomized algorithms is due to Yao [340]. This paper played a seminal role in complexity theory. The statement and proof of Yao's principle for unbounded cost minimization online problems is due to Borodin, Linial, and Saks [82]. The H_k lower bound proof for paging (Section 8.4) is a straightforward adaptation of the proof (also from [82]) for uniform metrical systems. A more direct proof of this theorem (without use of Yao's principle) is due to Fiat, Karp, Luby, McGeoch, Sleator, and Young [153] and can be found in Chapter 4. Example 8.4 is due to Pruhs (personal communication).

CHAPTER 9

Metrical Task Systems

In this chapter we study another abstract model for competitive analysis of online computation. This model, called metrical task systems (MTS), was formulated by Borodin, Linial, and Saks [82]. This abstract model captures particular online problems such as paging, (static) list accessing, and other general models such as the (finite space) k-server model, which is introduced in Chapter 10. Furthermore, within the MTS framework, we can introduce a number of general concepts and techniques.

Applications of the general MTS theory to particular online problems typically yield weak results. However, it is natural that a general model abstracts away special features of particular settings that must be exploited in order to obtain stronger results. Nevertheless, the existence of a general theory is an important fact in itself, and with respect to competitive analysis, the MTS results were the first evidence that a general theory of competitive online algorithms exists.

9.1 Formulation of (Metrical) Task Systems

A **metric space** $\mathcal{M}$ is a pair (S, d) where S is a set of points and $d : S \times S \rightarrow \mathbb{R}^+$ is a **metric** distance function that satisfies:

(i) $d(i, j) > 0$, $\quad \forall i \neq j$, $i, j \in S$ (positivity);

(ii) $d(i, i) = 0$, $\quad \forall i \in S$ (reflexivity);

(iii) $d(i, j) + d(j, k) \geq d(i, k)$, $\quad \forall i, j, k \in S$ (triangle inequality).

(iv) $d(i, j) = d(j, i)$, $\quad \forall i, j \in S$ (symmetry).

To understand how a metric space can be used to abstract online problems, we think of S as the set of all possible "configurations" that an online player can ever be situated in, while d becomes a **transition cost function** that measures the cost of transitions between these configurations (see Examples 9.1 and 9.2).

Suppose we have a *finite* metric space used to model configurations and the transition costs between them. What is missing is a formulation of "requests," and "answers" that service them. Requests are modeled in this framework as abstract tasks that should be "processed" by the player. A **task** r is defined as an N-ary vector of costs, $r = \langle r(1), r(2), \ldots, r(N) \rangle$, where for each i, $r(i) \in \mathbb{R}^+ \cup \{\infty\}$ is the cost of "processing" the task while in state i. A **metrical task system (MTS)** is a pair $(\mathcal{M}, \mathcal{R})$ where $\mathcal{M}$ is a metric space and $\mathcal{R}$ is a set of allowable tasks. When there are no restrictions on the set

123

of allowable tasks (i.e., any vector of costs is allowed), a task system is simply a metric space; throughout most of this chapter, we place no restrictions on the set of allowable tasks. In the context of task systems, by scaling processing and transition costs, we can always assume that $\min_{i \neq j} d(i, j) = 1$.

We consider a player (or an algorithm) that is given an initial state, s_0, and a finite sequence of tasks $\sigma = r_1, r_2, \ldots, r_n$, to be processed sequentially, one at a time starting from state s_0. If the player is currently in state s, upon arrival of the task r the player *first* changes the state to any desired state q (or stays in the same state), incurring a transition cost of $d(s, q)$. Then the player processes the task in state q, incurring a processing cost of $r(q)$.

ALG$[i] \in S$ denotes the state in which the ith task is processed by an algorithm ALG. By convention, we set ALG$[0] = s_0$. The total cost incurred by ALG for processing the task sequence σ is then

$$\text{ALG}(\sigma) = \sum_{i=1}^{n} d(\text{ALG}[i-1], \text{ALG}[i]) + \sum_{i=1}^{n} r_i(\text{ALG}[i]).$$

The left summation is called the **total transition cost** (to serve σ), and the right summation is called the **total processing cost**.

In this formulation, the player can, in principle, process any task from any state. In particular, the player may remain in the same state forever. However, since each task vector may include components with infinite weights, a player can be prevented from servicing a request in a particular state.

This abstraction captures particular online settings by the imposition of special restrictions on tasks and task sequences. We present some examples.

Example 9.1 Consider the paging problem with N slow memory pages and a fast memory of size $k, k \leq N$. We can model it as an MTS as follows. Suppose $p_1, p_2, \ldots, p_N$ are the pages. Let $S_1, S_2, \ldots, S_{\binom{N}{k}}$ be all the k-subsets of $\{p_1, \ldots, p_N\}$. Consider the following MTS. For $i = 1, 2, \ldots \binom{N}{k}$, let s_i be a state of S representing a configuration in which the pages of S_i are in the fast memory. For $j \neq i$, let $d(s_i, s_j) = k - |S_i \cap S_j|$, the cost of changing the contents of the fast memory from S_i to S_j. Clearly, d is a metric. A sequence of n requests for the pages $p_1, p_2, \ldots, p_n$ can be modeled by a task sequence $r_1, r_2, \ldots, r_n$ where for each $i = 1, \ldots, n$ and each $s_j \in S$,

$$r_i(s_j) = \begin{cases} 0 & \text{if } p_i \in S_j; \\ \infty & \text{otherwise.} \end{cases}$$

(That is, there are exactly $\binom{N-1}{k-1}$ 0-components in r_i.)

Example 9.2 Some problems are more subtle to model. Consider the static list accessing problem of Chapter 1. Assume that the list contains a (static) set of ℓ items, $\{x_1, x_2, \ldots, x_\ell\}$. As we have defined this problem (see Section 1.2.1), upon receiving a request to access an element x_i the online player is required to access x_i (i.e., to "process the task") and then the player may reorganize the list by performing a sequence of free and/or paid transpositions (i.e., "change states"). In contrast, a metrical task system *first* changes states and then processes the task (in the new state). Nevertheless, Exercise 1.2 shows that every list accessing algorithm (for this variant of the list accessing problem) that uses free and paid exchanges can be transformed to an algorithm that uses only paid exchanges (before the access) so this problem is circumvented.

Let the state set S of the MTS be $\{s_1, s_2, \ldots, s_{\ell!}\}$, where each state represents one ordering of the $\ell!$ possible orderings of the list. For each two states s_i and s_j let $d(i, j)$ be the number of transpositions (of consecutive items) required to transform the list from the ith ordering to the jth. Clearly, d is symmetric. A sequence of n requests $r_1, r_2, \ldots, r_n$ can be modeled by a task sequence $r_1, r_2, \ldots, r_n$ where for each $i = 1, \ldots, n$ and each $s_j \in S$,

$$r_i(s_j) = \text{the position of } x_i \text{ in the } j\text{th ordering.}$$

The preceding MTS succeeds in modeling this list accessing problem variant because the costs corresponding to a link traversal and a paid transposition are equal. This is not the case for other variants of the list accessing problem.

Remark 9.1 Consider the Δ-paid exchange model of the list accessing problem (with or without free transpositions). Recall that each transposition costs Δ and each link traversal (a search "step") costs 1 (see Section 1.2.1). In this case, it is not apparent how to model this problem as an MTS. The example, and the fact that metrical task systems fail to model dynamic list accessing problems, indicates that the MTS framework may not be sufficiently general. The Δ-paid exchange model and dynamic list accessing problems can be modeled as request–answer systems.

An online algorithm ALG for a task system is defined in a straightforward manner as an algorithm such that its ith state, ALG[i], depends only on the first i tasks and the initial state. An offline algorithm may, of course, choose its transitions based on the entire task sequence.

It is convenient to view the ith task as arriving at time i and being processed during the time interval $[i, i + 1)$. Thus, any algorithm may be specified as a sequence of state transitions and their transition times. Specifically, use $1 \leq t_1 < t_2 < \cdots < t_k$ to denote the times at which the algorithm changes states, and use $s_1, s_2, \ldots, s_k$ to denote the corresponding states.

9.1.1 Continuous Time Algorithms

Because of the discrete nature of task systems, all state transitions occur at integer times. Nevertheless, it is sometimes useful to consider "continuous time" algorithms, which may change states at arbitrary real times. Any such continuous time algorithm may be easily transformed to a "discrete" time algorithm that performs at least as well. The advantage of this extension is that some algorithms can be described more easily as continuous time algorithms.

Let (S, d) be a task system and let $\sigma = r_1, \ldots, r_n$ be any task sequence. A **continuous time algorithm** ALG is a function ALG[ ] : $[1, n + 1) \to S$, where ALG[t] gives the state at time t. Similar to discrete time algorithms, ALG can be described by two sequences: $s_1, \ldots, s_k$ of states, and $t_1 < \cdots < t_k$ of transition times. The difference is that the t_i's may be real numbers. The task processing cost incurred by ALG for the ith task is given by

$$\int_i^{i+1} r_i(\text{ALG}[t])dt.$$

Notice that this quantity is simply a sum $\sum_s \gamma_s r_i(s)$ where s ranges over all the states visited during the time interval $[i, i + 1)$ and γ_s is the proportion of time the algorithm spends in the state s with $\sum \gamma_s = 1$. Of course, the total cost incurred for this task must include the costs of all state transitions as well.

It is easy to transform any continuous time algorithm ALG to an ordinary discrete time algorithm ALG$'$ without increasing the total cost. For each task r_i, let S_i be the set of states visited by ALG while processing r_i (during the time interval $[i, i + 1)$). The algorithm ALG$'$ changes its state to that $j \in S_i$ that minimizes the task component; that is, $j = \arg\min\{r_i(j') : j' \in S_i\}$. Because d satisfies the triangle inequality, it is clear that the total cost ALG$'$ pays for processing r_i is no more than what ALG pays.

9.1.2 Nearly Oblivious and Traversal Algorithms

A continuous time algorithm ALG is called **nearly oblivious** if it is defined by two infinite sequences: $s_0, s_1, s_2, \ldots$ of states, and $c_0, c_1, c_2, \ldots$ of thresholds.[1] ALG remains in state s_i until it incurs a processing cost c_i while in that state; then it moves to s_{i+1}, and so on. It is clear that a nearly oblivious algorithm operates online.

A nearly oblivious algorithm is called a **periodic MTS algorithm** (with a period k) if for all $i \geq k$, $s_i = s_{i-k}$ and $c_i = c_{i-k}$.[2]

A periodic algorithm ALG is called a **traversal algorithm** if for each i, $c_i = d(s_i, s_{i+1})$. That is, the algorithm remains in state s_i until the processing cost in that state equals the cost of transition to the next state, at which point it changes states to s_{i+1}, and so on. Given an initial state, s_0, a traversal algorithm with a period k can be uniquely specified by a sequence of states

$$s_0 \to s_1 \to \cdots \to s_k(= s_0),$$

which is called **the traversal of** ALG. A **cycle** of ALG (with respect to some task sequence) is the time interval during which one traversal is completed. Clearly, a periodic algorithm ALG incurs a cost of exactly $2 \sum_{i=1}^k d(s_{i-1}, s_i)$ during each cycle.

Although the behavior of traversal algorithms depends rather weakly on the task sequence, these algorithms prove quite useful, as the following example demonstrates.

Example 9.3 Consider any MTS with two states s_1 and s_2. Suppose that the initial state is s_1. Then the only possibility for a traversal is $s_1 \to s_2 \to s_1$ and the corresponding traversal algorithm has a period 2.

The traversal algorithm starts in s_1, waits until it incurs a cost of $d(s_1, s_2)$, switches to s_2, waits until it incurs $d(s_2, s_1) = d(s_1, s_2)$, switches to s_1 (to complete a cycle), and so on. The algorithm incurs a total cost of $4d(s_1, s_2)$ per cycle. We claim that the optimal

---

[1] Although there is a similar basis for the terminology, the reader should not confuse "oblivious adversaries" and "nearly oblivious algorithms."

[2] Here we follow the definition in Borodin, Linial, and Saks [82], noting that the usual definition of "periodic" is as follows: there is a constant i_0 such that for all $i \geq i_0$, $s_i = s_{i-k}$ and $c_i = c_{i-k}$.

offline algorithm pays at least $d(s_1, s_2)$ during each cycle: if OPT moves during the cycle, then the claim is trivially true; otherwise, OPT stays in either s_1 or s_2 for the entire cycle and, according to the definition of a traversal algorithm, it incurs at least $d(s_1, s_2)$. It follows that this simple traversal algorithm is 4-competitive for any MTS with two states.[3]

9.2 An 8(N – 1)-Competitive Traversal Algorithm

It is not difficult to construct an $8(N-1)$-competitive traversal algorithm for any N-state MTS. This result is in fact inspired by Example 9.3. The idea is to construct a traversal by recursively partitioning the set of states into two components, traversing one component recursively until the cost incurred in that component is approximately that of moving to the other component, moving to the other component and traversing it (recursively), returning to the first component (and completing the cycle), and so on.

Let (S, d) be a metrical task system. To describe the traversal formally, it is useful to consider the task system as an undirected weighted (and complete) graph G on N vertices (the states) where the edge weights are given by d. For each edge weight w, we define the "rounded weight" w' as 2^i, where $2^{i-1} < w \le 2^i$.

Fix a minimum (cost) spanning tree $MST = (S, E)$ for G. We now define recursively a traversal $\mathcal{T}$ as follows: For the base case, $|E| = 0$ (no edges), the traversal is defined to be the empty one. Also, it may be instructive to consider another base case of E containing a single edge, (u, v). In this case, the traversal is defined to be $u \to v \to u$.

For $|E| > 1$, let (u, v) be an edge with maximum weight in MST. Suppose its rounded weight $d'(u, v)$ is 2^M. The removal of (u, v) partitions MST into two smaller trees, $MST_1 = (S_1, E_1)$ and $MST_2 = (S_2, E_2)$, with $u \in S_1$ and $v \in S_2$. Let $\mathcal{T}_1$ and $\mathcal{T}_2$ be the traversals constructed recursively for MST_1 and MST_2. Suppose that the maximum weight edge in MST_1 and MST_2 have rounded weights 2^{M_1} and 2^{M_2}, respectively.

The traversal $\mathcal{T}$ starts at u, followed by 2^{M-M_1} cycles of $\mathcal{T}_1$, followed by the edge (u, v), followed by 2^{M-M_2} cycles of $\mathcal{T}_2$, followed by the edge (v, u).

Theorem 9.1 *The traversal algorithm* ALG *specified by* $\mathcal{T}$ *is* $8(N-1)$-*competitive for any MTS with N states.*

PROOF. Let 2^M be the maximum rounded weight in MST. The theorem is clearly established by the following assertions:

(i) The total cost incurred by ALG during each cycle is at most $4(N-1)2^M$.
(ii) During the time that ALG completes a cycle, OPT incurs a cost of at least 2^{M-1}.

To prove (i), we claim that any edge in $\mathcal{T}$ of rounded weight 2^m is traversed exactly 2^{M-m} times in each direction. This claim, once established, proves that the total cost

---

[3] Example 9.3 is an abstraction of "Rudolph's ski rental problem" from Rudolph [297]: For how long should a novice skier rent skis before buying? We can think of a request as an irresistible urge to go skiing. The "competitive solution" to this problem is to continue renting until the cost of rental equals the purchase price, at which point the skier buys a pair of skis. This solution guarantees that the skier will not pay more than twice the optimal cost, even if the skier decides to retire from skiing at any point in time (see also Section 15.6).

resulting from transitions (in both directions) of any edge with rounded weight 2^m is at most $2 \cdot 2^{M-m} \cdot 2^m = 2 \cdot 2^M$. Since MST is a tree with N vertices, it contains exactly $N - 1$ edges. Hence, the total cost for a cycle, including the processing costs, is at most $4(N - 1)2^M$, as stated in (i). It remains to prove the above claim.

We prove the claim by induction on $|E|$ where E is the edge set of the minimum spanning tree, MST. For the base case, $|E| = 0$, there is nothing to prove. Assume that $|E| > 0$ and let (u, v), MST_1, and MST_2 be as in the construction of the algorithm. Clearly, (u, v) is traversed exactly once in each direction. By the induction hypothesis, each edge in MST_1 of rounded weight 2^m is traversed 2^{M_1-m} times in each direction, where 2^{M_1} is the maximum rounded weight of an edge in MST_1. However, by construction, the traversal defined by MST_1 is cycled 2^{M-M_1} times, which means that this edge is traversed 2^{M-m} times in all, as required. Exactly the same argument applies to MST_2, which completes the induction step. We conclude that (i) holds.

We prove (ii) also by induction on $|E|$. Suppose $|E| > 1$. Again, let (u, v), MST_1, and MST_2 be as in the construction of the algorithm. If, during a cycle of $\mathcal{T}$, OPT moves from some state in MST_1 to some state in MST_2, then since MST is a minimum spanning tree, there is no path connecting MST_1 to MST_2 with a total weight smaller than $d(u, v) > 2^{M-1}$. Otherwise, suppose that throughout the cycle of $\mathcal{T}$, OPT occupies only states in some MST_i (without loss of generality, say MST_1). We have two cases to consider:

1. MST_1 consists of a single node u. Then OPT remains at state u throughout the traversal $\mathcal{T}$. By the definition of a traversal algorithm, a task processing cost of at least $d(u, v) > 2^{M-1}$ is incurred by OPT while the traversal algorithm is in state u.
2. MST_1 consists of more than one node. According to the induction hypothesis, OPT incurs a cost of at least 2^{M_1-1} per cycle of $\mathcal{T}_1$. However, as $\mathcal{T}$ contains exactly 2^{M-M_1} cycles of $\mathcal{T}_1$, OPT incurs a cost of at least 2^{M-1} in all.

This completes the induction step, and we conclude that (ii) holds. ∎

9.3 A $2N-1$ Lower Bound

9.3.1 Elementary Tasks and Cruel Adversaries

In Chapters 1 and 3 we encountered "cruel" adversaries and used them to derive lower bounds. Recall that in the context of the list accessing problem, the cruel strategy was always to request the last item on the list. For paging, the cruel strategy was to make the paging algorithm fault on every request.

We now define a family of cruel adversaries for any MTS and then show how these adversaries can force a competitive ratio arbitrarily close to $2N - 1$ for any deterministic algorithm for a metrical task system with N states.

Let (S, d) be any metrical task system where $S = \{1, 2, \ldots, N\}$. An **elementary task** r is one whose task vector is 0 in all but one component. We let $\langle i, \tau \rangle = (0, 0, \ldots, \tau, 0, \ldots, 0)$ denote the elementary task with nonzero cost τ in the ith component.

For the purpose of competitive analysis, the following lemma shows that we need to consider only elementary tasks.

Lemma 9.1 *Let* ALG *be any MTS algorithm for an arbitrary metric space* $\mathcal{M} = (S, d)$. *For any task sequence* σ, *there is a task sequence* σ' *consisting of only elementary tasks* such that $\text{ALG}(\sigma') \geq \text{ALG}(\sigma)$ and $\text{OPT}(\sigma') = \text{OPT}(\sigma)$. *That is, an optimal competitive lower bound can be derived by using only elementary sequences. Furthermore, any online algorithm defined for only elementary tasks can be extended to all tasks. That is, for the purpose of the competitive analysis of any online algorithm* ALG, *we can restrict attention to sequences of elementary tasks.*

PROOF. Consider any task $r = \langle r(1), \ldots, r(N) \rangle$ in the sequence σ. To simplify notation, assume, without loss of generality, that $0 \leq r(1) \leq r(2) \leq \cdots \leq r(N)$. We chop each r into a large number of elementary tasks to form a task sequence r' as follows: let ρ_i be the elementary task $(0, 0, \ldots, \varepsilon, 0, \ldots, 0)$ with positive cost ε in the ith component, where $\varepsilon \leq 1$ is chosen so that for all i, $\frac{r(i)-r(i-1)}{\varepsilon}$ is a nonnegative integer. Let $r' = r'_1 \cdots r'_N$ where r'_i is the sequence $\rho_i \cdots \rho_N$ repeated $\frac{r(i)-r(i-1)}{\varepsilon}$ times. For the sequence r', the sum of the task costs in the ith state equals $r(i)$. Since we assume $\min\{d(j, k) | j \neq k \in S\} = 1$, each change of state will cost at least as much as the processing cost being avoided; therefore, even an offline algorithm cannot save any cost by changing states more than once to process r'. By the same reasoning that shows how to convert any continuous time algorithm to a discrete time algorithm, this conversion of any request r to a sequence of elementary tasks r' shows how any online algorithm defined for only elementary tasks can be extended to all tasks.   ■

Let ALG be any deterministic (discrete time) online algorithm for this system. For any positive real ε, define ADV_ε as the adversary that produces the task sequence $\sigma = r_1, r_2, \ldots$, where for each $s \in S$,

$$r_i(s) = \begin{cases} \varepsilon & \text{if } s = \text{ALG}[i-1]; \\ 0 & \text{otherwise.} \end{cases}$$

That is, the processing cost for ALG is ε for the ith task if and only if ALG remains in the previous state at which it processed the $(i-1)$st task. With respect to the algorithm ALG, we have thus defined the family $\{\text{ADV}_\varepsilon\}$ of **cruel adversaries**.

One simple property of "cruel" task sequences (which we will use later) is that the cost of any online algorithm is strictly increasing with the length of the cruel sequence. Moreover, if σ_n is the cruel sequence of length n, $\text{ALG}(\sigma_n) \to \infty$ with n. This follows from the definition of the cruel sequence and the positivity of the transition cost function d.

9.3.2 A Lower Bound

We are now in a position to state a theorem that directly yields the lower bound of $2N - 1$.

Theorem 9.2 *Let* ALG *be any deterministic online algorithm for the MTS (S, d) and let ε be any positive real. For each positive integer n, let $\sigma_n = r_1, r_2, \ldots, r_n$ be the task sequence of length n produced by the cruel adversary* ADV_ε *with respect to* ALG. *Then,*

$$\limsup_{n \to \infty} \frac{\text{ALG}(\sigma_n)}{\text{OPT}(\sigma_n)} \geq \frac{2N - 1}{1 + 2\varepsilon}. \tag{9.1}$$

The desired lower bound follows immediately from Theorem 9.2: assume that ALG is c-competitive with $c < 2N - 1$. By definition, there exists a constant α such that for each task sequence and in particular σ_n, $\text{ALG}(\sigma_n) - c \cdot \text{OPT}(\sigma_n) < \alpha$. This implies that

$$\frac{\text{ALG}(\sigma_n)}{\text{OPT}(\sigma_n)} \leq c + \frac{\alpha}{\text{OPT}(\sigma_n)}. \tag{9.2}$$

If $\limsup_{n \to \infty} \text{OPT}(\sigma_n)$ is bounded, then ALG is not at all competitive, since $\text{ALG}(\sigma_n) \to \infty$ with n. Otherwise, according to Theorem 9.2, there exist sufficiently large n and sufficiently small ε for which equation (9.2) does not hold. Hence, ALG is not c-competitive with respect to ADV_ε, and $2N - 1$ is indeed a lower bound.

Corollary 9.3 $2N - 1$ *is a lower bound on the competitive ratio of any deterministic algorithm for an MTS with N states.*

Proof of Theorem 9.2. Consider the cruel task sequence σ_n and suppose ALG changes states k times (i.e., $k \leq n$). Consistent with the definition of the cruel sequence, ALG pays ε for each unit time interval except for those intervals immediately after transitions. Hence, ALG pays a total processing cost of $(n-k)\varepsilon$. Thus, $\text{ALG}(\sigma_n) = (n-k)\varepsilon + \sum_{1 \leq i \leq k} d(s_{i-1}, s_i)$ where $s_0, s_1, \ldots, s_k$ are the states occupied by ALG (in this order).

Our goal now is to bound $\text{OPT}(\sigma_n)$ from above. We use the averaging technique (first used in Chapter 1): instead of considering OPT, we consider a finite set B of offline algorithms (not necessarily optimal) and calculate the sum of the costs incurred by each of the algorithms in B to process σ_n. Use $B(\sigma_n)$ to denote this total. At least one of the algorithms in B incurs a cost smaller than or equal to the average cost (over all the algorithms), $\frac{B(\sigma_n)}{|B|}$. Hence, it must be that $\text{OPT}(\sigma_n) \leq \frac{B(\sigma_n)}{|B|}$.

We now show how a wise choice of B yields the theorem. For convenience, use q to denote the state occupied by ALG during $[i, i+1)$, and use $q_1, q_2, \ldots, q_{N-1}$ to denote the other states in S. The set B includes exactly $2N - 1$ offline algorithms and preserves the following invariant at each time interval $[i, i+1)$, $i = 1, \ldots, n-1$.

> **Invariant:** During $[i, i+1)$, exactly two offline algorithms occupy state q_j, $j = 1, \ldots, N-1$ (a total of $2N - 2$ algorithms), and exactly one algorithm occupies state q.

Note that this invariant is easily maintained: when ALG changes its state to q', exactly one offline algorithm (among the two) previously occupying q' changes its state to q.

We now calculate $B(\sigma_n)$. For each transition made by ALG, exactly one offline algorithm performs the symmetric transition (and there are no other transition costs). Also, exactly one offline algorithm is always in the same state as ALG, so this processing cost totals to $(n-k)\varepsilon$. Finally, during those time intervals in which ALG does not pay ε (immediately after transitions), exactly two offline algorithms each pay ε. Since there are exactly k such intervals, this amounts to an additional processing cost of $2k\varepsilon$. Hence,

$$B(\sigma_n) = (n-k)\varepsilon + \sum_{1 \leq i \leq k} d(s_i, s_{i-1}) + 2k\varepsilon$$

$$= (n-k)\varepsilon + \sum_{1 \leq i \leq k} d(s_{i-1}, s_i) + 2k\varepsilon \quad \text{(using symmetry)},$$

which means that

$$\text{OPT}(\sigma_n) \leq \frac{2k\varepsilon + \text{ALG}(\sigma_n)}{2N - 1}. \tag{9.3}$$

Since

$$\text{ALG}(\sigma_n) \geq \sum_{1 \leq i \leq k} d(s_{i-1}, s_i) \geq k \cdot \min_{s \neq q} d(s, q) = k,$$

we have $2k\varepsilon \leq 2\varepsilon \text{ALG}(\sigma_n)$. Hence, using equation (9.3), we obtain

$$(2N - 1) \cdot \text{OPT}(\sigma_n) \leq 2\varepsilon \text{ALG}(\sigma_n) + \text{ALG}(\sigma_n)$$

$$= \text{ALG}(\sigma_n) (1 + 2\varepsilon),$$

from which the theorem follows. ∎

9.4 An Optimal Work Function MTS Algorithm

Work functions and work function algorithms play an important role in the competitive analysis of (deterministic) online algorithms.

Sometimes, in order to be competitive, an online player needs to keep track of the optimal offline cost thus far; this realization leads to the concept of "work function algorithms" that try in some sense to follow the optimal offline algorithm.

Here we present an analysis of a work function algorithm for MTSs that attains an optimal competitive ratio of $2N - 1$ for any N-state MTS.

Let (S, d) be any MTS and let s_0 be an initial state. Fix any task sequence $\sigma = r_1, r_2, \ldots, r_n$. For $i = 1, \ldots, n$, let $\sigma_i = r_1, r_2, \ldots, r_i$ be the prefix of σ containing the first i tasks. By convention we take $\sigma_0 = \varnothing$ (the empty sequence).

For each state $s \in S$, define $w_i(s)$ to be the minimum (offline) cost to process σ_i starting from s_0 and ending in state s. Clearly, $\text{OPT}(\sigma) = \min_{x \in S} w_n(x)$. A dynamic program that computes $w_n(s)$ (and thus $\text{OPT}(\sigma)$) is given by

$$w_{i+1}(s) = \min_{x \in S}\{w_i(x) + r_{i+1}(x) + d(x, s)\}, \tag{9.4}$$

$$w_0(s) = d(s_0, s).$$

The proof that this relation actually describes an optimal way to calculate w_{i+1} is based on a simple observation sometimes called the **principle of optimality**.[4] In our context, the principle of optimality can be stated as follows: *an optimal sequence of state transitions to process the task sequence has the property that no matter what the final transition is, and no matter what the state preceding the final state is, the sequence of transitions from the initial state to the state preceding the final one is optimal.*

Exercise 9.1 Prove that the work functions w_i can be defined by equation (9.4).

---

[4] This "principle" is usually attributed to Bellman (see Bellman [53], and Dreyfus [135]).

The way to go about calculating w_n is to compute a table of n rows and N columns such that the ith row contains the values $w_i(1)$, $w_i(2)$, ..., $w_i(N)$. Equation (9.4) shows that the computation of the $(i + 1)$st row can be based solely on the ith row, and so on. Thus the optimal offline cost, $\min_s w_n(s)$ (and schedule), can be computed using this method (which is commonly termed **dynamic programming**).

Exercise 9.2 Given an N-state MTS, an initial state, and a task sequence of length n, what are the time and space complexities to compute the optimal offline schedule and cost to serve the task sequence using the above work function method?

The functions $w_0, w_1, w_2, \ldots$ are called the **work functions** of σ with respect to s_0. Having defined the work functions, we are now ready to describe the MTS WORK FUNCTION ALGORITHM.

> **Algorithm WFA:** Suppose that the algorithm is in state s_i after processing the i tasks in σ_i. Then, to process r_{i+1}, the algorithm moves to a state
>
> $$s_{i+1} = \arg \min_x \{w_{i+1}(x) + d(s_i, x)\},$$
>
> with s_{i+1} satisfying
>
> $$w_{i+1}(s_{i+1}) = w_i(s_{i+1}) + r_{i+1}(s_{i+1}). \tag{9.5}$$

The WFA is well defined, as stated in the following lemma.

Lemma 9.2 *Let A be the set of all the states that satisfy both $s_{i+1} = \arg \min_x w_{i+1}(x) + d(s_i, x)$ and $w_{i+1}(s_{i+1}) = w_i(s_{i+1}) + r_{i+1}(s_{i+1})$. Then A is not empty (i.e., WFA can always choose an appropriate state s_{i+1}).*

PROOF. Define the set

$$A' = \left\{ y \ : \ y \in S \quad \text{and} \quad y = \arg \min_x \{w_{i+1}(x) + d(s_i, x)\} \right\}.$$

Clearly, A' is not empty because the set of states S is finite and not empty. We will prove that there is an element of A' that satisfies equation (9.5). This will prove that the set A is not empty.

For each state $x \in S$, $w_{i+1}(x) \leq w_i(x) + r_{i+1}(x)$. This is because the optimal way to process the sequence σ_{i+1} ending in state x is surely no more costly than optimally processing σ_i ending in x and then processing r_{i+1} from state x (without considering any other, perhaps better, option). Adding $d(x, s_i)$ to both sides of this inequality, we obtain

$$w_{i+1}(x) + d(x, s_i) \leq w_i(x) + r_{i+1}(x) + d(x, s_i). \tag{9.6}$$

Let z be any element of A' and let x^* be a state for which the minimum in equation (9.4) with $s = z$ is obtained. That is,

$$w_{i+1}(z) = w_i(x^*) + r_{i+1}(x^*) + d(x^*, z). \tag{9.7}$$

Adding $d(x^*, s_i)$ to both sides of equation (9.7) and rearranging terms, we obtain

$$w_i(x^*) + r_{i+1}(x^*) + d(x^*, s_i) = w_{i+1}(z) + d(x^*, s_i) - d(x^*, z). \tag{9.8}$$

Using the triangle inequality $d(x^*, s_i) - d(x^*, z) \leq d(z, s_i)$, inequality (9.6), and equality (9.8), we learn that

$$w_{i+1}(x^*) + d(x^*, s_i) \leq w_{i+1}(z) + d(z, s_i). \tag{9.9}$$

Therefore, since $z = \arg\min_x\{w_{i+1}(z) + d(x, s_i)\}$, it must be that $x^* \in A'$. Moreover, inequality (9.9) must be an equality. Therefore, when $x = x^*$, inequality (9.6) must also be an equality. Hence, x^* is an element of A. ∎

The work function algorithm is rather simple. However, notice that for processing the next task, the work function algorithm must compute the N values of the next work function. For applications that require a large number of states, this algorithm may be extremely time consuming.

Theorem 9.4 *The work function algorithm is* $(2N - 1)$*-competitive for any MTS with* N *states.*

Fix any initial state s_0 and a task sequence σ. Let $s_0, s_1, \ldots, s_n$ be the states occupied by WFA for processing σ. Define, for $i = 0, 1, \ldots, n$,

$$B_i = 2 \cdot \sum_{s \neq s_i} w_i(s) + w_i(s_i).$$

Also, define μ to be the maximum distance between any two states in S. The theorem follows according to Lemma 9.3, which establishes

$$\text{WFA}(\sigma) \leq (2N - 1) \cdot \text{OPT}(\sigma) + [(2N - 2)\mu - B_0].$$

Lemma 9.3 *For all* $0 \leq i \leq n$,

$$B_i \leq (2N - 1) \cdot \text{OPT}(\sigma_i) + (2N - 2)\mu; \tag{9.10}$$

$$\text{WFA}(\sigma_i) + B_0 \leq B_i. \tag{9.11}$$

PROOF. First, based on equation (9.4), for all $s \in S$, $w_i(s) \leq \min_x w_i(x) + \mu$. Then equation (9.10) follows from the fact that $\text{OPT}(\sigma_i) = \min_x w_i(x)$.

We now prove inequality (9.11). By the definitions of s_{i+1} and of the work function w_{i+1},

$$\begin{aligned}
w_{i+1}(s_{i+1}) + d(s_i, s_{i+1}) &= \min_x\{w_{i+1}(x) + d(s_i, x)\} \\
&\leq w_{i+1}(s_i) + d(s_i, s_i) \tag{9.12} \\
&= w_{i+1}(s_i).
\end{aligned}$$

Although it is not needed for our proof, we note that the inequality (9.12) can be replaced by equality. (Equality readily follows from the identity $\min_x\{w_{i+1}(x)\} = \min_x\{w_i(x) + r_{i+1}(x)\}$.)

Using inequality (9.12), we conclude that

$$w_{i+1}(s_i) - w_{i+1}(s_{i+1}) \geq d(s_i, s_{i+1}). \tag{9.13}$$

By definition, s_{i+1} satisfies

$$w_{i+1}(s_{i+1}) - w_i(s_{i+1}) = r_{i+1}(s_{i+1}). \tag{9.14}$$

Adding equations (9.13) and (9.14), we obtain

$$w_{i+1}(s_i) - w_i(s_{i+1}) \geq d(s_i, s_{i+1}) + r_{i+1}(s_{i+1}). \tag{9.15}$$

Notice that the right-hand side is the total cost (processing plus transition) that WFA incurs for the $(i + 1)$st task. Next we claim that

$$B_{i+1} - B_i \geq w_{i+1}(s_i) - w_i(s_{i+1}). \tag{9.16}$$

This inequality can be shown as follows: first notice that the work function is monotone increasing with i; that is, $\forall s, i, \ w_i(s) \leq w_{i+1}(s)$. Rearranging terms, the difference $B_{i+1} - B_i$ can be written as

$$\left(2 \sum_{\substack{s \neq s_{i+1} \\ s \neq s_i}} w_{i+1}(s) - 2 \sum_{\substack{s \neq s_i \\ s \neq s_{i+1}}} w_i(s) \right) + (2w_{i+1}(s_i) - w_i(s_i))$$

$$+ (w_{i+1}(s_{i+1}) - 2w_i(s_{i+1})).$$

Consistent with the monotonicity of w, the first term is nonnegative and we can subtract $w_{i+1}(s_i) - w_i(s_i)$ and $w_{i+1}(s_{i+1}) - w_i(s_{i+1})$, which are both nonnegative, from the second and third terms, respectively. It follows that equation (9.16) holds.

To conclude, based on equations (9.16) and (9.15), $B_{i+1} - B_i$ bounds from above the total cost for processing the $(i + 1)$st task and therefore, $\sum_{0 \leq j < i}(B_{j+1} - B_j) = B_i - B_0$ bounds above the total cost for processing σ_i, proving equation (9.11). ∎

9.5 A Randomized Algorithm for a Uniform MTS

An MTS (S, d) is called **uniform** if all state transitions have identical (say, unit) cost; that is, $\forall i \neq j, d(i, j) = 1$.

Since we do not restrict memory, without loss of generality we consider behavioral randomized MTS algorithms for which the change of state is now a probabilistic function of the configuration of the algorithm. We now describe a continuous time randomized algorithm attaining a competitive ratio of $2H_N$ for the uniform MTS against an oblivious adversary. As in the case of deterministic algorithms, a randomized continuous time algorithm can be transformed into a randomized discrete time algorithm.

It is useful to introduce the following notation and terminology. The algorithm proceeds in a sequence of phases. Use t_{i-1} to denote the starting time of the ith phase. A state s is called "saturated" for phase i at time $t > t_{i-1}$ if the cost to work continuously at state s during the time interval $[t_{i-1}, t]$ is at least 1.

Remark 9.2 Notice that by definition, during each time instance, several states may become saturated simultaneously. For the purposes of the proof, we can impose an arbitrary order (as to the time of saturation) on these states.

Randomized algorithm for uniform MTS: At the start of each phase, all the states are unsaturated and the algorithm enters a random state chosen uniformly among all the states. During a phase, the algorithm remains in the same state until that state becomes saturated. Then it enters a new state chosen randomly and uniformly among all the unsaturated states for that phase. When all the states become saturated, the phase ends and a new phase starts.

Theorem 9.5 *The above algorithm is $2H_N$-competitive against an oblivious adversary.*

PROOF. Let σ be any task sequence. The phases of the algorithm partition the task sequence into (nonstochastic) phases in the obvious manner. The first observation is that the optimal offline algorithm must incur a cost of at least 1 during each phase: either because of a state transition, or because it remains in some state during the entire phase and that state becomes saturated.

Therefore, it is sufficient to prove that the expected cost incurred by the algorithm during each phase is at most $2H_N$. Let $f(i)$ be the expected number of state transitions until the end of the phase, given that there are i unsaturated states remaining. First, $f(1) = 1$; simply, if the current state is the last unsaturated one, when it becomes saturated the phase ends and a transition is made. When there are i unsaturated states one of which, say, s, is currently occupied by the algorithm, we claim that the probability that s will be the first to saturate is $\frac{1}{i}$. This claim is easily established when we recall that the phase is not stochastic and the order in which states become saturated is independent of the random choices of the algorithm (see also the remark above). If this happens, the algorithm will pay 1; otherwise, the next saturated state will not result in a state transition. This means that $f(i) = \frac{1}{i} + f(i-1)$. Hence, $f(N) = H_N$. It follows that the total expected cost incurred by the algorithm during each phase is at most $2H_N$ (state transitions plus task processing). ∎

A lower bound of H_N on the competitive ratio of any algorithm against an oblivious adversary may be obtained similarly to the lower bound of H_k for paging (see Theorem 4.4).

9.6 A Randomized Polylogarithmic Competitive Algorithm for Any MTS

We have just seen that for the uniform metric space, randomization (against an oblivious adversary) allows for a significant reduction in the competitive ratio. Is it possible that there is an $O(\log N)$-competitive randomized MTS algorithm for every metric space? Such a result has not yet been established, although it remains the "popular" conjecture. Nevertheless, there is a weaker yet still remarkable result, namely, that for every metric space there is a polylogarithmic (i.e., $\log^{O(1)} N$)-competitive algorithm for every space. One idea necessary to achieve this result was originally observed in the context of the k-server problem (see Chapter 11): rather than work in a given metric space $\mathcal{M}$, it may be beneficial to embed $\mathcal{M}$ in a "nicer" space. If this embedding does not distort the metric too much, then a "good" competitive ratio for the nicer space will imply a good competitive ratio for the given space. We formalize this idea as follows.

Let $\mathcal{M} = (S, d)$ and $\tilde{\mathcal{M}} = (S, \tilde{d})$ be two metrics defined on the same set of points S. We say that $\tilde{\mathcal{M}}$ (**deterministically**) α-**approximates** $\mathcal{M}$ if $\forall u, v \in S$, we have $d_{uv} \leq \tilde{d}_{uv} \leq \alpha \cdot d_{uv}$. The proof of the following theorem is immediate.

Theorem 9.6 Let $\mathcal{M} = (S, d)$ and $\tilde{\mathcal{M}} = (S, \tilde{d})$ be two metric spaces defined on the same set of points S and let $\tilde{\mathcal{M}}$ α-approximate $\mathcal{M}$. If there exists a deterministic (respectively, randomized) c-competitive MTS algorithm for $(S, \tilde{d})$, then there exists a deterministic (respectively, randomized) $c\alpha$-competitive MTS algorithm for (S, d).

We need to generalize this concept of deterministic approximation to one of probabilistic approximation. Let $\mathcal{H} = (S, d^{(x)})$ be a class of metric spaces all of which are defined on the same point set S as the metric space $\mathcal{M} = (S, d)$. We say $\mathcal{H}$ **probabilistically λ-approximates** $\mathcal{M}$ if there is a probability distribution $D(x)$ on $\mathcal{H}$ such that for all $u, v \in S$:

1. $d_{uv} \leq d_{uv}^{(x)}$.
2. $\mathbf{E}_{D(x)}\left[d_{uv}^{(x)}\right] \leq \lambda \cdot d_{uv}$.

Theorem 9.6 is easily extended to probabilistic approximation to obtain the following theorem.

Theorem 9.7 Let (S, d) be a metric space and suppose $\mathcal{S} = (S, d^{(x)})$ probabilistically α-approximates (S, d). If there exists a deterministic (or randomized) c-competitive MTS algorithm for each $(M, \tilde{d})$, then there exists a randomized $c\alpha$-competitive MTS algorithm for (S, d).

We define a class $\mathcal{H}$ of hierarchically decomposable spaces with the following two informally stated properties:

- There is a randomized polylogarithmic (in N)-competitive MTS algorithm for any N-point space $T \in \mathcal{H}$.
- Let $\mathcal{M}$ be an arbitrary metric space. $\mathcal{M}$ can be probabilistically approximated (within a polylogarithmic factor) by $\mathcal{H}$.

It follows from the above properties and Theorem 9.7 that there is a polylogarithmic-competitive algorithm for every MTS. The proof of this result is quite substantial; Bartal, Blum, Burch, and Tomkins [44] and Bartal [43] provide complete proofs of the desired properties of $\mathcal{H}$. We only sketch these proofs here; in particular, we limit our discussion of the first property to the case in which the diameter of the space is polynomial in N.[5]

To motivate the first property and the definition of an appropriate $\mathcal{H}$, consider the case of a metric space $\mathcal{M}$ composed of b metric subspaces $\mathcal{M}_1, \ldots, \mathcal{M}_b$, pairwise separated by some distance D that is relatively large compared to the diameters of the subspaces.[6] If c_i denotes an achievable competitive ratio for the MTS on the subspace $\mathcal{M}_i$, we might expect to achieve a competitive ratio of $c = O(\max_i\{c_i\} \cdot \log b)$ on the entire space. Informally, the reason is that we can treat each subspace $\mathcal{M}_i$ as a node in a uniform metric space and use the uniform MTS algorithm to move randomly to different subspaces. While in a subspace $\mathcal{M}_i$, we remain on that subspace and use the c_i-competitive algorithm until an optimal offline algorithm would have incurred cost D if it had also been in this same

---

[5] The **diameter** $\mathrm{diam}(\mathcal{M})$ of a metric space $\mathcal{M} = (S; d)$ is the $\max\{d(u, v)|u, v \in S\}$.

[6] That is, for $i \neq j$, $d(u, v) = D$ for any $u \in \mathcal{M}_i$ and $v \in \mathcal{M}_j$ where $D \geq h \cdot \mathrm{diam}(\mathcal{M}_i)$ for some sufficiently large h. For the purpose of this motivating example, it is sufficient that h is a constant. For the desired competitive result (see Theorem 9.9 and Corollary 9.12), we will need h to be polylogarithmic in N.

subspace. Alternatively stated, we derive the stated ratio by "unfairly" charging the online algorithm c_i times the task vector while processing tasks in the subspace $\mathcal{M}_i$.

We would like to do even better! Suppose that for the above space $\mathcal{M}$, we could achieve a competitive ratio of $\max\{c_i\} + O(\log b)$. (Of course, to achieve such a good competitive ratio, we cannot simply remain in the same subspace until it has achieved sufficient processing cost.) Now assume we have a metric space that can be recursively decomposed into a "balanced" collection of subspaces separated by a relatively large distance, with the depth of this decomposition logarithmic in N. Letting $C(N)$ be the ratio for the N-state space, we then obtain $C(N) \leq C\left(\frac{N}{b}\right) + O(\log b)$, which implies $C(N) = O(\log N)$.

This informal argument suggests the following definition of the class $\mathcal{H}$ of **h-hierarchical separated tree spaces**. The parameter h quantifies the relative size of the separation between subspaces. The points of these constructed metric spaces are leaves in an edge-weighted rooted tree, and the metric is the metric induced by the weighted undirected tree path lengths between these leaves. Any such constructed space T is called an h-HST. We abuse notation and use T to denote both the metric space and the weighted tree, which induces this metric space. The inductive definition of h-HSTs is as follows:

1. Every one-node space is an h-HST.
2. Let $b \geq 1$ and let $T_1, \ldots, T_b$ be h-HSTs. Let D be an upper bound on the diameter of any of the subspaces T_i. For any $W \geq h \cdot D$, construct the tree T consisting of a root and the b subtrees $T_1, \ldots, T_b$ and let W be the weight of the edge from the root to the root of each subtree. Then the space induced by the leaves of T with the weighted path length metric is also an h-HST.

Obviously, the diameter D of an h-HST T is at least h times larger than the diameter of any of its subspaces, and the tree depth of T is at most $\log_h D$. We proceed in the next two subsections to show that h-HSTs satisfy the properties required to obtain a polylogarithmic competitive bound for all metric spaces.

9.6.1 An MTS Algorithm for Hierarchical Separated Spaces

In order to construct a competitive algorithm for h-HSTs, it is helpful to look at randomized algorithms as controlling the amount of probability that flows to and from states in the following sense.

Lemma 9.4 *Against an oblivious adversary, we can view any (behavioral) randomized MTS algorithm* ALG *as follows:* ALG *maintains a probability distribution* $(p_1, \ldots, p_N)$ *over the points of the metric space. (*ALG *may also maintain a "memory state" and base its decision on the probability distribution and the memory.) Given a task* $r = \langle r(1), \ldots, r(N) \rangle$, *first* ALG *is allowed to change this distribution to some* $\langle p'_1, \ldots, p'_N \rangle$. *For every* $\tilde{p}$ *units of probability being moved a distance of* δ, ALG *pays transition cost* $\tilde{p} \cdot \delta$. *Then, to service the task,* ALG *pays expected processing cost* $\sum_{i=1}^{N} p'_i r(i)$.

PROOF. It is clear that for every behavioral randomized algorithm and for every request sequence, the probability distribution described in the lemma is well defined. Conversely, to convert back to a behavioral algorithm, one simply needs to proceed state by state to show how to define the MTS move on a task in order to achieve the desired movement of probability mass.   ∎

Lemma 9.1 is easily extendable to randomized algorithms so that once again we can concentrate on elementary tasks. Without loss of generality, we can assume that given an elementary task $\langle i; \tau \rangle$, an online algorithm will not increase its mass p_i and will (possibly) decrease its mass p_i by distributing some of this mass to other states. For example, when $p_i = 0$, an online algorithm will not change its distribution when given a task $\langle i; \tau \rangle$. It follows that when an adversary issues a task $\langle i; \tau \rangle$ that causes the online algorithm to set $p_i = 0$, then τ is the minimum value needed to achieve this.

We introduce the **unfair MTS** problem, a generalization of the standard uniform task system problem. This generalization provides a good abstraction for our goal to construct a randomized algorithm for every h-HST space. Let $\mathcal{M}$ be a uniform b-point space with d pairwise distance between points. Associated with the ith point is a **cost ratio** c_i, and associated with the distance d is a **distance ratio** s. When a randomized online algorithm serves a task $(i; \tau)$ by decreasing its probability mass in state i from p_i to p_i', it pays a total cost of $p_i' c_i \tau + (p_i - p_i')sd$. The offline player pays τ if it serves $(i; \tau)$ in state i, or it pays d if it moves from state i to some other state $j \neq i$.

The cost ratios $\{c_i\}$ are introduced in order to apply recursively an algorithm for the unfair problem, with points on $\mathcal{M}$ becoming subspaces (with ratios $\{c_i\}$) of an h-HST. The distance ratio is introduced in order to compensate for the fact that the cost ratio in each subspace represents amortized costs and not worst-case cost per request. We also need to compensate for the fact that the distance between points (in different subspaces) is not uniform.

From Section 9.4, we recall the definition of the work function $w_i(\sigma)$ as the optimal offline cost to end in state i after processing σ. (We simply write w_i, since the context is clear.) We can now define a competitive randomized algorithm (with parameter t) for the unfair MTS problem.

Algorithm W-BALANCE$_t$: Let t be an odd positive integer. The algorithm W-BALANCE$_t$ sets its probability distribution $\langle p_1, \ldots, p_b \rangle$ so that

$$p_j = \frac{1}{b} + \frac{1}{b} \sum_{i=1}^{b} \left(\frac{w_i - w_j}{d} \right)^t.$$

Lemma 9.5 *For any odd positive integer t, the vector $\langle p_1, \ldots, p_N \rangle$ defined by the algorithm W-BALANCE$_t$ is a probability distribution; that is, after processing every task,*

$$0 \leq p_i \leq 1 \quad and \quad \sum_{i=1}^{N} p_i = 1.$$

PROOF. Since t is odd, it is easy to see that

$$\sum_{j=1}^{b} \sum_{i=1}^{b} \left(\frac{w_i - w_j}{d} \right)^t = 0.$$

and hence that

$$\sum_{i=1}^{b} p_i = 1.$$

By thinking of W-BALANCE$_t$ as a continuous time algorithm, the probability p_j becomes a continuous decreasing function of w_j (and increasing with all other w_i). Thus, if a p_j decreases to 0 by some task $\langle j; \tau \rangle$, then τ will be a minimum such cost and p_j will be set to zero and will not be further decreased. ∎

Note that W-BALANCE$_t$ sets its probability distribution as a function of (only) the $\{w_i\}$ values. We call such an algorithm a **w-based** algorithm. When $t = 1$, W-BALANCE$_t$ is perhaps the most natural w-based algorithm. Larger values of t cause W-BALANCE$_t$ to move more probability to states with small w values. We say that an online randomized algorithm is **reasonable** if for all states $i \neq j$, $p_i = p_j + d$ implies $p_i = 0$. A w-based algorithm must be reasonable if it is to be competitive. (Otherwise, the adversary can continue issuing $\langle i, \tau \rangle$ tasks that will not change the value of w_i.) We observe that W-BALANCE$_t$ is reasonable.

Lemma 9.6 *For any odd positive integer t, the algorithm W-BALANCE$_t$ is reasonable.*

PROOF. Suppose $w_j = w_k + d$. Consider the summation $\sum_{i=1}^{b}\left(\frac{w_i - w_j}{d}\right)^t$ in the definition of p_j. Since $w_i \leq w_k + d = w_j$ for all i, every term in this summation is at most 0. Moreover, the kth term of this summation is exactly -1. Therefore, the summation is at most -1 and p_j is at most 0. ∎

A reasonable w-based algorithm such as W-BALANCE$_t$ permits the following simplification on the nature of the adversary.

Lemma 9.7 *For a reasonable w-based algorithm, we can assume that after each task $\langle i; \tau \rangle$, w_i increases by τ.*

Exercise 9.3 Prove Lemma 9.7.

We are now ready to prove that W-BALANCE$_t$ is sufficiently competitive.

Theorem 9.8 *Consider the unfair MTS problem with $c_1 \geq c_2 \geq \cdots \geq c_b$. Then algorithm W-BALANCE$_t$ is $(c_1 + 2s \cdot b^{1/t} \cdot t)$-competitive. In particular, when $t = \log b$, W-BALANCE$_t$ is $(c_1 + O(\log b))$-competitive.*

PROOF. Let Φ be a nonnegative-valued potential function. Using the first style of the potential function method (see Section 1.4), it is sufficient to show for every request r that

$$\text{ALG}(r) + \Delta\Phi \leq c \cdot \Delta(\text{OPT})$$

$$= c \cdot \Delta(\min_i\{w_i\}).$$

As usual, $\Delta\Phi$ denotes the change in potential; similarly, $\Delta(\text{OPT})$ denotes the change in OPT's value or, equivalently, OPT's cost to process the request r. Since $|w_i - w_j| \leq d$ for all i and j, it is also sufficient for ALG to compete against *any* weighted average $\bar{w}$ of the $\{w_i\}$, rather than $\min_i\{w_i\}$. That is, we need to show

$$\text{ALG}(r) + \Delta\Phi \leq c \cdot \Delta(\bar{w}).$$

The potential function used here $\Phi = \Phi_l + \Phi_m$ is the sum of two sub-functions where Φ_l amortizes the local processing cost at each node and Φ_m amortizes the movement cost. Let $r = \langle k; \tau \rangle$ be an elementary task and assume that in response to this request, W-BALANCE$_t$ decreases its mass on state k from p_k to p_k'. Since W-BALANCE is reasonable, after processing $\langle k; \tau \rangle$, w_k increases by τ and w_i is unchanged for $i \neq k$. That is, $\Delta\bar{w} = \frac{\tau}{b}$.

By summing the amortized processing and movement costs, it suffices to show the following:

(1) $p_k' c_k \tau + \Delta\Phi_l \leq \frac{c_1\tau}{b} = c_1 \cdot \Delta\bar{w}$.

(2) $(p_k - p_k')sd + \Delta\Phi_m \leq 2sb^{1/t} \cdot t \cdot \frac{\tau}{b} = (2sb^{1/t}t) \cdot \Delta\bar{w}$.

We establish (1) as follows:
Define

$$\Phi_l = \frac{c_1 d}{2(t+1)b} \sum_{i=1}^{b} \sum_{j=1}^{b} \left(\frac{w_i - w_j}{d} \right)^{t+1},$$

so that

$$\frac{\partial\Phi_l}{\partial w_k} = -\left(p_k - \frac{1}{b} \right) c_1.$$

Suppose $w_k = y$ before the request.
Since p_k decreases as a function of w_k, we have

$$p_k' c_k \tau + \Delta\Phi_l \leq \int_y^{y+\tau} \left(p_k c_k + \frac{\partial\Phi_l}{\partial w_k} \right) dw_k$$

$$\leq p_k c_k \tau - \left(p_k - \frac{1}{b} \right) c_1 \tau$$

$$\leq c_1 \frac{\tau}{b}.$$

We establish item (2) as follows:
Define

$$\Phi_m = \frac{sd}{2b} \sum_{i=1}^{b} \sum_{j=1}^{b} \left| \frac{w_i - w_j}{d} \right|^t.$$

$$(p_k - p_k')sd + \Delta\Phi_m \leq \int_y^{y+\tau} \left(\frac{\partial p_k}{\partial w_k} sd + \frac{\partial\Phi_m}{\partial w_k} \right) dw_k.$$

We want to show that the integrand is upper bounded by $\frac{2sb^{1/t}t}{b}$. We have

$$\frac{\partial p_k}{\partial w_k} sd = \frac{st}{b} \sum_{i \neq k} \left(\frac{w_i - w_j}{d} \right)^{t-1},$$

and

$$\frac{\partial \Phi_m}{\partial w_k} = \frac{st}{b} \sum_{w_i < w_k} \left(\frac{w_k - w_i}{d} \right)^{t-1} - \frac{st}{b} \sum_{w_i > w_k} \left(\frac{w_i - w_k}{d} \right)^{t-1},$$

so that

$$\frac{\partial p_k}{\partial w_k} sd + \frac{\partial \Phi_m}{\partial w_k} = \frac{2st}{b} \sum_{w_i < w_k} \left(\frac{w_k - w_i}{d} \right)^{t-1}$$

$$\leq \frac{2st}{b} \sum_{i \neq u} \left(\frac{w_u - w_i}{d} \right)^{t-1} \qquad \text{(letting } w_u = \max_i \{w_i\}\text{)}.$$

We note that

$$\sum_{i \neq u} \left(\frac{w_u - w_i}{d} \right)^{t} \leq 1 \qquad \text{(by the definition of } p_u \text{ as a probability)}$$

and that each term of this sum is nonnegative. The maximum value of such a sum is obtained when all terms are equal; that is,

$$\left(\frac{w_u - w_i}{d} \right)^{t} = \frac{1}{(b-1)}.$$

It follows that

$$\sum_{i \neq u} \left(\frac{w_u - w_i}{d} \right)^{t-1} \leq (b-1)^{1/t} \leq b^{1/t}.$$

∎

We now recursively apply Theorem 9.8 in order to derive an algorithm for h-HSTs of polynomial diameter. We replace each point in the space of the unfair MTS problem by a smaller h-HST subspace. As already mentioned, we must overcome some technical problems. First, we use the cost ratio c_i to abstract the relative cost in the ith subspace; however, this abstraction must be reconciled with the fact that we have an amortized cost (and not a worst case per request) in each subspace.

The following lemma shows how we use the distance ratio and bounds on the potentials to compensate for this amortization.

Lemma 9.8 *Let $\{\mathcal{M}_i\}$ for $1 \leq i \leq b$ be subspaces such that for each $\mathcal{M}_i$ there is a c_i-competitive randomized algorithm* ALG$_i$ *established via a potential function Φ_i with $\Phi_i \leq \Phi_{\max}$. Furthermore, suppose each such competitive ratio c_i is obtained by competing against some weighted average $\hat{w}_i$ of work function values on the space $\mathcal{M}_i$. Suppose there is a c-competitive randomized algorithm* ALG *using some potential function Φ for the unfair MTS problem with cost ratios $\{c_i\}$, distance d, and distance ratio $s = \hat{s} + \frac{\Phi_{\max}}{d}$. Now consider a **modified unfair problem** on a space $\widehat{\mathcal{M}}$ where we replace the ith point by the subspace $\mathcal{M}_i$. In the modified problem, a request $(i; \tau)$ served at a state in $\mathcal{M}_i$ costs $p_i'(c_i\tau - (\Phi_i' - \Phi_i))$ where Φ_i' is the ith potential after serving the request. Then* *there exists a c-competitive algorithm* $\widehat{\text{ALG}}$ *for the modified unfair problem with distance ratio* $\hat{s}$; *furthermore, the competitive bound is established using the potential function* $\hat{\Phi} = \Phi + \sum_{j=1}^{b} p_j \Phi_j \leq \Phi + \Phi_{\max}$, *competing against the average of the* $\hat{w}_i$ *(which is a weighted average of work function values on the space* $\widehat{\mathcal{M}}$).

Lemma 9.8 indicates the need to bound the potential in Theorem 9.8.

Lemma 9.9 *Let* Φ *be the potential function in Theorem 9.8. Then* $\Phi \leq \left(\frac{c_1}{t+1}\right)d$.

Exercise 9.4 Prove Lemmas 9.8 and 9.9.

It is now clear that the choice of t is constrained in two ways. First, it must be set appropriately in order to achieve a sufficiently small competitive ratio in Theorem 9.8. Second, it must provide a bound on the potential that is small enough to enable the algorithm to be applied recursively. Some other technical obstacles must be overcome before we can recursively apply algorithm W-BALANCE$_t$ to obtain a competitive algorithm for h-HST spaces. We do not have a uniform distance between the subspaces; rather, the diameter of each subspace is at most a factor $\frac{1}{h}$ of the diameter of the entire space. We also need a strengthened version of the reasonableness property. Specifically, we need the online algorithm to be **hierarchically reasonable**, which means that whenever $w_u = w_v + d(u, v)$, for u and v in different subspaces, then the algorithm assigns zero probability to *any* state in the same subspace as state u.

We are now ready to state the competitive result for h-HSTs.

Theorem 9.9 *Let* $\mathcal{M}$ *be an* N-*point* h-*HST of depth* ℓ *with* $h > 9\ell$. *For* $t \geq \log N$, *there is a randomized algorithm* ALG *(i.e., a judicious recursive application of algorithm* W-BALANCE$_t$*) such that* $\overline{\mathcal{R}}(\text{ALG}) \leq 9\ell t + 1 = O(\log N \log_h D)$. *Furthermore, the proof of competitiveness uses a potential function* Φ *that is bounded above by* $\frac{9\ell}{h} D$.

PROOF. The proof is by induction on the depth ℓ. The basis ($\ell = 0$) is immediate. Consider an h-HST of depth ℓ and diameter D. The depth of each subspace is at most $\ell - 1$ and the diameter is at most $\frac{D}{h}$; therefore, according to the inductive hypothesis, there is a $9(\ell - 1)t + 1$-competitive algorithm via a potential function bounded by $\frac{9(\ell-1)}{h} D$.

We consider the modified unfair MTS problem with $d = \frac{D-2}{h} D$, cost ratios

$$9(\ell - 1)t + 1 \geq c_1 \geq c_2 \geq \cdots \geq c_b,$$

and distance ratio

$$\hat{s} = \frac{h}{h - 2}.$$

These parameters ensure that the maximum distance between any two points is $D = \hat{s}d$ (i.e., the online player is not undercharged), whereas the offline adversary pays d, a "little" less than necessary for moves between the subspaces. Moreover, it is not difficult to show that algorithm W-BALANCE$_t$ is hierarchically reasonable for this setting of the parameters.

According to Lemma 9.8, since the maximum potential needed for each subspace is $\frac{9(\ell-1)}{h} D \leq d$, we can use $s = \hat{s} + 1 \leq \frac{9}{4}$ in the unfair problem. We now calculate the competitive ratio and bound the potential by combining Theorem 9.8, Lemma 9.8, and Lemma 9.9. Since $t \geq \log N \geq \log b$, we have $b^{1/t} \leq 2$, and the competitive ratio satisfies

$$c_1 + 2sb^{1/t}t \leq 9(\ell - 1)t + 1 + 2 \cdot \frac{9}{4} \cdot 2 \cdot t$$
$$\leq 9\ell t + 1.$$

The potential is bounded by

$$\left(\frac{c_1}{t+1} + s\right)D + \frac{9(\ell - 1)}{h}D \leq \left[\frac{9(\ell - 1)t + 1}{t + 1} + \frac{9}{4} + 1\right]D$$
$$\leq 9\ell \cdot D.$$

This completes the induction step and the proof. ∎

Clearly, the depth ℓ is at most $\log_h D$; however, for unbalanced trees, ℓ is not bounded by a polynomial in $\log N$. We want to remove the dependence on the diameter of the h-HST. Some additional ideas are needed to prove a general result that does not depend on the diameter D. We state (without proof) the desired result.

Theorem 9.10 *Let $\mathcal{M}$ be an arbitrary N-point h-HST with $h = \Omega(\log^2 N)$. Then there is a randomized algorithm* ALG *such that* $\overline{\mathcal{R}}(\text{ALG}) = O(\log^2 N)$.

9.6.2   Embedding Arbitrary Metric Spaces into h-HSTs

We now turn to the second major result needed to establish a polylogarithmic competitive algorithm for *every* metric space. We need to show that every metric space can be probabilistically approximated by h-HSTs.

Theorem 9.11 *Let $\mathcal{M} = (S; d)$ be an N-point metric space of diameter D. For every $h \geq 2$, $\mathcal{M}$ can be α-probabilistically approximated by h-HSTs of diameter $O(D)$ with $\alpha = O(h \log N \log_h(\min\{N, D\}))$.*

Corollary 9.12 *For every N-point space $\mathcal{M}$ of diameter D, there is a c-competitive MTS algorithm with*

$$c = O\left(\frac{\log^3 N \log^2 D}{\log^3 \log D}\right).$$

For every N-point space $\mathcal{M}$, there is a c'-competitive MTS algorithm with

$$c' = O\left(\frac{\log^6 N}{\log \log N}\right).$$

PROOF. For the diameter-bounded result, we set $h = O\left(\frac{\log D}{\log \log D}\right)$, combine Theorems 9.9 and 9.11, and then apply Theorem 9.7. For the general result, we set $h = O(\log^2 N)$ and use Theorem 9.10 instead of Theorem 9.9. ∎

We sketch the proof of Theorem 9.11. Specifically, we sketch the proof of this result only for $\alpha = O(h \log N \log_h D)$. $\mathcal{M}$ can be viewed as a metric space induced by a weighted N-node graph $G = (V, E, d)$ with $d : E \to \mathbb{R}^+$. We first show how to construct probabilistic partitions of G; that is, how to construct an appropriate distribution on partitions of the node set V in which every block of each partition has "small diameter" and the probability that a small weighted edge is not contained in some block is sufficiently small. We can recursively apply these probabilistic partitions to construct probabilistically h-HSTs that approximate $\mathcal{M}$. Simply stated, the blocks of the partition become the subtrees of the h-HST.

We first need to define probabilistic partitions. Let G be an N-node graph. An m-**probabilistic partition of G** is a probability distribution over partitions $(V_1, \dots, V_s)$ of the node set V satisfying the following properties:

- $\operatorname{diam}(G(V_i)) \le m \cdot (2 \ln N + 1)$, where $G(V_i)$ is the subgraph induced by the block of nodes V_i.
- $\max_{e \in E} \Pr[e \notin G(V_i) \text{ for any } i, 1 \le i \le s] \le \frac{2 \cdot d(e)}{m}$.

To prove Theorem 9.11, we need the following two lemmas.

Lemma 9.10 *If for every weighted graph G of diameter D and every m, $1 \le m \le D$, there exists an m-probabilistic partition of G, then for all $h \ge 1$, G is α-probabilistically approximated by h-HSTs of diameter $O(D)$ with $\alpha = O(h \log N \log_h D)$.*

PROOF. We shall only describe the construction of the desired h-HSTs; we leave the proof of the required properties as an exercise. We construct the h-HST recursively (i.e., by induction on $|V|$). With every stage of the recursion there is an associated graph G_i ($G_1 = G$) and parameter m_i. The base case of the recursion is when $G_\ell = (V_\ell, E_\ell, d_\ell)$ with $|V_\ell| = 1$, where ℓ is the depth of the recursion. Consider the case $|V_i| > 1$. Set $m_i = \lfloor \frac{\operatorname{diam}(G_i)}{h(2 \ln N + 1)} \rfloor$. Compute an m_i-probabilistic partition of G_i, resulting, for example, in blocks $C_1, \dots, C_s$. Recursively compute h-HSTs for each C_j, $1 \le j \le s$. (That is, for each j, set $G_{i+1} = C_j$ and inductively apply the construction.) Suppose the resulting h-HSTs are the trees $T^1, \dots, T^s$ with roots $q^1, \dots, q^s$. Construct T by introducing a new root node q and edges $(q, q^1), \dots, (q, q^s)$, with the weight of every edge (q, q^j) set to $\frac{1}{2} \operatorname{diam}(G_i)$. This completes the construction. Using Exercise 9.5, for $G_1 = G$ we probabilistically construct $T_1 = T$, satisfying $\operatorname{diam}(T) \le (1 + \frac{1}{h-1}) \operatorname{diam}(G) = O(\operatorname{diam}(G))$, and for all $u, v \in V$, we have

- $d_G(u, v) \le d_T(u, v)$.
- $E[d_T(u, v)] \le 2(2 \ln N + 1) h (1 + \frac{1}{h-1})(\ell - 1) d_G(u, v) = O(h \log N \log_h D)$.

■

Exercise 9.5 For the construction in Lemma 9.10, inductively prove the following:

- $\operatorname{diam}(G_{i+1}) \le \frac{\operatorname{diam}(G_i)}{h}$ $1 \le i \le \ell - 1$.
- $\operatorname{diam}(T_i) \le (1 + \frac{1}{h-1}) \operatorname{diam}(G_i)$ $1 \le i \le \ell$.
- $d_{G_i}(u, v) \le d_{T_i}(u, v)$ for all $u, v \in U_i$.
- $E[d_{T_i}(u, v)] \le 2(2 \ln N + 1) h (1 + \frac{1}{h-1})(\ell - i) d_{G_i}(u, v)$ for all $u, v \in V_i$.

Let $G = (V, E, d)$ be an N-node weighted graph. The desired m-probabilistic partitions are constructed by the following randomized algorithm.

> **Algorithm** GRAPH-PARTITIONS$_m$: Proceed in stages $i = 1, 2, \ldots$ to construct blocks $B_1, B_2, \ldots, B_s$ of a partition of G. At stage i, there remains a subset of nodes $U_i \subseteq V$ and a subgraph $H_i = G(U_i)$. We begin with $U_0 = V$ and end when $U_{s+1} = \emptyset$.
>
> Stage i: Choose any node $u_i \in U_i$. If the connected component of H_i containing u_i has diameter $\leq 2m \ln N$, then let B_i be this component. Otherwise, choose a radius δ, $0 \leq \delta \leq m \cdot \ln N$ at random according to the continuous distribution with probability density function $q(z) = \left(\frac{N}{N-1}\right)\frac{1}{m}e^{-z/m}$.[7] Set $B_i = \{u \mid d_{H_i}(v_i, u) \leq \delta\}$ and set $U_{i+1} = U_i - B_i$.

Lemma 9.11 *For every weighted graph G and for every m, $1 \leq m \leq \operatorname{diam}(G)$, algorithm* GRAPH-PARTITIONS *constructs an m-probabilistic partition of G.*

PROOF. Clearly, each block B_i has diameter at most $2m \ln N$. It remains to show that small weight edges are likely to be included in some block. Define the metric $\hat{d} = \min\{d, m \ln N\}$. Fix a stage i in the GRAPH-PARTITIONS construction. Let $u_i \in U_i$ be the node chosen to begin this stage and let δ be the radius that is randomly chosen. Let $e = (v, w)$ be an arbitrary edge in E and suppose $d(u_i, v) \leq d(u_i, w)$. Consider the following random events:

- A_i is the event that $v, w \in U_i$. Hence, in this case, neither v nor w is in any block so far.
- M_i^X is the event that $\hat{d}(u_i, v) \leq \delta < \hat{d}(u_i, w)$ conditional on A_i. In this case, v but not w is placed in the block B_i, and edge (v, w) is excluded from all blocks in the partition.
- M_i^C is the event that $\delta < \hat{d}(u_i, v)$ conditional on A_i. In this case, neither v nor w is included in the block B_i and, hence, neither will be in the active node set U_{i+1} for the next stage.
- X_i is the event that edge (v, w) is not included in any block B_j for $j \geq i$ conditional on A_i.

We need to compute a bound on $\Pr[X_0]$, given that $\Pr[A_0] = 0$ and that the X_i satisfy the recurrence

$$\Pr[X_i] = \Pr[M_i^X] + \Pr[M_i^C]\Pr[X_{i+1}].$$

From the definition of the probability density function q, it is easy to verify that

$$\Pr[M_i^X] \leq \frac{N}{N-1}\frac{\hat{d}(v, w)}{m}e^{-(\hat{d}(u_i,v))/m}$$

and that

$$\Pr[M_i^C] = \frac{N}{N-1}\left(1 - e^{-(\hat{d}(u_i,v))/m}\right).$$

---

[7] That is, $\Pr[\text{choosing a radius } \delta \leq y] = \int_0^y q(z)dz$. Note that $\int_0^{m \ln n} p(z)dz = 1$.

Suppose stage s is the last stage (i.e., $U_{s+1} = \varnothing$). Then $\Pr[X_s] = 0$. Using the recurrence for $\Pr[X_i]$, it is also easy to show by induction on $s - i$ that

$$\Pr[X_i] \leq \left(2 - \frac{i}{N-1}\right) \frac{\hat{d}(v, w)}{m}.$$

This completes the proof.   ∎

9.7   Historical Notes and Open Questions

Deterministic MTS Results. The MTS framework was formulated in 1987 by Borodin, Linial, and Saks [81, 82]. It was the first model to propose an abstraction of competitive analysis for online computation, giving the first evidence (including the $2N - 1$ upper and lower bounds) of the somewhat surprising fact that there is a general phenomenon of "competitive" online algorithms. A number of principles and techniques for competitive analysis were developed and first presented within the MTS framework. Among them are: the first application of randomization and formalization of Yao's principle in the competitive analysis context; and the notions of cruel adversaries, traversal, and nearly oblivious algorithms. Also, the idea and motivation for an online work function algorithm was implicitly introduced in the proof of Theorem 9.4 from Borodin, Linial, and Saks [82]. The discrete work function algorithm of Theorem 9.4 (and its analysis) is due to Ricklin [293] and is significantly simpler than the nearly oblivious continuous-time algorithm presented in Borodin, Linial, and Saks [82]. The lower bound of Theorem 9.2 has also been simplified by using the explicit averaging technique introduced in Manasse, McGeoch, and Sleator [255].

Randomized MTS Results. For uniform metric spaces, the $2H_N$ upper bound and the H_N lower bound (of Section 9.5) were presented in Borodin, Linial, and Saks [82]. Irani and Seiden [202] improved the $2H_N$ upper bound for uniform task systems, giving a randomized algorithm attaining a competitive ratio of

$$H_N + O\left(\sqrt{\log N}\right)$$

against an oblivious adversary. Irani and Seiden [201] also constructed a randomized algorithm that achieves for every metric space a competitive ratio of $\frac{eN-1}{e-1} \approx 1.5820N - 0.5820$ against an oblivious adversary. For several years this remained the best randomized upper bound for an arbitrary MTS. Much of the subsequent development of randomized algorithms took place in the context of trying to obtain randomized algorithms for k-server problems (see Chapter 11), with the special case of $N = k + 1$ already posing a substantial problem. Blum, Raghavan, and Schieber [76] gave an $2^{O(\sqrt{\log N \log \log N})}$ upper bound for metric spaces defined by N equally spaced points on the line. Blum, Karloff, Rabani, and Saks [75] and Seiden [306] gave polylogarithmic upper bounds for some particular metric spaces; moreover, these studies provided important insights leading to the breakthrough studies by Bartal [43] and Bartal, Blum, Burch, and Tomkins [44]. First, Bartal proved Theorem 9.11, which shows how to probabilistically approximate within a polylogarithmic factor every metric space by h-HSTs. (Bartal also showed how to improve the approximation factor α in Theorem 9.11 by a $\log N$ factor if the space being approximated is itself a weighted tree or a mesh. This improved the earlier tree embedding result by Alon, Karp, Peleg, and West [12] and yielded an improved (but not yet polyloga-rithmic) upper bound for MTSs. Bartal et al. then showed how to obtain a polylogarithmic upper bound for HST spaces, and in conjunction with Bartal's result [43], they obtained the polylogarithmic upper bound for every metric space. Embedding of metric spaces is, of course, a classical area of research. In the context of online algorithms, the concept of probabilistic approximations was implicitly introduced by Karp [217] and further studied by Alon et al. [12]. In particular, they show that any N-point metric space can be α-approximated by a class of tree metrics (by uniformly choosing spanning trees) with $\alpha = 2O(\sqrt{\log N \log \log N})$. Bartal [43] explicitly defined the concept of probabilistic approximations and, in addition to the upper bound of Theorem 9.11, showed (as a lower bound) that there exist N-node graphs G that require $\alpha = \Omega(\log N)$ if G is to be α-approximated by any class of tree metrics. The probabilistic graph partitions presented by Bartal [43] are inspired by the deterministic partitions studied in Awerbuch and Peleg [30], and Linial and Saks [245].

With regard to randomized lower bounds, there are $\Omega(\log N)$ lower bounds for some special spaces such as the uniform space, studied by Borodin, Linial, and Saks [82], the "superincreasing space," studied by Karloff, Rabani, and Ravid [214], and any weighted star graph space (equivalently, the weighted paging problem for $N = k + 1$), studied by Blum, Furst, and Tomkins [72]. To date, the best-known lower bound for arbitrary spaces is $\Omega(\sqrt{\log N / \log N \log N})$, due to Blum et al. [75], which improved upon the earlier $\Omega(\log \log N)$ bound presented by Karloff, Rabani, and Ravid [214].

Nonsymmetric Spaces and Restricted Classes of Tasks. There are also a few results for nonsymmetric task systems. Consider a nonsymmetric task system (S, d) (i.e., the cost function d is nonsymmetric). Define the **cycle offset ratio** $\psi(d)$ as the maximum over all cycles $s_0, s_1, s_2, \ldots, s_k = s_0$ of the ratio

$$\frac{\sum_{1 \leq i \leq k} d(s_{i-1}, s_i)}{\sum_{1 \leq i \leq k} d(s_i, s_{i-1})}.$$

(When d is symmetric, $\psi(d) = 1$.) The proofs of Theorems 9.2 and 9.4 generalize to the nonsymmetric case. These generalizations show that the competitive ratio of a nonsymmetric task system is in the interval $[(2N - .1)/\psi(d), (2N - 1)\psi(d)]$. More recently, Saks and Tetali [298] showed that the upper bound is $2N - 1$, the same as for the symmetric case. Note that the new upper bound contrasts sharply with the corresponding nonsymmetric k-server model (Chapter 10), where the competitive ratio may depend on the cycle factor.

Manasse, McGeoch, and Sleator [256] gave a $(2K - 1)$-competitive deterministic algorithm for any MTS when restricted to **discrete tasks** of dimension K. Each discrete task is an integer combination of a basis set of K elementary tasks. The basis set is fixed and known to the online player in advance.

Motivated by the k-server model (see Chapter 10), Manasse, McGeoch, and Sleator considered another interesting and natural class of tasks. In this class, the components of each task vector are either 0 or ∞. This means that to process a task, the algorithm must be in a state for which the processing cost is 0 (see Example 9.1). Such tasks are called "forcing tasks." For an MTS with only forcing tasks, Manasse, McGeoch, and Sleator gave an $(N - 1)$-competitive (deterministic) algorithm.

Blum and Burch [71] identify and explore an interesting relation between MTS algorithms and expert learning algorithms.

Credit for Exercises. Exercise 9.1, the "principle of optimality," is due to Bellman [53]. Exercises 9.3 and 9.4 are due to Bartal et al. [44], and Exercise 9.5 is from Bartal [43].

9.7.1   Open Questions

As mentioned at the beginning of this chapter, although the ideas and techniques appearing here prove useful in many settings, the actual competitive ratios that can be derived by applying Theorem 9.4 to particular problems are rather disappointing. For example, both paging and static list accessing can be modeled as MTSs (see Examples 9.1 and 9.2); however, the competitive ratios that follow from Theorem 9.4 are excessively large compared to the specialized ratios that exist for these problems. The main conceptual open problem concerning the MTS framework is therefore to refine the task model to derive more meaningful competitive bounds. The main "technical" open problem relates to the gap between the known lower and upper bounds on randomized MTS algorithms for arbitrary metric spaces.

9.1 (*Value = I5/T4*) Give some natural restrictions on the collection of allowable tasks that result in better competitive online algorithms. For example, give a restriction that includes static list accessing (e.g., without any paid transpositions) and allows for online algorithms with constant competitive ratios.

9.2 (*Value = I3/T4*) Formalize a more general MTS-like framework that can model the static and/or the Δ-paid exchange list accessing problem variants, and determine which statements concerning the standard MTS framework apply to the new framework. For example, we might allow state transitions before and after processing a transaction. In this case, there are two metrics, d_1 and d_2, where d_1 determines the traversal costs before incurring the processing cost, and d_2 determines the traversal costs after incurring the processing cost. As in the next question, either d_1 or d_2 might be asymmetric. Try to adopt any of the results in this chapter (for the standard MTS) to the proposed model.

9.3 (*Value = I4/T2*) What is a tight lower bound for nonsymmetric task systems? In particular, is it the case that $2N - 1$ (or at least $\Omega(N)$) is a lower bound for every nonsymmetric task system?

9.4 (*Value = I5/T5*) Can the $O\left(\frac{\log^6 N}{\log \log N}\right)$ upper bound on the randomized competitive ratio for arbitrary MTSs be improved? In particular, does there exist an $O(\log N)$ upper bound for every MTS?

9.5 (*Value = I5/T5*) Can the $\Omega\left(\sqrt{\log N / \log N \log N}\right)$ lower bound on the randomized competitive ratio for arbitrary MTSs be improved? In particular, does there exist an $\Omega(\log N)$ lower bound for every MTS?

9.6 (*Value = I4/T4*) Give lower and upper bounds on the randomized competitive ratio of other specific task systems. In a particular task system suggested by Borodin, Linial, and

Saks [82], d is the graph distance on a cycle; that is,

$$d(s_i, s_j) = \min\{|j - i|, \ N - |j - i|\}.$$

In this case, the present upper bound is $O\left(\frac{\log^5 N}{\log\log N}\right)$, using the results of Karp [217] and Bartal [43]. Another system of interest is the one for which d is the graph distance on a weighted star graph. In this case, the present upper bound is $O(\log^2 N)$ and the lower bound is $\Omega(\log N)$ (see Blum, Furst, and Tomkins [72]).

CHAPTER 10

The k-Server Problem

A natural generalization of the paging problem is the **k-server problem** proposed by Manasse, McGeoch, and Sleator [256]. This model provides an interesting abstraction for a number of problems. Moreover, the model and the k-server conjecture has been a significant catalyst for the development of competitive analysis.

10.1   The Formulation of the Model

Let $k > 1$ be an integer, and let $\mathcal{M} = (M, d)$ be a metric space where M is a set of points with $|\mathcal{M}| > k$ and d is a metric over $\mathcal{M}$. An algorithm controls k mobile **servers**, which are located on points of $\mathcal{M}$. The algorithm is presented with a sequence $\sigma = r_1, r_2, \ldots, r_n$ of requests where a request r_i is a point in the space. We say that a request r is served if one of the servers lies on r. By moving servers, the algorithm must serve all requests sequentially. For any request sequence σ and any k-server algorithm ALG, ALG(σ) is defined as the total distance (measured by the metric d) moved by ALG's servers in servicing σ. The k-server problem revolves around the question of finding competitive online k-server algorithms for arbitrary and special metric spaces.

For convenience, we sometimes refer to and specify metric spaces as weighted graphs. In this case, we use the standard graph terminology, and we may interchange points with vertices, distance values with edge weights, and so on. $\mathcal{M}$ may be a finite or infinite space. When the metric space $\mathcal{M}$ is finite, we use $N = |\mathcal{M}|$ to denote the size of $\mathcal{M}$.

We define the **(h, k)-server problem** as we did the (h, k)-paging problem in Chapter 3. The performance of the online algorithm with k servers is compared against that of the optimal offline algorithm, which has only $h \leq k$ servers. **Asymmetric k-server problems** are also considered later in this chapter. In the asymmetric version of the problem the distance function d is not symmetric (therefore, the space is not metric). Unless otherwise specified, we assume symmetric problems throughout the chapter. Let $G = (V, E, w)$ be any edge weighted undirected (respectively, directed) graph. G induces a k-server (respectively, asymmetric k-server) problem by letting $d(x, y)$ be $w(x, y)$ if (x, y) is an edge in E; otherwise, it is the distance induced by the transitive closure of the relation w (i.e., the least cost path with respect to the edge weights w).

Over a finite metric space, every k-server problem is a special case of an MTS (see Chapter 9) where each configuration of k servers in the space corresponds to an MTS state and the transition cost between two MTS states is the cost of the minimum weight matching between the two corresponding server configurations. In addition, we must restrict the tasks to model the *k*-server game (i.e., the task vector has infinite processing costs for configurations that do not cover the request and zero cost otherwise). An immediate consequence of Theorem 9.4 is that every metric space with N points allows for a deterministic $(2\binom{N}{k} - 1)$-competitive *k*-server algorithm. This bound is independent of the distance function; however, it does depend on N as well as k. Note that the matching lower bound for an arbitrary MTS with unrestricted tasks (Theorem 9.2) does not apply to the *k*-server problem; therefore, even at the outset, there are possibilities for lower competitive ratios.

The *k*-server model provides an abstraction of various interesting problems. Listed below are some examples of problems that are captured by the *k*-server model.

- **Paging:** An instance of the *k*-server problem with a uniform metric space (all distances are 1) where the k servers represent the k memory slots in the cache and $N = |\mathcal{M}|$ is the number of slow memory pages.
- **Weighted paging:** A paging problem in which the cost of copying different pages into the cache varies. These problems naturally occur in computer systems. For example, in a distributed operating system that uses a distributed file system, page access costs may vary depending on communication costs and architectures of the various machines. A virtual memory management system in which "pages" can have different sizes (e.g., the bitmaps of fonts that must be cached by the display unit) provides another example of weighted paging. Weighted paging is an instance of an asymmetric *k*-server problem in which the cost of moving a server from point x to point y (i.e., evicting x in order to bring in y) can be different from the cost of moving the server from y to x. Alternatively, we can view weighted paging as a symmetric server system (see Corollary 10.6).
- **Two-headed (*k*-headed) disk:** Two (k) read/write heads move along a line segment that is a radius of the disk. When coordinated with the disk spin, they can access every location on each disk track. An algorithm must determine which of the two (k) heads to move in order to service the next read/write request from/to a certain location in a given track. One meaningful way to measure the performance of such a system is to measure the total distance moved by the heads. This is equivalent to the 2-server (*k*-server) problem on a line segment. (For some distributional studies of this problem, see Hofri [189], and Calderbank, Coffman, and Flatto [89].)

10.2 Some Basic Aspects of the *k*-Server Problem

In this section we present some basic concepts and observations concerning *k*-server problems.

10.2.1 The Optimal Offline Algorithm

For any request sequence σ, the optimal offline cost and the optimal offline schedule to serve σ can be computed by using dynamic programming. The straightforward dynamic programming approach to computing an optimal offline *k*-server schedule (for example, see Section 10.7) is not the most efficient algorithm. An alternative, faster method of computing the optimal offline cost and schedule is achieved by reduction to a minimum cost/maximum flow problem. When we use this method, the time needed to calculate the optimal offline cost and schedule is $O(kn^2)$, where n is the number of requests in σ.

10.2.2   The Greedy Policy is Not Competitive

For any request–answer system, we can define a **greedy online algorithm** as any algorithm that processes each request in order to minimize the cost (or maximize the profit) on the input sequence seen thus far. In general, there can be many greedy choices for a given request. Indeed, for the paging problem every demand paging algorithm is greedy, and for the list accessing problem every algorithm that does not use paid exchanges is greedy. For k-server problems, it is equivalent to say that greedy algorithms must process each request in order to minimize the individual cost for serving that request; that is, serve each request with a server that is nearest to the request.

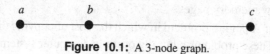

Figure 10.1: A 3-node graph.

It is easy to see why a greedy policy is not necessarily competitive. Consider the 2-server problem when the metric space is the 3-node graph shown in Figure 10.1. In the figure, $d(a, b) < d(b, c)$. No matter what the initial positions of the two servers are, the greedy algorithm will service the request sequence $c, b, a, b, a, b, a, \ldots$ as follows: one server will remain at c "forever," and all the requests for a and b will be served by a single server incurring an unbounded cost. Clearly, the optimal offline algorithm can serve this request sequence (from any starting configuration) with a total cost no greater than $d(a, b) + 2d(b, c)$.

10.2.3   Lazy Algorithms

A straightforward observation is that we may restrict our attention to server algorithms that move at most one server in response to each request, and we may do so only if the request is not presently covered by a server. We call such algorithms **lazy**. (Recall that in the special case of paging, a lazy algorithm is called demand paging; see Section 3.1). This reduction is easily justified: since each request can be serviced by one server, if an algorithm wants to move other servers to some new locations, it can store these locations in memory and move a server (according to the stored locations) only when it is its turn to service a request. According to the triangle inequality, the total distance incurred by the modified algorithm is no more than the total distance incurred by the original one.

10.2.4   The *k*-Server Conjecture

The following conjecture was formulated by Manasse, McGeoch, and Sleator [255]:

> **The *k*-server conjecture:** *Any metric space allows for a deterministic k-competitive, k-server algorithm.*

After considerable effort, researchers have "nearly" solved the k-server conjecture. Koutsoupias and Papadimitriou [232] have shown that there is a generic k-server algorithm (the work function algorithm) that is $(2k - 1)$-competitive in any metric space. The work function algorithm and its analysis are presented in Section 10.7. In addition, there are various examples of special metric spaces that allow for k-competitive server algorithms. Considering these results, we may believe that the conjecture is true. On the other hand, it may appear somewhat strange if this conjecture holds: most other natural generalizations of the results on paging (that hold for paging) are known to be false for k servers. Here are two examples:

- It is not true that any metric space allows for a deterministic $\frac{k}{k-h+1}$-competitive k-server algorithm for the (h, k)-server problem (in contrast, LRU and many other algorithms are $\frac{k}{k-h+1}$-competitive for paging).
- It is not true that in any metric space a randomized competitive ratio of H_k is attainable against an oblivious adversary. In contrast, there is an H_k-competitive for paging (see Chapters 4 and 11).

In addition, the k-server conjecture does not generalize to asymmetric spaces. In Section 10.8 we elaborate on these negative examples.

10.3 A Deterministic Lower Bound

In this section we prove a lower bound of k on the competitive ratio of any deterministic k-server algorithm in a metric space with at least $k + 1$ points. In fact, we have a stronger result, a lower bound of $\frac{k}{k-h+1}$ on the competitive ratio of any server algorithm for the (h, k)-server problem.

Theorem 10.1 *Let $\mathcal{M}$ be any metric space with at least $k + 1$ points. For any $1 \leq h \leq k$, $\frac{k}{k-h+1}$ is a lower bound on the competitive ratio of any online (h, k)-server algorithm for $\mathcal{M}$.*

PROOF. Let ALG be any k-server algorithm. We show that there exists an arbitrarily long (cruel) request sequence σ such that $\text{ALG}(\sigma) \geq \left(\frac{k}{k-h+1}\right) \cdot \text{OPT}(\sigma)$.

Without loss of generality, we assume that ALG is lazy. For the construction of the cruel request sequence, fix any set M of $k + 1$ points in the space. Let the initial configuration of ALG be $\{1, 2, \ldots, k\}$. Since ALG is lazy, it always occupies exactly k distinct points in M (assuming that ALG's initial configuration contains k distinct points). Let $\sigma = r_1, r_2, \ldots, r_n$ be a sequence requesting at each step the (unique) point unoccupied by ALG. This means that ALG serves r_i with the server positioned on the point r_{i+1} incurring a cost of $d(r_{i+1}, r_i)$. For such a (cruel) request sequence σ of length $n \geq 2$, the total cost incurred by ALG is

$$\text{ALG}(\sigma) = \sum_{i=1}^{n-1} d(r_{i+1}, r_i)$$

$$= \sum_{i=1}^{n-1} d(r_i, r_{i+1}) \quad \text{(using symmetry)}.$$

We now prove the existence of an offline h-server algorithm that serves σ while incurring a cost of no more than $\text{ALG}(\sigma)/\left(\frac{k}{k-h+1}\right)$.

We define a set $\mathcal{B}$ of particular h-server algorithms. For each h-subset $S \subset M$ with $r_1 \in S$ (recall that $r_1 = 0$ is the unique point not occupied by ALG in the initial configuration), let B$_S$ be an offline algorithm that operates as follows:

> Algorithm B$_S$ starts in the initial configuration S and serves an uncovered request r_i ($i = 2, 3, \ldots, n$) with the server occupying r_{i-1} (by definition $r_1 \in S$). Note that B$_S$ is well defined, since one of its servers must occupy r_{i-1} when r_i is requested. *Note:* If one assumes that the adversary starts from the same configuration as ALG, then B$_S$ will pay at most $\max_{p \in M} d(p, 0)$ to move to the initial configuration.

Let $\mathcal{B}$ be the set of all such algorithms B$_S$. We now claim that the number of algorithms in the set $\mathcal{B}$ is fixed throughout the game; that is, after each request is processed, different algorithms will always be in different configurations. To prove this claim, it is useful to use the following notation: for each algorithm B$_S$ (with an initial configuration S), let S^i, $i = 0, 1, 2, \ldots$ denote the configuration of B$_S$ after it serves the ith request ($S^0 = S$). We prove the claim by induction on i, where the induction statement is:

Induction statement: If $S_1 \neq S_2$, then the algorithms B$_{S_1}$ and B$_{S_2}$ are such that $S_1^i \neq S_2^i$ for all $i = 0, 1, \ldots, n$.

The base case ($i = 0$) is true by definition. A brief case analysis proves the induction step:

- *Case 1:* r_i is in S_1^{i-1} and S_2^{i-1}. In this case, both algorithms do not move; therefore, according to the induction hypothesis, $S_1^i = S_1^{i-1} \neq S_2^{i-1} = S_2^i$.
- *Case 2:* r_i is in, for example, S_1^{i-1} but not in S_2^{i-1}. B$_{S_1}$ does not move, and B$_{S_2}$ serves the request with the server located at r_{i-1}. Thus, $S_1^i = S_1^{i-1}$ contains r_{i-1} but S_2^i does not.
- *Case 3:* r_i is in neither S_1^{i-1} nor S_2^{i-1}. Clearly, $S_1^{i-1} - \{r_{i-1}\} \neq S_2^{i-1} - \{r_{i-1}\}$, and both algorithms serve the request with the server from r_{i-1}, so $S_1^i \neq S_2^i$.

We conclude that the configurations of the algorithms in $\mathcal{B}$ remain distinct throughout the game. Hence, at all times $\mathcal{B}$ contains exactly $\binom{k}{h-1}$ algorithms corresponding to all h-subsets of M that include the first request. Now, what is the total cost incurred by all algorithms in $\mathcal{B}$?

For each request r_i (except the first one), exactly $\binom{k-1}{h-1}$ algorithms move a server (from r_{i-1}) in order to serve this request. These algorithms correspond to all $(h-1)$-subsets of M that include r_{i-1} but not r_i. Hence, the total cost incurred by all algorithms in $\mathcal{B}$ is

$$\binom{k-1}{h-1} \cdot \sum_{i=2}^{n} d(r_{i-1}, r_i) = \binom{k-1}{h-1} \cdot \sum_{i=1}^{n-1} d(r_i, r_{i+1}).$$

It follows that the average performance of these algorithms is

$$\frac{\binom{k-1}{h-1}}{\binom{k}{h-1}} \cdot \sum_{i=1}^{n-1} d(r_i, r_{i+1}) = \left(\frac{k-h+1}{k} \right) \cdot \sum_{i=1}^{n-1} d(r_i, r_{i+1}).$$

Since at least one of these algorithms incurs costs no greater than this average, the proof is complete.   ∎

10.4 *k*-Servers on a Line and a Tree

For most natural geometric structures (e.g., the Euclidean plane or the circle), no simple *k*-competitive deterministic algorithms are known. In contrast, we do have a simple *k*-competitive algorithm for the Euclidean line, and this algorithm can be generalized to metric spaces defined by trees.

10.4.1 The Line Algorithm

We first consider the real line with Euclidean metric. This metric space allows for a simple deterministic *k*-competitive *k*-server algorithm. The algorithm is one of the more elegant *k*-server algorithms. This line algorithm naturally generalizes to trees and subsequently has several interesting applications. We now describe the algorithm for the real line called DOUBLE-COVERAGE or DC for short.

> **Algorithm DC:** If the request falls outside the convex hull of the servers, serve it with the nearest server. Otherwise, the request is in between two adjacent servers. In this case, move both these servers toward the request at equal speeds until (at least) one server reaches it. (If two servers occupy the same point, then choose one arbitrarily.)

Notice that DC is not a lazy algorithm; it may move one or two servers as a response to some requests. Of course, it may operate as a lazy algorithm by remembering the "virtual" locations of the servers as described before. However, sometimes (and, indeed, in this case) it is more intuitive and easier to analyze nonlazy algorithms, especially since the nonlazy moves have some intuitive meaning.

Example 10.1 Consider the response of DC (with two servers) to the request sequence that defeated the greedy algorithm (see Section 10.2.2 and Figure 10.1). Suppose that the two servers, s_1 and s_2, of DC are positioned on b and c, respectively. Assume, for this example, that $d(a, b) \ll d(b, c)$. Consider the behavior of DC in response to the sequence $a, b, a, b, a, b, \ldots$ of requests. The first request for a is served by s_1; then, the request for b is also served by s_1, but this time s_2 moves a distance $d(a, b)$ toward b. This pattern of response continues; consequently, DC does not fall for the greedy trap by gradually shuttling the server s_2 to help server s_1 on the "western front." Clearly, after sufficiently many such repetitions, DC positions its two servers on a and b.

Theorem 10.2 DC *is k-competitive.*

PROOF. Let $M_{\min}$ denote the minimum cost matching between OPT's and DC's servers. For $i = 1, 2, \ldots, k$, denote by s_i DC's servers. Let Σ_{DC} denote the sum of all interpoint distances between DC's servers: $\Sigma_{DC} = \sum_{i<j} d(s_i, s_j)$. The proof uses the following potential function:

$$\Phi = k \cdot M_{\min} + \Sigma_{DC}.$$

Note that Φ is nonnegative and, hence, bounded below as required for a potential function. Using the potential function method (with the "interleaving moves style"; see Section 1.4), it is sufficient to prove the following. (i) If the adversary moves a distance d, the potential is increased by *at most* kd. (ii) If DC moves d, the potential is decreased by *at least* d.

Proving that (i) holds is almost trivial (notice that the adversary's move does not affect the Σ_{DC}-component and, clearly, M_{min} cannot increase by more than d). To prove that (ii) holds, we consider two possible kinds of moves by DC. First, suppose DC moves a single server, say, a distance d. According to the definition of DC, this server is an extreme point of the convex hull of all the servers. Since this server is moving away from all other servers, Σ_{DC} increases by $(k-1)d$. However, there exists a minimum weight matching in which this moving server is matched to the request, so M_{min} decreases by at least d. Thus, the total decrease of potential is at least $kd - (k-1)d = d$, which is exactly the cost incurred by DC.

In the second case, suppose servers s_1 and s_2 move toward the request from opposite sides. Suppose also that each of these servers moves a distance d. Clearly, one of these servers is matched to the request (in some minimum weight matching), so its move decreases M_{min} by at least d. The other moving server may move away a distance d from its match. Hence, M_{min} does not increase overall. Now consider the change in Σ_{DC}. The change in the sum of distances from s_1 and s_2 to any other server q is zero: one of them is moving away a distance d from q, and the other is moving a distance d toward q. However, the distance between s_1 and s_2 is shortened by $2d$, which is the total online move. This proves (ii). ∎

10.4.2   The Tree Algorithm

Algorithm DC and its analysis can be generalized to work for trees (still attaining a competitive ratio of k). We now describe the tree algorithm and briefly indicate the necessary changes in the analysis.

We consider a tree network in which the distance between any two points on the tree is the length of the simple path between them. (Clearly, any edge-weighted tree can be embedded in the Euclidean plane so that the edge weights become edge lengths. We view these trees as being so embedded.) Consider any configuration of k servers and a request r on the tree. We say that a server s_i is a "neighbor" of the request if there is no other server on the (unique) simple path from s_i to the request. When two servers located in the same spot are neighbors of the request, we consider only one of them to be a neighbor (arbitrarily breaking the tie). The k-server tree algorithm is called DC-TREE.

> **Algorithm DC-TREE:** At each time, all the servers neighboring the request are moving in a constant speed toward the request.

Algorithm DC-TREE coincides with algorithm DC when the tree is simply a line. Notice that algorithm DC-TREE may move any number of its k servers. Also, the number of servers that move in response to a particular request may decrease during the service process since a moving server may become "blocked" by other servers (i.e., it may stop being a neighbor) while traveling toward the request.

We prove that algorithm DC-TREE is k-competitive by generalizing the proof for algorithm DC using the same potential function Φ from Theorem 10.2. When the adversary moves a distance d, it can increase the potential by at most kd. To analyze the change in potential that results from the online move, we break the behavior of algorithm DC-TREE into phases; in each phase, the set of neighbors (moving servers) is fixed. Consider a phase in which there are m neighbors. Suppose that during the phase, each of these servers moves a distance d (for a total of md). Again, it is clear that one of the neighbors is matched to the request in some minimum weight matching, thus decreasing M_{min} by d. The other $m - 1$ moving servers may increase M_{min} by at most $(m - 1)d$. The total increase in potential that results from a change in the minimum weight matching component is, therefore,

$$(m - 2)kd = mkd - 2kd. \tag{10.1}$$

The change of the Σ_{DC}-component during the phase can be broken down as follows. Consider any nonneighboring server s. Clearly, one of the m moving servers is traveling a distance d away from s, and the other $m - 1$ servers are moving toward s (each a distance d). Summing this change over all $k - m$ nonmoving servers results in a decrease of

$$(k - m)(m - 2)d = kmd - 2kd - m^2d + 2md. \tag{10.2}$$

Finally, each pair of moving servers is getting closer to the other by $2d$. Summing over all $\frac{m(m-1)}{2}$ pairs, we have an additional decrease of $dm(m - 1) = dm^2 - dm$, which, together with equation (10.2), gives an overall decrease of $kmd - 2kd + dm$ of the Σ_{DC}-component. Subtracting from this quantity the increase resulting from the change in M_{min} (equation 10.1), we obtain an overall decrease of

$$(kmd - 2kd + dm) - (mkd - 2kd) = dm.$$

However, this is exactly the total distance moved by algorithm DC-TREE during that phase. Hence, we have the following theorem.

Theorem 10.3 *Algorithm* DC-TREE *is k-competitive.*

10.4.3 Some Applications of the Tree Algorithm

We now mention several applications of algorithm DC-TREE. One simple application is for arbitrary finite graphs. Let G be any N-node graph. Fix any spanning tree T of G. We can use algorithm DC-TREE for T to service requests on G. That is, for the purpose of the analysis, the online servers move only on T (of course, these servers can cross edges not in T when there are shorter opportunities; this only improves the online performance). Let OPT-TREE denote the optimal offline algorithm restricted to the tree. A simple observation that follows from the minimality of the minimum spanning tree is that any edge of length d in G has a detour on the tree of length at most $(N - 1)d$. Using this observation, we obtain for any request sequence σ: OPT-TREE$(\sigma) \leq (N - 1) \cdot$ OPT(σ). From Theorem 10.3, we have DC-TREE$(\sigma) \leq k \cdot$ OPT-TREE(σ). Hence, we have the following corollary.

Corollary 10.4 *Algorithm* DC-TREE *is $(N - 1)k$-competitive on any N-node graph.*

Notice that this general result is much better than the competitive ratio $\left(2\binom{N}{k} - 1\right)$, which follows from an application of results on MTSs for k-servers.

Another interesting application of the tree algorithm is for paging. Consider a paging problem with N slow memory pages and a cache of size k. We can embed this paging

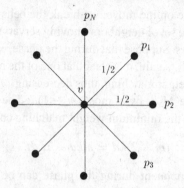

Figure 10.2: A star tree simulating paging.

problem into a tree and obtain a paging algorithm using the k-server tree algorithm as follows: the tree is a star with n arms, each of length $\frac{1}{2}$. There are N vertices labeled $p_1, p_2, \ldots, p_N$ that are connected by the arms to a central vertex labeled v (see Figure 10.2). In this star the vertex p_i represents the ith slow memory page. Call such a vertex a "page vertex." Moving a server from a page vertex to another page vertex costs 1, which is the cost of evicting a cache location and storing in its place a new page. It follows that any k-server algorithm for the star is equivalent to a paging algorithm (this connection is easy to make by considering the lazy version of the k-server algorithm). Hence, we obtain the following corollary.

Corollary 10.5 *Algorithm* DC-TREE *is k-competitive for paging.*

Consider the behavior of algorithm DC-TREE on the star tree. Suppose that initially the k servers are located on k different page vertices. When a request for a new page arrives, all the servers are traveling in a constant speed toward the central vertex v. Then, one (arbitrarily chosen) server continues and serves the request. All other servers remain on the central vertex v. Now, each of the following $k - 1$ requests for uncovered page vertices is served by one (arbitrarily chosen) server from the center. We have then returned to the beginning. It is quite surprising that this algorithm is equivalent to algorithm FWF (FLUSH-WHEN-FULL) in Chapter 3. Hence, we obtain an alternative proof of the fact that FWF is k-competitive for paging.

A construction similar to the star shown in Figure 10.2 extends to the **weighted paging** problem. In this problem each page p has some nonnegative weight $w(p)$: the cost of copying it into the cache. This asymmetric problem can be made essentially symmetric over arbitrarily long request sequences by charging $\frac{w(p)}{2}$ to bring p into the cache, and $\frac{w(p)}{2}$ to evict it. Thus, we have the following corollary.

Corollary 10.6 *Algorithm* DC-TREE *is k-competitive for the weighted paging problem.*

The following exercise explores another simple application of the tree algorithm.

Exercise 10.1 Show how to use algorithm DC-TREE to obtain a $k(\sqrt{N} + 1)$-competitive algorithm for the $(\sqrt{N} \times \sqrt{N})$-mesh. (We assume that nodes that are adjacent in the graph have distance 1 and that all other distances are induced by the transitive closure of the edge distances.)

After algorithm DC-TREE was discovered, it seemed plausible that there might be a simple generalization of this algorithm that could yield a low deterministic competitive ratio for general metric spaces. However, no such generalization has been proven, although tree embeddings have played an important role in the development of randomized algorithms against an oblivious adversary (see Chapters 9 and 11).

10.5 An Efficient 3-Competitive 2-Server Algorithm for Euclidean Spaces

The fact that there is such a simple and computationally efficient k-server algorithm for the line (i.e., the one-dimensional Euclidean space) immediately raises the question of whether or not such an algorithm exists for higher-dimensional spaces. Presently we do not have any good competitive bound for an efficient k-server algorithm for the two-dimensional plane. A reasonable definition of efficiency would at least require the computational cost per request to be independent of the length of the request sequence.

Here we present a simple and efficient 2-server algorithm that attains a competitive ratio of 3 in any Euclidean space. Let $\mathcal{M}$ be any Euclidean space. For any three points $x, y, r \in \mathcal{M}$, define their **slack**, slack(x, y, r), to be

$$\text{slack}(x, y, r) = d(x, y) + d(x, r) - d(y, r),$$

where $d(\cdot)$ is the Euclidean metric. According the triangle inequality, the slack is always nonnegative. Let γ be a nonnegative real, $\gamma \in [0, 1]$. We now define a 2-server algorithm SLACK-COVERAGE$_\gamma$ (SC$_\gamma$, for short). Let x and y be the two servers controlled by SC$_\gamma$. In particular contexts, it is clear that x and y will also denote the current locations of these servers.

> **Algorithm SC$_\gamma$:** Suppose r is the current request to be served and that x is closer to r. (If x and y are the same distance from r, choose x arbitrarily.) Move y toward x a distance $\gamma \cdot$ slack(x, y, r) and then serve the request with x.

The first observation is that when applied to the line (i.e., one-dimensional Euclidean space), SC$_{1/2}$ is equivalent to algorithm DC. Second, we observe that SC$_\gamma$ always moves the server y a distance at most $2\gamma d(x, r)$ to some point within the line segment $\overline{yx}$. Hence, if y moves to a new location, it moves closer to the request r.

For positive reals $a, b \in \mathbb{R}$, define the following potential function

$$\Phi = a \cdot M_{\min} + b \cdot d(x, y),$$

where $M_{\min}$ denotes (as before) the minimum weight matching between SC$_\gamma$'s servers and the adversary servers. Notice that Φ is nonnegative and (for the case of 2-servers) generalizes the potential function used for analyzing algorithms DC and DC-TREE. If we wish to prove some competitive ratio for SC$_\gamma$ using the potential function method (second style, with interleaving moves), the best competitive ratio we can prove is a: when a lazy optimal offline algorithm serves the request, it may increase the minimum weight component of Φ (that is, $aM_{\min}$) by a times the distance it moves. Using this method, in order to establish that SC$_\gamma$ is a-competitive, it remains to prove that when SC$_\gamma$ moves its servers (after the adversary moves) it decreases the potential by at least the total distance it moves, $d(x, r) + \gamma$ slack(x, y, r).

We then examine the change in potential that results from the online move. Use y' to denote the new location of the server y. Based on the above discussion, $d(y', r) \leq d(y, r)$; therefore, the change in the $d(x, y)$-component of Φ is

$$\Delta d(x, y) = d(y', r) - d(x, y) \leq d(y, r) - d(x, y).$$

Call the offline servers s_1 and s_2 and assume that s_1 has just served the request. We distinguish between two cases: (i) in $M_{\min}$, x is now matched to s_1; and (ii) in $M_{\min}$, y is now matched to s_1.

In case (i), $M_{\min}$ decreases by $d(x, r)$ as a result of x's move and may increase by $\gamma \operatorname{slack}(x, y, r)$ due to y's move. Hence, in this case, $\Delta \Phi$ satisfies

$$\Delta \Phi \leq a \cdot \left[\gamma \cdot \operatorname{slack}(x, y, r) - d(x, r) \right] + b \cdot \left[d(y, r) - d(x, y) \right]. \tag{10.3}$$

In case (ii), after sc_γ moves, x is matched to r, and y' is matched to s_2. Hence, using the triangle inequality, the change in $M_{\min}$ satisfies

$$\begin{aligned}
\Delta M_{\min} &= d(y', s_2) - d(s_2, x) - d(y, r) \\
&\leq d(y', x) - d(y, r) \\
&= d(y, x) - \gamma \cdot \operatorname{slack}(x, y, r) - d(y, r).
\end{aligned}$$

Therefore, in case (ii), the total change in potential, $\Delta \Phi$, satisfies

$$\Delta \Phi \leq a \cdot \left[d(x, y) - \gamma \cdot \operatorname{slack}(x, y, r) - d(y, r) \right] + b \cdot \left[d(y, r) - d(x, y) \right]. \tag{10.4}$$

To complete such a proof, we must prove that in either case, (i) or (ii),

$$\Delta \Phi \leq -(\text{distance moved by } \operatorname{sc}(\gamma)) = - \left[d(x, r) + \gamma \cdot \operatorname{slack}(x, y, r) \right]. \tag{10.5}$$

Substituting inequalities (10.3) and (10.4) for $\Delta \Phi$ in condition (10.5) and rearranging terms, we obtain the following two conditions, which are sufficient for proving the a-competitiveness of sc_γ:

$$\begin{aligned}
d(x, y) \left[\gamma(a + 1) - b \right] + d(x, r) \left[\gamma(a + 1) + 1 - a \right] \\
+ d(y, r) \left[b - \gamma(a + 1) \right] \leq 0;
\end{aligned} \tag{10.6}$$

$$\begin{aligned}
d(x, y) \left[\gamma(1 - a) + a - b \right] + d(x, r) \left[\gamma(1 - a) \right] \\
+ d(y, r) \left[\gamma(1 - a) + b - a \right] \leq 0.
\end{aligned} \tag{10.7}$$

It is easy to verify that conditions (10.6) and (10.7) are satisfied with $\gamma = \frac{1}{2}$, $a = 3$, and $b = 2$. We thus obtain the following theorem.

Theorem 10.7 *Algorithm* $\operatorname{sc}_{1/2}$ *is 3-competitive for 2 servers in any Euclidean space.*

Exercise 10.2 Prove that for any $a < 3$ there are no feasible values for γ and b (that satisfy conditions (10.6) and (10.7)).

Exercise 10.3 Consider the class of metric spaces $\mathcal{M}$ that satisfy the following properties: (i) for every pair of points $x, y \in \mathcal{M}$, $\mathcal{M}$ also includes the points along a real line segment between x and y; and (ii) for every $x, y, r \in \mathcal{M}$ on a line such that y is between x and r, and for every point p, if $d(x, p) \leq d(r, p)$ then $d(y, p) \leq d(r, p)$. Prove that (1) this class of metric spaces includes all Euclidean spaces; and (2) $SC_{1/2}$ is 3-competitive with respect to each metric space in this class.

Exercise 10.4 Consider the following 2-server algorithm. After serving each request, label the server at the request s_1 and the other server s_2 (if both servers are at the request, break ties arbitrarily). Consider the next request r and set $b = d(s_1, r)$. If $d(s_2, r) < 3b$, serve r with s_2. Otherwise, serve r with s_1 and also move s_2 a distance $3b$ toward r. Prove that this algorithm is $O(1)$-competitive in any Euclidean space.

It is possible to embed efficiently any N-point metric space in an $O(\log N)$-dimensional Euclidean space with logarithmic distortion (Bourgain [83], Linial, London, and Rabinovich [244]). Using this result, we apply the preceding 2-server algorithm to any N-point metric space to attain a competitive ratio of $O(\log N)$. Although this competitive ratio is not independent of N, the resulting algorithm is a fast online algorithm with a better competitive ratio than the ratio that can be obtained via the tree algorithm (see Section 10.4.2).

10.6 Balancing Algorithms

When $N = k + 1$, any lazy algorithm (including OPT) has exactly one node (called a **hole**) that is not covered by a server. The following simple lazy algorithm attains an optimal competitive ratio of k in any metric space with $N = k + 1$ points. The algorithm is called BALANCE (or BAL, for short).

> **Algorithm BAL:** For each server s_i, maintain its total distance traveled thus far, D_i. To serve a request r, shuttle the server s_i that minimizes $D_i + d(s_i, r)$ (break ties arbitrarily).

The following assumptions and notation are useful for the analysis of algorithm BAL. Consider any $(k + 1)$-node graph. Denote its vertices by $v_0, v_1, \ldots, v_k$. Assume, without loss of generality, that BAL starts from the initial configuration $\{v_1, \ldots, v_k\}$. After a request to v_0 is made, BAL moves a server to v_0 and opens a hole in a different vertex. At this stage we relabel the vertices so that after a request is serviced, v_1 always denotes the most recently covered vertex and v_0 always denotes the hole. We may assume that at all times the request is made to the hole (otherwise, BAL does not pay anything and the adversary may incur some cost). Finally, at all times $D(v_i)$, with $i \neq 0$, denotes the cumulative distance of the server currently located on v_i. Algorithm BAL, as its name suggests, moves its servers so that their cumulative distances are balanced. Specifically, we have the following lemma.

Lemma 10.1 *For all v_i and v_j (other than v_0),*

$$|D(v_i) - D(v_j)| \leq d(v_i, v_j).$$

PROOF. We prove the lemma by induction on the number of requests. The base case (no requests) trivially holds. Assume that the lemma holds up to some time when a new request for v_0 arrives. Suppose BAL serves the request with the server from v_l. Based on the above labeling convention, after the service we label the vertices so that v_1', the new, most recently serviced vertex, is set to v_0, and v_0', the new hole, is set to v_l. We need to prove for all $v_i', v_j' \neq v_0'$, that $|D(v_i') - D(v_j')| \leq d(v_i', v_j')$. The only change, in any of the cumulative distances, is that of the moving server, which before the move has cumulative distance $D(v_l)$ and after the move, has $D(v_1') = D(v_l) + d(v_l, v_0)$. To complete the induction step, it is necessary only to compare v_1' to any other vertex $v_j' \neq v_0'$ and prove

$$|D(v_j') - D(v_1')| \leq d(v_1', v_j'). \tag{10.8}$$

(The rest of the pairs are unchanged and thus satisfy the lemma by the induction hypothesis.) This is easily obtained as follows. On the one hand, we have

$$D(v_j') - D(v_1') = D(v_j) - (D(v_l) + d(v_l, v_0)),$$

by labeling convention and definition of $D(v_1')$;

$$\leq |D(v_j) - D(v_l)| - d(v_l, v_0)$$

by induction hypothesis;

$$\leq d(v_j, v_0),$$

by triangle inequality;

$$= d(v_j', v_1'),$$

labeling convention. $\tag{10.9}$

On the other hand, based on the definition of algorithm BAL (i.e., its choice of v_l) and the labeling convention, we have

$$D(v_1') - D(v_j') = D(v_l) + d(v_l, v_0) - D(v_j) \leq d(v_j, v_0) = d(v_j', v_1').$$

Combining these two cases we obtain equation (10.8). $\blacksquare$

Consider inequality (10.9) in the proof of Lemma 10.1. According to the labeling convention, we have $d(v_j, v_l) - d(v_l, v_0) = d(v_j', v_0') - d(v_0', v_1')$. Hence, we obtain the following result: at each stage after BAL serves the first request[1] and for every $j \neq 0$,

$$D(v_j) - D(v_1) \leq d(v_j, v_0) - d(v_0, v_1). \tag{10.10}$$

Equipped with the above lemma and inequality (10.10), we are now ready to prove the following theorem.

Theorem 10.8 BAL *is k-competitive in any metric space with $N = k + 1$ points.*

PROOF. Fix any optimal offline algorithm, OPT. We define the following potential function. With respect to the current configurations of BAL and OPT, set $S = \sum_{i \neq 0} D(v_i)$ and define the "current potential" as

$$\Phi = \begin{cases} k \cdot (D(v_1) - d(v_1, v_0)) - S & \text{if OPT's hole is on } v_0; \\ k \cdot D(v_i) - S & \text{if OPT's hole is on } v_i \neq v_0. \end{cases}$$

---

[1] The inequality uses the labeling convention, which is defined only after BAL's first move.

Note that Φ is defined for each stage only *after* BAL makes its first move because its definition uses the labeling convention. Lemma 10.1 makes it clear that at each time (after BAL's first move), the current potential is bounded below by a constant independent of the request sequence (hence, it can be used as a potential function).

It remains to prove that: (i) if OPT moves a distance d, the potential is increased by at most kd; and (ii) if BAL moves d, the potential is decreased by at least d. We start with (i). Assume that OPT does not cover v_0 (otherwise OPT does not move and there is nothing to prove), and suppose it moves the server from v_j, incurring a cost of $d(v_j, v_0)$. The potential before the move is $k(D(v_1) - d(v_1, v_0)) - S$. The potential after the move is $kD(v_j) - S$. Using inequality (10.10), it is easy to show that the increase in potential is bounded as required.

$$\Delta\Phi = (\Phi \text{ after}) - (\Phi \text{ before}) = k(D(v_j) - D(v_1) + d(v_1, v_0))$$
$$\leq k(d(v_j, v_0) - d(v_0, v_1) + d(v_1, v_0))$$
$$= kd(v_j, v_0).$$

We now prove (ii). Since after its move OPT's hole is on $v_j \neq v_0$, the potential prior to BAL's move is $kD(v_j) - S$. Use S' to denote the value of S after BAL's move. Clearly, $S' = S + d(v_l, v_0)$. The potential after BAL's move depends on the location of BAL's hole (which, according to our convention, is opened at v_l): if $l = j$, then since v_l is relabeled to v_0', the potential after the move is $k(D(v_1') - d(v_1', v_0')) - S' = k(D(v_l) + d(v_l, v_0) - d(v_0, v_l)) - S - d(v_l, v_0) = kD(v_l) - S - d(v_l, v_0)$. In the second case, where $l \neq j$, the potential after the move is $kD(v_j') - S' = kD(v_j) - S - d(v_l, v_0)$. In either case, the decrease in potential is exactly $d(v_l, v_0)$, as required.   ∎

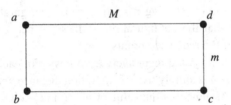

Figure 10.3: A 4-node graph that fails BAL.

Unfortunately, BAL is not competitive in metric spaces with $N > k + 1$ points. This can be shown even when there are only two servers and $N = 4$. Consider Figure 10.3. In this graph, $M > m$. Suppose that the two servers are initially located at c and d. Consider the request sequence $\sigma = a, b, c, d, a, b, c, d, \ldots, a, b, c, d$. BAL pays M for each request. On the other hand, OPT (starting from the same configuration) pays M for the first request and then will pay m for all subsequent requests. Clearly, the performance ratio approaches $\frac{M}{m}$, which means that BAL is not competitive at all.

It is somewhat surprising that a simple modification of the balancing rule yields a 10-competitive 2-server algorithm. Specifically, the balancing algorithm that serves the request r with a server s_i ($i = 1, 2$) that minimizes $D_i + 2d(s_i, r)$ is 10-competitive. In general, any 2-server balancing algorithm that serves with the server that minimizes $D_i + f(d(s_i, r))$, where f is any real-valued function, cannot attain a competitive ratio smaller than $\frac{5 + \sqrt{7}}{2} \approx 3.82$.

10.7   The k-Server Work Function Algorithm

In Chapter 9 we introduced a work function algorithm for MTSs. In this section we study a work function k-server algorithm. The analysis here yields a competitive ratio of $2k - 1$ for any metric space.

10.7.1   Work Functions for the k-Server Problem

Fix any metric space $\mathcal{M} = (\mathcal{M}, d)$. A configuration of any k-server algorithm is viewed in this section as a set of k (not necessarily distinct) points representing the locations of the servers. We denote configurations by capital letters and points of $\mathcal{M}$ by small letters. Throughout this section a configuration is a multiset, allowing configurations in which two or more servers occupy the same node. For configurations C_1 and C_2, we let $C_1 + C_2$ denote the multiset union; similarly, $C_1 - C_2$ denotes multiset exclusion. For a point p and configuration C, we abbreviate $C + \{p\}$ by $C + p$ and $C - \{p\}$ by $C - p$. So, for example, if $p \in C$ then the configuration $C + p$ contains at least two copies of p and $C - p + p = C + p - p$ contains p. However, if $p \notin C$ then $C - p = C$ and $C - p + p \neq C + p - p$. For every two configurations X and Y, we define $D(X, Y)$, the **configuration distance**, as the value of the minimum weight matching between X and Y.

Fix a request sequence, $\sigma = r_1, r_2, \ldots, r_n$, and use σ_i to denote the prefix, $r_1, r_2, \ldots, r_i$, of σ. Use $\emptyset$ to denote the empty request sequence. Similar to MTSs, k-server work functions are defined in terms of an initial configuration C_0 and a request sequence. Specifically, for each initial configuration C_0, configuration C, and i ($i = 0, 1, \ldots, n$), the k-server **work function** $w_{\sigma_i}(C) = w_{\sigma_i}(C_0, C)$ is defined as the optimal offline cost of (sequentially) servicing all the requests in σ_i, starting from the initial configuration C_0 and ending at configuration C. Notice that the configuration C does not necessarily contain the last request r_i of σ_i (or any of the requested points in σ_i).

Work functions can be computed recursively as follows. For each configuration C, the initial work function $w_\emptyset(C)$ is simply the configuration distance between C_0 and C. That is, $w_\emptyset(C) = D(C_0, C)$. Assume that the value of $w_{\sigma_i}(C)$ is known for any configuration C. Given the next request $r = r_{i+1}$ and a configuration C, the value of $w_{\sigma_i r}(C)$ is computed as follows. If $r \in C$, then clearly $w_{\sigma_i r}(C) = w_{\sigma_i}(C)$. Otherwise, $r \notin C$ and the optimal offline algorithm that must first serve the request r before ending up in configuration C can first process the sequence $\sigma_i r$ ending up in some configuration $B = C - x + r$ that contains r (and differs from C by one point) and then move to configuration C. In other words,

$$w_{\sigma_i r}(C) = \min_{x \in C}\{w_{\sigma_i r}(C - x + r) + d(r, x)\} = \min_{x \in C}\{w_{\sigma_i}(C - x + r) + d(r, x)\}.$$

The second equality in the above equation is due to the fact that $r \in C - x + r$. Whether or not $r \in C$, we use the notation

$$w(C) = w_{\sigma_i}(C),$$

$$w'(C) = w_{\sigma_i r}(C)$$

and obtain the following basic recurrence for work functions.

Lemma 10.2 *For any configuration C, and any request r,*

$$w_\emptyset(C) = D(C_0, C),$$

$$w'(C) = \min_{x \in C}\{w(C - x + r) + d(r, x)\}. \tag{10.11}$$

Lemma 10.2 provides the means for computing the work functions. This can be done efficiently using dynamic programming. Notice that since $r \in C - x + r$, $w'(C)$ can also be expanded and expressed as

$$w'(C) = \min_{x \in C}\{w'(C - x + r) + d(r, x)\}. \tag{10.12}$$

(We make some use of this expression later.) Given any initial configuration and any request sequence σ, we can use work functions to compute the optimal offline cost to serve σ, which is

$$\text{OPT}(\sigma) = \min_C w_\sigma(C). \tag{10.13}$$

Example 10.2 Let C be any configuration and x, y any two points. The expression $w(C - x + y) + d(y, x)$ can be interpreted as the cost of optimally serving the request sequence thus far while ending in the configuration $C - x + y$ and then moving to the configuration C (by moving a server from y to x). This cost is no smaller than the cost $w(C)$ of optimally serving the same request sequence while ending in the configuration C. That is,

$$w(C) \leq w(C - x + y) + d(y, x).$$

Such elementary arguments (and inequalities) are used throughout this section without explicit mention.

Example 10.3 Consider a 5-node weighted undirected graph with node set $\{a, b, c, d, e\}$. The graph is complete and the edge weights are as follows. Edges between any two nodes in the subset $\{a, b, c, d\}$ all have weight 1. All edges from nodes in this subset to e have weight 2.

Consider three servers on this graph initially located on the nodes a, b, and c. In Table 10.7.1 we specify values of work functions corresponding to all 3-node configurations and all prefixes of the request sequence

$$e, d, a, b, c, a, b, a, c, e.$$

The first row gives all values of initial work functions (empty request sequence) with respect to the initial configuration abc. For example, $D(abc, acd) = 1$; that is, the configuration distance between abc and acd is 1 (move the server from node b to node d) and $D(abc, cde) = 3$. The second row gives the values of work function after the first request e is introduced. For instance, let us calculate the value of $w_e(acd)$. Using equation (10.11), we have

$$w_e(acd) = \min_{x \in \{a,c,d\}}\{w_\emptyset(acd - x + e) + d(r, x)\}$$

$$= \min\{w_\emptyset(cde) + d(e, a), w_\emptyset(ade) + d(e, c), w_\emptyset(ace) + d(e, d)\}$$

$$= \min\{D(abc, cde) + 2, D(abc, ade) + 2, D(abc, ace) + 2\}$$

$$= \min\{5, 5, 4\}$$

$$= 4.$$

The rest of the values in the table can be computed similarly.

Table 10.1: Work function values for three servers in a 5-node graph example.

Request i		abc	abd	abe	acd	ace	ade	bcd	bce	bde	cde
ø	0	0	1	2	1	2	3	1	2	3	3
e	1	4	4	2	4	2	3	4	2	3	3
d	2	5	4	4	4	4	3	4	2	3	3
a	3	5	4	4	4	4	3	4	4	3	3'
b	4	5	4	4	5	5	5	5	5	4	5
c	5	5	6	6	5	5	6	6	6	7	6
a	6	5	6	6	5	5	6	6	6	7	6
b	7	5	6	6	6	7	7	6	6	7	7
a	8	5	6	6	6	7	7	6	7	7	8
c	9	5	6	7	6	7	8	6	7	8	8
e	10	9	9	7	9	7	8	9	7	8	8

Exercise 10.5 Given the conditions of Example 10.3, verify that $\text{OPT}(\sigma) = w_\sigma(ace) = 7$, where σ is the entire request sequence of that example.

Exercise 10.6 In Example 10.3 we dealt with a finite metric space (a 5-node graph); using equation (10.11), we computed work functions by considering all 10 possible 3-node configurations. How would you compute work functions when the metric space is infinite?

Exercise 10.7 In Example 10.3 we can see that work functions are always monotone (nondecreasing) in the length of the request sequence. Prove this (nonsurprising) fact. That is, prove that for any configuration C, $w(C) \le w'(C)$.

10.7.2 The Online k-Server Work Function Algorithm

We now describe the online k-server work function algorithm WFA.

Algorithm WFA: Let σ_i be the request sequence thus far and let C be the configuration of WFA after servicing σ_i. Then, given the next request $r = r_{i+1}$, WFA serves r with a server $s \in C$ satisfying

$$s = \arg\min_{x \in C}\{w(C - x + r) + d(x, r)\},$$

with ties broken arbitrarily.

Clearly, the cost of algorithm WFA to serve the request r is $d(s, r)$.

Exercise 10.8 Calculate the moves and total cost of the 3-server WFA with respect to the graph and request sequence of Example 10.3.

Exercise 10.9 Consider the WFA algorithm. The choice of the server s minimizes the sum of two terms: $w(C - x + r)$ and $d(x, r)$. Consider an online algorithm that chooses to serve the next request r with the server s that minimizes only the second term. This algorithm is exactly the greedy algorithm of Section 10.2.2. On the other hand, consider an online algorithm that chooses to serve with a server s that minimizes only the first term. This algorithm "mimics" the configuration of an optimal offline algorithm that serves the request sequence obtained thus far. We call this algorithm the "retrospective-greedy" algorithm. Compute the cost and schedule of the 3-server retrospective-greedy algorithm assuming the metric space (graph) of Example 10.3 with respect to (i) the request sequence of Example 10.3, and (ii) a cruel request sequence of length 10.

10.7.3   Analysis of Algorithm WFA

This section is devoted to proving the following theorem.

Theorem 10.9 *For any k and any metric space, algorithm* WFA *is* $(2k - 1)$-*competitive.*

Fix any request sequence $\sigma = r_1, r_2, \ldots, r_n$. Without loss of generality, we assume that both WFA and OPT start at the same initial configuration, C_0, and also that they end up in the same configuration, C_n. The latter assumption is valid, since the adversary can, without any extra cost, continue to request the points of C_n until WFA covers all the points of C_n.

Assume that WFA has just finished processing the request r_i and that it is now at configuration C. Consider the next request $r = r_{i+1}$ and assume that WFA serves r with the server currently on point $s \in C$. We let $C' = C - s + r$ be the next configuration of WFA. Define the current **offline pseudocost** to be

$$\text{offline pseudocost} = w'(C') - w(C).$$

The sum, over all requests, of all the offline pseudocosts telescopes and equals $w_\sigma(C_n) - w_\emptyset(C_0) = \text{OPT}(\sigma)$.

Since $r \in C'$ and since $w'(C) = w(C') + d(s, r)$ (by the definition of WFA and equation 10.11), we obtain

$$w'(C') = w(C') = w'(C) - d(s, r). \tag{10.14}$$

Using equation (10.14), we now consider the sum of the offline pseudocost and the online costs $d(s, r)$ for serving the next request.

$$w'(C') - w(C) + d(s, r) = w'(C) - d(s, r) - w(C) + d(s, r)$$
$$= w'(C) - w(C)$$
$$\leq \max_X \{w'(X) - w(X)\}.$$

Call $\max_X\{w'(X) - w(X)\}$ the current **extended cost**.

Using this terminology, we readily obtain the following lemma, which provides a useful condition for proving the c-competitiveness of algorithm WFA.

Lemma 10.3 *Let α be a constant independent of the request sequence σ. If the total sum over all moves of the extended costs is bounded above by $(c + 1) \cdot \text{OPT}(\sigma) + \alpha$, then algorithm* WFA *is c-competitive.*

According to Lemma 10.3, in order to prove Theorem 10.9, it remains to prove that

$$\text{total extended cost} \leq 2k \cdot \text{OPT}(\sigma) + \alpha \tag{10.15}$$

(for some constant α). The advantage of this reduction via the use of extended costs is that there is no longer a need to consider configurations of algorithm WFA.[2] To facilitate the proof of equation (10.15), we now introduce a few lemmas that reveal useful properties of work functions.

We say that a work function w is **quasi-convex** if for any configurations X and Y and any point $x \in X$,

$$\min_{y \in Y}\{w(X - x + y) + w(Y - y + x)\} \leq w(X) + w(Y). \tag{10.16}$$

Lemma 10.4 (Quasi-convexity lemma) *All work functions are quasi-convex.*

PROOF. In order to prove the lemma, we prove that work functions satisfy a more general quasi-convexity property.

> **Property GQ:** Let w be a work function and let X and Y be two configurations. Then there exists a bijection $g : X \to Y$ such that for all partitions of X into X_1 and X_2, the following holds
>
> $$w(X_1 + g(X_2)) + w(g(X_1) + X_2) \leq w(X) + w(Y). \tag{10.17}$$

By setting $X_1 = X - x$ and letting $y = g(x)$, we can see that the property GQ implies the quasi-convexity property. We prove that work functions satisfy the property GQ by relying on the following claim.

> **Claim:** If the bijection g satisfies equation (10.17), then there exists a bijection $\bar{g}$ such that $\bar{g}(x) = x$ for all $x \in X \cap Y$, which also satisfies equation (10.17).

Under the assumption that the preceding claim holds, we prove the following by induction on the length of the request sequence.

Induction hypothesis: Work functions satisfy the property GQ.

Base case. For $i = 0$ we have $w_\emptyset(X) + w_\emptyset(Y) = D(C_0, X) + D(C_0, Y)$. Consider two minimum weight matchings M_X and M_Y whose values are $D(C_0, X)$ and $D(C_0, Y)$, respectively. Each point $c_j \in C_0$ is mapped by M_X to some point $x_j \in X$ and by M_Y to some point $y_j \in Y$. It is easy to see that the bijection $g(x_j) = y_j$ satisfies equation (10.17).

Induction step. Assume that w satisfies the property GQ and let r be the new request. We show that w' now satisfies property GQ.

According to equation (10.11), there exists some $x \in X$ so that $w'(X) = w(X - x + r) + d(r, x)$. Similarly, $w'(Y) = w(Y - y + r)$ for some $y \in Y$. According to the induction hypothesis, for $(X - x + r)$ and $(Y - y + r)$, there exists a bijection

---

[2] On the other hand, the extended cost may overestimate the online cost and thus may give rise to nonoptimal bounds.

$g : (X - x + r) \to (Y - y + r)$ that satisfies property GQ. We can further assume, from the preceding claim, that $g(r) = r$. Define the bijection $g' : X \to Y$:

$$
g'(z) = \begin{cases} g(z), & \text{if } z \neq x; \\ y, & \text{otherwise.} \end{cases}
$$

To prove that w' satisfies property GQ, consider any partition (X_1, X_2) of X. Without loss of generality, assume that $x \in X_1$. Set $X_{xr} = X - x + r$ and $Y_{yr} = Y - y + r$. We have

$$
\begin{aligned}
w'(X) + w'(Y) &= w(X_{xr}) + w(Y_{yr}) + d(r, x) + d(r, y) \\
&= w((X_1 - x + r) \cup X_2) + w(Y_{yr}) + d(r, x) + d(r, y) \\
&\geq w((X_1 - x + r) \cup g(X_2)) \\
&\quad + w(g(X_1 - x + r) \cup X_2) + d(r, x) + d(r, y),
\end{aligned}
$$

by the induction hypothesis;

$$
\begin{aligned}
&= w(X_{xr} \cup g'(X_2)) + w((g'(X_1) - y + r) \cup X_2) + d(r, x) + d(r, y) \\
&\geq w'(X_1 \cup g'(X_2)) + w'(g'(X_1) \cup X_2),
\end{aligned}
$$

by equation (10.11).

This completes the induction step.

It remains to prove the preceding claim. Let $g : X \to Y$ be a bijection. Assume that among all such bijections, g maps the maximum number of elements from $X \cap Y$ to themselves. Assume, by contradiction, that there exists some $a \in X \cap Y$ such that $g(a) \neq a$. Define the bijection $\bar{g} : X \to Y$ that agrees with g everywhere but interchanges the values of g on a and $a^{-1} = g^{-1}(a)$. That is, set $\bar{g}(a) = a$ and $\bar{g}(a^{-1}) = g(a)$. By our assumption, $\bar{g}$ cannot satisfy property GQ.

Let (X_1, X_2) be any partition of X and assume, without loss of generality, that $a^{-1} \in X_1$. It cannot be the case that $a \in X_1$; if it were the case, then $g(X_1) = \bar{g}(X_1)$ and $g(X_2) = \bar{g}(X_2)$. Given that $a \notin X_1$, we have

$$
w(X) + w(Y) \geq w((X_1 + a) \cup g(X_2 - a)) + w(g(X_1 + a) \cup (X_2 - a)),
$$

since g satisfies equation (10.17);

$$
= w((X_1 + a) \cup \bar{g}(X_2 - a)) + w(\bar{g}(X_1 + a) \cup (X_2 - a)),
$$

by the definition of $\bar{g}$;

$$
= w(X_1 \cup \bar{g}(X_2)) + w(\bar{g}(X_1) \cup X_2).
$$

Hence, $\bar{g}$ does satisfy property GQ, which is a contradiction. ∎

Let w be the current work function and let r be any point. A configuration A is called a **minimizer of r with respect to w** if

$$
A = \arg\min_X \left\{ w(X) - \sum_{x \in X} d(x, r) \right\}.
$$

We now use the quasi-convexity lemma to prove the following two lemmas.

Lemma 10.5 *Let w be the current work function and let r be the next request. If A is a minimizer of r with respect to w, then A is also a minimizer of r with respect to w'.*

PROOF. It is sufficient to prove that for any configuration B,

$$w'(A) - \sum_{a \in A} d(a, r) \le w'(B) - \sum_{b \in B} d(b, r). \tag{10.18}$$

Applying the expansion (10.11) to $w'(A)$ and $w'(B)$, proving inequality (10.18) is equivalent to proving

$$\min_{a' \in A} \left\{ w(A - a' + r) + d(a', r) - \sum_{a \in A} d(a, r) \right\}$$

$$\le \min_{b' \in B} \left\{ w(B - b' + r) + d(b', r) - \sum_{b \in B} d(b, r) \right\}. \tag{10.19}$$

By removing the min operator from the right-hand side of inequality (10.19), proving this inequality (and therefore the lemma) is equivalent to proving that for all $b' \in B$,

$$\min_{a' \in A} \left\{ w(A - a' + r) + d(a', r) - \sum_{a \in A} d(a, r) \right\}$$

$$\le w(B - b' + r) + d(b', r) - \sum_{b \in B} d(b, r). \tag{10.20}$$

Since A is a minimizer of r with respect to w,

$$w(A) - \sum_{a \in A} d(a, r) \le w(B - b' + a') - \sum_{b \in B - b' + a'} d(b, r). \tag{10.21}$$

Substituting

$$\sum_{b \in B} d(b, r) - d(b', r) + d(a', r) \quad \text{for} \quad \sum_{b \in B - b' + a'} d(b, r)$$

in equation (10.21) and rearranging terms, we obtain

$$-w(B - b' + a') + w(A) + d(a', r) - \sum_{a \in A} d(a, r)$$

$$\le d(b', r) - \sum_{b \in B} d(b, r). \tag{10.22}$$

We now apply the quasi-convexity lemma with $X = B - b' + r$, $Y = A$, $x = r$, and $y = a'$. Thus,

$$\min_{a' \in A} \{ w(B - b' + a') + w(A - a' + r) \} \le w(B - b' + r) + w(A). \tag{10.23}$$

Finally, inequality (10.20) is obtained by summing equations (10.22) and (10.23) and then subtracting $w(A)$ from both sides.   ∎

Let w be the current work function, let r be the next request, and let w' be the resulting work function. Recall that the extended cost is defined as $\max_X\{w'(X) - w(X)\}$. Any configuration A satisfying

$$A = \arg\max_X\{w'(X) - w(X)\}$$

is called a **maximizer with respect to** w.

Lemma 10.6 (Duality lemma) *Any minimizer of r with respect to w is also a maximizer with respect to w.*

PROOF. Let A be a minimizer of r with respect to w. Proving the lemma is equivalent to proving that for any configuration B,

$$w'(B) + w(A) \le w(B) + w'(A).$$

Notice that if $r \in B$, this inequality trivially becomes an equality. Expanding $w'(A)$ and $w'(B)$ and using formula (10.11), it is sufficient to prove that for all B with $r \notin B$,

$$\min_{b' \in B}\{w(B - b' + r) + d(b', r) + w(A)\} \le \min_{a' \in A}\{w(A - a' + r) + d(a', r) + w(B)\},$$

or, equivalently, to prove that for all such B and for all $a' \in A$,

$$\min_{b' \in B}\{w(B - b' + r) + d(b', r) + w(A)\} \le w(A - a' + r) + d(a', r) + w(B). \quad (10.24)$$

Since A is a minimizer,

$$w(A) - \sum_{a \in A} d(a, r) \le w(A - a' + b') - \sum_{a \in A - a' + b'} d(a, r). \quad (10.25)$$

Substituting

$$\sum_{a \in A} d(a, r) - d(a', r) + d(b', r) \quad \text{for} \quad \sum_{a \in A - a' + b'} d(a, r)$$

in equation (10.25) and then subtracting $\sum_{a \in A} d(a, r)$ from both sides and rearranging terms, we obtain

$$w(A) + d(b', r) - d(a', r) \le w(A - a' + b'). \quad (10.26)$$

Applying the quasi-convexity lemma with $X = A - a' + r$, $Y = B$, $x = r$, and $y = b'$, we obtain

$$\min_{b' \in B}\{w(A - a' + b') + w(B - b' + r)\} \le w(A - a' + r) + w(B).$$

Together with an application of inequality (10.26), the proof of equation (10.24) is complete. ∎

Let A be a minimizer of r with respect to w. Define

$$\text{MIN}_w(r) = w(A) - \sum_{a \in A} d(a, r).$$

That is, $\text{MIN}_w(r)$ is the value of the minimizer configuration.

At this point we introduce a potential-like function that will be used in the proof of Theorem 10.9. Fix any k-server optimal offline algorithm OPT and denote by $U = \{u_1, u_2, \ldots, u_k\}$ the (current) configuration of OPT.

Define

$$\Phi(U, w) = \sum_{u \in U} \text{MIN}_w(u).$$

Consider the next request, r, and assume that OPT serves this request with the server currently located at u_j. Thus, the next configuration of OPT is $U' = U - u_j + r$.

Lemma 10.7 $\Phi(U', w) - \Phi(U, w) \geq -k \cdot d(u_j, r)$.

PROOF.

$$\Phi(U', w) - \Phi(U, w) = \sum_{u' \in U'} \text{MIN}_w(u') - \sum_{u \in U} \text{MIN}_w(u)$$

$$= \text{MIN}_w(r) - \text{MIN}_w(u_j). \tag{10.27}$$

Using the triangle inequality $d(a, r) \leq d(a, u_j) + d(u_j, r)$ (for any point a), we have

$$\text{MIN}_w(r) = \min_A \left\{ w(A) - \sum_{a \in A} d(a, r) \right\}$$

$$\geq \min_A \left\{ w(A) - \sum_{a \in A} (d(a, u_j) + d(u_j, r)) \right\}$$

$$= \text{MIN}_w(u_j) - k \cdot d(u_j, r).$$

Combined with equation (10.27), the proof is complete. ∎

Lemma 10.8

$$\Phi(U', w') - \Phi(U', w) \geq \max_X \{w'(X) - w(X)\}.$$

PROOF. Let A be a minimizer of r with respect to w. Based on the monotonicity of the work function (i.e., for all X, $w'(X) \geq w(X)$, see Exercise 10.7), for any point p,

$$\text{MIN}_{w'}(p) = \min_X \left\{ w'(X) - \sum_{x \in X} d(p, x) \right\}$$

$$\geq \min_X \left\{ w(X) - \sum_{x \in X} d(p, x) \right\} = \text{MIN}_w(p). \tag{10.28}$$

That is, similar to work functions, MIN is also monotone (nondecreasing) with respect to w. Hence,

$$\Phi(U', w') - \Phi(U', w) = \sum_{u \in U'} (\text{MIN}_{w'}(u) - \text{MIN}_w(u))$$

$$= \text{MIN}_{w'}(r) - \text{MIN}_w(r) + \sum_{u \in U : u \neq r} (\text{MIN}_{w'}(u) - \text{MIN}_w(u))$$

$$\geq \text{MIN}_{w'}(r) - \text{MIN}_w(r),$$

using equation (10.28);

$$= w'(A) - \sum_{a \in A} d(a, r) - \left(w(A) - \sum_{a \in A} d(a, r) \right),$$

A is also a minimizer w.r.t. w' (Lemma 10.5);

$$= \max_X \{ w'(X) - w(X) \},$$

according to the duality lemma. ∎

Finally, we are ready to prove the celebrated Theorem 10.9.

Proof of Theorem 10.9. It is sufficient to prove that inequality (10.15) holds. That is, we need to prove that

$$E = (\text{total extended cost}) \leq 2k \cdot \text{OPT}(\sigma) + \alpha.$$

According to Lemma 10.7 and (respectively) Lemma 10.8, we have

$$\Phi(U', w) - \Phi(U, w) \geq -k \cdot d(u_j, r), \tag{10.29}$$

$$\Phi(U', w') - \Phi(U', w) \geq \max_X \{ w'(X) - w(X) \}. \tag{10.30}$$

Summing inequalities (10.29) and (10.30), we obtain

$$\Phi(U', w') - \Phi(U, w) \geq \max_X \{ w'(X) - w(X) \} - k \cdot d(u_j, r). \tag{10.31}$$

Hence, if we sum inequality (10.31) over all requests, we obtain

$$\Phi(U_\sigma, w_\sigma) - \Phi(U_\emptyset, w_\emptyset) \geq E - k \cdot \text{OPT}(\sigma),$$

where $U_\sigma (= C_n)$ is the final configuration of OPT (and WFA) and $U_\emptyset = C_0$ is the initial configuration. To complete the proof, it is sufficient to prove that

(i) $\Phi(U_\sigma, w_\sigma) \leq k \cdot w_\sigma(U_\sigma) = k \cdot \text{OPT}(\sigma);$
(ii) $\Phi(U_\emptyset, w_\emptyset) \geq - \sum_{a, b \in C_0} d(a, b) = \text{constant}.$

By definition, $\Phi(U_\sigma, w_\sigma) = \sum_{u \in U_\sigma} \text{MIN}_{w_\sigma}(u)$. For each $u \in U_\sigma$ and point y, set $U(y) = U_\sigma - u + y$.

According to the definition of MIN, we have for each $u \in U_\sigma$,

$$\text{MIN}_{w_\sigma}(u) \le \min_{y \notin U_\sigma} \left\{ w_\sigma(U(y)) - \sum_{x \in U(y)} d(x, u) \right\}.$$

Let y^* be the y that minimizes the right-hand side. Hence,

$$\text{MIN}_{w_\sigma}(u) \le w_\sigma(U(y^*)) - \sum_{x \in U(y^*)} d(x, u)$$

$$\le w_\sigma(U(y^*)) - d(y^*, u)$$

$$= w_\sigma(U_\sigma - u + y^*) - d(y^*, u)$$

$$\le w_\sigma(U_\sigma),$$

which proves (i).

We now prove that (ii) holds. (Note that it is obvious that some constant bound must exist.) First, according to the definitions of Φ and MIN,

$$\Phi(U_\emptyset, w_\emptyset) = \sum_{u \in U_\emptyset} \text{MIN}_{w_\emptyset}(u)$$

$$= \sum_{u \in U_\emptyset} \min_X \left\{ w_\emptyset(X) - \sum_{x \in X} d(x, u) \right\}. \tag{10.32}$$

Consider $u \in U_\emptyset$, and let $X^* = \{x_1, x_2, \ldots, x_k\}$ be a configuration that minimizes the right-hand side of equation (10.32). The initial work function satisfies $w_\emptyset(X^*) = D(U_\emptyset, X^*)$. Without loss of generality, assume that in the minimum weight matching between $U_\emptyset$ and X^*, u_i is matched to x_i, $i = 1, 2, \ldots, k$. Therefore,

$$\text{MIN}_{w_\emptyset}(u) = \sum_{i=1}^k d(u_i, x_i) - \sum_{i=1}^k d(x_i, u)$$

$$= \sum_{i=1}^k (d(u_i, x_i) - d(x_i, u))$$

$$\ge \sum_{i=1}^k (d(u_i, x_i) - (d(x_i, u_i) + d(u_i, u))),$$

using the triangle inequalities $d(x_i, u) \le d(x_i, u_i) + d(u_i, u)$;

$$= - \sum_{i=1}^k d(u_i, u).$$

It follows that

$$\sum_{u \in U_\emptyset} \text{MIN}_{w_\emptyset}(u) \ge - \sum_{a,b \in U_\emptyset} d(a, b).$$

Putting all this together, we have, for $\alpha = \sum_{a,b \in U_\emptyset} d(a, b)$,

$$E \le \Phi(U_\sigma, w_\sigma) - \Phi(U_\emptyset, w_\emptyset) + k \cdot \text{OPT}(\sigma) \le 2k \cdot \text{OPT}(\sigma) + \alpha.$$

∎

We state without proof the following optimal bounds for the WFA.[3]

Theorem 10.10 *Prove that the k-server* WFA *algorithm is k-competitive when k = 2.*

Theorem 10.11 *Prove that the k-server* WFA *algorithm is k-competitive in any (k + 2)-point metric space.*

Exercise 10.10 Prove that the *k*-server WFA algorithm is *k*-competitive when the metric space is a real line segment.

Exercise 10.11 The definition of algorithm WFA may appear somewhat arbitrary. Consider the following generalization of algorithm WFA. Let γ be any real in [0, 1], and consider the following algorithm called WFA$_\gamma$: while in configuration C, choose to serve the next request r with the server s satisfying

$$s = \arg\min_{x \in X}\{\gamma \cdot w(C - x + r) + (1 - \gamma) \cdot d(x, r)\}.$$

Prove the following, somewhat surprising, result:

1. If $\gamma < \frac{1}{2}$, then WFA$_\gamma$ is not competitive.
2. If $\gamma \geq \frac{1}{2}$, then WFA$_\gamma$ is $\frac{\gamma}{1-\gamma}(2k - 1)$-competitive.

10.8   On Generalizations of the *k*-Server Conjecture That Fail

In this section we describe examples that defeat two natural generalizations of the *k*-server conjecture that were mentioned in Section 10.2.4. In Chapter 11 we will also see that the *k*-server conjecture does not easily generalize to randomized algorithms.

10.8.1   The *(h, k)*-Server Problem

Recall that for the (h, k)-paging problem we have several algorithms (e.g., LRU, FIFO) that attain the optimal competitive ratio of $\frac{k}{k-h+1}$. For instance, LRU with a cache of size 100 attains a competitive ratio of $\frac{100}{99} \approx 1.01$ with respect to an optimal offline algorithm with a cache of size 2. This is not surprising. After all, we are providing the online algorithm with many more resources. However, this result does not generalize to the (h, k)-server problem.

Theorem 10.12 *For any k, there exists a metric space (e.g., the line) in which 2 is the lower bound for the (2, k)-server problem.*

We now sketch the proof. First consider the case in which $h = 2$ and $k = 3$. We describe a metric space, a request sequence σ, and a 2-server offline algorithm ADV that will force a competitive ratio arbitrarily close to 2 for any deterministic online 3-server algorithm ALG. We rely on the lower bound of 2 for the (2, 2)-server problem (see Theorem 10.1).

---

[3] See Chrobak and Larmore [106] for the proof of Theorem 10.10, and Koutsoupias and Papadimitriou [233] for the proof of Theorem 10.11.

Consider (any) line interval. On the edges of this line, we maintain two "fronts": the "east" front and the "west" front, separated by a "large" distance D. Each "front" is an ε-length line interval for sufficiently small ε. Consider an initial configuration in which one offline and two online servers are on the west front and one offline and one online server are on the east front. We describe how to construct a sequence of requests consisting of an arbitrary number of phases such that for each phase the total cost incurred by ALG is twice as much as the total cost incurred by ADV. Each phase starts in a configuration similar to the initial one or the symmetric configuration (where one offline and two online servers are on the east). Examine the response of ALG to a sequence of many requests placed very close together within the eastern front. According to ALG's response to such a sequence, we devise the adversary's strategy for the phase: if ALG attains a competitive ratio smaller than 2, it must be that ALG eventually moves all three servers to the eastern front; otherwise, ADV immediately moves its two servers to the east and turns the situation into a $(2, 2)$-problem in the eastern front (where it can force a ratio arbitrarily close to 2).

Let e_1 be the total cost incurred by ALG for servicing requests within the eastern front just before it moves a second server to the east, and let $e_1 + e_2$ be the total cost incurred by ALG within the eastern front just before it moves its third server to the east. In these costs, we do not include the costs of moving servers across the long distance D.

If $e_1 \leq D$, then by keeping one server at each front, ADV pays e_1 and ALG pays $D + e_1$, and the phase ends with ALG paying at least twice as much as ADV; the next phase begins with a configuration symmetric to the initial one. Otherwise, if $e_1 > D$, ADV immediately moves its second server to the east and alternates requests in the east front between two close points where its servers are located. After ALG moves its second server to the east, ADV plays in the east front a game of 2 against 2, for which he can guarantee a cost ratio of 2. This continues until ALG incurs a cost of e_2 and then ALG brings its third server to the east. At this point ADV moves one of its servers to the west front, makes one request there (thus forcing ALG to move one server to the west as well), and brings the phase to a close. Notice that now the configuration is symmetric to the initial one so that the next (symmetric) phase can start immediately. A brief calculation of the total costs incurred by the two algorithms for this phase completes the analysis: the total cost incurred by ALG for this phase is: $e_1 + e_2 + 3D$. ADV, on the other hand, pays $2D + \frac{e_2}{2}$. Since $e_1 > D$, ADV pays less than half as much as ALG does for this phase.

Exercise 10.12 Complete the proof of Theorem 10.12. Use the above construction as a basis for a recursive construction of a metric space and a request sequence that forces a ratio of 2 against any number k of online servers for the $(2, k)$-server problem.

Exercise 10.13 Show that for every $h \geq 2$, there exists a metric space relative to which any online algorithm with $2h + 1$ servers cannot attain a smaller competitive ratio than an online algorithm with $2h$ servers (i.e., when they are both compared with an offline algorithm with h servers). Hint: The metric space is not necessarily a line segment.

On the positive side, Corollary 10.6 shows that there is a k-competitive algorithm for the weighted cache problem, a problem that can be formulated as a symmetric (or asymmetric) k-server problem. We note that an optimal competitive ratio of $\frac{k}{k-h+1}$ is obtainable for the (h, k) generalization of the weighted paging problem.

10.8.2   Asymmetric Spaces

The second example (demonstrating that the k-server conjecture does not allow for some natural generalizations) concerns asymmetric spaces. In general, with regard to asymmetric spaces, there is no one definite conclusion: some spaces allow for competitive server algorithms, and others do not. We present two examples: the first characterizes some easy spaces; the second is a particular asymmetric space that does not allow for competitive 2-server algorithms.

Asymmetric spaces are viewed as weighted, directed graphs. Consider a finite directed graph G. Recall that the cycle offset ratio ψ is the maximum over all cycles in G of the ratio of the cost of moving around the cycle in one direction to that in the other direction. The first observation is that any c-competitive k-server algorithm for a (general) symmetric space yields a $c\psi$-competitive algorithm for G. Specifically, construct an undirected (and thus, symmetric) graph G' on the vertices of G where each edge (u, v) has length $\frac{1}{2}(d(u, v) + d(v, u))$. Clearly, for any sequence requesting nodes in G, the c-competitive server algorithm running on G' yields a $c\psi$-competitive for G. Note that although G is asymmetric, the distance function is still required to satisfy the triangle inequality. Hence, for a graph with N vertices, $\psi \leq N - 1$.

Example 10.4   Consider a $(k + 1)$-cycle in which edges going clockwise have cost 1 and edges going counterclockwise have cost 2. Then we can use a k-competitive k-server algorithm (say, BAL) to obtain a $2k$-competitive algorithm for the asymmetric cycle with $(k + 1)$ points.

Exercise 10.14   Let G be an asymmetric space and suppose that c is a lower bound on the competitive ratio for the symmetric space G' (as defined above). Show that $\frac{c}{\psi}$ is a lower bound for the space G.

We now describe a negative result of a particular asymmetric space that does not allow for competitive 2-server algorithms. The graph is constructed by a sequence of "diamond" graphs as follows: each "diamond" D is a directed graph on vertices a, b, c, d with directed edges: (a, b), (a, c), (b, d), and (c, d) where all edges have length 1. We connect N diamonds $D_1, \ldots, D_N$ by identifying d_i with a_{i+1} for all i, $1 \leq i < N$, and identifying d_N with a_1. Notice that the resulting graph is strongly connected.

Consider any deterministic online 2-server algorithm ALG where both servers are initially on a_1. Request b_1 and then c_1. Assume that ALG answers these two requests with two different servers (otherwise we extract from ALG a cost of $2N$ and can continue with this construction). Request $a_2 = d_1$ and assume that ALG serves with the server from c_1. Now request c_1. ALG must go through the whole cycle to service this request, incurring a cost of at least $2N - 1$. OPT, on the other hand, does not move the server from c_1 and avoids any cost for this request. The adversary can reconstruct this trap on the diamond D_2 by moving both his servers to a_2, etc. Hence, OPT pays 4 for each time it forces ALG to have a cost of at least $2N$. This gives a lower bound $\Omega(N)$ on the competitive ratio of any 2-server algorithm.

Exercise 10.15   Let $k \geq 2$. Show that there is an asymmetric space induced by an $O(kN)$-node directed graph G for which the competitive ratio of the k-server problem on this space is $\Omega(N)$.

10.9   Historical Notes and Open Questions

The k-server problem was proposed by Manassé, McGeoch, and Sleator [255, 256] as a natural abstraction of the paging problem. The problem attracted a great deal of attention from researchers to the extent that it played a significant role in the development of competitive analysis. Although some of the early results on the k-server problem have been subsumed, the history of the k-server problem is quite interesting.

   Early Results and the k-Server Conjecture. In the initial paper introducing the server problem [255], Manasse, McGeoch, and Sleator presented several results. In partic-ular, they gave a 2-competitive algorithm for two servers in any metric space (see also McGeoch [262]). For each request, this algorithm must compute (using dynamic programming) the optimal offline schedule thus far. The second algorithm from Man-asse, McGeoch, and Sleator [255] is the simple and fast balancing algorithm BAL of Section 10.6, which is k-competitive for k servers in metric spaces with $k + 1$ points (Theorem 10.8). Manasse, McGeoch, and Sleator proved the fundamental lower bound (Theorem 10.1) of $\frac{k}{k-h+1}$ for k online servers against $h \leq k$ offline servers. This lower bound requires only that the metric space contain more than k points; therefore, it applies to any k-server problem. Manasse, McGeoch, and Sleator also posed the cel-ebrated k-server conjecture: any metric space allows for a k-competitive, k-server de-terministic algorithm. Given that this conjecture was posed when it was known to hold only for the paging problem (k-server in a uniform metric space) and for all spaces with $k = 2$ or $N = k+1$, it was indeed a brave conjecture. This simple but strong con-jecture contributed much to the appeal of the k-server problem and was a catalyst for the interest in competitive analysis. For a short time, there was no substantial progress in the direction of the k-server conjecture. Despite extensive efforts, researchers found algorithms only for special cases of the problem. Then, Fiat, Rabani, and Ravid [154] solved the "weak" k-server conjecture: there is a fixed function of k that bounds the competitive ratio of every server system. In particular, they constructed a determinis-tic algorithm for k servers that is $O((k!)^3)$-competitive in any metric space. In doing so, they were the first to show that there is a competitive ratio upper bound that is independent of the size of the metric space. This ratio was somewhat improved by a deterministic version of the randomized algorithms by Grove [178] and then Bartal and Grove [47]. (See also Chapter 11.) In 1994, Koutsoupias and Papadimitriou [232] proved that the work function algorithm is $(2k - 1)$-competitive in any metric space. To date, this $2k - 1$ bound is the best-known deterministic (or randomized) upper bound for general metric spaces. Koutsoupias and Papadimitriou [233] also proved that the k-server conjecture holds for any $(k + 2)$-point metric space. The finding that the k-server conjecture does not extend to the (h, k)-server problem is due to Bar-Noy and Schieber [38].

   The Work Function Algorithm. Sometimes, in order to be competitive, an online player must keep track of the optimal offline cost; this realization led several researchers to design algorithms that make use of the "optimal offline cost thus far." For instance, several interesting algorithms for the k-server problem are based on this concept. Among them are the "residue-based" 2-competitive algorithm for two servers, from Manasse, McGeoch, and Sleator [256] and McGeoch [262], and the $O((k!)^3)$-competitive algorithm due to Fiat, Rabani, and Ravid [154]. However, from our present perspective it seems that the simple (and generic) work function algorithm best captures this notion. The idea for an online work function algorithm was implicitly introduced by Borodin, Linial and Saks [82] in connection to MTSs (see Chapter 9). A work function algorithm for the k-server problem had been proposed by several researchers. In particular, Chrobak and Larmore [102] formally defined the k-server work function algorithm and established some of its basic properties. They also proved that this algorithm is 2-competitive for two servers. They also show (in [104]) that the work function algorithm is k-competitive against a "benevolent adversary," which is a "lazy adversary" (see Chapter 11) that announces whenever the online configuration matches the adversaries configuration. As noted above, Koutsoupias and Papadimitriou [232] proved that this algorithm is $(2k - 1)$-competitive (Theorem 10.9). Bartal [39] and Koutsoupias [230] have independently shown that the work function algorithm is k-competitive for the k-server problem on the line. The proof of Theorem 10.9 presented here is based on Koutsoupias's dissertation [229] and on a presentation of this proof due to Bartal [42] that offers a simpler potential-like function argument.

We note that work function algorithms have been applied to a number of other online problems. Chrobak, Larmore, Reingold, and Westbrook [107] use work functions to obtain results concerning the page migration problem. Burley [86] also uses a work function algorithm for the layered graph traversal problem.

Special Metric Spaces. There have also been a number of results for special metric spaces. Chrobak, Karloff, Payne, and Vishwanathan [100] constructed the elegant k-competitive DC algorithm for k servers on a real line. This algorithm was then generalized by Chrobak and Larmore [103] to trees while preserving optimality. The applications of the tree algorithm in Section 10.4.3 are due to Chrobak and Larmore [103].

Chrobak et al. [100] also proved that a simple balancing policy of choosing the server with minimum cumulative distance is k-competitive for the weighted paging problem. Young [344] obtained a $\frac{k}{k-h+1}$-competitive algorithm for the (h, k) version of the weighted paging problem. We note that Young's analysis employs a novel technique based on linear programming and duality.

Fiat, Rabani, Ravid, and Schieber [155] constructed an $O(k^3)$-competitive algorithm for k servers on a circle.

Two Servers, Three Servers, and Fast Algorithms. Other work has focused on two (and three) servers. Although the optimal deterministic competitive ratio for two servers had already been achieved (by Manasse, McGeoch, and Sleator), some of the work on 2-server algorithms has aimed at reducing the high time complexity required by the known algorithms for this case (e.g., the 2-server algorithm by Manasse, McGeoch, and Sleator). One of the goals has been to find "fast" (or real time) server algorithms: those that can compute each answer in "constant time." Chrobak and Larmore [101] constructed a (still slow) 2-competitive 2-server algorithm for general metric spaces. Then, they show in [106] that for three servers this algorithm, called EQUIPOISE, is 11-competitive, greatly improving upon the constant competitive ratio first achieved by Berman, Karloff, and Tardos [61] for three servers. The modification of the balancing algorithm (see Section 10.6) that yields a 10-competitive 2-server algorithm is due to Irani and Rubinfeld [200]. However, Chrobak and Larmore [105] showed that this version of the balancing algorithm is no better than 6-competitive. Kleinberg [225] showed that any 2-server balancing algorithm that serves with the server that minimizes $D_i + f(d(s_i, r))$ where f is any real-valued function, cannot attain a competitive ratio smaller than $\frac{5+\sqrt{7}}{2} \approx 3.82$. Chrobak and Larmore [105] also gave a constant time 4-competitive algorithm (that uses unbounded memory). We note that the idea and first use of "slack" (as defined in Section 10.5) is due to Chrobak and Larmore [105].

Karloff [213] constructed a simple, fast $O(1)$-competitive algorithm for two servers in Euclidean spaces (see Exercise 10.4). El-Yaniv and Kleinberg [142] constructed a fast 2-competitive algorithm for Euclidean spaces under the L_1 metric, which is $2\sqrt{d}$-competitive in $\mathbb{R}^d$ under the "Euclidean" metric (L_2). Bartal [41] discovered the fast SC$_{1/2}$ algorithm (Section 10.5), which is a 3-competitive 2-server algorithm for the class of metric spaces described in Exercise 10.3 (that includes all Euclidean spaces). The beautiful result of Bourgain [83] and Linial, London, and Rabinovich [244] shows that it is possible to embed efficiently any N-point metric space in an $O(\log N)$-dimensional Euclidean space with a logarithmic distortion. From this, it follows that any c-competitive algorithm for k servers in Euclidean space yields an $O(c \log N)$-competitive algorithm for k servers in an arbitrary N-point metric space. (See also the remark at the end of Section 10.5.)

Optimal Offline Algorithms. The computation of the optimal offline cost (and schedule) is important for several algorithms. Manasse, McGeoch, and Sleator [255, 256] observed that a straightforward dynamic programming algorithm can obtain the optimal offline cost (and schedule) for serving a request sequence of length n in time $O\left(nN\binom{N}{k}\right)$, where N is the number of distinct request points in σ. Chrobak et al. [100] reduced this problem to a minimum cost–maximum flow problem and obtained an optimal offline algorithm with running time $O(kn^2)$. Assuming the algebraic computation tree model of Ben-Or [57], Chrobak et al. show a lower bound of $\Omega(n \log n)$ on the time required for the computation of the optimal offline cost for servicing n requests on a line. Recall that for the special case of the uniform metric space (paging), there is a linear time algorithm for OPT (algorithm LONGEST-FORWARD-DISTANCE).

Asymmetric Spaces. Manasse, McGeoch, and Sleator [256] observed that any c-competitive algorithm ALG for general spaces attains a competitive ratio in $\left[\frac{c}{\psi}, c\psi\right]$ in an asymmetric space with cycle factor ψ (see Section 10.8.2). Chrobak et al. [100] discovered the class of asymmetric spaces in Section 10.8.2 that do not allow for 2-server algorithms with constant competitive ratio.

Variants of the k-Server Problem. There are a number of interesting generalizations and variants of the k-server model. The following list presents some examples.

- *The k-server problem with excursions, defined by Manasse, McGeoch, and Sleator [256]:*
  In this variant, there are two metrics, the distance function d as in the standard k-server problem and a smaller excursion function e. Upon a request for a point v, the algorithm can either serve the request by moving a server from u to v at cost $d(u, v)$ or make an excursion at cost $e(u, v)$. After its excursion to v, the server returns to the originating point u. This variant is nontrivial even for the case of $k = 1$.

- *The k-taxicab problem, defined by Fiat, Rabani, and Ravid [154]:*
  Here, requests are pairs of points in a metric space. If (s, t) is a request pair, then it is serviced by sending a server to s and then immediately shuttling the server to t. However, the point t is made known only *after* the server arrives at s. Their (exponential in k-) competitive k-server algorithm gives a competitive taxicab algorithm. Interestingly, the taxicab problem is not a special case of MTSs.

- *The k-server problem with jumping, introduced by Bern, Greene, Raghunathan, and Sudan [62]:*

In this variant, servers can jump to a location occupied by another server at no cost. Bern et al. consider a special case of this problem with application to online check-pointing.

- *The chasing problem, defined by Friedman and Linial [162]:*
  In this variant, requests come from some family of subsets of the space and a server now must move to some point in the subset being requested. For example, the family might be lines, hyperplanes, or convex regions in some Euclidean space. For convex regions in two-dimensional Euclidean space, Friedman and Linial obtain an $O(1)$-competitive algorithm for $k = 1$.

Credit for Exercises. Exercise 10.1 is due to Chrobak and Larmore [103]. Exercise 10.3 is due to Bartal [41]. Exercise 10.4 is due to Karloff [213]. Exercise 10.11 is due to Koutsoupias [230] and Exercise 10.10 is due independently to Bartal [39] and Koutsoupias [230].

10.9.1 Open Questions

The interest in the k-server model has inspired the formulation of many interesting open problems.

10.1 *(Value = I5/T5)* Prove or disprove the k-server conjecture. Alternatively, diminish the gap $[k, 2k - 1]$ in the competitive ratio of the k-server problem. Note that in light of the Koutsoupias–Papadimitriou result, the "popular" conjecture is that WFA is k-competitive.

10.2 *(Value = I3/T4)* Find a fast optimal offline algorithm for general or other special metric spaces such as the line. It would be especially useful to find an algorithm with a simple description (such as algorithm LONGEST-FORWARD-DISTANCE for paging).

10.3 *(Value = I3/T4)* Construct a simple $O(k)$-competitive deterministic k-server algorithm for the plane or for the circle. For the plane, we can consider various interesting metrics such as the L_1 "Manhattan" metric or the L_2 "Euclidean" metric, and so on. For the circle, consider the natural metric where the distance between two points is the length of the circle arc connecting them. Another metric for the circle is the "Euclidean 2-space distance"; we can view the circle k-server problem as a restricted form of the k-server problem on the plane problem.

10.4 *(Value = I4/T4)* Can the DC-TREE algorithm (or any other tree algorithm) be extended to give a deterministic algorithm for every metric space with competitive ratio depending only on k (and not N)?

10.5 *(Value = I3/T4)* Show a lower bound strictly greater than 2 on the competitive ratio of any deterministic 2-server algorithm that uses constant time and space per request. The model of computation needs to be formalized. For example, it is possible to encode unlimited amounts of information using real points in Euclidean spaces. Such models should be avoided. Perhaps it is appropiate to allow comparisons only between linear combinations of distances.

10.6 *(Value = I2/T3)* For particular and arbitrary metric spaces, give a more extensive characterization of upper and lower bounds for the (h, k)-server problem for $h > 2$ and varying values of k.

CHAPTER 11

Randomized *k*-Server Algorithms

We have already seen that randomization (against an oblivious adversary) dramatically reduces the competitive ratio for the paging problem and for any MTS problem. In this chapter we study randomization in the context of the *k*-server problem. Although substantial effort has been devoted to randomized *k*-server algorithms, the results thus far have not been nearly as conclusive as in the deterministic case. One of the initial goals in studying adaptive adversaries was to solve the (deterministic) *k*-server conjecture. Since the "almost" resolution of the *k*-server conjecture (see Chapter 10), we can now redefine the goal for *adaptive* adversaries as follows: to find a universal, simply stated, and efficient *k*-server algorithm with an optimal or near-optimal competitive ratio (for all metric spaces or for specific metric spaces of particular interest).[1] For oblivious adversaries, the goal is to determine if (similar to paging) randomization can dramatically reduce the competitive ratio for particular classes of metric spaces or, possibly, for all metric spaces. Most work thus far has focused on algorithms against adaptive-online adversaries; this work has led to results of independent interest such as the connection between random walks and electrical networks. We start with one example (other than paging) of randomization against an oblivious adversary before turning our attention to adaptive adversaries.

11.1   Oblivious Adversaries and Two Randomized *k*-Server Algorithms for the Circle

The fact that the paging problem has an (optimal) H_k-competitive randomized algorithm raises the obvious question of whether or not every *k*-server problem has an $O(\log k)$-competitive randomized algorithm against an oblivious adversary. As we have seen, any *k*-server problem on an *N*-point metric space can be viewed as an $\binom{N}{k}$-state MTS problem (with a restricted set of tasks). It follows immediately from Corollary 9.12 that for any *c*, there exists an $O\big(\frac{c \log^6 N}{\log\log N}\big) = O\big(\frac{c \log^6 k}{\log\log k}\big)$- competitive algorithm for a *k*-server problem on any $N = (k + c)$-point metric space. For some particular metric spaces, there are better *k*-server results for the case of $N = k + 1$. However, with the major exception of

---

[1]   See Chapter 5 for a brief discussion of the term "universal." Section 11.2 shows that the lower bound of *k* for deterministic adversaries extends to randomized algorithms against an adaptive adversary so that, indeed, against adaptive adversaries, simplicity and efficiency is the goal rather than a significantly improved competitive ratio. •

the paging problem, we do not have sublinear randomized competitive ratios for k-server problems when $N \geq 2k$ (and, in particular, when N is infinite).

In this section we present and analyze two k-server algorithms for the circle. Both algorithms work against oblivious adversaries. The first algorithm works in any metric space that can be embedded in a circle and attains a competitive ratio of $2k$. The second algorithm works in the metric space consisting of $k+1$ equally spaced points on the circle and attains the sublinear competitive ratio $O(\sqrt{k} \cdot \log k)$. Although this ratio is subsumed by Corollary 9.12, the construction is of some independent interest.

11.1.1   A $2k$-Competitive Circle Algorithm

For a (continuous) circle with circumference C, consider the following algorithm.

> **Algorithm CIRC:** The online player chooses randomly and uniformly a point P on the circumference of the circle. Think about the point P, which remains unknown to the (oblivious) adversary, as a roadblock that breaks the circle into a line segment. On this line segment the online player plays the k-server game according to the optimal (deterministic) line algorithm DC (DOUBLE-COVERAGE) of Section 10.4.1.

Clearly, the above algorithm is a mixed algorithm; it makes only a single random choice. Note, however, that this single random choice is a real number.[2] A more important feature is that this algorithm introduces a general approach for constructing randomized algorithms against an oblivious adversary.

Theorem 11.1 CIRC *is $2k$-competitive against an oblivious adversary.*

PROOF. Call OPT-LINE the optimal offline algorithm that serves a request within the line segment (as defined by P). OPT is the optimal offline algorithm for the circle. Clearly, for any request sequence σ,

$$\text{CIRC}(\sigma) \leq k \cdot \text{OPT-LINE}(\sigma). \tag{11.1}$$

We now bound OPT-LINE(σ) from above in terms of OPT(σ). Consider an algorithm OPT$'$ that behaves exactly as OPT does except that whenever OPT crosses the point P, OPT$'$ makes a detour along the circle, paying C. Since OPT$'$ is an algorithm for the line segment, OPT-LINE$(\sigma) \leq$ OPT$'(\sigma)$. Every distance d_i traveled by OPT's servers crosses P with probability at most $\frac{d_i}{C}$. Hence the expected cost for all detours is at most $D = \sum_i \frac{d_i}{C} \cdot C = \text{OPT}(\sigma)$. To summarize, we obtained

$$\text{OPT-LINE}(\sigma) \leq \mathbf{E}[\text{OPT}'(\sigma)] \leq \text{OPT}(\sigma) + D = 2 \cdot \text{OPT}(\sigma). \tag{11.2}$$

From equations (11.1) and (11.2),

$$\mathbf{E}[\text{CIRC}(\sigma)] \leq 2k\text{OPT}(\sigma).$$

■

---

[2] Alternatively, we can use finite precision and let CIRC converge to a real (random) point P by randomly generating one bit b_i of $P(= C \times .b_0 b_1 b_2 \cdots)$ after every request. At the ith request, CIRC would then use $\tilde{P} = C \times .b_0 b_1 \cdots b_i$ as the roadblock.

Algorithm CIRC suggests the following general approach for designing online k-server algorithms. We recall from Chapter 9 the definition of probabilistic approximation of one space by another. A closer look at the proof of Theorem 11.1 shows that the circle metric space can be probabilistically approximated by (a distribution on) lines. The following theorems are immediate analogues of Theorems 9.6 and 9.7.

Theorem 11.2 *Let $\mathcal{M} = (V, d)$ and $\tilde{\mathcal{M}} = (V, \tilde{d})$ be two metric spaces defined on the same set of points V, and let $\tilde{\mathcal{M}}$ λ-approximate $\mathcal{M}$. If there exists a deterministic (respectively, randomized) c-competitive k-server algorithm for $\tilde{\mathcal{M}}$, then there exists a deterministic (respectively, randomized) $c\lambda$-competitive k-server algorithm for $\mathcal{M}$.*

For example, the proof of Theorem 11.1 shows that the circle (say, of circumference C) can be randomly 2-approximated by a class of lines of length C. Each cut point j induces a "line metric" on the points of the circle, with the cut point being the endpoint of this line.

Theorem 11.3 *Let $\mathcal{M} = (V, d)$ be a metric space and let the class $\mathcal{S} = \{(V, d^{(x)})\}$ probabilistically λ-approximate $\mathcal{M}$. If there exists a deterministic (or randomized) c-competitive k-server algorithm for each $(V, d^x) \in \mathcal{S}$, then there exists a randomized $c\lambda$-competitive k-server algorithm for $\mathcal{M}$.*

In this terminology CIRC becomes the randomized algorithm guaranteed by Theorem 11.3. Further applications of this approach are discussed in Section 11.7.

11.1.2   A Sublinear Ratio for $k + 1$ Equally Spaced Points on the Circle

After the randomized algorithm for uniform spaces (i.e., paging), the following algorithm (and its variant for the line) was the first randomized k-server algorithm for which a sublinear competitive ratio was achieved. Consider N equally spaced points on a circle and suppose, without loss of generality, that the circumference of the circle is N. We describe an algorithm for $k = N - 1$ servers that serves requests in this space. The idea of this algorithm is to break the circle into a collection of equal-size "line" segments. Since there are k servers and only $k + 1$ points in the space, the algorithm "exposes" only one "hole" at each time. The algorithm uses a policy very similar to the uniform MTS algorithm (see Section 9.5) to keep the hole in some line segment until this segment becomes "saturated" (with requests). Then, the algorithm randomly chooses a new unsaturated line segment and moves the hole to the unsaturated segment, and so on. Inside each line segment, the algorithm applies any k-competitive deterministic algorithm (such as DOUBLE-COVERAGE or BALANCE).

Let us now describe this circle algorithm, called CIRC2, more carefully. Let $m = \lceil \sqrt{2N} \rceil$. Break the circle into $\lceil \frac{N}{m} \rceil$ intervals, each of m points (except maybe one interval). Label these intervals $I_0, I_1, \ldots, I_{\lceil N/m \rceil - 1}$. For each point $i = 1, 2, \ldots, N$, the algorithm maintains a variable $C(i)$ giving a lower bound on the optimal offline cost of serving the request sequence thus far (since the last "initialization") and ending with the hole sitting on i. The following simple rule updates the variable $C(i)$ appropriately: after a request is made at i, set $C(i) := \min\{C(i-1)+1, \; C(i+1)+1\}$ (where index additions are made mod N).

Algorithm CIRC2:

Step 1. Initialize the variables $C(i)$ to zero and all intervals to be "unsaturated."

Step 2. Randomly and uniformly choose an unsaturated interval I_j. Keep the hole within I_j while running DC within I_j until $C(i) \geq m$ for all $i \in I_j$. Mark "saturated" each interval I_l with $C(j) \geq m$ for all $j \in I_l$. If there are some unsaturated intervals remaining, repeat Step 2.

Step 3. All intervals are now saturated. Go to Step 1.

Theorem 11.4 CIRC2 *is* $O(\sqrt{N} \log N)$-*competitive against an oblivious adversary.*

PROOF. Let $R(N)$ be the competitive ratio attained by CIRC2 with $N - 1$ servers for a request sequence σ such that $\text{OPT}(\sigma) \geq N$. The first observation is that on average, each application of Step 2 costs CIRC2 at most $\left\lceil \frac{N}{2} \right\rceil + m^2 \frac{\text{OPT}(\sigma)}{N}$: "jumping" into a new line segment costs at most $\left\lceil \frac{N}{2} \right\rceil$, and serving requests within a randomly chosen line segment (using DC with $m - 1$ servers) costs on average at most $m \frac{\text{OPT}(\sigma)}{N/m} = m^2 \frac{\text{OPT}(\sigma)}{N}$.

The number of applications of Step 2 until all intervals become saturated is $O(\log N)$ (see a similar derivation in the proof of Theorem 9.5). Hence, for some constant c,

$$R(N) \leq \frac{c \cdot \frac{N}{m} \log N \left(m^2 \frac{\text{OPT}(\sigma)}{N} + \frac{N}{2} \right)}{\text{OPT}(\sigma)}$$

$$\leq c \cdot \frac{N}{m} \log N \left(\frac{m^2}{N} + \frac{1}{2} \right)$$

$$= c \cdot \log N \left(m + \frac{N}{2m} \right).$$

The theorem is obtained by our choice of $m = \left\lceil \sqrt{2N} \right\rceil$. ∎

This algorithm can also be applied to the line. When one considers the line the idea can be carried further to obtain a $2^{O(\sqrt{\log N \log\log N})}$-competitive algorithm for the line. It is sufficient to apply the algorithm recursively in each line segment and use as a basis any optimally competitive (deterministic) algorithm for $N = k + 1$ points.

Exercise 11.1 Use the above suggestion to construct a $2^{O(\sqrt{\log N \log\log N})}$-competitive k-server algorithm for $N = k + 1$ equally spaced points on the line against an oblivious adversary.

11.2 A Lower Bound Against an Adaptive-Online Adversary

Consider the proof of Theorem 10.1. In the proof, we have defined a class $\mathcal{B}$ of (online) algorithms for the adversary (each controlling $h \leq k$ servers) such that for every deterministic algorithm ALG the average competitive ratio of ALG, with respect to all algorithms in $\mathcal{B}$ is $\frac{k}{k-h+1}$. Recall that the set $\mathcal{B}$ was defined with respect to a cruel request sequence that was constructed specially for ALG. Notice that a cruel request sequence can still be constructed by an adaptive adversary against a randomized algorithm.

Since we are proving a lower bound, it is better to assume that the algorithms being considered do not have any memory limitations (i.e., are games of perfect recall) and that we can therefore appeal to Theorems 6.1 and 6.2 to obtain the equivalence between mixed and behavioral strategies. For the purpose of this result, it is convenient to consider the mixed strategy form.

Theorem 11.5 *Let G be a randomized algorithm for any (h, k)-server problem. Then $\overline{\mathcal{R}}_{\text{ADON}}(G) \geq \frac{k}{k-h+1}$.*

PROOF. Let $G = \{G_x\}$ be a randomized algorithm choosing randomly (with some distribution) a deterministic algorithm G_x. Imagine a table with the rows indexed by the deterministic algorithms G_x and the columns indexed by the algorithms in $\mathcal{B}$ where each entry $(G_{\hat{x}}, B_y)$ gives the competitive ratio of G_x with respect to B_y using a cruel request sequence for G_x. Now suppose that the rows are distributed according to the probability distribution of the randomized algorithm G, and that columns are distributed uniformly. Theorem 10.1 shows that the average competitive ratio over each row is $\frac{k}{k-h+1}$. The proof is completed by appealing to Theorem 7.1, which shows that randomization does not help the adversary. Alternatively, we can argue directly that there must be a column that attains this average (i.e., attains an average no smaller than $\frac{k}{k-h+1}$ with respect to the distribution of G). This means that there exists a strategy for the adversary that forces this competitive ratio on G (note that this proof is not constructive). ∎

11.3   The Cat and Rat Game and Applications to Randomized k-Server Algorithms

We now introduce a game based on random walks in a weighted graph. We use this game to establish some upper and lower bounds for "memoryless" randomized k-server algorithms. These upper bounds apply to randomized algorithms against an adaptive adversary; however, the lower bound (for lazy behavioral memoryless algorithms) also applies to an oblivious adversary.

Consider a k-server game on an N-node metric space $(\mathcal{M}, d)$. We recall from Section 10.2.3 that for unbounded memory it is sufficient to restrict attention to lazy server algorithms that move at most one server in response to each request and do so only if the request is not presently covered by a server. Throughout this section we assume that all online algorithms (and OPT) are indeed lazy. Specifically, the algorithm (and OPT) always has its k servers on k distinct nodes. We define ALG's current **server configuration** to be the *set* of k nodes occupied by ALG's servers.[3] Note that when $N = k + 1$, each player has exactly one node (called a hole) that is not covered by a server. In this case, the configuration of a player at any given time is completely determined by the location of its hole and we can view the operation of moving a server from point v to serve a request at point u as moving the hole from u to v.

A deterministic k-server algorithm can be defined as a function

$$\text{ALG} : \mathcal{S} \times \mathcal{C} \times \mathcal{M} \to \mathcal{S} \times \mathcal{C}.$$

---

[3] It is also reasonable to define the configuration as the *sequence* of nodes occupied by the servers, that is, the mapping of servers to nodes. However, for the purpose of defining memory bounded algorithms, it seems fairer to take the more restrictive notion of a configuration.

That is, based on its current state (in S) and configuration (in C) and the present request (from the metric space M), the algorithm changes state and (if the request is not in the current configuration) changes the configuration by evicting some node in order to include the present request. A k-server algorithm is called **bounded memory** if S is finite (i.e., independent of the length of the request sequence) and it is called **memoryless** if $|S| = 1$; that is, there is only one state, in which case

$$\text{ALG} : C \times M \to C.$$

The same definitions can be applied to randomized algorithms, in which case the function ALG is a probabilistic function. Consider a deterministic or randomized memoryless online algorithm ALG (e.g., the randomized paging algorithm RAND). Since ALG is memoryless, a request for a node that is already in the current configuration is ignored. Therefore, in the case of a deterministic algorithm or a randomized algorithm against an adaptive adversary, we can assume that the adversary is a cruel adversary that requests only those nodes not in the current cache of ALG. When $N = k + 1$, we can summarize the situation as follows: wherever a randomized memoryless algorithm ALG has its hole (e.g., at node u), the adversary requests u, causing ALG to move the hole to some node v (at a cost of $d_{uv} = d_{vu}$), according to some distribution, that depends only on u.

We can model this situation as a game between an online "blind"[4] CAT and an adversarial RAT on a weighted (strongly connected) directed $(k+1)$-node graph $G = (V, E, d)$ where the distance function d is symmetric.[5] The CAT is situated on some node of the graph, and the RAT requests ("threatens") that node, causing the CAT to move. The CAT's moves are defined by a stochastic matrix $P = (p_{ij})$ where p_{ij} is the probability that the CAT will move from i to j when i is requested. Note that in general, $p_{ij} \neq p_{ji}$.

Initially (at the start of a stage), both the CAT and the RAT are at the same node. Then, after generating a request for that node, the RAT moves to some other node. In every step, the adversary generates a request for the node on which the CAT is located. Then the CAT moves to another node, according to the probabilities on the outgoing edges, from its current node. That is, the CAT begins a random walk (determined by P) on the graph. When the CAT finally catches the RAT (i.e., moves to the node occupied by the RAT), the stage ends and a new stage begins.

11.3.1 Random Walks, Stretch Factors, and the Competitive Ratio

Consider the cat and rat game played on G. The cost to the online player (the CAT) to go from i to j is the weighted hitting time h_{ij} (see Appendix C) of going from i to j using a random walk (determined by the edge probabilities) in the graph. Note that the (weighted) hitting time depends on both the distance function d and P. The cost to the adversary (the RAT) to go from i to j is just the distance d_{ij}. Assume that initially both the CAT and RAT start at node i_0, and let the adversary request the sequence of nodes $\sigma = i_1, i_2, \ldots, i_t$. The RAT pays $\text{RAT}(\sigma) = \text{RAT}(\sigma, G) = \sum_{\ell=1}^{t} d_{i_{\ell-1}, i_\ell}$, and CAT pays $\text{CAT}(\sigma) = \text{CAT}(\sigma, G) = \sum_{\ell=1}^{t} h_{i_{\ell-1}, i_\ell}$. The competitive ratio (against an adaptive online adversary) for CAT in this game is naturally defined as $\overline{\mathcal{R}}_{\text{ADON}}(\text{CAT}) = \overline{\mathcal{R}}_{\text{ADON}}(\text{CAT}, G) = \sup_\sigma \frac{\text{CAT}(\sigma)}{\text{RAT}(\sigma)}$. This motivates the following

---

[4] We say "blind," since the CAT will never know when the CAT and RAT are occupying the same node.

[5] For the abstract cat and rat game defined here, we assume only that d is symmetric. For the application to the k-server problem, d is also a metric.

definitions for a random walk on a symmetric weighted graph G as determined by a stochastic matrix P:

- Let $e = (i, j)$ be an edge in the graph. The **stretch factor of an edge** e is the ratio $\frac{h_{ij}}{d_{ij}}$, that is, the ratio between the expected cost of a random walk from i to j and the weight of e.
- The **edge stretch factor** is the maximum stretch factor of any edge in the graph.
- The **stretch factor of a cycle** $\sigma = u_1, u_2, \ldots, u_\ell, u_1$ is the ratio $\frac{\text{CAT}(\sigma)}{\text{RAT}(\sigma)}$.
- The **cycle stretch factor** is the maximum stretch factor of any cycle in the graph.

It is easy to see that the cycle stretch factor is upper bounded by the edge stretch factor. It should also be clear (by definition of the cat and rat game) that the edge stretch factor of a graph G with respect to a stochastic P immediately gives an upper bound on the competitive ratio for a CAT (determined by P). The following theorem shows that the cycle stretch factor also gives an upper bound.

Theorem 11.6 *Let G be any symmetric weighted graph and let P be a stochastic matrix that determines an online algorithm* CAT. *If the cycle stretch factor of G with respect to P is c, then $\overline{\mathcal{R}}_{\text{ADON}}(\text{CAT}) \leq c$.*

PROOF. For a worst-case input sequence, consider the path of the RAT on the graph. By a process of eliminating cycles, we can view this path as a collection of cycles, and an additional simple path (with length $\leq |V| - 1$). Therefore, the expected cost of the game for the CAT is at most c times the cost of that path for the RAT, plus the expected cost of the additional simple path (which is bounded by some constant that is independent of the length of the request sequence). ∎

Conversely, the stretch factor is the best competitive ratio that can be achieved.

Theorem 11.7 *Let G be any symmetric weighted graph and let* CAT *be any online algorithm (i.e., let P be any stochastic matrix). If the cycle stretch factor of a graph with respect to P is c, then there exists an adaptive adversary that extracts a competitive ratio of c from the online player. That is, $\overline{\mathcal{R}}_{\text{ADON}}(\text{CAT}) \geq c$.*

PROOF. The graph contains a cycle with a stretch factor c, so the adaptive online adversary will move the RAT to some node on that cycle. Then, whenever the CAT meets the RAT, the adversary will move the RAT to the next node on that cycle. In this way, the expected cost of the online player for each round in that cycle will be c times the cost of the adversary. ∎

Corollary 11.8 *Let $(\mathcal{M}, d)$ be a $(N = k + 1)$-node metric space and let* ALG *be a lazy (behavioral) memoryless k-server online algorithm. Let P be the stochastic matrix defined by* ALG *(i.e., the matrix of probabilities for moving the online hole) and let P have cycle stretch factor c. Then $\overline{\mathcal{R}}_{\text{ADON}}(\text{ALG}) \geq \overline{\mathcal{R}}_{\text{OBL}}(\text{ALG}) \geq c$*

PROOF. The lower bound for an adaptive adversary follows directly from Theorem 11.7 and the observation that the cat and rat game models the game between a lazy memoryless randomized algorithm and an adversary on an $(N = k + 1)$-node metric space.

The problem with constructing an oblivious adversary, using the above approach, is that, in effect, the adversary does not know where the CAT has moved in any step. Let σ be a cycle with stretch factor c and, say, weight W. The oblivious adversary ADV will (like an adaptive adversary) have its hole traverse the cycle σ at cost $\text{ADV}(\sigma) = W$. Now suppose that the adversary moves its hole from, say, u to v (by requesting v and then moving a server from u to v, the next node on the cycle σ). The adversary will then request $c \cdot W$ repetitions of the request sequence $1, \ldots, v-1, v+1, \ldots, N$; that is, request every other node except v sufficiently many times. It follows that during one traversal of σ by the adversary, either the hole of ALG does a random walk on σ or ALG pays at least $c \cdot W = c \cdot \text{ADV}(\sigma)$ during the adversary's traversal of σ. ∎

The main technical result of this section is to show that for every symmetric weighted N-node graph and for every stochastic matrix P, the cycle stretch factor is at least $N-1$. We need some lemmas (of independent interest) concerning random walks on graphs.

Assume, without loss of generality, that the Markov chain determined by P is **irreducible** in the sense that for every pair of distinct nodes i, j, there is a positive probability that j will be reached (in some number of steps) from i. A Markov chain is **periodic** if there exists an $\ell \geq 2$ (the period) such that if $\Pr[j$ will be reached from i in exactly t steps$] > 0$, then t is a multiple of ℓ. For simplicity (and without loss of generality for what follows), we will assume that the Markov chain is aperiodic (i.e., not periodic). Then (in the limit[6]) the probability ϕ_i, called **the stationary probability**, of being at a node i in G is well defined.[7] The probabilities ϕ_i are those that solve the system $\phi_j = \sum_i \phi_i p_{ij}$. Then (again, in the limit) the probability of traversing an edge (i, j) is $\phi_i p_{ij}$, and the expected cost of leaving a node i (conditioned on being at node i) is $e_i = \sum_j p_{ij} \cdot d_{ij}$. We can then define the expected cost of a move to be $H = \sum_i \phi_i e_i$. As before, we use h_{ij} to denote the expected cost of a random walk from i to j.

The following lemma asserts that for every node i, the expected cost of a cycle that begins and ends in i is exactly the expected cost of a single move, divided by the probability of being in i.

Lemma 11.1 *For every node i in the graph, it holds that* $h_{ii} = \frac{H}{\phi_i}$.

PROOF. We give an informal proof here.[8] Let i be a node in the graph, and consider a long random walk in the graph that begins at i. If the length T of the walk is sufficiently long, then we expect to visit i about $\phi_i \cdot T$ times during this walk. Moreover, the expected cost of this walk is $H \cdot T$. Therefore, the average cost between two successive occurrences of i in the walk is $\frac{H \cdot T}{\phi_i T} = \frac{H}{\phi_i}$. ∎

The following lemma asserts that for a random walk on a graph, the expected cost to return (using a random walk) to a node (having just left it) is exactly $N-1$ times the expected cost of returning via the direct edge that goes back.

---

[6] Formally, given some initial state i_0, let $\phi_{i,t}$ denote the probability that the Markov chain will be in state i at time t. We consider the limit as $t \to \infty$. For an aperiodic irreducible Markov chain, this limit exists and is independent of the initial state.

[7] When the Markov chain is periodic, we can define ϕ_i as the ith component of the left eigenvector of P for the eigenvalue 1.

[8] A formal proof can be found in Kemeny, Snell, and Knapp [220].

Lemma 11.2 *For every symmetric cost matrix (d_{ij}) and every stochastic matrix $P = (p_{ij})$, it holds that*

$$\sum_{i,j} \phi_i p_{ij} h_{ji} = (N-1) \sum_{i,j} \phi_i p_{ij} d_{ji}. \tag{11.3}$$

PROOF. Notice that for any node i, the sum $\sum_j p_{ij} h_{ji}$ is the expected cost h_{ii} of a round trip of commuting from i to i minus the expected cost of the first move. That is, $\sum_j p_{ij} h_{ji} = h_{ii} - e_i$. Moreover, from Lemma 11.1 we have for every node i that $h_{ii} = \frac{H}{\phi_i}$. Therefore, we can write the left-hand side of equation (11.3) as

$$\sum_{i,j} \phi_i p_{ij} h_{ji} = \sum_i \phi_i \sum_j p_{ij} h_{ji}$$

$$= \sum_i \phi_i (h_{ii} - e_i)$$

$$= \sum_i \phi_i \left(\frac{H}{\phi_i} - e_i \right) \tag{11.4}$$

$$= N \cdot H - \sum_i \phi_i e_i = (N-1) \cdot H.$$

On the other hand, since (d_{ij}) is symmetric, we can write the summation in the right-hand side of equation (11.3) as

$$\sum_{i,j} \phi_i p_{ij} d_{ij} = \sum_{ij} \phi_i p_{ij} d_{ij} = \sum_i \phi_i \sum_j p_{ij} d_{ij} = H. \tag{11.5}$$

Combining equations (11.4) and (11.5), we complete the proof of the lemma. ∎

We now consider a flow in the graph, where each edge (j, i) carries $\phi_j p_{ji}$ units of flow. We claim that this induces a **circulation** where the flow into every node is equal to the flow out of every node. This holds for every node i, since the amount of flow entering i is $\sum_j \phi_i p_{ij} = \phi_i \sum_j p_{ij} = \phi_i$, and the amount of flow exiting i is $\sum_j \phi_j p_{ji} = \phi_i$. It is easy to see the following.

Lemma 11.3 *For any circulation, we can break the flow into a convex sum of cycles. That is, there exists a set of cycles in the graph $\{C_1, \ldots, C_r\}$ and a set of corresponding positive numbers $\{a_1, \ldots, a_r\}$ so that for every edge (i, j) it holds that*

$$\phi_j p_{ji} = \sum_{k:(i,j)\in C_k} a_k.$$

Theorem 11.9 *For every N-node graph G with symmetric cost matrix (d_{ij}), and for every stochastic matrix P, the cycle stretch factor of G with respect to P is at least $N-1$.*

PROOF. We need to show that there is some cycle C with stretch factor $N-1$. Using Lemma 11.3, we can rewrite equation (11.3) as follows:

$$\sum_{k=1}^{r} \sum_{(j,i)\in C_k} a_k h_{ji} = (N-1) \sum_{k=1}^{r} \sum_{(j,i)\in C_k} a_k d_{ji}. \tag{11.6}$$

Thus, there exists at least one cycle C_k for which $\sum_{(j,i)\in C_k} a_k h_{ji} \geq (N-1) \sum_{(j,i)\in C_k} a_k d_{ji}$; therefore, the stretch factor of that cycle is $\frac{\sum_{(j,i)\in C_k} h_{ji}}{\sum_{(j,i)\in C_k} d_{ji}} \geq N - 1$. ∎

Corollary 11.10 *For every* $(N = k+1)$-*node metric space* $(\mathcal{M}, d)$ *and every lazy behavioral memoryless randomized online algorithm* ALG, *the competitive ratio of* ALG *against an adaptive or oblivious adversary is at least* k.

PROOF. The proof follows directly from Corollary 11.8 and Theorem 11.9. ∎

Note that Theorem 6.5 shows that the same bound does not apply to memoryless algorithms defined as mixed strategies.

11.4 The Harmonic Random Walk

An obvious randomized strategy for the CAT is to take a harmonic random walk (see Appendix C) on the graph, choosing each edge with probability inversely proportional to its cost; that is,

$$p_{uv} = \Pr[u \to v \mid \text{at } u] = \frac{1/d_{uv}}{\sum_{w\in N(u)}(1/d_{uw})}.$$

In Section 11.5 we consider HARMONIC as a general k-server algorithm. When the metric space is the uniform metric space, the HARMONIC k-server algorithm reduces to algorithm RAND for paging. Here we consider the special case when $N = k + 1$, in which case HARMONIC is a harmonic random walk by the hole (i.e., the CAT).

Theorem 11.11 *Let* $G = (V, E, d)$ *be any undirected weighted graph. For the cat and rat game on* G, *the harmonic random walk on* G *is* $(2|E|)$-*competitive against any adaptive-online adversary.*

PROOF. It is sufficient to show that the edge stretch factor is at most $2|E|$. From Corollary C.2 we know that $h_{uv} \leq 2|E|d_{uv}$. That is, the stretch factor of any edge in E is less than $2|E|$. ∎

Corollary 11.12 *Let* $(\mathcal{M}, d)$ *be any* $(N = k+1)$-*node metric space. Then the competitive ratio of the* HARMONIC *algorithm in this metric space is at most* $k(k + 1)$.

PROOF. Note that HARMONIC is memoryless and clearly $|E| \leq \frac{k(k+1)}{2}$. The corollary follows immediately from the theorem. ∎

What about the k-server problem when $N > k + 1$? We should be able to exploit more efficiently the bound on the edge stretch factor for HARMONIC (or any other memoryless algorithm) based on the following reasoning. In the case $N = k + 1$ and a memoryless algorithm, we saw that we could assume that the adversary always requests a node (in this case, "the" node) where the online algorithm ALG has its hole. This trivially implies that whenever ALG has a hole on a node covered by the adversary, the adversary makes a cruel request without any cost to itself. It seems reasonable to believe that even if $N > k + 1$, the most effective strategy for the adversary is to remain "lazy" and avoid costs to itself whenever possible.[9] That is, we have the following conjecture.

The lazy adversary conjecture: *Let* ALG *be a memoryless randomized k-server algorithm. The following is an optimal strategy for the adversary: whenever the adversary and* ALG *have different configurations, the adversary requests a node that is in its configuration.*[10]

By the same reasoning that allows us to use the edge stretch factor as an upper bound for the competitive ratio in the $N = k + 1$ case, we have the following theorem.

Theorem 11.13 *Assume the lazy adversary conjecture. Let* $(\mathcal{M}, d)$ *be an arbitrary metric space and let* ALG *be a memoryless randomized algorithm (defined by a stochastic matrix* P*). Suppose that for any* $(k + 1)$*-node subspace* G *of* $(\mathcal{M}, d)$*, the edge stretch factor of* G *with respect to* P *is at most* c*. Then* ALG *is* c*-competitive against an adaptive adversary.*

Exercise 11.2 Prove Theorem 11.13.

Corollary 11.14 *If the lazy adversary conjecture is true, then* HARMONIC *is* c*-competitive for* $c \leq k(k + 1)$ *for any metric space* $(\mathcal{M}, d)$*.*

In fact, it can be shown that the upper bound of Corollaries 11.12 and 11.14 can be improved to $\frac{k(k+1)}{2}$, which is optimal according to Theorem 11.15.

11.5   The HARMONIC *k*-Server Algorithm on an Arbitrary Metric Space

The HARMONIC k-server algorithm operates as follows.

Algorithm HARMONIC: Serve an uncovered request r with a randomly chosen server where each server is chosen with probability inversely proportional to its distance from the requested node. More precisely, let $\mathcal{C} = \{s_1, s_2, \ldots, s_k\}$ be the set of online servers. Suppose that no online server is currently located on the request. For each $1 \leq i \leq k$, set $d_i = d(s_i, r)$. Then HARMONIC serves the request, with the server s_i chosen with probability

$$\frac{1/d_i}{\sum_{j=1}^{k} 1/d_j} = \frac{1}{d_i \sum_{j=1}^{k} 1/d_j}.$$

---

[9] We follow common notation and use the term of a "lazy adversary"; however, this should not be confused with the concept of a "lazy" algorithm. Whereas there is no loss in generality in assuming that an algorithm is lazy, there very well may be a loss of generality in assuming that the adversary is lazy even for memoryless algorithms.

[10] Of course, because the adversary and the optimal offline player are in fact the same entity, we only conceptually view the offline algorithm's moves as if they are taking place as the game is being played.

In a sense, HARMONIC can be viewed as a randomized version of the noncompetitive deterministic greedy algorithm that serves a request with the closest server. HARMONIC is clearly memoryless.

We start with a lower bound on the competitive ratio of HARMONIC. We first give a lower bound against an adaptive online adversary and then refine it to work with respect to an oblivious adversary.

Theorem 11.15 *There exists a $(k + 1)$-node graph for which the competitive ratio of* HARMONIC *against an adaptive online adversary is not smaller than $\frac{k(k+1)}{2}$.*

PROOF. Let $\{0, 1, 2, \ldots, k\}$ be the labels of the nodes of a complete graph such that $d_{01} = 1$ and all other distances are $B \gg k$. Let $\{1, 2, \ldots, k\}$ be the initial configuration. The adversary strategy is the following: with $k - 1$ of its servers, it covers the set of nodes $S = \{2, 3, \ldots, k\}$ until the end of the game. The adversary constructs a request sequence consisting of phases. In every odd phase he requests the node 0, answers this request with the server from node 1, and then makes (lazy) requests to nodes in S until HARMONIC converges to the offline configuration. In every even phase the adversary requests the node 1, answers this request with the server from node 0, and makes lazy requests to nodes in S until HARMONIC converges to the offline configuration.

Clearly, the adversary pays exactly 1 per phase. Now consider the activity of HARMONIC. At each time, HARMONIC leaves one node uncovered (the hole). On every two consecutive phases (odd and then even), the hole is performing a harmonic random walk from node 1 to node 0 and then back to node 1. What is the expected cost of this round trip? The answer comes from Theorem C.1. Using that result, it is easy to show that the expected cost of a round trip $1 \to 0 \to 1$ on our graph is $\frac{k(k+1)2B}{2B+k-1}$, which becomes arbitrarily close to $k(k+1)$ as B gets large. Hence, since the adversary incurs a cost of 2 for these two phases, we have completed the proof. ∎

As in Theorem 11.7, the lower bound of Theorem 11.15 can be easily strengthened to work with respect to oblivious adversaries. The problematic issue is again that the oblivious adversary cannot directly construct the cruel request sequence. Nevertheless, the oblivious adversary can produce a sequence that achieves the same effect. Let ℓ be a large integer, and consider the following request sequence partitioned into phases (we indicate three phases):

$$\sigma = (0, 2, 3, \ldots, k)^{\ell}, \ (1, 2, 3, \ldots, k)^{\ell}, \ (0, 2, 3, \ldots, k)^{\ell}, \ldots.$$

For sufficiently large ℓ, by the end of each phase HARMONIC will converge to the adversary configuration with very high probability. Thus for sufficiently large ℓ and B, we obtain the same result with respect to an oblivious adversary. Thus we have the following corollary.

Corollary 11.16 *There exists a $(k + 1)$-node graph for which the competitive ratio of* HARMONIC *against an oblivious adversary is not smaller than $\frac{k(k+1)}{2}$.*

Next we prove the main result of this section, an upper bound on the competitiveness of HARMONIC.

Theorem 11.17 HARMONIC *attains a competitive ratio of $(k + 1)(2^k - 1) - k$ against an adaptive online adversary.*

PROOF. Let A be the set of offline (adversary) servers and S the set of online servers. The proof is obtained by a potential function argument. To construct the potential function, we need the following definitions. For each online server s and offline server a, define $p(s, a)$ to be the sum of edge weights of a minimum weighted simple path from s to a going only through points in A; the weights of edges along this path are given by a special weight function $w : \{1, 2, \ldots, k\} \to \mathbb{R}^+$ that assigns the weight $w(i)$ to the ith edge in this path from s to a. The weight function $w(\cdot)$ is strictly decreasing, giving large weights to edges at the beginning of the path and smaller weights to further edges. For now we leave $w(\cdot)$ undetermined, and after obtaining some constraints on the best possible competitive ratio in terms of $w(\cdot)$, we determine the weight function that allows the best possible competitive ratio (given our particular potential function). More precisely, define

$$p(s, a) = \min_{\{a_1, \ldots, a_\ell = a\} \subseteq A} \left\{ w(1) \cdot d(s, a_1) + \sum_{2 \leq j \leq \ell} w(j) \cdot d(a_{j-1}, a_j) \right\}.$$

Then, the potential function is

$$\Phi = \min_M \sum_{s \in S} p(s, M(s)),$$

where $M : S \mapsto A$ is a one-to-one matching function. Let M_o be a matching M that achieves the minimum in the definition of Φ. We consider to what extent Φ is changed by the offline and online moves.

First, consider the offline move. What is the worst possible increase of potential that can be obtained? It is not difficult to see that a move of an offline server can increase the value of all paths from z to $M_o(z)$ where z is an online server. Since the weight function is decreasing, the worst possible situation is that the offline server that is moved, for example, a, appears in the first place after the source in paths from $z \to M_o(z)$. If the path $z \to M_o(z)$ contains more than one edge, the offline server will increase the value of the first two edges (with the largest weights, $w(1)$ and $w(2)$). This can be the case for every online server z except the online server that is matched to a, $M_o^{-1}(a)$. For the path $M_o^{-1}(a) \to a$, the worst possible situation is when a is directly connected to $M_o^{-1}(a)$ via an edge (with weight $w(1)$). Hence, the maximum increase in potential, which is a lower bound on the smallest possible competitive ratio, is

$$kw(1) + (k - 1)w(2). \tag{11.7}$$

We now consider the change in potential that results from the online move. Suppose a request r is placed on $M_o(x)$ for some online server $x \in S$. We examine the change in potential after an online server z serves the request. To obtain an upper bound on the value of the potential function after the online move (in order to prove a decrease in potential), we consider a new matching M_{new} in which z (the server that has answered the request) is matched to $M_o(x)$ (the request) and x is matched to $M_o(z)$. Of course, M_{new} may not be a minimum cost matching in this server configuration; however, it provides an upper bound on the new minimum cost matching after the online move.

Let $P(x) = \{x_1, x_2, \ldots, x_{\ell(x)}\}$ be the set of offline servers on the path from x to $M_o(x)$ and let $P(z) = \{z_1, z_2, \ldots, z_{\ell(z)}\}$ be the set of offline servers on the path from z to $M_o(z)$ (i.e., before z is moved). We consider two cases:

- *Case 1:* $M_o(z) \in P(x)$. Suppose there are j offline servers on the path from x to $M_o(z)$. It is easy to see that $j \geq \ell(z)$; otherwise, $j < \ell(z)$ and by matching z to $M_o(x)$ and x to $M_o(z)$ we could obtain a "smaller" minimum cost matching by strictly reducing the contribution of the segment from $M_o(z)$ to $M_o(x)$. This contradicts the minimality of M_o (recall that $w(\cdot)$ is decreasing).

Every edge from $P(z)$ has an index no greater than $\ell(z) \leq j \leq \ell(x)$. Consider the new matching function M_{new}. The potential decreases by the weighted sum of edge costs on a path from z to $M_o(x)$ for which every weight is at least $w(\ell(x))$. Hence, the potential decreases by at least $d(z, M_o(x)) \cdot w(\ell(x))$. Set $N(x) = \sum_{z \in S} \frac{1}{d}(z, M_o(x))$. The expected decrease in potential for this case is at least

$$
\begin{aligned}
D_1 &= \sum_{M_o(z) \in P(x)} \Pr[z \text{ is moved}] \cdot d(z, M_o(x)) \cdot w(\ell(x)) \\
&= \sum_{M_o(z) \in P(x)} \frac{d(z, M_o(x)) \cdot w(\ell(x))}{N(x) \cdot d(z, M_o(x))} = \frac{\ell(x) \cdot w(\ell(x))}{N(x)}.
\end{aligned}
$$

- *Case 2:* $M_o(z) \notin P(x)$. In this case, we may expect an increase of potential after the online move. We now construct a path from x to $M_o(z)$ that will be used in the new matching M_{new} (after z serves the request $M_o(x)$). Although the path we construct will not show an expected decrease of potential, it will guarantee that the expected increase is not too large.

Let $Q(x, z) = P(z) - P(x)$ and let the order of the nodes in the path $P(z)$ induce an order of the nodes in $Q(x, z)$. The path $P(x)$ followed by $Q(x, z)$ is a path from x to $M_o(z)$ such that every edge along this path has a weighting factor at most what it had for its contribution to the potential (via contributions to $P(x)$ and $P(z)$) before the move. However, in order to connect $P(x)$ and $Q(x, z)$ we added one new edge $(M_o(x), z)$ that has a weight $w(\ell(x) + 1) \cdot d(z, M_o(x))$. Hence, the new path has total weighted value at most $w(\ell(x) + 1) \cdot d(z, M_o(x))$ more than the sum of the previous values of the two paths $(P(x)$ and $P(z))$. Thus, the expected increase of potential for Case 2 is at most

$$
D_2 = \sum_{M_o(z) \notin P(x)} \frac{w(\ell(x) + 1) \cdot d(z, M_o(x))}{N(x) \cdot d(z, M_o(x))} = \frac{(k - \ell(x)) \cdot w(\ell(x) + 1)}{N(x)}.
$$

The expected distance moved by HARMONIC to serve the request $M_o(x)$ is

$$
D = \sum_{z \in S} \frac{d(z, M_o(x))}{N(x) \cdot d(z, M_o(x))} = \frac{k}{N(x)}.
$$

In order to guarantee that the expected decrease in potential after the online move will "cover" the expected distance D moved by HARMONIC, it must be that $D_1 \geq D + D_2$. This inequality is immediately simplified to

$$
i \cdot w(i) \geq (k - i) \cdot w(i + 1) + k.
$$

Taking $i = k$ in this inequality yields $w(k) \geq 1$. Since the competitive ratio is bounded below by an expression involving $w(1)$ and $w(2)$ with positive signs (see equation 11.7), we change inequalities to equalities and obtain the recurrence:

$$i \cdot w(i) = (k - i) \cdot w(i + 1) + k, \tag{11.8}$$

$$w(k) = 1. \tag{11.9}$$

A brief calculation yields the minimum possible value for $w(1) = 2^k - 1$. Then the competitive ratio (11.7) evaluates to $(k+1)(2^k - 1) - k$. Note that in order to complete the proof, we must verify that $w(i)$ is indeed decreasing (this assumption was used throughout the proof). We leave this as an exercise. ∎

Exercise 11.3 Complete the proof of Theorem 11.17. In particular, solve the recurrence (11.8) and prove that the weight function $w(\cdot)$ is strictly decreasing.

Since the proof of Theorem 11.17 is based on a computable potential function, we can use a constructive version of Corollary 7.5 to construct a deterministic k-server algorithm for an arbitrary metric space with competitive ratio $O(k^2 2^{2k})$. Using an improved bound for HARMONIC of $O(2^k \log k)$, one obtains the deterministic bound $O(2^{2k} \log^2 k)$.

11.6   The Resistive Approach

By using electrical networks to analyze random walks in weighted graphs, we not only derive an optimal cat algorithm in the cat and rat game but also suggest an approach that could lead to an efficient randomized k-server algorithm for any metric space. This development is rather substantial and somewhat technical. We limit ourselves here to a brief discussion of the approach, omitting all proofs.[11] This approach is based on the concept of a resistive network.

Let G be a symmetric positive weighted graph with node set V, and let $D = (d_{uv})$ be its cost matrix. G is said to be **resistive** if there exists an electrical network G^{RI} (called the **resistive inverse** of G) with node set V and branch resistances d'_{uv} such that for all $u \neq v$ the effective resistance R_{uv} between u and v is exactly d_{uv} (see Appendix C). We note without proof that when G is resistive, its resistive inverse can be computed.[12]

Not every metric space is resistive. In fact, there is a metric space $(\mathcal{M}, d)$ consisting of four points in two-dimensional Euclidean space (with d the Euclidean distance between points) such that $\mathcal{M}$ is not resistive; moreover, for every λ, there is a finite space contained in two-dimensional Euclidean space that cannot be λ-approximated by any resistive space. Examples of resistive metric spaces include the following: any 3-node metric space, any uniform metric space, the metric space induced by points on the Euclidean real line, or, more generally, the metric space induced by a weighted tree.[13] An example of a space that

---

[11] The reader is referred to Coppersmith, Doyle, Raghavan, and Snir [115], where these ideas are introduced and developed. Bollobás [78] and Biggs [67] provide excellent texts describing the relation between random walks and electrical networks. A detailed exposition of the resistive approach of Coppersmith et al. [115] can be found in Ponzio [277].

[12] See Coppersmith et al. [115] and Ponzio [277].

[13] All these examples can be viewed as tree closures, and Theorem 10.3 shows that the deterministic algorithm DC-TREE is k-competitive for the k-server problem on any such space. An example of a resistive space that is not a tree closure is also given in Coppersmith et al. [115].

is not resistive but can be 2-approximated by a resistive graph is any set of points on the circle (the metric space considered in Section 11.1).

To motivate the "resistive random walk" (and, later, the resistive k-server algorithm), we recall the k-server algorithm DC for the line. This deterministic algorithm and its analysis suggests the following memoryless randomized algorithm.

> **Algorithm RDC:** If the request r falls outside the convex hull of the servers, serve it with the nearest server. Otherwise, the request is in between two adjacent servers, for example, s_1 and s_2. Serve r using server s_i with probability
> $$\frac{1/d(s_i,r)}{(1/d(s_1,r))+(1/d(s_2,r))}.$$

Exercise 11.4 Using the same potential function as in Theorem 10.2, show that for all k, RDC is k-competitive (against an adaptive adversary) for the k-server problem on the line.

Consider algorithm RDC when applied to an N-point line L with the Euclidean distance d between points. Consider the graph L' with the same node set as L and distance matrix D' where $d'_{ij} = d_{ij}$ if the points i and j are adjacent in L, and $d'_{ij} = \infty$ otherwise. It is not difficult to see that $L' = L^{RI}$, the resistive inverse of L. That is, when we view L' as an electrical network with branch resistances d', the effective resistance between points i and j is simply the sum of the branch resistances between these points since these resistances are in series. Thus, algorithm RDC can be viewed as a harmonic walk, except that we do not use the matrix D as the weights but, instead, the matrix D', which forces us to serve a request by using an adjacent server.

We are led to the following resistive walk: if the graph G is resistive, then compute its resistive inverse G^{RI} having, for example, distance matrix D'. Now we define the random walk using the stochastic matrix P' where

$$p'_{uv} = \Pr[u \to v \mid \text{at } u] = \frac{1/d'_{uv}}{\sum_{w \in N(u)}(1/d'_{uw})}.$$

The following result provides an optimal strategy for any resistive graph.

Theorem 11.18 *Let G with cost matrix D be an N-node resistive graph. Let G^{RI} with distance matrix D' be its resistive inverse, and define P' as above. Then the stretch factor of G with respect to P' is exactly $N - 1$. As a consequence, the optimal competitive ratio for a cat and rat game on any resistive graph G is $N - 1$.*

In fact, even when G is not resistive, there is a way to obtain an optimal resistive walk.

Theorem 11.19 *Let (G, d) be any weighted graph with positive symmetric distance matrix D. There is a unique resistive matrix $\hat{G}$ with cost matrix $\hat{D}$ and resistive inverse $\hat{G}^{RI}$ with distance matrix D' that satisfies the following properties:*

- *For every $i \neq j$, d'_{ij} is positive (or infinite).*
- *For all $i \neq j$, $\hat{d}_{ij} \leq d_{ij}$.*
- *For all $i \neq j$, if $d'_{ij} \neq \infty$, then $\hat{d}_{ij} = d_{ij}$.*

The graph $\hat{G}^{RI}$ is called the **generalized resistive inverse** of G. Given that this generalized resistive inverse always exists (and is computable from G), we can obtain the following result.

Theorem 11.20 *Let (G, d) be an arbitrary graph with positive symmetric weight function d. Let P' be the stochastic matrix obtained by the Harmonic walk applied to the graph $\hat{G}^{RI}$. Then the cycle (respectively, the edge) stretch factor of G with respect to P' is $N - 1$ (respectively, at most $2N - 3$). Consequently, the optimal competitive ratio for a cat and rat game on any graph G is $N - 1$. Hence, for every $(N = k + 1)$-node k-server problem, there is an (optimal) k-competitive randomized algorithm and, assuming the lazy adversary conjecture, there is a $(2k - 1)$-competitive algorithm for the k-server problem on any metric space.*

For "resistive metric spaces," Theorem 11.18 can be extended to an optimal algorithm for the k-server problem as follows. The metric space $(\mathcal{M}, d)$ is said to be k-**resistive** if every $(k + 1)$-node subgraph G of $\mathcal{M}$ is resistive, and $\mathcal{M}$ is called a **resistive space** if it is k-resistive for every $k \geq 2$.

For a resistive metric space $(\mathcal{M}, d)$, the RHARMONIC k-server algorithm operates as follows.

> **Algorithm RHARMONIC (RESISTIVE-HARMONIC):** Let r be the current request and let $\mathcal{C} = \{s_1, s_2, \ldots, s_k\}$ be the configuration of the online servers. If $r \in \mathcal{C}$, then do nothing. Otherwise, compute the resistive inverse G^{RI} of the subgraph G defined by $\mathcal{C} \cup \{r\}$. For simplicity denote the nodes of G by $\{1, 2, \ldots, k + 1\}$ with r being node $k + 1$. Let P' be the stochastic matrix defined by the harmonic random walk on the graph G^{RI}. Serve r by server s_i with probability $p'_{i,k+1}$.

The concluding result (thus far) of this development is the following theorem.[14]

Theorem 11.21 *Let $(\mathcal{M}, d)$ be a resistive metric space. Then the RHARMONIC algorithm is k-competitive for the k-server problem on the metric space $(\mathcal{M}, d)$.*

In the same way, we obtain the following corollary.

Corollary 11.22 *If every $(k + 1)$-node subgraph of $(\mathcal{M}, d)$ can be λ-approximated by a resistive graph, then there is a $(\lambda \cdot k)$-competitive algorithm for the k-server problem on $(\mathcal{M}, d)$.*

Since the circle can be 2-approximated by a resistive graph, we have the following improvement of Theorem 11.1.

Corollary 11.23 *There is a randomized $2k$-competitive algorithm against an adaptive adversary for the circle metric space. (That is, the $2k$ upper bound for the circle against an oblivious adversary is now achieved by a memoryless algorithm against an adaptive adversary.)*

---

[14] The proof in Coppersmith et al. [115] uses the same potential function as in Theorem 10.2. See also Exercise 11.4. We also note that Coppersmith et al. present an example of a 3-server problem on a (nonresistive) 5-node metric space for which RHARMONIC is not 3-competitive.

11.7 Historical Notes and Open Questions

Oblivious Adversaries. Algorithm CIRC and its analysis are from Karp [217]. With this result began the study of probabilistic approximations of metric spaces (in particular, by tree metrics) as developed in the work of Alon, Karp, Peleg, and West [12] and Bartal [43]. (See the discussion in the Historical Notes of Chapter 9.) Since there is a deterministic k-competitive algorithm for every tree metric space, it follows that for every metric space there is a $O(k \cdot \log^2 N)$-competitive randomized k-server algorithm against an oblivious adversary. This bound is, of course, dependent on N and not as good as the deterministic $2k - 1$ of Koutsoupias and Papadimitriou [232]; however, it does show how sublinear bounds (in k) for the k-server problem on tree metrics could be used to construct algorithms with sublinear competitive ratio for any space with N subexponential in k. Algorithm CIRC2 is an adaptation of a line algorithm by Blum, Raghavan, and Schieber [76]. For this space there is an $\Omega\left(\frac{\log k}{\log \log k}\right)$ lower bound presented in Blum, Karloff, Rabani, and Saks [75]. In addition to the uniform space (and spaces well approximated by the uniform space), there are a few special metric spaces (all with $N = k + 1$ points) where sublinear competitive ratios are obtained. For example, Blum, Furst, and Tomkins [72] obtain an $O(\log^2 k)$-competitive algorithm for the $N = k+1$ weighted paging problem (i.e., star tree metric). For this space they also obtain an $\Omega(\log k)$ lower bound, and we might conjecture (based on the uniform case, which appears to be the easiest metric space) that there is an $\Omega(\log k)$ lower bound for every metric space. The best lower bound $\Omega\left(\sqrt{\log k / \log \log k}\right)$ presently known for an arbitrary metric space is from Blum et al. [75]. The best general upper bound is provided by the $O\left(\frac{\log^6 N}{\log \log N}\right)$-competitive result for the MTS problem, from which the analogous bound follows for all k-server problems on an $N = (k + c)$-point metric space, for any constant c. The fact that not every metric space allows for an H_k-competitive randomized algorithm is demonstrated by Karlin, Manasse, McGeoch, and Owicki [210].

Adaptive Adversaries. The $\frac{k}{k-h+1}$ lower bound for any metric space is from Raghavan and Snir [284], based on the analogous lower bound for deterministic algorithms in Manasse, McGeoch, and Sleator [256]. Raghavan and Snir introduce the concept of bounded memory and memoryless k-server algorithms as well as stating the lazy adversary conjecture. They also define the HARMONIC algorithm, obtain the $\frac{k(k+1)}{2}$ lower bound for HARMONIC (noting that this bound also holds for an oblivious adversary), and show that HARMONIC is k-competitive for the weighted paging problem. The $k(k + 1)$ upper bound for the case of $N = k + 1$ and lazy adversaries is also from Raghavan and Snir, and the improvement to the optimal $\frac{k(k+1)}{2}$ was independently observed by Raghavan [281] and Bartal [40]. The cat and rat game was introduced by Coppersmith, Doyle, Raghavan, and Snir [115], who establish the optimal bound of k for every symmetric distance cat and rat game. They also provide the relation of this game to memoryless k-server algorithms (in particular, proving Corollary 11.10) and to arbitrary k-server algorithms under the lazy adversary conjecture. The $O(k2^k)$ upper bound for HARMONIC is originally from Grove [179]. An improved $O(2^k \log k)$ upper bound was obtained independently by Bartal and Grove and appears in [47]. Our presentation of the $(k + 1)(2^k - 1) - k$ bound is also from Bartal and Grove [47].

The Resistive Approach. The resistive approach is from Coppersmith et al. [115], and all the results in Section 11.6 are obtained in this paper. Specifically, they show that under the lazy adversary conjecture, there is a k-competitive randomized algorithm for every metric space. An excellent exposition of this development can be found in Ponzio [277]. Turpin [329] presents a more intuitive, yet still rigorous, explanation for the case $k = 2$.

Credit for Exercises. Exercise 11.1 is from Blum, Raghavan, and Schieber [76]. Exercise 11.2 is from Raghavan and Snir [284]. Exercise 11.3 is from Bartal and Grove [47]. Exercise 11.4 is from Coppersmith et al. [115].

11.7.1   Open Questions

11.1 (*Value = 15/T5*) Does there exist a randomized k-server algorithm for arbitrary or particular metric spaces (e.g., the line or the circle) that achieves a polylogarithmic (in k-) competitive ratio?

One special case of interest is the weighted paging problem (itself a special case of metric spaces induced by weighted trees).

11.2 (*Value = 14/T4*) Determine the optimal competitive ratio for randomized algorithms against an oblivious adversary for the weighted paging problem.

The example of $k = 2$ servers and an isosceles triangle metric space (see [210]) provides a case in which the competitive ratio $\frac{e}{e-1}$ is provably different from $H_2 = 1.5$. Hence, in contrast to the deterministic k-server conjecture, there cannot be a single function that is the randomized competitive ratio for all metric spaces. However, can there be a better space than the uniform space?

11.3 (*Value = 14/T4*) Does there exist a metric space and a k such that the randomized competitive ratio against an oblivious adversary is less than H_k?

Although HARMONIC cannot be optimal, the following question continues to be of considerable interest.

11.4 (*Value = 14/T5*) Determine the competitive ratio of HARMONIC (against an adaptive adversary) or, at least, improve on the $O(2^k \log k)$ bound.

Although algorithm RHARMONIC has competitive ratio k is any resistive space, the following question is still open.

11.5 (*Value = 14/T5*) Determine the competitive ratio for RHARMONIC for an arbitrary metric space. In particular, does RHARMONIC have a competitive ratio (against an adaptive adversary) that is bounded by a function of k (i.e., independent of the size of the metric space)? If so, is the competitive ratio of RHARMONIC at least as good as HARMONIC for every metric space?

11.6 (*Value = 14/T4*) Prove or disprove the lazy adversary conjecture.

11.7 (*Value = 14/T4*) Can the lower bound of Corollary 11.10 be extended to nonlazy algorithms? Note that in this case there is no immediate way to associate a random walk on the metric space with the online algorithm.

11.8 (*Value = 14/T5*) Consider an arbitrary or particular k-server problem. Let ALG be a (lazy or nonlazy) bounded memory behavioral randomized algorithm with s memory states. Derive a lower bound (as a function of k and s) on the competitive ratio for such an algorithm.

CHAPTER 12

Load Balancing

The term "load balancing" has different (but related) meanings in different research communities. One of the most common meanings comes from the area of parallel processing, where processes are assigned and periodically reassigned to processors in order to balance the load over all processors. We also use the term "load balancing" to mean the assignment of jobs to machines or processors (in order to balance load in some sense) but, in our case, disallowing any later reassignment.

12.1 Defining the Problem

In the **machine assignment** problem, there is a finite set of (perhaps different) machines. In the online version of this problem, a sequence of jobs is arriving where each job is specified by its processing cost, called the **load**. Each job must be either refused or assigned to one of the machines upon arrival. If the machines are not identical, then each job may have different loads depending on the machine to which the job is assigned. In this chapter, we primarily consider the **load balancing** problem in which jobs cannot be refused and one is trying to minimize the maximum load on any machine. Moreover, we emphasize nonidentical machine models for which the most natural greedy algorithms may be far from optimal. In Section 12.5 we also briefly consider a different machine assignment optimization problem, namely, the bin packing problem. For both load balancing on identical machines and the bin packing problem, greedy algorithms are quite reasonable; however, their nonoptimality has inspired an extensive body of research.

Classical problems in scheduling such as load balancing and bin packing provide perhaps the earliest implicit and explicit uses of competitive analysis for online algorithms. For scheduling and other combinatorial optimization problems, we can view online algorithms as a particular class of approximation algorithms; thus, the competitive ratio naturally becomes the approximation ratio for such algorithms. We note that it is NP-hard to compute the optimal solution for any of the problems considered in this chapter. It is likely that interest in such problems will be renewed as a result of active research in the areas of approximation algorithms and competitive analysis.

There are so many variants of scheduling problems that it is beyond the scope of this text to attempt a comprehensive survey of online scheduling problems.[1] It is illustrative,

---

[1] For a recent survey, see Sgall [308].

however, to define some prototypical problems. Section 12.3 shows how the load balancing problem is naturally related to edge congestion minimization in **virtual circuit routing**. In virtual circuit routing, a call arrives with a specified bandwidth requirement, and this call must be routed from its origin to its destination in a network where each of the links (i.e., edges) has limited capacity. The call is routed on a dedicated path in the network, thereby consuming the required bandwidth on each edge of the path (i.e., virtually obtaining a dedicated path in the network). For congestion minimization, the goal is to minimize the load on any edge relative to the edge capacity. It is possible to view some simple machine assignment problems as a special case of routing in which the network consists of two nodes connected by an edge for each possible machine. Conversely, we can view virtual circuit routing as a generalized machine assignment problem, as presented in Section 12.3.

12.1.1   Load Balancing Versus Call Admission

For either machine assignment or virtual circuit routing, we can consider many types of optimizations. In the case of load balancing or edge congestion minimization, jobs are not refused and one is trying to minimize the maximum load on any machine (respectively, the "relative load" or "congestion" on any edge). If this cost is identified with time, then machine assignment load balancing is perhaps the most classical optimization problem; it is the job scheduling problem for which one wants to optimize the **makespan**, defined as the completion time for all jobs.[2] In the terminology of offline approximation algorithms, load balancing (similar to bin packing, as discussed in Section 12.5, and path coloring, as discussed in Section 13.7) is a "covering problem" in which all requests must be covered and one wants to minimize the cost (e.g., the number of bins for bin packing, and the maximum load on any processor for load balancing) in doing so. It is perhaps easier to motivate this optimization problem in the machine assignment context than in the circuit routing context. We can think of any machine as being able to serve unlimited demand by incurring degradation of service. In the circuit routing problem, what does it mean to exceed the capacity of an edge? We can envisage a situation in which someone is designing a network and trying to estimate how much more capacity is needed (equivalently, what fraction of the bandwidth request can be met), or a situation in which the total bandwidth required does not exceed the capacities, so that the excess capacity can be used for other routing modes.

Another important optimization problem is called the **call admission/throughput** problem. Here each job or call can be rejected, and the goal is to maximize the number of (or profit accrued from) jobs that are scheduled or calls that are routed. In the terminology of offline approximation algorithms, call admission is a "packing problem" in which, informally, one tries to maximize the profit (e.g., throughput) obtained from packing requests into a constrained environment. The knapsack problem is perhaps the most basic and well-known packing problem. Covering and packing problems can be formulated as particular

---

[2] We should also note that in the classical job scheduling problem, even if all jobs arrive at once, one usually does not need to schedule any jobs until some processor is available (i.e., has completed its latest job). For our interest in online problems, we insist that a job must be scheduled upon arrival. For the classical offline makespan problem, there may or may not be precedence constraints among the jobs. In the online setting, the precedence is already inherent in the order in which jobs arrive, since we assume that a job must be scheduled immediately upon arrival.

classes of integer or linear programming.[3] Call admission for virtual circuit routing is studied in Chapter 13.

12.1.2 Load Balancing Variations

There are many variants for the load balancing problem. Here are some of the issues and conditions that are relevant. First, we can consider either identical machines or different varieties of nonidentical machines. Second, we can consider jobs that are either permanent (equivalently, all requests are for the same finite time slot) or of limited duration; in the latter case, we must distinguish between durations that are known initially and those that are unknown. Note that, in general, any competitive algorithm for the limited known duration case must also imply a competitive algorithm for the permanent case, since in the former case the algorithm must be able to work when all jobs arrive (almost) simultaneously and have unit duration. Conversely, it is generally the case that a competitive algorithm for the permanent job case can be used to derive a competitive bound for the limited but known duration case. In some cases, we see bounds for the limited but known duration case that depend on T, the maximum duration, or the ratio of the maximum to the minimum duration. Another issue is whether or not (limited) reassignment is allowed and at what cost. Throughout this text, we assume that once scheduled, jobs cannot be rescheduled. Finally, there is always the distinction between deterministic and randomized algorithms.

12.1.3 Different Machine Models

Suppose that we have N machines. In order to distinguish the ways in which machines can vary, we can describe the jth job r_j as an N-tuple $r_j = \langle r_j(1), \ldots, r_j(N) \rangle$ where $r_j(i)$ is a positive real (or infinite) value denoting the additional load incurred if r_j is placed on processor i. For **identical machines**, for all i, $r_j(i)$ is some single value v_j. For **related machines**, there are constants $\alpha_1, \ldots, \alpha_N$ such that for every j and for all i, $r_j(i) = \frac{v_j}{\alpha_i}$; that is, the α_i can be thought of as indicating the speed or power of machine i. For **unrelated machines**, the load vectors r_j are arbitrary. A special case of the unrelated machines model is that of the **restricted (subset of) machines model** in which for every j there is a v_j such that $r_j(i)$ is in $\{v_j, \infty\}$ for all i; that is, every job can be run on only a subset of the machines, and for every machine in that subset the cost is the same.

12.1.4 Scalable Problems

We note that load balancing problems are **scalable** problems in the following sense: let σ' be a scaled version of input sequence σ where every job request r_j in the input sequence σ is multiplied by some fixed value s (i.e., $r_j = \langle r_j(1), \ldots, r_j(N) \rangle$ becomes $r'_j = \langle s \cdot r_j(1), \ldots, s \cdot r_j(N) \rangle$); then, $\text{OPT}(\sigma) = s \cdot \text{OPT}(\sigma')$.[4] For another scalable problem, see the discussion of one-way currency trading in Chapter 14. We note that for scalable problems, there is no essential difference between competitiveness and strict competitiveness. To see

---

[3] See Plotkin, Shmoys, and Tardos [276].

[4] Indeed, OPT can use the same assignment of jobs for σ' as it does for σ.

Table 12.1: Summary of known bounds for the online competitive ratio for machine load balancing of permanent jobs.

	Deterministic	Randomized
Identical	$1.852 \le \rho \ (N \ge 80)$	$\frac{e}{e-1} \le \rho$ (N sufficiently large)
	$\rho \le 1.923$	$\rho = \frac{4}{3}$ for $N = 2$
	$\rho \le 2 - \frac{1}{N}$ (optimal for $N = 2, 3$)	For $N > 2$, no better upper bound than for deterministic algorithms
Related	$2.25 \le \rho \le 5.828$	$1.8 \le \rho \le 4.311$
Restricted	$\log(N + 1) \le \rho \le \log N + 1$	$\ln N \le \rho$
		No better upper bound than for deterministic algorithms
Unrelated	$\rho = \Theta(\log N)$	$\rho = \Theta(\log N)$

Note: ρ is the deterministic or randomized competitive ratio for the indicated problem, and N denotes the number of machines.

this, let ALG be an online algorithm satisfying $\mathrm{ALG}(\sigma) \le c \cdot \mathrm{OPT}(\sigma) + \alpha$ for all σ. Then, for any ε, there is an online algorithm $\mathrm{ALG}'(\sigma)$ satisfying $\mathrm{ALG}'(\sigma) \le c \cdot \mathrm{OPT}(\sigma) + \varepsilon$ for all σ. We simply let ALG$'$ on input σ simulate ALG on a suitably scaled input σ' where the scaling factor s is sufficiently large. Then, clearly, $s \cdot \mathrm{ALG}'(\sigma) = \mathrm{ALG}(\sigma') \le c \cdot \mathrm{OPT}(\sigma') + \alpha = cs \cdot \mathrm{OPT}(\sigma) + \alpha$, so that

$$\mathrm{ALG}'(\sigma) \le c \cdot \mathrm{OPT}(\sigma) + \frac{\alpha}{s}.$$

12.2   Online Algorithms for Load Balancing of Permanent Jobs

We begin with the problem of online job scheduling on identical machines; that is, in the terminology of the machine assignment load balancing problem we assign (upon arrival) permanent jobs to identical machines, with each job having a certain fixed load. Sections 12.2.2 and 12.3 then show how the problem becomes more complicated as one allows nonidentical machines. This difference becomes much more pronounced when we consider limited duration jobs in Section 12.4. Table 12.1 (respectively, Table 12.2) summarizes known results for load balancing of permanent (respectively, limited duration) jobs.

12.2.1   Identical Machines

We consider the following natural greedy algorithm for the load balancing problem:

Algorithm GREEDY: Assign each incoming job r_j to the machine that, after assigning r_j, will have the least load (breaking ties arbitrarily).[5]

---

[5] For identical machines, it is equivalent to assign the job to the machine that has the least load *before* assigning the current job. This alternative formulation seems less natural as a greedy algorithm for the cases of related or unrelated machines that will follow.

Table 12.2: Summary of bounds for the deterministic competitive ratio for machine load balancing of jobs having limited duration.

	Unknown duration	Known duration (no better lower bounds than for permanent jobs)
Identical	$\rho = 2 - \frac{1}{N}$	No better upper bound than for unknown duration
Related	$3 \leq \rho \leq 20$	No better upper bound than for unknown duration
Restricted	$\rho = \Theta(\sqrt{N})$	$\rho = O(\log NT)$
Unrelated	$\rho \leq N$ No better lower bound than for restricted machines	$\rho = O(\log NT)$

Note: The $\Omega(\sqrt{N})$ lower bounds for the case of unknown durations in the restricted machines model hold for randomized algorithms.

Graham [175] proved the following classical result, which we state in the language of competitive analysis:

Theorem 12.1 *The competitive ratio of algorithm* GREEDY *for assigning jobs on N identical machines is exactly* $2 - \frac{1}{N}$.

PROOF. For the GREEDY lower bound, consider a sequence of $N(N-1)$ jobs, each with load 1 followed by a single job with load N. The GREEDY algorithm incurs a maximum load of $2N - 1$, while an offline algorithm can achieve a maximum load of N by placing the last job (having load N) on some machine and smoothing out all the other requests equally on the $N - 1$ remaining machines.

For the upper bound, let σ be an arbitrary input sequence. Without loss of generality, assume that machine 1 incurs the maximum load in GREEDY(σ), and that the last item placed on this machine has load w and is placed on top of an existing load of s on machine 1. Clearly, GREEDY(σ) is exactly $w + s$. The load on every machine must be at least s, since at the time the last job is placed on machine 1, every machine load must be at least as great as that on machine 1. Hence the total load must be at least $w + Ns$. Thus, OPT(σ) must be at least $\frac{w+Ns}{N}$ and, obviously, also at least w. Therefore,

$$\text{GREEDY}(\sigma) = w + s \leq w + \text{OPT}(\sigma) - \frac{w}{N}$$

$$= \text{OPT}(\sigma) + \left(1 - \frac{1}{N}\right) \cdot w$$

$$\leq \text{OPT}(\sigma) + \left(1 - \frac{1}{N}\right) \cdot \text{OPT}(\sigma)$$

$$= \left(2 - \frac{1}{N}\right) \cdot \text{OPT}(\sigma).$$

Exercise 12.1 Show that the upper bound still holds even if the jobs have (known or unknown) limited duration. Hint: Consider the above inequalities at the time that the worst competitive ratio is achieved by the adversary.

In contrast to Exercise 12.1, the analysis or the results for permanent jobs cannot usually be extended to that of limited duration jobs (especially in the unknown duration case).

The greedy algorithm can be shown to be optimal for $N = 2$ and 3. As N grows, the competitive ratio for the greedy algorithm approaches 2. There are deterministic algorithms whose competitive ratio is bounded below 2 for all N. The best bound is presently 1.923. For randomized algorithms, the optimal bound for $N = 2$ is $\frac{4}{3}$, showing that (at least in one case) randomization can help.

12.2.2   The Restricted Machines Model

For the restricted machines model (and permanent jobs), a greedy algorithm (to which we again refer as GREEDY) that schedules a job on an allowable processor having the least load is not only asymptotically optimal but also almost exactly optimal: GREEDY achieves a competitive ratio of $\lceil \log_2 N \rceil + 1$, whereas the lower bound (even when each job has unit load on all its allowable machines) for any deterministic online algorithm is $\lceil \log_2(N+1) \rceil$. It is also known that for the case of unit load jobs, a randomized greedy algorithm (against an oblivious adversary) improves this ratio by a constant factor. The randomized greedy algorithm initially chooses a random ordering of the machines and then breaks ties among equally loaded machines according to this ordering. For unit load jobs, the upper bound for the randomized greedy algorithm (against an oblivious adversary) is $\ln N + 1$, and there is an almost matching lower bound of $\ln N$. However, unlike the case for identical machines, for jobs with limited but unknown duration, algorithm GREEDY is no longer asymptotically optimal; furthermore, all online algorithms (deterministic or randomized) have a rather poor competitive ratio (see Section 12.4).

Theorem 12.2 *For the assignment of permanent jobs in the restricted machines model,* GREEDY *achieves a competitive ratio of* $\lceil \log_2 N \rceil + 1$.

PROOF. Let $\sigma' = r_1, \ldots, r_n$ and let job r_k have load w_k on any of its allowable machines. We can think of GREEDY's assignment to each machine as partitioned into layers, each layer having assigned exactly load OPT(σ) with the possible exception of the last layer. In order to do so, some jobs r_k are split over two adjacent layers. Clearly,

$$\text{OPT}(\sigma) \geq \sum_{1 \leq k \leq n} \frac{w_k}{N}.$$

Let W_i denote the total load of jobs assigned by GREEDY in layer i (with the understanding that the load of some jobs is split between two layers), and set

$$W = \sum_{1 \leq i \leq N} W_i = \sum_{1 \leq k \leq n} w_k.$$

Let $R_i = W - \sum_{1 \leq l \leq i} W_l$ be the total load that has not yet been assigned by GREEDY within the first i layers. The crux of the proof is to show that $W_i \geq R_i$ for each layer i;

that is, GREEDY assigns more load in layer i than it leaves over. From this, it easily follows that $R_i \leq R_{i-1} - R_i$; that is, $R_i \leq \frac{R_{i-1}}{2}$. Then

$$R_{\lceil \log N \rceil} \leq \frac{R_0}{N} = \frac{W}{N} \leq \text{OPT}(\sigma).$$

Thus, any load remaining after level $\lceil \log N \rceil$ will be assigned in level $\lceil \log N \rceil + 1$, which yields the desired result: $\text{GREEDY}(\sigma) \leq (\lceil \log N \rceil + 1) \cdot \text{OPT}(\sigma)$.

It remains to prove $W_i \geq R_i$ for each layer i. Let $A_i = \{j |$ machine j is an allowable machine for some job r_k that has not been completed by level i; that is, r_k contributes to $R_i\}$. Let N_i denote the cardinality of A_i. Clearly, $R_i \leq N_i \cdot \text{OPT}(\sigma)$. Let $AFULL \subset A_{i-1}$ be those machines in A_{i-1} that are full in layer i; that is, GREEDY assigns load $\text{OPT}(\sigma)$ to each $j \in AFULL$. Thus, $W_i \geq |AFULL| \cdot \text{OPT}(\sigma)$. The proof is completed by observing that $N_i \leq |AFULL|$. This observation follows from the definition of the GREEDY algorithm. If a non-full machine j in A_{i-1} were an allowable machine for some job r_k being assigned after layer i, then machine j would have a load less than any machine in A_i and hence would be assigned job r_k; that is, either machine j would become full or r_k would not contribute to R_i. Summarizing, we have

$$R_i \leq |AFULL| \cdot \text{OPT}(\sigma)$$

$$\leq N_i \cdot \text{OPT}(\sigma)$$

$$\leq W_i.$$

$\blacksquare$

Theorem 12.3 *Consider the restricted machines model and assume that every job has unit load on any of its allowable machines;[6] that is, the load vector $\langle r_j(1), \ldots, r_j(N) \rangle$ is in $\{1, \infty\}^N$. The competitive ratio of any online algorithm for this problem is at least $\lceil \log(N+1) \rceil$.*

PROOF. Under the given assumption, the problem can be viewed as an online "many-to-one" bipartite graph assignment problem in which one set of nodes U represents the input jobs and the other set V represents a fixed set of N machines. A job or node $u \in U$ is input by giving its adjacent edges (i.e., its allowable machines). The algorithm must assign each $u \in U$ to one $v \in V$; the goal is to minimize the maximum load, that is, to minimize the maximum number of nodes $u \in U$ assigned to any $v \in V$.

Let ALG be any online algorithm. We input N jobs so that the resulting graph has a perfect matching and OPT can thus achieve a maximum load of 1; however, ALG will have a maximum load of $\lceil \log_2(N+1) \rceil$. Thus we force a competitive ratio of $\lceil \log_2(N+1) \rceil$.

For simplicity, we assume that $N = 2^k$ for some integer k. We input the jobs in $k+1$ "batches." For $1 \leq i < k$, the ith batch U_i consists of $\frac{N}{2^i}$ jobs. U_k and U_{k+1} each consist of one job. The neighborhood set for each $u \in U_i$ is a distinct pair of nodes in V_i, with $|V_i| = \frac{N}{2^{i-1}}$ and $V_{i+1} \subseteq V_i$ for $1 \leq i \leq k+1$. The adversary determines V_{i+1} by choosing those nodes in V_i that ALG used in assigning batch i. For example, if a job $u \in U_i$ has neighbors $\{v', v''\}$ and if ALG assigns u to v', then $v' \in V_{i+1}$; otherwise, $v'' \in V_{i+1}$. It follows by induction that just before the ith batch is input, the load on every node in V_i

---

[6] The unit load assumption strengthens the lower bound.

is precisely $i - 1$. If $V_{k+1} = \{v\}$, then v has load $k + 1$ after assignment of the last job comprising U_{k+1}. However, since $|V_i - V_{i+1}| = \frac{N}{2^i} = |V_i|$, U_i can be perfectly matched to $V_i - V_{i+1}$, and the resulting final graph has a perfect matching.   ■

Remark 12.1 Note that in the case of identical machines, if all jobs have load ≤ 1, then the "greedy" competitive ratio can be stated as $\text{GREEDY}(\sigma) \leq 1 \cdot \text{OPT}(\sigma) + 1$. On the other hand, for the restricted machines model it is not the case that $\text{GREEDY}(\sigma) \leq 1 \cdot \text{OPT}(\sigma) + \log N$. In order to obtain a multiplicative $\frac{\log N}{2}$ lower bound for the restricted machines case even when all jobs have load at most 1, the above argument can be modified so that batch i is repeated M times for M arbitrarily large.

12.2.3   The Related Machines Case

The fact that a simple greedy algorithm performs so well in the case of identical and restricted machines does not extend to the other machine assignment models. Consider the following exercise.

Exercise 12.2 For the related machines model, show that GREEDY is $\Theta(\log N)$-competitive.

In contrast to Exercise 12.2, we present an $O(1)$-competitive algorithm for the related machines case. For both the related and unrelated machines cases, we first show how to assign jobs under the assumption that there is a known bound on the cost (i.e., maximum load) of an optimal algorithm OPT. This assumption is then removed in Theorem 12.5.

Suppose $\text{OPT}(\sigma) \leq \Lambda$. Then the following algorithm, called SLOWFIT_Λ, assigns jobs to the slowest machine possible in order to maintain maximum load $\leq 2\Lambda$ on every (related) machine.

> **Algorithm** SLOWFIT_Λ: Without loss of generality, assume the machines $\{M_i\}$ are ordered so that M_1 is the slowest; thus, for all requests r_j, $r_j(1) \geq r_j(2) \geq \cdots \geq r_j(N)$. Let $l_j(i)$ denote the present load on machine i for the assignment of $r_1, \ldots, r_j$ by SLOWFIT_Λ. Upon input request r_{j+1}, assign this job to machine i where
>
> $$i = \arg\min_k \{l_j(k) + r_{j+1}(k) \leq 2\Lambda\}. \tag{12.1}$$

If there is no such machine, the algorithm outputs "failure," indicating that $\text{OPT}(\sigma)$ exceeds Λ.

Theorem 12.4 *Let σ be any input sequence. Assume that $\text{OPT}(\sigma) \leq \Lambda$. Then SLOWFIT_Λ does not fail and $\text{SLOWFIT}_\Lambda(\sigma) \leq 2\Lambda$.*

PROOF. First, note that if SLOWFIT_Λ does not fail then, clearly, $\text{SLOWFIT}_\Lambda(\sigma) \leq 2\Lambda$ (see equation 12.1). The proof is by contradiction. We assume $\text{OPT}(\sigma) \leq \Lambda$ but that $\text{SLOWFIT}_\Lambda(\sigma)$ fails on the last input r_n of σ. Let f be the fastest machine (i.e., the largest index by our ordering of machines) such that $l_{n-1}(f) \leq \text{OPT}(\sigma)$. (We will show that f must exist.) We have $f < N$ since otherwise $l_{n-1}(N) + r_n(N) \leq \text{OPT}(\sigma) + \text{OPT}(\sigma) \leq 2\Lambda$ and r_n could have been assigned to (the fastest) machine N. Let $\Gamma = \{i \mid i > f\}$ be the set of "overloaded" machines. Since $f < n$, $\Gamma \neq \emptyset$. Letting S_i (respectively, S_i^*) denote the set of jobs assigned to machine i by SLOWFIT$_\Lambda$ (respectively, OPT), we have

$$\sum_{i\in\Gamma, s\in S_i} v_s = \sum_{i\in\Gamma, s\in S_i} \frac{v_s}{r_s(i)} \cdot r_s(i)$$

$$= \sum_{i\in\Gamma} \alpha_i \sum_{s\in S_i} r_s(i),$$

recalling that for related machines $r_s(i) = \frac{v_s}{\alpha_i}$;

$$> \sum_{i\in\Gamma} \alpha_i \text{OPT}(\sigma), \tag{12.2}$$

by definition of Γ as the set of overloaded machines;

$$\geq \sum_{i\in\Gamma} \alpha_i \sum_{s\in S_i^*} r_s(i)$$

$$= \sum_{i\in\Gamma, s\in S_i^*} \frac{v_s}{r_s(i)} \cdot r_s(i)$$

$$= \sum_{i\in\Gamma, s\in S_i^*} v_s. \tag{12.3}$$

Hence, since inequality (12.3) is a proper inequality, $\Gamma \neq \{1, 2, \ldots, N\}$ and $f \geq 1$ exists. Moreover, this proper inequality implies that there exists a job r_s ($s < n$) that is assigned to some $i \in \Gamma$ by SLOWFIT$_\Lambda$ but assigned by OPT to a slower machine $i' \notin \Gamma$ with $i' \leq f$. This implies $r_s(f) \leq r_s(i') \leq \text{OPT}(\sigma) \leq \Lambda$. Furthermore, since $f \notin \Gamma$ and r_s occurred before r_n, $l_{s-1}(f) \leq l_{n-1}(f) \leq \text{OPT}(\sigma) \leq \Lambda$. However, then $l_{s-1}(f) + r_s(f) \leq 2\Lambda$, and SLOWFIT$_\Lambda$ should have assigned r_s to machine f (or a slower machine) instead of the faster machine $i \in \Gamma$. ∎

Exercise 12.3 Show why this proof does not extend to the case of limited duration jobs when we consider the inequality (12.3) at the time t that SLOWFIT$_\Lambda$ fails.

We now show how to remove the assumption that a "good" bound Λ is known a priori. Instead, we continuously update Λ (by doubling) whenever it is detected that $\text{OPT}(\sigma) > \Lambda$. Although testing whether or not $\text{OPT}(\sigma) > \Lambda$ can be exactly (or approximately) computed, it is more efficient simply to determine whether the online algorithm SLOWFIT$_\Lambda$ (σ) exceeds 2Λ, which is sufficient (but not necessary) to determine that $\text{OPT}(\sigma) > \Lambda$. This "doubling trick" is applicable to many problems; however, we state only the following result for load balancing.

Theorem 12.5 *Let Π be any load balancing problem. Let* ALG$_\Lambda$ *be a parameterized online algorithm for Π satisfying* $\text{OPT}(\sigma) \leq \Lambda \Rightarrow \text{ALG}_\Lambda(\sigma) \leq c \cdot \Lambda$ *(e.g., $c = 2$ for* SLOWFIT$_\Lambda$ *when applied to related machines). Then there is an algorithm* ALG *such that for all σ,* $\text{ALG}(\sigma) \leq 4c \cdot \text{OPT}(\sigma)$ *(i.e.,* ALG *is strictly $4c$-competitive).*

PROOF. The algorithm ALG executes in stages, each stage corresponding to the most recent estimate of Λ. Initially (stage 0), Λ is set to $\Lambda_0 = $ OPT's cost for the first request. In stage k, Λ is set to $2^k \Lambda_0$.

Suppose an input r arrives while the algorithm ALG is in stage j, and let σ_j denote the input subsequence that has thus far been processed while the algorithm is in stage j. ALG attempts to process r using algorithm ALG_Λ, ignoring the assignment of inputs occurring in all previous stages. We say that ALG_Λ "succeeds in assigning r" if $\text{ALG}_\Lambda(\sigma_j r) \leq c \cdot \Lambda$. If ALG_Λ succeeds in assigning r, then ALG uses this assignment. If ALG_Λ fails in assigning r, then stage j terminates and stage $j + 1$ begins, with Λ being increased to $2^{j+1}\Lambda_0$.

We now argue that $\text{ALG}(\sigma) \leq 4c \cdot \text{OPT}(\sigma)$ for any input sequence σ. Suppose ALG terminates in stage h. If $h = 0$, then clearly $\text{ALG}(\sigma) \leq c \cdot \text{OPT}(\sigma)$, since $\Lambda_0 = $ OPT's cost for the first request and ALG_{Λ_0} does not fail on σ. Otherwise, let $h > 0$, and now let σ_j denote the entire input subsequence that was processed while ALG was in stage j. Since stage $h - 1$ must have failed on $\sigma_{h-1}r$ (where r is the first request of stage h), and given the assumption on ALG_Λ when $\Lambda = 2^{h-1}\Lambda_0$, we have $\text{OPT}(\sigma) \geq \text{OPT}(\sigma_{h-1}r) > 2^{h-1}\Lambda_0$. Finally, we easily bound

$$\text{ALG}(\sigma) = \sum_{j=0}^{h} \text{ALG}(\sigma_j) \leq \sum_{j=0}^{h} c \cdot 2^j \Lambda_0 = c(2^{h+1} - 1)\Lambda_0.$$

∎

Corollary 12.6 *Let* SLOWFIT *be the algorithm resulting from* SLOWFIT_Λ *using Theorem 12.5. Then,* SLOWFIT *is 8-competitive for the related machines model.*

12.3 Formulating the Machine Assignment Problem as a Generalized Virtual Circuit Routing Problem

First, we note that the GREEDY algorithm performs quite poorly in the unrelated machines case.

Exercise 12.4 For the unrelated machines model, show that GREEDY (as defined in Section 12.2.1) is exactly N-competitive.

In order to develop an asymptotically optimal algorithm for the case of load balancing on unrelated machines, we now introduce the idea of an exponential weighting function on the "relativized" load assigned to a given machine thus far.

Recall that the jth job is denoted by a vector of loads $\langle r_j(1), \ldots, r_j(N) \rangle$. Consider that a greedy algorithm would assign each job in order to minimize the maximum load on any machine. Instead, we weight the present load relative to an estimate Λ on the maximum load used by the offline algorithm and then assign jobs in order to minimize the increase in the weighted load. Using Theorem 12.5 again, the estimate for Λ can be dynamically updated (by doubling) whenever it becomes known to the algorithm that the present estimate is insufficient.

The algorithm and analysis for unrelated machine load balancing can be extended to the virtual circuit routing problem. Consider load balancing in the context of virtual circuit routing. We have an edge labeled multigraph $G = (V, E, u)$ where $u : E \to \mathbb{R}^+$ is the capacity bound of an edge; that is, $u(e)$ denotes the capacity of an edge $e \in E$. A **call** $r_j = (s_j, t_j, b_j)$ is a request to route a call using bandwidth b_j on some path from s_j to t_j. In the load balancing (i.e., congestion minimization) problem, we must route all calls and therefore risk exceeding the "capacity" of an edge. Our goal is to minimize the maximum relative congestion (i.e., relative to edge capacity) whether or not the capacity is exceeded. Namely, let $b'_j : E \to \mathbb{R}$ be defined as

$$b'_j(e) = \frac{b_j}{u(e)}.$$

Routing a call on a path P_j increases the relativized load on edge e by $b'_j(e)$. For any routing algorithm ALG and any call request sequence $\sigma = r_1, r_2, \dots, r_n$, we can define

$$L_j(e) = \sum_{\substack{i \leq j \\ P_i : e \in P_i}} b'_i(e)$$

as the relativized load on edge e incurred by algorithm ALG after routing $r_1, \dots, r_j$ on paths $P_1, \dots, P_j$. Our competitive analysis goal is to construct an online algorithm ALG that attempts to minimize $\max_{\sigma} lo \max_e \frac{L_n(e)}{\text{OPT}(\sigma)}$, where $n = |\sigma|$.

We now consider circuit routing in a slightly more general framework that also includes the unrelated machine assignment problem as a special case. We no longer have capacities on each edge; rather the bandwidth requirement of a call $r_j = (s_j, t_j, b_j)$ is now a function $b_j : E \to \mathbb{R}^+$ instead of a constant b_j. The call r_j must be routed on some path P_j, and the load on every edge e in P_j is then increased by $b_j(e)$. Obviously, this generalizes the circuit routing problem above for which

$$b_j(e) = \frac{b_j}{u(e)}.$$

It also includes the machine assignment problem as a special case by the following reduction: consider a 2-node uniform capacity network $\{s, t\}$ with N edges between s and t, one edge per machine; minimizing the edge congestion on this network corresponds directly to minimizing the load.

Consider the following routing algorithm, which first assumes a bound Λ on the load of the optimal algorithm:

Algorithm ROUTE-EXP$_\Lambda$: Let $\gamma > 0$ and $a = (1 + \gamma)$. Given $r_j = (s_j, t_j, b_j)$, route r_j on a path P_j that minimizes $\sum_{e \in P_j} a^{\tilde{L}_{j-1}(e) + \tilde{\rho}_j(e)} - a^{\tilde{L}_{j-1}(e)}$, where

$$L_j(e) = \sum_{\substack{i \leq j \\ P_i : e \in P_i}} b_i(e),$$

$$\tilde{L}_j(e) = \frac{L_j(e)}{\Lambda},$$

and

$$\tilde{\rho}_j(e) = \frac{b_j(e)}{\Lambda}.$$

That is, route r_j along a shortest path with respect to the distances $c_j(e) = a^{\tilde{L}_{j-1}(e) + \tilde{\rho}_j(e)} - a^{\tilde{L}_{j-1}(e)} = a^{\tilde{L}_{j-1}(e)} [a^{\tilde{\rho}_j(e)} - 1]$.

Theorem 12.7 *Let $G = (V, E)$ be an arbitrary m-edge multigraph. If* OPT$(\sigma) \leq \Lambda$, *then* ROUTE-EXP$_\Lambda(\sigma) = O(\log m) \cdot \Lambda$.

PROOF. By choosing $a = (1 + \gamma)$, we have

$$a^x - 1 \leq \gamma x \quad \text{for all } x \in [0, 1]. \tag{12.4}$$

We let $P_1, \ldots, P_n$ (respectively, $P_1^*, \ldots, P_n^*$) denote the edges used by ROUTE-EXP$_\Lambda$ (respectively, OPT) in order to route request r_j.[7]

$$\sum_{e \in P_j} a^{\tilde{L}_{j-1}(e)}[a^{\tilde{\rho}_j(e)} - 1] \leq \sum_{e \in P_j^*} a^{\tilde{L}_{j-1}(e)}[a^{\tilde{\rho}_j(e)} - 1],$$

since P_j is a shortest path with respect to
the distance $c_j(e)$;

$$\leq \sum_{e \in P_j^*} a^{\tilde{L}_n(e)}[a^{\tilde{\rho}_j(e)} - 1],$$

since $\tilde{L}_k(e)$ is nondecreasing in k;

$$\leq \gamma \sum_{e \in P_j^*} a^{\tilde{L}_n(e)} \tilde{\rho}_j(e),$$

by equation (12.4).

Therefore,

$$\sum_{j=1}^{n} \sum_{e \in P_j} a^{\tilde{L}_{j-1}(e)} \big[a^{\tilde{\rho}_j(e)} - 1\big] \leq \gamma \sum_{j} \sum_{e \in P_j^*} a^{\tilde{L}_n(e)} \tilde{\rho}_j(e).$$

Exchanging summations,

$$\sum_{e} \sum_{j : e \in P_j} a^{\tilde{L}_{j-1}(e)} \big[a^{\tilde{\rho}_j(e)} - 1\big] \leq \gamma \sum_{e} a^{\tilde{L}_n(e)} \sum_{j : e \in P_j^*} \tilde{\rho}_j(e). \tag{12.5}$$

The inner summation in the left-hand side of inequality (12.5) "telescopes" so that the left-hand side becomes

$$\sum_{e} (a^{\tilde{L}_n(e)} - 1) = \sum_{e} a^{\tilde{L}_n(e)} - m.$$

The second summation in the right-hand side of inequality (12.5) is at most 1 when we assume OPT$(r_1, \ldots, r_n) \leq \Lambda$. Therefore,

$$\sum_{e} a^{\tilde{L}_n(e)} - m \leq \gamma \sum_{e} a^{\tilde{L}_n(e)}.$$

---

[7] For machine load balancing, P_j and P_j^* are singleton sets.

Equivalently, by choosing a fixed $\gamma < 1$, we have

$$\sum_e a^{\tilde{L}_n(e)} \le \frac{m}{1 - \gamma}$$

$$\tilde{L}_n(e) \le \log_a\left(\frac{m}{1 - \gamma}\right)$$

$$L_n(e) \le \log_a\left(\frac{m}{1 - \gamma}\right) \cdot \Lambda$$

$$= \log_a\left(\frac{1}{1 - \gamma}\right) \log_a m \cdot \Lambda$$

$$= O(\log m) \cdot \Lambda.$$

■

Corollary 12.8 ROUTE-PERM *is* $O(\log m)$-*competitive where* ROUTE-PERM *is the algorithm derived by the construction of Theorem 12.5.*

Exercise 12.5 Prove an $\Omega(\log N)$ lower bound for edge congestion in the standard (i.e., not generalized) circuit routing problem in which each call has a fixed bandwidth. Hint: Construct a directed network with $\binom{N}{2}$ source nodes $s_{i,j}$, N intermediate nodes u_i, and one sink node t. The edge set consists of edges from each $s_{i,j}$ to u_i and u_j as well as edges from each u_i to t. Now reduce the machine load balancing problem for the restricted machine model (with two machines per job) to routing on this network.

12.4   Load Balancing of Temporary Jobs

For load balancing problems (and obviously also for the call admission/routing problems that follow in Chapter 13), it is natural to assume that requests have a limited duration. The jth request arrives at some time s_j, and we assume it must be scheduled immediately. (We do not consider the case that requests need to be scheduled within some allowable period of delay. In the context of call admission, see Feldman [147].) The completion time f_j (or, equivalently, the **duration** $d_j = f_j - s_j$) may or may not be known at the time of arrival; for either case, there may or may not be a given bound on the maximum duration of a request. The cost ALG(σ) of an algorithm ALG on a sequence of requests is the maximum load on any machine at any point in time.

We have already noted that the GREEDY remains $\left(2 - \frac{1}{N}\right)$-competitive for identical machines even in the case of unknown limited duration. In fact, it can be shown that in the case of identical machines and unknown limited durations, $2 - \frac{1}{N}$ is optimal. It is also true (although we do not prove it here) that a somewhat modified SLOWFIT algorithm remains $O(1)$-competitive for the related machines case. The situation for the restricted and unrelated machines models is substantially different.

12.4.1   Known Durations

We begin with an example that is most similar to the permanent duration case (equivalently, all requests occur in the same unit of time), namely, the case of known limited durations where a bound T on the maximum duration of any job is initially given. More precisely, T is a bound on the ratio of the maximum job duration to the minimum job duration. It can be shown that it is not necessary to know T in advance in the case of known durations.

We consider the general model of unrelated machines and show how the circuit routing perspective can be exploited.

Theorem 12.9 *For the unrelated machine model (and hence for the restricted machine model), if the duration of any job is at most T (discrete time units), then there is an algorithm* ROUTE-KNOWN$_T$ *that is $O(\log NT)$-competitive.*

PROOF. Jobs are partitioned according to their arrival time; jobs arriving during the interval $[(k-1)T, kT)$ are placed in "group" k. Jobs in any group (e.g., group k) are assigned (ignoring all other jobs) in the following way. Construct a network G^k with $2TN + 3T$ nodes composed of

$$\text{nodes } u_{i,h}^k \text{ for } 0 \le i < 2T \text{ and } 1 \le h \le N,$$

$$\text{nodes } t_{i+1}^k \text{ for } 0 \le i < 2T - 1, \text{ and}$$

$$\text{nodes } s_i^k \text{ for } 0 \le i < T.$$

In G^k, there are $5NT - 2N$ edges composed of

$$2NT - N \text{ edges } e_{i,h}^k = (u_{i,h}^k, u_{i+1,h}^k),$$

$$2NT - N \text{ edges } (u_{i+1,h}^k, t_{i+1}^k) \text{ for } 0 \le i < 2T - 1 \text{ and } 1 \le h \le N, \text{ as well as}$$

$$NT \text{ edges } (s_i^k, u_{i,h}^k) \text{ for } 0 \le i < T \text{ and } 1 \le h \le N.$$

A machine assignment request $r_j = \langle r_j(1), \ldots, r_j(N) \rangle$ with duration d_j arriving at time $(k-1)T + l$ $(0 \le l < T)$ is viewed as a routing request r_j' with source s_l^k, destination $t_{l+d_j}^k$, and edge costs $b_j(e_{i,h}^k) = r_j(h)$ for $l \le i < l + d_j$, and $b_j(e) = 0$ for all other edges e. We now use algorithm ROUTE-PERM from Corollary 12.8 to route r_j'.

It is easily seen that the assignment of routing request r_j' in group k in the network G^k corresponds to an assignment of r_j to some machine h. Moreover, the load on a machine h at any time t (e.g., $t = (k-1)T + i$) is equal to the sum of the loads on edges $e_{i+T,h}^{k-1}$ and $e_{i,h}^k$. Since the routing of requests on every G^k is accomplished within an $O(\log(NT))$-competitive factor, it follows that ROUTE-KNOWN$_T$ is also $O(\log(NT))$-competitive. ∎

Exercise 12.6 The proof of Theorem 12.9 assumes that T is known in advance. Show how this assumption can be removed.

12.4.2 Unknown Durations

As already suggested, for the restricted machines model (and hence also the unrelated machines model), the case of unknown limited durations is substantially more problematic for online algorithms.

Theorem 12.10 *Consider the restricted machines model and assume that every job has unit load on any of its allowable machines. The competitive ratio of any online algorithm for this problem is $\Omega(\sqrt{N})$.*

PROOF. Let $L_i(t)$ denote the ALG's load on machine i at time t. (Specifically, suppose $L_i(t)$ is the load just prior to any arrivals at time t but after all departures at times $t' \leq t$.) At any time t, reorder the machines so that $L_1(t) \geq L_2(t) \geq L_{q(t)}(t)$ and $L_i(t) = 0$ for $i > q(t)$. When the context is clear, we simply let q denote $q(t)$. The goal of the adversary is to construct a request sequence σ of unit load tasks satisfying the following conditions:

1. At any point in time, there are at most N jobs and OPT never assigns more than one job to any machine; that is, $\text{OPT}(\sigma) \leq 1$.
2. After the last job of σ has been assigned, there are N active jobs and $L_i(t) \geq L_{i+1}(t)+1$ for $1 \leq i \leq q - 1$.

If these conditions hold, then for $\ell = L_1(t) = \text{ALG}(\sigma)$, we have

$$N = \sum_{i=1}^{q} L_i(t) \leq \sum_{i=0}^{q-1} (\ell - i) = q\ell - \frac{q(q-1)}{2} \qquad (12.6)$$

and $q \leq \ell$ (since $\ell - (q-1) \geq L_q(t) > 0$). The minimal ℓ satisfying equation (12.6) is obtained by maximizing $q = \ell$; then we obtain $\frac{\ell(\ell+1)}{2} \geq N$; that is, $\ell \geq \sqrt{2N}(1 + o(1))$.

It remains to show how to construct σ. Given two vectors of loads

$$L = \langle L_1(t), \ldots, L_{q(t)}(t) \rangle$$

and

$$L' = \langle L_1(t'), \ldots, L_{q(t')}(t) \rangle,$$

we say $L < L'$ if $L_j(t) = L_j(t')$ for $j < i$ and $L_i(t) < L_i(t')$ for some $1 \leq i \leq q(t')$. The adversary inductively constructs σ in stages.

Base case. The initial stage creates N jobs that are forced (by having only one allowable machine for each job) onto N different machines.

Inductive step. Let σ_k be the input constructed by the end of the kth stage and let

$$L^{(k)} = \langle L_1^{(k)}, \ldots, L_{q_k}^{(k)} \rangle$$

denote the vector of loads *after* the last job of σ_k has been assigned. If $L^{(k)}$ satisfies the required conditions (e.g., $L_i^{(k)} \geq L_{i+1}^{(k)} + 1$), then $\sigma = \sigma_k$ and we are done. Otherwise, we want to show how to terminate jobs and extend σ_k to σ_{k+1} so that $L^{(k)} < L^{(k+1)}$. Since $\sum_{i=1}^{q_k} L_i^{(k)} = N$ and all loads are integral, this is a finite ordering and the construction must eventually terminate (in at most $2^{\sqrt{N}}$ stages).[8]

We need one more condition concerning the assignment of jobs in each stage. Namely, if OPT is currently processing a job r on machine i and if $L_i^{(k)} > 0$, then ALG has also assigned job r to machine i.

---

[8] The maximum number of stages is clearly bounded by $P(N)$, the number of ways to represent the number N as the sum of not necessarily distinct positive integers. A good approximation for $P(N)$ is

$$P(N) \approx \frac{1}{4\sqrt{3}N} e^{\pi\sqrt{2/3}\sqrt{N}}.$$

(See Andrews [14].) Furthermore, it can be shown that $2^{\sqrt{N}}$ is a lower bound on the maximum number of stages.

We are now ready to describe the $(k + 1)$st stage under the assumption that

$$L_i^{(k)} = L_{i+1}^{(k)} > 0$$

for some $i \geq 1$. The stage consists of the following substeps:

1. The adversary terminates the jobs currently running on OPT's machines i and $i + 1$ (and by the last condition, also running on ALG's machines i and $i + 1$).
2. A new job r is then created whose allowable set of machines is $\{i, i + 1\}$. Without loss of generality, assume ALG assigns r to machine i. Then OPT assigns r to machine $i + 1$.
3. Next, all jobs currently assigned by ALG to machine $i + 1$ are terminated.
4. Finally, for each of OPT's idle machines, a new job is created and forced onto this idle machine (i.e., there is only one allowable machine for the jobs now being created).

This completes stage $k + 1$.

At the end of substep 2, $L_i(t) = L_i^{(k)}$. At the end of substep 4, $L_i^{(k+1)} = L_i^{(k)} + 1$. Thus, $L^{(k)} < L^{(k+1)}$, since $L_j^{(k)} \leq L_j^{(k+1)}$ for $1 \leq j < i$. ∎

Exercise 12.7 Extend Theorem 12.10 to randomized algorithms (against an oblivious adversary). Hint: In the construction of Theorem 12.10, there are at most two allowable machines for each job. The adversary proceeds as before by acting as if ALG assigns a job r to that machine having highest probability of being assigned r.

Exercise 12.8 Use Theorem 12.10 to derive an $\Omega(N^{1/4})$ lower bound for the competitive ratio of any online algorithm for minimizing edge congestion when routing calls of unknown duration in a directed routing network. Hint: See Exercise 12.5.

Exercise 12.9 Modify the proof of Theorem 12.10 to show that the competitive ratio of GREEDY is $\Omega(N^{2/3})$. Hint: Instead of the conditions $L_i(t) \geq L_{i+1}(t) + 1$, we need the stronger condition that $L_i(t) \geq L_{i+1}(t) + i - 1$.

In contrast to Theorems 12.2 and 12.3 (for the problem of permanent jobs), it is no longer the case that the GREEDY algorithm is optimal for unknown limited durations in the restricted machines model. Rather, Exercise 12.9 shows that the competitive ratio of GREEDY is $\Omega(N^{2/3})$. We now present an algorithm that achieves the asymptotically optimal $O(\sqrt{N})$-competitive ratio.

We say that job r_j arrives at time s_j, having load l_j on any machine in M_j, the set of allowable machines for job r_j. Let $L_i(s_j)$ denote the present load on machine i just *prior* to the assignment of r_j (assuming that any jobs terminating at time $t \leq s_j$ have been removed). Let σ_j denote the first j jobs $r_1, r_2, \ldots, r_j$. We have an obvious lower bound $B(s_j)$ on OPT(σ_j), where $B(s_0) = 0$ and $B(s_j) = \max\{B(s_{j-1}), l_j, \frac{1}{N}(l_j + \sum_i L_i(s_j))\}$, noting that the last term is the average load per machine.

Machine i is called **hard-working** at time s_j if $L_i(s_j) \geq \sqrt{N} \cdot B(s_j)$.[9] Note that we recompute B for each job arrival, and when $B(s_{j-1}) < B(s_j)$, some machines cease to

---

[9] In the terminology of Azar, Kalyanasundaram, Plotkin, Pruhs, and Waarts [34], a hard-working machine is called a "rich" machine. The following algorithm ROBIN-HOOD tries to give jobs to the poor rather than to the rich.

be hard-working. Also, machines can become (respectively, cease to be) hard-working as jobs are assigned (respectively, terminated).[10]

Algorithm ROBIN-HOOD: Assign r_1 to any machine. Upon arrival of r_j at time s_j, assign r_j to any allowable machine $i \in M_j$ that is *not* hard-working at time s_j; that is, $L_i(s_j) < \sqrt{N} B(s_j)$. If there is no such machine, then assign r_j to that machine that most recently became hard-working (breaking ties arbitrarily).

Theorem 12.11 *Algorithm ROBIN-HOOD is strictly $(2\sqrt{N} + 1)$-competitive.*

PROOF. As r_j arrives, the total load on all machines is $\sum_i L_i(s_j) \leq N \cdot B(s_j)$; there can be at most $\sqrt{N}$ hard-working machines at any time. Suppose ROBIN-HOOD assigns r_j to machine m. We want to show that

$$L_m(s_j) + l_j \leq \sqrt{N}(B(s_j) + \text{OPT}(\sigma_j)) + \text{OPT}(\sigma_j).$$

If machine m is not hard-working at time s_j then, clearly, $L_m(s_j) + l_j < \sqrt{N} \cdot B(s_j) + \text{OPT}(\sigma_j)$. Suppose then that machine m most recently becomes hard-working at time $s_{t(j)}$ and let S denote the jobs assigned to machine m during the time interval $[s_{t(j)}, s_j)$. For any $k \in S$, all machines in M_k are hard-working since at least time $s_{t(k)}$ (since r_k was assigned to the most recently hard-working machine m). Because there are at most $\sqrt{N}$ hard-working machines at time $s_{t(k)}$ and all machines in each M_k remain hard-working throughout the time interval $[s_{t(j)}, s_j)$, we have

$$h = \left| \bigcup_{k \in S} M_k \right| \leq \sqrt{N}.$$

Since $\sum_{k \in S} \frac{l_k}{h}$ can be thought of as the "ideal average load" per allowable machine, we have

$$\sum_{k \in S} l_k \leq h \cdot \text{OPT}(\sigma_j) \leq \sqrt{N}\text{OPT}(\sigma_j).$$

Therefore, the load on machine m after assigning r_j is

$$L_m(s_j) + l_j \leq L_m(s_{t(j)}) + \sum_{k \in S} l_k + l_j$$

$$< \sqrt{N} \cdot B_{t(j)} + \sum_{k \in S} l_k + l_j,$$

since machine m was hard-working after the assignment of $r_{t(j)}$ and was not hard-working before this assignment;

$$\leq (2\sqrt{N} + 1)\text{OPT}(\sigma_j),$$

since $\sum_{k \in S} l_k \leq \sqrt{N}\text{OPT}(\sigma_j)$ and $l_k \leq \text{OPT}(\sigma_j)$, for any $k \leq j$. ∎

---

[10] In particular, a machine i can cease to be hard-working at time t because of the recomputation of B and then immediately become hard-working again if r_j is assigned to machine i.

For the unrelated machines model, it is not too difficult to see that the GREEDY algorithm is N-competitive. No better lower bound than Theorem 12.10 is known for the unrelated machines model.

12.5   Bin Packing

The **bin packing** problem concerns a different machine assignment optimization.[11] Assume that we have an unbounded number of identical machines (called bins), each having a bounded identical capacity (e.g., without loss of generality, assume that this bound is 1).[12] Given a sequence σ of requests $r_1, r_2, \ldots$ with each request $r_i \leq 1$ representing a load or size that must be (permanently) assigned to some bin, the goal in the bin packing problem is to minimize the number of bins needed to assign all the requests without exceeding the capacity of any bin.

As we did in the case of load balancing on uniform machines, in this section we limit the discussion to the analysis of the natural greedy algorithm. In fact, for bin packing there are (at least) two natural greedy algorithms called FIRST-FIT (**FF**) and BEST-FIT (**BF**). FF considers each request and places it in the *first* bin in which it fits. BF instead places item r_i in the bin whose load thus far is closest to, but not exceeding, $1 - r_i$.

Theorem 12.12 *The competitive ratio of algorithms* FF *and* BF *is* $\frac{17}{10}$. *More precisely, for every input sequence* σ,

$$\text{FF}(\sigma) \leq \tfrac{17}{10}\text{OPT}(\sigma) + 1,$$

and there are sequences of arbitrary size such that

$$\text{FF}(\sigma) \geq \tfrac{17}{10}\text{OPT}(\sigma) - 8.$$

The same bounds hold for BF.

PROOF.   For simplicity, we show only the weaker lower bound of $\frac{5}{3}$. The optimal lower bound of $\frac{17}{10}$ is similar but more detailed. Consider the following request sequence $\sigma = r_1, \ldots, r_{3n}$ with

$$r_i = \begin{cases} \tfrac{1}{6} - 2\varepsilon & \text{if } i = 1, \ldots, n; \\ \tfrac{1}{3} + \varepsilon & \text{if } i = n+1, \ldots, 2n; \\ \tfrac{1}{2} + \varepsilon & \text{if } i = 2n+1, \ldots, 3n. \end{cases}$$

[11] More precisely, we are defining the one-dimensional bin packing problem in which each request is a one-dimensional size or load. More generally, we can consider multidimensional bin packing problems in which each request is a vector (of some fixed dimension) of loads; these requests must be packed into bounded volume rectangular solids of the corresponding dimension. In fact, there are many variants of the multidimensional bin packing problem depending on the physical constraints that must be solved in a legal packing. Bin packing problems are also called "cutting stock" problems.

[12] Traditionally, the bin packing problem refers to the case of uniform machines each having the same capacity bound. Of course, we could also consider the case in which the machines are not identical or the capacity bounds are different for each machine. Similarly, we could also consider limited duration jobs; again, however, the traditional assumption in bin packing is that the jobs are permanent.

Clearly, OPT can pack one item of each different size in each different bin; therefore, OPT$(\sigma) = n$. When we execute FF (or BF) on this particular example, the result is that for sufficiently small ε, the algorithm is forced to use $\frac{n}{6}$ bins on the first n items, $\frac{n}{2}$ on the second n items, and n on the last n items, for a total of $\frac{5n}{3}$ bins.

We present the upper bound FF$(\sigma) \leq \frac{17}{10}OPT(\sigma) + 2$. The technique used for proving this theorem is an accounting (or potential) method similar to a style of proof often found in amortized analysis. (For a simple proof of a somewhat weaker bound, see Exercise 12.10.) Define the following weight function:

$$w(r) = \begin{cases} \frac{6}{5}r & \text{if } 0 \leq r \leq \frac{1}{6}; \\ \frac{9}{5}r - \frac{1}{10} & \text{if } \frac{1}{6} \leq r \leq \frac{1}{3}; \\ \frac{6}{5}r + \frac{1}{10} & \text{if } \frac{1}{3} \leq r \leq \frac{1}{2}; \\ 1 & \text{if } \frac{1}{2} < r. \end{cases}$$

For any list $\sigma = r_1, r_2, \ldots, r_n$, define $W(\sigma) = \sum_{i=1}^{n} w(r_i)$, and for any bin B, define $W(B) = \sum_{j=1}^{t} w(r_{i_j})$ where $\{r_{i_j} | j = 1, \ldots, t\}$ are the items assigned to bin B. It is not hard to see that the following two lemmas imply the upper bound.

Lemma 12.1 *For any bin B, we have $W(B) \leq \frac{17}{10}$ and thus $W(\sigma) \leq \frac{17}{10}OPT(\sigma)$.*

Lemma 12.2 *If FF uses $k = $ FF(σ) bins $B_1, \ldots, B_k$, then*

$$\sum_{j=1}^{k} W(B_i) \geq k - 2,$$

so that FF$(\sigma) \leq W(\sigma) + 2$.

We now sketch the proof of these lemmas.

Proof of Lemma 12.1. If every item has size $\leq \frac{1}{2}$, then

$$\frac{w(r_i)}{r_i} \leq \frac{3}{2} < \frac{17}{10},$$

and this is sufficient for completing the proof. Therefore, assume that some $r_i > \frac{1}{2}$ and use $r_{i_1}, \ldots, r_{i_t}$ to denote the items that are packed in the same bin as r_i. Thus,

$$\sum_{j=1}^{t} r_{i_j} < \frac{1}{2}.$$

Therefore, we need to prove that

$$\sum_{j=1}^{t} w(r_{i_j}) < \frac{7}{10}.$$

Without loss of generality, we assume that each $r_{i_j} \leq \frac{1}{3}$, since if $r_{i_j} > \frac{1}{3}$, we can regard r_{i_j} as two items:

$$r_{i_j}^{1} = \frac{1}{3}$$

and

$$r_{i_j}^2 = r_{i_j} - \tfrac{1}{3} < \tfrac{1}{6}.$$

Since the weight function w is (piecewise) linear and has the same slope for $r < \tfrac{1}{6}$ and $\tfrac{1}{3} \le r < \tfrac{1}{2}$,

$$w(r_{i_j}) = w(r_{i_j}^1) + w(r_{i_j}^2).$$

Similarly, we can assume without loss of generality that for at most one index j, $r_{i_j} < \tfrac{1}{6}$. In fact, if two items $r_{i_1}, r_{i_2} < \tfrac{1}{6}$, we can combine them into a single item r with $r < \tfrac{1}{3}$ such that

$$w(r) \ge w(r_{i_1}) + w(r_{i_2}).$$

We conclude with the following case analysis:

- If $t = 1$, we have two subcases:
  - (i) If $r_{i_1} < \tfrac{1}{6}$, then $w(r) < \tfrac{1}{5} < \tfrac{7}{10}$;
  - (ii) If $\tfrac{1}{6} \le r_{i_1} \le \tfrac{1}{3}$, then $w(r) < \tfrac{3}{5} - \tfrac{1}{10} < \tfrac{7}{10}$.
- If $t = 2$, we have two subcases:
  - (i) If $r_{i_1} < \tfrac{1}{6} \le r_{i_2} \le \tfrac{1}{3}$, then $w(r) \le \tfrac{1}{5} + \tfrac{3}{5} - \tfrac{1}{10} = \tfrac{7}{10}$;
  - (ii) If $\tfrac{1}{6} \le r_{i_1}, r_{i_2} \le \tfrac{1}{3}$, we have $w(r) < \tfrac{9}{5}(r_{i_1} + r_{i_2}) - \tfrac{2}{10} < \tfrac{7}{10}$, since $(r_{i_1} + r_{i_2}) < \tfrac{1}{2}$.
- If $t = 3$, we again have two subcases:
  - (i) if $r_{i_1} < \tfrac{1}{6} \le r_{i_2}, r_{i_3} \le \tfrac{1}{3}$, we have $w(r) \le \tfrac{6}{5}r_{i_1} + \tfrac{9}{5}(r_{i_2} + r_{i_3}) - \tfrac{2}{10} < \tfrac{7}{10} - \tfrac{3}{5}r_{i_1} < \tfrac{7}{10}$, since $(r_{i_2} + r_{i_3}) < \tfrac{1}{2} - r_{i_1}$;
  - (ii) if $\tfrac{1}{6} \le r_{i_1}, r_{i_2}, r_{i_3} \le \tfrac{1}{3}$, we have $w(r) < \tfrac{9}{5}(r_{i_1} + r_{i_2} + r_{i_3}) - \tfrac{3}{10} < \tfrac{7}{10}$, since $(r_{i_1} + r_{i_2} + r_{i_3}) < \tfrac{1}{2}$.
- The case $t > 3$ is impossible.

∎

Proof of Lemma 12.2. If a bin B (packed by FF) contains an item $r > \tfrac{1}{2}$, then the weight $W(B)$ of this bin is at least 1, so that it is sufficient to prove the desired inequality by considering only those bins B with $W(B) < 1$, containing only items $r \le \tfrac{1}{2}$. Let $B_1, \ldots, B_l$ be a listing (in the order that they became nonempty) of such nonempty bins. For any such bin B, let $s(B)$ denote the (unweighted) load packed into B. We define the **coarseness** of a bin B_i as the number α, such that there exists a bin B_j, $j < i$ with $s(B_j) = 1 - \alpha$, and for each bin b_k, $k < i$, $s(B_k) \ge 1 - \alpha$. (By definition, the coarseness of the first bin is 0.)

Clearly, if B has coarseness α, then any item packed in B has size greater than α. Otherwise, it would have been packed in one of the previous bins. If a bin has coarseness $\alpha \ge \tfrac{1}{2}$, it means that in this bin there is only one item of size larger than $\tfrac{1}{2}$. Hence, it follows that all bins have coarseness smaller than $\tfrac{1}{2}$.

We make use of the following two claims, which will be proven later.

Claim 1: Suppose bin B is packed with items $a_1 \ge \cdots \ge a_m$. If $\sum_{i=1}^m a_i \ge 1 - \alpha$, where α is the coarseness of bin B, then $\sum_{i=1}^m w(a_i) \ge 1$.

Claim 2: Suppose bin B is packed with items $a_1 \geq \cdots \geq a_m$. If $\sum_{i=1}^{m} w(a_i) = 1 - \beta$ with $\beta > 0$, then either (i) $m = 1$ and $a_1 \leq \frac{1}{2}$, or (ii) $\sum_{i=1}^{m} a_i \leq 1 - \alpha - \frac{5}{9}\beta$, where α is the coarseness of B.

Let $W(B_i) = 1 - \beta_i$ with $\beta_i > 0$ and let $\alpha_i < \frac{1}{2}$ be the coarseness of B_i. Use $r_1^i, r_2^i, \ldots$ to denote the elements packed in B_i.

Suppose that $l > 1$. According to the definition of coarseness and using Claim 2, for $1 < i \leq l$:

$$\alpha_i \geq 1 - \sum_j r_j^{i-1} \geq \alpha_{i-1} + \frac{5}{9}\beta_{i-1}.$$

Here we use the fact that if case (i) of Claim 2 holds for bin B_{i-1}, then $\alpha_i \geq \frac{1}{2}$, contradicting our assumption about the coarseness of the bins.

Thus,

$$\sum_{i=1}^{l-1} \beta_i \leq \frac{9}{5} \sum_{i=2}^{l} (\alpha_i - \alpha_{i-1}) = \frac{9}{5}(\alpha_l - \alpha_1) \leq \frac{9}{5} \cdot \frac{1}{2} < 1.$$

Since $\beta_l \leq 1$, we have $\sum_{1=1}^{l} \beta_i \leq 2$. Clearly, if $l = 1$, we immediately have $\sum_{i=1}^{l} \beta_i \leq 2$.

Let m be the number of the bins other than $B_1, \ldots, B_l$ used by FF (so $m + l =$ FF(σ)). Applying Claim 1, we obtain that the weight of those bins is larger than 1. Therefore,

$$W(\sigma) = \sum w(r_i) \geq m + \sum_{i=1}^{l} W(B_i) = \text{FF}(\sigma) - \sum_{i=1}^{l} \beta_l \geq \text{FF}(\sigma) - 2.$$

That is, FF$(\sigma) \leq W + 2$ as desired. This fact combined with Lemma 12.1 yields

$$\text{FF}(\sigma) \leq \tfrac{17}{10}\text{OPT}(\sigma) + 2.$$

It remains to prove Claims 1 and 2.

Proof of Claim 1. If $a_1 > \frac{1}{2}$, the claim is immediate ($w(a_1) = 1$). Assume that $a_1 \leq \frac{1}{2}$. By the definition of coarseness, this means that $a_1 \geq a_2 \geq \alpha$. The following is a case analysis depending on the value of α:

- If $\alpha \leq \frac{1}{6}$, then $\sum_{i=1}^{m} a_i > 1 - \alpha \geq \frac{5}{6}$. Since the slope of w is greater than $\frac{6}{5}$ for items smaller than $\frac{1}{2}$, we have the claim.
- If $\frac{1}{6} \leq \alpha \leq \frac{1}{3}$, we have three subcases depending on the value of m:
  - (i) $m = 1$: Since $a_1 \leq \frac{1}{2}$, we must have $1 - \alpha \leq \frac{1}{2}$, which contradicts the hypothesis $\alpha \leq \frac{1}{3}$;
  - (ii) $m = 2$: If $a_1 \geq a_2 \geq \frac{1}{3}$, then $w(a_1) + w(a_2) \geq 2\left(\frac{6}{5}\frac{1}{3} + \frac{1}{10}\right) = 1$. If both are less than $\frac{1}{3}$, then $a_1 + a_2 < \frac{2}{3} < 1 - \alpha$, which contradicts our hypothesis on α. If $a_1 \geq \frac{1}{3} > a_2$, since $a_2 > \alpha$ and $\alpha \leq \frac{1}{3}$, we obtain

$$w(a_1) + w(a_2) = \tfrac{6}{5}a_1 + \tfrac{9}{5}a_2 = \tfrac{6}{5}(a_1 + a_2) + \tfrac{3}{5}a_2 > \tfrac{6}{5}(1 - \alpha) + \tfrac{3}{5}\alpha > 1;$$

  - (iii) $m \geq 3$: Very similar to case (ii).

- If $\frac{1}{3} \le \alpha \le \frac{1}{2}$, we have two subcases depending on the value of $m = 1, 2$. The analysis of these two subcases is similar to the analysis of the previous subcases.

Proof of Claim 2. If $m = 1$ and $a_1 > \frac{1}{2}$, it is impossible that $\beta > 0$. If $m \ge 2$, by the definition of coarseness, $a_1 \ge a_2 \ge \alpha$. Let $\sum_{i=1}^{m} a_i = 1 - \alpha - \gamma$. Then we can construct a bin $\tilde{B}$ packed with $a_3, \dots, a_m$ and two other items δ_1 and δ_2, such that $\delta_1 + \delta_2 = a_1 + a_2 + \gamma$, and $\delta_i \ge a_i$. Applying Claim 1 to B, we obtain

$$\sum_{i=3}^{m} w(a_i) + w(\delta_1) + w(\delta_2) \ge 1.$$

Because the slope of w is $\le \frac{9}{5}$ for items of size less than $\frac{1}{2}$, we obtain

$$w(\delta_1) + w(\delta_2) \le w(a_1) + w(a_2) + \frac{9}{5}\gamma.$$

Hence, $\gamma \ge \frac{5}{9}\beta$ and the claim holds.   ∎

Exercise 12.10 If we are willing to settle for a somewhat weaker upper bound, then there is a simple proof that $\mathrm{FF}(\sigma) \le \frac{7}{4}\mathrm{OPT}(\sigma) + 2$ for every input sequence σ. Prove this weaker bound by expressing $\mathrm{FF}(\sigma)$ as $b_1 + b_2 + b_3$, where

$b_1 = $ number of bins where FF packs only one item of size larger than $\frac{1}{2}$;

$b_2 = $ number of bins containing more than one item whose load is larger than $\frac{2}{3}$;

$b_3 = $ number of other bins.

12.6   Historical Notes and Open Questions

Azar [31] provides an excellent survey of online load balancing. The "near" optimality of GREEDY for scheduling permanent jobs on identical machines (Theorem 12.1) is due to Graham [175]. Graham's 1966 result might be considered the first result in competitive analysis, although it was not stated within the terminology or motivation of online algorithm analysis. Explicit interest in the competitive analysis of such scheduling algorithms begins with the paper of Shmoys, Wein, and Williamson [315], who consider a type of preemptive scheduling model for unknown duration jobs where the online algorithm is allowed to discontinue a job that has been assigned already and then reassign and restart (from the beginning) this job at a later time. Phillips and Westbrook [274] (respectively, Awerbuch, Azar, Plotkin, and Waarts [27]) study the tradeoff between the number of reassignments and the competitive ratio for load balancing of jobs with unknown duration for the restricted (respectively, unrelated) machines model. There are a number of excellent surveys for scheduling problems including load balancing problems with and without reassignment (for example, restarting) of jobs; see Hall [180] and Lawler, Lenstra, Rinnooy Kan, and Shmoys [239]. The results of Azar, Naor, and Rom [35] for the restricted machines model constitute the first explicit study of competitive analysis within the nonpreemptive model of load balancing, which is considered in this chapter. These results are related to earlier results concerning online graph matching algorithms, in particular, the randomized greedy bipartite matching algorithm of Karp, Vazirani, and Vazirani [218].

Results for machine load balancing are directly related to circuit routing and edge congestion. The virtual circuit routing problem is related, in turn, to the **multicommodity flow problem**. In multicommodity flow, we view the ith "call" as a request to establish a flow of b_i units (e.g., bandwidth) of commodity i from a source s_i to a sink t_i. The difference between virtual circuit routing and multicommodity flow is that in the latter problem the flow can be distributed among several paths, whereas in virtual circuit routing a call must be routed via a single path. In some integer programming formulations of virtual circuit routing problems, the related linear programming relaxation becomes the multicommodity flow problem. For the study of multicommodity flow, load balancing becomes the **concurrent multicommodity flow** problem (see Shahrokhi and Matula [310]).

As we have defined it, in load balancing the goal is to minimize the maximum load on any machine. This is, of course, tantamount to saying that we wish to minimize the L_∞ norm. Online load balancing in the L_p norm is studied by Awerbuch, Azar, Grove, Kao, Krishnan, and Vitter [25].

Identical Machines. After more than 25 years, we now know that (the competitive ratio of) GREEDY is not optimal for identical machines. The first improvement is due to Galambos and Woeginger [163], who obtain a ratio $2 - \frac{1}{N} - o(1)$. Bartal, Fiat, Karloff, and Vohra [45] achieve the first bound $2 - \varepsilon$ (for all N); specifically, the bound is $2 - \frac{1}{70} \approx 1.986$. Karger, Phillips and Torng [209] achieve the bound of 1.945, and Albers [5] achieves the current best bound of 1.923. It is not clear if these new algorithms and constant bounds (which are independent of N) can be extended to the case of known limited duration jobs. Faigle, Kern, and Turán [146] have shown that no deterministic online algorithm can achieve a competitive ratio better than $\frac{3}{2}$ for $N = 2$, $\frac{5}{3}$ for $N = 3$, and $1 + (1/\sqrt{2}) \approx 1.707$ for $N \geq 4$. Using Theorem 12.1, the first two bounds are optimal. Independently, Chen, van Vliet, and Woeginger [95] and Bartal, Karloff, and Rabani [48] increased the general lower bound to (respectively) 1.8319 and 1.837... for N sufficiently large. The current best deterministic lower bound is due to Albers [5], who shows that the competitive ratio is at least 1.852 for $N \geq 80$. Some lower bounds have also been established for randomized algorithms (against an oblivious adversary). For all N, Chen, van Vliet, and Woeginger [94] and, independently, Sgall [307] show a lower bound of $1 + \frac{1}{(N/N-1)^N - 1}$, which has as a special case the optimal bound of $\frac{4}{3}$ for $N = 2$ established by Bartal et al. [45]. For identical machines, the case $N = 2$ is thus far the only known instance in which randomization provably helps in scheduling on identical machines. Note that as $N \to \infty$, the general lower bound approaches the limit of $\frac{e}{e-1} \approx 1.58$.

Permanent Jobs on Nonidentical Machines. For the restricted machines model, Azar, Naor, and Rom [35] proved the almost exact optimality of the deterministic greedy algorithm and the almost exact optimality of the randomized greedy algorithm in the case of unit load jobs (see Theorems 12.2 and 12.3). The proof of Theorem 12.2 presented here is due to Ivrii (personal communication). In contrast, Aspnes, Azar, Fiat, Plotkin, and Waarts [19] show that GREEDY is not optimal for either the related machine model or unrelated machine model. Aspnes et al. introduce the idea of an exponential weighting of present cost (i.e., load) in the context of online algorithms, proving what is perhaps the most general result of this chapter, namely that algorithm ROUTE-PERM has a (asymptotically optimal) competitive ratio of $O(\log N)$. The idea of an exponential weighting of the present load can be found in the development of offline approximation algorithms for the concurrent maximum flow problem starting with the work of Shahrokhi and

Matula [310]. Aspnes et al. introduce the "doubling trick," which is used to avoid the
assumption that an upper bound is known on OPT's cost.[13] They also present and analyze
the SLOWFIT algorithm, noting that the idea of scheduling jobs on the slowest machine
possible (in the context of scheduling jobs with unknown durations using restarts) is due to
Shmoys, Wein, and Williamson [315]. For the related machines model, Berman, Charikar,
and Karpinski [60] present the current best upper and lower bounds for deterministic and
randomized algorithms (see Table 12.1).

Limited Duration Jobs. Azar, Broder, and Karlin [32] began the study of limited and
unknown duration jobs for preemptive load balancing models. They show that GREEDY
is $\Theta(N^{2/3})$-competitive for the restricted machines model and that $\Omega(N^{1/2})$ is a lower
bound for any (even randomized) algorithm for this problem. Azar, Kalyanasundaram,
Plotkin, Pruhs, and Waarts [34] provide a matching $O(N^{1/2})$ upper bound for the restricted
machines case, and they also show that a slightly modified version of SLOWFIT remains
(when assuming jobs of limited and unknown duration) $O(1)$-competitive for the related
machines model. The reduction of the limited but known duration jobs to that of permanent
jobs is also due to Azar et al. [34]. Azar and Epstein [33] provide lower bounds for
deterministic and randomized algorithms for load balancing of limited duration jobs in
the identical machines model. In particular, they show that the greedy algorithm is the
optimal deterministic algorithm for jobs of unknown duration.

Bin Packing. Ullman [330] and Garey, Graham, and Ullman [167] introduced the study
of bin packing (competitive) analysis. They show that the competitive ratio of FIRST-FIT (FF)
and BEST-FIT (BF) satisfy: $\mathcal{R}(\text{FF}) = \frac{17}{10}$ and $\mathcal{R}(\text{BF}) \geq \frac{17}{10}$. The corresponding upper bound
for BF was proven by Johnson [205]. The precise statement and proof of Theorem 12.12 is
due to Johnson, Demers, Ullman, Garey, and Graham [207]. In 1980 Yao [341], in what
may be the first explicitly stated result in competitive analysis (albeit one that does not use
the terminology of competitive analysis), proved a general lower bound for any online bin
packing algorithm ALG; he showed $\mathcal{R}(\text{ALG}) \geq 1.5$, and gave a modified version of FF called
REFINED-FIRST-FIT (RFF) for which $\mathcal{R}(\text{RFF}) = \frac{5}{3}$. Liang [243] and, independently, Brown
[85] improved the lower bound to $\mathcal{R}(\text{ALG}) \geq 1.536$. The current best lower bound 1.540
is due to van Vliet [331]. An algorithm that attains a competitive ratio closer to this lower
bound is a variant of a harmonic partitioning algorithm HARM. HARM takes a parameter M
and divides items into M classes, where the items in the ith class have size in $\left[\frac{1}{i+1}, \frac{1}{i}\right)$ (except for the Mth class, in which we pack items with size in $\left(0, \frac{1}{M}\right]$). Items are packed in the
same bin only if they are in the same class (using FF within each class). Ramanan, Brown,
Lee, and Lee [287] proved that $\mathcal{R}(\text{HARM}(M)) \leq G_M$ with $\lim_{M\to\infty} G_M = 1 + \frac{1}{2} + \frac{1}{6} + \frac{1}{42} +$
$\frac{1}{42 \cdot 43} = 1.6910\ldots$.[14] In the same paper, Ramanan et al. propose some modifications to

---

[13] As reported in Berman, Charikar, and Karpinski [60], Indyk uses a "randomized doubling trick" to reduce
the resulting competitive ratio from $4 \cdot c$ to $e \cdot c$ (see Theorem 12.5).

[14] G_M is defined as follows. First define k_i:

$$k_1 = 1 \text{ and } k_{i+1} = k_i(k_i + 1).$$

If i is such that $k_i \leq M < k_{i+1}$, then let

$$G_M = \frac{M}{k_{i+1}(M-1)} + \sum_{j=1}^{i} \frac{1}{k_j}.$$

this idea and, in particular, present an algorithm called MODIFIED-HARMONIC-2 (**MHARM2**), which is 1.612-competitive. Another variant of HARM yields the current best upper bound 1.5887, due to Richey [292]. The history of offline bin packing algorithms is even more extensive. For both online and offline results, see the comprehensive survey by Coffman, Garey, and Johnson [113].

   Credit for Exercises. Exercises 12.2, 12.4, and 12.5 are due to Aspnes et al. [19]. Exercises 12.3 and 12.6 are due to Azar et al. [34]. Exercises 12.7 and 12.9 are due to Azar, Broder, and Karlin [32]. Exercise 12.10 is due to Goemans [172].

12.6.1   Open Questions

12.1 (*Value = I3/T3*) Can the $\ln N + 1$ upper bound for load balancing of permanent unit load jobs in the restricted machines model be extended to nonunit loads?

12.2 (*Value = I3/T3*) The competitive ratio lower bounds for the problem of congestion minimization (permanent and limited unknown duration jobs) in the standard circuit routing model was proven for directed graph networks in exercises 12.5 and 12.8. Bartal and Leonardi [49] establish an $\Omega(\log N)$ lower bound for congestion minimization of permanent jobs on the undirected $(N \times N)$ array. For what other networks do the $\Omega(\log N)$ and $\Omega(N^{1/4})$ lower bounds hold for (respectively) permanent and limited unknown duration jobs? Can the $\Omega(N^{1/4})$ lower bound be improved?

12.3 (*Value = I3/T3*) For the identical machines model and the load balancing of known limited duration jobs, does there exist a deterministic or randomized algorithm with competitive ratio $2 - \varepsilon$ for all N?

12.4 (*Value = I3/T4*) For the identical machines model and the load balancing of permanent jobs, is it the case that the competitive ratio is monotone nondecreasing as a function of the number of machine N?

12.5 (*Value = I4/T3*) For the case of assigning known limited duration jobs in either the restricted or unrelated machine models (see Theorem 12.9), must the competitive ratio be a function of T (e.g., $\log T$)? More generally, is there any machine model for which we can prove a lower bound for the case of limited but known durations that exceeds the best upper bound for the case of permanent jobs?

12.6 (*Value = I4/T3*) Eliminate or reduce the gap between the lower bound ($\sqrt{N}$) and upper bound (N) for assigning limited duration jobs with unknown durations in the unrelated machines model.

CHAPTER 13

Call Admission and Circuit Routing

We turn our attention to the problems of **call admission** and **routing** on networks having limited edge capacities that cannot be violated. Upon each request for a new call, an algorithm must decide whether or not to accept the call; if it is accepted, the algorithm must then allocate a route in the network. Each call comes with some specification of its bandwidth and duration requirements, as well as the profit derived from accepting the call. We assume throughout this chapter that, once accepted, a call cannot be preempted. For convenience, throughout this chapter, we refer to the call admission/routing problem simply as the routing problem.

13.1 Specifying the Problem

As in the load balancing (congestion minimization) problem, we distinguish between permanent calls and calls of (known or unknown) limited duration. We again begin with the more basic case of permanent calls (equivalently, all calls take place in a fixed time slot), noting that (as in congestion minimization), we can modify algorithms for this case so that they apply to the limited but known duration case (see Section 13.3). We denote the ith **call** by $r_i = (s_i, t_i, b_i, p_i)$, where p_i is the **(call) profit** (to the routing company) obtained by routing the ith call from the source s_i to the destination t_i, and b_i is the **bandwidth requirement** for the ith call.

"Real world" pricing might be quite complicated (i.e., it might depend on priority, time of the day, etc.); therefore, we first consider the case in which the profit of a call is proportional to the **throughput** (or information flow) of the call, defined as follows.

- For the unlimited duration case, throughput is the required bandwidth of the call.
- For the limited duration case, throughput is defined to be the product of the bandwidth and the duration.

We ignore the fact that certain types of calls might have bandwidth requirements that vary over the duration of the call and simply assume that the bandwidth requirement of every call remains constant throughout the call.[1]

---

[1] These simplifications are not essential for the development that follows. The algorithms and analysis presented here can be stated in a more general setting of profits and time varying bandwidth demands, as is done in Awerbuch, Azar, and Plotkin [26].

If all edge capacities and all bandwidth requests are identical (e.g., $= 1$), then the problem reduces to the classical one of finding the maximum number of edge disjoint paths for a set of calls (i.e., a set of source–destination pairs). As an offline problem, this **maximum disjoint paths problem** remains (at the time of this writing) one of the major open problems in the area of approximation algorithms for NP-hard optimization problems.

We often assume that routing networks are directed graphs. Undirected graphs, such as trees and arrays, can also be viewed as routing networks in one of two ways. In the "bidirectional mode" we simply replace each undirected edge (u, v) by two directed edges $\langle u, v \rangle$ and $\langle v, u \rangle$; if (u, v) has capacity c, then both $\langle u, v \rangle$ and $\langle v, u \rangle$ have capacity c. In the "undirected mode" we consider an undirected edge as a single edge capable of routing calls in either direction while requiring that the bandwidth sum of all calls (in either direction) is less than or equal c. Thus, for example, if all calls have bandwidth 1 and edge (u, v) has capacity c, then (u, v) is capable of being part of a total of c different paths. In general, for a fixed graph G, we do not know how to reduce routing in the bidirectional mode to the undirected mode (or conversely), although certain upper and lower bounds can be extended to either model. See, for example, the results for arbitrary networks in Section 13.2 and the results concerning trees in Section 13.5. On the other hand, as suggested in Open Question 13.2, it is quite reasonable to conjecture that the lower bound in Theorem 13.17 does not extend to brick wall graphs in the bidirectional mode.

Exercise 13.1 Let G be an undirected graph. Show that there is a directed graph G' such that a routing problem in the undirected mode on G can be reduced to a routing problem on G'.

13.2 Throughput Maximization for Permanent Calls in Networks with Large Edge Capacities

Consider an arbitrary directed network and the online routing problem. This problem is considerably easier if the bandwidth of each call is a "small fraction" of the minimum edge capacity. We present an algorithm due to Awerbuch, Azar, and Plotkin [26] that exploits this bandwidth restriction along with an exponential weighting function of edge loads (similar to the use of the exponential function for the case of load balancing/edge congestion discussed in Section 12.3) in order to construct an online routing algorithm in an arbitrary network. The exponential weighting emphasizes the cost of a heavily loaded edge so that when the edges in a path are not equally loaded, the exponential weighting tends to "protect" the heavily loaded edge.

Consider any online circuit routing algorithm ALG. Following the notation in Chapter 12 (Section 12.3), we let $u(e)$ be the capacity of edge e and define $L_j(e)$ as the "total normalized load on edge e" incurred by the online algorithm ALG having processed (i.e., rejected, or accepted and routed) the first j calls. Specifically, let A_j be the set of indices among the first j calls accepted by the online algorithm and let P_k denote the route assigned to $r_k, k \in A_j$. Then,

$$L_j(e) = \frac{1}{u(e)} \cdot \sum_{\substack{k \in A_j \\ e \in P_k}} b_k.$$

For any input sequence $\sigma = r_1, \ldots, r_n$, a call admission algorithm must guarantee that $L_n(e) \leq 1$ for all edges e. Define the **exponential edge cost function**

$$c_j(e) = u(e)[\mu^{L_j(e)} - 1], \tag{13.1}$$

where μ is a constant (to be defined below) depending on the maximum length D of any routing path. Since we are now considering the maximization of profit where profit is defined as proportional to the throughput (i.e., total bandwidth routed), we can scale the profit (i.e., change the units of currency) so that for every call $r_i = (s_i, t_i, b_i, p_i)$, $p_i = D \cdot b_i$. We then make a significant restriction on the allowable bandwidth. Specifically, let $0 \leq \varepsilon \leq 1$ and assume for every call r_i, $i = 1, 2, \ldots, n$, that

$$b_i \leq \min_e \frac{u(e)}{\varepsilon \log D + 1 + \varepsilon} = b^*(\varepsilon).$$

Note that for fixed ε,

$$b_i = O\left(\frac{u(e)}{\log D}\right).$$

We use $\varepsilon \leq 1$ to parameterize the extent to which a bandwidth request may exceed a $\frac{1}{\log D}$ fraction of the minimum edge capacity.

We are now ready to state algorithm AAP_ε.

> **Algorithm AAP_ε:** Let D be a bound (e.g., the number of nodes in the routing network) on the length of any routing path and let $0 \leq \varepsilon \leq 1$. Assume $b_i \leq b^*(\varepsilon)$ and $p_i = D \cdot b_i$ for every call r_i. Let $\mu = 2^{1 + 1/\varepsilon} D$. Upon arrival of the jth call $r_j = (s_j, t_j, b_j, p_j)$ if there exists *any* path P between s_j and t_j such that
>
> $$\sum_{e \in P} \frac{b_j}{u(e)} \cdot c_{j-1}(e) \leq p_j,$$
>
> then route r_j on such a path. Otherwise, reject the call. In either case, update $L_j(e)$ and $c_j(e)$ appropriately. Note: When the context is clear, we typically drop the subscript ε and write AAP.

We first prove that algorithm AAP is a proper call admission algorithm; that is, it guarantees the invariant that no edge constraints are violated. We then derive an asymptotically optimal upper bound on its competitiveness. (See Exercise 13.10 for a corresponding lower bound.)

Theorem 13.1 *Under the stated bandwidth and profit assumptions, the AAP algorithm never violates an edge capacity constraint.*

PROOF. Fix an input sequence $\sigma = r_1, \ldots, r_n$. We can clearly ignore rejected calls. Let A be the indices of calls r_j that are accepted and routed by AAP (on some path P_j). Since all calls are permanent, it is sufficient to prove that $L_n(e) \leq 1$ for every edge e.

Consider the routing of the kth call for $k \in A$. According to the definition of AAP, in order for r_k to be routed on P_k, it must be that

$$\sum_{e \in P_k} \frac{b_k}{u(e)} c_{k-1}(e) \leq p_k = Db_k,$$

which implies

$$\sum_{e \in P_k} \frac{c_{k-1}(e)}{u(e)} \leq D.$$

In particular, for any edge $e \in P_k$, we have

$$D \geq \tfrac{c_{k-1}(e)}{u(e)} = \mu^{L_{k-1}(e)} - 1$$

$$= \mu^{L_k(e) - b_k/u(e)} - 1$$

$$\geq \mu^{L_k(e) - 1/(\varepsilon \log D + 1 + \varepsilon)} - 1,$$

$$\text{since } \tfrac{b_k}{u(e)} \leq \tfrac{1}{\varepsilon \log D + 1 + \varepsilon};$$

$$= \mu^{L_k(e) - 1/(\varepsilon \log \mu)} - 1,$$

$$\text{since } \varepsilon \log \mu = (1 + \varepsilon) + \varepsilon \log D;$$

$$= \frac{\mu^{L_k(e)}}{2^{1/\varepsilon}} - 1.$$

Therefore, $\mu^{L_k(e)} \leq 2^{1/\varepsilon} D + 2^{1/\varepsilon} \leq 2^{1+1/\varepsilon} D = \mu$, implying $L_k(e) \leq 1$. ∎

Theorem 13.2 *Under the stated bandwidth and profit assumptions, algorithm* AAP *attains a competitive ratio of*

$$2^{1+1/\varepsilon} \log \mu + 1 = O\big(2^{1/\varepsilon} + 2^{1/\varepsilon} \log D\big).$$

PROOF. Let $r_1, r_2, \ldots, r_n$ be any sequence of requests. Define A as in the proof of Theorem 13.1, and define $\bar{A}$ as the set of indices of those calls in the input sequence σ that are rejected by the AAP algorithm but routed by some fixed optimal offline algorithm OPT. Consider the total online exponential edge cost $C = \sum_e c_n(e)$. It suffices to show that the following two inequalities hold:

(i) $C \leq (2^{1+1/\varepsilon} \log \mu) \displaystyle\sum_{j \in A} p_j$

   (that is, the online profit is a sufficiently large fraction of the total online exponential edge cost);

(ii) $\displaystyle\sum_{j \in \bar{A}} p_j \leq C$

   (that is, any possible additional profit gained by the optimal offline algorithm is sufficiently bounded).

The two inequalities complete the proof, since

$$\text{AAP}(\sigma) = \sum_{j \in A} p_j \quad \text{and} \quad \text{OPT}(\sigma) \leq \text{AAP}(\sigma) + \sum_{j \in \bar{A}} p_j.$$

Inequality (i) is proven by induction on $|A|$, the number of calls accepted by the AAP algorithm. (Clearly, rejected calls do not change either side of this inequality.) The base case of no calls is trivial. Therefore, let r_k be the last accepted call, and let P_k be the path used to route r_k.

By the induction hypothesis,

$$\sum_e c_{k-1}(e) \le 2^{1+1/\varepsilon} \log \mu \sum_{j \in A - \{k\}} p_j. \tag{13.2}$$

We want to show that

$$\sum_e c_k(e) \le 2^{1+1/\varepsilon} \log \mu \sum_{j \in A} p_j. \tag{13.3}$$

Using the induction hypothesis and subtracting equation (13.2) from equation (13.3), it is sufficient to prove that

$$\sum_e c_k(e) - \sum_e c_{k-1}(e) = \sum_{e \in P_k} (c_k(e) - c_{k-1}(e)) \le 2^{1+1/\varepsilon} p_k \log \mu. \tag{13.4}$$

For every $e \in P_k$,

$$
\begin{aligned}
[c_k(e) - c_{k-1}(e)] &= u(e) \left[\mu^{L_{k-1}(e) + b_k/u(e)} - \mu^{L_{k-1}(e)} \right] \\
&= u(e) \mu^{L_{k-1}(e)} \left[\mu^{b_k/u(e)} - 1 \right] \\
&\le u(e) \cdot \mu^{L_{k-1}(e)} \left[\log \mu \cdot \frac{b_k}{u(e)} \right] 2^{1/\varepsilon} \\
&= 2^{1/\varepsilon} \log \mu \cdot \left[\frac{c_{k-1}(e)}{u(e)} + 1 \right] \cdot b_k \\
&= 2^{1/\varepsilon} \log \mu \cdot \left[\frac{b_k}{u(e)} c_{k-1}(e) + b_k \right].
\end{aligned}
\tag{13.5}
$$

To obtain the inequality (13.5), we observe that

$$f(x) = \mu^x - 1 = 2^{x \log \mu} - 1, \qquad \frac{b_k}{u(e)} \log \mu \le \frac{1}{\varepsilon},$$

and clearly, $2^y - 1 \le y 2^{1/\varepsilon}$ for $y \in \left[0, \frac{1}{\varepsilon}\right]$. Therefore,

$$
\begin{aligned}
\sum_{e \in P_k} [c_k(e) - c_{k-1}(e)] &\le \log \mu \sum_{e \in P_k} \left[\frac{b_k}{u(e)} c_{k-1}(e) + b_k \right] \cdot 2^{1/\varepsilon} \\
&= \log \mu \left(\sum_{e \in P_k} \frac{b_k}{u(e)} c_{k-1}(e) + \sum_{e \in P_k} b_k \right) \cdot 2^{1/\varepsilon} \\
&\le \log \mu \left(p_k + \sum_{e \in P_k} b_k \right) \cdot 2^{1/\varepsilon},
\end{aligned}
$$

since r_k is routed on P_k by AAP;

$$\le \log \mu (p_k + D \cdot b_k) \cdot 2^{1/\varepsilon}$$
$$= \log \mu \cdot 2 p_k \cdot 2^{1/\varepsilon}.$$

This completes the proof for inequality (i).

Inequality (ii) is established as follows. For any call r_j accepted by OPT, let P_j^* be the path that OPT uses to route this call. Notice that, by definition, for each call r_j that was rejected by AAP and admitted by OPT,

$$p_j < \min_{s_j\text{-}t_j \text{ path } P} \sum_{e \in P} \frac{b_j}{u(e)} c_{j-1}(e) \le \sum_{e \in P_j^*} \frac{b_j}{u(e)} c_{j-1}(e).$$

Hence,

$$\sum_{j \in \bar{A}} p_j < \sum_{j \in \bar{A}} \sum_{e \in P_j^*} \frac{b_j}{u(e)} c_{j-1}(e)$$

$$\le \sum_{j \in \bar{A}} \sum_{e \in P_j^*} \frac{b_j}{u(e)} c_n(e),$$

since $c_\ell(e)$ is nondecreasing with ℓ, and r_n is the last request;

$$= \sum_{e} \sum_{j \in \bar{A}: e \in P_j^*} \frac{b_j}{u(e)} c_n(e)$$

$$= \sum_{e} c_n(e) \sum_{j \in \bar{A}: e \in P_j^*} \frac{b_j}{u(e)}$$

$$\le \sum_{e} c_n(e),$$

since the offline algorithm cannot exceed the capacity constraints;

$$= C.$$

This completes the proof of inequality (ii). ∎

Exercise 13.2 Suppose we want to compare AAP against an "impoverished optimal offline algorithm" whose edge capacity is only $\frac{u(e)}{\log \mu}$ for each edge e. Show that against such an adversary, AAP is now $(2^{1+1/\varepsilon} + 1)$-competitive.

Exercise 13.3 Suppose we want to compare AAP against the **fractional optimal offline algorithm**, which is allowed to accept and route a fraction of each bandwidth requested; moreover, it can fractionally assign a call to many different routes. Show that Theorem 13.2 still applies to such a fractional optimal offline algorithm and hence the same competitive ratio holds for AAP in this context. (This extension is necessary for the proof of Theorem 13.14.)

Exercise 13.4 Suppose the bandwidth b_j for every call satisfies $1 \le b_j \le F$. Let every call now have constant profit (rather than profit proportional to the bandwidth), and let AAP' be the AAP algorithm modified so that $\varepsilon = 1$ and $\mu = 4DF$. Show that AAP' is $O(\log \mu)$-competitive if we assume the bandwidth restriction $b_i \le \min_e \frac{u(e)}{\log \mu + 2}$.

Exercise 13.5 Verify that Theorems 13.1 and 13.2 apply to the case of undirected networks where $u(e)$ bounds the capacity of edge e for calls that are routed in either direction on this edge (i.e., the undirected mode discussed at the end of Section 13.1).

13.3   Throughput Maximization for Limited Duration Calls

Section 12.4.2 showed that the case of limited but unknown durations results in a very poor competitive ratio for any online algorithm for load balancing in the restricted machines model (which corresponds to edge congestion in a routing network). For the throughput maximization routing problem the situation is even worse. In particular, there can be no online competitive algorithm for unknown durations even for the simplest networks.

Exercise 13.6 Consider a graph consisting of a single edge with a fixed capacity u. Show that for the case of unknown durations, there is no competitive (deterministic or randomized) algorithm for the call admission problem.

This is rather disappointing, because the case of unknown durations is quite natural and of practical importance. However, although we may not know the duration of any particular call at the time of arrival, we may have a reasonable statistical model for call durations. When this is the case, it is possible to look at an expected competitive ratio under the assumption that although both the online and optimal offline algorithms do not have a priori knowledge of call durations, they both know the distribution on the duration of any particular type of call. We consider this approach in Section 13.4. Another way around the negative result for unknown durations is to assume that the algorithm can make a "small" number of route reassignments, or **preemptions**, where a scheduled call is removed from the network at some cost. Algorithms that allow rescheduling or preemption are beyond the scope of this text. For the remainder of this section, we consider only the case of known durations.

Suppose

$$T = \frac{\text{longest duration of any call}}{\text{shortest duration of any call}}.$$

We want to show that at the cost of introducing randomization and a $\log T$ multiplicative factor in the competitive ratio, any call admission algorithm for permanent calls can be used to derive a call admission algorithm for known durations.

Theorem 13.3 *Let* ALG *be a c-competitive (deterministic or randomized) online algorithm for call admission and routing of permanent calls (on any network and under any assumptions on the capacity of edges, the size of bandwidth requests, the profit function, etc.).*

(i) *Then there exists a $(3c \cdot \lceil \log T \rceil)$-competitive randomized algorithm ALG$_T$ for call admission and routing of known duration calls where T is a known bound on the ratio of the longest to shortest duration.*

(ii) *If T is not known in advance, then there is an $O(c_\varepsilon \cdot c \cdot \log T \log \log^{1+\varepsilon} T)$-competitive randomized algorithm ALG$'$ for any $\varepsilon > 0$ where c_ε is increasing as ε decreases to 0.*

PROOF. For simplicity, we assume that $T = 2^h$ for some h. First assume that T is known a priori. A call is of duration type i if its duration t satisfies $2^i \leq t < 2^{i+1}$. Here we assume some unit of time and allow i to be any positive or negative integer so that durations can be arbitrarily long or arbitrarily short. Note, however, that there can be at most $\log T$ types. The algorithm ALG$_T$ is defined as follows.[2]

> **Algorithm** ALG$_T$: Initially (before any calls arrive), choose uniformly at random a number $k \in \{0, 1, \ldots, \log T\}$, and an integer $l \in \{0, 1, 2\}$. A call r is a "candidate call" if and only if (i) r is of type i_k where type i_k is the kth distinct type of call that is encountered in σ; and (ii) r arrives during a time interval $I_m = [(3m + l)2^{i_k}, (3m + l + 1)2^{i_k})$ for some positive integer m. ALG$_T$ accepts a call r if and only if r is a candidate call and r would be accepted by ALG given the candidate calls already accepted.

Since any candidate call has duration at least 2^{i_k} and accepted calls arriving during time period I_m cannot overlap with accepted calls (which must be of the same type) arriving during time period I_{m+1}, we can consider candidate calls arriving in period I_m as if they were permanent calls. Since l and k (and, therefore, i_k) are chosen randomly, the expected profit of candidate calls is at least $\frac{\text{OPT}(\sigma)}{3 \log T}$. Then, since ALG is c-competitive, it follows that ALG$_T$ is $(3c \cdot \log T)$-competitive.

If T is not known a priori, then we need to modify the probability of selecting a type i_k. Instead of selecting type i_k with probability $\frac{1}{\log T}$, ALG$'$ selects type i_k with probability

$$p_k = \frac{1}{f_\varepsilon} \frac{1}{k \cdot \log^{1+\varepsilon}(k)},$$

where f_ε is chosen so that $\sum_{1 \le k} p_k = 1$.[3] We leave the remainder of the proof as an exercise. ∎

Exercise 13.7 Complete the proof that ALG$'$ is $O(c_\varepsilon \cdot \log T \log \log^{1+\varepsilon} T)$-competitive.

For maximizing throughput in large capacity networks, it is possible to extend Theorems 13.1 and 13.2 to apply to known limited duration calls. The $\log T$ multiplicative factor now becomes an additive factor (although the allowable bandwidth of a call must be somewhat more restricted). We now denote the jth call by $r_j = (s_j, t_j, b_j, p_j, a_j, f_j)$ where a_j and f_j, respectively, denote the arrival and finishing times for this call. We assume that profit is proportional to throughput, which in this case is defined as (bandwidth × duration). Again, without loss of generality, we can scale the profit so that it is now equal to $D \cdot$ (bandwidth × duration). Set the minimum duration of any call to be 1 (in some unit of time) and suppose that T is a known bound on the maximum duration of any call. For simplicity, we can view time as discrete and say that the duration of every call is an integer satisfying $1 \le f_j - a_j + 1 \le T$. Generalizing the definition of $L_j(e)$, we define $L_j(e, t)$ as the *present* normalized load on edge e incurred by the online algorithm during the time unit $[t, t+1)$ after having processed the first j requests. (Note that $L_j(e, t)$ can increase or decrease as t increases, since calls will arrive and terminate.) The definition of $c_j(e, t)$ is then defined as in the case of permanent calls by modifying equation (13.1), with $L_j(e, t)$ replacing $L_j(e)$. It remains only to increase the bandwidth restriction appropriately. The AAP algorithm for the known duration variant can now be presented as follows.

---

[2] Note that this algorithm rejects "most" calls; we present it mainly for its theoretical interest.

[3] For a different application of this idea, see Section 14.1.2.

Algorithm AAP-KNOWN$_\varepsilon$: Let D be a bound on the length of any routing path (e.g., the diameter of the routing network), and let $\varepsilon > 0$ be any constant. Assume that

$$b_i \leq \min_e u(e)\left(\varepsilon \log DT + 1 + \frac{1}{\varepsilon}\right),$$

and that $p_i = Db_i(f_i - a_i)$ for every call r_i. Let $\mu = 2^{1+1/\varepsilon}DT$.

Upon arrival of the jth call $r_j = (s_j, t_j, b_j, p_j, a_j, f_j)$, if there exists any path P between s_j and t_j such that

$$\sum_{a_j \leq t < f_j} \sum_{e \in P} \frac{b_j}{u(e)} c_{j-1}(e, t) \leq p_j,$$

then route r_j on such a path. Otherwise, reject the call. In either case, update $L_j(e, t)$ and $c_j(e, t)$ appropriately; that is, if r_j is accepted and $a_j \leq t < f_j$, then

$$L_j(e, t) := L_{j-1}(e, t) + \frac{b_j}{u(e)};$$

otherwise,

$$L_j(e, t) := L_{j-1}(e, t).$$

The following theorems are analogous to Theorems 13.1 and 13.2.

Theorem 13.4 *Under the stated assumptions, the* AAP-KNOWN$_\varepsilon$ *algorithm never violates an edge capacity constraint.*

Theorem 13.5 *Under the stated assumptions, the* AAP-KNOWN$_\varepsilon$ *algorithm is*

$$O(2^{1/\varepsilon} \log \mu) = O\left(\frac{2^{1/\varepsilon}}{\varepsilon} + 2^{1/\varepsilon} \log DT\right)\text{-competitive.}$$

Exercise 13.8 Modify the proofs of Theorems 13.1 and 13.2 to prove Theorems 13.4 and 13.5.

13.4 Experimental Results

In the spirit of Section 5.2, we once again view competitive (worst-case) analysis as a starting point for the development of algorithms that are potentially competitive in the commercial sense of the word. We continue to study call admission and circuit routing in large capacity networks and consider the AAP algorithm as a basis for the development of an algorithm that will perform well "in practice." The fact is, however, that currently the meaning of "in practice" is not well understood when one considers the emerging use of high capacity, multipurpose (e.g., data, voice, video, etc.) networks. In particular, neither the traffic patterns nor the topology (or switching technology) of the networks is well understood. Also, charging schemes must evolve with the technology and use of these networks.[4]

---

[4] To paraphrase a euphemism of the software industry, all these problematic aspects of network technology and its application are opportunities for innovative algorithm design.

What are some of the aspects of the AAP algorithm that negate its use as a "practical algorithm"?

- In the (practical) case of limited durations, the AAP algorithm needs to know the duration a priori and uses this information in a computationally intensive manner. That is, for each edge AAP needs to identify each call (and its time interval) that is occupying this edge. When considering a new call, the algorithm sums (or integrates) path costs over the entire duration of the new call.
- The AAP algorithm is to a large extent a call admission algorithm and only implicitly routes calls by limiting the choice of possible routes.
- The AAP algorithm chooses the parameter μ to optimize the (worst-case) competitive ratio and therefore may not be the best choice if, for example, one is trying to optimize performance at some expected level of network utilization.
- The AAP algorithm does not exploit the call bandwidth restriction beyond the logarithmic fraction threshold. That is, intuitively, the smaller the relative bandwidth to edge capacity ratio, the easier it should be to balance network utilization.

The first criticism (the need for known call duration) can be finessed by a standard assumption in communications and queuing networks: the duration of calls is exponentially distributed with some known mean duration. One can then analytically bound the expected competitive ratio for worst-case inputs or for source–destination inputs generated according to, for example, some Poisson distribution (also standard in network analysis). We do not discuss this type of analysis here; instead, we use such distributional assumptions to help in the algorithm design. (Of course, we can also use these assumptions for generating test data in experimental studies).[5]

Using the notation of algorithms AAP and AAP-KNOWN, we introduce a more "aggressive" and computationally simpler version of the AAP algorithm that (according to one interesting set of experimental studies) shows the promise of the underlying call admission approach of AAP.

Algorithm SAAP$_\mu$ (**SHORTEST-AAP**): Upon arrival of the jth call $r_j = (s_j, t_j, b_j, p_j, a_j, f_j)$, determine if there exists a path P between s_j and t_j such that

$$\sum_{e \in P} b_j \mu^{L_{j-1}(e)} \leq p_j$$

and for every $e \in P$,

$$L_{j-1}(e) + \frac{b_j}{u(e)} < 1.$$

If such a path exists, then route r_j on a *shortest* such path P. Otherwise, reject r_j. In either case, update $L_j(e)$ appropriately. Similarly, when a call terminates (e.g., after input r_{j-1} but before input r_j), update $L_{j-1}(e)$ appropriately.

Before discussing how to set μ and presenting some experimental studies of SAAP$_\mu$, we consider the ways in which SAAP differs from AAP. The most obvious difference is that

---

[5] See Feldman [147] for an interesting study.

SAAP$_\mu$ chooses a shortest path, since short paths use fewer resources. Furthermore, we have simplified the path acceptance condition and we are not explicitly restricting b_j in terms of μ, so we must indeed check that the capacity of each edge is not exceeded.

We now consider a more simplified scenario than in Sections 13.2 and 13.3. We assume every call r_j has a fixed (but substantially small) bandwidth requirement (e.g., $b_j = b$) and every edge has a fixed capacity. We also assume a fixed exponential distribution for the duration of calls; it follows, then, that these durations are sufficiently concentrated around their mean so we can assume that the profit associated with every call is identical (e.g., $p_j = p$). Under these assumptions, we can then scale the profit p so that if a call r can be accommodated by a single edge path, it will be accepted. That is, for single edge paths, we ignore the condition $b \cdot \mu^1 \leq p$ by setting $p = b\mu$. This is the sense in which SAAP is aggressive.

It remains to choose μ so that it will utilize longer paths unless it is "probable" (given some assumptions on the input arrival process) that such a path will help to saturate certain edges and preclude their later use. Here is one way to do this. Consider a length 2 path and suppose each of its edges has the same relativized load $L < 1$. We set μ so that if L exceeds some critical utilization L^*, then the call will be rejected. Namely, set μ to be the least value such that $2b\mu^{L^*} \geq b\mu = p$; that is, set $\mu = 2^{1/(1-L^*)}$. (Recall that the exponential weighting emphasizes the cost of a heavily loaded edge so that when the edges in a path are not equally loaded, the setting of μ tends to "protect" the heavily loaded edge.) Thus the setting of μ is reduced to a setting of L^*.

A setting of L^* might be determined experimentally (and dynamically) or we could use a heuristic analysis to guide in the setting of L^*. For example, suppose that we again assume that the inputs are Poisson distributed and that the durations are exponentially distributed. Consider a request for a two-link path where each edge is equally loaded at the maximum utilization L^*. That is, the number of calls on each edge (call the edges e_1 and e_2) of this path is $\frac{L^*}{b}$. From queuing systems analysis, we can calculate the probability that a new call requiring only a single edge (e.g., e_1) will be rejected if we accept the two-edge path. We then set L^* so that this probability is less than some $\beta < 0.5$. This ensures that the probability "that a selected two-edge path will block a later arriving one-edge call" is less than 1. Finally, we note that this calculation of L^* depends on the expected means of the assumed Poisson and exponential distributions. The mean duration time is not network dependent; however, the mean arrival rate (call it λ) of requests routable on a single edge path is very dependent on the network. One suggestion for setting (in a network-independent way) the value of λ (for the purpose of calculating a value of L^*) is to set the mean arrival time of a single edge routable call at the largest rate that still guarantees that the rejection rate for such calls (in the absence of any other calls) will be less than some target rejection rate ρ. This type of heuristic reasoning (based on probabilistic assumptions about the nature and independence of calls) and queuing systems analysis provides an approach for setting L^* (and hence μ) as a function of a desired maximum rejection rate.

Figure 13.1 illustrates the simulated performance of this SAAP based approach on a network topology of an existing commercial network having 25 nodes and 65 edges.[6] Here performance is measured as the experimentally observed rejection rate of calls as a function

---

[6] This figure was provided by S. Plotkin.

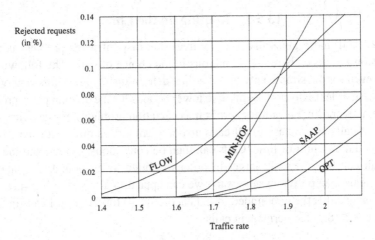

Figure 13.1: Simulation of routing algorithms on a commercial network.

of an aggregate arrival rate of calls.[7] Such simulations have been performed for both relatively static and relatively dynamic simulated traffic patterns using various settings for the desired maximum rejection rate ρ. This figure represents a desired maximum rejection rate of 0.033 (3.3%). The curve "Optimum" refers to a lower bound for the offline OPT using a fractional optimal multicommodity based solution. Hence, this "Optimum" is an underestimate of OPT. The curve "EXP" refers to SAAP using a desired maximum rejection rate of 3.3% to set the utilization threshold L^*. The curve "greedy min-hop" is the (perhaps most commonly used) algorithm that uses a shortest path that satisfies the (unweighted) edge capacity constraints. Finally, the curve "Proportional flow-based" refers to an offline approximation algorithm using multicommodity flows with randomized rounding. Such preliminary studies (as promising as they may be) are only suggestive at this point in time. However, the field of large capacity (multipurpose) network design and analysis is so new and evolving so quickly that new algorithms (such as SAAP and other variations based on competitive algorithms) are likely to influence commercial network design and analysis.

13.5 Call Admission for Particular Networks: The Disjoint Paths Problem

In this section we consider some standard networks: a line, a tree, and an array. For simplicity, we consider each of these networks in the undirected mode but claim that all results (both upper and lower bounds) can be extended to the bidirectional view of undirected graphs.

Algorithm AAP has the advantage that it applies to all networks. However, on the negative side, the competitiveness of algorithm AAP requires the capacity of each edge to be large in comparison to the bandwidth needed for a call. The classic problem of **disjoint path allocation** is simply the problem instance of routing and call admission of permanent calls where all calls have bandwidth 1 and each edge has capacity 1.

---

[7] The input calls were randomly generated according to a fixed matrix specifying the rate for each source–destination pair. To vary the aggregate rate, the matrix is multiplied by a constant.

13.5.1   Routing on the Line

For the line (and, more generally, for any tree), the disjoint paths problem is purely a call admission problem; there are no options in the choice of path. The following result shows that even for the simple network of a line, deterministic algorithms cannot be very competitive. In order to discuss asymptotic lower bounds for the disjoint paths problem on a fixed size network (that is, a finite, profit maximization problem), we can view the case of permanent calls as the case of all calls arriving "almost" simultaneously and having a duration equal to 1 unit of time. Calls can then be continuously input, and the optimal offline profit can be arbitrarily large. In order to obtain lower bounds for randomized algorithms against an oblivious adversary, we can appeal to Yao's principle, presented in Chapter 8, using either the unbounded form (Theorem 8.4) for duration 1 calls or the finite version (Theorem 8.3) for permanent calls.

Theorem 13.6 *Consider an N-node (i.e., diameter $D = N-1$) line. Then any deterministic online algorithm* ALG *for the disjoint paths problem has competitive ratio $\geq D = N-1$. In particular, there exists a request sequence σ such that* OPT$(\sigma) = N - 1$ *and* ALG$(\sigma) = 1$ *(or* OPT$(\sigma) = 1$ *and* ALG$(\sigma) = 0$).

PROOF. The adversary requests a unit duration call from node 0 to node D (i.e., using every edge on the line). If ALG rejects this call, then OPT accepts the call. If ALG accepts the first call, then (i) OPT rejects this call and (ii) the adversary then requests D additional calls, one for each edge of the line, with OPT accepting these D calls. Thus, for every call accepted by ALG, OPT accepts at least D calls. This is repeated for each time step. ∎

Exercise 13.9 Assume that every edge on the line has capacity K and that every call is permanent and has bandwidth 1. Show that any deterministic online algorithm for this call admission problem has competitive ratio at least $D^{1/K}$. Thus, the capacity assumption used in proving that the deterministic algorithm AAP is $O(\log D)$-competitive (see Section 13.2) is necessary. Similarly, consider the case of a single edge line of capacity K and every call having known limited duration and bandwidth 1. Show that $T^{1/K}$ is a lower bound for the competitive ratio of any deterministic algorithm where, as in Section 13.3, T is the ratio of the maximum to minimum duration.

Theorem 13.6 suggests the use of randomization for the disjoint paths problem. For the case of a line, it is easy to describe a randomized algorithm that achieves a competitive ratio of $\lceil \log N \rceil = \lceil \log(D + 1) \rceil$. For simplicity, assume $N = 2^k$ for some integer k. Let e_1 be the edge whose removal separates the line into two equal length sublines, each having 2^{k-1} nodes. Now separate each of these sublines by a separating edge. Let $E_2 = \{e_{21}, e_{22}\}$ be these separating edges. We continue recursively, and obtain "separating sets" $E_1 = \{e_1\}, E_2, \ldots, E_k$. The sets $\{E_i\}$ constitute a partition of the edges, and we can classify every call by saying that a call is a **level i call** if $i = \min_j E_j \cap E' \neq \varnothing$ where E' are the edges constituting the path requested by the call. (See Figure 13.2.)

Algorithm CRS (**CLASSIFY-AND-RANDOMLY-SELECT**): Randomly select a level i^* uniformly in $\{1, 2, \ldots, \log N\}$. Accept any level i^* call that does not conflict with a previously accepted call. Reject all level j calls for $j \neq i^*$.

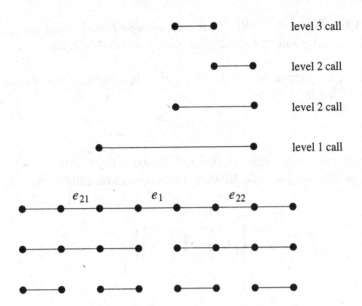

Figure 13.2: Partitioning the edges of the line into levels.

We obtain the following result.

Theorem 13.7 *Algorithm* CRS *is strictly* $\lceil \log N \rceil = \lceil \log(D + 1) \rceil$*-competitive for the disjoint paths problem on the line.*

PROOF. Again, for simplicity, assume $N = 2^k$ for some integer k. We first observe that if an input sequence of calls is restricted to one-level class, then greedy scheduling (i.e., accepting any call that does not conflict with a previously accepted call) is 1-competitive on such a restricted set of inputs. This follows simply because either any two-level i calls are edge disjoint or their intersection includes a unique edge in E_i. Thus, for every level i call accepted by greedy, there is at most one level i call accepted by an optimal algorithm.

Given any input sequence of calls σ, let OPT route o_i calls from level i and let CRS route c_i calls from level i (if $i = i^*$). Clearly, $o_i = c_i$; therefore,

$$
\mathbf{E}[\text{CRS}(\sigma)] = \sum_{i=1}^{\log N} \Pr[\text{CRS chooses level } i] \cdot c_i
$$

$$
\geq \sum_{i=1}^{\log N} \frac{1}{\log N} \cdot o_i
$$

$$
= \frac{1}{\log N} \sum o_i
$$

$$
= \frac{1}{\log N} \text{OPT}(\sigma).
$$

Conversely, we have the following theorem.

Theorem 13.8 $\left\lfloor \frac{\log(N)}{2} \right\rfloor = \left\lfloor \frac{\log(D+1)}{2} \right\rfloor$ *is a lower bound on the randomized (oblivious adversary) competitive ratio for the disjoint paths problem on the line.*

PROOF. Again, for simplicity, assume $N = 2^k$. We construct a distribution on input sequences σ such that

$$\mathbf{E}[\text{OPT}(\sigma)] = \frac{\log N}{2},$$

whereas for any online algorithm ALG, we have $\mathbf{E}[\text{ALG}(\sigma)] \leq 1$.

Consider the following sets of calls where $[u, v]$ denotes the call from node u to node v:

$$C_1 = \{[1, N]\}$$
$$C_2 = \left\{ \left[1, \frac{N}{2}\right], \left[\frac{N}{2}, N\right] \right\}$$
$$\vdots$$
$$C_{\log D} = \{[1, 2], [2, 3], \ldots, [N - 1, N]\}.$$

Clearly, all calls in C_i are level i calls and C_i uses all the edges of the line. Moreover, each call in C_i interferes with two calls in C_{i+1}, four calls in C_{i+2}, and so on. The distribution is generated as follows: choose ℓ in $\{1, 2, \ldots, \log N\}$ with probability $\frac{2^{-\ell}}{1-1/N}$, generate all calls in $C_1, C_2, \ldots, C_\ell$, and then end the input sequence.

We first consider OPT on a random input σ. If the input terminates with level i calls, then OPT accepts exactly the calls in level i, rejecting all calls in levels $j < i$. Therefore,

$$\mathbf{E}[\text{OPT}(\sigma)] = \sum_{i=1}^{\log N} 2^{i-1} \cdot \frac{2^{-i}}{1 - 1/N}$$
$$> \frac{\log N}{2}.$$

Now for any deterministic online algorithm ALG we have the following claims:

Claim 1: $\Pr[\text{ALG will see calls from } C_i \mid \text{ALG has seen the calls from } C_{i-1}] \leq \frac{1}{2}$.

Claim 2: If ALG rejects a call r in C_i that does not conflict with previously accepted calls, then $\mathbf{E}[\text{ALG's eventual benefit gained by rejecting } r] \leq 1 = \text{ALG's benefit gained by accepting } r$.

Claim 1 is immediate. Using Claim 1, we prove Claim 2 by (backward) induction on $i = \log N, \log N - 1, \ldots, 1$. Clearly, for the base case of $i = \log N$, if the algorithm rejects r, the expected eventual benefit is 0, since there will be no further calls that conflict with r; hence, the claim is true. Suppose the claim is true for level j. We show that it is true for level $j - 1$. If we reject a call r at level $j - 1$, we have the potential benefit of calls at level j that intersect with r. Thus ALG's expected benefit from rejecting r is at most $\frac{1}{2}(\mathbf{E}[r_1] + \mathbf{E}[r_2])$, where r_1 and r_2 are the two calls (i.e., the intervals) whose union is r, and $\mathbf{E}[r_i]$ is the maximum expected benefit from accepting or rejecting r_i. That is, with probability $\frac{1}{2}$, the algorithm will see both calls r_1 and r_2 and will have an opportunity to accept or reject these calls. However, since r_1 and r_2 are at level j, we know by the inductive hypothesis that $\mathbf{E}[r_1] = \mathbf{E}[r_2] \leq 1$, whether or not the algorithm accepts or rejects r_1 or r_2.

We conclude the proof as follows. ALG can either accept or reject the first call. If it accepts the first call then clearly $\text{ALG}(\sigma) = 1$. If it rejects the first call r, then by Claim 2 (with $i = 1$ and noting that there are no previously accepted calls with which r can conflict), we have $\mathbf{E}[\text{ALG}(\sigma)] \leq 1$. ∎

Exercise 13.10 As in Exercise 13.9, consider the line where every edge has a fixed capacity and every call has bandwidth 1. Show that the proof of the $\lfloor \frac{\log(D+1)}{2} \rfloor$ lower bound in Theorem 13.8 can be extended to this call admission problem. Hence, when $\varepsilon = 1$ and therefore $\mu = 4D$, we have a corresponding (randomized) lower bound for the (deterministic) upper bound of Theorem 13.2.

13.5.2 Routing on Trees

It is not difficult to extend the "classify and randomly select" idea to trees. One complication is that we cannot always equally partition a tree by removing an edge. (Consider a "star" tree with only one internal node.) However, for any N-node tree, we can remove a *node* v_1 so that each resulting disconnected subtree has at most $\frac{N}{2}$ nodes. We then continue this process in order to partition the nodes into classes $V_1 = \{v_1\}, V_2, V_3, \ldots, V_{\log N}$. The nodes in V_i are called level i node separators. A call is a **level i call** if $i = \min_j(V_j \cap V' \neq \varnothing)$ where V' is the set of nodes in the call path.

Theorem 13.9 *Algorithm* CRS *for the tree (based on node separators) is strictly* $(2 \log N)$-*competitive.*

PROOF. Edge (u, v) is called a level i edge if $i = \min(\text{level } u, \text{level } v)$. Following the proof of Theorem 13.7, here we first prove that when calls are restricted to one class, then greedy scheduling is 2-competitive. To see this, observe that any level i call intersects at most one level i node (otherwise, it would also intersect a level $i - 1$ node and hence be a level j call for some $j < i$). Furthermore, each level i call intersects at most two level i edges (which are adjacent to v_i). Thus, any two-level i calls either are edge disjoint or (i) share a unique level i separator v_i and (ii) share at least one and at most two level i edges. It follows that for every level i call r accepted by online greedy scheduling, there can be at most two calls accepted by OPT that edge intersect r (and hence may be rejected by the greedy algorithm), that is, at most one for each of the possibly two level i edges in the path used by the online algorithm for call r. Following the same argument as the one presented in the proof of Theorem 13.7, we can then obtain $\mathbf{E}[\text{CRS}(\sigma)] \geq \frac{1}{2 \log N} \text{OPT}(\sigma)$. ∎

Theorem 13.9 applies in a more general setting, as explored in the following exercises.

Exercise 13.11 Consider N-node trees with arbitrary integer capacities on the edges and calls that all have bandwidth 1. We want to maximize the number of accepted calls subject to the edge capacity constraints. Show that the CRS algorithm achieves a competitive ratio of $2 \log N$.

Exercise 13.12 Consider N-node trees with arbitrary positive capacities on the edges and calls that have arbitrary bandwidth. As in the previous exercise, we want to maximize the number of accepted calls. Using the previous exercise and the basic idea of Theorem 13.3, show that there is a randomized $O(\log N \log B)$-competitive algorithm where B is the ratio of the largest to smallest bandwidth.

Obviously, the $\log D$ lower bound in Theorem 13.8 also applies to trees. We now show that an $O(\log D)$ upper bound is also possible. In order to establish this optimal $O(\log D)$-competitive ratio for call admission on trees, it is helpful to make some observations about the intersection graph of paths on trees. Let T be a tree and $\mathcal{P}$ a set of paths on T. The **intersection graph** $I[T, \mathcal{P}] = (\mathcal{P}, E_\mathcal{P})$ is simply the graph whose nodes are the paths and whose edges correspond to intersecting paths. Our first observation is that for the study of routing problems on trees, we can assume without loss of generality that all paths are leaf to leaf. To see this, consider a tree T and a set of paths $\mathcal{P}$. We construct a new tree T' and a new set of leaf to leaf paths $\mathcal{P}'$ such that the intersection graphs $I[T, \mathcal{P}]$ and $I[T', \mathcal{P}']$ are the same. We construct T' by adding edges and leaves to T as follows. For every internal node v in T with edges $e_1, \ldots, e_d$, we add edges $e_i' = (v, w_i)$, with each w_i being a new leaf. Let P be a path with endpoint v, and let e_i be the first edge in this path. We construct $\mathcal{P}'$ by extending each such path P so that it ends at the leaf w_i. It should be clear that $I[T, \mathcal{P}] = I[T', \mathcal{P}']$; consequently, routing problems on trees can be restricted to leaf to leaf calls. For the remainder of this chapter we make this assumption.

Our second observation is a result of independent graph theoretic interest. We need the following definition. A graph $G = (V, E)$ is a **d-inductive graph** if there is an ordering of the vertices $v_1, \ldots, v_N$ in V such that for all i, $|\{(v_i, v_j)|i < j$ and $(v_i, v_j) \in E\}| \le d$.

Theorem 13.10 *Let $T = (V, E)$ be a tree and $\mathcal{P}$ a set of paths on T having maximum edge congestion g. Then the intersection graph $I[T, \mathcal{P}]$ is $2(g - 1)$-inductive.*

PROOF. The proof is by induction on $|\mathcal{P}|$ (and, strictly speaking, for a given $|\mathcal{P}|$ by induction on $|V|$). The basis $|\mathcal{P}| = 1$ is immediate. If $|V| = 2$, then the theorem is also immediate, so we can assume that there are at least three nodes in V. Therefore, T has at least one interior node. An interior node of T is called "central" if it has at most one nonleaf neighbor. It is easy to prove (by induction on $|V|$) that every tree with $|V| \ge 3$ has at least one central node. Now assume that the theorem holds for $|\mathcal{P}| = k$. For the induction step, we only need to show how to choose the first node for the inductive ordering of the intersection graph and then remove that path (= node in the intersection graph). If a central node v has degree 2, then we can eliminate the leaf ℓ adjacent to v and replace any path with endpoint ℓ by the one edge shorter path with endpoint v (which is now a leaf). If a central v has no paths intersecting it, then we can remove this node and all its leaf neighbors. We continue doing this until we find a central node v that has degree larger than 2 and that has at least one path passing through it (or until $|V| = 2$, in which case we are done). Let $\ell_1, \ldots, \ell_f$ be the leaves adjacent to v. If there is a length 2 path $P \in \mathcal{P}$ with endpoints in $\{\ell_1, \ldots, \ell_f\}$, then this path can be the first node in the inductive ordering, since P can intersect at most $2(g - 1)$ other paths. Otherwise, all paths with endpoints in $\{\ell_1, \ldots, \ell_f\}$ must intersect the unique edge $e = (v, w)$ for which w is not a leaf. Again, we can shorten all paths with endpoints in $\{\ell_1, \ldots, \ell_f\}$ and remove the leaves neighboring v.   ∎

Corollary 13.11 *The intersection graph has at most* $2(g-1) \cdot |V|$ *edges.*

We are ready to define a randomized $O(\log D)$-competitive call admission (i.e., disjoint paths) algorithm for any tree of diameter D.

> **Algorithm TREE-AAP:** Let σ be a sequence of calls.
> 1. Simulate algorithm AAP (with $\varepsilon = 1$) on T, assuming that each call has bandwidth 1 and that each edge has capacity $2 + \log D$. If a path r is accepted by AAP, then r becomes a **candidate**.
> 2. If r is a candidate and if it does not intersect some previously accepted path, then with probability $\frac{1}{4(1+\log D)}$ TREE-AAP accepts r.

Theorem 13.12 *There exists a constant c such that for every tree T of diameter D, and for every input sequence σ of paths on T,* TREE-AAP$(\sigma) \geq \frac{c}{\log D} \cdot$ OPT(σ). *That is,* TREE-AAP *is $O(\log D)$-competitive.*

PROOF. Let $\sigma = r_1, \ldots, r_n$ be an input sequence of paths. By an easy modification of the proof of Theorem 13.2, we claim that

$$|\{r_i | r_i \text{ is a candidate}\}| = \Omega(\text{OPT}(\sigma)).$$

This follows (as in Exercise 13.2) because the offline adversary is given only a fraction $\frac{1}{\log D + 2}$ of the bandwidth constraint of the online algorithm. Hence, inequality (ii) in the proof of Theorem 13.2 becomes

$$\sum_{j \in \bar{A}} p_j \leq \frac{C}{2 + \log D}.$$

We complete the proof by showing that

$$|\{r_i | r_i \text{ is accepted}\}| \geq \frac{1}{8(1 + \log D)} |\{r_i | r_i \text{ is a candidate}\}|.$$

Consider the intersection graph $(\mathcal{P}, E_{\mathcal{P}})$ corresponding to the set $\mathcal{P}$ of candidate calls. Clearly, the congestion number g of this set of paths is at most $2 + \log D$. We say that a path is a "lucky candidate" if it is a candidate and the probability $\left(\frac{1}{4(1+\log D)}\right)$-coin toss is successful. Let $X = \{r_i | r_i \text{ is a lucky candidate}\}$ and let $Y = \{(r_i, r_j) | \text{ both } r_i \text{ and } r_j \text{ are lucky candidates}\}$. Clearly,

$$|\{r_i | r_i \text{ is accepted}\}| \geq |X| - |Y|.$$

We calculate

$$\mathbf{E}[|X|] = |\mathcal{P}| \cdot \frac{1}{4(1 + \log D)}$$

and

$$\mathbf{E}[|Y|] = |E_{\mathcal{P}}| \cdot \frac{1}{16(1 + \log D)^2} \leq |\mathcal{P}|(2 + 2\log D)\frac{1}{16(1 + \log D)^2},$$

since the intersection graph is $2(g-1) = 2\log D + 2$ inductive and, therefore, $|E_{\mathcal{P}}| \leq (2\log D + 2)|\mathcal{P}|$. Thus

$$\mathbf{E}[|X| - |Y|] \geq \frac{|\mathcal{P}|}{8(1 + \log D)}.$$

13.5.3   Routing on Arrays

In considering the disjoint paths problem on arrays, we return to the more general call admission and routing problem, since (unlike trees) once again we must decide how to route every accepted call. We construct an $O(\log N)$-competitive randomized online algorithm for the disjoint paths problem on an $(N \times N)$-array network. Asymptotically, this is an optimal bound and randomization is necessary, with $\Theta(\sqrt{N})$ being the (asymptotically) optimal bound for deterministic algorithms. Note that the randomized $\Omega(\log N)$ lower bound for the line does not immediately apply to arrays, since now there are alternative paths even if all calls are restricted to a single row. However, the proof of Theorem 13.6 does lead to the following analogous result.

Theorem 13.13 *Let* ALG *be any randomized algorithm for the disjoint paths problem on an $(N \times N)$ array. Then,* $\overline{\mathcal{R}}_{\mathrm{OBL}}(\mathrm{ALG}) \geq \frac{\log(N)}{2}$.

PROOF. The proof is motivated by the proof of Theorem 13.8. We now describe the changes required for the array. First, we need to construct appropriate sets of calls, $C_1, \ldots, C_{\log N}$. Again assume $N = 2^k$ for some positive integer k. For each i ($1 \leq i \leq \log N$), partition the array into 4^{i-1} subarrays each of size $\frac{N}{2^{i-1}} \times \frac{N}{2^{i-1}}$. The class C_i consists of the following calls: for each of the 4^{i-1} subarrays, request $\frac{N}{2^{i-1}}$ "vertical calls" between the top and bottom of the subarray, and $\frac{N}{2^{i-1}}$ "horizontal calls" between the left and right boundaries of the subarray.

The request sequences are randomly generated as follows: choose l in $\{1, 2, \ldots, \log N\}$ with probability $\frac{2^{-l}}{1 - 1/N}$, and request all calls in $C_1, \ldots, C_l$ (in this order). Note that there are $2 \cdot \frac{N}{2^{i-1}} \cdot 4^{i-1}$ calls in C_i.

For any deterministic online algorithm ALG, we need to argue by the Yao principle (Theorem 8.3) that

$$\frac{\mathbf{E}[\mathrm{OPT}(\sigma)]}{\mathbf{E}[\mathrm{ALG}(\sigma)]} \geq \frac{\log N}{2}.$$

We first consider OPT. If the input sequence ends with class i, then OPT accepts all (and only) the calls in C_i. The expected benefit of OPT is then

$$\sum_{i=1}^{\log N} 2 \cdot \frac{N}{2^{i-1}} \cdot 4^{i-1} \cdot \frac{2^{-i}}{1 - 1/N} = \sum_{i=1}^{\log N} \frac{N}{1 - 1/N} > N \log N.$$

It remains to show that $E[\mathrm{ALG}(\sigma)] \leq 2N$. Let

$$A(i, k) = \max \mathbf{E} \left[\begin{array}{l|l} \text{number of calls in} & \sigma \text{ terminates in class } j \geq i, \text{ and} \\ \text{classes } j = i, i+1, \ldots & \text{there are at most } k \text{ free edges after} \\ & \text{calls in classes } C_1, \ldots, C_{i-1} \\ & \text{have been accepted} \end{array} \right].$$

The maximum operator is taken over all possible ways to accept calls in classes $C_1, \ldots, C_{i-1}$. Since a call in C_i requires a path of length at least $\frac{N}{2^{i-1}} - 1$, $A(i, k)$ satisfies the recurrence

$$A(i, k) \leq \max_{j \leq k / \frac{N}{2^{i-1}} - 1} \left(j + \frac{1}{2} A \left(i + 1, k - j \cdot \left(N/2^{i-1} - 1 \right) \right) \right).$$

We need to prove (by induction on $j = 1, 2, \ldots, \log N$) that $A(i, k) \leq \frac{k}{(N/2^{i-1}-1)}$.

Base case. $A(\log N, k) \leq k$, since every call in $C_{\log N}$ requires at least one edge.

Inductive step. Follows immediately from recurrence and induction hypothesis by setting j to its maximum value.

The proof is completed by observing that $\mathbf{E}[\text{ALG}(\sigma)] \leq A(1, 2N(N-1)) \leq 2N$. ∎

The basic idea for an $O(\log N)$-competitive algorithm is reasonably intuitive; however, the precise algorithm and its analysis are sufficiently complex that a complete proof would be prohibitively long. Here we describe only the basic approach. In Appendix F we provide a more detailed description of the algorithm and the basic ideas for the analysis so that this discussion can be extended to form a rigorous proof.

The main idea is as follows. Let c be a suitable constant to be chosen later. An $(N \times N)$ array G is viewed as a $\left(\frac{N}{c \log N} \times \frac{N}{c \log N}\right)$ array whose "supernodes" are $(c \log N \times c \log N)$ subarrays of the given array G. Since there are $c \log N$ common points between adjacent supernodes, we envision a pair of adjacent supernodes as if they were connected by a $c \log N$ capacity "superedge." For "long distance calls" whose source and destinations are several superedges apart, we hope that much of the superedge capacity can be utilized; thus, algorithm AAP of Section 13.2 is able to route long distance calls. "Local calls" are accommodated by exploiting the fact that the diameter, boundary, and size of a subarray are relatively small.

Of course, the above intuition ignores many important details. Perhaps the most important of these missing details is a proof that these large capacity superedges can actually be used to route a set of $O(\log N)$ long distance calls. Another crucial missing detail is a proof guaranteeing that local calls can be routed competitively and that the routing of local calls and long distance calls will not interfere with each other. To see that these details are nontrivial, we observe that for the "somewhat similar" brick wall graph (see Section 13.6), there is an $\Omega(N^\varepsilon)$ lower bound for the competitive ratio of any randomized online algorithm for disjoint paths.

Theorem 13.14 *Let G be an $(N \times N)$ array. Then there exists a randomized algorithm for the disjoint paths problem with competitive ratio $O(\log N)$.*

13.6 The Disjoint Paths Problem: A Lower Bound for a Difficult Network

We now show that there is a (perhaps pathological) network for which the competitive ratio of the maximum disjoint paths problem is provably large. The difficult network is based on the odd degree undirected **brick wall graph** W, as depicted in Figure 13.3.

For simplicity, we consider W in the undirected mode. (For a directed version of W with the desired properties, we could direct all vertical edges from north to south and alternate the direction of horizontal edges; i.e., edges in the topmost row are directed east to west, edges in the next row are directed west to east, etc.). From left to right, let $s_1, s_2, \ldots, s_N$ (respectively, $t_1, \ldots, t_N$) denote the source (respectively, sink) nodes of W. We say that the width of such a W is N and the height of W is the number of rows. Calls (s_{i_1}, t_{j_1}) and (s_{i_2}, t_{j_2}) are called **compatible** if $i_1 < i_2$ and $j_1 < j_2$ or $i_1 > i_2$ and $j_1 > j_2$. Basic properties of the brick wall graph are expressed in the following lemmas.

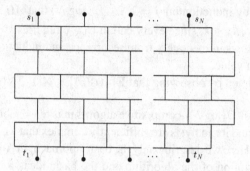

Figure 13.3: The brick wall graph.

Lemma 13.1 *In the brick wall graph, any two source to sink paths P_1 and P_2 are node disjoint if and only if they are edge disjoint.*

PROOF. Clearly, node disjoint paths are edge disjoint. Suppose paths P_1 and P_2 intersect at a node v. If P_1 and P_2 enter v on the same edge, then clearly P_1 and P_2 are not edge disjoint. If they enter v on distinct edges, then one must exit on one of the entering edges, or both exit v on the remaining edge. Hence, P_1 and P_2 are node disjoint if and only if they are edge disjoint. ∎

Exercise 13.13 More generally, consider any graph with maximum degree 3 and let P_1 and P_2 be two paths whose endpoints are at degree 2 vertices. Show that P_1 and P_2 are node disjoint if and only if they are edge disjoint.

Lemma 13.2 *A pair of source to sink calls (s_{i_1}, t_{j_1}) and (s_{i_2}, t_{j_2}) with $i_1 \neq i_2$, $j_1 \neq j_2$ have edge disjoint paths if and only if the calls are compatible.*

PROOF. If (i_1, j_1) and (i_2, j_2) are compatible with $i_1 < i_2$, then route (i_1, j_1) on a "leftmost" path P_1 and route (i_2, j_2) on a "leftmost" path P_2 that does not intersect P_1. If (i_1, j_1) and (i_2, j_2) are not compatible, then any paths P_1 for (i_1, j_1) and P_2 for (i_2, j_2) must intersect at some node, since path P_1 disconnects i_2 from j_2. ∎

Lemma 13.3 *Let h (respectively, w) denote the height (respectively, the width) of a brick wall graph. Let $\{(i_1, j_1), \ldots, (i_r, j_r)\}$ with $r \leq \min\{h, w\}$ be a set of pairwise compatible calls. Then this set of calls can be routed by a set of edge disjoint paths.*[8]

PROOF. Suppose $i_1 < i_2 < \cdots < i_n$. Informally, the proof of this lemma seems to follow easily from the previous lemma. Having routed $(i_1, j_1), \ldots, (i_{k-1}, j_{k-1})$ on $P_1, \ldots, P_{k-1}$, route (i_k, j_k) on a leftmost path that does not intersect P_{k-1}. Each path P_i effectively uses up one row and (zig-zag) column. We leave a formal inductive proof as an exercise. ∎

Exercise 13.14 Give a rigorous induction proof for Lemma 13.3.

---

[8] Note that according to the definition of the brick wall graph, the condition $r \leq w$ is required for any set of calls. The condition $r \leq h$ can be deemed necessary when considering a set of calls whose eastmost source is west of the westmost sink.

In order to obtain a competitive lower bound for the disjoint paths problem, we first consider the following online maximum independent set problem.[9] Given a known graph G, an adversary presents G one node at a time (with any of its incident edges that are adjacent to previous nodes) in some order not known to the online algorithm. The online algorithm is then constructing an independent set one node at a time, and must either add the new node to its current independent set or reject the node (from membership in the independent set being constructed). The adversary can stop inputting vertices at any time (i.e., before all of the graph has been input).

The basic idea of the disjoint paths lower bound proof is first to show that, for every N, there is an N-node undirected graph G such that the online maximum independent set problem for graph G is difficult (in the sense that there is an N^ε lower bound for the competitive ratio). We then reduce the problem of "maximum independent set in G" to the problem of "maximum number of disjoint paths in a brick wall graph W."

For simplicity, we consider only $N = 4^i$ for some i. We construct the $(N = 4^i)$-node graph G_i by induction on i.

Basis. G_0 consists of a single node.

Inductive step. Let

$$G_{i-1}^{(j)} = \left(V_{i-1}^{(j)}, E_{i-1}^{(j)}\right)$$

for $1 \le j \le 4$ denote four disjoint copies of the graph G_{i-1}. Then $G_i = (V_i, E_i)$ is defined as follows:

$$V_i = \bigcup_{1 \le j \le 4} V_{i-1}^{(j)},$$

and

$$E_i = \bigcup_{1 \le j \le 4} E_{i-1}^{(j)} \cup E^{12} \cup E^{13} \cup E^{24},$$

where

$$E^{k\ell} = \left\{(u, v) \mid u \in V_{i-1}^{(k)}, v \in V_{i-1}^{(\ell)}\right\}.$$

(See Figure 13.4.)

Note that a maximum independent set in G_i is composed of the union of maximum independent sets in $G_{i-1}^{(1)}$ and $G_{i-1}^{(4)}$, maximum independent sets in $G_{i-1}^{(2)}$ and $G_{i-1}^{(3)}$, or maximum independent sets in $G_{i-1}^{(3)}$ and $G_{i-1}^{(4)}$. Our adversary will always input exactly 3^i of the 4^i vertices in G_i. Thus, G_i has 4^i nodes and maximum independent sets of size 2^i.

Theorem 13.15 *Let* ALG' *be a randomized online algorithm for constructing an independent set S in the graph G_i. Then*

$$\mathcal{R}_{\text{OBL}}(\text{ALG}') \ge \left(\tfrac{4}{3}\right)^i.$$

That is, for $N = 4^i$, any randomized algorithm ALG' *is at best $(N^{1-\log_4 3})$-competitive against an oblivious adversary.*

---

[9] An "independent set" in a graph G is a set of pairwise nonadjacent vertices.

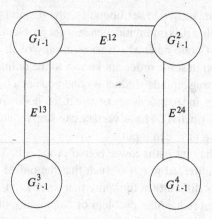

Figure 13.4: Difficult graph for online independent set problem.

PROOF. By the Yao principle, it is sufficient to construct a probability distribution D_i on the input sequences σ (i.e., on the order of the vertices in G_i presented by the adversary) such that $\mathbf{E}_\sigma[\text{OPT}(\sigma)] = 2^i$ and $\mathbf{E}_\sigma[\text{ALG}(\sigma)] \leq \left(\frac{3}{2}\right)^i$ for any deterministic algorithm ALG. The distribution D_i is constructed inductively.

Base case. D_0 is the single vertex of G_0 that is input with probability 1.

Inductive step. The vertices are input in two stages.

1. Input the vertices for $G_{i-1}^{(1)}$ and $G_{i-1}^{(2)}$ each according to D_{i-1}.

2. Choose a bit b uniformly at random. If $b = 0$, input the vertices for $G_{i-1}^{(3)}$ according to D_{i-1}. If $b = 1$, then input the vertices for $G_{i-1}^{(4)}$ according to D_{i-1}.

Clearly, for any σ in D_i, OPT can choose a maximum independent set in G_i and we have $\text{OPT}(\sigma) = 2^i$; hence, $\mathbf{E}_\sigma[\text{OPT}] = 2^i$.

Now consider the independent set being constructed by ALG. Since every node in $G_{i-1}^{(1)}$ is adjacent to every node in $G_{i-1}^{(2)}$, ALG must choose to accept nodes only from $G_{i-1}^{(1)}$ or only from $G_{i-1}^{(2)}$. In either case, by induction we can assume that the expected size of the independent set constructed from stage 1 vertices σ_1 satisfies $\mathbf{E}_{\sigma_1}[\text{ALG}] \leq \left(\frac{3}{2}\right)^{i-1}$. Regardless of whether ALG chooses $G_{i-1}^{(1)}$ or $G_{i-1}^{(2)}$ vertices, with probability $\frac{1}{2}$, the independent set constructed after stage 1 can be extended by the vertices input in stage 2 (and with probability $\frac{1}{2}$, it cannot be extended at all). Then

$$\mathbf{E}_\sigma[\text{ALG}] \leq \left(\tfrac{3}{2}\right)^{i-1} + \tfrac{1}{2}\left(\tfrac{3}{2}^{i-1}\right)$$

$$= \left(\tfrac{3}{2}\right)^i.$$

∎

We return to the circuit routing problem for the brick wall graph. It remains to embed the $N = 4^i$-node graph $G_i = G_{\log_4 N}$ into a routing problem on a brick wall graph $W_{\sqrt{N} \times N}$ of height $\sqrt{N}$ and width N. Each vertex u of G_i is associated with a call $(s_{k(u)}, t_{l(u)})$, so that $(u, v) \notin E_i$ (i.e., u and v not adjacent in G_i) if and only if $(s_{k(u)}, t_{l(u)})$ and $(s_{k(v)}, t_{l(v)})$ are compatible.

Theorem 13.16 *Let $i = \log_4 N$. There is a mapping of vertices u in G_i to calls $(s_{k(u)}, t_{l(u)})$ in the brick wall graph $W_i = W_{\sqrt{N} \times N}$ such that $(u, v) \notin E_i$ if and only if $(s_{k(u)}, t_{k(u)})$ and $(s_{k(v)}, t_{l(v)})$ are compatible.*

PROOF. Let S_i (respectively, T_i) denote the sources (respectively, the sinks) of W_i. For each i ($0 \le i \le \log_4 N$), we construct a mapping $\mu_i : V_i \to S_i \times T_i$. That is, for each node $u \in V_i$, we create a call $\mu_i(u) = (s_{k_i(u)}, t_{l_i(u)})$. The mapping is defined inductively. For $i = 0$, the mapping is trivial; there is only one source s_1 and sink t_1. For the induction step, we partition the sources S_i (and sinks T_i) into four blocks, each containing 4^{i-1} nodes. Recall that

$$V_i = \bigcup_{1 \le j \le 4} V_{i-1}^{(j)}.$$

Let $S_{i-1}^{(j)}$ represent the source nodes $s_{1+(j-1)4^{i-1}}, \ldots, s_{j4^i}$ (for $1 \le j \le 4$). Similarly, we define $T_{i-1}^{(j)}$ as the sink nodes $t_{1+(j-1)4^{i-1}}, \ldots, t_{j4^i}$. Then the mapping μ_i is defined by using μ_{i-1} in each of the following maps: (see Figure 13.5):

1. $V_{i-1}^1 \to S_{i-1}^1 \times T_{i-1}^3$;
2. $V_{i-1}^2 \to S_{i-1}^4 \times T_{i-1}^2$;
3. $V_{i-1}^3 \to S_{i-1}^2 \times T_{i-1}^1$;
4. $V_{i-1}^4 \to S_{i-1}^3 \times T_{i-1}^4$.

It is easy to verify (by induction) that the mapping is one-to-one and that every independent set of vertices in the graph G_i is mapped to a set of pairwise compatible calls in the brick graph W_i. ∎

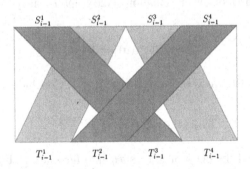

Figure 13.5: The inductive construction of the mapping μ_i.

This one-to-one mapping clearly shows that no matter how we try to route accepted calls, by itself the call admission aspect of online routing on the brick wall graph is difficult, since any set of r (edge disjoint) routable calls in a ($\sqrt{N} \times N$) brick wall graph determines (online) an independent set of r vertices in the N-node graph G_i. Thus, we have the following theorem.

Theorem 13.17 *Let ALG$'$ be a randomized online algorithm for the disjoint paths problem in the brick wall graph W_i. Then*

$$\overline{\mathcal{R}}_{\text{OBL}}(\text{ALG}') \ge \left(\frac{4}{3}\right)^i.$$

That is, for $N = 4^i$ and the $(\sqrt{N} \times N)$ brick wall graph, any randomized algorithm ALG$'$ *is at best $N^{(1-\log_4 3)}$-competitive against an oblivious adversary. In terms of $M = O(N^{3/2})$, the number of nodes (or edges) in the network, the lower bound is $\Omega(M^{2/3(1-\log_4 3)})$.*

Exercise 13.15 We want to improve the lower bound of Theorem 13.15 and as a corollary also improve Theorem 13.17. Consider the class of graphs H_i inductively defined as follows:

Basis. H_i consists of a single node.

Induction step. Let

$$H_{i-1}^{(j)} = \left(V_{i-1}^{(j)}, E_{i-1}^{(j)} \right)$$

for $1 \le j \le 3$ denote three disjoint copies of the graph H_{i-1}. Then $H_i = (V_i, E_i)$ is defined as follows:

$$V_i = \bigcup_{1 \le j \le 3} V_{i-1}^{(j)},$$

and

$$E_i = \bigcup_{1 \le j \le 3} E_{i-1}^{(j)} \cup E^{12} \cup E^{13},$$

where

$$E^{1k} = \left\{ (u, v) \mid u \in v_{i-1}^{(1)}, v \in v_{i-1}^{(k)} \right\}.$$

Show how to embed the class of graphs H_i into the class of brick wall graphs. Inductively construct a distribution D_i on the presentation of the graph H_i such that for the independent set problem

$$\mathbf{E}_{D_i(\sigma)}[\text{OPT}(\sigma)] = \left(\tfrac{3}{2}\right)^i,$$

whereas for any deterministic ALG, $\mathbf{E}_{\sigma \in D_i}[\text{ALG}(\sigma)] \le 1$. Conclude

$$\overline{\mathcal{R}}_{\text{OBL}}(\text{ALG}) \ge \left(\tfrac{3}{2}\right)^i = N^{1-\log_3 2}.$$

Show how to embed the class of graphs H_i into the class of brick wall graphs and deduce an improved version of Theorem 13.17.

13.7   Routing on Optical Networks

We consider one particular model for optical routing. We view optical routing as path selection plus path coloring. Each call is routed along a path that is then colored by an optical wavelength. Edge intersecting paths cannot have the same color (that is, wavelength). When there is only one wavelength, the throughput problem is exactly the disjoint paths problem; however, for multiple wavelengths the problem is not equivalent to routing in a network with edge capacities. For example, in the brick graph of Figure 13.3, if s_i is being routed to t_{N+1-i} for $1 \le i \le N$, then every two calls are not compatible and hence must intersect in at least one edge by Lemma 13.1. Thus, with two allowable wavelengths, the throughput is at most two calls, whereas with capacity 2 it is not difficult to see that all N calls can be routed.

In an optical network, we can study the maximum throughput question (i.e., a "packing problem") or the question of the minimum number of bandwidths necessary to route all calls (i.e., a "covering problem"). Fortunately, we have the following reductions.

Theorem 13.18 *Let G be an arbitrary network with m edges and let* ALG *be a c-competitive online algorithm for throughput maximization on G using one wavelength (i.e., the disjoint paths problem). Then,*

(i) *For all χ there is a $(c + 1)$-competitive algorithm* $\text{FFC}_\chi\{\text{ALG}\}$ *for throughput on G using χ wavelengths.*

(ii) *There is a (cH_m)-competitive algorithm* FFC$\{$ALG$\}$ *for minimizing the number of wavelengths in order to route all calls, where m is the number of edges in G and H_m is the mth harmonic number.*[10]

PROOF. For both results, the algorithm is a "relativized" greedy first fit approach. Consider the following two algorithms.

Algorithm $\text{FFC}_\chi\{\text{ALG}\}$ **(RELATIVIZED-FIRST-FIT-COLORING with χ Colors):** Upon arrival of the jth call r_j, if r_j can be routed by algorithm ALG on some wavelength i $(1 \leq i \leq \chi)$, then (using ALG) route r_j on the minimum such i. Otherwise, reject the call.

Algorithm FFC$\{$ALG$\}$ **(RELATIVIZED-FIRST-FIT-COLORING):** Upon arrival of the jth call r_j, suppose χ is the largest wavelength used to route $r_1, \ldots, r_{j-1}$. To route r_j, if r_j can be routed by ALG on some wavelength i $(1 \leq i \leq \chi)$, then route r_j on the minimum such i. Otherwise, route r_j on wavelength $\chi + 1$.

We now show that $\text{FFC}_\chi\{\text{ALG}\}$ (respectively, FFC$\{$ALG$\}$) is $(c + 1)$-competitive (respectively, cH_m-competitive). For any algorithm A (i.e., $\text{FFC}_\chi\{\text{ALG}\}$, FFC$\{ALG\}$, and OPT), let $A[i, \sigma]$ be the calls in σ assigned by A to wavelength i. Note that $\text{FFC}_\chi\{\text{ALG}\}[i, \sigma] = $ FFC$\{$ALG$\}[i, \sigma]$ for $1 \leq i \leq \chi$ and $\text{FFC}_\chi\{\text{ALG}\}[i, \sigma] = \varnothing$ for $i > \chi$; hence, depending on the context, we use FFC$\{$ALG$\}[i, \sigma]$ to denote either FFC$\{$ALG$\}[i, \sigma]$ or $\text{FFC}_\chi\{\text{ALG}\}[i, \sigma]$. Let

$$R[i, \sigma] = \sigma - \bigcup_{j<i} \text{FFC}\{\text{ALG}\}[j, \sigma]$$

denote the sequence of calls considered by $\text{FFC}_\chi\{\text{ALG}\}$ and FFC$\{$ALG$\}$ for wavelength i (i.e., not assigned to a wavelength $j < i$).

- Proof of statement (i):

  Clearly,

$$\text{OPT}[i, \sigma] - \bigcup_{j<i} \text{FFC}\{\text{ALG}\}[j, \sigma] \subset R[i, \sigma].$$

---

[10] Recall $\ln m \leq H_m \leq \ln m + 1$.

Hence, based on the competitiveness of ALG, we have

$$|\text{FFC}\{[\text{ALG}]\}[i, \sigma]| \geq \frac{1}{c}\left|\text{OPT}[i, \sigma] - \left(\bigcup_{j<i}\text{FFC}\{\text{ALG}\}[j, \sigma]\right)\right|$$

$$= \frac{1}{c}|\text{OPT}[i, \sigma]| - \frac{1}{c}\left|\left(\bigcup_{j<i}\text{FFC}\{\text{ALG}\}[j, \sigma]\right) \cap \text{OPT}[i, \sigma]\right|.$$

Therefore,

$$\text{FFC}_\chi\{\text{ALG}\}(\sigma) = \sum_{i=1}^{\chi}|\text{FFC}\{\text{ALG}\}[i, \sigma]| \geq \frac{1}{c}\sum_{i=1}^{\chi}|\text{OPT}[i, \sigma]| - \frac{1}{c}\left|\left(\bigcup_{i=1}^{\chi-1}\text{FFC}\{\text{ALG}\}[i, \sigma]\right)\right|$$

$$= \frac{1}{c}\text{OPT}(\sigma) - \frac{1}{c}\left|\bigcup_{i=1}^{\chi-1}\text{FFC}\{\text{ALG}\}[i, \sigma]\right|$$

$$\geq \frac{1}{c}\text{OPT}(\sigma) - \frac{1}{c}\text{FFC}_\chi\{\text{ALG}\}(\sigma).$$

We conclude that $\text{FFC}_\chi\{\text{ALG}\}(\sigma) \geq \frac{1}{c+1}\text{OPT}(\sigma)$.

• Proof of statement (ii):

Obviously, there are at most m calls that can be routed on any wavelength. To each request r_j, we assign a charge $c_j = 1/|\text{FFC}\{\text{ALG}\}[i, \sigma]|$, where i is the wavelength to which r_j was assigned by ALG. (Note that this charge is solely for the purpose of analysis and is not part of the algorithm.)

Clearly,

$$\text{ALG}(\sigma) = \sum_{1\leq j\leq n} c_j$$

$$= \sum_{1\leq i\leq \text{OPT}(\sigma)}\sum_{j\in \text{OPT}[i,\sigma]} c_j.$$

It suffices to show that

$$\sum_{j\in \text{OPT}[i,\sigma]} c_j \leq cH_m,$$

because this implies

$$\text{ALG}(\sigma) \leq \sum_{1\leq i\leq \text{OPT}(\sigma)} cH_m$$

$$= (cH_m) \cdot \text{OPT}(\sigma).$$

Claim: For any wavelength i and any positive integer k, $\text{OPT}[i, \sigma]$ can contain at most $c \cdot k$ calls r_j with charge $c_j \geq \frac{1}{k}$.

To prove the claim, let $T = \{r_j \mid c_j \geq \frac{1}{k}$ and $r_j \in \text{OPT}[i, \sigma]\}$. Let i^* be the highest-numbered wavelength such that $T \subset R[i^*, \sigma]$; that is, $\text{FFC}\{\text{ALG}\}$ considers all of T for wavelength i^* and assigns at least one call in T to wavelength i^*.

Note that ALG must assign some request $r_l \in T$ to wavelength i^*, otherwise i^* would not be the maximum wavelength considered for all of T. Since ALG is a c-competitive algorithm (for the call admission problem on a single wavelength), if OPT had assigned all requests in T to wavelength i, with $|T| > c \cdot k$, then ALG would have assigned more than k calls to wavelength i^*.

Since at least one of these calls is $r_l \in T$, we would have

$$c_l = \frac{1}{|\text{FFC}\{\text{ALG}\}[i, \sigma]|} < \frac{1}{k}$$

contradicting the fact that every call $r_l \in T$ has charge $\geq \frac{1}{k}$, It then follows that

$$\sum_{r_j \in \text{OPT}[i, \sigma]} c_j \leq c \left(1 + \frac{1}{2} + \frac{1}{3} + \cdots + \frac{1}{m}\right) = c H_m.$$

(Of the at most $c \cdot k$ calls of charge $\leq \frac{1}{k}$, the sum is maximized if $c(k-1)$ of these have charge $\leq \frac{1}{k-1}$ and c calls have charge $\frac{1}{k}$.) ∎

We can apply Theorem 13.18 to any of the upper bounds in Sections 13.2, 13.3, and 13.5. By using part (ii) of this theorem, these upper bounds will be degraded by an $O(\log N)$ factor. In the following section, we obtain improved results for path coloring corresponding to the particular graphs studied for call admission.

Exercise 13.16 Verify that part (i) of Theorem 13.18 also applies when we are given χ different networks and are trying to maximize the total number of calls that can be routed on these networks subject to the paths being edge disjoint in each network.

13.8 Path Coloring for Particular Networks

13.8.1 Path Coloring on the Line

For the line, the path coloring problem is an easier problem than the disjoint paths problem (i.e., improved competitive ratio). Path (i.e., interval) coloring on the line corresponds to node coloring of an **interval graph** where the intervals are the nodes of the graph and nodes are adjacent if the corresponding intervals intersect.[11] As such, path coloring on the line is a well-studied problem that precedes the more recent interest in optical routing.

Since an interval graph is a "perfect graph," the chromatic number of an interval graph is equal to its clique number. In terms of path coloring on the line, this means that the minimum (i.e., offline optimum) number of colors needed is equal to the maximum congestion on any subinterval. For offline path coloring on the line (interval graph coloring), there is a simple optimal offline greedy algorithm.[12] The most natural online greedy algorithm for

---

[11] More precisely, we need to be careful about how this interval graph is presented to an algorithm; that is, is it simply presented as a graph by, for example, an adjacency matrix or is it presented in terms of its line intervals representation? Note that it is not possible to construct *online* an interval representation from the graph representation. Hence upper bounds (respectively, lower bounds) are stronger when the graph is presented simply as a graph (respectively, when it is presented in terms of the interval representation).

[12] The offline optimal algorithm sorts intervals according to their left endpoints and then greedily colors the intervals by first fit.

path coloring on a line or on a tree is FFC (FIRST-FIT-COLORING). Given an input path P, FFC colors P with the first color that has not been used to color any previous path intersecting P. The greedy FFC is $O(1)$-competitive, as shown in the following (nontrivial) theorem, which we state without proof.[13]

Theorem 13.19 *For all σ, $\text{FFC}(\sigma) \leq 26\text{OPT}(\sigma)$. There exists σ such that $\text{FFC}(\sigma) > 4.4545 \cdot \text{OPT}(\sigma)$.*

We now present an optimally competitive online algorithm. To do so, we first inductively define a class of algorithms $\{\text{RECG}_w\}$, where RECG_w is an online algorithm that is specified for input sequences (i.e., intervals) whose maximum edge congestion is exactly w.

> **Algorithm RECG_w (BOUNDED-RECURSIVE-GREEDY):** The algorithms are defined by induction on the maximum edge congestion w among the intervals input thus far.
>
> *Base case* (RECG_1). Color the intervals with the first color.
>
> *Inductive step* (RECG_{k+1}). Assume that the input $\sigma = r_1, \ldots, r_n$ has been colored by RECG_w where $w \leq k+1$ is the maximum edge congestion among the intervals in σ. Consider a new input r_{n+1}. We suppose that σr_{n+1} has maximum edge congestion $k+1$. Let $\{r_{j_1}, \ldots, r_{j_s}\}$ be a minimal set of intervals such that $\sigma' = \sigma - \{r_{j_1}, \ldots, r_{j_s}\}$ has maximum edge congestion k. If $\sigma' r_{n+1}$ has maximum congestion k, then color r_{n+1} using RECG_k. Otherwise, use FFC on input sequence $A = r_{j_1}, \ldots, r_{j_s}, r_{n+1}$ to color r_{n+1}.

The unbounded (RECURSIVE GREEDY) RECG algorithm is as follows:

> **Algorithm RECG:** Initialize $w = 1$. While the maximum edge congestion of the input sequence is $w = k$, apply RECG_k to each input interval. If a new input interval r causes (for the first time) maximum edge congestion $k+1$, then increment w and apply RECG_{k+1} to r.

Theorem 13.20 *For every input sequence σ of intervals, $\text{RECG}(\sigma) \leq 3\text{OPT}(\sigma) - 2$. Furthermore, no deterministic online algorithm ALG is better than 3-competitive. More precisely, for every $w \geq 2$, there is an input σ with $w = \text{OPT}(\sigma)$ and $\text{ALG}(\sigma) \geq 3\text{OPT}(\sigma) - 2$.*

PROOF. Let $\sigma = r_1, \ldots, r_n$, and say $w = \text{OPT}(\sigma)$ is the maximum edge congestion for σ. We prove that $\text{RECG}_w(\sigma) \leq 3w - 2$ by induction on w.

Base case. $w = 1$ is immediate.

Induction step. Assume that the statement is true for $w = k$ and let the maximum edge congestion be $k+1$. Say that $r_1, \ldots, r_{n-1}$ has been properly colored. Suppose that A and σ' are as in the definition of the algorithm. According to the induction hypothesis, r_n is properly colored if $\sigma' r_n$ has congestion k. Otherwise, according to the induction hypothesis, σ' has been colored with $3k - 2$ colors. We need to show that no interval in A intersects more than two other intervals in A. From this, it immediately follows that the intervals in A can be colored by FFC using three colors and, hence, that $\text{RECG}_k(\sigma) \leq 3k - 2 + 3 = 3(k+1) - 2$.

---

[13] See Kierstead [222], and Kierstead and Qin [223].

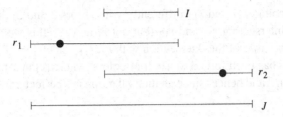

Figure 13.6: An illustration of why there cannot be three intervals in set A that pairwise intersect. The symbol ● indicates edge congestion $k + 1$ among the intervals already colored.

We first observe that there cannot be three intervals in A that pairwise intersect. Suppose r_1, r_2, r_3 were such intervals. Clearly, no interval r_i can be contained within another interval r_j, since r_i forces a congestion of $k + 1$ with σ', and r_j, in turn, would force a congestion of $k + 2$. Without loss of generality, suppose r_1 and r_2 are depicted as in Figure 13.6.

Here the symbol ● on intervals r_1 and r_2 indicates a **congestion point** where there is a total edge congestion of $k + 1$ (because of the intersection with intervals in σ'). Note that neither congestion point ● can be located in the intersection I between intervals r_1 and r_2; otherwise, we once again have edge congestion $k + 2$. Now r_3 must intersect I. If r_3 has a congestion point (relative to σ') within the union J of intervals r_1 and r_2, then once again this necessitates a total congestion of $k + 2$. Therefore, r_3 must have a congestion point outside of J, and r_3 extends past either r_1 or r_2, in which case it intersects the depicted congestion point of either r_1 or r_2; this again implies congestion $k + 2$.

Now we are ready to show that no interval r in A can intersect more than two other intervals in A. Suppose r intersects r_1, r_2, r_3. Then, by the above argument, r_1, r_2, and r_3 do not pairwise intersect. Without loss of generality, say r_1 is to the left of r_2, which is to the left of r_3. Thus interval r_2 must be contained in interval r; however, this again causes edge congestion $k + 2$.

This completes the proof of the upper bound. Although we express this upper bound in terms of the interval coloring, we note that the proof uses only the (interval) graph representation.

For the lower bound, we present only the case of $w = 2$, which is the base case of the general inductive argument for any $w \geq 2$. Suppose ALG is restricted to three colors. The adversary inputs ten nonintersecting intervals. Then there are at least four nonintersecting intervals, say (without loss of generality r_1, r_2, r_3, r_4) that ALG colors with color 1. Now the adversary inputs intervals r_{11} and r_{12}, as shown in Figure 13.7.

If ALG identically colors r_{11} and r_{12} by color 2, then the adversary inputs r_{13}, r_{14} as depicted in Figure 13.7. Clearly, r_{13} must receive a new color 3 and, consequently, r_{14} requires a color 4.

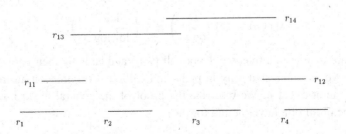

Figure 13.7: Input intervals for lower bound.

Finally, if ALG colors r_{11} and r_{12} differently with colors 2 and 3, then the adversary inputs an interval intersecting r_{11} and r_{12} (but not r_1 and r_4); this would require ALG to use a fourth color because of the intersection with r_2, r_{11}, and r_{12}.

In all cases, ALG has been forced to use four colors, whereas the set of input intervals has edge congestion 2 and hence (since an interval graph is a perfect graph) can be colored with two colors. ∎

13.8.2 Path Coloring on Trees

For any tree, it is easy to modify the CRS algorithm and proof of Theorem 13.9 to derive the following $O(\log N)$-competitive path coloring algorithm.

> **Algorithm CGC (CLASSIFY-AND-GREEDILY-COLOR):** Classify calls exactly as in Theorem 13.9. Using a different set of colors for each level, greedily (i.e., by first fit) color calls for any level using a distinct set of colors for each level.

Theorem 13.21 *For any N-node tree, CGC is $(2 \log N)$-competitive.*

PROOF. As in Theorem 13.9, it is easy to see that for any class i and level i node v, when CGC colors a level i call r passing through v by a certain color, there can be at most two calls that OPT can color that intersect with r. It follows that for every fixed class i, CGC is 2-competitive and hence $2 \log N$-competitive on any input. ∎

FFC attains the same competitive ratio although the proof is more substantial and is based on the following interesting result, which we state without proof.[14]

Theorem 13.22 *Every N-node, d-inductive graph can be greedily colored by FFC using at most $d \cdot \log N$ colors.*

Corollary 13.23 *For any N-node tree T, FFC is $(2 \log N)$-competitive.*

PROOF. Let σ be any set of calls (paths) and let g be its maximum edge congestion. Clearly, $\text{OPT}(\sigma) \geq g$. From Theorem 13.10 we know that the intersection graph induced by these paths on T is a $2(g-1)$-inductive graph. Hence, these paths (which are the nodes of the intersection graph) can be greedily colored using at most $2(g-1) \log N \leq 2 \log N \cdot \text{OPT}(\sigma)$ colors. ∎

Theorem 13.25 provides a "nearly" corresponding lower bound for path coloring on trees. Let T be a complete D level binary tree with $N = 2^D - 1$. For any deterministic online algorithm ALG, we want to construct a sequence of calls σ that can be 2-colored by an optimal algorithm while

$$\text{ALG}(\sigma) = \Omega\left(\frac{D}{\log D}\right) = \Omega\left(\frac{\log N}{\log \log N}\right).$$

Since paths are unique in a tree, we denote all paths and calls by their endpoints (v, u); furthermore, we are interested only in paths and calls that originate at an interior node v and terminate at a leaf u. We motivate the proof of the general lower bound by first presenting the proof of a lower bound for FFC.

---

[14] See Irani [194].

Theorem 13.24 *The deterministic* FFC *algorithm is at best $\frac{D}{2}$-competitive on the complete binary tree T of height D (i.e., T has $N = 2^D - 1$ nodes).*

PROOF. We prove by induction on i ($1 \leq i \leq \frac{D}{2}$) that for each height $2i$ subtree, we can construct a path π of length $2i$ terminating at a leaf u_i and a sequence σ_i of i nonintersecting calls that are all colored differently by the first i colors and that all intersect π.[15] The base case is immediate. Let T_{i+1} be a height $2(i + 1)$ subtree and consider, for example, its left child v. Now let T_i^1 and T_i^2 be the two depth $2i$ subtrees of v.

Let $\pi_i^1, \sigma_i^1, u_i^1$ (respectively, $\pi_i^2, \sigma_i^2, u_i^2$) be the path, sequence of calls and leaf satisfying the inductive hypothesis for T_i^1 (respectively, for T_i^2). Generate a call r from the root of T_{i+1} to, for example, u_i^1. This call r requires an $(i + 1)$st color by the inductive hypothesis. Now π_{i+1} is chosen to be the path from the root of T_{i+1} to u_i^2, σ_{i+1} is σ_i^2, r, and u_{i+1} is u_i^2. Clearly, $(\pi_{i+1}, \sigma_{i+1}, u_{i+1})$ satisfies the induction statement for depth $i + 1$.

Hence, on a depth D complete tree, FFC is forced to use $\frac{D}{2}$ colors for the input sequence σ_D. It only remains to show that OPT$(\sigma_D) = 2$. We claim (by induction on i) that σ_i can be colored with two colors and that all the calls on the path π_i are colored with a single color. The base case is again immediate. For the induction step, color π_i^1 by color 1 and π_i^2 by color 2. Color the new call r by color 2. This coloring satisfies the inductive statement and the proof is now complete. ∎

The general lower bound (for an online algorithm) is similar to the proof of Theorem 13.24 but requires substantially more work. We state the result without proof.[16]

Theorem 13.25 *For the complete binary tree on N nodes, any deterministic algorithm for path coloring has competitive ratio at least $\Omega\left(\frac{\log N}{\log \log N}\right)$.*

Note that the lower bound is established for the complete tree of depth $\log N$ so that (unlike Theorem 13.12 for disjoint paths) we cannot obtain an $O(\log D)$-competitive ratio where D is the depth of the tree.

13.8.3 Path Coloring on Arrays

Path coloring for arrays follows the approach used for the disjoint paths problem for arrays. We partition the array into ($c \log N \times c \log N$) subarrays and, once again, we partition calls into long distance and short distance calls. For path coloring, we need to accept all calls; we use different colors for each type of call, thus allowing us to consider short and long calls separately.

For short distance calls, we classify calls according to the size of the minimal block (see Appendix F) that contains both endpoints. Specifically, a call from u to v is of class l if the smallest block containing both u and v has size $2^l \times 2^l$. The algorithm uses distinct colors for each class, and within a class it simply routes the call by any shortest path and then greedily colors the call.

Following the idea used to construct disjoint paths for long distance calls (see Section 13.5.3), we view the blocks as nodes in a simulating network $\mathcal{N}$ with edges corresponding to the block adjacencies. We now need a strengthening of the congestion

---

[15] In the case of FFC, the intersection with π is a single edge.
[16] See Bartal and Leonardi [49].

minimization algorithm used in Section 12.3 to exploit the inherent $O(\log N)$ edge capacity of the simulating network. This strengthening allows us to path color any set of calls on the network $\mathcal{N}$ using $O(\Lambda)$ colors (on each of the $O(\log N)$ parallel edges that constitute the bandwidth) where Λ is the maximum congestion used by OPT to route these calls. Clearly, the congestion is a lower bound on the number of colors needed by the optimal algorithm.

We ignore all the details and state the following theorem.

Theorem 13.26 *Let G be an $(N \times N)$ array. There is a deterministic online algorithm that is $O(\log N)$-competitive for path coloring in G.*

We have a corresponding lower bound that also provides a lower bound for the problem of edge congestion on an undirected graph (see Exercise 12.5 for the case of directed graphs).

Theorem 13.27 *Let G be an $(N \times N)$ array and let ALG be any randomized online algorithm for path coloring in G. Then $\overline{\mathcal{R}}_{\mathrm{OBL}}(\mathrm{ALG}) \geq \Omega(\log N)$.*

PROOF. Appealing to the Yao principle (Theorem 8.5), we construct a distribution on input sequences $\{\sigma\}$ such that $\mathrm{OPT}(\sigma) = 18$ and the expected congestion (and, hence, the minimal number of colors used) for any deterministic online algorithm is $\Omega(\log N)$.

Without loss of generality, let $N = 3^L$ for some L. The distribution is constructed in L stages. For the ith stage ($1 \leq i \leq L$), the calls originate and terminate within a $(3^{L-i+1} \times 3^{L-i+1})$ subarray S_i. The subarrays S_i ($1 \leq i \leq L$) are randomly chosen by induction as follows:

Base case. $S_1 = G$.

Induction step. Partition S_i into 9 subarrays of size $3^{L-i} \times 3^{L-i}$. Choose S_{i+1} uniformly at random to be one of these 9 subarrays.

We can now specify the calls for the ith stage. Let C_i be the center subarray of S_i and let $S(x, y)$ denote the node at the xth row and yth column of C_i. For each y ($0 \leq y \leq 3^{L-i}$), input 18 vertical calls from $S(0, y)$ to $S(3^{L-i}, y)$.

The following two claims complete the proof.

Claim 1: For every input sequence σ generated by the distribution, $\mathrm{OPT}(\sigma) = 18$.

Claim 2: At the end of the ith stage, $\mathbf{E}[\text{congestion on edges in } S_i] \geq i$.

The first claim follows by observing that OPT routes the ith stage calls by a direct vertical line if $S_{i+1} \neq C_i$, and if $S_{i+1} = C_i$, then OPT routes the calls using the edges in $S_i - C_i$.

For the second claim, note that any algorithm must use $18 \times 3^{L-i}$ paths and at least $18 \times 3^{L-i} \times 3^{L-i}$ edges to route the calls in the ith stage. There are $2 \times (3^{L-i+1})^2$ edges in S_i and, hence, the ith stage increases the average edge congestion in S_i by at least 1. Finally, since S_{i+1} is chosen as a random subarray in S_i, the expected congestion on edges in S_{i+1} prior to the $(i + 1)$st stage is equivalent to the expected congestion on edges in S_i after the ith stage. ∎

13.9 A Lower Bound for Path Coloring on the Brick Wall Graph

Following the approach in Section 13.6, we now show that for the brick wall graph (see Figure 13.3), the randomized competitive ratio for path coloring is provably large. Whereas the proof of Theorem 13.17 is based on a reduction of the maximum independent set problem (for the class of graphs G_i) to the disjoint paths problem (for the brick wall graphs W_i), we now need to reduce the node coloring problem (for G_i) to the path coloring problem (for W_i).

We use the same class of graphs $\{G_i\}$ defined in Section 13.6 and the same embedding as in Theorem 13.16. The counterpart of Theorem 13.15 is the lower bound for node coloring presented in the following theorem.

Theorem 13.28 *Let* ALG' *be a randomized online algorithm for constructing a node coloring of* G_i. *Then*

$$\overline{\mathcal{R}}_{\mathrm{OBL}}(\mathrm{ALG'}) \geq \left(\tfrac{4}{3}\right)^i ;$$

that is, for $N = 4^i$, *any randomized algorithm* ALG' *is at best* $N^{1-\log_4 3}$*-competitive against an oblivious adversary.*

PROOF. As we did in the proof of Theorem 13.15, here we need to construct a distribution D_i on the presentation of the graphs G_i. We construct D_i so that the expected number of colors used by any online algorithm is at least 2^i, whereas the expected number of colors used by OPT is $\left(\tfrac{3}{2}\right)^i$. Once again, the distribution D_i is constructed inductively.

Base case. D_1 is the single vertex of G_1.

Inductive step. The vertices are input in two stages.

1. Input the vertices for G^3_{i-1} and G^4_{i-1}, each according to D_{i-1}.
2. Choose a bit b uniformly at random. If $b = 0$, then input the vertices for G^1_{i-1} and G^2_{i-1} according to D_{i-1}. If $b = 1$, then no other vertices are input.

We first show that

$$\mathbf{E}_{D_i(\sigma)}[\mathrm{OPT}(\sigma)] = \left(\tfrac{3}{2}\right)^i$$

by induction on i. The basic case $i = 1$ is obvious. Since OPT knows (a posteriori) the value of b, it can color $G^{(3)}_{i-1}$ and $G^{(4)}_{i-1}$ using the same set of colors if $b = 1$ and using two distinct sets of colors if $b = 0$. In the latter case, $G^{(1)}_{i-1}$ (respectively, $G^{(2)}_{i-1}$) is colored with the same set of colors as $G^{(4)}_{i-1}$ (respectively, $G^{(3)}_{i-1}$). Thus,

$$\mathbf{E}_{D_i(\sigma)}[\mathrm{OPT}(\sigma)] = \tfrac{1}{2}\mathbf{E}_{D_{i-1}(\sigma_1)}[\mathrm{OPT}(\sigma_1)] + \tfrac{1}{2}\cdot 2 \cdot \mathbf{E}_{D_{i-1}(\sigma_2)}[\mathrm{OPT}(\sigma_2)]$$

$$= \tfrac{1}{2}\left(\tfrac{3}{2}\right)^{i-1} + \tfrac{1}{2}\left(\tfrac{3}{2}\right)^{i-1} = \left(\tfrac{3}{2}\right)^i.$$

Finally, we show $\mathbf{E}_{\sigma \in D_i}[\mathrm{ALG}(\sigma)] \geq 2^i$ by induction on i. The base case is again obvious. Suppose the expected number of colors used by ALG to color $G^{(3)}_{i-1}$ and $G^{(4)}_{i-1}$ (in the first stage of the input) is $(1 + \alpha)2^{i-1}$ with $0 \leq \alpha \leq 1$. Then the expected number of colors used to color both $G^{(3)}_{i-1}$ and $G^{(4)}_{i-1}$ is $(1 - \alpha)2^{i-1}$. If $b = 0$, then ALG must also color $G^{(1)}_{i-1}$

and $G_{i-1}^{(2)}$. The expected number of colors used to color $G_{i-1}^{(1)}$ (or $G_{i-1}^{(2)}$) is at least 2^{i-1}, and all the colors used for $G_{i-1}^{(1)}$ (respectively $G_{i-1}^{(2)}$) must be distinct from the set of $i-1$ colors used by both $G_{i-1}^{(3)}$ and $G_{i-1}^{(4)}$. That is, the expected number of new (i.e., different from $G_{i-1}^{(3)}$ and $G_{i-1}^{(4)}$) colors for $G_{i-1}^{(1)}$ is at least $(1-\alpha)2^{i-1}$, and this expected number of new (i.e., different from $G_{i-1}^{(3)}$, $G_{i-1}^{(4)}$ and $G_{i-1}^{(1)}$) colors for $G_{i-1}^{(2)}$ is at least $(1-\alpha)2^{i-1}$. Thus,

$$\mathbf{E}[\text{ALG}(\sigma)] = (1+\alpha)2^{i-1} + \tfrac{1}{2}\big(2 \cdot (1-\alpha)2^{i-1}\big) = 2^i.$$

∎

Using the reduction of Theorem 13.16, we obtain the following analogue of Theorem 13.17.

Corollary 13.29 *Let* ALG' *be a randomized online algorithm for the disjoint paths problem in the brick wall graph* W_i. *Then,*

$$\overline{\mathcal{R}}_{\text{OBL}}(\text{ALG}') \geq \left(\tfrac{4}{3}\right)^i.$$

That is, for $N = 4^i$ *and the* $(\sqrt{N} \times N)$ *brick wall graph, any randomized algorithm* ALG' *is at best* $(N^{(1-\log_4 3)})$*-competitive against an oblivious adversary. In terms of* $M = O(N^{3/2})$, *the number of nodes (or edges) in the network, the lower bound is* $\Omega(M^{2/3(1-\log_4 3)})$.

13.10   Historical Notes and Open Questions

Call Admission. The first explicit competitive analysis of call admission and circuit routing for the purpose of maximizing the number or benefit of calls accepted is due to Garay and Gopal [164] and Garay, Gopal, Kutten, Mansour, and Yung [165]. The focus of both these papers is a line graph (specifically, a single edge graph) and an online model that allows preemption (but at different costs). Garay and Gopal also show that without preemption, there cannot be a competitive algorithm for calls of unknown limited duration. Awerbuch, Azar, and Plotkin [26] provide the first comprehensive study of online call admission and circuit routing without preemption. They consider deterministic online call admission/routing algorithms in arbitrary networks in cases where the bandwidth of each call is a small ("logarithmic") fraction of the minimum edge capacity. Their general goal is to maximize the "profit" obtained from the accepted calls. From the perspective of offline approximation algorithms, this bandwidth restriction has good precedent. When the profit of each call is the same, then the $\{0, 1\}$ case of unit capacities and bandwidth requests is a difficult optimization problem for which presently there are only good approximation algorithms for special networks. Raghavan and Thompson [285] and Raghavan [282] showed that such a bandwidth restriction makes it possible to use linear programming with randomized rounding to achieve a constant factor offline approximation algorithm for maximizing the number of calls that can be routed on an edge capacity–constrained network. Awerbuch, Azar, and Plotkin use the bandwidth restriction along with an exponential weighting function of edge loads (similar to the use of the exponential function by Aspnes, Azar, Fiat, Plotkin, and Waarts [19] in the case of edge congestion minimization) in order to construct the online call admission/routing algorithm AAP (which is applicable to any network topology). Their algorithm (as extended by Kleinberg and Tardos [227]) achieves an $O(\log D)$ deterministic competitive ratio when the bandwidth of each call is an O(log D) fraction of the smallest capacity and the profit of a call is defined as the throughput (i.e., the bandwidth requested), where D is a bound on the length of any simple path. Assuming a somewhat stronger assumption on the allowable bandwidth of any call, Awerbuch, Azar, and Plotkin establish the deterministic algorithm AAP-KNOWN for throughput (i.e., bandwidth × duration) with competitive ratio $O(\log(DT))$ for calls having a limited but known duration, where T is the ratio of the longest to the shortest duration of a call. These results all extend to arbitrary profits. Again, at the cost of a somewhat more restrictive assumption on the allowable bandwidth of a call, the stated competitive ratio for permanent (respectively, for known limited duration) calls becomes $O(\log DP)$ (respectively, $O(\log(DPT))$) where P is the ratio of the maximum to minimum profit of a call. We note that Awerbuch, Azar, and Plotkin state their algorithm for the known limited duration case in terms of continuous-time and time-varying bandwidth requirements. In general, for T and P, as above, Awerbuch, Bartal, Fiat, and Rosén [28] show that *any* c-competitive call admission algorithm for permanent calls with identical profits can be used to derive an $O(c \log P \log T)$-competitive randomized algorithm for calls of known limited duration. This result assumes that P and T are known in advance, and a slightly weaker result is established without any a priori assumptions using a technique developed in Lipton and Tomkins [246]. This technique has been used in other fields, and we present another application in Chapter 14. For deterministic algorithms and the disjoint paths problem (i.e., the call admission problem when all edges have capacity 1 and all calls have bandwidth 1), the bandwidth restriction is shown to be essential by Awerbuch, Azar, and Plotkin [26]; they show, for example, that D is a lower bound for the competitive ratio of the disjoint paths problem on the line. Similarly, Awerbuch et al. [28] establish lower bounds for randomized algorithms: again, for the disjoint paths problem on the line, they show $\Omega(\log D)$, $\Omega(\log P)$, and $\Omega(\log T)$ randomized lower bounds. Algorithm SAAP and the discussion in Section 13.4 is due to Gawlick, Kamath, Plotkin, and Ramakrishnan [169].

Preemption. Results concerning preemption and rescheduling can be found in Awerbuch, Azar, Plotkin, and Waarts [27], Bar-Noy, Canetti, Kutten, Mansour, and Schieber [37], and Canetti and Irani [90]. These results assume no penalty for preemption other than the loss (of profit) of the job that was preempted. In some cases, this assumption greatly underestimates the true cost of preemption (e.g., what is the cost of having an irate customer?); however, in other situations this may be a reasonable assumption or even an overestimate of the cost (e.g., when the transmission of a low priority file is interrupted). Given that the cost of preemption is at least the loss of the job, it is clear that an optimal offline algorithm would never schedule a job that eventually is preempted. Hence, the competitive ratio achieved by algorithms that cannot preempt scheduled jobs can only improve with preemption.

Disjoint Paths Problem. As noted above, even for a network as simple as a D-edge line, there are deterministic $\Omega(D)$ and randomized $\Omega(\log D)$ lower bounds for the disjoint paths problem. Awerbuch et al. [28] show that the CLASSIFY-AND-RANDOMLY-SELECT algorithm CRS is $O(\log N)$-competitive for any N node tree. The classify and randomly select paradigm is independently studied in Lipton and Tomkins [246]. In an unpublished version of their paper, Awerbuch et al. [28] also suggest an $O(\log D)$ algorithm for any diameter D tree. Awerbuch, Gawlick, Leighton, and Rabani [29] present a different $O(\log D)$-competitive algorithm for any diameter D tree (and show that their algorithm applies to any uniform edge capacity). Leonardi, Marchetti-Spaccamela, Presciutti, and Rosén [240] provide another $O(\log D)$-competitive algorithm (TREE-AAP) for trees that, in contrast to the algorithms based on the classify and randomly select paradigm, gives good competitive performance "with good probability." Awerbuch et al. [29] provide a randomized $O(\log N \log \log N)$-competitive algorithm when the network is an $(N \times N)$ array, and they show that $\Omega(\log N)$ is a lower bound for any randomized algorithm. The optimal $O(\log N)$ upper bound for the array is due to Kleinberg and Tardos [227]. For arbitrary networks (in particular, for the brick wall graph), the N^ε randomized lower bound is due to Bartal, Fiat, and Leonardi [46]. They also prove the lower bound for the online maximal independent set problem, which is used as a lemma in the lower bound proof for the disjoint paths problem.

Path Coloring. The path coloring problem provides another historical reference point for competitive analysis. The field of "recursive combinatorics" is concerned with the effective computability of problems whose inputs are "effectively represented" infinite objects such as infinite graphs. One effective way to represent graphs is to input them in an online manner and then insist that an algorithm (approximately) compute properties (e.g., the chromatic number) of the graph in an online fashion. For example, Kierstead [221] studies an online version of Dilworth's theorem for partial orders. Dilworth's theorem states that the number of chains (i.e., colors) needed to cover any partial order is the maximal size (i.e., the width) of any antichain. One "classic" special case is the problem of computing the chromatic number of an interval graph that (as an offline problem) is equivalent to the path (i.e., interval) coloring problem on the line. Kierstead and Trotter [224] give a 3-competitive algorithm for path coloring on the line and show that this is optimal. The fact that the greedy FFC algorithm is $O(1)$-competitive for path coloring on the line is presented by Kierstead [222], with the best-known bounds to date presented by Kierstead and Qin [223]. As observed by Bartal and Leonardi [49], the fact that the CLASSIFY-AND-GREEDILY- COLOR algorithm (CGC) is $O(\log N)$-competitive for trees follows quite easily from the analogous result for the CRS algorithm for disjoint paths on trees. Bartal, Kleinberg, and Molloy (personal communication) independently observed that the path intersection graph of a tree is a "d-inductive graph" for $d \leq 2 \cdot \omega$ where the congestion number ω is the maximum number of paths intersecting on an edge. Clearly, ω is a lower bound on the number of colors needed to color the intersection graph. Irani [194] showed for that any N-node d-inductive graph G, the online greedy FFC algorithm colors G using at most $d \cdot \log N$ colors. From this it follows that for path coloring on trees, FFC is at least $(2 \log N)$-competitive. The general lower bound of $\frac{\log N}{\log \log N}$ for path coloring on trees is due to Bartal and Leonardi [49]. Bartal and Leonardi also construct the optimal $O(\log N)$-competitive algorithm for path coloring on arrays. The fact that path coloring for arbitrary graphs (again, specifically for the brick wall graph) has a competitive ratio lower bound of N^ε is presented by Bartal, Fiat, and Leonardi [46]. The reduction of the multiple bandwidth problem to the single bandwidth problem (i.e., the disjoint paths problem) is due to Awerbuch, Azar, Fiat, Leonardi, and Rosén [24]. In fact, a somewhat better reduction can be derived from earlier results by Cornuejols, Fisher, and Nemhauser [117] and Bertsimas and Vohra [65]. They studied the general problem of optimizing the choice of χ sets (from some set system) to maximize the size of the set union. The improved competitive ratio is $\frac{e^{1/c}}{e^{1/c}-1} \leq c+1$; however, unlike the reduction presented by Awerbuch et al. [24], this bound does not apply to the case of χ different networks (see Exercise 13.16). The reduction of path coloring to disjoint paths is due to Kleinberg and Sudan [226] and is based on an analogous result for offline set cover approximation algorithms due independently to Chvátal [111], Lovász [248], and Johnson [206].[17]

Credit for Exercises. Exercise 13.1 was suggested by Kleinberg (personal communication). Exercise 13.3 is due to Kleinberg and Tardos [227]. Exercise 13.6 is due to Garay and Gopal [164]. Exercises 13.4, 13.8, and 13.9 are due to Awerbuch, Azar, and Plotkin [26]. Exercises 13.7, 13.11, and 13.12 are due to Awerbuch et al. [28]. Exercise 13.15 is due to Bartal, Fiat, and Leonardi [46].

13.10.1   Open Questions

13.1 *(Value = I2/T3)* Can algorithm AAP-KNOWN be extended to apply to situations in which the maximum to minimum duration ratio T is not known a priori?

13.2 *(Value = I2/T3)* Can the algorithm for the disjoint paths problem for arrays be modified to yield a log N randomized disjoint paths algorithm for *bidirectional* brick wall graphs?

13.3 *(Value = I4/T3)* The reduction of Theorem 13.18 introduces an additional $O(\log N)$ factor in the competitive ratio of the path coloring problem relative to the ratio for the disjoint paths problem. Does there exist a class of networks for which this $O(\log N)$ factor is necessary?

13.4 *(Value = I3/T3)* Is CGC optimal (i.e., can the lower bound in Theorem 13.25 be improved) or is $\Theta\left(\frac{\log N}{\log\log N}\right)$ optimal for path coloring on trees?

13.5 *(Value = I3/T4)* We note that the lower bound in Theorem 13.25 is an "additive" rather than "multiplicative" lower bound. That is, this lower bound does not preclude the possibility that there is an online algorithm ALG such that for every input sequence σ, $\text{ALG}(\sigma) \le \text{OPT}(\sigma) + \log N$. Is there a multiplicative lower bound where the ratio holds for arbitrarily large values of $\text{OPT}(\sigma)$? Note that this same additive versus multiplicative issue applies also to the lower bound for FFC in Theorem 13.24.

13.6 *(Value = I4/T3)* Does there exist a path coloring problem for which randomization provably helps? More specifically, what is the randomized competitive ratio for path coloring on trees? (At present, we know of no lower bound for randomized path coloring on trees.)

---

[17] We can view the wavelength assignment problem as a set covering problem in which the universe is the set of call requests and the covering sets are the sets of calls routable using only one wavelength.

CHAPTER 14

Search, Trading, and Portfolio Selection

Financial problems are very attractive candidates for competitive analysis. Such problems are typically online in nature in that information about the future is often scarce and/or unreliable. In this chapter we focus on two problems that are both related to trading. In the first problem the online player is searching for the maximum or minimum price in the market. This problem is closely related to a one-way trading problem in which the online player wishes to trade some initial amount of money to another asset or currency. In the second problem, called the portfolio selection problem, the player wishes periodically to reallocate his wealth among a number of investment opportunities in the most profitable way. A particular case of interest is the two-way trading problem in which there are only two investment possibilities: cash and one risky security.

In Chapter 5 we explored various alternative approaches to "pure" competitive analysis in the context of the paging problem. In this chapter we encounter two frameworks of analysis that relax pure competitive analysis. In one such framework we assume a weaker kind of opponent called a "statistical adversary." Such an adversary must generate request sequences that conform to particular statistical constraints (see Section 14.3). In the other framework we measure the performance ratio of some online portfolio selection algorithms not with respect to OPT but with respect to an optimal member of a restricted class of offline algorithms (in particular, the "constant rebalanced" algorithms in Section 14.5). The latter framework somewhat resembles the relaxation in the (h, k)-paging and (h, k)-server problems in Chapters 3 and 10 and the comparison of online list accessing algorithms to a static optimal offline algorithm (in Appendix B).[1]

14.1 Online Search and One-Way Trading

Consider the following time series **search problem**. An online player is searching for the maximum (or minimum) price in a sequence of prices that unfolds sequentially. At the beginning of each time period i, the player obtains a price quotation p_i. Then the player must decide whether to accept p_i or continue sampling more prices. The game ends when the player accepts some price p_j and the return is p_j.

---

[1] As discussed in Chapter 3, the performance of a given algorithm with respect to an optimal member of a class of (not necessarily offline) algorithms is called the "comparative ratio"; see Koutsoupias and Papadimitriou [232].

Search is a fundamental feature of economic markets with applications such as job and employee search, and search for the lowest price of goods. Another important application of search is one-way trading. In the **one-way trading problem**, the online player is a trader whose goal is to trade some initial wealth D_0, given in some currency (e.g., dollars), to some other asset or currency (e.g., yen). Each period starts when a new price quotation is obtained. This **price** gives the exchange rate, yen per dollar. Given the current exchange rate, the trader must decide on the fraction of the remaining dollars to be exchanged for yen using the current exchange rate. The need for one-way trading strategies arises in various economic situations, for instance, when a fund manager decides to change the position of a portfolio and enter (or exit) some market (in which case, D_0 is the part of his wealth allocated to the new position). Another natural example, related to foreign exchange, is when the player, for the purpose of emigrating to a foreign country, sells his local property in order to exchange the local currency received to the foreign one.

14.1.1 The Relationship Between Randomized Search and One-Way Trading Algorithms

In the search problem, the online player must accept one price, whereas in the one-way trading problem the trader can partition his initial wealth and trade the parts sequentially, each part at a different exchange rate. That is, we can *define* a search algorithm as a one-way trading algorithm that must trade its entire wealth at once. Nevertheless, these problems are equivalent in the following sense. Any deterministic (or randomized) one-way trading algorithm that trades the initial wealth in parts can be interpreted as a randomized search algorithm, and vice versa. This follows from the fact that any one-way trading algorithm is equivalent, in terms of expected returns, to a randomized trading algorithm that trades the entire wealth at once at some randomly chosen period. Further, any randomized trading algorithm that trades the entire wealth at once is equivalent to a deterministic algorithm that trades the initial wealth in parts. Formally, we have the following theorem.

Theorem 14.1 *(i) Let* ALG$_1$ *be any randomized one-way trading algorithm. Then there exists a deterministic one-way trading algorithm* ALG$_2$ *such that for any price sequence* σ, ALG$_2(\sigma) = \mathbf{E}[\text{ALG}_1(\sigma)]$. *The reverse statement is also true: (ii) let* ALG$_2$ *be any deterministic one-way trading algorithm. Then there exists a randomized search algorithm* ALG$_1$ *such that* $\mathbf{E}[\text{ALG}_1(\sigma)] = \text{ALG}_2(\sigma)$ *holds for all* σ.

PROOF. Let ALG$_1$ be any randomized one-way trading algorithm. In particular, on each day, ALG$_1$ may trade any amount using any distribution (perhaps conditioned on the history thus far). According to Kuhn's theorem (Theorem 6.2), there exists a mixed algorithm ALG$_1'$, achieving the same expected return as ALG$_1$ for any price sequence σ, which is a probability distribution $\{\mu(a)\}$ over $\mathcal{A}$, the set of all deterministic algorithms. For any sequence of prices $\sigma = p_1, p_2, \ldots, p_n$, the expected return of ALG$_1'$ is $\mathbf{E}_\mu[\text{ALG}_1'(\sigma)] = \int_{\mathcal{A}} a(\sigma) d\mu(a)$. Consider a deterministic algorithm ALG$_2$ that spends a fraction $\int_{\mathcal{A}} s(i, a) d\mu(a)$ of its initial wealth in period i, where $s(i, a)$ is the amount spent by the deterministic algorithm a in period i. Thus, the return of ALG2 is

$$
\begin{aligned}
\text{ALG}_2(\sigma) &= \sum_{i=1}^{n} p_i \int_{\mathcal{A}} s(i, a) d\mu(a) \\
&= \int_{\mathcal{A}} \sum_{i=1}^{n} s(i, a) p_i d\mu(a) \\
&= \int_{\mathcal{A}} a(\sigma) d\mu(a) = \mathbf{E}_{\mu}[\text{ALG}'_1(\sigma)].
\end{aligned}
$$

To prove part (ii) consider a deterministic algorithm that trades a fraction s_i of its initial wealth at the ith period, $\sum_i s_i = 1$. Now consider a randomized algorithm ALG1 that, with probability s_i, trades its entire wealth at the ith period. Clearly, the expected return of ALG1 equals the return of the deterministic algorithm ALG2. ∎

It follows that an optimal deterministic one-way trading algorithm has the same return as an optimal randomized search algorithm. This implies that randomization cannot improve the competitive performance in one-way trading. In contrast, Theorem 14.2 shows that randomization is advantageous for search.

We note that in general, both in the search and one-way trading problem, the online player is often required to pay a sampling cost, a transaction cost, or both. Depending on the application, there are many different types of costs that can be levied. For example, in the one-way trading problem the transaction fees can be a function of the amount traded (i.e., dollars spent) or of the price rate (equivalently, the amount of yen received). Additionally, the transaction fees can include a fixed or minimum fee per transaction. Any of the above schemes can be progressive with respect to the amount traded, and so on.

Here we simplify the problem and ignore such costs.[2] As discussed in the following exercise, the nature of the sampling/transaction fees can affect the analyses.

Exercise 14.1 Prove the following:

(i) The competitive ratio of any one-way trading algorithm is independent of transaction costs determined by a fixed percentage applied to the amount spent. In this case, the equivalence of Theorem 14.1 obviously holds.

(ii) When we introduce transaction fees determined by a fixed percentage applied to the price rates, the competitive ratio improves but Theorem 14.1 still holds.

(iii) When fixed transaction costs are introduced, the deterministic competitive ratio increases and there is no longer an equivalence between deterministic one-way trading algorithms and randomized search algorithms.

14.1.2   Competitive Search Algorithms

In this section we describe competitive solutions to a few variants of the above search and one-way trading problems. In all the variants we consider, we assume that prices (exchange

---

[2] Also, we make the assumption that arbitrary fractions of money units can be traded; when large amounts are traded, this assumption is not significant.

rates) are drawn from some real interval $[m, M]$ with $0 < m \leq M$. Set $\varphi = \frac{M}{m}$ and call φ the **global fluctuation ratio**. In all the variants, we assume that time is discrete and the horizon is finite. We distinguish between known and unknown duration. In the known duration case, the online player knows the number of trading periods in advance. In the unknown duration case, we assume that the player is informed immediately prior to the last period that the game ends after the following period. The duration, or the number of periods played, is always denoted by n. In both the known and unknown duration variants of the trading (respectively, search) game, the player can always end the game after trading his remaining dollars at an exchange rate of at least m (respectively, accepting the price m).

Suppose that m and M are known to the player.[3] The optimal deterministic search solution is the following RESERVATION-PRICE-POLICY (RPP):

Algorithm RPP: Accept the first price greater than or equal to $p^* = \sqrt{Mm}$.

Call p^* the **reservation price**. Algorithm RPP is $\sqrt{\varphi}$-competitive and its analysis is simple. By a "balancing argument," p^* should be chosen to equate the return ratio, offline to online, corresponding to the two events: (i) the (posteriori) maximum price encountered, $p_{\max}$, will be greater than or equal to p^*, in which case the performance ratio, offline to online, will be $\frac{M}{p^*}$; and (ii) $p_{\max} < p^*$, in which case the ratio is $\frac{p_{\max}}{m}$. It follows that p^* is the solution p of $\frac{M}{p} = \frac{p}{m}$. The above reservation strategy is optimal for infinite and finite time horizons and when duration is known or unknown.

Exercise 14.2 Prove that if only φ is known, then no competitive ratio smaller than the trivial φ is achievable by any deterministic algorithm.

A dramatic improvement is obtained by using randomization. First we show how a simple randomized search algorithm called EXPO attains a competitive ratio of $O(\log \varphi)$. For simplicity, assume that $\varphi = 2^k$ for some integer k. For $i = 0, 1, \ldots, k - 1$, use RPP$_i$ to denote the deterministic reservation price policy with reservation price $m2^i$. Algorithm EXPO is a uniform probability mixture over $\{\text{RPP}_i\}$.

Algorithm EXPO: With probability $\frac{1}{k}$, choose algorithm RPP$_i$, $i = 1, \ldots, k$.

Theorem 14.2 *Algorithm EXPO is $(c(\varphi) \log \varphi)$-competitive, with $c(\varphi)$ approaching 1 when $\varphi \to \infty$.*

PROOF. Let $p_{\max}$ be the (posteriori) maximum price obtained and let j be an integer such that $m2^j \leq p_{\max} < m2^{j+1}$ (note that $j \leq k$).[4] Clearly, the optimal offline return is $p_{\max}$. The particular choice of the interval $[m2^j, m2^{j+1})$ and the exact value of $p_{\max}$ in this interval are controlled by the adversary. For any particular choice of j, it is advantageous to the adversary to choose $p_{\max}$ arbitrarily close to $m2^{j+1}$ because it increases the offline return and does not change the online return at all. Hence, in the worst case, $p_{\max} = m2^{j+1} - \varepsilon$ for some j and arbitrarily small $\varepsilon > 0$. Now, for each $i \leq j$, the strategy RPP$_i$

---

[3] At various times, binational and multinational agreements have set m and M for some duration in time. More generally, a trader can choose m and M based on expert predictions.

[4] When $j = k$, $p_{\max} = M$, by the underlying constraint that all prices are in $[m, M]$. We can argue that the choice of $j = k$ (and, therefore, of $p_{\max} = M$) is not advantageous to the adversary, so one may further assume that $j \leq k - 1$.

chooses the threshold price $m2^i$, and for all $i > j$, RPP_i obtains at least m. It follows that EXPO will return, on average,

$$\frac{m}{k}\left(k - j + \sum_{1 \le i \le j} 2^i\right) = \frac{m}{k}(2^{j+1} + k - j - 2).$$

For each particular choice of j, we use $R(j)$ to denote the offline to online ratio obtained. Thus, ignoring ε,

$$R(j) = k\frac{2^{j+1}}{2^{j+1} + k - j - 2}.$$

It is not difficult to show that the real-valued function $R(j)$ obtains its maximum at $j^* = k - 2 + \frac{1}{\ln 2}$. It follows that the coefficient of k in $R(j)$ is approximately 1, resulting in a competitive ratio that is greater than but approaching $k = \log \varphi$ as φ (and k) grow. ∎

Exercise 14.3 Extend algorithm EXPO and its analysis to the case in which φ is not a power of 2.

The bound of Theorem 14.2 holds even if the player does not know the values of m and M and knows only the global fluctuation ratio φ. Here, however, the strategies RPP_i are set after the first price p_1 is revealed (in which case, RPP_i has reservation price $p_1 2^i$).

Algorithm EXPO can be modified to work even without the knowledge of φ. Let $\mu = \{q(i)\}_{i=0}^{\infty}$ be a probability distribution over the natural numbers (i.e., $q(i)$ is the probability of choosing i). Assume that the first price revealed is p_1. Consider the following algorithm, EXPO$'_\mu$.

Algorithm EXPO$'_\mu$: Choose the reservation price $p_1 2^i$, with probability $q(i)$, $i = 0, 1, \ldots$.

Theorem 14.3 *Algorithm* EXPO$'_\mu$ *is* $\left(\frac{2}{q(\lfloor \log \varphi \rfloor)}\right)$*-competitive against an oblivious adversary, where φ is the posteriori global fluctuation ratio.*

PROOF. Let $p_{\max}$ be the maximum price obtained and assume that $p_1 2^j \le p_{\max} < p_1 2^{j+1}$ for some integer j. In the worst case, OPT's return is less than, but arbitrarily close to, $p_1 2^{j+1}$ and the expected return of algorithm EXPO$'_\mu$ is at least $q(j)p_1 2^j$. It follows that the competitive ratio of EXPO$'_\mu$ is not smaller than $\frac{2}{q(j)}$. ∎

We can apply Theorem 14.3 using slowly converging infinite sums. As a first example, consider the Riemann zeta function $\zeta(x) = \sum_{i=1}^{\infty} \frac{1}{i^x}$. Specifically, for every positive ε, the infinite sum $\sum_{i=1}^{\infty} \frac{1}{i^{1+\varepsilon}}$ converges to the constant $\zeta(1 + \varepsilon)$. It follows that

$$\mu_\varepsilon = \left\{\frac{1}{\zeta(1 + \varepsilon)(i + 1)^{1+\varepsilon}}\right\}_{i=0}^{\infty}$$

is a probability distribution over the natural numbers. Hence, according to Theorem 14.3, EXPO$'_{\mu_\varepsilon}$ attains a competitive ratio of $2\zeta(1 + \varepsilon)(\log \varphi + 1)^{1+\varepsilon} = O(\log^{1+\varepsilon} \varphi)$, where φ is the posteriori global fluctuation ratio. However, we can do better. The infinite sum

$\sum_i \frac{1}{i\log^{1+\varepsilon}(i)}$ converges more slowly than the zeta function and, according to Theorem 14.3, yields the competitive ratio of

$$O\big(\log(\varphi) \cdot \log^{1+\varepsilon}(\log\varphi)\big). \tag{14.1}$$

Notice, however, that as ε decreases, the constant in the "big-oh" notation increases. Hence, the particular choice of the distribution μ_ε can be optimized only if some bounds on φ are known.

Exercise 14.4 Generalize the upper bound given by equation (14.1) and show how, for every integer k, to achieve an upper bound of

$$O\left(\log(\varphi) \cdot \log^{1+\varepsilon} \underbrace{(\log\log\cdots\log\varphi)}_{k} \right)$$

on the competitive ratio for some EXPO'_μ.

14.1.3   The "Threat-Based" Policy

The competitive ratio $O(\log\varphi)$ is attained by a very simple strategy. This competitive bound is within a constant factor of the best possible result. Nevertheless, to obtain an optimal competitive ratio requires a somewhat more involved strategy.

The optimal performance is obtained by algorithms that obey a **threat-based policy**. Let c be any competitive ratio that can be attained by some one-way trading algorithm. First, assume that c is known to the trader. For each such c, the corresponding THREAT-BASED algorithm consists of the following two rules:

Rule 1: Consider converting dollars to yen only when the current rate is the highest seen thus far.

Rule 2: When converting dollars, convert *just enough* to ensure that a competitive ratio c would be obtained if an adversary dropped the exchange rate to the minimum possible rate and kept it there throughout the game.[5]

At the outset it is not clear how to follow such a policy – specifically, how to follow Rule 2. For the moment, assume that it is possible to compute the quantity "just enough" dollars prescribed by Rule 2 and consider an algorithm that follows this policy. (We soon show how to remove this assumption.) Thus, such an algorithm converts dollars to yen based on the threat that the exchange rate will drop permanently to the minimum possible rate. Under the above assumptions, for each attainable competitive ratio c the corresponding threat-based algorithm can be shown to be c-competitive. This assertion can be intuitively justified as follows. Consider the first trade (at exchange rate p_1). Since the current exchange rate is the highest seen thus far, the algorithm considers a trade. Since the competitive ratio c is attainable by some deterministic trading algorithm, there exists some $s \geq 0$ such that the ratio c continues to be attainable if s dollars are traded to yen.

---

[5] The "minimum possible rate" is defined with respect to the information known to the trader. That is, it is m if m is known, and it is $\frac{p}{\varphi}$ if only φ is known and p is the highest price seen thus far.

Further, the chosen amount of dollars s is such that the ratio c is thus far guaranteed even if there is a permanent drop of the exchange rate and no further trades are conducted (except for one last trade converting the remaining dollars under the minimum possible exchange rate). Specifically, there is no need to consider any exchange rate smaller than p_1. Similar arguments can be used to justify the choice of the amounts for the remaining trades; thus, intuitively, this policy induces a c-competitive algorithm. A more formal analysis follows.

Assume a known duration n, and known m and M. We now show how the optimal threat-based algorithm, denoted THREAT, can be derived. Initially, assume that the optimal competitive ratio c^* attainable by THREAT is known. A simple observation is that any exchange rate that is not a global maximum at the time it is revealed to the trader is ignored (Rule 1). Hence, we can assume, without loss of generality, that the exchange rate sequence consists of an initial segment of successive maxima of length $k \leq n$. In order to realize a threat, the adversary chooses $k < n$ and chooses $p_{k+1} = p_{k+2} = \cdots = p_n = m$.

For each $i = 0, 1, \ldots, n$ let D_i and Y_i be the number of remaining dollars and the number of accumulated yen, respectively, immediately after the ith period. By assumption, the trader starts with $D_0 = 1$ dollar and $Y_0 = 0$ yen. Let $s_i = D_{i-1} - D_i$ be the number of dollars traded at the ith period, $i = 1, 2, \ldots, n$. Thus, $Y_i = \sum_{j=1}^{i} s_j p_j$. Since the ratio c^* is attained by algorithm THREAT, according to Rule 2 it must be that the amounts s_i are chosen such that for any $1 \leq i \leq n$,

$$\frac{p_i}{Y_i + m \cdot D_i} = \frac{p_i}{(Y_{i-1} + s_i p_i) + m \cdot (D_{i-1} - s_i)} \leq c^*. \tag{14.2}$$

Here the denominator on the left-hand side represents the return of THREAT if an adversary drops the exchange rate to m, and the numerator on the left-hand side is the return of OPT for such an exchange rate sequence. According to Rule 2, THREAT must spend the minimal s_i that satisfies inequality (14.2). Since the left-hand side is decreasing with s_i, and since s_i is chosen to achieve the target competitive ratio c^*, we must spend the minimum possible amount (in order to leave as much as possible for higher rates); therefore, we replace the inequality in equation (14.2) with equality. Solving the resulting equality for s_i, we obtain

$$s_i = \frac{p_i - c^* \cdot (Y_{i-1} + m D_{i-1})}{c^* \cdot (p_i - m)}. \tag{14.3}$$

From equation (14.2) (with equality) we also obtain the following relation:

$$Y_i + m \cdot D_i = \frac{p_i}{c^*}. \tag{14.4}$$

Closed form expressions for the s_i's can now be obtained. From equation (14.3) at $i = 1$, we get

$$s_1 = \frac{1}{c^*} \frac{p_1 - mc^*}{p_1 - m}.$$

From equation (14.4), with $i - 1$ replacing i, we obtain

$$Y_{i-1} + m D_{i-1} = \frac{p_{i-1}}{c^*}.$$

Hence, from equation (14.3), we have

$$s_i = \frac{1}{c^*} \frac{p_i - p_{i-1}}{p_i - m}$$

for $i > 1$.

It remains, of course, to determine c^*, the optimal competitive ratio attainable by algorithm THREAT. For any sequence of k exchange rate maxima it must be that the s_i satisfy $\sum_{1 \leq i \leq k} s_i \leq D_0 = 1$. Further, if the value of k is known to the trader, then the optimal choice of the s_i's is such that there will be no dollars remaining after the last transaction. That is, the optimal competitive ratio has the property that $\sum_{1 \leq i \leq k} s_i = 1$. Substituting into this equation the expressions determined for the s_i's, we obtain

$$1 = \frac{1}{c^*} \frac{p_1 - mc^*}{p_1 - m} + \frac{1}{c^*} \sum_{i=2}^{k} \frac{p_i - p_{i-1}}{p_i - m},$$

and solving it for c^*, we obtain

$$c^* = c^*(k, m, p_1, p_2, \ldots, p_k) = 1 + \frac{p_1 - m}{p_1} \cdot \sum_{i=2}^{k} \frac{p_i - p_{i-1}}{p_i - m}.$$

Use $c_n^*(m, M)$ to denote the optimal competitive ratio for the n-day game. Thus,

$$c_n^*(m, M) = \max_{\substack{k \leq n \\ m \leq p_1 < p_2 < \cdots < p_k \leq M}} c^*(k, m, p_1, p_2, \ldots, p_k).$$

An explicit expression for $c_n^*(m, M)$ cannot be obtained; however, the following lemma holds.

Lemma 14.1 $c_n^*(m, M)$ is the unique root, c^*, of the equation

$$c = n \cdot \left(1 - \left(\frac{m(c-1)}{M-m} \right)^{1/n} \right). \tag{14.5}$$

Exercise 14.5 Prove Lemma 14.1. Hint: Fix k, m, and M and maximize over the p_i's.

Exercise 14.6 Find one optimal price generation strategy for the adversary. Hint: There exists a sequence against which the optimal threat-based algorithm trades $\frac{1}{n}$ of its initial wealth in each trading period.

Thus, $c_n^*(m, M)$ is the minimum competitive ratio attainable by algorithm THREAT for an n-day game. Moreover, $c_n^*(m, M)$ is the optimal competitive ratio for this problem variant.

Theorem 14.4 (One-way trading lower bound) *No one-way trading algorithm (deterministic or randomized) can obtain a competitive ratio smaller than $c_n^*(m, M)$.*

Exercise 14.7 Prove Theorem 14.4. Hint: Consider Exercise 14.6.

It follows that $c_n^*(m, M)$ is the exact competitive ratio for the trading problem of known duration and known bounds (m and M). The fact that randomization cannot help in this problem was established in Theorem 14.1. Theorem 14.4 refines that result by providing an explicit deterministic online optimal algorithm.

Exercise 14.8 (Lenient adversary) In the above known duration one-way trading model, the optimal threat-based algorithm computes all its trading amounts based on one competitive ratio c that is calculated prior to the start of the game (based on the worst-case exchange rate sequence). Nevertheless, a more clever strategy could recalculate the worst-case ratio every period and exploit any deviation of the adversary from its best price generation strategy. Determine such a dynamic online (threat-based) algorithm, and prove that it optimally takes advantage of any deviation from the worst possible price sequence.

The threat-based solution for the known duration case implies a solution for trading with unknown duration. On the one hand, algorithm THREAT, computed with $c_\infty^*(m, M) = \lim_{n\to\infty} c_n^*(m, M)$, can handle any finite number of time periods while attaining a competitive ratio of $c_\infty^*(m, M)$. On the other hand, when the duration is not known until the last day, the adversary can choose any n and force a competitive ratio approaching $c_\infty^*(m, M)$ (Exercise 14.7). It not difficult to show that $c_\infty^*(m, M)$ is the unique root c^* of the equation

$$c = \ln \frac{M - m}{m(c - 1)}.$$

Here again, it is not possible to obtain $c_\infty^*(m, M)$ explicitly. However, it is not difficult to see that $c_\infty^*(m, M) = \Theta(\ln \varphi)$.

Exercise 14.9 Consider the one-trading problem variant in which the trader knows only the global fluctuation ratio $\varphi = \frac{M}{m}$ but not m and M. Prove that when the duration n is known, the threat-based algorithm obtains an optimal competitive ratio of $c_n^*(\varphi)$ where

$$c_n^*(\varphi) = \varphi \left(1 - (\varphi - 1) \left(\frac{\varphi - 1}{\varphi^{n/(n-1)} - 1} \right)^n \right). \tag{14.6}$$

Using equation (14.6), prove that for the unknown duration variant, algorithm THREAT obtains an optimal competitive ratio of

$$c_\infty^*(\varphi) = \varphi - \frac{\varphi - 1}{\varphi^{1/(\varphi-1)}} = \Theta(\ln \varphi).$$

Table 14.1 summarizes the competitive ratio of the algorithms discussed in this section for some values of φ. We see that the optimal threat-based algorithm for the variant where m and M are known is always significantly superior to all other algorithms. The deterministic reservation price algorithm is better than EXPO for small values of φ, but the growth rate of the competitive ratio of EXPO is approximately the logarithm of the growth rate of the competitive ratio of the optimal deterministic RPP algorithm.

Exercise 14.10 Prove that

$$\lim_{\varphi\to\infty} \frac{\overline{\mathcal{R}}(\text{EXPO})}{\mathcal{R}(\text{THREAT})} = \frac{1}{\ln 2} \approx 1.44,$$

where $\overline{\mathcal{R}}(\text{EXPO})$ and $\mathcal{R}(\text{THREAT})$ are the competitive ratios of algorithms EXPO and THREAT for the problem variant where only φ is known.

Table 14.1: Numerical examples of competitive ratios for some search and one-way trading algorithms (unknown duration).

Algorithm	Value of φ					
	1.5	2	4	8	16	32
RPP (m, M known)	1.22	1.41	2	2.82	4	5.65
EXPO (only φ known)	1.5	2	2.66	3.42	4.26	5.16
THREAT (only φ known)	1.27	1.50	2.11	2.80	3.53	4.28
THREAT (m, M known)	1.15	1.28	1.60	1.97	2.38	2.83

It is also interesting to consider the rate of increase of the optimal competitive ratio as a function of the number of trading days n. For some examples, consider the graph in Figure 14.1. As indicated in this figure, the function $c_n^*(m, M)$ grows very quickly to its asymptote. Nevertheless, there is still a slight advantage to playing short games. For instance, already at the $n = 20$th period, $c_n^*(1, 2)$ has almost reached its asymptote, $c_\infty^*(1, 2) \approx 1.278$ (which is equivalent to guaranteeing 78.2% of the optimal offline return); at $n = 10$, the ratio achieved is 1.26 (79.3%); and at $n = 5$, the ratio is 1.24 (80.6%).

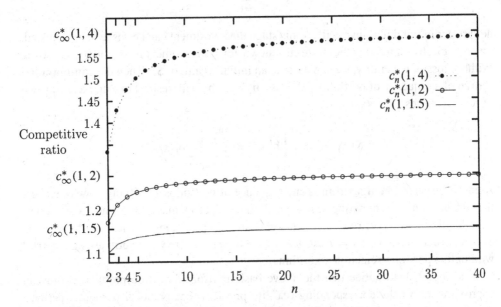

Figure 14.1: Three examples of the optimal competitive ratio (attained by threat-based algorithms) as functions of the number of trading periods. (*Note:* $c_\infty^*(1, 1.5) \approx 1.157$, $c_\infty^*(1, 2) \approx 1.278$, and $c_\infty^*(1, 4) \approx 1.604$.)

14.2   Online Portfolio Selection

Consider a market of s securities (assets). These can be stocks, bonds, foreign currencies, or commodities. Let $\mathbf{p}_i = (p_{i1}, p_{i2}, \ldots, p_{is})$ denote a vector of prices where for each $j = 1, 2, \ldots, s$, the price p_{ij} denotes the number of units of the jth security that can be bought for one dollar at the start of the ith period, $i = 1, 2, \ldots$.[6] The "local" currency, for example, dollars, may or may not be one of the s securities. This local currency is also called **cash**. The "price" of cash is constantly equal to 1. The change in security prices during the ith period is represented as a column vector $\mathbf{x}_i = (x_{i1}, x_{i2}, \ldots, x_{is})$, where for each i, $i = 1, 2, \ldots$, and for each j, $j = 1, \ldots, s$,

$$x_{ij} = \frac{p_{ij}}{p_{(i+1)j}}.$$

The quantity x_{ij} is called the **relative price** of security j (for the ith period). Thus, an investment of d dollars in the jth security just before the start of the ith period yields dx_{ij} dollars by the end of the ith trading period. Any sequence of price vectors or relative price vectors is called a **market sequence**.

An investment in the market, or **portfolio**, is specified as the proportion of dollar wealth currently invested in each of the s securities. Specifically, we represent a portfolio as a probability distribution $\mathbf{b} = (b_1, b_2, \ldots, b_s)$, where $b_i \geq 0$ and $\sum_i b_i = 1$. Consider a portfolio $\mathbf{b}_1 = (b_{11}, b_{12}, \ldots, b_{1s})$ invested just before the first period. By the start of the second period, this portfolio yields

$$\mathbf{b}_1^t \cdot \mathbf{x}_1 = \sum_{j=1}^{s} b_{1j} x_{1j}$$

dollars per initial dollar invested. At this stage the investment can be cashed and adjusted, for example, by reinvesting the entire current wealth in some other proportion $\mathbf{b}_2$, and so on. Without loss of generality, we can assume an initial wealth of $1. Then the **compounded return** of a sequence of portfolios, $B = \mathbf{b}_1, \mathbf{b}_2, \ldots, \mathbf{b}_n$ with respect to a market sequence of relative prices $X = \mathbf{x}_1, \mathbf{x}_2, \ldots, \mathbf{x}_n$ is

$$R(B, X) = \prod_{i=1}^{n} \mathbf{b}_i^t \cdot \mathbf{x}_i = \prod_{i=1}^{n} \sum_{j=1}^{s} b_{ij} x_{ij}.$$

A **portfolio selection algorithm** is any sequence of portfolios specifying how to reinvest the current wealth from period to period. With respect to a market sequence X, the compounded return of a portfolio selection algorithm ALG producing a sequence of portfolios ALG[X] is denoted ALG(X) = R(ALG[X], X). Of course, here we are primarily concerned with online portfolio selection algorithms.

It is important to notice that the above basic portfolio selection problem is only an approximation of the corresponding real-life problem. For practical purposes, perhaps the most important factors missing in this model are *transaction fees* and *risk management*. Later, in Section 14.5.4 we extend the portfolio selection model to include transaction fees. In Section 14.6 we briefly discuss the issue of risk management in the context of the one-way trading problem. The above model also makes the assumption that money and units of securities are arbitrarily divisible. Other important missing factors are taxes and interest rates, which typically are crucial factors involved in investment planning (here we assume that the interest rate is 0). The model does not consider

---

[6] Notice that in this definition of "price," a downward change in a security's price corresponds to an increase in its value (i.e., fewer units of the security can be bought with $1).

many investment instruments that exist in a modern market, starting with "short selling" and ending with myriad "derivative securities" such as futures, options, and so on, although such financial instruments, as well as other factors such as interest rates, can be incorporated into this model. Nevertheless, this model is rich enough in itself and contitutes a reasonable foundation for studying some of the essential questions related to investment planning.

14.2.1 Buy-and-Hold Versus Market Timing

Financial agents study and use a large variety of trading strategies. Some of these are "slow," almost static strategies, typically used by mutual fund managers who select and buy some portfolio and then hold it for a relatively long time. Such strategies rely on the natural tendency of securities to increase in value as a result of natural economic forces. For instance, stocks pay dividends and increase their prices as the underlying firms succeed in their businesses. Such slow strategies are generally called BUY-AND-HOLD (**BAH**). In contrast, some financial agents use aggressive strategies that buy and sell securities very frequently, sometimes even many times during one day. Such strategies primarily attempt to take advantage of security price fluctuations and are called **market timing** strategies. Of course, in the long run every buy-and-hold strategy is also a market timing strategy; after all, sooner or later owners of securities want to realize the monetary value of the assets they hold. Hence, whether a strategy is buy-and-hold or market timing is relative to the time horizon considered.

Market timing strategies have the potential for enormous returns. Consider the following illustration.[7] A \$1 portfolio invested in the Dow Jones Industrial Average in January 1946 was worth \$116 at the end of 1991 (including reinvestment of dividends but excluding tax deductions). This is equivalent to an 11.2% compound annual gain. A market timing strategy that, fortunately, was not in the market during the 50 weakest months during that period (spanning 552 months) but was otherwise fully invested using the same fixed portfolio would return \$2541, or a 19% annual gain. Further, an offline strategy that was in a short position during the 50 weakest months would have returned \$44,967, or a 26.9% annual gain.

14.2.2 Constant Rebalanced Algorithms

A strategy that is sometimes used in practice is **constant rebalancing**, which is defined by a fixed portfolio $\mathbf{b} = (b_1, b_2, \ldots, b_s)$ used for each trading period. That is, prior to each trading period the algorithm invests in the portfolio $\mathbf{b}$. This means that the algorithm must rebalance the portfolio after any price changes. For example, if a portfolio $\mathbf{b} = \left(\frac{1}{2}, \frac{1}{2}\right)$ is invested prior to some trading period and the first security appreciates, then prior to the start of the next period the algorithm must rebalance its portfolio by selling some portion of the first security and buying some portion of the second security. Informally, we can think of this rebalancing as a "flow of investment" from security 1 to security 2.

This CONSTANT-REBALANCED algorithm, denoted CBAL$_\mathbf{b}$, is clearly a market timing strategy. Use **CBAL-OPT** to denote the optimal offline constant rebalanced algorithm. That is, CBAL-OPT = CBAL$_{\mathbf{b}^*}$, where for any market sequence $X = \mathbf{x}_1, \ldots, \mathbf{x}_n$, the fixed portfolio

---

[7] This illustration is due to Shilling [314].

$\mathbf{b}^*$ used by CBAL-OPT is

$$\mathbf{b}^* = \arg\max_{\mathbf{b}} \prod_{1 \le i \le n} \mathbf{b} \cdot \mathbf{x}_i.$$

The performance of the optimal offline CBAL-OPT is always at least as good as that of the optimal offline BAH and is usually significantly better because the optimal offline BAH performs only as the best security in the market; however, CBAL-OPT also takes advantage of fluctuations in the market, giving rise to exponential returns.

Example 14.1 (Constant rebalanced) Consider a market consisting of cash and one stock. The relative prices of the cash are always 1. Suppose that the relative prices of the stock follow the sequence: $\frac{1}{2}, 2, \frac{1}{2}, 2, \dots$. Clearly, the optimal offline BAH strategy, which buys the stock after the first period and sells after the second (or after any even period), will double its investment. We calculate the return of CBAL$_{\mathbf{b}}$ with $\mathbf{b} = \left(\frac{1}{2}, \frac{1}{2}\right)$.

The multiplicative cash increase of CBAL$_{\mathbf{b}}$ that results from any odd period is $\frac{1}{2}1 + \frac{1}{2}\frac{1}{2} = \frac{3}{4}$. The multiplicative cash increase that results from any even period is $\frac{1}{2}1 + \frac{1}{2}2 = \frac{3}{2}$. Therefore, after every pair of odd and even periods, the multiplicative cash increase is $\frac{3}{4}\frac{3}{2} = \frac{9}{8}$. Thus, after n periods, CBAL$_{\mathbf{b}}$ exponentially increases its initial investment by a factor of $\left(\frac{9}{8}\right)^{n/2}$.

We now examine the performance of CBAL$_{\mathbf{b}}$ versus that of BAH with respect to some real data. Consider the stocks of Iroquois Brands Ltd (IBL) and Kin Ark Corp. (KAC) during the 22-year period ending in 1985. IBL increased its price by a factor of 8.91, and KAC increased its price by a factor of 4.12.[8] An investor who was lucky enough to buy IBL and hold it during this period would have made a return of 891%, equivalent to an annual an annual return of 6.6%. Now consider the performance of the CBAL$_{(b,1-b)}$ algorithms, $b \in [0, 1]$. The returns of these algorithms are plotted in the graph of Figure 14.2. For

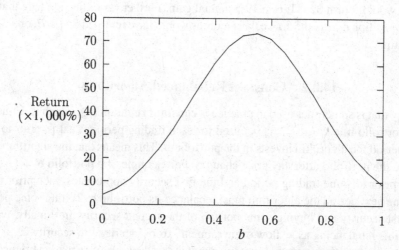

Figure 14.2: The returns ($\times 1000\%$) of the constant rebalanced algorithms CBAL$_{(b,1-b)}$, where b denotes the fraction invested in Iroquois Brands Ltd and $1 - b$ denotes the fraction invested in Kin Ark Corp.

---

[8] These figures have been adjusted to include dividends.

example, the constant rebalanced vector $(0.55, 0.45)$ could make a return of $73,619\%$, equivalent to an annual return of 149.8%.[9]

Of course, CBAL$_b$ makes as many as s transactions at the start of each trading period to adjust its portfolio, whereas BAH performs at most $2s$ transactions during the entire trading period (s to enter the market and s to exit). In the models considered here, this large number of transactions is not a consideration; however, this number does become significant when transaction costs are introduced.

14.3 Two-Way Trading: Statistical Adversaries and "Money Making" Algorithms

The portfolio selection problem when there are two securities, and one of the two securities is cash, is called the **two-way trading** problem. This problem receives special attention in this section. Recall that the relative prices of cash are always 1.

The two-way trading problem is a relatively specialized task in terms of the transactions that a general portfolio trader might want to undertake. Any sequence of two-way trading decisions can be viewed as a sequence of one-way trading tasks, and we have the following easily derivable exponential bounds.

Theorem 14.5 *Assume that all prices are drawn from $[m, M]$ and that $\varphi = \frac{M}{m}$ is known to the online player.*

(i) *$c_2^*(\varphi)^{n/2}$ is a lower bound on the competitive ratio for the n-period two-way trading problem (and hence for online portfolio selection with two or more securities), where the constant $c_2^*(\varphi) > 1$ is the optimal bound for a one-way two-period trading game in which the online player knows the global fluctuation φ.*

(ii) *There is a two-way trading algorithm that is $c_\infty^*(\varphi)^n$-competitive for any n-period game.*

Exercise 14.11 Prove Theorem 14.5.

Define the **profit** of a trading strategy as its final compounded return minus its initial wealth (a negative profit is called **loss**). An unfortunate but simple observation is that any competitive two-way trading algorithm may end the trading game with a loss.

Motivated by this observation, we now study models that allow for (competitive) algorithms that never lose. It is not surprising that in order to achieve this property, we must make sufficiently strong assumptions. Indeed, throughout this section we consider **statistical adversaries** that choose their worst-case market sequence while conforming to certain constraints that are specified by a "few" parameters (statistics).[10] The adversaries considered in Section 14.1 conformed to very weak constraints such as the global fluctuation ratio and the minimum and maximum price bounds; they also can be thought of as statistical adversaries. In this section we consider statistical adversaries conforming to stronger constraints.

---

[9] The graph of Figure 14.2 is based on a similar graph in Cover [119].

[10] This description is intentionally vague; the reader can decide whether or not restricted adversaries such as those found in the graph access and Markov paging models of Chapter 5 should be considered as statistical adversaries.

An online trading algorithm is called **money making** if it returns positive profit in any market sequence for which the optimal offline algorithm accrues positive profit.

For the remainder of this section we consider finite market sequences prescribed by a sequence of security prices $p_1, p_2, \ldots, p_n$ or, alternatively, by a sequence of the relative prices $x_1, x_2, \ldots, x_{n-1}$, where

$$x_i = \frac{p_i}{p_{i+1}}, \quad i = 1, 2, \ldots, n-1.$$

When referring to a market sequence, we usually use the relative price representation.

14.3.1 The (n, ϕ)-Adversary

Fix some $n \geq 2$. Assume that each feasible price sequence is of length n, and impose the restriction that the optimal offline return associated with a feasible sequence is at least ϕ (clearly, $\phi \geq 1$). The underlying assumption here is that true (n, ϕ) pairs exist in relevant real price sequences in that such pairs can be statistically estimated from past markets with some degree of confidence. An adversary that is constrained to generate only such feasible sequences is called the **(n, ϕ)-adversary**. Let $X = x_1, x_2, \ldots, x_{n-1}$ be a feasible sequence of relative prices. It is not difficult to see that the optimal offline return ϕ is given by

$$\phi = \prod_{1 \leq i \leq n-1} \max\{1, x_i\}. \tag{14.7}$$

It follows that for any such sequence of (relative) prices, an online player knowing ϕ and n at the start of the game can determine at the start of the $(i+1)$st period, just after the $(i+1)$st price is revealed ($i = 1, 2, \ldots$), what the optimal offline return ϕ_{n-i} would be for a new $(n-i)$-period game starting in that period; that is, if the optimal offline algorithm were to start in that period, a "new game" (with initial wealth of 1) with respect to the suffix $x_{i+1}, \ldots, x_n$ of the original market sequence. Specifically, using equation (14.7), we have $\phi_{n-1} = \min\{\phi, \frac{\phi}{x_1}\}$, and in general,

$$\phi_{n-j-1} = \min\left\{\phi_{n-j}, \frac{\phi_{n-j}}{x_{j+1}}\right\}.$$

Hence, when playing against the (n, ϕ)-adversary, the online player can track the current wealth accrued by the optimal offline algorithm with a delay of one day. This special property allows for the following continuous dynamic programming derivation of the optimal online algorithm for this problem. Consider the following algorithm, called MONEY-MAKING (MM), which is defined recursively in terms of the parameters n and ϕ. Use $R_n(\phi)$ to denote the return of algorithm MM for an n-period game with a corresponding optimal offline return of ϕ.

Algorithm MM$_{n,\phi}$: If $n = 2$, invest the entire wealth in yen (in which case, the return is $R_2(\phi)$). Otherwise, invest b dollars in yen where

$$b = \arg\max_{0 \leq b' \leq 1}\left\{\inf_{x_1 \leq \phi}\left\{(b'x_1 + 1 - b')\, R_{n-1}(\phi_{n-1})\right\}\right\}$$

(in which case, the return is $R_n(\phi)$).

Clearly, $R_2(\phi) = \phi$ as the adversary must generate an exchange rate sequence of length 2 with a relative price of $x_1 = \phi$. Therefore, we have the following recurrence relation for $R_n(\phi)$.

$$R_2(\phi) = \phi,$$

$$R_n(\phi) = \max_{0 \le b \le 1} \inf_{x \le \phi} \{(bx + 1 - b) R_{n-1}(\phi_{n-1})\}. \tag{14.8}$$

Algorithm MM attempts to choose its best investment b against the worst possible relative price x. The wealth obtained from the investment bx plus the remaining cash $1 - b$ are then reinvested optimally with respect to an $(n - 1)$-period game in which the optimal offline return is ϕ_{n-1}, and so on.

Exercise 14.12 Prove that algorithm MM achieves the highest return among all deterministic online algorithms for this model.

Although a closed form for $R_n(\phi)$ seems to be beyond reach it is still quite easy to obtain the following result.

Theorem 14.6 *Algorithm* MM *is money making.*

Exercise 14.13 Prove Theorem 14.6.

Unfortunately, although MM is money making, its performance is poor.

Lemma 14.2 *For any $\phi > 1$ and $n \ge 2$,*

$$R_n(\phi) \le \frac{1}{1 - (1 - 1/\phi)^{n-1}}. \tag{14.9}$$

PROOF. The bound (14.9) can be obtained by considering the following restricted version of the (n, ϕ)-adversary. In each period, this adversary has two options: either to decrease the price by a factor of ϕ or to increase the price by a huge factor so that the dollar value of the previous investment is negligible. (Recall from our definition of "price" that the downward movement is the profitable one.) Once this restricted adversary exercises the first option, there can be no further downward fluctuations, since the optimal offline return of ϕ has been realized. Hence, if this is the case, the game is over. In the former case, an investment of b returns $b\phi + 1 - b$. In the latter case, the adversary makes the dollar worth of the investment b arbitrarily small so that by the next period the dollar worth of the current portfolio is $1 - b + \varepsilon$ (with ε arbitrarily small). This amount can now be reinvested. Hence, in the limit as $\varepsilon \to 0$, we have the following recurrence relation for $R'_n(\phi)$:

$$R'_n(\phi) = \max_{0 \le b \le 1} \min\{b\phi + 1 - b, (1 - b)R'_{n-1}(\phi)\}. \tag{14.10}$$

(Here again, $R'_2(\phi) = \phi$.) Clearly, the optimal choice of b must equate both arguments of the minimum operator. Solving for b in the equation

$$b\phi + 1 - b = (1 - b)R'_{n-1}(\phi)$$

and then substituting the solution into equation (14.10), we obtain that the right-hand side of equation (14.9) is an approximate closed form for R'_n. Clearly, for any $n \geq 2$ and $\phi > 1$, $R'_n(\phi)$ is an upper bound on $R_n(\phi)$. ∎

Using the approximation

$$\left(1 - \frac{1}{\phi}\right)^{n-1} = \left(1 - \frac{1}{\phi}\right)^{\phi(n-1)/\phi} \approx e^{-(n-1)/\phi},$$

for large ϕ, we have

$$R'_n(\phi) \approx \frac{1}{1 - e^{-(n-1)/\phi}}.$$

The following relations can now be easily derived.

- If $\phi = \omega(n)$, then $e^{-(n-1)/\phi} \approx 1 - \frac{n-1}{\phi}$ and $R'_n(\phi) \approx \frac{\phi}{n-1}$.
- If $\phi = \Theta(n)$, then $R'_n(\phi) \approx \frac{1}{1-e^{-c}}$, where c is some positive constant.
- If $\phi = o(n)$, then $R'_n(\phi)$ approaches 1 as $n \to \infty$.

Hence, although MM is money making, the optimal online return $R_n(\phi)$ against the (n, ϕ)-adversary can be a minuscule fraction of ϕ. In terms of competitiveness, the above bounds easily yield the following corollary.

Corollary 14.7 $\mathcal{R}(\text{MM}) \geq \max\{n - 1, \phi\}$.

Exercise 14.14 Consider the following two variations of the above model. In one variation, the online player knows only n and does not know ϕ. In the second, the player knows only ϕ. Prove that online deterministic algorithms corresponding to either variant are not money making.

14.3.2   More Restricted Statistical Adversaries and the General Money Making Scheme

The derivation of an optimal online algorithm against the (n, ϕ)-adversary gives rise to a general scheme for obtaining money making optimal online algorithms with respect to any statistical adversary that is at least as restricted as the (n, ϕ)-adversary. For any collection of constraints C that subsume the (n, ϕ) constraint, a similar relation to equation (14.8) yields the corresponding optimal online algorithm when the constraints in C are appropriately included in the recurrence.

Intuitively, we would expect better online performance with respect to more restricted adversaries. For example, against the (n, ϕ)-adversary the online player is forced to invest very small amounts in most trading periods, since the adversary can depreciate the value of most investments by increasing the subsequent prices arbitrarily. Such threats can be made until period $n - 1$ (eventually, the optimal offline algorithm must realize a return of ϕ). Such market sequences are of course unrealistic. By imposing one or more of the following additional constraints, it is possible to reduce substantially these unrealistic threats: (i) upper bounds on relative prices; (ii) minimum and maximum bounds on prices; (iii) upper bounds on the length of runs of monotonically increasing or decreasing prices; and (iv) other statistical parameters such as mean and higher moments of the empirical distribution observed.

14.4 Two-Way Trading and the Fixed Fluctuation Model

In the **fixed fluctuation model** all relative prices x_i are in $\{\alpha, \alpha^{-1}\}$ where $\alpha > 1$. Assuming, without loss of generality, that the initial price is 1, it follows that each possible price is an element of $\{\alpha^k : k \text{ integer}\}$. We now add the restriction that each feasible sequence of relative prices is of length n and the number of downward (i.e., profitable) α^{-1}-fluctuations is exactly k, $0 \leq k \leq n$. Hence, the number of upward α-fluctuations is $n - k$. Call the adversary that produces such feasible sequences the (α, n, k)-**adversary**. This (α, n, k)-constraint subsumes the (n, ϕ)-constraint of Section 14.3.1, since the implied optimal offline return for each feasible market sequence is exactly $\phi = \alpha^k$. Hence, it is possible to obtain the optimal online money making two-way trading algorithm (against the (α, n, k)-adversary) using the money making scheme of Section 14.3.2. In what follows, we study this optimal online algorithm against the (α, n, k)-adversary and characterize some of its properties.

14.4.1 On the Fixed Fluctuation Model and Time Scaling

Before we continue with the analysis let us take note of the practical relevance of the fixed fluctuation model. Clearly, relative prices are variable. In order to apply algorithms designed for the fixed fluctuation model, we can use a **time scaling** approach in which each trading period is of variable length such that the $(i + 1)$st price tick occurs at the first time instance after the ith price tick when a price that approximates $p_i \alpha$ or $\frac{p_i}{\alpha}$ is encountered (with p_i denoting the price at the ith tick).[11] One advantage of this fixed fluctuation model is that the player may choose a suitable α that will filter out noise – that is, very small fluctuations that can be avoided, for example, when transaction costs are taken into consideration.

14.4.2 The Optimal Online Algorithm Against the (α, n, k)-Adversary

Denote by FMM the optimal online money-making algorithm against the (α, n, k)-adversary and let $R(n, k) = R_\alpha(n, k)$ be its return. Specializing the general scheme described in Section 14.3.2 for the (α, n, k)-adversary, we easily obtain the following recurrence for $R(n, k)$.

$$R(n, k) = \max_{0 \leq b \leq 1} \min \left\{ \begin{array}{l} (b\alpha^{-1} + 1 - b) \cdot R(n - 1, k), \\ (\alpha b + 1 - b) \cdot R(n - 1, k - 1) \end{array} \right\}, \qquad (14.11)$$

$$R(n, 0) = 1,$$

$$R(n, n) = \alpha^n.$$

Here again, the b that minimizes equation (14.11) is the first investment made by algorithm FMM. The remainder of the transactions performed by FMM can be determined by expanding the recurrence.

The recurrence (14.11) can be easily simplified. The upper operand in the minimum operator in (14.11) is decreasing with b, and the lower one is increasing with b. Hence,

---

[11] Of course, to allow for such time scaling the choice of α must be made in accordance with observed properties of the market in question. Specifically, α cannot be too large.

by using a balancing argument, we know that the optimal choice of b, denoted b^*, must equate both operands. Therefore,

$$b^* = \frac{R(n-1,k) - R(n-1,k-1)}{(\alpha-1)R(n-1,k-1) - (\alpha^{-1}-1)R(n-1,k)}.$$

Substituting b^* for b in either operand of the minimum in equation (14.11) and rearranging, we obtain the following expression for the reciprocal $R^{-1}(n,k)$.

$$R^{-1}(n,k) = \frac{\alpha}{\alpha+1} \cdot R^{-1}(n-1,k) + \frac{1}{\alpha+1} \cdot R^{-1}(n-1,k-1). \tag{14.12}$$

Our goal now is to study this recurrence and derive some of its properties. We do this in two steps. In the first step, we express $R^{-1}(n,k)$ in terms of partial binomial sums. These sums can be approximated in closed form, so in the second step we provide an asymptotic closed form approximation for $R^{-1}(n,k)$ (and $R(n,k)$). We then use the approximate expression for $R(n,k)$ to derive some financial interpretations.

Define $B_p\left\{{n \atop k}\right\} = \sum_{0 \le i \le k} \binom{n}{i} p^i (1-p)^{n-i}$, the partial binomial sum. Note that $B_p\left\{{n \atop k}\right\}$ is the probability that at most k successes occur in a series of n Bernoulli trials with success probability p.[12] Also set $p = \frac{\alpha}{1+\alpha}$ and $q = 1 - p = \frac{1}{1+\alpha}$.

Lemma 14.3 Let $c = \frac{k}{n}$. Then,

$$R^{-1}(n, cn) = B_p\left\{{n-1 \atop n(1-c)-1}\right\} + \alpha^{n(1-2c)} \cdot B_p\left\{{n-1 \atop cn-1}\right\}.$$

PROOF. Artificially extend the domain of $R^{-1}(n,k)$ such that

$$R^{-1}(n,j) = \begin{cases} 1 & j \le 0; \\ \alpha^{n-2k} & j \ge n. \end{cases} \tag{14.13}$$

Although $R^{-1}(n,j)$, with negative values of j or values of j that are greater than n, does not have a meaningful interpretation, it is still well defined and can be shown by induction on n to be consistent with recurrence (14.12).

Consider the graph in Figure 14.3. This graph is called a **binomial tree** and corresponds to an expansion of the extended recurrence $R^{-1}(n,k)$.[13] Each node in the graph is labeled by a pair (x,y) that corresponds to $R^{-1}(x,y)$. The root is labeled (n,k). Each internal node (x,y) has two outgoing edges, one to its lower child $(x-1, y-1)$, and the other to its upper child $(x-1, y)$. All the leaves are of the form $(1, k-(n-i))$, $i = 1, \ldots, n$. According to equation (14.12), the value of $R^{-1}(x,y)$ corresponding to the node (x,y) is computed from the values of its children, $(x-1, y-1)$ and $(x-1, y)$. In each node (x,y), x corresponds to the level of the node (where the leaves are at level 1 and the root is at level n) and y corresponds to the edge distance from the line connecting the

---

[12] Using standard notation $B_p\left\{{n \atop k}\right\} = \Pr[S_n \le k]$, where S_n denotes the number of successes in n Bernoulli trials (with success probability p).

[13] This graph is in essence a "weighted" Pascal triangle. The term "binomial tree" is typically used in finance for such graphs as those shown in Cox and Rubinstein [123], although clearly these graphs are not trees in the graph theoretic sense.

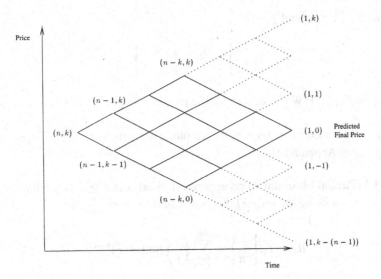

Figure 14.3: A binomial tree illustrating the expansion of the recurrence (14.12). The solid-line lattice corresponds to the original recurrence, and the dotted-line extension corresponds to the artificial expansion in equation (14.13).

root and uppermost leaf $(1, k)$. All the paths to a leaf have the same number of up and down moves. In particular, the path to the leaf $(1, k - (n - i))$ has $n - i$ down edges and $(n - 1) - (n - i) = i - 1$ up edges (there is a total of $n - 1$ edges in each path). According to equation (14.12), when we calculate the value $R^{-1}(n, k)$, each up move contributes a factor $q = \frac{1}{1+\alpha}$ and each down move contributes a factor $p = \frac{\alpha}{1+\alpha}$. Hence, the "weight" of any path to the leaf $(1, k - (n - i))$ is $p^{i-1}q^{n-i}$. Abbreviating $z_i = k - (n - i)$, we have

$$R^{-1}(n, k) = \sum_{\text{leaf}(1, z_i)} R^{-1}(1, z_i) \cdot \left[\# \text{ of paths to } (1, z_i)\right] \cdot \left[\text{weight of a path to } (1, z_i)\right]$$

$$= \sum_{1 \le i \le n} R^{-1}(1, z_i) \binom{n-1}{i-1} p^{i-1} q^{n-i}$$

$$= \sum_{z_i \le 0} R^{-1}(1, z_i) \binom{n-1}{i-1} p^{i-1} q^{n-i} + \sum_{z_i \ge 1} R^{-1}(1, z_i) \binom{n-1}{i-1} p^{i-1} q^{n-i}$$

$$= \sum_{z_i \le 0} 1 \binom{n-1}{i-1} p^{i-1} q^{n-i} + \sum_{z_i \ge 1} \alpha^{n-2k} \binom{n-1}{i-1} p^{i-1} q^{n-i}$$

$$= \sum_{i=1}^{n-k} \binom{n-1}{i-1} p^{i-1} q^{n-i} + \alpha^{n-2k} \sum_{i=n-k+1}^{n} \binom{n-1}{i-1} p^{i-1} q^{n-i}$$

$$= \sum_{i=0}^{n-k-1} \binom{n-1}{i} p^i q^{n-i-1} + \alpha^{n-2k} \cdot \sum_{i=0}^{n-k} \binom{n-1}{i} q^i p^{n-i-1}$$

$$= B_p \left\{ \begin{matrix} n-1 \\ n-k-1 \end{matrix} \right\} + \alpha^{n-2k} \cdot B_q \left\{ \begin{matrix} n-1 \\ n-k \end{matrix} \right\}.$$

Clearly, for all n, $k \leq n$, and p,

$$B_p \begin{Bmatrix} n \\ k \end{Bmatrix} = B_{1-p} \begin{Bmatrix} n \\ n-k \end{Bmatrix}, \qquad (14.14)$$

so $B_q \begin{Bmatrix} n-1 \\ n-k \end{Bmatrix} = B_p \begin{Bmatrix} n-1 \\ k-1 \end{Bmatrix}$, which completes the proof. ∎

The following lemma provides useful asymptotic properties of $B_p \begin{Bmatrix} n \\ k \end{Bmatrix}$. The proof of this lemma appears in Appendix H.

Lemma 14.4 (Partial binomial sums approximation) *Let $n \geq 2$ be an integer and let $0 < c < 1$ (with cn being an integer). Let $\alpha > 1$ and set $p = \frac{\alpha}{1+\alpha}$. Set*

$$B_n = B_p \begin{Bmatrix} n \\ cn \end{Bmatrix} = \sum_{i=0}^{cn} \binom{n}{i} p^i (1-p)^{n-i}.$$

Define

$$W(x) = \frac{x^x (1-x)^{(1-x)} (1+\alpha)}{\alpha^{(1-x)}}, \qquad (14.15)$$

and to simplify notation, let $W^n(x)$ denote $(W(x))^n$. Then, the following conditions hold.

(i) *If $c > p$, then $B_n \to 1$ almost surely.*
(ii) *If $c = p$, then $B_n \to \frac{1}{2}$.*
(iii) *If $c < p$, then $B_n = \Theta\left(\frac{1}{\sqrt{n}} \cdot W^{-n}(1-c)\right)$.*

Lemma 14.4 can now be used to prove the following theorem that characterizes $R(n, cn)$ in terms of regions of c.

Theorem 14.8 (Characterization of FMM) *Let $c \in [0, 1]$ with cn being an integer. Then*

(i) *If $0 \leq c < q$, then $R(n, cn) \to 1$.*
(ii) *If $c = q$, then $R(n, cn) \to 2$.*
(iii) *If $q < c < p$, then $R(n, cn) = \Theta(\sqrt{n} W^n(c))$.*
(iv) *If $c = p$, then $R(n, cn) \to 2W^n(c) = 2\alpha^{(2c-1)n}$.*
(v) *If $p < c \leq 1$, then $R(n, cn) \geq \alpha^{(2c-1)n}$ and $R(n, cn) \to \alpha^{(2c-1)n}$.*

PROOF. The proof is easily obtained via a straightforward case analysis using Lemma 14.4. Recall that

$$R^{-1}(n, cn) = B_p \begin{Bmatrix} n-1 \\ n(1-c)-1 \end{Bmatrix} + \alpha^{n(1-2c)} \cdot B_p \begin{Bmatrix} n-1 \\ cn-1 \end{Bmatrix}.$$

Set

$$B_1 = B_p \begin{Bmatrix} n-1 \\ n(1-c)-1 \end{Bmatrix},$$

$$B_2 = B_p \begin{Bmatrix} n-1 \\ cn-1 \end{Bmatrix}.$$

Thus, $R^{-1}(n, cn) = B_1 + \alpha^{n(1-2c)} B_2$. As an example, we now prove that condition (i) holds. First, notice that in order to prove (i), it is sufficient to prove that $B_1 \to 1$. The reason is that since FMM is money making, $R(n, cn) > 1$ and, therefore, $R^{-1}(n, cn) < 1$. Hence, $B_1 \to 1$ implies $R(n, cn) \to 1$. Since $c < q$ if and only if $1 - c > p$, based on Lemma 14.4 (i) (applied with $1 - c$ instead of c and with $n - 1$ instead of n), $B_1 \to 1$.

As a second example, we prove that condition (iii) holds. Here $q < c < p$. Since $q < c$, we have $1 - c < p$. Hence, Lemma 14.4 (iii) shows that

$$B_1 = \Theta \left(\frac{1}{\sqrt{n} W^n(c)} \right).$$

Since $c < p$, we also have, based on Lemma 14.4 (iii), that B_2 is exponentially small. Specifically,

$$B_2 = \Theta \left(\frac{1}{\sqrt{n} W^n(1 - c)} \right).$$

Hence,

$$R^{-1}(n, cn) = \Theta \left(\frac{1}{\sqrt{n} W^n(c)} \right),$$

and the bound follows. The remaining cases are left as an exercise. ∎

Exercise 14.15 Complete the proof of Theorem 14.8.

Theorem 14.8 entails an interesting corollary. Consider the optimal offline BAH. If $c > \frac{1}{2}$, BAH invests its entire wealth on the first period and cashes it at the end of the game. Otherwise, BAH keeps its wealth in cash. The return of BAH, $R(\text{BAH})$, is

$$R(\text{BAH}) = \begin{cases} 1 & \text{if } c \leq \frac{1}{2}; \\ \alpha^{n(2c-1)} & \text{if } c \geq \frac{1}{2}. \end{cases} \tag{14.16}$$

Corollary 14.9 *Algorithm* FMM *always outperforms* BAH. *Moreover, if* $q < c < p$, FMM *performs exponentially better than* BAH.

PROOF. Whenever $c \in \left[0, \frac{1}{2}\right]$ or $c \in [p, 1]$, the proof readily follows from Theorem 14.8 and equation (14.16). Hence, to complete the proof it remains to show that whenever $c \in \left(\frac{1}{2}, p\right)$, $W(c) > \alpha^{2c-1}$. It is not difficult to see that the function

$$f(c) = \frac{W(c)}{\alpha^{2c-1}} = \left(\frac{c}{\alpha} \right)^c (1 - c)^{1-c}(1 + \alpha)$$

is strictly decreasing in $\left(\frac{1}{2}, p\right)$ and that $f(p) = 1$. ∎

Thus, whenever the market is stable (in the sense that it does not exhibit a "major" trend) but nevertheless active (i.e., there are many fluctuations), algorithm FMM performs remarkably well relative to BAH. Moreover, even when the market exhibits a slight unfavorable trend (i.e., $c \in \left(q, \frac{1}{2}\right)$), algorithm FMM continues to yield exponential returns. Notice that the size of this profitable interval (q, p) increases with α and thus can be controlled by the online player. Nevertheless, for larger values of α, algorithm FMM may overlook many prices (and price fluctuations), because of the time scaling required to approximate the fixed fluctuation model.

It is interesting to consider the performance of the optimal constant rebalanced algorithm (CBAL) within the same model.

Exercise 14.16 For $\text{CBAL}_{(b,1-b)}$ prove that the optimal balancing constant $b = \frac{c(\alpha+1)-1}{\alpha-1}$ against the $(n, k = cn, \alpha)$-adversary (within the fixed fluctuation model). Then prove that the return of the optimal CBAL-OPT, $R_c(\text{CBAL-OPT})$, is characterized by

$$
R_c(\text{CBAL-OPT}) = \begin{cases}
1 & \text{if } 0 \leq c \leq q; \\
W^n(c) & \text{if } q \leq c \leq p; \\
\alpha^{n(2c-1)} & \text{if } p \leq c \leq 1.
\end{cases}
$$

Thus the optimal CBAL-OPT is also exponentially better than BAH in the interval (q, p) but does not give any advantage over BAH for other values of c. In contrast, algorithm FMM always outperforms BAH and CBAL-OPT.

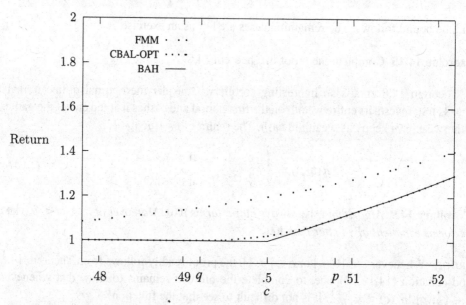

Figure 14.4: The theoretical returns of FMM, CBAL-OPT, and BAH ($\alpha = 1.03$, $n = 200$).

The results of Corollary 14.9 and Exercise 14.16 are illustrated in Figure 14.4, where the theoretical returns of FMM, CBAL-OPT, and BAH are plotted as a function of c with respect to fixed $\alpha = 1.03$ and fixed $n = 200$. In particular, it is possible to see that within the profitable interval (q, p), CBAL outperforms BAH. In Figure 14.5 we plot the returns of OPT and FMM.

According to Theorem 14.8, whenever $c \notin (q, p)$, the return of algorithm FMM is larger than, but approaching, that of BAH for large n. If transaction costs are introduced, then it is quite possible that the large number of transactions performed by FMM will wipe out the advantage. Hence, even if the trader has a perfect prediction of c (and $c > q$), the use

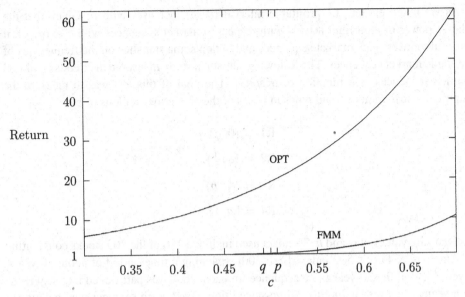

Figure 14.5: The returns of OPT and FMM, $\alpha = 1.03$, $n = 200$.

of FMM or any other market timing strategy could result in inferior returns compared to BAH.

14.4.3   On the Empirical Performance of FMM

Consider the following preliminary experimental results regarding the performance of algorithm FMM. These experiments included two data sets, both of which consisted of "intraday" prices for both U.S. dollars (USD) versus Japanese yen (JY), and U.S. dollars versus deutsche marks (DM). Data set A spanned one month and included all price quotations,[14] and data set B included prices at six-minute intervals during one year. In both cases, α was set to $1 + 5/$(initial exchange rate), since almost all changes in these data occurred in five-point increments.[15] Such changes are small relative to the exchange rates; therefore, the additive changes can be reasonably well approximated by multiplicative changes of α. The value of n varied between 100 and 1,000, thus breaking the trading period into a sequence of short games with reinvestment. Finally, c was naively chosen to be $\frac{1}{2}$ for all games. The returns of FMM with respect to data set A were enormous (223% and 167% for USD/DM and USD/JY, respectively). The results with respect to data set B were marginal (104% and 111%). When transaction costs of 0.02% were introduced, the returns against data set A remained very high (133% and 134%); however, against data set B, FMM suffered severe losses (73% and 89%). Examination of these data sets reveals that in data set A the assumption $c = \frac{1}{2}$ was quite closely satisfied, whereas in data set B this assumption was violated many times. These experimental results suggest that FMM is quite robust with respect to the parameter c, although no theoretical results exist to substantiate this robustness.

---

[14] In such data a new price tick occurs every 10–120 seconds.

[15] A "point" is the smallest unit used to measure prices.

As we noted earlier, the profitable interval (q, p) increases with α. Given that the relative power of algorithm FMM is with respect to market sequences with $c \in (q, p)$, it is useful to investigate market sequences and obtain some statistics on the frequencies of profitable market sequences. The following statistical study measured the trends exhibited in price sequences as a function of α and n. The goal of this test was to measure the empirical distribution of trend types in terms of the above four regions of c,

$$R1 = [0, q]$$
$$R2 = \left(q, \tfrac{1}{2}\right)$$
$$R3 = \left(\tfrac{1}{2}, p\right)$$
$$R4 = [p, 1],$$

with varying values of α and n. The data used included 486 of the 500 stocks constituting the Standard & Poor's 500 index (S&P 500), spanning a time period of about 30 years. Given α and n, the 30-year price sequence for each stock was partitioned into segments, each segment corresponding to n time-scaled ticks. Each such segment then belongs to one of the four regions. Call regions R2 and R3 the "nontrendy" regions and regions R1 and R4 the "trendy" regions. The tests revealed the following relations. As α or n grows, the fraction of segments of length n in the nontrendy regions grows. (As expected, as a result of economic growth, the fraction of segments in region R3 is larger than that in R2.) For small values of α (e.g., $1.005 \leq \alpha \leq 1.05$), the majority of sequences are in the trendy regions. For larger values of α, the majority of sequences are in the nontrendy regions. These results may suggest that with respect to the stock market, the practical advantage of market timing strategies such as FMM or CBAL, using a fixed fluctuation model, can be obtained only when large values of α and n are used (clearly, when time scaling is used). On the other hand, if a particular market does not allow for large values of α, it might be wiser to remain static using BAH. Note that for large values of α, for example, $\alpha \geq 1.1$, transaction points cannot occur too often, which may be considered an advantage by some investors.

14.4.4   Binomial Risk-Neutral Valuation and Adversarial Analysis

The adversarial analysis of FMM is intimately related to a classical approach to valuation of financial portfolios called **binomial risk-neutral valuation**.[16] In fact, this approach is a combination of three fundamental financial concepts: "binomial trees," "risk-neutral valuation," and "arbitrage arguments." We now briefly describe these concepts and their connection with our adversarial model.

Define the **value** (or the per unit price) of a security as the reciprocal of its price, that is, the number of dollars required to purchase one unit of the security. In contrast to the price (as used throughout this chapter), when we use the security value, the "profitable direction" of a value change is upward. A **probabilistic binomial tree** models stock value evolution via a graph such as the one shown in Figure 14.3. As before, it is assumed that each upward change is by a factor of α and each downward change is by a factor

---

[16] (Binomial) risk-neutral valuation is typically used for pricing derivatives of securities such as options (for a comprehensive treatment of this topic, see Hull [190]).

of $\frac{1}{\alpha}$. However, in contrast to the previously stated adversarial model, in the traditional binomial model it is assumed that an upward change occurs with some probability β and a downward change occurs with probability $1 - \beta$ (see Figure 14.6). It is widely accepted that if each change occurs during some small time period, Δt, this binomial model for the evolution of security prices is sufficiently realistic.[17]

An **arbitrage opportunity** arises when, with "zero investment," an investor can conduct transactions that yield a risk-free profit. In order to construct such transactions, the investor must be able to sell short at least one asset.[18] An obvious instance of an arbitrage opportunity arises when a security is traded at two different prices in two different markets. In this case, an arbitrager can simultaneously sell short the security in the higher-priced market, buy the asset in the lower-priced market, and immediately cover the short position (i.e., return the borrowed asset). There are, of course, arbitrage opportunities that are not as obvious as this one and require sophisticated methods to be detected. Arbitrage opportunities do not last long. The exploitation of such opportunities by arbitragers quickly causes the forces of supply and demand to drive down the higher price and simultaneously drive up the lower price until they reach an equilibrium. Hence, it is natural to assume that for most investors the market is free of arbitrage opportunities.

We define a **risk-neutral** investor as one who is indifferent to any two portfolios as long as they have the same expected returns.[19] We say that a risk-neutral investor considers an arbitrage opportunity to be any opportunity to make an expected profit.

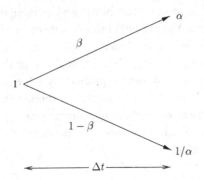

Figure 14.6: One-period binomial model.

Assume that all investors are risk-neutral. Consider a market with a **risk-free** interest rate of $r \geq 0$; that is, any cash amount d deposited in the bank will return with certainty $(1 + r)d$ after one Δt time period. We make the common, albeit unrealistic, simplifying assumption that r is the interest rate for both saving and borrowing. Now consider a stock whose initial value is 1. As illustrated in Figure 14.6, the value of the stock after Δt time is either α or $\frac{1}{\alpha}$. The investor has two investment alternatives. The first alternative is to invest his wealth in the stock and sell it after one period. The second is to deposit the

---

[17] It can be shown that in the limit, as $\Delta t \to 0$, this binomial model of security price movements becomes the geometric Brownian motion model.

[18] In a **short sale**, an investor borrows shares of an asset and sells the shares. Later, the investor must repurchase shares of the same asset in order to replace the borrowed shares (see, e.g., Bodie, Kane, and Marcus [77], pp. 99–101).

[19] More generally, the definitions of risk neutrality, risk aversion, and risk seeking are based on the concept of utility functions (discussed in Chapter 15). Specifically, a risk-neutral investor has a linear utility function.

money in the bank (thus investing in the risk-free interest) and cash it after one period. The return b of the first alternative is the expected value of the stock, which is $\beta\alpha + \frac{1-\beta}{\alpha}$. The return of the second alternative is $1 + r$. Combining the risk-neutrality assumption and the no-arbitrage argument, it must be that

$$b = \beta\alpha + \frac{1 - \beta}{\alpha} = 1 + r \tag{14.17}$$

Specifically, if there were an inequality in equation (14.17), for example, $b < 1 + r$, then a risk-neutral arbitrager could sell one stock short and invest the cash at the bank for one time period. After that, he would buy the stock and close his short position. This transaction would give him a risk-neutral expected profit of $1 + r - b > 0$. On the other hand, if $b > 1 + r$, an arbitrager would borrow \$1 from the bank and buy the stock. At the end of the period he would sell the stock for (an expected amount) b and return his debt to the bank, which by now would grow to $1 + r$. This would give him a risk-neutral expected profit of $b - (1 + r) > 0$.

Given the risk-free interest rate r and α, equation (14.17) is solved for the **risk-neutral probability** β, giving

$$\beta = \frac{1}{1 + \alpha} + \frac{r\alpha}{\alpha^2 - 1}.$$

Having determined this risk-neutral probability, we can compute the return of portfolios and financial derivatives (such as options) involving this underlying stock. Indeed, this is exactly the underlying principle of the binomial risk-neutral pricing method.

When $r = 0$, we obtain $\beta = \frac{1}{1+\alpha}$. Recall that in the analysis of algorithm FMM we assumed that $r = 0$. Hence, the risk-neutral probability β is exactly q (see page 282). The fact that $\beta = q$ immediately yields an alternative interpretation of equation (14.12) as the (reciprocal of the) return of a risk-neutral (no-arbitrage) strategy within the traditional (and distributional) binomial model. In this sense, our adversarial model and the risk-neutral pricing approach are equivalent.[20]

14.5 Weighted Portfolio Selection Algorithms

We now return to the general problem of investing in an arbitrary number of securities. Throughout this section we consider unrestricted adversaries; however, we measure performance relative to a restricted class of offline algorithms.

14.5.1 The Family of μ-Weighted Portfolio Selection Algorithms

We now define a very general class of online portfolio selection algorithms. Every algorithm in the class is specified by a probability measure μ over the set of all portfolios and starts by hedging (i.e., distributing one's wealth) uniformly on all possible portfolios. Then it rebalances the weight it gives to various securities according to the past performance of constant rebalanced portfolios while putting more weight on the better-performing ones.

---

[20] It is interesting to note that in the limit, as $\Delta t \to 0$, the binomial risk-neutral valuation model approaches the well-known Black–Scholes continuous pricing model (see Hull [190]).

The probability measure μ provides an additional weighting mechanism that can favor particular portfolios.

Fix some positive integer m. Let $\mathcal{B}$ be the set of all possible portfolios over m securities (i.e., $\mathcal{B}$ is an $(m-1)$-dimensional simplex). Let $\mathbf{b} \in \mathcal{B}$ denote a portfolio and let $\mathbf{b}^t$ denote the transpose of the vector $\mathbf{b}$. With respect to a market sequence $X = \mathbf{x}_1, \ldots, \mathbf{x}_n$, define $X_i = \mathbf{x}_1, \ldots, \mathbf{x}_i$, $i = 1, 2, \ldots, n$, the prefix of X consisting of the first i market vectors. With respect to X_i, define

$$R_i(\mathbf{b}) = R(\mathbf{b}, X_i) = \prod_{j=1}^{i} \mathbf{b}^t \cdot \mathbf{x}_j. \tag{14.18}$$

That is, $R_i(\mathbf{b})$ is the compounded return of a fixed portfolio $\mathbf{b}$ after i trading periods. By convention, set $R_0(\mathbf{b}) = 1$, the initial wealth. (Alternatively, $R_i(\mathbf{b}) = \text{CBAL}_\mathbf{b}(X_i)$.)

Fix any market sequence X, and let μ be a probability measure over $\mathcal{B}$. An algorithm is a μ-**weighted portfolio selection algorithm** if its ith-period portfolio $\mathbf{b}_i$ is specified by[21]

$$\mathbf{b}_i = \frac{\int_\mathcal{B} \mathbf{b} R_{i-1}(\mathbf{b}) d\mu(\mathbf{b})}{\int_\mathcal{B} R_{i-1}(\mathbf{b}) d\mu(\mathbf{b})}. \tag{14.19}$$

Clearly, any μ-weighted algorithm operates online.

Let X be any market sequence of length n, and let $\mathbf{b}_1, \mathbf{b}_2, \ldots, \mathbf{b}_n$ be the portfolios obtained by a μ-weighted algorithm ALG_μ. The expression for the compounded return $\text{ALG}_\mu(X)$ of ALG_μ can be simplified as follows.

$$\begin{aligned}
\text{ALG}_\mu(X) &= \prod_{1 \leq i \leq n} \mathbf{b}_i^t \cdot \mathbf{x}_i \\
&= \prod_{1 \leq i \leq n} \frac{\left(\int_\mathcal{B} \mathbf{b}^t R_{i-1}(\mathbf{b}) d\mu(\mathbf{b})\right) \cdot \mathbf{x}_i}{\int_\mathcal{B} R_{i-1}(\mathbf{b}) d\mu(\mathbf{b})} \\
&= \prod_{1 \leq i \leq n} \frac{\left(\int_\mathcal{B} \mathbf{b}^t \cdot \mathbf{x}_i R_{i-1}(\mathbf{b}) d\mu(\mathbf{b})\right)}{\int_\mathcal{B} R_{i-1}(\mathbf{b}) d\mu(\mathbf{b})} \\
&= \prod_{1 \leq i \leq n} \frac{\int_\mathcal{B} R_i(\mathbf{b}) d\mu(\mathbf{b})}{\int_\mathcal{B} R_{i-1}(\mathbf{b}) d\mu(\mathbf{b})}. \tag{14.20}
\end{aligned}$$

Hence, since the last product telescopes, we have

$$\text{ALG}_\mu(X) = \int_\mathcal{B} R_n(\mathbf{b}) d\mu(\mathbf{b}) = \int_\mathcal{B} \text{CBAL}_\mathbf{b}(X) d\mu(\mathbf{b}). \tag{14.21}$$

---

[21] Here the integral is a Lebesgue integral, which provides the analytical tool for dealing with arbitrary probability measures. For our purposes, these integrals can be considered to be the usual Riemann integrals or even finite sums. When the probability measure μ has a density function, d_μ, the Lebesgue integral can be expressed in terms of ordinary multiple integrals. Specifically, set $b_m = 1 - b_1 - b_2 - \cdots - b_{m-1}$. For any integrable function $f(x_1, x_2, \ldots, x_m)$, we have

$$\int_\mathcal{B} f(\mathbf{b}) d\mu(\mathbf{b}) = \int_0^1 \int_0^{1-b_1} \cdots \int_0^{1-b_1-\cdots-b_{m-2}} f(b_1, \ldots, b_m) d_\mu(b_1, \ldots, b_m) db_1 db_2 \cdots db_{m-1}.$$

A concise treatment of Lebesgue integration may be found in Williamson [337]. (For a thorough exposition of Lebesgue integration and measure theory, see Halmos [181].)

Although the μ-weighted algorithm dynamically adapts its portfolio online (see equation 14.19) and gives more weight to the better-performing (constant rebalanced) portfolios, its final return is simply a μ-average of the returns of all constant rebalanced portfolios in $\mathcal{B}$. It follows that the expected return of an algorithm that chooses randomly one portfolio $\mathbf{b}$ with probability measure μ, is equal to the return of ALG_μ.

14.5.2   The Uniform Weighted Algorithm

Use UNI to denote the μ-weighted algorithm corresponding to the uniform distribution μ over $\mathcal{B}$.

Exercise 14.17 Assuming the market and market sequence of Example 14.1, compute the return of algorithm UNI for n periods.

The remainder of this section is devoted to proving the following theorem.

Theorem 14.10 *Let X be any market sequence of length n. Then,*

$$\frac{\text{CBAL-OPT}(X)}{\text{UNI}(X)} \leq \binom{n+m-1}{m-1}.$$

Furthermore, there is a market sequence X for which the upper bound is achieved.

It is easy to see that $\binom{n+m-1}{m-1} \leq (n+1)^{m-1}$. (This follows from Theorem G.1 in Appendix G but can easily be proven directly.) Therefore, in a restricted sense of competitiveness, algorithm UNI is $(n+1)^{m-1}$-competitive (with respect to CBAL-OPT).

In fact, we present two proofs of Theorem 14.10. The first proof relies on some techniques from information theory and has the advantage that it has been extended to other distributions such as the Dirichlet distribution (obtaining the best-known bounds; see Section 14.5.3). Appendix G provides the relevant results from information theory. The second proof is more direct and has the advantage that it has been extended to markets with commissions.

In preparation for the first proof, we need some notation and a simple lemma. Let $[m] = \{1, 2, \ldots, m\}$. Denote by $J_n = (j_1, j_2, \ldots, j_n)$ any sequence of indices from $[m]$ (i.e., $J_n \in [m]^n$). Let $X = \mathbf{x}_1, \ldots, \mathbf{x}_n$ be a market sequence, and let $\mathbf{b}$ be any portfolio. In the analysis, we use the following manipulation, which gives a different representation for the compounded return of the constant rebalanced algorithm with a (fixed) portfolio $\mathbf{b}$ (i.e., CBAL$_\mathbf{b}$).

$$\text{CBAL}_\mathbf{b}(X) = \prod_{1 \leq i \leq n} \mathbf{b}^t \cdot \mathbf{x}_i$$

$$= \prod_{1 \leq i \leq n} \sum_{1 \leq j \leq m} b_j x_{ij}$$

$$= \sum_{J_n \in [m]^n} \prod_{1 \leq i \leq n} b_{j_i} x_{ij_i}. \tag{14.22}$$

Lemma 14.5 *Let* $\alpha_1, \ldots, \alpha_N \geq 0$ *and* $\beta_1, \ldots, \beta_N \geq 0$. *Then,*

$$\frac{\sum_{1 \leq i \leq N} \alpha_i}{\sum_{1 \leq i \leq N} \beta_i} \leq \max_j \frac{\alpha_j}{\beta_j}.$$

PROOF. Set $k = \arg\max_j \frac{\alpha_j}{\beta_j}$. Assume that both $\alpha_k > 0$ and $\beta_k > 0$ (otherwise, the lemma trivially holds). By the choice of k, for each j, $\frac{\alpha_j}{\beta_j} \leq \frac{\alpha_k}{\beta_k}$. Hence, $\frac{\alpha_j}{\alpha_k} \leq \frac{\beta_j}{\beta_k}$. Therefore,

$$\frac{\sum_j \alpha_j}{\sum_j \beta_j} = \frac{\alpha_k \left(1 + \sum_{j \neq k} \frac{\alpha_j}{\alpha_k}\right)}{\beta_k \left(1 + \sum_{j \neq k} \frac{\beta_j}{\beta_k}\right)} \leq \frac{\alpha_k}{\beta_k} = \max_j \frac{\alpha_j}{\beta_j}.$$

∎

First Proof of Theorem 14.10. Fix any market sequence X of length n. Let $\mathbf{b}^*$ be the portfolio used by CBAL-OPT. Using the representation (14.22) for CBAL-OPT and UNI, we have

$$\text{CBAL-OPT}(X) = \sum_{J_n \in [m]^n} \prod_{i=1}^{n} b^*_{j_i} x_{i j_i};$$

$$\text{UNI}(X) = \sum_{J_n \in [m]^n} \int_{\mathcal{B}} \prod_{i=1}^{n} b_{j_i} x_{i j_i} d\mu(\mathbf{b}),$$

where μ is the uniform probability measure over $\mathcal{B}$. The ratio of compound returns, $\frac{\text{CBAL-OPT}(X)}{\text{UNI}(X)}$, is now a ratio of two finite summations each involving $N = m^n$ nonnegative terms. According to Lemma 14.5, we have

$$\frac{\text{CBAL-OPT}(X)}{\text{UNI}(X)} \leq \max_{J_n \in [m]^n : \Pi_i x_{j_i} > 0} \frac{\prod_{i=1}^{n} b^*_{j_i} x_{i j_i}}{\int_{\mathcal{B}} \prod_{i=1}^{n} b_{j_i} x^i_{i j_i} d\mu(\mathbf{b})}$$

$$= \max_{J_n \in [m]^n : \Pi_i x_{j_i} > 0} \frac{\prod_{i=1}^{n} b^*_{j_i}}{\int_{\mathcal{B}} \prod_{i=1}^{n} b_{j_i} d\mu(\mathbf{b})}$$

$$\leq \max_{J_n \in [m]^n} \frac{\prod_{i=1}^{n} b^*_{j_i}}{\int_{\mathcal{B}} \prod_{i=1}^{n} b_{j_i} d\mu(\mathbf{b})}. \tag{14.23}$$

Our goal now is to bound from above the right-hand side of inequality (14.23). This can be done using Lemma 14.6 and some elementary results from the "method of types" of information theory.

Fix a vector $J_n = (j_1, \ldots, j_n) \in [m]^n$. For each $i \in [m]$, use $n_i = n_i(J_n)$ to denote the number of occurrences of i in J_n, and let $\nu_i(J_n) = \frac{n_i}{n}$. The distribution $D(J_n) = (\nu_1(J_n), \nu_2(J_n), \ldots, \nu_m(J_n))$ specifies the "type" of the sequence J_n (see Appendix G). According to Theorem G.2, for any distribution (portfolio) $\mathbf{b}$ and any such J_n,

$$\prod_{i=1}^{n} b_{j_i} \leq 2^{-n H(D(J_n))}, \tag{14.24}$$

where $H(D(J_n))$ is the Shannon entropy of D (i.e., $H(D) = \sum_i -v_i(J_n) \log v_i(J_n)$). Equality is obtained at $\mathbf{b} = D(J_n)$. This upper bounds the numerator in (14.23).

We need the following lemma, whose proof is given in Appendix H.

Lemma 14.6

$$\int_{\mathcal{B}} \prod_{i=1}^{n} b_{j_i} d\mu(\mathbf{b}) = \frac{n_1! n_2! \ldots n_m! (m-1)!}{(m-1+n_1+n_2+\cdots+n_m)!}.$$

Noticing that $n_1 + n_2 + \cdots + n_m = n$, we have

$$\int_{\mathcal{B}} \prod_{i=1}^{n} b_{j_i} d\mu(\mathbf{b}) = \frac{n_1! n_2! \ldots n_m! (m-1)!}{(n+m-1)!}$$

$$= \left(\frac{(n+m-1)!}{(m-1)! n!} \cdot \frac{n!}{n_1! n_2! \cdots n_m!} \right)^{-1}$$

$$= \left(\binom{n+m-1}{m-1} \cdot \binom{n}{n_1 n_2 \cdots n_m} \right)^{-1}$$

$$= \left(\binom{n+m-1}{m-1} \cdot |C(D)| \right)^{-1}$$

according to Theorem G.3. Here, $|C(D)| = |C(v_1(J_n), \ldots, v_m(J_n))|$ is the number of sequences of type D. Hence, according to Theorem G.3,

$$|C(D)| \leq 2^{n H(v_1(J_n), \ldots, v_m(J_n))},$$

and we have

$$\int_{\mathcal{B}} \prod_{i=1}^{n} b_{j_i} d\mu(\mathbf{b}) \geq \frac{1}{\binom{n+m-1}{m-1}} 2^{-n H(D)}. \tag{14.25}$$

Combining the bounds (14.24) and (14.25), we have

$$\frac{\text{CBAL-OPT}(X)}{\text{UNI}(X)} \leq \max_{J_n} \binom{n+m-1}{m-1} \frac{2^{-n H(D(J_n))}}{2^{-n H(D(J_n))}}$$

$$= \binom{n+m-1}{m-1}.$$

This completes the proof of the desired inequality. A worst-case market sequence is left as an exercise. ∎

Exercise 14.18 Find a market sequence X such that

$$\frac{\text{CBAL-OPT}(X)}{\text{UNI}(X)} = \binom{n+m-1}{m-1}.$$

Exercise 14.19 Design an $O(n^{m-1})$ time and space algorithm that computes the portfolios for algorithm UNI.

Exercise 14.20 Consider the following randomized approximation to algorithm UNI. From the set of all portfolios $\mathcal{B}$, choose k portfolios $\mathbf{b}_1, \ldots, \mathbf{b}_k$, randomly and uniformly. Then invest $\frac{1}{k}$ of the initial wealth in each of the constant rebalanced strategies CBAL$_{\mathbf{b}_1}, \ldots,$ CBAL$_{\mathbf{b}_k}$.

Use $\mathcal{R}(\text{UNI})$ to denote the "competitive ratio" of UNI (relative to the optimum constant rebalanced portfolio). Prove that for each $0 < \varepsilon, \delta < 1$, by choosing $k = \frac{\mathcal{R}(\text{UNI})-1}{\varepsilon\delta^2}$, one can guarantee with probability at least $1 - \delta$ a return that is at least as large as $1 - \varepsilon$ times the return of algorithm UNI.

14.5.3 Dirichlet-Weighted Algorithms

In this section we consider a family of μ-weighted algorithms where μ is a Dirichlet distribution. A random vector $\mathbf{b} = (b_1, b_2, \ldots, b_m)$ has a **Dirichlet distribution**[22] Dirichlet($\boldsymbol{\alpha}$), with parametric vector $\boldsymbol{\alpha} = (\alpha_1, \alpha_2, \ldots, \alpha_m)$, $\alpha_i > 0$, if the probability density function (p.d.f.) of $\mathbf{b}$ with respect to $\boldsymbol{\alpha}$, $f_{\boldsymbol{\alpha}}(\mathbf{b})$, satisfies the following conditions:

- At any point $\mathbf{b} \in \mathcal{B}$ (with $b_i \geq 0$, $\sum_i b_i = 1$),

$$f_{\boldsymbol{\alpha}}(\mathbf{b}) = \frac{\Gamma(\alpha_1 + \cdots + \alpha_m)}{\Gamma(\alpha_1) \cdots \Gamma(\alpha_m)} b_1^{\alpha_1 - 1} \cdots b_m^{\alpha_m - 1},$$

where Γ is the Gamma function.[23]
- At any other point $\mathbf{b}' \in \mathbb{R}_m$, $f_{\boldsymbol{\alpha}}(\mathbf{b}') = 0$.

Thus $f_{\boldsymbol{\alpha}}(\mathbf{b})$ is positive only when the vector $\mathbf{b}$ is a distribution function, $\sum_i b_i = 1$. Hence, counter to its appearance, $f_{\boldsymbol{\alpha}}(\mathbf{b})$ is not an m-dimensional p.d.f. but rather gives the joint p.d.f. of any $(m - 1)$-subset of the m random variables $b_1, b_2, \ldots, b_m$, satisfying $\sum_i b_i = 1$. Notice that the Dirichlet distribution with $\frac{\alpha_i}{\alpha_i - 1} = (1, 1, \ldots, 1)$ is the uniform distribution on the $(m - 1)$-dimensional simplex.

For $m = 2$, the graph in Figure 14.7 plots three Dirichlet density functions corresponding to the parameters $(1, 1)$ (i.e., uniform), $(\frac{3}{4}, \frac{3}{4})$ and $(\frac{1}{2}, \frac{1}{2})$. Notice that the two nonuniform densities are convex. This means that if they are used by a μ-weighted algorithm, "skewed" portfolios that invest most of the wealth in one security have larger weights.

Use **DIR$_{\boldsymbol{\alpha}}$** to denote the μ-weighted portfolio selection algorithm with an m-dimensional parametric vector $\boldsymbol{\alpha}$. Thus, DIR$_{(1,1,\ldots,1)}$ is exactly algorithm UNI. We now state, without proof, the following theorem.[24]

Theorem 14.11 *For any market sequence* X,

$$\frac{\text{CBAL-OPT}(X)}{\text{DIR}_{(1/2,1/2,\ldots,1/2)}(X)} \leq \frac{\Gamma(1/2)\Gamma(n + m/2)}{\Gamma(m/2)\Gamma(n + 1/2)} \leq 2(n + 1)^{(m-1)/2}.$$

---

[22] The Dirichlet distribution is sometimes referred to as the **multinomial beta distribution**.

[23] The Gamma function $\Gamma(x) = \int_0^\infty e^{-t} t^{x-1} dt$ plays an important role in calculus. It can be shown that $\Gamma(1) = 1$ and that $\Gamma(x + 1) = x\Gamma(x)$. Therefore, if $n \geq 1$ is an integer, $\Gamma(n + 1) = n!$. Note also that $\Gamma(\frac{1}{2}) = \sqrt{\pi}$ (consult Courant and John [118] for a comprehensive treatment).

[24] See Cover and Ordentlich [121].

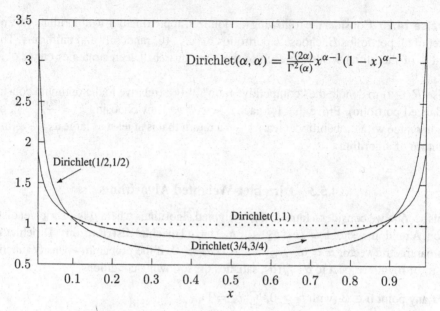

$$\text{Dirichlet}(\alpha, \alpha) = \frac{\Gamma(2\alpha)}{\Gamma^2(\alpha)} x^{\alpha-1}(1-x)^{\alpha-1}$$

Figure 14.7: Three Dirichlet density functions ($m = 2$).

Thus, $\text{DIR}_{(1/2,1/2,\ldots,1/2)}$ is $\left(2(n+1)^{(m-1)/2}\right)$-competitive with respect to CBAL. Theorem 14.11 can be proven following the same lines as the proof of Theorem 14.10 but is somewhat more technical (since the integrals involved are more complex).

Exercise 14.21 Prove Theorem 14.11.

14.5.4   Portfolio Selection with Transaction Costs

So far in our analyses of portfolio selection, we have ignored transaction costs (called commissions). We now consider such costs and show that the online uniform weighted algorithm is competitive (with CBAL-OPT) for markets with commissions.

We focus on the following transaction cost charging model. There is a fixed multiplicative cost, $\gamma \in [0, 1]$, called the **commission rate**.[25] We charge only upon purchases (equivalently, only upon sales). So, for example, for purchasing $\$d$ worth of some security, the trader must pay a commission of $\$\gamma d$. This charging scheme is equivalent to charging a commission rate of $\frac{\gamma}{2}$ for *both* buying and selling.[26] For example, for selling $\$d$ worth of security i, the trader must pay $\$\frac{\gamma d}{2}$. Then, for buying $\frac{d}{p_j}$ units of security j, a trader again must pay a commission of $\$\frac{\gamma d}{2}$, for a total commission of $\$\gamma d$ for the entire transaction.

Now consider a constant rebalanced algorithm CBAL$_\mathbf{b}$ in a market with a commission rate γ. Despite the commissions that CBAL$_\mathbf{b}$ must pay, it adjusts its portfolio so that it is **b**-balanced at the start of every trading period. Suppose that a **b**-balanced portfolio changes to $\mathbf{b}'$ by the end of some period. For the new trading period, CBAL$_\mathbf{b}$ rebalances as

---

[25] In practice, the value of γ depends on the market. For example, in the stock market a full-service broker might charge (a negotiable) 3%, which is typically larger than the rates encountered in foreign exchange markets.

[26] There are numerous variations of this charging model. Also, in markets such as the foreign exchange, there often are no explicit transaction costs but a similar effect results because of the bid–ask price spreads.

follows. For all $j = 1, 2, \ldots m$, a fraction $|b'_j - b_j|$ of the entire investment must flow into or out of the jth security. Hence, the overall (per dollar) rebalancing commission factor com$(\mathbf{b}, \mathbf{b}')$, for rebalancing from portfolio $\mathbf{b}$ to portfolio $\mathbf{b}'$, is

$$\text{com}(\mathbf{b}, \mathbf{b}') = \frac{\gamma}{2} \sum_{j=1}^{m} |b'_j - b_j|. \tag{14.26}$$

Clearly, com$(\mathbf{b}, \mathbf{b}') = $ com$(\mathbf{b}', \mathbf{b})$. Equivalently, when we charge only for purchases,

$$\text{com}(\mathbf{b}, \mathbf{b}') = \gamma \sum_{j:b_j > b'_j} (b_j - b'_j).$$

Example 14.2 Consider the same conditions of Example 14.1, and now assume an excessive commission rate $\gamma = \frac{3}{5}$. At the end of the first period, CBAL$_\mathbf{b}$, $\mathbf{b} = (\frac{1}{2}, \frac{1}{2})$, rebalances from $\mathbf{b}' = (\frac{2}{3}, \frac{1}{3})$ to $(\frac{1}{2}, \frac{1}{2})$ Therefore, this transaction must be covered by paying a commission factor of

$$\text{com}\left(\left(\frac{2}{3}, \frac{1}{3}\right), \left(\frac{1}{2}, \frac{1}{2}\right)\right) = \frac{\gamma}{2}\left(\left|\frac{2}{3} - \frac{1}{2}\right| + \left|\frac{1}{3} - \frac{1}{2}\right|\right) = \frac{\gamma}{6} = \frac{1}{10}.$$

That is, CBAL$_\mathbf{b}$ pays 10% of its total portfolio value to close the deal. By symmetry, the rebalancing commission factor of the second day is exactly the same, $\frac{1}{10}$.

It follows that for each pair of days, odd and even, CBAL$_\mathbf{b}$ increases its investment by a factor of

$$\frac{9}{8} \cdot \frac{9}{10} \cdot \frac{9}{10} = \frac{731}{800} < 1.$$

That is, now CBAL$_\mathbf{b}$ loses.

Exercise 14.22 With respect to the market and market sequence of Example 14.2, determine the commission rate γ for which CBAL$_\mathbf{b}(X) = 1$, with $\mathbf{b} = (\frac{1}{2}, \frac{1}{2})$ and $X = \frac{1}{2}, 2, \frac{1}{2}, 2, \ldots, \frac{1}{2}, 2$.

Our goal now is to analyze the performance of the uniform weighted portfolio selection algorithm in a market with commissions. To this end, we first present the promised second proof of Theorem 14.10 (for a market without commissions). This proof is later extended to markets with commissions.

Second Proof of Theorem 14.10. Fix any market sequence X of length n and let $\mathbf{b}^* = (b_1^*, \ldots, b_m^*)$ be the portfolio used by CBAL-OPT. For any portfolio $\mathbf{b} = (b_1, \ldots, b_m) \in \mathcal{B}$, let

$$r(\mathbf{b}) = r_{\mathbf{b}^*}(\mathbf{b}) = \min_j \frac{b_j}{b_j^*}.$$

(Whenever $\mathbf{b}$ is understood from the context, we use $r = r(\mathbf{b})$.) Let $\mu(\mathbf{b})$ be the uniform probability measure on all portfolios. Clearly, with respect to $\mu(\mathbf{b})$, $r = r(\mathbf{b})$ is a random variable. It is sufficient to prove the following two properties.

Claim 1: UNI$(X) \geq \mathbf{E}_{\mu(\mathbf{b})}[r^n] \cdot$ CBAL-OPT(X).

Claim 2: $E_{\mu(\mathbf{b})}[r^n] = 1/\binom{n+m-1}{m-1}$.

We start by proving Claim 1. By definition, for any $\mathbf{b}$ and for all $j = 1, \ldots, m$, $b_j \geq r \cdot b_j^*$, and we have the following bound on the multiplicative return growth of CBAL$_\mathbf{b}$ for the ith period

$$\sum_{j=1}^m b_{ij} x_{ij} \geq r \sum_{j=1}^m b_{ij}^* x_{ij}.$$

Aggregated over all n periods of the market sequence X, we have

$$\text{CBAL}_\mathbf{b}(X) \geq r^n \cdot \text{CBAL-OPT}(X). \tag{14.27}$$

Using equation (14.27) and representation (14.21) for UNI, we have

$$\text{UNI}(X) = \int_\mathcal{B} \text{CBAL}_\mathbf{b}(X) d\mu(\mathbf{b})$$

$$\geq \int_\mathcal{B} r^n \cdot \text{CBAL-OPT}(X) d\mu(\mathbf{b})$$

$$= \text{CBAL-OPT}(X) \int_\mathcal{B} r^n d\mu(\mathbf{b})$$

$$= E_{\mu(\mathbf{b})}[r^n] \text{CBAL-OPT}(X).$$

To prove Claim 2, we rely on simple properties of multidimensional volumes in Euclidean spaces. For any d-dimensional Euclidean subspace B, let $\text{Vol}_d(B)$ be its volume. Recall that $\mathcal{B}$ is an $(m-1)$-dimensional simplex. Thus, for any $B \subseteq \mathcal{B}$, we have

$$\text{Pr}_{\mu(\mathbf{b})}[\mathbf{b} \in B] = \frac{\text{Vol}_{m-1}(B)}{\text{Vol}_{m-1}(\mathcal{B})}.$$

Let $B \subset \mathbb{R}^d$, $\mathbf{b} \in \mathbb{R}^d$, and $x \in \mathbb{R}$, and define

$$xB + \mathbf{b} = \{(xv_1 + b_1, xv_2 + b_2, \ldots, xv_d + b_d) : (v_1, v_2, \ldots, v_d) \in B\}.$$

We now claim that for any real $z \in [0, 1]$,

$$(1-z)\mathcal{B} + z\mathbf{b}^* = \{\mathbf{b} : \mathbf{b} \in \mathcal{B} \text{ and } b_j \geq zb_j^*, \ j = 1, \ldots, m\}. \tag{14.28}$$

This is true, since, by definition, $(1-z)\mathcal{B} + z\mathbf{b}^*$ equals

$$\mathcal{B}' = \{(1-z)v_1 + zb_1^*, \ldots, (1-z)v_m + zb_m^* : (v_1, \ldots, v_m) \in \mathcal{B}\}.$$

Thus, every vector in $\mathcal{B}'$ is a probability vector, since $(1-z)\sum_j b_j + z\sum_j b_j^* = 1$. Moreover, since $(1-z)b_j$ is nonnegative, we have $(1-z)b_j + zb_j^* \geq zb_j^*$ for all j; therefore, any vector in $\mathcal{B}'$ is also in the set of the right-hand side of equation (14.28). The converse is true, since the linear equation $(1-z)v_j + zb_j^* = b_j$ can always be solved for v_j such that $\sum_j v_j = 1$. This proves equation (14.28).

Now, for any $B \subseteq \mathcal{B}$, we clearly have

$$\text{Vol}_d(xB + \mathbf{b}) = x^d \text{Vol}_d(B). \tag{14.29}$$

Applying this volume formula (14.29) and the identity (14.28), we learn that for every $z \in [0, 1]$,

$$\Pr_{\mu(\mathbf{b})}\left[r(\mathbf{b}) \geq z\right] = \frac{\text{Vol}_{m-1}\left((1-z)\mathcal{B} + z\mathbf{b}^*\right)}{\text{Vol}_{m-1}(\mathcal{B})} = (1-z)^{m-1}. \tag{14.30}$$

For our next derivation we need the following basic result, which we state without proof.[27]

Lemma 14.7 *Let X be a continuous random variable with support $[0, 1]$ and distribution F that has a density function f. Then,[28]*

$$\mathbf{E}[X] = \int_0^1 [1 - F(x)]\,dx = \int_0^1 \Pr[X \geq x]\,dx.$$

Using Lemma 14.7 and equation (14.30), we have

$$\mathbf{E}_{\mu(\mathbf{b})}[r^n(\mathbf{b})] = \int_0^1 \Pr_{\mu(\mathbf{b})}\left[r(\mathbf{b}) \geq z^{1/n}\right] dz$$

$$= \int_0^1 \left(1 - z^{1/n}\right)^{m-1} dz$$

$$= \int_0^1 n(1-y)^{m-1} y^{n-1}\,dy,$$

$$\text{by a change of variable } z \to y^n;$$

$$= \int_0^1 n(1-y)^{n-1} y^{m-1}\,dy.$$

To complete the proof of Claim 2, we claim that

$$\int_0^1 n(1-y)^{n-1} y^{m-1}\,dy = \frac{1}{\binom{n+m-1}{m-1}}. \tag{14.31}$$

The identity (14.31) is obtained by considering the following probability exercise. Suppose we pick $n + m - 1$ numbers in $[0, 1]$ uniformly at random. What is the probability that each of the first n numbers is smaller than each of the last $m - 1$ numbers? On the one hand, each of the $\binom{n+m-1}{m-1}$ subsets of size $m - 1$ has equal probability of containing the $m - 1$ largest numbers. On the other hand, a direct calculation shows that the conditional probability that any particular number y among the first n numbers is the maximum of the first n numbers and is smaller than the last $m - 1$ numbers, equals $y^{n-1}(1-y)^{m-1}$. Therefore, the desired probability equals $n \int_0^1 y^{n-1}(1-y)^{m-1}$. This completes the proof. ∎

We return to markets with commissions. In particular, for the remainder of this section we consider markets with commission rate $\gamma > 0$. Let $\mathbf{x}_1, \ldots, \mathbf{x}_n$ be a market sequence.

---

[27] See Grimmett and Stirzaker [176] (Section 4.3) for a proof.
[28] The discrete version of this identity is $\mathbf{E}[X] = \sum_j j \cdot \Pr[X = j] = \sum_j \Pr[X \geq j]$. See p. 371 in Appendix E.

Consider the holdings of CBAL$_b$ before and after some trading period i. By definition, before this period CBAL$_b$ is **b**-balanced. After this period, the wealth of CBAL$_b$ is increased by a factor of $R(\mathbf{b}, \mathbf{x}_i) = \mathbf{b}^t \cdot \mathbf{x}_i$ and the portfolio changes to $\mathbf{b}'$ where

$$\mathbf{b}' = \mathbf{b}'_{\mathbf{x}_i} = \frac{1}{\mathbf{b}^t \cdot \mathbf{x}_i}(b_1 x_{i1}, \dots, b_m x_{im}).$$

(We use $\mathbf{b}'$ whenever the subscript x_i is understood from the context.) To rebalance to **b**, CBAL$_b$ pays a rebalancing factor of $\mathrm{com}(\mathbf{b}', \mathbf{b})$ of its current wealth.

Use $R_\gamma(\mathbf{b}, \mathbf{x}_i)$ to denote the multiplicative increase of CBAL$_b$ for the ith period when the commission rate is γ. As in equation (14.18), we have the following expression $R_{\gamma,n}(\mathbf{b})$ for the compounded return of CBAL$_b$ after n trading periods, given a market sequence $X = \mathbf{x}_1, \dots, \mathbf{x}_n$ and a commission rate γ,

$$R_{\gamma,n}(\mathbf{b}) = R_{\gamma,n}(\mathbf{b}, X) = \prod_{i=1}^{n} R_\gamma(\mathbf{b}, \mathbf{x}_i)$$

$$= \prod_{i=1}^{n} R(\mathbf{b}, \mathbf{x}_i)\big(1 - \mathrm{com}(\mathbf{b}', \mathbf{b})\big)$$

$$= \prod_{i=1}^{n} \mathbf{b}^t \cdot \mathbf{x}_i \big(1 - \mathrm{com}(\mathbf{b}'_{\mathbf{x}_i}, \mathbf{b})\big)$$

$$= \prod_{i=1}^{n} \left(\mathbf{b}^t \cdot \mathbf{x}_i - \frac{\gamma}{2} \sum_{j=1}^{m} \big| b_j x_{ij} - b_j (\mathbf{b}^t \cdot \mathbf{x}_i) \big| \right).$$

(By definition, in a market with commission rate γ, CBAL$_b(X) = R_{\gamma,n}(\mathbf{b})$.) We require the following basic lemmas.

Lemma 14.8 ("Triangle inequality" for commissions) *An investor who invests in the portfolio* **u** *and then, at the end of the trading period (with market vector* **x**), *rebalances from* $\mathbf{u}' = \mathbf{u}'_{\mathbf{x}}$ *to the portfolio* **b** *is returning at least as much as an investor who invests in* **u** *and then, at the end of the period, rebalances first to* **u** *and then to* **b**. *That is,*

$$R(\mathbf{u}, \mathbf{x})(1 - \mathrm{com}(\mathbf{u}', \mathbf{b})) \geq R(\mathbf{u}, \mathbf{x})(1 - \mathrm{com}(\mathbf{u}', \mathbf{u}))(1 - \mathrm{com}(\mathbf{u}, \mathbf{b})).$$

PROOF. Clearly, by combining the rebalancing from $\mathbf{u}' \to \mathbf{u}$ and then $\mathbf{u} \to \mathbf{b}$ to one transaction, $\mathbf{u}' \to \mathbf{b}$, an investor can save on commissions by offsetting opposite flows to and from securities. ∎

Lemma 14.9 *Let* **x** *be any market vector. Given two portfolios* **u** *and* **v**, *let*

$$\mathbf{w} = \lambda \mathbf{u} + (1 - \lambda)\mathbf{v}$$

be their mixture, $0 \leq \lambda \leq 1$. *Then,*

(i) $\mathrm{com}(\mathbf{w}, \mathbf{u}) \leq \gamma(1 - \lambda).$

(ii) $R(\mathbf{w}, \mathbf{x})(1 - \mathrm{com}(\mathbf{w}', \mathbf{w})) \geq \lambda R(\mathbf{u}, \mathbf{x})(1 - \mathrm{com}(\mathbf{u}', \mathbf{w}))$
$+ (1 - \lambda)R(\mathbf{v}, \mathbf{x})(1 - \mathrm{com}(\mathbf{v}', \mathbf{w})).$

PROOF. We prove property (i) as follows.

$$\text{com}(\mathbf{w}, \mathbf{u}) = \frac{\gamma}{2} \sum_j \left| u_j - \lambda u_j - (1 - \lambda) v_j \right|$$

$$\leq \frac{\gamma}{2} \sum_j \left| u_j(1 - \lambda) \right| + \frac{\gamma}{2} \sum_j \left| -(1 - \lambda) v_j \right|$$

$$= \frac{\gamma}{2}(1 - \lambda) + \frac{\gamma}{2}(1 - \lambda)$$

$$= \gamma(1 - \lambda).$$

Property (ii) is obvious, since the investor can save only on commissions (using the same argument as in the proof of Lemma 14.8). ∎

For markets without commissions, we know from equation (14.21) that the return of algorithm UNI is a uniform average of the returns of all constant rebalanced algorithms. We now proceed to adapt algorithm UNI for markets with commissions. The following theorem considers the average return of all constant rebalanced algorithms that pay commissions.

Theorem 14.12 *Consider a market with a commission rate γ. Let X be any market sequence of length n, and let μ be the uniform probability measure over $\mathcal{B}$. Then,*

$$\mathbf{E}_{\mu(\mathbf{b})}\left[R_{\gamma,n}(\mathbf{b}, X)\right] \geq \binom{(1 + \gamma)n + m - 1}{m - 1} \cdot R_{\gamma,n}(\mathbf{b}^*, X).$$

PROOF. The proof closely follows the line of the second proof of Theorem 14.10.

First, note that since we now consider a uniform average of constant rebalanced portfolios (that pay commissions), we obtain for free the representation analogous to equation (14.21), which is used in the proof of Theorem 14.10 to show that UNI returns exactly the uniform average return of all constant rebalanced portfolios.

Having modified equation (14.21), the proof here differs from the second proof of Theorem 14.10 in only one respect: property (i). Specifically, when facing commissions, we are able to show only that

$$\mathbf{E}_{\mu(\mathbf{b})}\left[R_{\gamma,n}(\mathbf{b}, X)\right] \geq \mathbf{E}_{\mu(\mathbf{b})}\left[r^{(1+\gamma)n}(\mathbf{b})\right]\text{CBAL-OPT}(X). \tag{14.32}$$

It is easy to see that given equation (14.32) and using the remaining arguments in the proof of Theorem 14.10, we can conclude the proof.

Let $\mathbf{b}$ be any portfolio such that for all $j = 1, \ldots, m$, $b_j \geq r b_j^*$. We show that for any period i,

$$R_\gamma(\mathbf{b}, \mathbf{x}_i) \geq r(1 - \gamma(1 - r)) \cdot R_\gamma(\mathbf{b}^*, \mathbf{x}_i).$$

That is, we need to show that

$$R(\mathbf{b}, \mathbf{x}_i)(1 - \text{com}(\mathbf{b}', \mathbf{b})) \geq r(1 - \gamma(1 - r))R(\mathbf{b}^*, \mathbf{x}_i)(1 - \text{com}(\mathbf{b}^{*'}, \mathbf{b}^*)). \tag{14.33}$$

Since $b_j \geq r b_j^*$ for all j, we have, for some $z_j \in [0, 1]$,

$$b_j = r b_j^* + (1 - r) z_j.$$

Denoting $\mathbf{z} = (z_1, \ldots, z_m)$, we thus have $\mathbf{b} = r\mathbf{b}^* + (1 - r)\mathbf{z}$. Now,

$$
\begin{aligned}
R_\gamma(\mathbf{b}, \mathbf{x}_i) &= R(\mathbf{b}, \mathbf{x}_i)(1 - \mathrm{com}(\mathbf{b}, \mathbf{b}')) \\
&\geq rR(\mathbf{b}^*, \mathbf{x}_i)(1 - \mathrm{com}(\mathbf{b}^{*\prime}, \mathbf{b})) + (1 - r)R(\mathbf{z}, \mathbf{x}_i)(1 - \mathrm{com}(\mathbf{z}', \mathbf{b})),
\end{aligned}
$$

by Lemma 14.9(ii) with $\mathbf{w} = \mathbf{b}, \mathbf{u} = \mathbf{b}^*, \mathbf{v} = \mathbf{z}, \lambda = r$;

$$
\begin{aligned}
&\geq rR(\mathbf{b}^*, \mathbf{x}_i)(1 - \mathrm{com}(\mathbf{b}^{*\prime}, \mathbf{b})) \\
&\geq rR(\mathbf{b}^*, \mathbf{x}_i)(1 - \mathrm{com}(\mathbf{b}^{*\prime}, \mathbf{b}^*))(1 - \mathrm{com}(\mathbf{b}^*, \mathbf{b}^*)),
\end{aligned}
$$

by Lemma 14.9(i) with $\mathbf{w} = \mathbf{b}, \mathbf{u} = \mathbf{b}^*, \lambda = r$;

$$
\geq r(1 - \gamma(1 - r))R(\mathbf{b}^*, \mathbf{x}_i)(1 - \mathrm{com}(\mathbf{b}^{*\prime}, \mathbf{b}^*)),
$$

by Lemma 14.8;

$$
= r(1 - \gamma(1 - r))R_\gamma(\mathbf{b}^*, \mathbf{x}_i).
$$

Now, based on the concavity of the log function, we have

$$
\begin{aligned}
\log(1 - \gamma(1 - r)) &= \log((1 - \gamma)1 + \gamma r) \\
&\geq (1 - \gamma)\log 1 + \gamma \log r = \log r^\gamma.
\end{aligned}
$$

Hence, when we aggregate upon all n periods, we get

$$
R_{\gamma,n}(\mathbf{b}) \geq r^{(1+\gamma)n}R_{\gamma,n}(\mathbf{b}^*),
$$

which proves equation (14.32).   ∎

Using the expression $R_{\gamma,i}(\mathbf{b}, \mathbf{x})$ for the compound return of CBAL$_\mathbf{b}$ after i periods, it is straightforward to define the uniform weighted algorithm UNI$_\gamma$, which pays commissions (see equation 14.19). Also, for any market sequence X of length n, let

$$
\text{CBAL-OPT}_\gamma(X) = R_{\gamma,n}(\mathbf{b}^*, X).
$$

We have the following somewhat surprising corollary, showing that the introdution of commission rates does not result in a significant deterioration in the competitive bound.

Corollary 14.13 *Consider a market with commission rate γ. Let X be any market sequence of length n. Then,*

$$
\text{UNI}_\gamma(X) \geq \binom{(1 + \gamma)n + m - 1}{m - 1} \cdot \text{CBAL-OPT}_\gamma(X).
$$

Exercise 14.23 Prove Corollary 14.13. Hint: Prove that $\text{UNI}_\gamma(X) \geq \mathbf{E}_{\mu(\mathbf{b})}[R_{\gamma,n}(\mathbf{b}, X)]$.

14.5.5 Portfolio Selection with Side Information

We return to the portfolio selection problem without commissions. Now, consider how a more sophisticated trader can incorporate additional knowledge into her trading decisions.

Typically, a trader may have "(in)side information" based on various kinds of predictions of future values of market vectors. To model side information, we consider an "oracle" that announces a number $info_i \in \mathcal{I} = \{1, 2, \ldots, k\}$ at the start of the ith trading period. The number announced represents an abstract state of some prediction apparatus. For example, in the ideal case, $info_i$ identifies the best security in the ith period. Nevertheless, we assume that the online player does not know in advance the quality of the side information provided to him and, moreover, that the quality of the side information may vary during the trading period. Therefore, in order to benefit from such side information the trader must learn about the quality of this information during the trading period. Formally, with respect to an n-period trading game we define **side information** as any sequence $info_1, info_2, \ldots, info_n$ with $info_i \in \mathcal{I}$.

Example 14.3 Here we consider a market of two securities and a simple (online) side information function with two states. Let $\mathcal{I} = \{1, 2\}$. Set $info_1 = 1$, and for all $j > 1$, set $info_j = 1$ if the total multiplicative growth of the first security up until period $j - 1$ exceeds the total multiplicative growth of the second security. Set $info_j = 2$ otherwise. That is, with respect to a market sequence X, for $j > 1$,

$$
info_j = \begin{cases} 1 & \text{if } \prod_{i < j-1} x_{i1} > \prod_{i < j-1} x_{i2}; \\ 2 & \text{otherwise.} \end{cases}
$$

Now, consider the market and market sequence of Example 14.1; that is, the market consists of cash and one stock and the relative price sequence of the stock is $\frac{1}{2}, 2, \frac{1}{2}, 2, \ldots$. Clearly, the side information sequence is $1, 2, 1, 2, \ldots$.

Let $X = \mathbf{x}_1, \ldots, \mathbf{x}_n$ be any market sequence and let $I = info_1, info_2, \ldots, info_n$ be any side information. As usual, use I_i to denote the prefix of I consisting of the first i elements. We use $\text{ALG}(X|I)$ to denote the return of the algorithm ALG with respect to X given the side information I. Let $\mathbf{b}$ be any portfolio and $\ell \in \mathcal{I}$. With respect to the side information I_i and market sequence X_i, define

$$
R_i(\mathbf{b}|\ell) = \prod_{j \leq i \,:\, info_j = \ell} \mathbf{b}^t \mathbf{x}_j.
$$

That is, $R_i(\mathbf{b}|\ell)$ is the compounded return of a constant rebalanced algorithm that is out of the market at all periods where the side information is not ℓ and is fully invested, using the portfolio $\mathbf{b}$, at all other periods.

Let μ be any probability measure. Using $R_i(\mathbf{b}|\cdot)$, we now define the **μ-weighted algorithm with side information** as the algorithm that at the ith period uses the portfolio

$$
\mathbf{b}_i(info_i) = \frac{\int_B \mathbf{b} R_{i-1}(\mathbf{b}|info_i) d\mu(\mathbf{b})}{\int_B R_{i-1}(\mathbf{b}|info_i) d\mu(\mathbf{b})}.
$$

This is a generalization of the definition of the μ-weighted algorithm. Clearly, when $k = 1$ (i.e., no side information), this definition reduces to equation (14.19).

In a way analogous to the simplification obtained by formula (14.20), we now simplify the expression for the compounded return $\text{ALG}_\mu(X|I)$:

$$
\begin{aligned}
\text{ALG}_\mu(X|I) &= \prod_{i=1}^{n} \mathbf{b}_i^t(info_i)\mathbf{x}_i \\
&= \prod_{j=1}^{k} \prod_{i \le n \,:\, info_i = j} \mathbf{b}_i^t(j)\mathbf{x}_i \\
&= \prod_{j=1}^{k} \int_{\mathcal{B}} R_n(\mathbf{b}|j)\,d\mu(\mathbf{b}).
\end{aligned}
\tag{14.34}
$$

Although we do not know how to determine the performance ratio of the μ-weighted algorithm with side information with respect to the optimal offline constant rebalanced algorithm (it is heavily dependent on the side information), we can determine the performance ratio with respect to a more powerful offline algorithm that is also dependent on the side information. The advantage of this approach is that the dependence on the side information factors out and we obtain a performance ratio that is dependent only on the cardinality of $\mathcal{I}$.

Fix $\mathcal{I}$. Let $B : \mathcal{I} \to \mathcal{B}$ be any mapping from side information to portfolios. Define the **state-constant rebalanced algorithm** (with mapping B), denoted SCBAL_B, as the algorithm that at each period uses one of the portfolios $B(1), B(2), \ldots, B(k)$. Specifically, the algorithm invests according to the portfolio $B(info_i)$ during the ith trading period (for which the side information is $info_i$). The return of algorithm SCBAL_B for a market sequence X and side information sequence I is thus given by

$$
\text{SCBAL}(X|I) = \prod_{i=1}^{n} B^t(info_i) \cdot \mathbf{x}_i.
$$

Exercise 14.24 Assuming the market and market sequence of Example 14.1, compute the return of the best state-constant rebalanced algorithm corresponding to the side information of Example 14.3.

The optimal offline state-constant rebalanced algorithm, denoted **SCBAL-OPT**, is a state-constant rebalanced algorithm that optimizes its choice of the mapping B based on advance knowledge of the market sequence X and the side information I. That is, this algorithm uses the portfolio B^* where

$$
B^* = \arg\max_{B} \prod_{i=1}^{n} B^t(info_i) \cdot \mathbf{x}_i.
$$

Use $\text{UNI}(X|I)$ and $\text{SCBAL-OPT}(X|I)$ to denote the compounded returns of the online uniform weighted algorithm and the optimal offline state-constant rebalanced algorithm, respectively, for a market sequence X given side information I. For each $j = 1, 2, \ldots, k$, set $n_j(I)$ to be the number of j's in I.

Theorem 14.14 *For each market sequence X and side information I,*

$$\frac{\text{UNI}(X|I)}{\text{SCBAL-OPT}(X|I)} \le \prod_{j=1}^{k} \left(n_j(I) + 1\right)^{(m-1)} \le (n+1)^{k(m-1)}.$$

PROOF. For each $j = 1, 2, \ldots, k$, denote by $X(j)$ the subsequence $\mathbf{x}_{j_1}, \mathbf{x}_{j_2}, \ldots, \mathbf{x}_{j_l}$ of X, where $info_{j_r} = j$ for all $1 \le r \le l$. By the definition of SCBAL-OPT and equation (14.34), we have

$$\frac{\text{UNI}(X|I)}{\text{SCBAL-OPT}(X|I)} = \prod_{j=1}^{k} \frac{\text{UNI}(X(j))}{\text{SCBAL}(X(j))}.$$

Hence, according to Theorem 14.10, applied with sequences $X(j)$, we have

$$\prod_{j=1}^{k} \frac{\text{UNI}(X(j))}{\text{SCBAL}(X(j))} \le \prod_{j=1}^{k} \left(n_j(I) + 1\right)^{(m-1)} \le \prod_{j=1}^{k} (n+1)^{(m-1)}.$$

∎

With respect to a market sequence X and side information I, use $\text{DIR}_{(1/2,\ldots,1/2)}(X|I)$ to denote the compounded return of the Dirichlet-weighted $\left(\frac{1}{2}, \ldots, \frac{1}{2}\right)$ algorithm. We leave the proof of the following theorem as an exercise.

Theorem 14.15 *For each market sequence X and side information I,*

$$\frac{\text{DIR}_{(1/2,\ldots,1/2)}(X|I)}{\text{SCBAL-OPT}(X|I)} \le \prod_{j=1}^{k} \left(n_j(I) + 1\right)^{(m-1)/2} \le 2^k (n+1)^{(k(m-1))/2}.$$

Exercise 14.25 Prove Theorem 14.15.

14.5.6 Extremal Mixture Algorithms

Equation (14.22) suggests the following interpretation. Fix some $J_n = (j_1, j_2, \ldots, j_n) \in [m]^n$ and consider the following "extremal" algorithm, denoted EXT_{J_n}.

Algorithm EXT_{J_n}: At time i, invest the entire wealth in the j_ith security.

Let $\mathbf{b} = (b_1, \ldots, b_m)$. It is possible to represent the constant rebalanced algorithm $\text{CBAL}_{\mathbf{b}}$ in terms of extremal algorithms as follows. Partition $\text{CBAL}_{\mathbf{b}}$'s initial wealth into m^n portions, one for each of the m^n sequences J_n in $[m]^n$. The number of dollars in the part corresponding to J_n is $w(J_n) = \prod_{i=1}^{n} b_{j_i}$. Notice that

$$\sum_{J_n \in [m]^n} w(J_n) = 1.$$

That is, $\{w(J_n)\}$ is a probability distribution (and a proper partition of the initial wealth). For each of the extremal algorithms EXT_{J_n}, maintain a separate investment "account" starting with an initial wealth of $w(J_n)$. For a market sequence X, the wealth accrued by EXT_{J_n} is therefore,

$$\text{EXT}_{J_n}(X) = w(J_n) \prod_{i=1}^{n} x_{j_i} = \prod_{i=1}^{n} b_{j_i} x_{j_i}.$$

Equation (14.22) shows that the sum of the wealth accrued by all the extremal algorithms is exactly $\text{CBAL}_\mathbf{b}(X)$.

Exactly as in Theorem 14.1, we can interpret and apply this algorithm as a mixed randomized algorithm. Simply choose the extremal algorithm EXT_{J_n} with probability $w(J_n)$. In this case, of course, $\text{CBAL}_\mathbf{b}(X)$ is the expected return of this algorithm. From a computational point of view, using this mixture of extremal algorithms saves the relatively large "daily" computational costs required for operating the deterministic algorithm. As a mixed randomized algorithm, only one of the extremal mixture algorithms is computed (before the start of the game).

Using equation (14.21), we can interpret algorithms UNI and DIR (and any μ-weighted algorithm) analogously. All that is needed is to partition the initial wealth so that algorithm EXT_{J_n} is assigned

$$w(J_n) = \int_{\mathcal{B}} \prod_{i=1}^{n} b_{j_i} d\mu(\mathbf{b})$$

(where μ is the corresponding probability measure).

The preceding interpretation of the constant rebalanced (and μ-weighted algorithms) gives rise to the following general class of extremal mixture algorithms. For each n, an **extremal mixture** strategy is specified by a probability distribution w over the set J_n. Such a strategy invests in the extremal algorithm EXT_{J_n} a fraction $w(J_n)$ of its initial wealth. From the above discussion, it follows that for each n, an optimal online extremal mixture algorithm performs at least as well as the best μ-weighted algorithm.

Fix n and let OEXT be the extremal mixture algorithm specified by the following probability distribution over the extremal algorithms. For each $J_n \in [m]^n$, set $q(J_n) = \prod_{i=1}^{m} \nu_i(J_n)^{n_i(J_n)}$. The distribution w is then

$$w(J_n) = \frac{q(J_n)}{\sum_{J_n \in [m]^n} q(J_n)}.$$

We now state without proof the following theorem.

Theorem 14.16 *For each market sequence X of length n,*

$$\frac{\text{CBAL-OPT}(X)}{\text{OEXT}(X)} \leq \sum_{J_n \in [m]^n} \frac{n!}{\prod_{1 \leq i \leq m} n_i(J_n)!} \prod_{1 \leq i \leq m} \left(\frac{n_i(J_n)}{n}\right)^{n_i(J_n)}. \tag{14.35}$$

Furthermore, in the worst case, this bound is tight and hence OEXT is optimal in this regard.

Exercise 14.26 Prove Theorem 14.16.

Given the equivalence of deterministic and mixed randomized extremal mixture algorithms in this setting, since the inequality of Theorem 14.16 is tight in the worst case, we have the following.

Corollary 14.17 *For every n, the right-hand side of inequality (14.35) is a lower bound on the competitive ratio (with respect to* CBAL-OPT*) of any randomized extremal mixture algorithm (or deterministic μ-weighted algorithm) against an oblivious adversary.*

For the case $m = 2$, this competitive ratio (14.35) of OEXT with respect to CBAL reduces to

$$\sum_{0 \le k \le n} \binom{n}{k} \cdot \left(\frac{k}{n}\right)^k \cdot \left(\frac{n-k}{n}\right)^{n-k},$$

and using the Stirling approximation, it can be shown to be approximately $\sqrt{\pi n/2} \approx 1.253\sqrt{n}$. Note that the competitive ratio of the DIR$_{(1/2,...,1/2)}$ algorithm for $m = 2$ is not larger than $2\sqrt{n+1}$, so the Dirichlet algorithm attains a competitive ratio that is (approximately, for large n) within a factor 1.6 of algorithm OEXT.

14.6 Historical Notes and Open Questions

This chapter studies only a few financial problems and is mainly restricted to one perspective, that of competitive analysis. The subject of mathematical finance is, of course, a much wider and mature discipline. A greater appreciation of this important discipline can be gained by reading two basic and excellent textbooks: *Investments*, by Bodie, Kane, and Marcus [77], and *Options, Futures, and Other Derivative Securities*, by Hull [190].

The first results related to portfolio selection in the spirit of competitive analysis are due to Cover (see, e.g., Cover and Gluss [120]). This development took place independent of computer scientists' interest in online algorithms.

Search and One-Way Trading. El-Yaniv, Fiat, Karp, and Turpin [140] studied one-way trading and proved the optimality of the threat-based algorithms for several problem variants. The family of EXPO algorithms were suggested by Levin [241]. The paper by El-Yaniv et al. [140] also studied several other variants of the one-way trading game: a continuous time model, and a model in which the adversary chooses a probability distribution that determines the exchange rates (this probability distribution is made known to the online trader).

Two-Way Trading. The term "statistical adversary" was coined by Raghavan [283], who studied the two-way trading problem and analyzed constant rebalanced and "dollar cost average strategies" with respect to a "mean-variance" minimax adversary. Specifically, in this setting feasible market sequences must exhibit a particular mean and variance.

The "money making" algorithm MM and the money making scheme was defined and studied by Chou, Cooperstock, El-Yaniv, Klugerman, and Leighton [98]. This paper also introduced the adversarial fixed fluctuation model and studied the optimal online strategy for the fixed fluctuation model. The bounds obtained in [98] for algorithm FMM were later improved by Chou, Shrivastava, and Sidney [99], who also obtained the bounds for the optimal offline CBAL-OPT (Exercise 14.16). In this paper, Chou, Shrivastava, and Sidney also analyzed the performance of an online algorithm within a distributional model analogous to the fixed fluctuation model. Empirical results for algorithm FMM (Section 14.4.3) were obtained by Chou [97]. The statistical classification of trends exhibited in historical price sequences was obtained by Chou, Shrivastava, and Sidney [99].

Portfolio Selection. The class of μ-weighted portfolio selection algorithms discussed in Section 14.5.1 was introduced by Cover and Ordentlich [121]. They studied the performance of algorithms UNI and DIR (see Sections 14.5.2 and 14.5.3). Cover and Ordentlich also introduced the concepts of side information, μ-weighted algorithms with side information, and state-constant rebalanced algorithms. They also introduced the class of extremal mixture algorithms. The optimal extremal mixture algorithm is presented by Ordentlich and Cover in [270].

There are various other portfolio selection results that were not discussed in this chapter. Cover and Gluss [120] consider a model in which the set of possible market vectors of relative prices is finite, for example, with cardinality k. Using the game-theoretic approachability-excludability theorem of Blackwell [70], they obtain an online portfolio selection algorithm whose exponential growth rate approaches that of the optimal offline constant rebalanced algorithm at convergence rate $(L\sqrt{k}+1)\sqrt{2L^2+1}/\sqrt{n}$, where L is a bound on the logarithm of the maximum relative price, and n is the length of the game.[29] In the long run, it is possible in this model to track approximately the performance of the optimal offline constant rebalanced algorithm and, in particular, to outperform the optimal offline BAH strategy.

Cover and Ordentlich's μ-weighted algorithms as presented here are a generalization of a result by Cover [119] in which it is shown that the competitive ratio of the uniform weighted algorithm with respect to CBAL-OPT is bounded above by a polynomial in n, the number of trading periods. This result assumes that all relative prices are bounded away from zero. In the same paper, Cover presents a more refined analysis and bounds the competitive ratio of the uniform weighted UNI with respect to CBAL-OPT in terms of a sensitivity matrix A measuring the "empirical volatility" (defined in Cover and Ordentlich's paper) of prices exhibited in the market sequence presented to the algorithm. Specifically, the upper bound on the competitive ratio is $\sqrt{|A|}\,(n/(2\pi))^{(m-1)/2}\,/(m-1)!$. The value of the determinant $|A|$ can be bounded by a constant if the prices of all securities are sufficiently volatile so that CBAL-OPT gives positive weights to all securities. Cover also provides some interesting experimental results demonstrating the performance of this algorithm. Jamshidian [204] analyzes the performance of the uniform universal portfolio selection algorithm in a continuous time model. The results obtained are similar to those obtained by Cover [119].

Following Cover and Ordentlich, Helmbold, Schapire, Singer, and Warmuth [185] presented an online portfolio selection algorithm based on techniques from statistical inference. Specifically, their algorithm chooses an $(i+1)$st portfolio, $\mathbf{b}_{i+1}$, that maximizes $\eta \log(\mathbf{b}_{i+1}^t \cdot \mathbf{x}_i) - D(\mathbf{b}_{i+1}\|\mathbf{b}_i)$, where η is some constant (that determines the adaptation rate) and $D(\cdot\|\cdot)$ is the Kullback–Leibler dissimilarity measure (see Appendix G). Thus, this algorithm attempts to adapt to the recent history while keeping its next portfolio "close" to the previous portfolio. They present several variants of this algorithm for the cases in which n is known or unknown and for a model with side information. All their theoretical bounds are comparable but inferior to the (respective) bounds obtained by Cover and Ordentlich. Nevertheless, it is shown that this algorithm empirically outperforms the Dirichlet-weighted algorithm (with and without side information) on several historical data sets obtained from a twenty-two-year period of the New York Stock Exchange.

---

[29] A similar algorithm and bound can be obtained using the results of Hart and Mas-Collel [183].

Recently, Blum and Kalai [73] presented the alternative analysis of the uniform weighted portfolio selection algorithm of Cover and Ordentlich [121] yielding the same $\binom{n+m-1}{m-1}$ bound (see Theorem 14.10). Moreover, they showed how their analysis extends to markets with constant commission rate γ giving a competitive ratio of at most $\binom{(1+\gamma)n+m-1}{m-1}$ for the uniform μ-weighted algorithm. Blum and Kalai [74] present preliminary performance tests on the same New York Stock Exchange historical data for the uniform weighted portfolio selection algorithm with various commission rates and rebalancing frequencies. Not surprisingly, they discover that rebalancing less frequently is beneficial, especially with higher commission rates. In the tests in which rebalancing occurs monthly, the algorithm performs better than the average stock when the commission rate is smaller than 4%, but deteriorates below the average stock when commissions rates are higher. Although these results are suggestive, it is important to note that more conclusive results must include also risk analysis. Interestingly, as reported by Blum and Kalai, the portfolio selection algorithm by Helmbold et al. (mentioned above) usually outperformed the uniform-weighted algorithm even though theoretical competitive bounds for the algorithm by Helmbold et al. have yet to be established when transaction fees are introduced.

Awerbuch, Azar, Fiat, and Leighton [23] consider the following setting. The online player wishes to invest his entire wealth in one of the m securities, hoping that the chosen security will be a "winner" that yields high dividends. The decision is irreversible, and after the player has chosen one security the game is essentially over. If D is the posteriori dividend return of the best security, then the optimal expected return of the player is trivially $\Theta\left(\frac{D}{m}\right)$. Now consider a game such that in each period, each of the securities may issue a dividend of exactly \$1. Under the assumption that the yield of the best security is $D \geq 3 \log m$, and that D is known to the online player, Awerbuch et al. provide a selection strategy obtaining a return of at least $\frac{D}{3 \log m}$ with probability at least $1 - \frac{3 \log m}{D} - \frac{2}{m}$. This basic result is extended for multiple choices of securities. Finally, in the case in which D is not known in advance, the player can retain the same yield but the probability of success is decreased.

Portfolio Selection, Prediction, and Compression. There are striking relationships between portfolio selection (and gambling), prediction, and universal data compression. Cover and Thomas [122] (Chaps. 6 and 15 and references therein) study the relationships between gambling and data compression and optimal distributional portfolio selection and optimal source coding. Ordentlich [269] (and Cover and Ordentlich [121]) explore the relationships between worst-case portfolio selection algorithms and universal data compression algorithms.

Portfolio selection algorithms can also be reduced to prediction algorithms that combine expert advice. Recent studies of this reduction are by Cover and Ordentlich [121] and Blum and Kalai [73].

Competitive Analysis and Risk Management. A financial agent can manage his risk if he controls the natural tradeoff between risk and return. One desirable and, in fact, indispensable feature of modern financial instruments is **risk management**. This element is, of course, missing from pure competitive analysis, which elicits only risk-averse strategies. Indeed, the access graph approach (for paging), statistical adversaries, and other Bayesian compromises can be viewed as an attempt to overcome this aspect of extreme risk aversion; however, these approaches do not offer a quantifiable and controllable risk management mechanism.

Recently, al-Binali [3] offered a framework that incorporates risk management into competitive analysis. Essentially, this is done as follows. The risk of an algorithm ALG is defined as the ratio of ALG's competitiveness to the optimal competitive ratio. A user specifies a bound on the allowable risk; that is, the user accepts only those algorithms that satisfy this risk constraint. The second aspect of this framework is that the user also has some forecast that is defined as a subset of all request sequences (exactly as in the access graph model for paging and the statistical adversary for the one- and two-way trading problems). Given a risk bound and a forecast, the user then attempts to optimize the competitive ratio, assuming the forecast is correct but still subject to the risk bound condition (which, in particular, applies when the forecast does not hold).

As an example, al-Binali applies this framework to the one-way trading problem and derives optimal algorithms with respect to a class of forecasts predicting that some exchange rate will exceed a given threshold (within the known lower and upper bounds, m and M).

Credits for Exercises. Exercises 14.5, 14.6, 14.7, 14.8, 14.9, and 14.11 are due to El-Yaniv et al. [140]. Exercises 14.12, 14.13, and 14.14 are due to Chou et al. [98]. Exercises 14.15 and 14.16 are due to Chou, Shrivastava, and Sidney [99]. Exercises 14.21, 14.19, and 14.25 are due to Cover and Ordentlich [121]. Exercises 14.20 and 14.23 are due to Blum and Kalai [73], Exercises 14.26 and 14.18 are due to Ordentlich and Cover [270], and Exercise 14.24 is due to Ordentlich [269].

14.6.1   Open Questions

14.1 (*Value = I3/T3*) Consider the search problem with sampling costs. Specifically, assume that for obtaining the ith price quotation p_i, the player must pay a sampling cost s_i. Assuming that all s_i are equal to some constant, determine the optimal randomized online algorithm for this problem.

14.2 (*Value = I2/T2*) Considering the two variations discussed in Exercise 14.14, can there be a randomized online algorithm corresponding to either variant that is money making?

14.3 (*Value = I2/T4*) Determine the optimal μ-weighted portfolio selection algorithm when μ is Dirichlet.

14.4 (*Value = I4/T3*) Determine the optimal algorithm within the fixed fluctuation model that allows for "short selling" and a nonzero fixed interest rate.

14.5 (*Value = I5/T4*) Extend other models and algorithm analyses (such as Dirichlet-weighted and extremal mixture algorithms and side information) considered in this chapter to include commissions.

14.6 (*Value = I5/T5*) Consider other transaction cost models such as a bid-ask price spread, which is essentially a variable commission rate per security and per period.

14.7 (*Value = I2/T4*) Determine the true competitive ratio (with respect to OPT, not CBAL-OPT) of the algorithm UNI and DIR (with and without commissions).

14.8 (*Value = 15/T3*) Evaluate the empirical performance of the portfolio selection algorithms presented in this chapter against historical data. Note that in order to obtain meaningful results, the performance must be related to the empirical risk and the results must attain substantial statistical significance. There are many commonly used measures of risk. For example, one measure of empirical risk is Sharpe's ratio, given by

$$\frac{\mathbf{E}[R(\text{ALG})] - R(\text{risk-free})}{\sqrt{\text{Var}(\text{ALG})}},$$

where $\mathbf{E}[R(\text{ALG})]$ and $\text{Var}(\text{ALG})$ are the mean and variance, respectively, of ALG's return and $R(\text{risk-free})$ is the risk-free rate of return (see, e.g., Sharpe [311] and Bodie, Kane, and Marcus [77], Chaps. 23 and 24).

CHAPTER 15

On Decision Theories and the Competitive Ratio

A key ingredient required for any evaluation of online algorithms is an optimality criterion. For nontrivial online problems the choice of optimality criterion is crucial, since different criteria generally give rise to different (optimal) algorithms. It is therefore important to be familiar with known optimality criteria, understand their various properties, and assess their appropriateness.

Of course, the ultimate success of any theory is judged by its ability to explain and predict outcomes (e.g., algorithmic performance) in "real-life" settings; therefore, any comprehensive evaluation of an optimality criterion requires empirical studies. Nevertheless, through theoretical studies we can understand the special properties of decision criteria and compare the suitability of the criteria in various settings. Thus, a treatment of online problems and their optimality criteria (e.g., the competitive ratio) would not be complete without placing them within the context of decision theory.

In this chapter, we familiarize ourselves with some concepts and ideas from classical and more contemporary decision theory, and we discuss some of the basic issues. What are reasonable decision criteria for online problems? What justifies the choice of a particular criterion? Is the competitive ratio a reasonable criterion? The goal is to provide the reader with a better perspective on competitive analysis and its decision theoretic foundations.

A decision making approach very similar to the competitive ratio was known almost 50 years ago. However, for the most part it was superseded by the "Bayesian approach," which evolved to be the main tool for most online applications in economics and finance, statistics, and operations research. Although this text is essentially about applications of the competitive ratio, we do not believe that the competitive ratio (or any other decision making approach) is the most appropriate criterion under all circumstances. By tracing the background of some older and some more recent approaches to decision making, we account for some of the difficulties and controversies related to the issue of choosing a decision making criterion for online problems. However, the subject of decision theory is so extensive that we must limit ourselves to an incomplete and somewhat anecdotal discussion.

15.1 Certainty, Risk, and Strict Uncertainty

Throughout this chapter we are concerned with **single-person decision making problems**; that is, the decision maker is a person or organization (without internal conflicts). Of course, this is an idealization that abstracts what we believe to be the essence of many online problems. However, the assumption of no internal conflicts is sometimes inaccurate. For example, the choice of a paging algorithm in a multitasking environment or a routing algorithm for a communication network does in principle involve internal conflicts (for example, as a result of different system design philosophies).

15.1.1 A Simple Decision Theoretic Model

Consider the following "one-shot" decision problem. There is a set $\mathcal{A}$ of **actions** and a set $\mathcal{S}$ of **states of nature**. Associated with the sets $\mathcal{A}$ and $\mathcal{S}$ is a **cost** function $C : \mathcal{A} \times \mathcal{S} \to \mathbb{R}$. Whenever the sets $\mathcal{A}$ and $\mathcal{S}$ are finite, we can view the cost function as a matrix $C = (c_{ij})$, where i and j range over the indices of actions and states of nature (with respect to some fixed enumerations of $\mathcal{A}$ and $\mathcal{S}$) and $c_{ij} = C(a_i, s_j)$. A **decision problem** P is defined as a triplet, $P = (\mathcal{A}, \mathcal{S}, C)$. Given a decision problem P, a decision maker must choose one action a in $\mathcal{A}$. After the choice is made, "nature" chooses one of the states s and the decision maker incurs a cost of $C(a, s)$. Which state nature chooses is beyond the control of the decision maker.

Example 15.1 Consider the following problem:

$$P = (\{a_1, a_2\}, \{s_1, s_2, s_3, s_4\}, C),$$

where the cost function is defined by the matrix of Figure 15.1. Assume that the costs are given in some currency, for example, dollars. Now imagine that the decision maker is forced to choose one action (a_1 or a_2).

$$P = \quad \begin{array}{c|c|c|c|c|} & s_1 & s_2 & s_3 & s_4 \\ \hline a_1 & 70 & 80 & 90 & 1 \\ \hline a_2 & 1 & 1 & 1 & 10{,}000 \\ \hline \end{array}$$

Figure 15.1: A simple decision problem.

Given a decision problem such as P in Figure 15.1, our goal is to rank the actions in $\mathcal{A}$ in a way that is best (i.e., in some sense optimal) for the decision maker. Obviously, the answer to such a question depends on the information available to the decision maker regarding the "relative likelihood" of the various states of nature. It will become apparent that such a ranking should, in principle, also depend on the character of the decision maker.

15.1.2 Preference Relations and Decision Criteria

In order to discuss how different decision makers might rank the available actions in a decision problem, we need a general definition of preference.

Let X be a set. Given a binary relation $\preccurlyeq$ over the set X, we define two new binary relations $\prec$ and $\backsim$ over X:

$$x \prec y \text{ if } y \not\preccurlyeq x;$$

$$x \approx y \text{ if } x \preccurlyeq y \text{ and } y \preccurlyeq x.$$

We say that the binary relation $\prec$ is a **preference relation** if $\preccurlyeq$ is complete (i.e., for all x, y in X, either $x \preccurlyeq y$ or $y \preccurlyeq x$) and transitive.

Define a **decision criterion** for a class $\mathcal{P}$ of decision problems as a mapping that assigns to each problem $P = (\mathcal{A}, \mathcal{S}, C) \in \mathcal{P}$ a complete and transitive order relation $\preccurlyeq_P$ over $\mathcal{A}$. When $a \prec_P b$, we say that a is **strictly preferred** to b, and when $a \approx_P b$, we say that a and b are **indifferent**. An **optimal algorithm** for a problem P is an algorithm $a \in \mathcal{A}$ such that for all other $b \in \mathcal{A}$, $a \preccurlyeq_P b$.

15.1.3   Certainty and Uncertainty

With respect to our simplified decision theoretic model, we classify various types of decision problems. When the decision maker knows which state of nature will obtain (before having to make a choice of action), we say that the problem is **under certainty**. Such problems correspond to classical optimization problems in which the issue is the identification and efficient computation of the optimal (offline) action. In this case, the decision issue is essentially nonexistent because the problem is formulated in terms of a single real-valued cost function. In more general formulations of decision problems, the range of the cost function[1] can be arbitrary "commodity bundles" (i.e., collections of commodities) or resource allocations. Hence, in these more general formulations, there is the added complication that the decision maker must have a (consistent) preference relation between the various commodity bundles or resource allocations.

Whenever there is incomplete information on which of the states of nature will prevail, we say that the problem is **under uncertainty**. Within this class of decision problems under uncertainty, we distinguish two extreme subclasses. Problems for which the probabilities of the various states of nature are completely known (in principle, such as casino games) are called **problems under pure risk**. In contrast, problems for which absolutely nothing is known about the relative likelihood of the states of nature are called problems under **strict uncertainty**.[2] The vast majority of real-life decision problems we encounter are under uncertainty; however, they are not under strict uncertainty or under pure risk. Theoretical modeling of such problems is much more difficult than modeling problems of pure risk or of strict uncertainty, since it is difficult to devise a rigorous (yet practically useful) model of partial information.

In this chapter we discuss various methods of dealing with problems under risk and problems under strict uncertainty. One natural approach to deal with problems that combine risk and (strict) uncertainty is to transform them into problems in either one of the extreme subclasses. For example, in its essence, "pure" competitive analysis belongs to the family of approaches that "deliberately" ignores all available (partial) information regarding the relative likelihood of the states of nature. On the other hand, in the **Bayesian approach**, the partial information available is somehow extended so that all uncertainty is entirely replaced by "risk," which means that all states of nature are assigned probabilities. We begin with some of the approaches used for decisions under strict uncertainty (which is the main theme of this chapter). We then discuss decision problems under pure risk and conclude with a brief discussion of some Bayesian approaches in the context of nonstrict uncertainty.

---

[1] In these more general formulations, the cost function is called an outcome function.

[2] The term "complete ignorance" is also used in the literature, for example, by Luce and Raiffa [251].

15.1.4   Descriptive Theories Versus Prescriptive Theories

Under the realistic assumption that decision makers are not perfectly rational, there are at least two different incentives for studying theories regarding decision making under uncertainty. The first incentive is to provide a realistic explanation and prediction of how individuals make their choices under uncertainty. The second is to describe how an idealized rational individual *should* act, thus advising individuals how to act more "rationally," sometimes even against their intuitive understanding. Theories of the former type are called **descriptive**, and theories of the latter type are called **prescriptive** (or **normative**).

Much of modern economic theory and its applications in finance, marketing, and other areas is concerned with descriptive theories of decision making applied as follows. Descriptive models are constructed to approximate the way various agents (i.e., individuals or organizations) make decisions. Then a theory regarding the entire economy (of interest) is devised based on the assumption that all agents conform to these descriptive models.

In contrast, for algorithmic online optimization, we are concerned with prescriptive theories of decision making. That is, our primary goal is to be able to advise an individual concerning which online algorithms are "best" to employ.

There is a fuzzy middle ground between the descriptive and prescriptive approaches. In fact, they can even be employed simultaneously. For example, (prescriptive) advice for a certain action in the stock market (respectively, for the utilization of a particular routing algorithm) might be substantially improved if it takes into account the (descriptive) actions of the other investors in the market (respectively, other parties in the communication network).

15.2   Decision Making Under Strict Uncertainty

The primary goal of this chapter is to study the rationality of the competitive ratio and compare it to other decision criteria for strict uncertainty. Although strict uncertainty conditions are difficult to envision (we almost always know *something* about the likelihood of the states of nature), there are situations in which our knowledge is very limited. Such situations are particularly frequent when we consider request sequences whose stochastic characteristics are extremely complex and/or dynamically changing.

15.2.1   Some Criteria for Strict Uncertainty

Using the simplified decision model of Section 15.1.1, we describe various decision criteria. Let $P = (\mathcal{A}, \mathcal{S}, C)$ be a cost minimization decision problem. Each of the following decision criteria assigns to each action $a \in \mathcal{A}$ a real value $V(a)$. If $V(a) < V(b)$ for $a, b \in \mathcal{A}$, then a is strictly preferred to b; if $V(a) = V(b)$, then a and b are indifferent. Thus, such a function $V : \mathcal{A} \to \mathbb{R}$ defines a preference relation over $\mathcal{A}$.

The function $V(a) = \max_s \left\{ \frac{C(a,s)}{\min_x C(x,s)} \right\}$ essentially (ignoring the issue of additive constants) defines the deterministic competitive ratio. In this case, the decision maker's best choice should be $a^* = \arg\min_x V(x)$. A straightforward interpretation of the competitive ratio is as follows: there is an adversary that, based on the knowledge of the decision maker's choice of action, will choose a state of nature in the worst possible way in order to increase the decision maker's posteriori multiplicative "regret."

The following is a list of some of the classical decision criteria for strict uncertainty. Note that some of these criteria assume that $\mathcal{A}$ and/or $\mathcal{S}$ are finite. (See Section 15.9 for some further examples of decision criteria.)

- The **minimax cost** from Wald [334]: Minimize $V(a) = \max_s C(a, s)$.
- The **pessimism–optimism index** due to Hurewicz [191]: Let $\alpha \in [0, 1]$ be a subjective pessimism–optimism index. Minimize

$$V(a) = \alpha \cdot \max_s C(a, s) + (1 - \alpha) \cdot \min_s C(a, s).$$

Notice that when $\alpha = 1$, this criterion is identical to the above minimax cost criterion.[3]

- The **minimax regret** due to Niehans [268] and (independently) Savage [300]: Minimize

$$V(a) = \max_s \left\{ C(a, s) - \min_x C(x, s) \right\}.$$

Notice the striking similarity to the competitive ratio. The minimax regret could be called "minimax additive regret," whereas the competitive ratio would then be called the "minimax multiplicative regret."[4]

- The **principle of insufficient reason** (which dates back to Bayes and Laplace): Minimize

$$V(a) = \sum_s \frac{C(a, s)}{|\mathcal{S}|}.$$

Using this criterion, the decision maker assumes that all states occur with equal probability and chooses an action with the lowest average cost.

These criteria are significantly different in that they give rise to different optimal algorithms.

Example 15.2 Consider the decision problem P in Figure 15.2. It is not difficult to see that the minimax cost, minimax regret, competitive ratio, pessimism–optimism criterion (with $\alpha = \frac{1}{2}$), and principle of insufficient reason will choose a_1, a_2, a_3, a_4, and a_5, respectively, as optimal actions.

In Section 15.6 we consider a more natural problem that distinguishes between the criteria.

Exercise 15.1 For the decision problem of Figure 15.2, prove that the composite decision criterion that takes a weighted majority of the above criteria is not necessarily a preference relation over $\mathcal{A}$.

Thus far we have assumed that the choice of action is deterministic. Nevertheless, all the above criteria are naturally generalized for randomized (mixed) actions. Let $P = (\mathcal{A}, \mathcal{S}, C)$ be any decision problem, and let $\Delta(\mathcal{A})$ denote the set of all probability measures

---

[3] When $\alpha = 0$, the pessimism–optimism index reduces to a criterion called the "minimin" cost (or "maximax," for profit maximization problems).

[4] Alternatively, one could name the minimax regret the "competitive difference."

	s_1	s_2	s_3	s_4	s_5
a_1	6	5	5	4	5
a_2	3	8	2	5	7
a_3	1	7	4	1	8
a_4	3	5	1	7	7
a_5	7	4	5	2	3

Figure 15.2: A decision problem P that distinguishes between five criteria for strict uncertainty.

over the set $\mathcal{A}$. The **randomized extension** of $\mathcal{A}$ can be defined as $P' = (\Delta(\mathcal{A}), \mathcal{S}, C')$, where for each $\mu \in \Delta(\mathcal{A})$, $s \in \mathcal{S}$, $C'(\mu, s) = \mathbf{E}_{\mu(a)} C(a, s)$. With respect to the competitive ratio, the minimax regret, and the minimax cost, the optimal decision is, in general, a mixed strategy (see Chapter 8). It is easy to see from Lemma 8.2 that randomization cannot help with regard to the principle of insufficient reason.

15.2.2 Some Problematic Examples

Each criterion has some obvious deficiencies. Consider first the minimax cost. If we assume that events will be chosen by an adversary whose only goal is to maximize the decision maker's regret, then for many nontrivial decision problems the adversary will easily succeed and the minimax will prescribe extremely poor choices. For instance, in the decision problem shown in Figure 15.3, according to the minimax cost criterion the optimal action is a_2. Nevertheless, because action a_1 is significantly better than a_2 in three of the states and only marginally worse in one state, a choice of a_2 may cause a serious regret.

	s_1	s_2	s_3	s_4
a_1	1	1	1	$10^6 + 1$
a_2	10^6	10^6	10^6	10^6

Figure 15.3: A bad example for the minimax cost.

The minimax regret criterion will avoid the poor choice made by the minimax cost in the above example. However, this criterion overlooks another issue. The importance or "utility" of a given cost or profit depends on the individual's wealth and attitudes (see Section 15.7). For example, as wealth increases, the increment to utility becomes progressively smaller so that we derive less and less satisfaction with each subsequent unit of incremental wealth. For example, it is reasonable to believe that a loss or gain of $10 is more significant to a pauper than to a billionaire. This is called the principle of

diminishing marginal utility (returns). In the decision problem depicted in Figure 15.4, the optimal choice of the minimax regret is a_2. However, we can argue in favor of a_1 by noting that in most states we are going to pay almost nothing and if s_4 occurs we increase our cost by only 10%.[5]

	s_1	s_2	s_3	s_4
a_1	1	1	1	11,000
a_2	1,000	1,000	1,000	10,000

Figure 15.4: A bad example for the minimax regret.

One obvious deficiency regarding the competitive ratio is that it cannot handle zero or negative costs. This deficiency excludes the modeling of many interesting problems (e.g., insurance problems; see Example 15.6). However, perhaps a more severe criticism is illustrated in the decision problem of Figure 15.5. It is likely that a decision maker would choose a_2. The optimal action prescribed by the competitive ratio is a_1, which appears unreasonable.

	s_1	s_2	s_3	s_4
$P' = \quad a_1$	70	80	90	1/10,000
a_2	1	1	1	1

Figure 15.5: A bad example for the competitive ratio.

The pessimism–optimism index leaves the choice of the subjective parameter α open. Hence, it is not clear how to implement this index in theoretical analyses of algorithms. However, the following fundamental issue is more problematic. Consider the decision problem presented in Figure 15.6 and a decision maker with a pessimism–optimism index $\alpha = \frac{1}{2}$. The values for the three actions are $V(a) = V(b) = \frac{1}{2}$ and $V(z) = \frac{3}{4}$. Hence, both a and b are optimal and z is suboptimal. Nevertheless, action z is a probability mixture of a and b. In particular, $z = \frac{1}{2}a + \frac{1}{2}b$. Notice that any probability mixture of optimal actions will eventually choose one of the optimal actions, so how can z be suboptimal?

The principle of insufficient reason can be criticized for being extremely vague. In particular, the "basic events" are not well defined. The principle thus allows for pathological cases that lead to ambiguous or meaningless results, as in the following example. An urn is known to contain two balls. Each ball is known to be either black or white. What is the probability of drawing two balls of different colors? One possibility is that there are three

---

[5] From the discussion in Section 15.7, it will become apparent that we can address this issue by using an appropriate utility function. Specifically, if we take a logarithmic utility function in this example, the minimax regret will choose a_1. In general, it is easy to see that using the minimax regret on the transformed problem with logarithmic utilities instead of costs is equivalent to using the competitive ratio.

	s_1	s_2	s_3
a	1	0	1
b	0	1	1
z	$\frac{1}{2}$	$\frac{1}{2}$	1

Figure 15.6: A bad example for the pessimism–optimism index.

basic events in this problem that thus correspond to the three sets describing the possible states of the urn:

$$\{\text{black, black}\}, \{\text{black, white}\}, \{\text{white, white}\}.$$

Since nothing is known about these three events, according to the principle of insufficient reason, each event should be assigned a probability of $\frac{1}{3}$. Obviously, there is another possible partition according to the order of the draw, if we draw one ball at a time. Now there are four basic events, represented by the tuples:

$$\langle\text{black, black}\rangle, \langle\text{black, white}\rangle, \langle\text{white, black}\rangle, \langle\text{white, white}\rangle.$$

According to this partition, the probability of drawing balls of different color is $\frac{1}{2}$.[6]

Other criticisms of the principle of insufficient reason involve partitions of the states of the world into basic events of varying "complexities," depending on our current state of knowledge (e.g., an organism's eye may be partitioned into many small components but its brain into only a few, since relatively less is known about the brain).

Obviously, none of the above criteria is perfect. However, is any one of them reasonable or at least more reasonable than the others? How does one systematically compare decision criteria? Instead of searching in a somewhat ad hoc fashion for "counterexamples" and peculiarities of the above criteria, we proceed in a more systematic manner. One useful approach is to characterize the criteria with respect to a set of axioms. By focusing on the most basic features of decision criteria, we can better understand their strengths and weaknesses and the relation between them.

15.2.3 Algorithmic Decision Problems

Although the decision model of Section 15.1.1 is sufficient for describing simple one-shot decision problems, it does not in general capture algorithmic decision problems and criteria. We need a model within which we can refer to online and offline algorithms, request sequences, and so on. A simple and straightforward extension of this model that employs the request–answer framework of Chapter 7 is sufficient.

---

[6] One possible recovery of this problem by Sinn [316] suggests that if we do not have a sufficient explanation for why one partition is more plausible than the other, we should give equal probability to each partition. Using this idea, the probability of drawing balls of different colors is $\frac{1}{2} \cdot \frac{1}{3} + \frac{1}{2} \cdot \frac{1}{2} = \frac{5}{12}$.

Let $G = (R, \{A_i\}, \{cost_i\})$ be any request–answer system where R is the request set and A_i are the answer sets (see Chapter 7). Here, for notational simplicity, we assume that all answer sets are equal and we use A to denote this one common answer set.

With respect to G, we can refer to online and offline algorithms and request sequences. Let $\mathcal{A}$ be any nonempty set of algorithms, and let $\mathcal{S}$ be any nonempty subset of R^* (the finite sequences over R). Define the function $C : \mathcal{A} \times \mathcal{S} \to \mathbb{R}$ such that for all $a \in \mathcal{A}$ and $s \in \mathcal{S}$,

$$C(a, s) = cost_{|s|}(s, a[s]),$$

where $a[s] \in A^*$ is the sequence of answers in response to the request sequence s. For a randomized algorithm a we denote by $C(a, s)$ its expected cost. The triplet $P = (\mathcal{A}, \mathcal{S}, C)$ is called an **algorithmic decision problem (over G)**. $\mathcal{A}$ is the choice set from which the decision maker must choose an algorithm. $\mathcal{A}$ may include any (deterministic or randomized) online or offline algorithm, and the sets $\mathcal{A}$ and $\mathcal{S}$ may be finite or infinite. Recall from Chapter 7 that an offline algorithm b is optimal if for all s,

$$C(b, s) = cost_{|s|}(s, b[s]) = \inf_{x \in A^*} \{cost_{|s|}(s, x)\}.$$

As usual we let OPT denote a generic optimal offline algorithm. OPT may or may not be a member of $\mathcal{A}$; however, in either case, it is always defined with respect to G.

Let G be any request-answer system, and let $P = P_G = (\mathcal{A}, \mathcal{S}, C)$ be a decision problem over G. P is **bounded** if the function C is bounded. A bounded problem P is **closed** if for all $a \in \mathcal{A}$, $\min_s C(a, s)$ and $\max_s C(a, s)$ exist. P is ε_P-**bounded away from zero** if there is a positive constant ε_P such that for all $a \in \mathcal{A}, s \in \mathcal{S}, C(a, s) \geq \varepsilon_P$. If $\mathcal{A}$ and $\mathcal{S}$ are finite, then P is **finite**.

Let a be any algorithm (online or offline). If for some $s \in \mathcal{S}$, $C(a, s) = C(\text{OPT}, s)$, then we say that algorithm a is s-**wise optimal** (or **pointwise optimal**). Clearly, for any s, OPT is s-wise optimal. P is **well-represented** if for each $s \in \mathcal{S}$, there exists an s-wise optimal algorithm in $\mathcal{A}$. With respect to any request–answer system G, any nonempty set $\mathcal{P} = \{P_G\}$ of algorithmic decision problems is called a **problem class**.

Example 15.3 (The competitive ratio) Consider the class of decision problems $P = (\mathcal{A}, \mathcal{S}, C)$ that are well-represented and bounded away from zero. For each $s \in \mathcal{S}$, define $C^*(s) = \inf_{a \in \mathcal{A}} C(a, s)$. Since P is well-represented, $C^*(s)$ is always the optimal offline cost for the sequence s. For each algorithm $a \in \mathcal{A}$, define the value $V(a)$ as

$$V(a) = \sup_{s \in \mathcal{S}} \frac{C(a, s)}{C^*(s)}. \tag{15.1}$$

Clearly, $V(a) \geq 1$ for any algorithm a. For algorithms a, b such that $V(a)$ and $V(b)$ are not finite, we use the convention $V(a) = V(b)$. Thus, the function V assigns cardinal (real) values for algorithms and induces a preference relation $\preccurlyeq_P$ over $\mathcal{A}$, where $a \preccurlyeq_P b$ if and only if $V(a) \leq V(b)$. This preference relation defines the **competitive ratio** criterion.

Example 15.4 (The max/max ratio) Let P be an algorithmic decision problem over a request–answer system with a finite request set.[7] For any algorithm a and a positive

---

[7] The assumption that R is finite guarantees that $M_n(a)$ is well defined. Otherwise, $M_n(a)$ is defined with sup instead of max.

integer n, define

$$M_n(a) = \max_{s \in S: |s|=n} \frac{1}{n} C(a, s).$$

For each algorithm a, define its **max/max ratio** value

$$V(a) = \lim_{n \to \infty} \sup \frac{M_n(a)}{M_n(\text{OPT})}.$$

The preference relation defined by $V(\cdot)$ is called the **max/max ratio criterion**. For a finite or bounded P, the max/max ratio is identical to the minimax cost criterion.

Since the minimax cost is defined only with respect to bounded problems, the max/max ratio generalizes the minimax cost for unbounded problems. Under suitable assumptions (e.g., finiteness), all the other criteria presented in Section 15.2.1 can be defined within this algorithmic decision model.

15.3 The Competitive Ratio Axioms

In this section we present an axiom set that is shown to characterize the competitive ratio. We require the following definitions.

- Let $P = (\mathcal{A}, \mathcal{S}, C)$ and $P' = (\mathcal{A}', \mathcal{S}', C')$ be algorithmic decision problems. P and P' are **isomorphic** if there exist bijections $h : \mathcal{A} \to \mathcal{A}'$ and $g : \mathcal{S} \to \mathcal{S}'$ such that for every $a \in \mathcal{A}, s \in \mathcal{S}, C(a, s) = C'(h(a), g(s))$. In this case, we use the notation

$$P \overset{h,g}{\cong} P'.$$

- Let $a, b \in \mathcal{A}$. We say that a **strongly dominates** b if for all $s \in \mathcal{S}, C(a, s) < C(b, s)$; a **weakly dominates** b if for all s, $C(a, s) \leq C(b, s)$.
- Let E be a nonempty set of algorithms. The problem $P' = (\mathcal{A} \cup E, \mathcal{S}, C)$ is an **algorithmic extension** of $P = (\mathcal{A}, \mathcal{S}, C)$. Let $P' = (\mathcal{A}', \mathcal{S}, C)$ be an algorithmic extension of a problem $P = (\mathcal{A}, \mathcal{S}, C)$. We say that $\preccurlyeq_P$ is **equivalent to** $\preccurlyeq_{P'}$ **over** $\mathcal{A}$ if $\preccurlyeq_P$ agrees with $\preccurlyeq_{P'}$ over $\mathcal{A}$; that is, for all $a, b \in \mathcal{A}, a \preccurlyeq_P b$ if and only if $a \preccurlyeq_{P'} b$.
- For algorithms a and b and a real $p \in [0, 1]$, denote by $pa + (1 - p)b$ an algorithm whose cost, for each $s \in \mathcal{S}$, is $pC(a, s) + (1 - p)C(b, s)$ (that is, this algorithm is a probability mixture of a and b).
- Let $\{P_k = (\mathcal{A}, \mathcal{S}, C_k)\}$ be a sequence of decision problems. The sequence $\{P_k\}$ **uniformly converges** to $P = (\mathcal{A}, \mathcal{S}, C)$ if for all $a \in \mathcal{A}$, and for all $\varepsilon > 0$, there exists K such that for all $k \geq K$,

$$\sup_{s \in S} |C_k(a, s) - C(a, s)| < \varepsilon.$$

Fix any problem $P = (\mathcal{A}, \mathcal{S}, C)$. Our first axiom requires that the decision maker has a preference relation $\preccurlyeq_P$ over the algorithm set of $\mathcal{A}$.

Axiom 0 (Completeness): There exists a preference relation $\preccurlyeq_P$ over $\mathcal{A}$.

The following axioms prescribe conditions on the characteristics of $\preccurlyeq_P$.

Axiom 1 (Algorithm labeling): $\preccurlyeq_P$ is invariant under algorithm labeling. Specifically, let $P' = (\mathcal{A}', \mathcal{S}, C')$ such that

$$P \overset{h,g}{\cong} P'$$

and g is the identity. Then, for all $a, b \in \mathcal{A}$, $a \preccurlyeq_P b$ if and only if $h(a) \preccurlyeq_{P'} h(b)$.

This axiom merely states that our preference relation among algorithms should not be dependent on how we choose to label the involved algorithms. We are not familiar with any argument against this axiom.

Axiom 2 (Request sequence labeling): $\preccurlyeq_P$ is invariant under request sequences labeling. Specifically, let $P' = (\mathcal{A}, \mathcal{S}', C')$ such that

$$P \overset{h,g}{\cong} P'$$

and h is the identity. Then $\preccurlyeq_P$ is equivalent to $\preccurlyeq_{P'}$.

At the outset, Axiom 2 appears as natural as Axiom 1. However, this axiom is not quite as innocuous. Together with Axiom 5, which follows, Axiom 2 entails Lemma 15.2, which has strong consequences (as discussed after the proof of Lemma 15.2). Nevertheless, it is difficult to argue against Axiom 2 by itself.

Axiom 3 (Weak domination): If a weakly dominates b, then $a \preccurlyeq_P b$.

This axiom is perhaps the most fundamental rational requirement for *any* decision criteria.[8]

Axiom 4 (Uniform continuity): Let $\{P_k = (\mathcal{A}, \mathcal{S}, C_k)\}$ be a sequence of decision problems such that $\{P_k\}$ uniformly converges to $P = (\mathcal{A}, \mathcal{S}, C)$. Let $a, b \in \mathcal{A}$ be such that for all k, $a \preccurlyeq_{P_k} b$. Then, $a \preccurlyeq_P b$.

We require the essentially technical concept of uniformity because the axiom variant that relaxes uniformity and requires only pointwise convergence is not consistent with the competitive ratio. Consider the following sequence of problems $P_k = (\mathcal{A}, \mathcal{S}, C_k)$, where $\mathcal{A} = \{a, b\}$, $\mathcal{S} = \{s_1, s_2, s_3, \ldots\}$, and $C_k(a, s_j) = 1 + \frac{j}{k}$, $C(b, s_j) = 2$. Clearly, using the competitive ratio, the unique optimal choice is b in P_k, for each k. The sequence $\{P_k\}$ converges pointwise to $P = (\mathcal{A}, \mathcal{S}, C)$, where $C(a, s_j) = 1$ and $C(b, s_j) = 2$. However, in P, the unique optimal choice is a.

Axiom 5 (Independence of weakly dominated alternatives): Let $P' = (\mathcal{A} \cup E, \mathcal{S}, C')$ be any algorithmic extension of $P = (\mathcal{A}, \mathcal{S}, C)$ such that for all $a \in \mathcal{A}$, $s \in \mathcal{S}$, $C'(a, s) = C(a, s)$ and for all $b \in E$ and all $s \in \mathcal{S}$, there exists $a \in \mathcal{A}$ such that $C(a, s) \leq C(b, s)$. Then, $\preccurlyeq_{P'}$ is equivalent to $\preccurlyeq_P$ over $\mathcal{A}$.

---

[8] If we also accept the following Axiom 4, this weak domination axiom can be replaced by its strong dominance analogue (simply replace "weakly" with "strongly" in Axiom 3), which is a weaker requirement.

In other words, Axiom 5 states that we can add a new algorithm x to the algorithm set $\mathcal{A}$ and the preference relation between algorithms in $\mathcal{A}$ will remain the same provided that the new algorithm x is pointwise weakly dominated. Figure 15.7 illustrates this axiom. In Figure 15.7(a) we see a "legal" addition. Although the cost of the new algorithm x is a minimum in the left column, it is weakly dominated by algorithm a. The addition of y in Figure 15.7(b) is "illegal" according to Axiom 5.

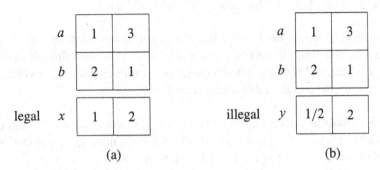

Figure 15.7: Illustration of Axiom 5.

Axiom 5 is problematic in that the weak dominance requirement seems somewhat contrived. After all, why should the addition of a new (arbitrary) algorithm to $\mathcal{A}$ alter the relative order of the other algorithms in $\mathcal{A}$? Paradoxically, it may be easier to argue in favor of a stronger (more universal) axiom, stating that $\preccurlyeq_P$ should be invariant under the addition of *any* algorithm (not necessarily a dominated one), which is precisely what is prescribed by the following axiom:

Axiom 5' (Independence of irrelevant alternatives): Let $P' = (\mathcal{A} \cup E, \mathcal{S}, C')$ be any algorithmic extension of $P = (\mathcal{A}, \mathcal{S}, C)$ such that for all $a \in \mathcal{A}$, $s \in \mathcal{S}$, $C'(a, s) = C(a, s)$. Then, $\preccurlyeq_{P'}$ is equivalent to $\preccurlyeq_P$ over $\mathcal{A}$.

Axiom 5' cannot replace Axiom 5 in any characterization of the competitive ratio. For example, in Figure 15.7 the addition of algorithm y changes the preference relation between algorithms a and b as prescribed by the competitive ratio.

One argument in favor of the weak domination condition in Axiom 5 is that in its absence, the introduction of a new algorithm that is not weakly dominated contributes new information to the decision maker because the new algorithm outperforms any of the older ones with respect to at least one input sequence. In this sense, the availability of the new algorithm may add information regarding the plausibility of the occurrence of some input sequences. Consider the following well-known hypothetical story:

> A man walks into a restaurant and sees from the menu that there are only two possible dinner main courses, roast chicken and steak. He orders the chicken. Soon after, the waiter returns from the kitchen and, after apologizing politely, says that he forgot to mention today's special, steamed Pacific salmon in a creamed dill and vodka sauce served with potatoes Dauphinois. Immediately the man changes his mind and orders the steak.

This story is based on the assumption that although mediocre restaurants tend to serve terrible steaks, they usually manage to serve a reasonable roast chicken. In more algorithmic terms, the addition of a dominating algorithm (Pacific salmon) fundamentally changes the underlying request–answer system; therefore, one cannot assume that the preference relation corresponding to the original request–answer system is maintained. This supports and motivates the domination requirement and, thus, Axiom 5.

Axiom 6 (Convexity): Let $a_1, a_2 \in \mathcal{A}$ with $a_1 \approx_P a_2$. For any $p \in [0, 1]$, let $b = pa_1 + (1 - p)a_2$. Use $P' = (\mathcal{A}', \mathcal{S}, C')$ to denote the algorithmic extension of P with $\mathcal{A}' = \mathcal{A} \cup \{b\}$. Then, $b \preccurlyeq_{P'} a_1$ and $b \preccurlyeq_{P'} a_2$.

In particular, this axiom implies that the set of optimal algorithms is convex. Axiom 6 appears to be compelling. Indeed, any probability mixture of two algorithms eventually yields one of them, and if they are both equally preferable, the outcome (which is one of them) is certainly not less desirable than any of them.[9]

Axiom 7 (Redundancy): Let $P' = (\mathcal{A}', \mathcal{S}', C')$, where $\mathcal{S}' = \mathcal{S} - E$ and C' is identical to C at all $a \in \mathcal{A}$, $s \in \mathcal{S}'$. If for all $s \in E$, there exists some $s' \in \mathcal{S}'$ such that for all $a \in \mathcal{A}$, $C'(a, s') = C(a, s)$, then $\preccurlyeq_P$ is equivalent to $\preccurlyeq_{P'}$.

Figure 15.8 illustrates Axiom 7. The axiom simply states that the two problems in Figure 15.8 are identical in the sense that the preference relations of these problems (over the algorithm set $\{a, b\}$) are identical. Axiom 7 is persuasive once we accept the underlying assumption of strict uncertainty. Indeed, given no information whatsoever about the relative likelihood of two input sequences that yield exactly the same outcomes with respect to all algorithms, we might as well strategically consolidate them into one. Axiom 7 is the axiom most closely identified with the concept of strict uncertainty. Specifically, the acceptance of Axiom 7 immediately eliminates the principle of insufficient reason.

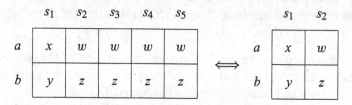

Figure 15.8: Illustration of Axiom 7.

Axiom 8 (Proportionality): Let $P = (\mathcal{A}, \mathcal{S}, C)$ be a problem ε_P-bounded away from zero (i.e., $\inf_{a,s} C(a, s) \geq \varepsilon_P > 0$). Let c be any positive real number, and let s^* be any element of $\mathcal{S}$. Set $P' = (\mathcal{A}, \mathcal{S}, C')$ such that for all $a \in \mathcal{A}$, $s \in \mathcal{S}$,

$$
C'(a, s) = \begin{cases} c \cdot C(a, s) & \text{if } s = s^*; \\ C(a, s) & \text{otherwise.} \end{cases}
$$

Then if P' is ε_P-bounded away from zero, $\preccurlyeq_{P'}$ is equivalent to $\preccurlyeq_P$.

---

[9] Luce and Raiffa [251] present, but do not advocate, the following argument against this axiom: although the final outcome of the randomized algorithm is that of one of the two underlying deterministic algorithms, the anticipation the decision maker experiences until the outcome of the random choice is determined may reduce the preferability of the randomized algorithm.

With regard to finite problems, this axiom essentially states that our preference relation is invariant under multiplication of all the elements of a column by a positive constant.

Axiom 8 is one of the more difficult axioms to justify. First, note that the requirement that P' remains εP-bounded away from zero is necessary once we also assume the continuity axiom (Axiom 4). Otherwise, it is easy to construct a sequence of decision problems that converges to a problem that has zero costs (with which the competitive ratio cannot cope). Nevertheless, the technical εP-boundedness requirement is not likely to raise conceptual objections once decision problems have been formulated in terms of a positive cost function.

One justification of Axiom 8 relates to the strict uncertainty assumption. Suppose it is known that there is a prior probability measure that will determine the choice of the input sequence but this probability measure is completely unknown. By allowing the multiplication by an arbitrary constant of all outcomes in a given column (corresponding to some input sequence), the decision maker recognizes and accepts the possibility that any probability measure can prevail.

Another justification of the proportionality axiom is that the decision maker is interested only in the relative performance of the various algorithms (in fact, this is exactly what this axiom contemplates). The axiom is perhaps related to people's tendency to measure quantities (and progress) relative to other already known or "universal" quantities.

A strong argument against Axiom 8 is based on the principle of marginal decreasing worth. Consider the two decision problems P and P' depicted in Figures 15.1 and 15.5, respectively. For many individuals the "rational" choice is: algorithm a_1 in problem P, and a_2 in problem P'. Nevertheless, if we accept Axiom 8, the relations $\preccurlyeq_P$ and $\preccurlyeq_{P'}$ are equivalent.

These are the competitive ratio axioms. The axioms that may be considered as "strict uncertainty axioms" are: Axioms 2 and 5 combined (see Lemma 15.2); Axiom 5, to some extent (although its relaxed variant, Axiom 5', is not related to strict uncertainty); Axiom 7; and, depending on its preferred justification, perhaps Axiom 8. The remaining axioms (1, 3, 4, and 6) do not appear to be related to the notion of strict uncertainty.

15.4 Characterization of the Competitive Ratio

We say that a problem $P = (\mathcal{A}, \mathcal{S}, C)$ is in **canonical form** if there exists $a^* \in \mathcal{A}$ such that for all $s \in \mathcal{S}$, $C(a^*, s) = 1$ and for all $a \in \mathcal{A}, s \in \mathcal{S}, C(a, s) \geq 1$. Notice that if P (in canonical form) is also well-represented with respect to the underlying request–answer system G, then such an algorithm a^* is an optimal offline algorithm for P.

Consider the problem class $\mathcal{P}^*$ containing all decision problems P such that P is well-represented, closed, and bounded away from zero. Notice that $\mathcal{P}^*$ contains every bounded (and, therefore, every finite) problem.

The main result of this section states that with respect to each problem in the class $\mathcal{P}^*$, the competitive ratio criterion is characterized by Axioms 0–8. For simplicity, we choose to state and prove the characterization theorem in terms of $\mathcal{P}^*$, which is a restricted class of algorithmic decision problems. The characterization can be extended (see Theorem 15.3) to a more general class of problems that captures all specific problems discussed in this text.

Theorem 15.1 (Competitive ratio characterization) *Let $P = (\mathcal{A}, \mathcal{S}, C)$ be any algorithmic decision problem in $\mathcal{P}^*$. Then the preference relation $\preccurlyeq_P$ is equivalent (i.e., defines the same preference relation) to the competitive ratio if and only if Axioms 0–8 hold.*

Theorem 15.1 is proven in two parts. The easy direction (only if) is proven in the following exercise. To prove the other (if) direction, we will need several lemmas.

Exercise 15.2 Prove that for any $P = (\mathcal{A}, \mathcal{S}, C)$ in $\mathcal{P}^*$, the preference relation over $\mathcal{A}$, defined by the competitive ratio (see Example 15.3), is consistent with Axioms 0–8.

For the remainder of this section, $P = (\mathcal{A}, \mathcal{S}, C)$ represents any problem in the class $\mathcal{P}^*$. Assuming Axioms 5 and 8, we can transform every decision problem $P = (\mathcal{A}, \mathcal{S}, C)$ that is well-represented and bounded away from zero into a problem $Q = (\mathcal{A}_Q, \mathcal{S}, C_Q)$ in canonical form such that $\mathcal{A} \subseteq \mathcal{A}_Q$ and the preference relation $\preccurlyeq_Q$ is equivalent to the preference relation $\preccurlyeq_P$ over $\mathcal{A}$. We illustrate this straightforward transformation on the following finite problem P:

	s_1	s_2
a_1	x	y
a_2	w	z

Without loss of generality, assume that a_1 is s_1-wise optimal and that a_2 is s_2-wise optimal. Now consider the following problem P':

	s_1	s_2
a_1	1	$\frac{y}{z}$
a_2	$\frac{w}{x}$	1

According to Axiom 8, the preference relation $\preccurlyeq_{P'}$ is equivalent to the preference relation $\preccurlyeq_P$. Now consider the following problem Q:

	s_1	s_2
a_1	1	$\frac{y}{z}$
a_2	$\frac{w}{x}$	1
OPT	1	1

Clearly, Q is in canonical form. Q is obtained from P' by adding OPT to its algorithm set. Since the costs of OPT in Q are (pointwise) dominated, by Axiom 5, the preference relation $\preccurlyeq_Q$ is equivalent to $\preccurlyeq_{P'}$ over $\{a_1, a_2\}$. Hence, the relation $\preccurlyeq_Q$ is equivalent to $\preccurlyeq_P$ over $\{a_1, a_2\}$. The problem Q is called "the canonical form of P."

Remark 15.1 Suppose that P is defined over a request answer system G. The constructed problems Q (and P') are, in general, no longer defined over G; nevertheless, there exists a request–answer system G' upon which they can be defined.

We have illustrated this transformation for a particular finite problem. The same transformation can be applied to any algorithmic decision problem in $\mathcal{P}^*$. We thus have the following simple lemma.

Lemma 15.1 *Assume Axioms 5 and 8. Let $P = (\mathcal{A}, \mathcal{S}, C)$ be a well-represented problem, and assume that P is ε_P-bounded away from zero ($\varepsilon_P > 0$). Then, P has an algorithmic extension in canonical form $Q = (\mathcal{A}_Q, \mathcal{S}, C_Q)$ such that $\preccurlyeq_Q$ is equivalent to $\preccurlyeq_P$ over $\mathcal{A}$.*

For the remainder of this section whenever we refer to the canonical form of a problem P, we refer to the canonical form of P as constructed in the statement of Lemma 15.1, with OPT $\in \mathcal{A}$ denoting the algorithm with $C_Q(\text{OPT}, s) = 1$ for all s. Clearly, if $P \in \mathcal{P}^*$ then the canonical form of P is also in $\mathcal{P}^*$.

The following lemma reveals the power of Axioms 2 and 5 when they are combined. For a finite problem given in a matrix form, the lemma states that we can permute any row while keeping the preference relation invariant. Although the proof of this lemma is very simple, the result is strong (and surprising).

Lemma 15.2 *Assume Axioms 2 and 5. Let $P = (\mathcal{A}, \mathcal{S}, C)$ be a problem in canonical form. Let π be any permutation of any finite subset $S' \subseteq \mathcal{S}$. Then an algorithm a is indifferent to any algorithm b if the following holds: $C(b, \pi(s)) = C(a, s)$ for all $s \in S'$ and $C(b, s) = C(a, s)$ for all $s \notin S'$.*

PROOF. We illustrate the proof with the following "small" problem $P = (\mathcal{A}, \mathcal{S}, C)$, where $\mathcal{A}$ is an arbitrary algorithm set and $\mathcal{S} = \{s_1, s_2\}$. A finite permutation of costs in this problem corresponds to one transposition, since we have only two request sequences. Using Axiom 5, it is sufficient to prove the lemma for the following problem P.

	s_1	s_2
a	x	z
b	z	x
OPT	1	1

We need to prove that $a \approx_P b$. Without loss of generality, assume that $a \preccurlyeq_P b$. Consider the three problems in Figure 15.9. These three problems are isomorphic where the isomorphisms are depicted by the arrows. Notice that the problem in the right-hand side is exactly P. Therefore, according to the first isomorphism, we have $b' \preccurlyeq_Q a'$, and by the second isomorphism, we have $b \preccurlyeq_P a$. Hence, $a \approx_P b$.

This idea can be easily extended to an arbitrary request sequence set $\mathcal{S}$ and an arbitrary finite permutation π. ∎

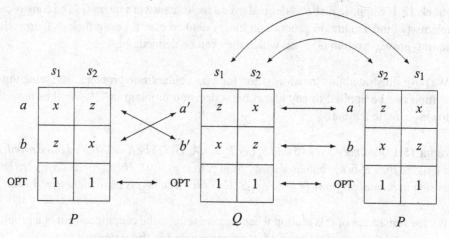

Figure 15.9: An illustration of the proof of Lemma 15.2.

Lemma 15.2 has several striking corollaries. For a problem with a finite $\mathcal{S}$, the lemma excludes all probability distributions except for the uniform distribution. Hence, once we accept Axioms 2 and 5, any other "distributional" decision making approach is essentially out of the question!

The same conclusions hold even when we replace Axiom 5 by the weaker Axiom 5′ since nowhere in the proof do we need the stronger requirement of pointwise domination.

We use Lemma 15.2 to prove that any two algorithms that attain the same minimum and the same maximum are indifferent. Formally, we state the following lemma.

Lemma 15.3 *Assume Axioms 1–3, 5, and 7. Let $P = (\mathcal{A}, \mathcal{S}, C)$ be a closed problem in canonical form. Let $a, b \in \mathcal{A}$ such that $m = \min_s C(a, s) = \min_s C(b, s)$ and $M = \max_s C(a, s) = \max_s C(b, s)$. Then $a \approx_P b$.*

PROOF. We illustrate the proof with the following finite problem P. The generalization of the proof for an arbitrary (closed) problem is straightforward.

	s_1	s_2	s_3	s_4
a		m		M
$P = b$	M		m	
OPT	1	1	1	1

Using Lemma 15.2, we can permute the first row so that the minimum and maximum costs of a and b occur on the same column. Specifically, we permute the first row so that both minimums occur at s_3 and both maximums occur at s_1. The preference relation $\preccurlyeq_P$ remains the same. We now construct the following algorithmic extension of P where we add to $\mathcal{A}$ the two algorithms χ_m and χ_M.

	s_1	s_2	s_3	s_4
a	M		m	
b	M		m	
$P' = \chi_m$	M	m	m	m
χ_M	M	M	m	M
OPT	1	1	1	1

According to Axiom 5, the preference relation $\preccurlyeq_{P'}$ is equivalent to $\preccurlyeq_P$ over $\{a, b, \text{OPT}\}$. According to the weak domination axiom (Axiom 3), we have

$$\chi_m \preccurlyeq_{P'} a, b \preccurlyeq_{P'} \chi_m.$$

To complete the proof of the lemma, it is now sufficient to prove that $\chi_m \approx_{P'} \chi_M$. Consider the following "subproblem" of P':

	s_1	s_2	s_3	s_4
χ_m	M	m	m	m
$P'' = \chi_M$	M	M	m	M
OPT	1	1	1	1

According to Axiom 5, the preference relation $\preccurlyeq_{P''}$ is equivalent to $\preccurlyeq_{P'}$ over $\{\chi_m, \chi_M, \text{OPT}\}$. Transpose the first and third elements of P'' in the row corresponding to χ_M. According to Lemma 15.2, the resulting row is indifferent to χ_M. Now delete the third and fourth columns. According to Axiom 7, this transformation keeps the preference relation invariant. We are left with the following problem.

	s_1	s_2
χ_m	M	m
χ_M	m	M
OPT	1	1

According to Lemma 15.2, in this problem χ_m is indifferent to χ_M. The proof is complete. ∎

Lemma 15.3 implies that for any closed problem in canonical form, the preference relation between algorithms depends only on the maximums and minimums obtained by the algorithms.

We need one more lemma for the proof of the characterization theorem.

Lemma 15.4 *Assume Axioms 1–7. Consider the following finite problem* $P = (\mathcal{A}, \mathcal{S}, C)$, *where* $\mathcal{A} = \{a, b, \text{OPT}\}$, $\mathcal{S} = \{s_1, s_2\}$, *and* C *are given by the following cost matrix:*

	s_1	s_2
a	m	M
b	M	M
OPT	1	1

where $M \geq m$. *Then,* $a \approx_P b$.

PROOF. We first prove the following claim.

Claim: Let y and Y be any real numbers such that $y \leq Y$. Consider the following problem:

		s_1	s_2
	c	y	Y
$P(y, Y) =$	d	Y	$\frac{y+Y}{2}$
	OPT	1	1

Then, in $P = P(y, Y)$, $d \preccurlyeq_P c$.

The proof of the claim is easily obtained by considering the following problem P':

		s_1	s_2	s_3
	a	Y	Y	y
	b	Y	y	Y
$P' =$	c	y	Y	Y
	d	Y	$\frac{y+Y}{2}$	$\frac{y+Y}{2}$
	OPT	1	1	1

According to Lemma 15.2, $a \approx_{P'} b \approx_{P'} c$. Applying Axiom 6 to a and b with $p = \frac{1}{2}$, we have $d \preccurlyeq_{P_1} a$ and $d \preccurlyeq_{P_1} b$. By transitivity, $d \preccurlyeq_{P_1} c$. The claim is then obtained by Axioms 5 and 7.

Using the claim, we can now prove the lemma. Let $m \leq M$, and consider the following infinite sequence of problems $\{Q_k\}$ where the the general (kth) element is

		s_1	s_2
	c_k	m	M
$Q_k =$	d_k	M	$\left(1 - \frac{1}{2^k}\right)M + \frac{m}{2^k}$
	OPT	1	1

It is easy to see that the sequence $\{Q_k\}$ converges uniformly to

		s_1	s_2
	c	m	M
$Q =$	d	M	M
	OPT	1	1

It is now sufficient to prove that for every k, we have $d_k \preccurlyeq_{Q_k} c_k$, since Axiom 4 implies $d \preccurlyeq_Q c$, while Axiom 3 shows $c \preccurlyeq_Q d$. Hence, $c \approx_Q d$, and the proof is complete using Axiom 1.

It remains to prove that $d_k \preccurlyeq_{Q_k} c_k$ for every k. This is easily established by induction on k. The base case, $k = 1$, holds according to the preceding claim. Assume the induction hypothesis for $k = j$. Set

$$m' = \left(1 - \frac{1}{2^j}\right) M + \frac{m}{2^k}.$$

Now consider the following problem:

		s_1	s_2
	a	m	M
	b	m'	M
$P =$	c	M	$\frac{y+M}{2}$
	OPT	1	1

According to the claim, with $Y = M$ and $y = m'$ and using Axioms 5, 1, and 2 and Lemma 15.2, we have $c \preccurlyeq_P b$. From the induction hypothesis, it follows that $b \preccurlyeq_P a$, so $c \preccurlyeq_P a$.   ∎

Lemma 15.4 implies the following simple but very important corollary stating that the preference relation among algorithms depends only on the maximums they obtain.

Corollary 15.2 *Assume Axioms 1–7. Let $P = (\mathcal{A}, \mathcal{S}, C)$ be a closed problem in canonical form. Let $a, b \in \mathcal{A}$ such that $M = \max_s C(a, s) = \max_s C(b, s)$. Then $a \approx_P b$.*

PROOF. Using Axioms 1, 2, 5, and 7 and Lemma 15.3, proving the indifference of a and b in P is equivalent to proving the indifference of a' and b' in the following finite problem:

$$
P' = \quad
\begin{array}{c|c|c|}
 & s_1 & s_2 \\
\hline
a' & M & m_1 \\
\hline
b' & M & m_2 \\
\hline
\chi & M & M \\
\hline
\text{OPT} & 1 & 1 \\
\hline
\end{array}
$$

where $m_1 = \min_s C(a, s)$ and $m_2 = \min_s C(b, s)$. Based on Lemma 15.4, $a' \approx_{P'} \chi$ and $\chi \approx_{P'} b'$, so by transitivity, $a' \approx_{P'} b'$. ∎

We are now ready to prove the second part of Theorem 15.1.

Proof of Theorem 15.1 (if direction). Given any problem $P \in \mathcal{P}^*$, consider its canonical form $P' = (\mathcal{A}', \mathcal{S}, C')$. According to Lemma 15.1, $\preccurlyeq_{P'}$ is equivalent to $\preccurlyeq_P$ over $\mathcal{A}$. Note that P' is closed, since P is closed. Hence, for each $a \in \mathcal{A}'$, $M_a = \max_s C(a, s)$ exists. Using Corollary 15.2, we can modify C' so that for each algorithm $a \in \mathcal{A}'$, the cost function $C'(a, s) = M_a$ for all s. This transformation preserves the preference relation $\preccurlyeq_{P'}$. In this modified problem, for any $a, b \in \mathcal{A}'$, either a weakly dominates b or b weakly dominates a. Therefore, according to Axiom 3, for each $a, b \in \mathcal{A}'$, $a \preccurlyeq_{P''} b$ if and only if a weakly dominates b if and only if $M_a \leq M_b$. This preference relation is clearly equivalent to the competitive ratio. ∎

Theorem 15.1 can be strengthened in terms of how it applies to nonclosed problems. This extension is somewhat technical, and we leave the proof of the following theorem as an exercise.

Theorem 15.3 *Consider any problem $P = (\mathcal{A}, \mathcal{S}, C)$. For each algorithm $a \in \mathcal{A}$, abbreviate*

$$\sup^{(P)}(a) = \sup_s C(a, s);$$

$$\inf^{(P)}(a) = \inf_s C(a, s).$$

Similarly, whenever $\max_s C(a, s)$ and $\min_s C(a, s)$ are defined, abbreviate

$$\max^{(P)}(a) = \max_s C(a, s);$$

$$\min^{(P)}(a) = \min_s C(a, s).$$

Let $P' = (\mathcal{A}', \mathcal{S}, C')$ be the canonical form of a problem $P = (\mathcal{A}, \mathcal{S}, C)$. We say that P is sup-bounded if $\sup^{(P')}(a) < \infty$ for all $a \in \mathcal{A}'$. Let $\hat{\mathcal{A}} \subset \mathcal{A}'$ be the set of algorithms a for which either $\max^{(P')}(a)$ or $\min^{(P')}(a)$ is not defined (but with $\sup^{(P')}(a) < \infty$). P is approximable if and only if

$$\inf_{a \in \hat{\mathcal{A}}} \left\{ \sup^{(P)}(a) - \inf^{(P)}(a) \right\} > 0. \tag{15.2}$$

Define $\mathcal{P}^{**}$ as the class of all algorithmic decision problems P such that (i) P is well-represented; (ii) P is bounded away from zero; (iii) P is sup-bounded; and (iv) P is approximable.

For any problem $P \in \mathcal{P}^{**}$, the preference relation $\preceq_P$ is equivalent to the competitive ratio if and only if Axioms 0–8 hold.

Exercise 15.3 Prove Theorem 15.3.

15.5   Characterizations of the Classical Criteria for Strict Uncertainty

In this section we present and discuss characterizations of the classical criteria for strict uncertainty (see Section 15.2.1). Some of these characterizations are based on axioms that are different from the competitive ratio axioms; however, in general, there is much overlap between the various axiom sets, which allows us to compare the various criteria.

15.5.1   Characterization of the Minimax Cost

For problems in canonical form, the competitive ratio preference relation is identical to the minimax cost. Hence, it is easy to modify the proof of Corollary 15.2 and its underlying lemmas so that the minimax cost is characterized by the assumptions of Axioms 0–7. Further, in this characterization of the minimax cost, Axiom 5 can be replaced by the stronger Axiom 5'. Thus, we have the following theorem.

Theorem 15.4 (Characterization of minimax cost) Let $P = (\mathcal{A}, \mathcal{S}, C)$ be any bounded algorithmic decision problem, and consider any preference relation over $\mathcal{A}$. Then this preference relation is equivalent to the minimax cost if and only if Axioms 0–4, 5', 6, and 7 hold.

15.5.2   Characterization of the Minimax Regret

Obviously, the essential difference between the competitive ratio and the minimax regret criterion is that of multiplication versus addition. For the characterization of the minimax regret, we therefore consider the following axiom, presented in terms of a finite problem.

Axiom 8' (Column linearity): $\preceq_P$ is invariant under the addition of a constant to all the elements of a column.

Axiom $8'$ is the additive analogue of Axiom 8. Assuming Axiom $8'$ instead of Axiom 8, a characterization of the minimax regret can essentially be obtained by using the ideas in Theorem 15.1. All that is needed is to modify the definition of the canonical form of a problem. Specifically, for each column, instead of dividing each element of the column by its minimum element, we subtract this minimum element. Then we add to the cost matrix a new row consisting of 0's instead of 1's. The rest of the proof (relying on Corollary 15.2) is essentially the same. Of course, the costs must be bounded below by some constant (that may be negative).

Theorem 15.5 (Characterization of minimax regret) *Let* $P = (\mathcal{A}, \mathcal{S}, \mathcal{C})$ *be any bounded (below) algorithmic decision problem, and consider any preference relation over* $\mathcal{A}$. *Then this preference relation is equivalent to the minimax regret if and only if Axioms 0–7 and $8'$ hold.*

From the viewpoint of a rational decision maker, the choice between the competitive ratio and the minimax regret depends upon which axiom is accepted: Axiom 8 or Axiom $8'$.

Axiom $8'$ has the same drawback as Axiom 8 with regard to marginal decreasing worth. As with the example that demonstrated this weakness in Axiom 8 (Section 15.3), it is easy to construct examples in which an addition (or subtraction) of large constants to some columns may drastically change the decision maker's desired preference relation over the rows.

However, here is one justifying argument for Axiom $8'$. Suppose that a decision maker is promised that no matter what his choice is, if $s^* \in \mathcal{S}$ occurs, he will obtain a bonus of x dollars. Under such circumstances (and ignoring problems that result from marginal decreasing worth!), it is very reasonable for a rational decision maker to maintain his preferences independent of the value of x.[10]

15.5.3   Characterization of the Principle of Insufficient Reason

A characterization of the principle of insufficient reason is obtainable based on Axioms 1–3, $5'$, and $8'$. Of course, this criterion requires that the set $\mathcal{S}$ of request sequences (states of nature) is finite.

Theorem 15.6 (Characterization of the principle of insufficient reason) *Let $P = (\mathcal{A}, \mathcal{S}, \mathcal{C})$ be any algorithmic decision problem with a finite $\mathcal{S}$. Consider any preference relation over $\mathcal{A}$. Then this preference relation is equivalent to the principle of insufficient reason if and only if Axioms 1–3, $5'$, and $8'$ hold.*

Exercise 15.4 Prove Theorem 15.6.

We previously argued that Axioms 1–3, $5'$, and $8'$ are well-motivated. Moreover, the principle of insufficient reason is compatible with Axioms 4 and 6, which also appear to be compelling. Nevertheless, the principle of insufficient reason is not consistent with the noncontroversial Axiom 7. Hence, the rationality of the principle of insufficient reason with respect to problems with finite $\mathcal{S}$ depends upon the acceptance or rejection of Axiom 7.

---

[10] Chernoff [96] presents a more elaborate defense of Axiom $8'$.

15.5.4 Characterizations of the Pessimism–Optimism Index

Consider the following axiom.

> **Axiom 9 (Linearity):** The ordering of algorithms is invariant under positive linear transformation of the cost function. Specifically, let $P' = (\mathcal{A}, \mathcal{S}, C')$, where $C' = \lambda C + \beta$ ($\lambda > 0$). Then, $\preceq_{P'}$ is equivalent to $\preceq_P$.

This axiom states that our preference relation is invariant under scaling and translation of the cost function. For instance, if costs are given by temperatures, it should not matter if we choose the Fahrenheit or the Celsius scale. This axiom appears to be fundamentally compelling. Note that the competitive ratio is inconsistent with this axiom (it is consistent only with scaling). In contrast, the minimax cost, the minimax regret, and the principle of insufficient reason are compatible with this axiom. This is one of the more compelling arguments favoring, for example, the minimax regret over the competitive ratio. (See also the discussion preceding Open Question 15.3 for another argument favoring the minimax regret.)

Theorem 15.7 (Characterization of the pessimism–optimism index) *Let* $P = (\mathcal{A}, \mathcal{S}, C)$ *be any bounded algorithmic decision problem. Consider any preference relation over* $\mathcal{A}$. *Then this preference relation is equivalent to the pessimism–optimism index if and only if Axioms 1–4, 5', 7, and 9 hold.*

Exercise 15.5 Prove Theorem 15.7.

Although the Axiom set 1–4, 5', 7, and 9 is appealing, the resulting criterion contradicts the fundamental convexity axiom (Axiom 6), which significantly diminishes its attractiveness (see the counterexample shown in Figure 15.6).

Table 15.1 summarizes the above results regarding consistency versus inconsistency with the axioms and the characterizations of the various criteria for strict uncertainty.

Table 15.1: Axioms and criteria for strict uncertainty.

Criterion											
	Axiom										
	1	2	3	4	5	5'	6	7	8	8'	9
Competitive ratio	⊕	⊕	⊕	⊕	⊕	−	⊕	⊕	⊕	−	−
Minimax cost	⊕	⊕	⊕	⊕	+	⊕	⊕	⊕	−	+	+
Minimax regret	⊕	⊕	⊕	⊕	⊕	−	⊕	⊕	−	⊕	+
Insufficient reason	⊕	⊕	⊕	+	+	⊕	+	−	−	⊕	+
Pessimism–optimism	⊕	⊕	⊕	⊕	+	⊕	−	⊕	−	−	⊕

Note: + denotes consistency with an axiom; − denotes inconsistency; and ⊕ denotes characterization.

15.6 An Example – The Leasing Problem

In this section we focus on a simple **leasing problem**, known in the computer science literature as "the ski rental problem" (see Example 9.3). For this decision problem, we construct the optimal algorithms dictated by the various criteria discussed in this chapter.

The finite leasing problem can be stated as follows. Let $N > 1$ be an integer. A decision maker needs to use some equipment for some number n of periods, $1 \le n \le N$. We assume that the bound N is known to the decision maker but n is unknown. At the start of each time period, it becomes known whether or not the equipment will be needed for the current period; the decision maker must choose between two options:

(i) Renting the equipment during the current period for a rental fee r.
(ii) Purchasing the equipment for a larger amount p.

Of course, once the decision maker has purchased the equipment, he no longer has to pay rental fees; however, he may no longer need the equipment in subsequent periods. For simplicity, we assume that $k = \frac{p}{r} > 1$ is an integer. The total cost incurred by the decision maker is the sum of all rentals plus, perhaps, one purchase cost.

This model provides a reasonable abstraction to leasing problems in which the equipment, once bought, cannot be sold after some periods of use (or can be sold, but for a negligible amount). In what follows, we analyze and identify optimal deterministic algorithms for the leasing problem, using the various criteria for strict uncertainty.

First, we explicitly describe the leasing problem as a decision problem $(\mathcal{A}, \mathcal{S}, C)$ in terms of the parameters N, p, and r. Clearly, $\mathcal{S} = \{1, 2, \ldots, N\}$ and $\mathcal{A} = \{s(t) \mid 1 \le t \le N + 1\}$, where for $t \le N$, $s(t)$ is the following deterministic strategy:

$$s(t) = \text{rent } t - 1 \text{ periods and then buy,}$$

and $s(N + 1)$ is the strategy that always rents. Thus, the cost function is

$$C(s(t), n) = \begin{cases} nr & \text{if } n < t; \\ (t - 1)r + p & \text{otherwise.} \end{cases}$$

Finally, notice that $C(\text{OPT}, n) = \min\{p, nr\}$.

15.6.1   The Principle of Insufficient Reason

For $t = 1, 2, \ldots, N + 1$, let $V(s(t))$ denote the average cost of $s(t)$ with respect to a uniform probability distribution over $\mathcal{S}$. Thus, for $1 \le t \le N$,

$$V(s(t)) = \frac{1}{N} \sum_{n=1}^{N} C(s(t), n)$$

$$= \frac{1}{N} \left(\sum_{n=1}^{t-1} nr + \sum_{n=t}^{N} ((t - 1)r + p) \right)$$

$$= \frac{1}{N} \left(\frac{1}{2} rt(t - 1) + (N + 1 - t)(tr - r + p) \right)$$

$$= \frac{1}{N} \left(-\frac{1}{2} rt^2 + \left(\frac{3}{2} r + Nr - p \right) t + (N + 1)(p - r) \right). \tag{15.3}$$

In equation (15.3) only the first two terms depend on t, and the parabola $-\frac{1}{2} rt^2 + (\frac{3}{2} r + Nr - p)t$ obtains its minimums at the boundaries, $t = 1$ and $t = N$. At these points, the values of $V(s(t))$ are $V(s(1)) = p$ and $V(s(N)) = \frac{rN(N+1)+2p-2r}{2N}$. Now consider $V(s(N+1))$. Clearly,

$$V(s(N+1)) = \sum_{n=1}^{N} rn = \frac{r(N+1)}{2N}.$$

It is easy to see that for all $N > 1$, $V(s(1)) < V(s(N))$. Also, $V(s(1)) \leq V(s(N+1))$ if and only if $k \leq \frac{1}{2}N(N+1)$. Hence, the optimal strategy, according to the principle of insufficient reason, is to buy immediately (i.e., use $s(1)$) if $k \leq \frac{1}{2}N(N+1)$ and always to rent (i.e., use $s(N+1)$) otherwise.

15.6.2 The Minimax Regret

For each n and t, the maximum regret, if $s(t)$ is chosen, is

$$V(s(t)) = \max_{n} \{C(s(t), n) - C(\text{OPT}, n)\}.$$

It is not difficult to see that

$$V(s(t)) = \begin{cases} p - r & \text{if } t \in [1, k]; \\ p + (i-1)r & \text{if } t = k+i, i = 1, 2, \ldots, N-k; \\ p\left(\frac{N}{k} - 1\right) & \text{if } t = N+1. \end{cases}$$

Hence, whenever $k < \frac{N+1}{2}$, the set of optimal algorithms, according to the minimax regret, is $S = \{s(1), s(2), \ldots, s(k)\}$. Otherwise, if $k > \frac{N+1}{2}$, the unique optimal strategy is $s(N+1)$, and when $k = \frac{N+1}{2}$, the set of optimal strategies is $S \cup \{s(N+1)\}$.

15.6.3 The Competitive Ratio

For each n and t, the maximum competitive ratio if $s(t)$ is chosen is

$$V(s(t)) = \max_{n} \left\{ \frac{C(s(t), n)}{C(\text{OPT}, n)} \right\},$$

which is given by

$$V(s(t)) = \begin{cases} 1 + \frac{k-1}{t} & \text{if } t \in [1, k]; \\ 2 + \frac{i-1}{k} & \text{if } t = k+i, i = 1, 2, \ldots, N-k; \\ \frac{N}{k} & \text{if } t = N+1. \end{cases}$$

Clearly, when $t \in [1, k]$, $V(s(t))$ is decreasing and attains its minimum at $t = k$, with $V(s(k)) = 2 - \frac{1}{k}$. When $t \in [k+1, N]$, $V(s(t))$ is increasing and attains its minimum at $t = k+1$, with $V(s(k+1)) = 2$. Hence, according to the competitive ratio, whenever $k < \frac{N+1}{2}$, the unique optimal algorithm is $s(k)$. Whenever $k > \frac{N+1}{2}$, the unique optimal algorithm is $s(N+1)$, and if $k = \frac{N+1}{2}$, they are both optimal.

15.6.4   The Pessimism–Optimism Index

For each t, the worst possible events when $s(t)$ is chosen are those where $n \geq t$, in which case, $C(s(t), n) = C(s(t), t) = (t - 1)r + p$. The best possible event for $s(t)$, $t > 1$, is when $n = 1$, in which case, $C(s(t), 1) = r$. For $t = 1$, the worst case is also the best case. Hence, for each pessimism–optimism index $\alpha \in [0, 1]$, and $t > 1$, we have

$$V(s(t)) = \alpha ((t - 1)r + p) + (1 - \alpha)r$$
$$= \alpha r(t - 2) + \alpha p + r.$$

For $t = 1$, we have

$$V(s(1)) = \alpha p + (1 - \alpha)p = p.$$

For $t = N + 1$, we have

$$V(s(N + 1)) = \frac{p}{k} (\alpha(N - 1) + 1).$$

Hence, for all α, it follows that $s(N + 1)$ is the unique optimal algorithm if $k > N - 1$. Otherwise, the best alternative is either $s(1)$ or $s(2)$ (notice that $V(s(t))$ is increasing with t when $t > 1$ and the minimum is obtained at $t = 2$). It is not difficult to see that whenever $k < N - 1$, for all $\alpha > 1 - \frac{r}{p}$, $s(1)$ is the unique optimal algorithm, and for all $\alpha < 1 - \frac{r}{p}$, $s(2)$ is the unique optimal algorithm. Both $s(1)$ and $s(2)$ are optimal when

$$\alpha = 1 - \frac{r}{p},$$

and whenever $k = N - 1$, $s(N + 1)$ is optimal.

15.6.5   The Minimax Cost

Since the minimax cost value is equivalent to the pessimism–optimism index with $\alpha = 1$, we deduce that the optimal solution, according to the minimax cost criterion, is $s(1)$ if $k \leq N - 1$ and $s(N + 1)$ if $k > N - 1$.

15.6.6   A Specific Instance of the Leasing Problem

Although it is not reasonable to assess the overall rationality of the various criteria based on one example, it is interesting to examine the various "optimal" algorithms suggested for the leasing problem. For concreteness, we focus on the case $k = \frac{p}{r} = 16$. With respect to periods measured in days, this ratio roughly approximates real-life rental problems, such as ski rentals.[11]

The choice of N is somewhat complicated. Notice, however, that the only crucial factor in all the above solutions is the relation between N and k. In any case, the strategy

---

[11] For comparable equipment, the 1997 cost of a full set of reasonable-quality ski equipment (skis, bindings, poles, boots) is between $500 and $550 (Canadian dollars), whereas the daily rental costs between $30 and $35. Price quotation is courtesy of Humber Trails Bicycle and Ski Shoppe, Toronto.

$S(N + 1)$ will never be involved in the optimal solution if $N > 15$, which is a very reasonable assumption, since N is an upper bound on the number of possible ski days.

According to the principle of insufficient reason, the decision maker must immediately buy the ski equipment.

The minimax regret recommends buying the equipment after 0–15 rental periods. This criterion is unable to distinguish between the first k strategies, which appears to be a serious drawback. Nevertheless, recall that we have restricted ourselves in this exercise to deterministic strategies and, in general, for the minimax regret (as well as the minimax cost and the competitive ratio) better strategies (i.e., smaller values of V) are possible with the use of randomization (see Chapter 6). Hence, it seems reasonable to break the symmetry by randomizing among the first k algorithms. Indeed, this is the optimal randomized algorithm according to the minimax regret (see Exercise 15.6).

The competitive ratio recommends renting the ski equipment for 15 periods and then buying. This strategy provides a "performance guarantee" factor of less than 2.

The optimal choices of the pessimism–optimism index and the minimax cost are essentially to buy immediately.

Hence, we observe two qualitatively different solutions: either buy immediately, or buy somewhere in the middle, with the randomized minimax regret in some sense bridging the two solutions. Which one of these solutions is more sensible? Clearly, the answer depends on the application.[12]

Exercise 15.6 Determine the optimal randomized strategies with respect to the competitive ratio, minimax cost, and minimax regret.

Exercise 15.7 With respect to the competitive ratio, determine the optimal (deterministic and randomized) algorithm according to the various decision criteria for the following generalization of the leasing problem.

Leasing with discounting. Assume a fixed discounting factor (or interest rate) i.

15.7 Decision Making Under Risk

Decision problems under risk are perhaps the most studied class of decision problems under uncertainty. Although the consequences of decisions are uncertain, the uncertainties are unambiguously quantifiable in the form of probabilities. Throughout this section we are not concerned with how these probabilities are obtained; we simply assume that there are correct, "objective" probabilities. Two fundamental concepts relevant to risk problems are utility functions and risk aversion. After introducing these concepts, we discuss several decision criteria for problems under risk. Following the literature in this area, we formulate these concepts in terms of profit maximization problems.

---

[12] The leasing problem is, of course, an abstraction of various practical problems. For example, a repeated version of this leasing problem (called "snoopy caching," see Karlin, Manasse, Rudolph, and Sleator [212]) has an application for maintaining memory coherency in shared memory computer systems. An empirical study of snoopy caching heuristics by Eggers and Katz [137] found that with respect to inputs that simulated some real applications, the better strategies were always to rent or to buy immediately.

15.7.1   Utility Functions and Attitudes Toward Risk

Define a **lottery** as any probability distribution over a set of prizes (or outcomes). Now suppose that in a lottery L there are n monetary (dollar) prizes $z_1, z_2, \ldots, z_n$, and assume that a player that participates in this lottery will receive z_i dollars with probability p_i, where $\sum_i p_i = 1$. The central question now is how much one is willing to pay in order to participate in such a lottery and thus be able to rank all probability distributions (over this set of prizes) according to their desirability.

During the seventeenth century, when the development of modern probability theory took place, mathematicians such as Pascal and Fermat believed that the "fair value" of such lotteries is given by their expected dollar return. That is, the value of the lottery L was assumed to be $\sum_i p_i z_i$. Later, it was realized that the expected dollar return is not necessarily the fair value of a lottery.

Suppose the following two lotteries are offered. In the first lottery an individual can participate for $1. This (risky, but very familiar) lottery pays $1,000,000 with probability $\frac{1}{2,000,000}$ and $0 otherwise. The participation price of the second lottery is again $1, and it returns $1 with certainty. Although the expected value of the second lottery is twice that of the first lottery, many individuals will choose the first lottery.

In contrast, consider the following two lotteries. The participation price for both lotteries is $1,000,000. The first (risky) lottery returns $12,000,000 with probability $\frac{1}{4}$ and $0 otherwise, whereas the second lottery returns $1,500,000 with certainty.

The second set of lotteries is somewhat reminiscent of the more dramatic St. Petersburg paradox posed by Nicholas Bernoulli in 1728.

Example 15.5 (The St. Petersburg paradox) There is a story about a casino in St. Petersburg that was willing to run any lottery, provided that the management could "appropriately" set the participation price. The following lottery was proposed. In a (fair) coin game, the gambler receives 2^n dollars if the first heads occurs on the nth trial. What should be the participation price for this lottery? How much would *you* be willing to pay in order to participate in this lottery?

It is easy to see that the expected dollar return of this lottery is infinite, namely,

$$\tfrac{1}{2} \cdot 1 + \tfrac{1}{4} \cdot 2 + \tfrac{1}{8} \cdot 4 + \cdots = \tfrac{1}{2} + \tfrac{1}{2} + \tfrac{1}{2} + \cdots.$$

Nevertheless, it is difficult to believe that there is anyone who would be willing to pay an arbitrarily large amount for the privilege of participating in this gamble.

In fact, the unbounded prizes offered in the St. Petersburg lottery are not essential for making the point. Redefining this lottery so that the number of coin tosses is at most 1,000,000 results in an expected return of $500,000. However, it would still be difficult to find individuals who would be willing to pay a sum close to $500,000 for participating in the modified lottery.

In order to resolve the St. Petersburg "paradox" and defend the principle that people try to behave according to expected values, Daniel Bernoulli (Nicholas' cousin) suggested that the "true" value of money grows at a diminishing rate (see Bernoulli [63, 64]); that is, the value of money is an increasing but concave function. Specifically, he suggested that the intrinsic value of x is $\log x$ (to some base) and then the paradox appears to be solved. For example, when we use $\ln x$ for the intrinsic value of x, the expected intrinsic value of the St. Petersburg lottery becomes $\sum_i \ln \frac{2^i}{2^i} = 2\ln 2 \approx 1.39$. The (monetary) **certainty equivalent** of this value is the number of \$$x$ such that $\ln(x) = 2\ln 2$; that is, $x = \$4$, which is the value an individual would be willing to pay to participate in the St. Petersburg lottery. The (log) function that gives this "intrinsic" value of money is called a **utility function**. Independently, Cramer [124] also resolved this paradox and suggested using $\sqrt{x}$ to measure the utility of \$$x$, which gives an expected utility of

$$\sum_i \frac{\sqrt{2^i}}{2^i} = \sum_i \frac{1}{\sqrt{2^i}} = \frac{1}{1 - (1/\sqrt{2})} \approx 3.41,$$

and a certainty equivalent of approximately \$11.65.

Both these solutions are based on simple but profound ideas. First of all, it is assumed that individuals prefer more money to less money. Second, as discussed in Section 15.2.2, the principle of diminishing marginal utility argues that the determination of the value of a prospect must not be based on its price but rather on the utility it yields, and the utility of a gain depends on one's wealth.

The use of either Bernoulli's logarithmic or Cramer's square root utility function seems to provide an elegant way out of the paradox. However, consider the following variation of the St. Petersburg lottery. Given a decision maker with a Bernoulli or Cramer utility function $U(x)$, assume that for every integer n there is some amount x_n such that $U(x_n) = 2^n$. Modify the St. Petersburg lottery so that the prize corresponding to a first head in the nth trial is x_n. Both Bernoulli and Cramer are now willing to pay all they have in order to participate in the modified gamble!

The paradox seems to have reappeared. Nevertheless, there are various ways out. Perhaps the most obvious is to consider *bounded* utility functions. Recalling that utilities are supposed to represent the "amount of satisfaction," the idea that all utilities are bounded makes some sense. Undervaluation of *small probabilities* also resolves this "paradox"; that is, we may regard events whose probability is smaller than some critical value to be "impossible." Since the probability that head will not appear until the nth trial becomes negligible very quickly, the resulting expectation is finite. However, underevaluation is in general problematic, since we may have a finite partition into events all of which have probability smaller than some proposed critical value. It would be contradictory (to basic probabilistic reasoning) to claim that all events are impossible.

We turn again to *unbounded* marginal decreasing utility functions as in the original Bernoulli–Cramer solutions. A different conceptual problem with these solutions is that they are fundamentally ad hoc. There is no obvious reason why the utility, among all monotone and concave functions that give diminishing worth for money, should be measured by the logarithm or the square root. In particular, it would be reasonable to assume that the satisfaction from gains (and the rate at which this satisfaction diminishes) is a subjective quantity. Further, we cannot exclude the possibility that for some individuals this satisfaction does not diminish with the gain, or that for some, it even increases. Indeed, this seems plausible and we shall pursue this idea somewhat further.

An individual who is not willing to pay the expected monetary return of the lottery and requires some price reduction is called **risk-averse**. This price reduction is called a **risk premium**. That is, in any nontrivial lottery the certainty equivalent of a risk-averse player is smaller than the expected monetary value of the lottery (i.e., its fair value). Similarly, a player whose certainty equivalent is larger than the fair value of any lottery is called

risk-seeking. Finally, when the certainty equivalent equals the fair value, the player is called **risk-neutral**. As we see in the following exercise, these notions are well captured by concavity/convexity. (See also Section 15.7.4.)

Exercise 15.8 Suppose that a player uses a utility function U and evaluates the price of a lottery by its expected utility. Prove that (i) the player is risk-averse if and only if U is strictly concave; (ii) the player is risk-neutral if and only if U is linear; and (iii) the player is risk-seeking if and only if U is strictly convex.

Example 15.6 (Risk versus insurance) Consider a player endowed with a wealth of $\$w$. The player has the option of insuring his wealth. In case of a disaster, the player without insurance will lose his entire wealth. For a premium of $\$b$, the player can insure his wealth so that in case of a disaster the insurance company will compensate him for the amount of $\$w - \$b$ (his wealth after paying the premium). The player must decide whether to insure himself or take the risk of losing everything. This problem is summarized in the following decision matrix.

	Disaster	No disaster
Insurance	$\$w - \$b$	$\$w - \$b$
No insurance	$\$0$	$\$w$

Suppose that the probability of a disaster is exactly p and known to the player. The choice of no insurance is a choice to play the lottery specified by the second row (i.e., outcomes $\$0$ and $\$w$ with probabilities p and $1 - p$, respectively). Choosing to insure is therefore a choice of opting out of the risk situation (the lottery) by choosing the "lottery," giving a sure outcome of $\$w - \$b$. Now suppose that the player knows his utility function U. The choice of whether or not to insure reduces to whether or not the monetary certainty equivalent of the lottery, $U^{-1}((1 - p)U(w))$, is larger or smaller than $\$w - \$b$. The more that the player is risk-averse, the smaller this certainty equivalent is, which means that the player will be willing to pay a larger premium and purchase the insurance.

Clearly, a personal utility function can be quite complex: concave in some regions and convex in others. Furthermore, there can be various (personal) degrees of risk aversion (risk seeking).

Exercise 15.9 (Measuring Risk Aversion) Let $U(x)$ be a utility function. The curvature index

$$I_U(x) = \frac{-U''(x)}{U'(x)}$$

of $U(x)$ is a popular measure for risk aversion called the **Arrow–Pratt measure of risk aversion**. Specifically, the utility function U_1 is at least as risk-averse as U_2 if $I_{U_1}(x) \geq I_{U_2}(x)$ for all x. Prove that if this inequality holds, then an individual using U_1 would be willing to pay at least as much for insurance against any risk as would someone using the function U_2.

15.7.2   von Neumann–Morgenstern Expected Utility Theory

The idea of measuring monetary quantities via a personal utility function is the entire basis of modern **utility theory**, as was further developed by von Neumann and Morgenstern [333]. In particular, they show that if an individual can consistently specify his preferences between all pairs of lotteries, then there exists a (subjective) utility function that takes into account his personal attitude toward risk by ranking all probability distributions (over the given set of possible prizes) according to their expected utility. Moreover, this utility is unique (up to a positive linear transformation). After the determination of the utility function, it is sufficient to optimize decisions simply by maximizing the expected utility.

Fix any set $\mathcal{Z}$ of prizes (or "outcomes"), and let $\mathcal{L} = \mathcal{L}(\mathcal{S})$ be the set of all lotteries with prizes in $\mathcal{Z}$. For simplicity, we assume that $\mathcal{Z} = \{z_1, z_2, \ldots, z_n\}$ is finite. Each lottery $L \in \mathcal{L}$ is specified by a probability distribution $L = (p_1, p_2, \ldots, p_n)$ where the p_i's sum to 1. The interpretation is that if the lottery L is played, the decision maker obtains prize z_i with probability p_i.

The underlying assumption of the theory is that the decision maker has a "preference relation" over elements of $\mathcal{L}$. Basically, this means that the decision maker can compare between any two lotteries and that the order relation defined by such comparisons is consistent in the sense that it does not lead to intransitivities. Note that some of the lotteries in $\mathcal{L}$ are complex to the extent that they may look "incomprehensible" to the decision maker (in fact, the decision maker cannot even observe all of them since $\mathcal{L}$ is infinite). Nevertheless – and this is a crucial point – the theory still assumes that the decision maker can elicit a consistent preference relation over the set of lotteries. The goal is now to characterize uniquely the decision maker's preference relation in terms of a standard order relation (over real numbers) so that a lottery $L = (p_1, \ldots, p_n)$ is preferred to lottery $L' = (p'_1, \ldots, p'_n)$ if and only if

$$\sum_i p_i U(z_i) < \sum_i p'_i U(z_i),$$

where $U(\cdot)$ is a personal utility function of the decision maker.

We now state and discuss the von Neumann–Morgenstern (NM) axioms for a decision maker's preferences over the set of lotteries $\mathcal{L}$. Since we are formulating these axioms in terms of profit maximization, we use $\succ$ to denote a preference relation.

> **Axiom NM0 (Completeness):** The decision maker has a preference relation $\succ$ over the set of all lotteries.

This is clearly an analogue of Axiom 0 in Section 15.3. A decision maker who accepts this axiom must be prepared, if forced, to compare and choose between any two lotteries in $\mathcal{L}$ in a consistent way (i.e., so that $\succeq$ is complete and transitive).

Given two lotteries L_1 and L_2 and a real $\alpha \in [0, 1]$, we use $\alpha L_1 + (1 - \alpha) L_2$ to denote the following (compound) lottery: with probability α play L_1, and with probability $1 - \alpha$ play L_2.

> **Axiom NM1 (Independence):** For all $L, L_1, L_2 \in \mathcal{L}$ and $\alpha \in (0, 1]$, $L_1 \succ L_2$ implies
>
> $$\alpha L_1 + (1 - \alpha)L \;\succ\; \alpha L_2 + (1 - \alpha)L.$$

Initially, this independence axiom looks quite compelling, at least as a prescriptive rule. However, we will soon be presented with a direct attack on this axiom (mainly from the descriptive point of view).

Axiom NM2 (Continuity): For all L, L_1 and L_2 such that $L_1 \succ L \succ L_2$, there exist $\alpha, \beta \in (0, 1)$ such that

$$\alpha L_1 + (1 - \alpha)L_2 \;\succ\; L \;\succ\; \beta L_1 + (1 - \beta)L_2. \qquad (15.4)$$

Consider the following lotteries. In L_1 one obtains \$100 with certainty; in L one obtains \$10 with certainty; in L_2 one is killed with certainty. Most individuals will surely exhibit the preference $L_1 \succ L \succ L_2$. If the continuity axiom holds, there must be a probability $\alpha \in (0, 1)$ such that $\alpha L_1 + (1 - \alpha)L_2 \succ L$. In other words, one is willing to risk one's life to trade \$10 for \$100! Of course, α may be so small that even upon reflection, one may still be willing to risk one's life for these \$100. For example, an individual is given \$10 and told that in a certain location, six blocks away, this \$10 can be traded for \$100. It does not sound like such a bad idea to drive to this location and trade the \$10, even though it is clear that driving this distance involves some nonzero chance of death. Hence, Axiom NM2 appears convincing, from both a descriptive and a normative point of view.

Theorem 15.8 (von Neumann–Morgenstern expected utility) *A binary relation $\succ$ over $\mathcal{L}$ satisfies Axioms NM0–NM2 if and only if there exists a function $U : \mathcal{L} \to \mathbb{R}$ such that*

$$L \succ L' \quad \text{if and only if} \quad \sum_i p_i U(z_i) > \sum_i p_i' U(z_i).$$

Moreover, U is unique up to a positive affine transformation.[13]

An important point is that Theorem 15.8 is existential. It does not construct the personal utility U. Since the knowledge of the utility function can resolve any decision problem under risk (for NM decision makers), applied decision consultants and decision theory experimenters are often interested in eliciting their clients' (subjects') NM utility function.[14]

Although many applications of the expected utility theory have been concerned with monetary outcomes, the domain of the utility function can clearly be any particular set of outcomes. In particular, the theory can be applied to online problems posed in terms of arbitrary cost/profit functions such as distances moved by a server or numbers of page faults in a virtual memory system.

---

[13] That is, U represents $\succ$ if and only if $U'(x) = c \cdot U(x) + d$ also represents $\succ$ for any real $c > 0$ and real d. See Kreps [234] or French [161] for a proof. We note that the theorem holds even when the set of prizes $\mathcal{Z}$ is uncountably infinite; however, in this case, the definition of the "set of all lotteries" and the proof of the theorem are more subtle and involved.

[14] Whenever the prizes in $\mathcal{Z}$ are monetary, an approximation of the utility function can be recursively determined using the so-called **fractile method**. Assuming that the utility function is "normalized" so that $U(0) = 0$ and $U(M) = 1$ for some large M, we start by eliciting our certainty equivalent of the lottery with prizes $(0, M)$ with probabilities $(\frac{1}{2}, \frac{1}{2})$. Suppose that this certainty equivalent is E_1. That is, $U(E_1) = \frac{1}{2}U(M) + \frac{1}{2}U(0) = \frac{1}{2}$. Next we find the certainty equivalents E_{21} and E_{22} of the two lotteries $(0, E_1)$ and (E_1, M), both with probabilities $(\frac{1}{2}, \frac{1}{2})$. Clearly $U(E_{21}) = \frac{1}{4}$ and $U(E_{22}) = \frac{3}{4}$. We recursively continue with E_{31}, E_{32}, E_{33}, and E_{34}, and so on. After obtaining sufficiently many values of our utility function one can attempt to interpolate U.

Note, however, that using the expected utility theory to its fullest extent (with the exact *personal* utility function) for theoretical (and practical) analyses is sometimes very difficult if not impossible. Indeed, in a great many applications either the assumption taken is that the utility function is some "nice" concave function (often the logarithm) or the issue of risk aversion is completely ignored by assuming that the player is risk-neutral (see also Section 14.4.4).

15.7.3 The Allais Paradox and Other Violations of the Expected Utility Theory

The von NM expected utility theory is widely accepted among decision theorists and economists as a descriptive as well as normative framework for rational choice under risk.[15] Nevertheless, there are many pieces of empirical evidence of classes of choice problems that systematically violate the axioms of expected utility theory, thus reducing the attractiveness of the theory (as a descriptive tool). The first and perhaps most famous violation of the NM framework is the so-called **Allais paradox** [10]. This violation has been observed in many experimental studies.[16] Consider the four lotteries shown in Figure 15.10. In the first choice problem, one is supposed to choose between lottery A and lottery B. In the second problem, one is supposed to choose between lottery C and lottery D.

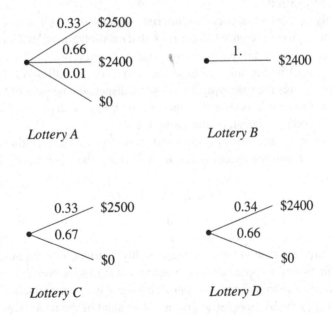

Figure 15.10: The Allais paradox.

It was found that most people prefer lottery B in the first problem and, simultaneously, lottery C in the second. This pattern of preference violates expected utility theory: say U is the utility of an individual exhibiting such preferences, and assume for convenience

---

[15] See Keeney and Raiffa [219] and Arrow [17].
[16] Here we present one empirical example of the Allais paradox that was obtained by Kahneman and Tversky [208].

that $U(0) = 0$. The first preference (B over A) implies that $U(2400) > 0.33U(2500) + 0.66U(2400)$, which means that $0.34U(2400) > 0.33U(2500)$. Since C is preferred to D, we have $0.33U(2500) + 0.67U(0) > 0.34U(2400) + 0.66U(0)$, so $0.33U(2500) > 0.34U(2400)$.

Exercise 15.10 Prove that the preference relation $B \succ A$ and $C \succ D$ in the Allais paradox violates the independence axiom (Axiom NM1).

Although the Allais paradox was initially dismissed as an isolated example, it is now known to be a special case of a more general violation pattern of the independence axiom (and thus of expected utility theory). Moreover, various empirical violations of the other axioms have been observed. For example, most people who are risk-averse in the positive domain are risk seekers in the negative domain, so that most risk-averse subjects prefer an 80% risk of losing $4000 to a sure loss of $3000 (see Kahneman and Tversky [208] and also Example 15.6).[17]

15.7.4   Other Approaches to Decision Making Under Risk

The von Neumann–Morgenstern expected utility theory is by no means the only optimality criterion for decision problems under risk. There are numerous other approaches to risk problems. Here we shall only sketch one of the more prominent (and practical) approaches that have been considered.

A large family of criteria that concerns lotteries over *monetary* prizes is of the following "parametric" form: give preference to lotteries L that maximize an index $U(k_1(L), k_2(L))$, where $k_i(L)$ are characteristic parameters of the underlying probability distribution of L. Specifically, $k_1(L)$ is typically the expected (monetary) payoff and $k_2(L)$ is another parameter that measures the risk, typically via some dispersion measure of the underlying distribution. The function U is chosen to increase with k_1 and, depending on the attitude toward risk, U is concave, linear, or convex with k_2.

The most common choice for k_2 is the standard deviation. The resulting decision procedure is called the **mean-variance criterion**. In this case, the criterion is of the following form:

$$U(L) = \mathbf{E}(L) - \delta \cdot \sigma(L).$$

Here $\mathbf{E}(L)$ is the expected return, $\sigma(L)$ is the standard deviation of the return, and δ is a risk-aversion coefficient. This criterion was first proposed by Fisher [159], who seems to have had in mind the case in which the probability distribution is normal. In this case, of course, the mean and standard deviation determine the entire probability distribution. For other probability distributions, this approach gives a first approximation to the "true" utility function (in general, in order to give a full account of the underlying distribution, one must consider all its moments).

15.8   Bayesian Approaches for Decision Making Under Uncertainty

We briefly discuss various approaches to decision problems that attempt to utilize partial information that the decision maker may have. The dominating approach here is

---

[17] For other examples of violations of expected utility, see the excellent survey by Machina [253].

"distributional" or "Bayesian," where the general idea is to transform the uncertainties to risks (i.e., probabilities). In fact, the term "Bayesian decision making" refers to a large class of approaches in which the decision maker assigns probabilities to the various states of nature and then solves the resulting decision problem under risk. The assigned probability model is called a **prior distribution** (or, simply, "a prior"). The name "Bayesian" reflects the idea that, given further observations, the decision maker updates his prior distribution using Bayes' formula for conditional probabilities.[18] The resulting distribution is called a **posterior**. This "iteration" is continued whenever a new sample is obtained and the new prior probabilities are the posterior probabilities of the preceding round.

What are these prior probabilities, and where do they come from? In the case of a true lottery, for example, the problem of choosing a color to bet on in an unbiased roulette, there is a well-defined notion of objective probabilities that can be assigned to the various states of nature. On the other hand, in the case of an investor who must choose between several investment opportunities whose returns depend upon complex events in the economy, the determination of objective probabilities is not obvious (and the definition of probabilities is not necessarily meaningful!).

There are many heuristics and theories regarding the assignment of a prior distribution. A crucial subtlety related to determination of prior distributions concerns the definition of probabilities. Indeed, the various methods of obtaining a priori probabilities are directly tied with two main schools of probability theory.

In principle, **objectivists** require that one can sample the "true" underlying probability distribution. The objectivists then have myriad techniques for recovering a prior (e.g., empirical distribution, maximum likelihood, maximum entropy).[19] If such observations do not exist, an objectivist will often resort to the principle of insufficient reason or other variants based on symmetry, or they will even assign an arbitrary probability distribution as the prior, assuming that further sampling of the underlying distribution will quickly provide them with sufficient information to determine a better estimate that will converge to the true distribution.

On the other hand, each **subjectivist** has a set of qualitative beliefs that is based on personal experience and is consistent with a certain set of axioms. These beliefs include a preference relation over the set of probability distributions and induce a unique (personal) probability prior and a unique (personal) utility function.

One important property common to all Bayesian approaches is that Bayes' optimal strategy is always deterministic. Specifically, the Bayesian decision problem can be viewed as a two-person zero-sum game between Nature and the decision maker in which the payoff to Nature is the negative reward of the decision maker. The prior distribution assumed for Nature is a randomized mixed strategy. Hence, using elementary game theoretic results (see Lemma 8.2), randomized strategies for the decision maker are superfluous at best.[20]

---

[18] For an event a and mutually exclusive and exhaustive events $b_1, b_2, \ldots$, **Bayes' formula** states that

$$\Pr[b_k|a] = \frac{\Pr[a|b_k]\Pr[b_k]}{\sum_i \Pr[a|b_i]\Pr[b_i]}$$

(see Feller [148], p. 124).

[19] See, for example, DeGroot [128].

[20] This property may cause a conceptual problem for (Bayesian) statisticians with regard to statistical design problems, in which random sampling is usually considered to be a very important feature.

To present the Bayesian approach (objective or subjective) while doing justice to these extensive theories would require several textbooks. To end this discussion we must at least mention Savage's [301] theory of maximizing expected utility with subjective probabilities. This theory proposes a set of axioms that imply, for every decision maker, a unique subjective prior and a unique subjective utility function according to which the decision maker can (and, in fact, *must* if he accepts the axioms) make choices by maximizing his expected utility with respect to the prior. Following the initial ideas of Ramsey, Savage's theory essentially supersedes and combines two preceding theories, the theory of subjective probabilities of de Finetti and the von Neumann–Morgenstern theory of expected utility. This doctrine is considered by many decision theorists to be one of the major achievements of modern decision theory.[21]

15.9   Historical Notes and Open Questions

Decision making under uncertainty is so pervasive that it is not an exaggeration to say that it pertains to almost every choice we make. This is perhaps the reason why for centuries mathematicians, economists, statisticians, philosophers, and psychologists have studied related issues. Just over 250 years ago, the main concern was the concept of utility, also referred to as "subjective value," "psychic satisfaction," and so on. Starting with Bernoulli's [63] initial concept of utility, the subject eventually matured with the introduction of the von Neumann–Morgenstern theory of maximizing expected utility [333]. Although the core of the concept of utility is similar in both works, von Neumann and Morgenstern's motivation for studying utility functions is fundamentally different from that of Bernoulli. In particular, Bernoulli's starting point is that of utility functions for riskless quantities, and von Neumann and Morgenstern's starting point is that of a preference relation over risky lotteries.

In addition to the NM approach, there is the large family of "parametric" risk criteria. The most common choice for a risk parameter is the standard deviation, which gives rise to the well-known "mean-variance" criterion. This criterion became widely accepted after its successful application to portfolio selection by Markowitz [257] and Tobin [327]. Two other choices considered for the risk parameter are the probability (or magnitude) of loss (see Domar and Musgrave [133]), and semivariance (see Markowitz [259]). Sometimes, more than two parameters of the underlying distribution are used to obtain a more accurate representation. In particular, the third and fourth moments were considered in Stange [322]. However, there are those such as Samuelson [299] who assert that moments higher than the second are not essential.

Finally, we note that there are other criteria for risk problems that are based on lexicographic ordering of distributions with respect to some sequence of "critical thresholds," which are typically subjective quantities (see Encarnación [144], Nachtkamp [266], Cramér [125], Roy [296], and Haussmann [184]). There is an extensive literature that compares, supports, and criticizes the various approaches to decision making under risk. For further details, see Arrow [16], Markowitz [259], Sinn [316], and Yaari [339].

Von Neumann–Morgenstern expected utility theory had a seminal influence on the area of decision making under risk. Also, it encouraged further studies in the more general

---

[21] See, for example, Kreps [234].

(and conceptually more difficult) area of decision making under uncertainty. One of the seminal works of that time was Wald's *Statistical Decision Functions* [334], which formulated and set forth the field of statistics as a branch of decision theory under uncertainty. One aspect of Wald's work promoted the idea of strict uncertainty and, in particular, the use of the minimax criterion (which had previously been employed by von Neumann and Morgenstern in two-person games). Wald considered the minimax criterion in the context of statistical estimation and hypothesis testing (two of the more important statistical routines). Soon after Wald published his book, several other criteria for strict uncertainty were offered (e.g., the minimax regret, by Savage [300], and the pessimism–optimism index, by Hurewicz [191]). The state of the art at that time, regarding decision under risk and uncertainty, is well-described in a critical survey by Arrow [16]. In addition to these classical criteria, there are other proposals, such as the following:

- The **domain criterion**, due to Starr [323, 324]. Let $\mathcal{D} \subset \mathbb{R}^{|\mathcal{S}|}$ be the set of all probability distributions over $\mathcal{S}$ (assuming $\mathcal{S}$ is finite). Assume a uniform distribution over $\mathcal{D}$, and for each $a \in \mathcal{A}$ define $D(a)$ as the set of all distributions $d \in \mathcal{D}$ with respect to which a yields the smallest expected cost (among all elements of $\mathcal{A}$). Note that for each a, $D(a)$ can be shown to be a convex polyhedron. Set $V(a)$ to be the volume of $D(a)$ (in the usual Euclidean sense), and choose a with the highest volume.
- Arrow and Hurewicz [18] suggest the following variation of the pessimism–optimism index: a is preferred to b if and only if

$$\max_s C(a, s) \leq \max_s C(b, s)$$

and

$$\min_s C(a, s) \leq \min_s C(b, s)$$

(in which case, a is preferred to b also by the pessimism–optimism criterion). They define an optimal algorithm as one that is preferred to any other algorithm in $\mathcal{A}$. Note that this criterion induces only a partial order, and an optimal algorithm may not exist.
- Other more sophisticated (and not easily describable) criteria were offered. Shackle's "potential surprise" theory [309] is a kind of generalization of the above Arrow–Hurewicz criterion. Milnor [264] offered a criterion that is a variation of the minimax regret.

Following Wald's book, axiomatizations of all the classical criteria for strict uncertainty were obtained by Milnor [264] and, independently (for some criteria), by Chernoff [96]. These were followed by Savage's profound and influential book *The Foundations of Statistics* [301], which characterizes the maximization of expected utility with a subjective prior criterion. This characterization resulted in a "paradigm shift" for decision making under uncertainty. Savage's theory was essentially a merging of earlier ideas by Ramsey [288] (subjective expected utility), de Finetti [127] (qualitative and subjective probability theory), and the von Neumann–Morgenstern expected utility theory. Indeed, Savage's work ignited a rich and very active theory upon which economic theories of uncertainty could be built. As a result of the sophistication and success of this subjective approach for uncertainty, the (relatively "primitive") theories and approaches for studying decision making under strict uncertainty were superseded and, for the most part, abandoned.[22] Nevertheless, note that minimax costs (or "losses") are still considered important in statistical inference (although they are far from being universally accepted). An excellent discussion of the 1950s literature can be found in Luce and Raiffa [251]. Recent experimental studies (of descriptive aspects) of strict uncertainty criteria were performed by Seale and Rapoport [305].

Until the 1970s, Savage's doctrine was the most prominent theory of decision making under uncertainty. Indeed, this doctrine was considered one of the more impressive success stories of economic theory. Resting on a solid axiomatic basis, it provided the foundation for numerous applications and theories.

The Allais paradox [10] was initially dismissed but later received recognition when similar evidence was obtained by Markowitz [258] and Williams [336]. The accumulation and recognition of evidence against the NM theory lead to a growing tension between those who preferred to view decision models as descriptive and those who preferred to view them as normative. New challenges were created for the advocates in descriptive theories. Indeed, these violations revived interest in theories of decision making under risk that depart from the original NM axioms (especially from the independence axiom), and the field benefited from a large number of generalizations and variations of the NM expected utility theory. To confuse matters more, it was found by Yaari [338] that violations of the independence axiom necessarily imply that the decision maker is vulnerable to a "Dutch book"; this means that the decision maker exhibits nontransitivity (and therefore can lose his entire wealth). In addition, based on an argument by de Finetti [126], Yaari observed that in order to be immune against Dutch books, the decision maker must satisfy another axiom called the "dual independence axiom." Then he showed that if a decision maker satisfies both the independence and dual independence axioms, he must be risk-neutral! Fishburn [158] provides a survey of more recent alternative theories of expected utility.

Violations of Savage's axioms were first observed and reported in the seminal paper of Ellsberg [143]. These were replicated many times, in particular by Kahneman and Tversky [208], who presented other violations of expected utility theory (with subjective prior) as well as an alternative theory based on the idea that "utility" should be measured through *changes* in wealth rather than by the final wealth. Machina [253] published a survey of negative empirical results. The Ellsberg paradox and the ideas of uncertainty aversion motivated several researchers to modify the Savage doctrine (see Gilboa [170], Schmeidler [303], Gilboa and Schmeidler [171], Chateauneuf [93], Machina and Schmeidler [254], and Epstein and Le Breton [145]). In the ensuing controversy, numerous alternative theories emerged and the field became very active (see, e.g., Anscombe and Aumann [15], Fishburn [157], Dreze [136], and Karni [215]).

We briefly describe two relatively recent and prominent works. The first approach, of maximizing expected utility with *nonadditive* (subjective or objective) probability measures, was developed by Schmeidler [303]. This approach requires that the likelihood of the events in question (based on facts or beliefs) be measured by using probabilities that do not necessarily sum to unity. For example, if there are only two mutually exclusive events,

---

[22] French [161] writes: "Savage renounced the use of minimax regret ideas and it is far from certain that Laplace, Hurewicz, or Wald would still champion the decision rules that bear their names" (p. 57). He also writes: "The Bayesian school of decision theory is not the only school: there are many others. But, as you have no doubt gathered, I believe all to be inferior to the Bayesian" (p. 352).

e_1 and e_2, they may be assigned probabilities p_1 and p_2 such that $p_1 + p_2 \leq 1$. Thus, the quantity $1 - p_1 - p_2$ would indicate the decision maker's lack of confidence in the probability assessment. The idea of nonadditive probability distributions is not new and has been used extensively in physics.[23] In order to use the idea of nonadditive probability measures, one must give precise mathematical formulation of such measures. In particular, the expectation must be defined. In his paper, Schmeidler gives an axiomatic support of his approach as well as a mathematical formulation of the nonadditive probability measure. With this formulation the decision maker's attitude toward uncertainty as well as his attitude toward risk are accommodated automatically by choosing the action that maximizes the (nonadditive) expected utility. Gilboa and Schmeidler [171] proposed an axiomatic foundation of a criterion that combines the minimax criterion with the Savage criterion. This generalized maximin criterion, called "minimax with nonunique prior distribution," bridges these two approaches. The resulting criterion is the expected value of the maximin, where the minimum is taken with respect to a subset of the possible priors. Interestingly, Schmeidler in [302] shows that under certain conditions on the set of possible priors, the nonadditive approach coincides with this "generalized maximin" criterion. See Karni and Schmeidler's [216] thorough survey of the present state of the art regarding subjective probability and utility.

Detached from all these developments and debates, theoretical computer scientists indirectly revived the study of decision making under strict uncertainty by considering the competitive ratio and applying it to many online problems. For (some) computer scientists, the natural appeal of the competitive ratio comes from its intimate relation to the well-accepted "approximation factor" used to evaluate offline approximation algorithms. Moreover, the extensive use of the fundamental approach to worst-case analysis of offline optimization algorithms, which is the backbone of classical complexity theory, has proven to be extremely useful in theoretical analyses of algorithms because of its "universality" (i.e., independence of particular assumptions on the input). Through worst-case analysis, we can obtain a kind of universal but nevertheless quantitative performance measure. (The use of Bayesian approaches is typically nonuniversal or only qualitative.) This advantage applies also to the worst-case analysis of online algorithms (through the competitive ratio).

The competitive ratio was not the only criterion that was used for online applications. The minimax regret and other classical criteria were also occasionally used for applications in statistics and economics and, recently, by machine learning theorists (see, e.g., the papers by Auer, Cesa-Bianchi, Freund, and Schapire [20] and Briys and Louberge [84]). The max/max criterion, a generalization of the minimax cost, was proposed by Ben-David and Borodin [54] as a possible decision criterion.

The characterization of the competitive ratio was obtained by El-Yaniv [138]. The algorithmic decision model on which this result is built is a straightforward extension of Wald's classical decision model using the request–answer model for online computation. The result itself is an extension of Milnor's characterization of the minimax (regret) criterion. The axiom set of the competitive ratio (see Sections 15.3) is essentially based (except for Axiom 8) on the axioms proposed by Milnor [264], Chernoff [96], Arrow and Hurewicz [18], and Luce and Raiffa [251].

---

[23] See, for example, Feynman, Leighton, and Sands [150].

Credits for Exercises. Exercises 15.2 and 15.3 are due to El-Yaniv [138]. Exercise 15.4 is due to Chernoff [96], Milnor [264], and French [161]. Exercise 15.5 is due to Milnor [264]. Exercise 15.7 is due to El-Yaniv, Kaniel, and Linial [141]. Exercise 15.9 is due to Pratt [279].

15.9.1   Open Questions

A subjective refinement of the competitive ratio. Consider the contrasting examples in Figures 15.1 and 15.5, which made a case against Axiom 8. Apparently, the root of such problems is that our perception of very large or very small quantities is too crude to be reliable. Of course, "very large" and "very small" are subjective quantities. Consider the following problem:

$$
P'' = \quad
\begin{array}{c|cccc}
 & s_1 & s_2 & s_3 & s_4 \\
\hline
a_1 & 70 & 80 & 90 & \frac{1}{50} \\
\hline
a_2 & 1 & 1 & 1 & 1 \\
\end{array}
$$

The only difference between P'' and P' (in Figure 15.5) is the value of $C(a_1, s_4) = \frac{1}{50}$ (which is $\frac{1}{10,000}$ in P'). We saw that for P', the optimal choice with respect to the competitive ratio is a_1, whereas for many decision makers the "natural" choice seems to be a_2. Although the problem P'' is slightly less favorable to the decision maker than P' (one of the outcomes is higher by less than two cents), it is likely that many rational individuals would believe that the optimal choice should not be affected if we replace P' with P''. However, with respect to the competitive ratio there is a drastic change; in P'' the unique optimal choice is a_2, which is now consistent with our preferences, assuming that we still prefer a_2 to a_1.

Such examples inspire the following refinement of the competitive ratio, which may overcome such deficiencies. With respect to subjective positive thresholds m and M, define the following (subjective) threshold function f,

$$
f(x) = \begin{cases} m & \text{if } x \le m; \\ x & \text{if } m < x < M; \\ M & \text{if } x \ge M. \end{cases}
$$

Then, instead of solving the problem $P = (\mathcal{A}, \mathcal{S}, C)$ (e.g., using the competitive ratio), solve the problem $P' = (\mathcal{A}, \mathcal{S}, f \circ C)$.

15.1 (*Value = 14/T5*) Establish an axiomatization of this criterion; that is, construct a unique, subjective function f so that its use, in conjunction with the competitive ratio, is characterized by a certain axiom set.

Characterization of the max/max ratio. The max/max ratio of Ben-David and Borodin [54] generalizes the minimax cost from finite "one-shot" problems to (infinite) algorithmic decision problems. Since the rationality of the minimax cost criterion can be as well justified as the competitive ratio, it is useful to characterize the max/max ratio criterion. The max/max ratio is defined in terms of "amortized" cost functions (where each cost is divided by the length of the corresponding request sequence). Assuming that the initial problem is previously given in terms of such amortized cost functions, it is possible to characterize the max/max ratio (based on Axioms 1–4, 5′, 6, and 7) by using techniques similar to those used for the minimax cost and the competitive ratio. Nevertheless, it is not clear how to justify the transformation from the initial cost function to the amortized cost function.

15.2 (*Value* = *l4/T3*) Characterize the max/max ratio criterion.

The competitive ratio and nonstrict uncertainty. Gilboa and Schmeidler [171] generalized the maximin cost and the maximum expected utility criteria by characterizing their "expected utility with multiple priors" criterion. In essence, this criterion maintains that after incorporating the known (subjective or objective) probabilistic information (thus eliminating some distributions), one should use Wald's minimax cost approach for the remaining (perhaps infinite) subset of possible distributions of the input sequences. This appealing idea is rather old (see Hurewicz [192]) and has been reinvented quite a few times, as in Chapter 5, where we discuss the restricted Bayesian compromise. One of the positive features of this criterion is that it establishes a continuous transition from the maximin cost to expected utility theory. Note that a similar continuous transition between the competitive ratio and expected utility cannot be established; the minimization of the "expected competitive ratio" is not consistent with the minimization of expected cost. To see this, consider the following decision problem:

	s_1	s_2
a_1	6	1
a_2	2	4

Suppose that we know the prior distribution on the states that yields s_1 (respectively, s_2) with probability p (respectively, $1 - p$). Then, for p such that $\frac{3}{7} < p < \frac{3}{5}$, conflict arises. Specifically, for such p it is not difficult to see that $\mathbf{E}[a_1] = 6p+q > 2p+4q = \mathbf{E}[a_2]$ and $\mathbf{E}_{\text{ratio}}[a_1] = 3p+1 < p+4q = \mathbf{E}_{\text{ratio}}[a_2]$, where $\mathbf{E}[a_i]$ and $\mathbf{E}_{\text{ratio}}[a_i]$ are the expected cost and expected competitive ratio, respectively, with respect to p. Interestingly, the minimax regret does not have this problem. Hence, we pose the following question.

15.3 (*Value* = *l4/T3*) Obtain a characterization of "minimax regret with multiple priors" that bridges the minimax regret and expected utility theory.

As with the leasing example in which we determined the various optimal algorithms according to various criteria, it may be revealing to obtain similar results with respect to other online problems. It can be especially beneficial to consider problems that have also been studied empirically.

15.4 (*Value* = *l4/T4*) Consider any online problem and determine the various optimal algorithms, according to the various criteria for strict uncertainty.

Most of the recent research activity concerning decision making under uncertainty is based on Savage-like models. It is therefore important to consider the following problem.

15.5 (*Value* = *l4/T3*) Extend the characterization of the competitive ratio to a Savage-like decision model. (See Savage [301].)

APPENDIX A

Glossary

This glossary contains symbols unique to this text as well as common, but possibly non-standard, mathematical notation.

$\mathcal{P}$	(optimization) problem
$\mathcal{I}$	input set
$\mathcal{O}$	output set
$F(I)$	feasible solutions for I, subset of $\mathcal{O}$
ALG	generic online algorithm
ALG[I]	output computed by ALG for input I
ALG(I)	cost incurred or profit gained by ALG for input I
OPT	optimal offline algorithm
ADV	generic adversary
OBL	oblivious adversary
ADON	adaptive-online adversary
ADOF	adaptive-offline adversary
$\sigma = r_1, \ldots, r_n$	request sequence
$\sigma_i = r_1, \ldots, r_i$	length i prefix of σ
$\mathcal{R}(\text{ALG})$	deterministic competitive ratio of ALG
$\overline{\mathcal{R}}_{\text{ADV}}(\text{ALG})$	expected competitive ratio of ALG against adversary of type ADV
$\overline{\mathcal{R}}(\text{ALG})$	expected competitive ratio of ALG when adversary type is understood
Φ	potential function
ALG$_i$	actual cost for ith request (event)
$S_1 + S_2$	multiset union
$S + x$	multiset union with a singleton $(= S + \{x\})$
$S - x$	multiset difference with a singleton $(= S - \{x\})$
$S - T$	set or multiset difference
$\mathcal{M} = (\mathcal{M}, d)$	metric space with metric d
$B_p\{{}^n_k\}$	partial binomial sum

$\langle x_1, \ldots, x_n \rangle$	n-tuple
$\approx$	approximate equality
$\gg, \ll$	much greater and much less than
$\succsim, \precsim, \succ, \prec, \sim$	preference and indifference relations
$\arg\min_x \{ f(x) : x \in S \}$	an $x^* \in S$ such that $f(x^*) = \min_x \{ f(x) : x \in S \}$
$\arg\max$	similar to $\arg\min$ for maximum
$\lceil x \rceil$	minimum integer $n \geq x$
$\lfloor x \rfloor$	maximum integer $n \leq x$
$\varnothing$	empty set
$\emptyset$	empty sequence
$\ln$	natural logarithm
$\log$	logarithm base 2
$\mathbf{E}[\cdot]$	mathematical expectation
$\Pr[\mathcal{E}]$	probability of event $\mathcal{E}$
$\Pr[\mathcal{E}_1 \mid \mathcal{E}_2]$	conditional probability of $\mathcal{E}_1$ given $\mathcal{E}_2$
$O(f)$	big-oh notation
$\Omega(f)$	big-omega notation
$\Theta(f)$	big-theta notation
$o(f)$	little-oh notation
$\omega(f)$	little-omega notation
$\mathbb{N}$	nonnegative integers
$\mathbb{R}$	real numbers

APPENDIX B

Stochastic Analyses for List Accessing Algorithms

The list accessing problem was first studied as part of an area called **self-organizing data structures**. The most studied of such data structures were lists and search trees that implement a dictionary data type (see, e.g., Allen and Munro [11], Bitner [69], McCabe [260], Rivest [294], and Sleator and Tarjan [319]). The traditional perspective has been that there is some unknown but fixed probability distribution that determines future accesses to items on the list (or tree). The item access probabilities are typically assumed to be independent. Under these assumptions, a good algorithm is expected to transform the data structure so that it "learns" the distribution, and operations on the (transformed) data structure are efficient, as if the data structure were originally designed for the particular distribution. The issue under question is how well and how fast it learns the distribution, which is never completely known. Although this stochastic approach is inherently different from competitive analysis and, in general, outside the scope of this text, we feel that in order to appreciate the perspective and origins of competitive analysis it is important to present a few stochastic results. Hence, for completeness, we devote this appendix to a miniature overview of selected stochastic results for the list accessing problem. Except for this appendix, we do not attempt to present or survey stochastic results related to the problems we study.[1]

There are several very interesting stochastic results concerning the static list accessing problem, a problem that has been studied since at least 1965 (see McCabe [260]). Here we state results concerning, primarily, MTF, TRANS, and FC. See the excellent introduction by Bentley and McGeoch [58] and the survey by Hester and Hirschberg [188] for summaries of other (mainly distributional) results concerning the above and other algorithms.

We begin with a short technical discussion of the stochastic approach, as was typically used for the list accessing problem. Let $\{x_1, x_2, \ldots, x_\ell\}$ be the (fixed) set of items on the list. In the stochastic analysis of the list accessing problem, one typically assumes that each request for an access is an independent observation of a probability distribution $D = \{p_1, \ldots, p_\ell\}$, where p_i is the probability of accessing item x_i. Let ALG be any list

---

[1] Nevertheless, we encounter the stochastic approach twice more in this text: in Chapter 5, we consider the Markov paging model, which is essentially a stochastic model for paging in which the fixed but unknown distribution is a Markov process; in Chapter 15, we compare various approaches to decision making under uncertainty.

update algorithm. Then one measures the performance of ALG with respect to D via the asymptotic expected search cost for a single item, derived as follows. Suppose that the list is currently situated in some random ordering τ so that a request for item x_i costs $\tau(i)$ (its position on the list). Define $L(\tau, D) = \sum_{i=1}^{\ell} p_i \cdot \tau(i)$, the expected cost of servicing the next request. Let $\Pr(\tau, j)$ be the probability that the list is in order τ just before the jth request. Hence, the expected cost for serving the jth request is

$$\sum_{\tau} \Pr(\tau, j) \cdot L(\tau, D). \tag{B.1}$$

Stochastic analyses have considered the list search as a Markov process, where the configurations of the list are the states and the distribution D together with ALG define the transition probabilities. Then, the asymptotic expected search cost (for an individual request) of ALG with respect to D is

$$\text{ALG}(D) = \lim_{j \to \infty} \text{ALG}(j, D).$$

Let S-OPT be the **static optimal offline** algorithm that initially arranges the list in decreasing order of request probabilities and never reorders them thereafter. Although S-OPT is not as powerful as OPT, which is dynamic in its nature (i.e., typically we expect that $\text{OPT}(D) < \text{S-OPT}(D)$), because of its simplicity S-OPT has been used as a benchmark for comparison to other (online) algorithms. Notice that $\text{S-OPT}(D) = \sum_{i=1}^{\ell} i p_i$.

For the sake of completeness, we present a relatively simple example of stochastic analysis.[2] (Note, however, that the following result is subsumed by Theorem 1.1.)

Theorem B.1 *Let $D = \{p_1, \ldots, p_{\ell}\}$ be any probability distribution. Then,* $\text{MTF}(D) \leq 2 \cdot \text{S-OPT}(D)$

PROOF. Assume that the list has been processed by MOVE-TO-FRONT so that all items have been accessed several times and the reorganization process has reached a steady state.

For any two distinct items x_i and x_j, let $p(i, j)$ be the probability that x_i appears before x_j on the list. It is easy to express $p(i, j)$ in terms of the probabilities p_is: in order for x_i to appear in front of x_j on the list, x_i must have been requested more recently than the last x_j. The probability of this event is exactly $\frac{p_i}{p_i + p_j}$.

Let us now calculate the expected search cost for x_j. The expected number of items preceding x_j is exactly $\sum_{i \neq j} p(i, j)$. Hence, the expected cost for accessing x_j is 1 plus this quantity. Therefore,

$$\begin{aligned}
\text{MTF}(D) &= \sum_{j=1}^{\ell} p_j \left(1 + \sum_{i \neq j} p(i, j) \right) \\
&= \sum_{j=1}^{\ell} p_j + \sum_{j=1}^{\ell} p_j \sum_{i \neq j} p(i, j) \\
&= 1 + \sum_{i \neq j} p_j p(i, j)
\end{aligned}$$

---

[2] The presentation here is based on Lewis and Denenberg [242].

$$= 1 + \sum_{i \neq j} \frac{p_i p_j}{p_i + p_j}$$

$$= 1 + 2 \sum_{i < j} \frac{p_i p_j}{p_i + p_j}.$$

In order to compare S-OPT(D) with MTF(D), we abbreviate $\Pi = \frac{\sum_{i<j} p_i p_j}{p_i + p_j}$. Then, since $\frac{p_i}{p_i + p_j} \leq 1$ for each i and j, we obtain

$$\Pi = \sum_{j=1}^{\ell} p_j \sum_{1 \leq i < j} \frac{p_i}{p_i + p_j}$$

$$\leq \sum_{j=1}^{\ell} p_j (j - 1)$$

$$= \text{S-OPT}(D) - 1.$$

To conclude,

$$\frac{\text{MTF}(D)}{\text{S-OPT}(D)} \leq \frac{1 + 2\Pi}{1 + \Pi} = 2 - \frac{1}{1 + \Pi} < 2.$$

∎

The asymptotic expected search cost for different algorithms was derived with respect to several probability distributions and was derived explicitly for any D, in a closed form formula, for MOVE-TO-FRONT (see Gonnet, Munro, and Suwanda [174], McCabe [260], Burville and Kingman [88], Knuth [228], Hendricks [186], Rivest [294], and Bitner [69]). As shown above, this formula can be used to show that MTF$(D) \leq 2 \cdot$ S-OPT(D) for any D. Through a more sophisticated analysis obtained by Gonnet, Munro, and Suwanda [173], it was shown that MTF$(D) \leq \frac{\pi}{2} \cdot$ S-OPT(D).[3] Gonnet, Munro, and Suwanda also proved that this $\frac{\pi}{2}$ bound is tight.

Rivest [294] obtained a formula (not in a closed form) for the asymptotic expected search cost for TRANSPOSE and showed that TRANS$(D) \leq$ MTF(D) with a strict inequality, except when D is a uniform distribution or $\ell = 2$ (in which case, the two algorithms are identical). He conjectured that TRANSPOSE has the lowest asymptotic expected search cost for every probability distribution D. Yao showed (reported in Bitner [68]) that if an optimal online algorithm does exist, it must be TRANSPOSE. (Here optimality is with respect to all probability distributions.) Nevertheless, Anderson, Nash, and Weber [13] found a counterexample to Rivest's conjecture: an algorithm that is better than TRANSPOSE with respect to a particular probability distribution.

There is an intuitive explanation for Rivest's result: once the list is in some semblance of a correct order, an occasional reference to a low-probability item does not substantially disturb the order if TRANSPOSE is used. However, MOVE-TO-FRONT will move such an item to the front, where it will delay searches for more frequent items. On the other hand, Bitner [69] showed, while TRANSPOSE has a better asymptotic cost, MOVE-TO-FRONT converges to its asymptote more quickly.

---

[3] This result appears also in Chung, Hajela, and Seymour [109].

The FREQUENCY-COUNT algorithm, which orders item x_i according to its frequency count, received much less attention (recall that it requires an unbounded space). By the law of large numbers, if $p_i > p_j$, the frequency count for x_i may be smaller than the frequency count for x_j for only a finite number of requests and, therefore, its expected search cost asymptotically approaches that of S-OPT.

For the more recent TIMESTAMP algorithm, Albers and Mitzenmacher [6] proved that for any distribution D, TIMESTAMP$(D) \leq 1.34 \cdot$ S-OPT(D). They also showed that with high probability TIMESTAMP$(D) \leq 1.5 \cdot$ OPT(D). So far, the latter result is the only known distributional result that compares an online algorithm to OPT.

The above underlying probabilistic assumption of identically and independently distributed (i.i.d.) requests is not well justified, and it is natural to consider Markov models. For the particular case of (ergodic) first-order Markov chains, Lam, Leung, and Siu [237] determined the asymptotic expected search cost for MTF. Chassaing [92] characterized a large class of stochastic matrices (of first-order Markov chains) for which MOVE-TO-FRONT achieves the lowest asymptotic expected search cost among all online algorithms. Schulz and Schömer [304] consider variants of MTF under Markov chains, determine their asymptotic expected search costs, and also provide insights for other classes of online list accessing algorithms in this setting.

APPENDIX C

The Harmonic Random Walk and Its Connection to Electrical Networks

Explicit connections between random walks and electrical networks can be found in Doyle and Snell [134], with origins of this topic dating back to the nineteenth century. The main result presented in this appendix (Theorem 11.11) is from Chandra, Raghavan, Ruzzo, Smolensky, and Tiwari [91].

Consider a symmetric weighted graph $G = (V, E, d)$. A case of particular interest is when $d(e) = 1$ for all $e \in E$, in which case we have (in effect) an unweighted graph. A stochastic matrix $P = (p_{uv})$ defines a probability distribution on the edges leaving each node; that is,

$$\sum_{w \in N(u)} p_{uw} = 1,$$

where the neighborhood $N(u)$ denotes the nodes adjacent to u. Any such matrix defines a **random walk** on the graph G. That is, we can visualize a "marker" that walks along the nodes of G according to the probabilities specified by P. Various random events can be associated with such a random walk. For example, one random event we might want to study is the total distance traversed in walking *from* some node i *to* another node j. This random event has an expectation, which we call the **weighted hitting time**, denoted by h_{ij}.[1] Given a starting node u_0, another event is the total distance traversed until all nodes have been visited. The expectation of this event is called the **cover time**. If we are interested in minimizing the hitting time or cover time, it seems reasonable to have a small probability associated with an edge of large weight. We are led to consider the following **harmonic random walk**: choose each edge with probability inversely proportional to its weight; that is,

$$p_{uv} = \Pr[u \to v \mid \text{at } u] = \frac{1/d_{uv}}{\sum_{w \in N(u)}(1/d_{uw})}.$$

When G is undirected, we assume that d is symmetric. When the graph is unweighted,

---

[1] The term "hitting time" is quite appropriate in the case of an unweighted graph, since in this case each edge traversal can be viewed as taking one time step. We abuse this terminology and continue to refer to the hitting time in the context of a weighted graph.

then the Harmonic walk reduces to the well-studied case of a **uniform random walk** on a graph where $p_{uv} = \frac{1}{\text{degree}(u)}$. [2]

We would like to be able to analyze hitting times for a random walk on an undirected graph. Even for the uniform random walk on an unweighted undirected graph, we can have $h_{ij} \neq h_{ji}$. It is easier to characterize the symmetric **commute time** $c_{ij} = c_{ji} = h_{ij} + h_{ji}$. By convention, when $i = j$, $c_{ii} = h_{ii}$ = the expected time to return to i having started at i. In order to analyze c_{ij}, we use an analogy between weighted undirected graphs and electrical systems. We consider the weights on the edges of G to be an electrical (branch) resistance between these two nodes. That is, the branch resistance (in ohms) between u and v is d_{uv}. We define the **effective resistance** between nodes u and v as the potential that would result between u and v if one ampere of current were injected at u and withdrawn at v, and we denote this effective resistance by R_{uv}. Notice that for any two nodes $u, v \in V$, $R_{uv} = R_{vu} \leq d_{uv} = d_{vu}$.

For every node $u \in V$, denote the degree of u by δ_u. Let Φ_{uv} denote the electrical potential difference from u to v, when δ_w units of current are injected into every node $w \in V$, and $2 \cdot |E|$ units of current are extracted out of node v.

Lemma C.1 *Let $G = (V, E, d)$ be any undirected weighted graph and consider a harmonic walk on G. For all $u, v \in V$, $\Phi_{uv} = h_{uv}$.*

PROOF. For all $u, v \in V$, the expected cost of a walk from u to v is

$$h_{uv} = \sum_{w \in N(u)} \Pr[u \to w] \cdot (d_{uw} + h_{wv}) = \sum_{w \in N(u)} \frac{1/d_{uw}}{\sum_{w'} 1/d_{uw'}} \cdot (d_{uw} + h_{wv}).$$

Simplifying this equation, we get

$$h_{uv} \cdot \sum_{w' \in N(u)} \frac{1}{d_{uw'}} = \sum_{w \in N(u)} \frac{1}{d_{uw}} \cdot (d_{uw} + h_{wv}) = \delta_u + \sum_{w \in N(u)} \frac{h_{wv}}{d_{uw}}.$$

Therefore,

$$\forall\, u, v \in V, \; \delta_u = \sum_{w \in N(u)} \frac{h_{uv} - h_{wv}}{d_{uw}}. \tag{C.1}$$

Now consider the situation in which δ_w units of current are injected into every node $w \in V$, and $2|E|$ units of current are extracted out of node v. The amount of current that leaves node u toward a node $w \in N(u)$ equals the electrical potential difference between u and w (which is $\Phi_{uv} - \Phi_{wv}$) divided by the resistance d_{uw}. Because the total current injected into u is δ_u units, δ_u units must leave u. Therefore, we have

$$\forall\, u, v \in V, \; \delta_u = \sum_{w \in N(u)} \frac{\Phi_{uv} - \Phi_{wv}}{d_{uw}}. \tag{C.2}$$

Notice that equations (C.1) and (C.2) are identical. There is a (unique) solution to this system of equations (since these are equations of a physical system); therefore, it follows that for all $u, v \in V$, $\Phi_{uv} = h_{uv}$. ∎

---

[2] If we do not otherwise specify, a random walk on an unweighted graph refers to the uniform random walk.

Theorem C.1 *Let $G = (V, E, d)$ be any undirected weighted graph, and consider a harmonic walk on G. Then*

$$c_{uv} = 2 \cdot |E| \cdot R_{uv}.$$

PROOF. Notice that we can view Φ_{vu} as *minus* the electrical potential difference from v to u, when δ_w units of current are extracted out of every node $w \in V$, and $2|E|$ units of current are injected into the node u. This means that Φ_{vu} is the electrical potential difference from u to v in this scenario.

Therefore, $\Phi_{uv} + \Phi_{vu}$ is the electrical potential difference from u to v when $2|E|$ units of current are injected into u, and $2|E|$ units are extracted from v. Hence, the effective resistance between u and v is $\frac{\Phi_{uv} + \Phi_{vu}}{2|E|}$. Thus, we have

$$c_{uv} = h_{uv} + h_{vu} = \Phi_{uv} + \Phi_{vu} = 2 \cdot |E| \cdot R_{uv}.$$

∎

We also have the following immediate corollary.

Corollary C.2 *For the harmonic walk on any undirected weighted graph $G = (V, E, d)$, we have*

$$h_{uv} \le 2 \cdot |E| \cdot d_{uv}.$$

APPENDIX D

Proof of Lemmas 5.4 and 5.5 in Theorem 5.11: FAR Is a Uniformly Optimal Online Paging Algorithm

D.1 Proof of Lemma 5.4: *Type 1* Reps and the Construction of T'

Since there can be at most five type 1 rep chain nodes on any chain, and there is a unique terminal nonchain node on every chain, there must be at least $\frac{R_1}{6}$ nonchain nodes. (The construction of T' applies to any marking algorithm and does not depend on FAR or on the definition of a rep.) We have two cases to consider. Let $\tilde{T}$ be the undirected tree corresponding to T.

- *Case 1:* At least half of the nonchain nodes in T either
  - (i) are leaves in $\tilde{T}$,
  - (ii) have degree ≥ 3 in $\tilde{T}$, or
  - (iii) have degree 2 in $\tilde{T}$, but their parent in T has degree $\neq 2$ in $\tilde{T}$.

For every nonchain node v satisfying (iii), there is a unique node v' satisfying (i) or (ii). We simply let v' be the first descendent of v in T that does not have degree 2 in $\tilde{T}$. Clearly, at most one such v becomes associated with a given v'. Hence, at least one-fourth (i.e., at least $\frac{R_1}{24}$) of the nonchain nodes must satisfy (i) or (ii). However, since the average degree of a node in *any* undirected tree is less than 2, at least one half of the nodes with degree $\neq 2$ in $\tilde{T}$ must have degree 1 (i.e., they must be leaves) in $\tilde{T}$. That is, there are at least $\frac{R_1}{48}$ leaves in $\tilde{T}$, and we can let T' be $\tilde{T}$ extended by one additional node so that

$$|T'| = k + 1.$$

- *Case 2:* If Case 1 does not hold, then more than half of the nonchain nodes in $\tilde{T}$ have degree ≥ 3 in G and degree 2 in $\tilde{T}$, and their parent (in T) also has degree 2 in $\tilde{T}$. Choose a maximal set of nodes S in $\tilde{T}$ with degree ≥ 3 in G and degree 2 in $\tilde{T}$, where their parent in T has degree 2 in $\tilde{T}$ but not in S. (That is, we essentially take every other node on certain paths in $\tilde{T}$ of degree 2 nodes.) We still have $|S| = \Omega(R_1)$, so it suffices to show that the required tree T' has $\Omega(|S|)$ leaves. We define T' by first augmenting $\tilde{T}$ to a tree $\hat{T}$ with at most $k + s$ nodes and at least s leaves where $\frac{|S|}{2} \leq s \leq |S|$. To form $\hat{T}$, for every node v in S, choose a node $a(v)$ that is adjacent to v in G but not in $\tilde{T}$. If a node w is chosen for this neighbor for exactly one node in S, then add w (as a leaf) to the tree $\tilde{T}$ by creating an edge to this node in S. If w is chosen as this neighbor for at least two nodes in S, then add w to the tree by creating an edge to each of these nodes in S and then for each such node $v \in S$ (except for one whose distance to the root of $\hat{T}$ is minimal), we delete the edge from v to its parent in $\hat{T}$ in order to make v a leaf. We now prune $\hat{T}$ (back to a $(k+1)$-node tree T') so that

$$\ell(T') \geq \frac{\ell(\hat{T})}{4} = \Omega(|S|) = \Omega(R_1).$$

Clearly, $|S| \leq k$ so that $\hat{T}$ has at most $2k$ nodes. It is then easy to see that there is a node w on $\hat{T}$ whose removal will result in component subtrees with at most k nodes. By coalescing subtrees, we can divide the nodes of $\hat{T} - \{w\}$ into at most five graphs. Any of these graphs becomes a subtree (when connected by the eliminated node w), and one of these subtrees must then contain at least $\Omega(R_1)$ leaves. It is then easy to extend the subtrees to a $(k+1)$-node tree T' with the same number of leaves.

D.2   Proof of Lemma 5.5: *Type 2* Reps and the Construction of H

The analysis of type 2 reps has three main parts. In Part 1, we show that the number of type 2 reps on any chain is at most $2\log$ (length of the chain). Thus, if we could make *every* chain a vine in some vine decomposition $\mathcal{V}(T)$, then $val(\mathcal{V}(T)) \geq \frac{1}{2} \cdot R_2$. However, (nodes on) some chains may be needed to create the tree part of a vine decomposition. Part 2 (which is somewhat more delicate) shows how to construct a vine decomposition $\mathcal{V}(S)$ (possibly augmenting T by some nodes in G outside of T) on at most $\frac{3k}{2}$ nodes S so that the summed value of the chains that do become vines is still $\Omega(R_2)$. Finally, Part 3 uses $\mathcal{V}(S)$ to construct either a cycle H or a vine decomposition $\mathcal{V}(H)$ on $k+1$ nodes such that $val(H) = \Omega(R_2)$.

D.2.1   Part 1

The number of type 2 reps on any (directed) path P in T is at most $2 \cdot \lfloor \log \ell_1 \rfloor$, where ℓ_1 is the length of this first (in terms of the direction) chain in P containing a type 2 rep.

Note that the internal nodes of a chain are "isolated" in that they can be accessed only by a path of node requests within the chain. Let P be a directed path in T. We need to establish two claims pertaining to reps (of any type) on a path P in T.

> **Claim 1:** If v, w, z are three consecutive reps in some chain, then $n(z) \leq \frac{n(v)}{2}$, where $n(u)$ represents the distance of a chain node u to the last (nonchain) node on the chain. According to the definition of a rep, v is marked before w is evicted. Let w' be the last node on this chain that is marked before w is evicted. Clearly, w' lies between v and w. Let w_{mid} be the node midway between w' and the end of the chain. If w occurs before w_{mid}, then, since FAR evicts the unmarked node farthest from the set of marked nodes, it must be the case that every node between

w and w_{mid} is not in the cache and, furthermore, that none of these nodes can be reps (since they would have been evicted before w is marked). This implies that z must occur after the midpoint w_{mid}. That is,

$$n(z) \leq \frac{n(w')}{2} \leq \frac{n(v)}{2}.$$

Claim 2: If y is the next to last rep on a chain in the path P and c is the third rep in the next (or any later) chain of P, then $n(c) \leq n(y)$. Consider the subsequence of reps y, z, a, b, c. Since y is marked before z is evicted, the distance from z to y is at most $n(y)$. At the time z is evicted, the nodes from a to the end of the chain containing a, b, c are all unmarked. Hence if $n(c)$ were greater than $n(y)$, the distance from c to the set of marked nodes (at the time of z's eviction) would be greater than z's distance to the set of marked nodes (since y is marked); hence, FAR would have evicted c before evicting z and, thus, c would not be a rep.

We conclude Part 1 as follows. Let $v_1, \ldots, v_m$ be the sequence of type 2 reps on the path P. Let v_0 be the fifth type 1 rep on the first chain in P that contains at least one type 2 rep. From Claim 1, $n(v_0) \leq \ell_1$. From Claims 1 and 2,

$$n(v_{i+2}) \leq \frac{n(v_i)}{2}$$

for $0 \leq i \leq m - 2$. It follows that

$$1 \leq n(v_m) \leq \frac{n(v_0)}{2^{\lfloor m/2 \rfloor}} \leq \frac{\ell_1}{2^{\lfloor m/2 \rfloor}}$$

and, hence, $m \leq 2\lfloor \log \ell_1 \rfloor$.

D.2.2　Part 2

We now show how to construct a vine decomposition $\mathcal{V}(S)$ on at most $\frac{3k}{2}$ nodes with $val(\mathcal{V}(S)) = \Omega(R_2)$. More precisely, the number of additional nodes in S is at most half the number of nodes in chains of T that have been selected to be vines in this vine decomposition.

The construction of $\mathcal{V}(S)$ takes place in stages. At the start of each stage, we have a tree $\tilde{T}$ whose edges are contractions of paths in G.[1] Initially, we have $\tilde{T} = T$ and contract all edges that do not occur in chains or which occur in chains without any type 2 reps. During each stage, we choose one chain to be a vine in the decomposition being constructed, and we choose other chains (plus one additional path in $G - T$) to be in the tree portion of the decomposition. In order to continue this process, we contract all the chosen chains. We continue until there is only one supernode in $\tilde{T}$.

A stage is defined as follows. Consider any pair of supernodes v_1 and v_2 in $\tilde{T}$ for which there is a path in G from some node (in G) contained in v_1 to some node in v_2 that does not contain any edges in T. (It is not difficult to see that there is always at least one such pair in which one supernode is a leaf in $\tilde{T}$.) We find that pair for which the length of this

---

[1] We contract an edge $e = (u, v)$ by merging u and v into a "supernode" and then replacing edges to u or v with edges to the supernode (eliminating multiple edges).

connecting path (call it SP) is minimal. Let r be the root of $\tilde{T}$, and consider (in $\tilde{T}$) the paths P_1 to v_1 and P_2 to v_2. Let P_1' and P_2' be the resulting paths after deleting the path (if any) common to both P_1 and P_2.[2] Suppose, without loss of generality, that P_1' has more type 2 reps than P_2'. Then we choose the first chain in P_1' to be a vine and we choose all other chains (i.e., edges in $\tilde{T}$) in P_1' and P_2' and the path SP for the tree portion of the decomposition.

We need to establish the following claims:

Claim 3: If C is the chain chosen as a vine and SP is the corresponding path in $G - T$ during any stage of this construction, then $|SP| \leq \frac{|C|}{2}$.

Claim 4: At the end of the construction, the sum of the values of the chosen vines is at least $\frac{R_2}{4}$.

For Claim 3, consider the last three reps x, y, z in the last chain of P_1'. Then we show that

$$|SP| \leq n(x) \leq \frac{|C|}{2}.$$

Based on an argument (using the nature of FAR) similar to that of Part 1, at the time y is evicted, there must be a path Q of length at most $n(x) - n(y)$ from z to some previously marked node w. Path Q is composed of a path (away from y) in this last chain of P_1', followed by a path that does not use any edges in T until it reaches the supernode in $\tilde{T}$ containing the previously marked node w. From Part 1 it follows that $|Q| \leq \frac{|C|}{2}$, and by the minimality of SP, we have the desired bound

$$|SP| \leq |Q| \leq \frac{|C|}{2}.$$

For the proof of Claim 4, let C, the first chain in P_1', be a selected vine and let $r(C)$ be the number of type 2 reps in P_1'. Then, consistent with Part 1, since the chosen vine C is a first chain, we have

$$val(C) = \log |C| \geq \frac{r(C)}{2},$$

and since P_1' has at least as many type 2 reps as does P_2', it follows that the number of type 2 reps incorporated into the decomposition (by the contraction process) during a stage is at most 4 times the value of the chosen vine.

D.2.3   Part 3

Finally, we need to construct either an appropriate cycle H or a vine decomposition $\mathcal{V}(H)$ on $k + 1$ nodes. Let $\mathcal{V}$ be the decomposition constructed in Part 2. Consider a vine C in $\mathcal{V}$, let P_1', P_2', and SP be the paths in $\tilde{T}$ as defined in the selection of C as a vine. Again let $r(C)$ be the number of type 2 reps in the path P_1'. Note that based on Part 1, $r(C) \leq 2 \log |C|$. We have two cases to consider.

---

[2] If v_1 and v_2 lie on the same path, then one of the P' paths is empty.

• *Case 1:* There is a single vine C in $\mathcal{V}$ with $r(C) \geq \frac{R_2}{16}$. We then have two subcases to consider, depending on the length α of the smallest cycle in $\mathcal{V}$ containing C. Note that P_1', P_2', SP is such a cycle.

(a) $\alpha \leq k + 1$. Then we simply extend this cycle to a vine decomposition $\mathcal{V}(H)$ on $k + 1$ nodes with value $\geq \log |C| \geq \frac{r(C)}{2} = \Omega(R_2)$.

(b) $\alpha > k + 1$. In this case, consider the stage in which C became a vine. Consider the cycle $H = P_1', SP, P_2'$ containing C. We claim the length of this cycle is $\leq k(1 + 2^{-r(C)/4})$. Let $v_1, \ldots, v_{r(C)}$ be the $r(C)$ type 2 reps on P_1'. Recalling the definition of type 1 and type 2 reps, let v_0 denote the type 1 rep immediately preceding v_1 and let $v_{r(C)+1}$ denote the last (type 1) rep in P_1'. From the argument in Part 2, we have

$$|SP| \leq n(v_{r(C)-1}),$$

and from Part 1, we have

$$n(v_{i+2}) \leq \frac{n(v_i)}{2}$$

for $0 \leq i \leq r(C) - 1$, and

$$n(v_0) \leq \frac{|C|}{4} \leq \frac{|P_1'|}{4},$$

with the last inequality following from the fact that there are four type 1 reps preceding the first type 2 rep. Hence,

$$|SP| \leq \frac{|P_1'|}{[2^{\lfloor r(C)-1 \rfloor /2}]} \leq \frac{|P_1'|}{2^{r(C)/4}}.$$

Now $|P_1'| + |P_2'| \leq k$, since P_1' and P_2' are part of T, the tree of marked nodes during a phase. It follows that the length $|H|$ of the cycle H is at most $k + \frac{k}{[2^{r(C)}]}$, and from the definition of the value of a cycle, we have

$$val(H) \geq \frac{r(C)}{8} = \Omega(R_2).$$

• *Case 2:* Every vine C in $\mathcal{V}$ has $r(C) \leq \frac{R_2}{16}$ type 2 reps. We order the vines according to nondecreasing ratios $\frac{r(C)}{|C|}$ and then (using this ordering) eliminate one vine at a time until there are at most $k + 1$ nodes. Let there be q vines in $\mathcal{V}$. Since

$$\frac{R_2}{2} \leq \sum_{i=1}^{q} r(C_i) \leq \sum_{i=1}^{q} 2 \cdot val(C_i)$$

and since $r(C_i) \leq \frac{R_2}{16}$, the elimination of the smallest ratio $\frac{r(C)}{|C|}$ vines still leaves the summed value of the vines to be $\Omega(R_2)$. Finally, we add back nodes from some eliminated vine in order to produce a vine decomposition on exactly $k + 1$ nodes.

APPENDIX E

Some Tools from Renewal Theory

The contents of this appendix are drawn from Ross: *Applied Probability Models with Optimization Applications* [295]. The appendix gives a self-contained exposition of essential material up to and including the elementary renewal theorem.

E.1   Renewal Processes

A **stochastic process**, $\{X(t) : t \in T\}$, is a family of random variables where T is an index set (for our applications, T is typically the positive integers). In applications, t often represents time; hence, $X(t)$ represents the *state* of the process at time t.

Let $\{X_i : i = 1, 2, \ldots\}$ be a sequence of nonnegative independent and identically distributed random variables. We assume that $\Pr[X_i = 0] < 1$ (otherwise the theory will be trivial). Let $S_n = \sum_{i=1}^{n} X_i$ where $n \geq 1$. Also let $S_0 = 0$. Define

$$N(t) = \sup\{n : S_n \leq t\}.$$

The process $\{N(t) : t \geq 0\}$ is called a **renewal process**. Intuitively, a renewal process represents a kind of a process that counts the number of times a certain event restarts itself within some time interval. We say that a renewal occurs at time t if $S_n = t$ for some n. After each renewal, the process begins again. X_n is the time between the $(n - 1)$st and nth renewal, S_n is the time of the nth renewal, and $N(t)$ is the number of renewals in the interval $[0, t]$.

Let $m(t) = \mathbf{E}[N(t)]$. We call $m(t)$ the **renewal function**. Much of renewal theory revolves around characterizing the renewal function.

Lemma E.1 *For all $t \geq 0$, $m(t) < \infty$.*

PROOF. By assumption, $\Pr[X_n = 0] < 1$. Hence, there exists some real $\alpha > 0$ such that $\Pr[X_n \geq \alpha] > 0$. We define a "truncated" renewal process based on the X_i's as follows:

$$X_n' = \begin{cases} 0 & \text{if } X_n < \alpha; \\ \alpha & \text{if } X_n \geq \alpha. \end{cases}$$

Also, let $N'(t) = \sup\{n : X_1' + \cdots + X_n' \leq t\}$. We call the process $\{N'(t), t \geq 0\}$ the truncated process. It is not difficult to see that for the truncated process, renewals can occur only at times $t = j\alpha$, $j = 0, 1, 2, \ldots$. Under our assumptions on the X_i's, the number of renewals at each of these times are independent random variables whose expectations are $\frac{1}{\Pr[X_n \geq \alpha]}$: simply, consider a sequence of Bernoulli trials, each with a success probability of

$$p = \Pr[X_n \geq \alpha].$$

The expected number of failures until the first success is the expected number of successive X_i''s assuming zeros, all occurring in the same renewal time.

Hence,

$$\mathbf{E}[N'(t)] \leq \frac{\lceil t/\alpha \rceil}{\Pr[X_n \geq \alpha]} < \infty.$$

Since $X_n' \leq X_n$, it must be that $N'(t) \geq N(t)$ and the lemma is complete. ∎

E.2   Wald's Equation

Let $X_1, X_2, \ldots$ be a sequence of independent random variables. An integer-valued positive random variable N is a **stopping time** for the sequence $X_1, X_2, \ldots$ if the event $[N = i]$ is independent of $X_{i+1}, X_{i+2}, \ldots$ for all $i = 1, 2, \ldots$.

Intuitively, we observe the X_i's one at a time and N denotes the time at which we stop. This way, if $N = i$, we have stopped after observing $X_1, \ldots, X_i$ and before observing $X_{i+1}, X_{i+2}, \ldots$.

Example E.1 (i) Let $X_i, i = 1, 2, \ldots$, be independent such that

$$\Pr[X_i = 0] = \Pr[X_i = 1] = \tfrac{1}{2}, \quad i = 1, 2 \ldots.$$

Let $N = \min\{n : X_1 + \cdots + X_n = 10\}$. Then N is a stopping time.

(ii) Let $X_i, i = 1, 2, \ldots$, be independent such that

$$\Pr[X_i = -1] = \Pr[X_i = 1] = \tfrac{1}{2}, \quad i = 1, 2 \ldots.$$

Let $N = \min\{n : X_1 + \cdots + X_n = 1\}$. Then N is a stopping time.

Theorem E.1 (Wald's equation) *Let $X_1, X_2, \ldots$ be independent and identically distributed random variables having finite expectations, and let X denote any X_i. If N is a stopping time for the X_i's such that $\mathbf{E}[N] < \infty$, then*

$$\mathbf{E}\left[\sum_{i=1}^{N} X_i\right] = \mathbf{E}[N] \cdot \mathbf{E}[X].$$

PROOF. For $i = 1, 2, \ldots$, let

$$Y_i = \begin{cases} 1 & \text{if } i \leq N; \\ 0 & \text{if } i > N. \end{cases}$$

Then

$$\sum_{i=1}^{N} X_i = \sum_{i=1}^{\infty} X_i Y_i.$$

Therefore,

$$\mathbf{E}\left[\sum_{i=1}^{N} X_i\right] = \mathbf{E}\left[\sum_{i=1}^{\infty} X_i Y_i\right] = \sum_{i=1}^{\infty} \mathbf{E}[X_i Y_i]. \tag{E.1}$$

(Justification for the last equality will follow.)

For all i, $Y_i = 1$ if and only if we have not stopped after successively observing $X_1, \ldots, X_{i-1}$. Therefore, Y_i is determined by $X_1, \ldots, X_{i-1}$ and is thus independent of X_i. Hence, we obtain

$$\mathbf{E}\left[\sum_{i=1}^{N} X_i\right] = \sum_{i=1}^{\infty} \mathbf{E}[X_i]\mathbf{E}[Y_i]$$

$$= \mathbf{E}[X]\sum_{i=1}^{\infty} \mathbf{E}[Y_i]$$

$$= \mathbf{E}[X]\sum_{i=1}^{\infty} \Pr[N \geq i]$$

$$= \mathbf{E}[X]\mathbf{E}[N]. \tag{E.2}$$

The equality

$$\mathbf{E}[N] = \sum_{i=1}^{\infty} \Pr[N \geq i]$$

in equation (E.2) is a standard trick obtained by changing the order of summation. It can be seen as follows:

$$\mathbf{E}[N] = \sum_{k=1}^{\infty} k\Pr[N = k] = \sum_{k=1}^{\infty}\sum_{i=1}^{k} \Pr[N = k]$$

$$= \sum_{i=1}^{\infty}\sum_{k=i}^{\infty} \Pr[N = k]$$

$$= \sum_{i=1}^{\infty} \Pr[N \geq i].$$

To complete the theorem, it remains only to justify the interchange of expectation and summation at the last equality of equation (E.1). We make use of the dominated convergence theorem (see Theorem E.2).

First, notice that if we replace X_i by $|X_i|$ throughout the proof, the interchange is valid because all the terms involved are nonnegative. This leads to the following conclusion:

$$\mathbf{E}\left[\sum_{i=1}^{N} |X_i|\right] = \mathbf{E}[N]\mathbf{E}[|X|] < \infty. \tag{E.3}$$

(The finiteness of the above expression follows from our assumptions on the X_i's and N.)

For $n = 1, 2, \ldots$, let

$$W_n = \sum_{i=1}^{n} X_i Y_i.$$

Let

$$Z = \sum_{i=1}^{\infty} |X_i| Y_i.$$

Clearly, $W_n \leq Z, n = 1, 2, \ldots$.

$$\mathbf{E}[Z] = \mathbf{E}\left[\sum_{i=1}^{\infty} |X_i| Y_i\right] = \sum_{i=1}^{N} \mathbf{E}[|X_i|].$$

According to equation (E.3), $\mathbf{E}[Z]$ is finite. Hence, we can apply Theorem E.2 to obtain

$$\mathbf{E}\left[\lim_{i \to \infty} W_i\right] = \lim_{i \to \infty} \mathbf{E}[W_i].$$

Notice that the left-hand side is exactly $\mathbf{E}\left[\sum_i X_i Y_i\right]$ and the right-hand side is $\sum_i \mathbf{E}[X_i Y_i]$.

∎

Example E.2 We apply Wald's equation to calculate the expected stopping times in Example E.1. For part (i), Wald's equation implies that

$$\mathbf{E}[X_1 + \cdots + X_N] = \tfrac{1}{2} \mathbf{E}[N].$$

However, since by the definition of N, $\sum X_i = 10$; therefore, $\mathbf{E}[N] = 20$.

Similarly, an application of Wald's equation to part (ii) is expected to yield

$$\mathbf{E}[X_1 + \cdots + X_N] = \mathbf{E}[N] \cdot \mathbf{E}[X].$$

However, based on the definition of N, the left-hand side is 1, whereas the right-hand side must be 0, since $\mathbf{E}[X] = 0$. Hence, it must be that the conditions of the theorem are violated and we deduce the somewhat surprising conclusion that $\mathbf{E}[N] = \infty$.

A generalization of part (ii) to the case in which $\Pr[X_i = 1] = p$, $\Pr[X_i = -1] = q$, $p \leq \tfrac{1}{2}$ yields the same unbounded stopping time. This result has several interesting interpretations. For instance, no stopping rule can affect the overall ratio of males to females in a population. This contradicts a popular (but erroneous) argument for family planning, such as encouraging families to have children until a boy is born, and so on.

In the proof of Wald's equation, we have used the following theorem the proof of which can be found in probability or analysis texts (e.g., Chung [110] and Lang [238]).

Theorem E.2 (Dominated convergence theorem) *Let $X_1, X_2, \ldots$ be a sequence of random variables. If there exists a random variable Y with finite expectation such that $|X_i| \leq Y$ for all i, then*

$$\mathbf{E}\left[\lim_{i \to \infty} X_i\right] = \lim_{i \to \infty} \mathbf{E}[X_i].$$

E.3 The Elementary Renewal Theorem

In this section we apply Wald's equation to prove the elementary renewal theorem. In order to apply Wald's equation, we must first identify a stopping time to the renewal process. The obvious choice for the stopping time is the random variable $N(t)$. Unfortunately, $N(t)$ cannot be a stopping time; the event $[N(t) = i]$ occurs if and only if both $X_1 + \cdots + X_i \leq t$ and $X_1 + \cdots + X_i + X_{i+1} > t$ occur. This means that the event $[N(t) = i]$ is not independent of X_{i+1}; therefore, it is not a stopping time.

Fortunately, the random variable $N(t) + 1$ is a stopping time for the renewal process because the event $[N(t) = i - 1]$ occurs if and only if $X_1 + \cdots + X_{i-1} \leq t$ and $X_1 + \cdots + X_i > t$.

According to Lemma E.1, $\mathbf{E}[N(t) + 1] = m(t) + 1 < \infty$, and we can apply Wald's equation to obtain

$$\mathbf{E}[X_1 + \cdots + X_{N(t)+1}] = \mathbf{E}[X] \cdot \mathbf{E}[N(t) + 1].$$

Using our notation and letting $\mu = \mathbf{E}[X]$, this is equivalent to saying that

$$\mathbf{E}[S_{N(t)+1}] = \mu \cdot (m(t) + 1). \tag{E.4}$$

We are now ready to prove the following theorem.

Theorem E.3 (Elementary renewal theorem)

$$\lim_{t \to \infty} \frac{m(t)}{t} = \frac{1}{\mu}.$$

PROOF. We divide the proof into two parts depending on whether μ is finite or not. Assume first that $\mu < \infty$. According to the definition of $N(t)$, $S_{N(t)+1} > t$, so from equation (E.4), $\mu(m(t) + 1) > t$, and we obtain a lower bound on the limit of $\frac{m(t)}{t}$:

$$\liminf_{t \to \infty} \frac{m(t)}{t} > \frac{1}{\mu}. \tag{E.5}$$

We now want to bound the limit from above. Fix a positive constant M and define a truncated renewal process based on the X_i's and M as follows: for $i = 1, 2, \ldots$,

$$X_i' = \begin{cases} X_i & \text{if } X_i \leq M; \\ M & \text{if } X_i > M. \end{cases}$$

Let $S_n' = \sum_{i=1}^n X_i'$, $N'(t) = \sup\{n : S_n' \leq t\}$, and $m'(t) = \mathbf{E}[N'(t)]$.

Since the X_i''s are bounded above by M, it is clear that $S_{N'(t)+1}' \leq t + M$. Therefore, from equation (E.4),

$$\mu' \cdot (m'(t) + 1) \leq t + M,$$

where $\mu' = \mathbf{E}[X_i']$. Hence,

$$\limsup_{t \to \infty} \frac{m'(t)}{t} \leq \frac{1}{\mu'}.$$

Since $S_n' \leq S_n$, it must be that $N'(t) \geq N(t)$, so $m'(t) \geq m(t)$, and we obtain

$$\lim_{t \to \infty} \sup \frac{m(t)}{t} \leq \frac{1}{\mu'}. \qquad \text{(E.6)}$$

Letting $M \to \infty$, we derive

$$\lim_{t \to \infty} \sup \frac{m(t)}{t} \leq \frac{1}{\mu}. \qquad \text{(E.7)}$$

Combining equations (E.5) and (E.7), we obtain the theorem for the case $\mu < \infty$.

When $\mu = \infty$, we prove the theorem by considering the same truncated process. This time we need to consider only the inequality (E.6); surely, $\mu \to \infty$ as $M \to \infty$, and the result follows. ∎

APPENDIX F

Proof of Theorem 13.14: Disjoint Paths in an Array

We present a more detailed sketch of the proof of Theorem 13.14, which states that there is a randomized $O(\log N)$-competitive algorithm for the disjoint paths problem on an $(N \times N)$ array G.[1] If a $(d \times d)$ subarray is located so that its boundary row and column falls on a multiple of d, then the subarray is called a **block**. We consider subarrays of size $c \log N \times c \log N$ for some suitable constant c. A call from u to v in array G is defined as a **long distance call** if $dist_G(u, v) \geq 16c \log N$; otherwise, it is a **short distance call**. The simplest way to avoid conflicts between long and short distance calls is to decide (randomly) to accept only one type of call. The disjoint paths problem is thus reduced to two separate disjoint paths problems at a cost of at most a factor of 2 in the competitive ratio.

For both long distance and short distance calls, we need a way to choose subarrays that are sufficiently spread out. To do so, we use a randomized version of Luby's [249] maximal independent set algorithm.

> **Algorithm MIS:** Let $G = (V, E)$ be an arbitrary graph. MIS constructs a maximal independent set V' in stages as follows. After any stage, there are nodes determined to be in V', nodes rejected from the independent set, and still "active" nodes. In a stage, each active node chooses a random integer in some range $[1, R]$ where R is sufficiently large to make ties "unlikely." If a node chooses a larger number than all its neighbors, then it is added to V' and its neighbors are eliminated. This continues until all nodes have been either eliminated or placed in V'.

We now develop disjoint paths algorithms for short and long distance calls, starting with the easier case of short distance calls.

F.1 Short Distance Calls

For short distance calls, we select subarrays X_u (centered around certain nodes u randomly chosen by MIS) that are sufficiently separated. The separation ensures that a somewhat

---

[1] For a complete proof, see Kleinberg and Tardos [227].

larger subarray Y_u, also centered at u, will be disjoint from any other Y_v. (Thus, routing in one Y_u does not interfere with routing within another Y_v.) Moreover, Y_u will be sufficient for routing a fraction of short distance calls originating and terminating in X_u. Finally, we guarantee with constant probability that the origin and destination of a short distance call will reside in one of the selected X_u.

The following algorithm and lemmas allow us to exploit the locality of short calls.

Lemma F.1 *Let H be a graph of diameter d with e edges. Then there is a deterministic online algorithm for disjoint paths in H that is $(2 \max\{d, \sqrt{e}\})$-competitive.*

Lemma F.2 *Let X (respectively, Y) be a $2d \times 2d$ (respectively, $4d \times 4d$) block centered at some node (i, j). Suppose that $\{r_1, \ldots, r_t\}$ are t calls that all originate and terminate in X and can be simultaneously routed by disjoint paths in G. Then at least $\frac{t}{4}$ of these calls can be routed within Y.*

We are now ready to describe the short distance algorithm.

Algorithm SHORT-CALL: Let $G = (V, E)$ be the array. Let $d = 32c \log N$ (i.e., twice the maximum distance of a short call). Run the randomized MIS algorithm to find a set $V' \subseteq V$ such that for any $u \neq v$ in V', the horizontal and vertical distance between u and v is at least $4d$. For $u \in V'$, let X_u denote the $(2d \times 2d)$ subarray centered at the node u and let Y_u be the $(4d \times 4d)$ subarray with the same center u.

Let $\sigma = r_1, r_2, \ldots, r_n$ be an input sequence of short (distance $\leq \frac{d}{2}$) calls. If r_i originates and terminates in some X_u ($u \in V'$), then attempt to route r_i within Y_u using Lemma F.1; otherwise, reject the call.

Theorem F.1 *Algorithm SHORT-CALL is $O(\log N)$-competitive for short distance calls on the $(N \times N)$ array.*

PROOF. We first claim that if (s, t) is a short call, then

$$\Pr[s \text{ and } t \text{ are both located within some } X_u] \geq \tfrac{1}{64}.$$

For this claim, we need consider only the probability that the MIS algorithm includes a node u (i.e., gives highest random number) to a node within distance $\frac{d}{2}$ of, for example, s. If it does, then t must also be within the block X_u. The MIS algorithm ensures that $Y_u \cap Y_v = \varnothing$ for $u \neq v$ in V'. Hence, routing in Y_u and Y_v will not conflict. Y_u has diameter $d = 4p = O(\log N)$, and the number of edges $e = O(\log^2 N)$. Lemma F.2 shows that it is not too restrictive to route within a Y_u, and Lemma F.1 shows that there is an $O(\log N)$-competitive routing (within Y_u) for the calls in X_u. ∎

F.2   Long Distance Calls

For long distance calls, we need a way to select certain blocks randomly as "call centers"; then we consider only those calls that originate and terminate in (different) call centers. Thus we need to ensure with constant probability that a long distance call originates in a call center and terminates in a call center. These centers, when surrounded by some "enclosing sub-arrays," will become the supernodes for the AAP simulation.

We define a simulation network $\mathcal{N}$ and a mapping from G into $\mathcal{N}$. A collection of (adjacent) blocks in G is mapped into a node in $\mathcal{N}$. The routing of long distance calls consists of three main components. First, we construct the mapping (before the inputs are processed). Second, we simulate the routing of certain calls in G within the network $\mathcal{N}$. Finally, we show how each disjoint path in $\mathcal{N}$ can be realized by a disjoint path in G.

Constructing the mapping. Partition G into $(c \log N \times c \log N)$ blocks. Let u be the center of such a subarray. Let C_u be the subarray centered at u, and let B_u denote C_u and the immediate eight neighboring subarrays that share $c \log N$ boundary walls with C_u. We run the MIS algorithm on the set of center nodes, selecting a subset $V' \subseteq V$ such that $u, v \in V'$ implies $B_u \cap B_v = \varnothing$. Every block C not included in some B_u ($u \in V'$) must node intersect (and share a boundary wall of) at least one B_u. Add C to such a B_u, and call the resulting collection (called a **cluster**) of subarrays $\{D_u\}$. Now $\mathcal{N}$ is the network with node set $\{D_u\}$ and edge set

$$\big\{(D_u, D_v) \mid D_u \text{ and } D_v \text{ intersect in a boundary wall}\big\}.$$

The following lemma shows that the MIS chosen set V' is sufficiently dense for our purposes.

Lemma F.3 *If u and v are centers of $(c \log N \times c \log N)$ subarrays, and if $\mathrm{dist}_G(u, v) \geq 11c \log N$, then $\Pr[u \text{ and } v \text{ are both in } V'] \geq \frac{1}{25}$.*

Selecting calls to route in $\mathcal{N}$. The online algorithm attempts to route (using $\mathcal{N}$) only certain long distance calls. First, we set the capacity of each edge in $\mathcal{N}$ to be $\rho \log N$ for some sufficiently small ρ. That is, we use only a constant fraction of the $c \log N$ capacity that a priori seems to be present between adjacent clusters (i.e., nodes in $\mathcal{N}$). However, we need to limit this capacity of edges in $\mathcal{N}$ so that later, when we actually need to route in G, we can limit the way calls enter and leave blocks.

Next, we attempt to route only those calls that originate in some C_u and terminate in some C_v with $u, v \in V'$; furthermore, we route at most one call originating or terminating in a given C_u.

We thus have the following "high level" long distance algorithm.

Algorithm LONG-CALL: Construct the network $\mathcal{N}$ with edge capacity $\rho \log N$. Accept a long distance call originating at s and terminating at t if and only if:

1. s resides in some C_u and t resides in some C_v.
2. For this u and v, no other calls have been routed that originate or terminate in either C_u or C_v.
3. Algorithm AAP would accept a call originating in (the image of) D_u and terminating in (the image of) D_v.

If LONG-CALL accepts this call, then the routing in $\mathcal{N}$ in turn determined by AAP provides a "high level" routing for routing the call in G. The call follows the sequence of clusters determined by AAP.

The algorithm is completed when we describe how each of these accepted calls can actually be routed by edge disjoint paths in G.

Note that since the boundary size of any D_u is $O(\log N)$, the optimal algorithm can route at most $O(\log N)$ calls that originate or terminate in some C_u. A call can be rejected either because some other call with the same originating block or terminating block has been accepted or because it will not be accepted by the AAP algorithm running on $\mathcal{N}$ (but only assuming a fraction of the implicit capacity of edges in $\mathcal{N}$). Each of these criteria accepts an $O\left(\frac{1}{\log N}\right)$ fraction of the optimal number of calls accepted. (Note that optimality against a fractional optimal means that the value of an optimal solution using $c \log N$ capacity edges is at most a constant factor better than that which can be achieved using only $\rho \log N$ capacity edges.)

The following (informally stated) "meta" algorithm and lemma show that the combined process still accepts an $O\left(\frac{1}{\log N}\right)$ fraction of the optimal.

> **Algorithm INTERSECT:** Consider any kind of "call admission" problem where we are trying to maximize the number of accepted requests.
>
> Let $\text{ALG}_1, \text{ALG}_2, \ldots, \text{ALG}_k$ be a finite number of online algorithms, each defined for some particular subproblem (i.e., defined on certain input subsequences). Let σ be an input sequence, and let INTERSECT denote the following algorithm. Given a request r, INTERSECT accepts r if and only if r is accepted by every ALG_i that considers r. In order to maintain the "state" of each algorithm ALG_i, we simulate each ALG_i as if it processed a subsequence σ_{ALG_i} of the sequence σ. Whenever a request r is accepted by INTERSECT, r is appended to each σ_{ALG_i} such that ALG_i considered (and accepted) it. For a rejected request r, append r to exactly one (arbitrarily chosen) sequence σ_{ALG_j} such that ALG_j considered and rejected r.

Lemma F.4 *Let* $\text{ALG}_1, \text{ALG}_2, \ldots, \text{ALG}_k$ *be deterministic online algorithms and let* ALG_i *be* c_i-*competitive. Then* INTERSECT *is* Σc_i-*competitive.*

Routing a call in G that has been routed by AAP *in* $\mathcal{N}$. This is the most technical step needed to complete the description of algorithm LONG-CALL. We only hint at the idea required. We use the neighboring blocks surrounding a C_u to effect a $\rho \log N$ "crossbar" connection between the clusters D_u. The idea is to use channels (i.e., cycles at a fixed radius from the center of the cluster and outside of the center block C_u, plus horizontal and vertical paths to the boundary) in each of these clusters to do the routing. In each cluster (on the AAP determined route) a call essentially remains in one channel and can switch channels (in order to enter a new cluster) at a unique intersecting node between the two channels.

We conclude that LONG-CALL is $O(\log N)$-competitive on long distance calls.

APPENDIX G

Some Tools from the Theory of Types

In this appendix we briefly present a few elementary information theoretic results related to the **theory of types**.[1] We note that all the results stated here can be proven using elementary probability and combinatorics. Nevertheless, the proofs given here, stated in terms of information theoretic concepts, are perhaps more revealing.

Let $P = (p_1, p_2, \ldots, p_n)$ be a probability distribution, $p_i \geq 0$, $\sum_i p_i = 1$. The **Shannon entropy** of P, $H(P)$, is

$$H(P) = -\sum_{i=1}^{n} p_i \log p_i,$$

where the logarithm is to the base 2. Fix any alphabet $\Sigma = \{s_1, s_2, \ldots, s_m\}$ of m symbols. Let $\mathbf{x} = x_1, x_2, \ldots, x_n$ be any sequence from Σ^n. Use $n_i(\mathbf{x})$ to denote the number of occurrences of s_i in $\mathbf{x}$ and set $v_i(\mathbf{x}) = \frac{n_i(\mathbf{x})}{n}$. The **type** of $\mathbf{x}$, denoted $T(\mathbf{x})$, is the empirical distribution of $\mathbf{x}$; that is,

$$T(\mathbf{x}) = \left(\frac{n_1(\mathbf{x})}{n}, \frac{n_2(\mathbf{x})}{n}, \ldots, \frac{n_m(\mathbf{x})}{n}\right) = (v_1(\mathbf{x}), v_2(\mathbf{x}), \ldots, v_m(\mathbf{x})).$$

Use $\mathcal{T}(n)$ to denote the set of all possible types of sequences of length n. Our first theorem states that there are at most a polynomial number of types.

Theorem G.1 $|\mathcal{T}(n)| \leq (n+1)^m$.

PROOF. Consider any type $\tau \in \mathcal{T}(n)$. That is, for some sequence $\mathbf{x} = x_1, \ldots, x_n$,

$$\tau = T(\mathbf{x}) = \left(\frac{n_1(\mathbf{x})}{n}, \ldots, \frac{n_m(\mathbf{x})}{n}\right).$$

Each numerator in this type vector can obtain at most $n + 1$ values. ∎

For the next theorem we need the following definition. Let $P = (p_1, \ldots, p_m)$ and $Q = (q_1, \ldots, q_m)$ be two probability distributions. The **Kullback–Leibler dissimilarity**

---

[1] The results presented in this appendix are drawn from chap. 12 of Cover and Thomas [122]. The presentation here is minimized to cover results essential only for the development of Chapter 14 of this text.

between P and Q, denoted $D(P\|Q)$, is

$$D(P\|Q) = \sum_{i=1}^{m} p_i \log \frac{p_i}{q_i}.$$

(Based on continuity, the standard convention is that $0 \log \frac{0}{q} = 0$ and $p \log \frac{p}{0} = \infty$.) Using convexity arguments, it is possible to prove that, always, $D(P\|Q) \geq 0$ and equality is obtained if and only if $P = Q$.

Suppose that the sequence $\mathbf{x} = x_1, x_2, \ldots, x_n$ is chosen randomly, with each symbol x_i chosen identically and independently using the probability distribution $P = \{p(s_i)\}_{i=1}^{m}$ defined over Σ. The probability of obtaining a particular sequence $\mathbf{x}$ is thus

$$P(\mathbf{x}) = \prod_{i=1}^{n} p(x_i).$$

Clearly, all sequences of the same type have the same probability. The next theorem expresses this probability in terms of the type.

Theorem G.2 *Assume that* $\mathbf{x} = x_1, \ldots, x_n$ *is chosen i.i.d. according to P. Then,*

$$P(\mathbf{x}) = \prod_{i=1}^{n} p(x_i) = 2^{-n(H(T(\mathbf{x}))+D(T(\mathbf{x})\|P))}.$$

PROOF.

$$\prod_{i=1}^{n} p(x_i) = \prod_{s_i \in \Sigma} p(s_i)^{n_i(\mathbf{x})}$$

$$= \prod_{s_i \in \Sigma} p(s_i)^{n\nu_i(\mathbf{x})}$$

$$= \prod_{s_i \in \Sigma} 2^{n\nu_i(\mathbf{x}) \log p(s_i)}$$

$$= \prod_{s_i \in \Sigma} 2^{n(\nu_i(\mathbf{x}) \log p(s_i) - \nu_i(\mathbf{x}) \log \nu_i(\mathbf{x}) + \nu_i(\mathbf{x}) \log \nu_i(\mathbf{x}))}$$

$$= 2^{n \sum_{s_i} \left(-\nu_i(\mathbf{x}) \log \frac{\nu_i(\mathbf{x})}{p(s_i)} + \nu_i(\mathbf{x}) \log \nu_i(\mathbf{x})\right)}$$

$$= 2^{n(-D(T(\mathbf{x})\|P) - H(T(\mathbf{x})))}.$$

■

It follows that in the particular case in which $T(\mathbf{x}) = P$, $P(\mathbf{x}) = 2^{-nH(T(\mathbf{x}))}$.

Let τ be any type in $\mathcal{T}(n)$. Use $C(\tau)$ to denote the set of all sequences of length n that have type τ. $C(\tau)$ is called the **type class** of τ. The last theorem of this appendix gives an upper bound on the size of the type class.

Theorem G.3 *Let* $\tau = (\tau(s_1), \tau(s_2), \ldots, \tau(s_m))$ *be any type in* $\mathcal{T}(n)$. *Then*

$$|C(\tau)| = \binom{n}{n\tau(s_1) \, n\tau(s_2) \, \cdots \, n\tau(s_m)} \leq 2^{nH(\tau)}.$$

PROOF. The equality is easily proved by the observation that $|C(\tau)|$ is the number of ways to arrange $n\tau(s_1)$ s_1-symbols, $n\tau(s_2)$ s_2-symbols, and so on, in a sequence of length n. To prove the inequality, first note that

$$\sum_{x \in C(\tau)} \prod_{i=1}^{n} \tau(x_i) \leq 1.$$

Simply, the left-hand side is the probability of choosing at least one element of $C(\tau)$ (assuming that the elements in Σ are chosen according to the distribution τ). Hence, from Theorem G.2, we have

$$\sum_{x \in C(\tau)} \prod_{i=1}^{n} \tau(x_i) = \sum_{x \in C(\tau)} 2^{-nH(\tau)}$$

$$= |C(\tau)| 2^{-nH(\tau)}.$$

∎

APPENDIX H

Two Technical Lemmas

In this appendix we prove two technical lemmas related to Chapter 14.

H.1 Proof of Lemma 14.4

In this section we (re)state and prove Lemma 14.4, which is required for the analysis of the two-way trading algorithm FMM of Chapter 14.

For the proof of the lemma, we require the following approximation formula for the binomial coefficient $\binom{n}{xn}$, $x \in (0, 1)$ (where xn is an integer).

$$\binom{n}{xn} \approx \frac{1}{\sqrt{2\pi(1-x)}} \cdot \frac{1}{\sqrt{n}} \cdot \left(x^{-x}(1-x)^{(1-x)}\right)^n. \tag{H.1}$$

This approximation can be easily derived using Stirling's approximation of $n!$.[1]

Lemma 14.4 provides useful asymptotic properties of $B_p\{{n \atop k}\}$. For convenience, we restate the lemma.

Lemma 14.4 (Partial binomial sums approximation) *Let $n \geq 2$ be an integer and let $0 < c < 1$ (with cn an integer). Let $p = \frac{\alpha}{1+\alpha}$ for some $\alpha > 1$. Set*

$$B_n = B_p\left\{{n \atop cn}\right\} = \sum_{i=0}^{cn} \binom{n}{i} p^i (1-p)^{n-i}.$$

Define

$$W(x) = \frac{x^x(1-x)^{(1-x)}(1+\alpha)}{\alpha^{(1-x)}}.$$

Then, the following conditions hold:

- (i) *If $c > p$, then $B_n \to 1$ almost surely.*
- (ii) *If $c = p$, then $B_n \to \frac{1}{2}$.*
- (iii) *If $c < p$, then $B_n = \Theta\left(\frac{1}{\sqrt{n}} \cdot W^{-n}(1-c)\right).$*

---

[1] Stirling's formula is: $n! \approx \sqrt{2\pi} n^{n+(1/2)} e^{-n}$ (see Feller [148], p. 52).

PROOF. Condition (i) readily follows from the strong law of large numbers.[2] Condition (ii) is a consequence of the DeMoivre–Laplace limit theorem.[3] More specifically, recall that $B_c\{{}^n_{cn}\} = \Pr[S_n \le cn]$, where S_n denotes the number of successes in n Bernoulli trials (with success probability c). The DeMoivre–Laplace limit theorem approximates this probability via the normal distribution. Thus, as n increases

$$\Pr[S_n \le cn] \to \mathcal{N}_{0,1}(0) = \tfrac{1}{2},$$

where $\mathcal{N}_{0,1}(x)$ is the normal distribution, with mean 0 and standard deviation 1.

We now prove condition (iii). Use a_i to denote the ith term of B_n. That is, $a_i = \binom{n}{i} p^i (1-p)^{(n-i)}$. For $i = 1, 2, \ldots, n$, set $r_i = \frac{a_{i-1}}{a_i}$. The first observation is that r_i strictly increases with i. Specifically, it is easy to see that

$$r_i = \frac{1-p}{p} \cdot \frac{i}{n-i+1},$$

which is clearly increasing with i. Now,

$$
\begin{aligned}
r_{cn} &= \frac{1-p}{p} \cdot \frac{cn}{n-cn+1} \\
&= \frac{1-p}{p} \cdot \frac{cn}{n(1-c)+1} \\
&< \frac{c}{p} \cdot \frac{1-p}{1-c} \qquad\qquad\qquad\qquad\qquad\qquad (\mathrm{H.2}) \\
&< 1 \qquad\qquad\qquad (\text{since } c < p).
\end{aligned}
$$

Using inequality (H.2) and the fact that $r_1 < r_2 < \cdots < r_{cn} < 1$, we now derive an upper bound on B_n.

$$
\begin{aligned}
B_n &= a_{cn} + a_{cn-1} + a_{cn-2} + \cdots + a_0 \\
&= a_{cn} + (r_{cn})a_{cn} + (r_{cn}r_{cn-1})a_{cn} + \cdots + (r_{cn}\cdots r_1)a_{cn} \\
&< a_{cn}\left(1 + r_{cn} + r_{cn}^2 + \cdots + r_{cn}^{cn}\right) \\
&< a_{cn} \sum_{i=0}^{\infty} r_{cn}^i \\
&= a_{cn}(1 - r_{cn})^{-1} \\
&< a_{cn}\left(1 - \frac{c(1-p)}{p(1-c)}\right)^{-1}, \qquad \text{using inequality (H.2);} \\
&= a_{cn}\left(1 - \frac{c}{\alpha(1-c)}\right)^{-1}, \qquad \text{using the identity } \tfrac{1-p}{p} = \tfrac{1}{\alpha}; \\
&= a_{cn} \cdot \frac{\alpha(1-c)}{\alpha(1-c) - c}.
\end{aligned}
$$

On the other hand, we have the obvious lower bound $B_n > a_{cn}$.

---

[2] See Feller [148], pp. 202–204.
[3] See Feller [148], p. 186.

Using the approximation formula for the binomial coefficient (H.1), it is not difficult to see that

$$a_{cn} \approx \frac{1}{\sqrt{2\pi c(1-c)}} \cdot \frac{1}{\sqrt{n}} \cdot W^{-n}(1-c).$$

Hence, combining the lower and upper bounds, we have

$$\frac{1}{\sqrt{2\pi c(1-c)}} < \sqrt{n} W^{n}(1-c) \cdot B_{n} < \frac{1}{\sqrt{2\pi c(1-c)}} \cdot \frac{\alpha(1-c)}{\alpha(1-c)-c}.$$

That is,

$$B_{n} = \Theta\left(\frac{1}{\sqrt{n}} \cdot W^{-n}(1-c)\right).$$

∎

H.2 Proof of Lemma 14.6

We restate and then prove the lemma:

Lemma 14.6: $\displaystyle\int_{B} \prod_{i=1}^{n} b_{j_i} d\mu(\mathbf{b}) = \frac{n_1! n_2! \cdots n_m! (m-1)!}{(m-1+n_1+n_2+\cdots+n_m)!}.$

Define

$$\beta_i = \sum_{j=1}^{i} b_j.$$

With respect to any nonnegative real c, define

$$K_m(c, n_1, n_2, \ldots, n_m)$$

$$= \int_0^c \int_0^{c-\beta_1} \int_0^{c-\beta_2} \cdots \int_0^{c-\beta_{m-2}} \left(\prod_{i=1}^{m-1} b_i^{n_i}\right) (1-\beta_{m-1})^{n_m} db_1 db_2 \cdots db_{m-1}.$$

The proof of Lemma 14.6 is established by using the following three lemmas.

Lemma H.1 *Let $m \geq 2$ be any integer and let $c > 0$ be any real. Then,*

$$K_m(c, 0, 0, \ldots, 0) = \frac{c^{m-1}}{(m-1)!}.$$

PROOF. We prove the lemma by induction on m.
  Base case. For $m = 2$, we have

$$K_2(c, 0, 0) = \int_0^c db_1 = x \Big|_0^c = c = \frac{c^1}{(2-1)!}.$$

Induction step. Let $b \leq c$. Using the induction hypothesis,

$$K_{m-1}(c-b, 0, 0, \ldots, 0) = \frac{(c-b)^{m-2}}{(m-2)!}.$$

We then have

$$K_m(c, 0, 0, \ldots, 0)$$

$$= \int_0^c \left(\int_0^{(c-b)} \int_0^{(c-b)-b_2} \cdots \int_0^{(c-b)-b_2-\cdots-b_{m-2}} 1 \cdot db_2 \cdots db_{m-1} \right) db$$

$$= \int_0^c \frac{(c-b)^{m-2}}{(m-2)!} db$$

$$= -\frac{(c-b)^{m-1}}{(m-1)(m-2)!} \Big|_0^c$$

$$= \frac{c^{m-1}}{(m-1)!}.$$

∎

Lemma H.2 *Let r and s be nonnegative integers. Define*[4]

$$I(r, s) = \int_0^1 x^r (1-x)^s dx.$$

Then,

$$I(r, s) = \frac{r! s!}{(r+s+1)!}.$$

PROOF. We first show that

$$I(r, s) = \frac{s}{r+s+1} \cdot I(r, s-1).$$

We use integration by parts. That is, $\int_0^1 u \cdot dv = uv \Big|_0^1 - \int_0^1 v \cdot du$, with $u = x^r(1-x)^s$ and $dv = dx$. Notice that

$$v \cdot du = x(rx^{r-1}(1-x)^s - sx^r(1-x)^{s-1})dx$$

$$= \left((r+s-s)x^r(1-x)^s - sx^{r+1}(1-x)^{s-1} \right) dx$$

$$= (r+s)x^r(1-x)^s dx - s \left(x^r(1-x)^{s-1}(1-x+x) \right) dx$$

$$= (r+s)x^r(1-x)^s dx - sx^r(1-x)^{s-1} dx.$$

Hence,

$$I(r, s) = x^r(1-x)^s x \Big|_0^1 - (r+s)I(r, s) + sI(r, s-1).$$

Rearranging, we obtain the recurrence $I(r, s) = \frac{s}{r+s+1} I(r, s-1)$. Note that $I(r, 0) = \int_0^1 x^r dx = \frac{1}{r+1}$. It follows that

$$I(r, s) = \frac{s!}{(r+s+1)(r+s)\cdots(r+1)} = \frac{r! s!}{(r+s+1)!}.$$

∎

---

[4] $I(r, s)$ is called the Beta function when r and s are reals.

Using Lemma H.2, we prove the following lemma.

Lemma H.3 *Let $m \geq 2$, and let $n_1, n_2, \ldots, n_m$ be nonnegative integers. Then,*

$$K_m(1, n_1, \ldots, n_m) = \frac{n_1! n_2! \cdots n_m!}{(m - 1 + n_1 + n_2 + \cdots + n_m)!}.$$

PROOF. We prove the lemma by induction on m.

Base case. According to Lemma H.2, the case $m = 2$ holds. Specifically,

$$K_2(1, n_1, n_2) = \int_0^1 x^{n_1}(1-x)^{n_2} dx = I(n_1, n_2) = \frac{n_1! n_2!}{(1 + n_1 + n_2)!}.$$

Induction step. Based on the induction hypothesis,

$$K_{m-1}(1, n_1, n_2, \ldots, n_{m-2}, 1 + n_{m-1} + n_m) = \frac{n_1! n_2! \cdots n_{m-2}!(1 + n_{m-1} + n_m)!}{(m + n_1 + n_2 + \cdots + n_m)!}.$$

Using the substitution,

$$b_{m-1} = x(1 - b_1 - b_2 - \cdots - b_{m-2}) = x(1 - \beta_{m-2}),$$

and using Lemma H.2, we have

$$
\begin{aligned}
& K_m(1, n_1, \ldots, n_m) \\
&= \int_0^1 \int_0^{1-\beta_1} \cdots \int_0^{1-\beta_{m-2}} \left(\prod_{i=1}^{m-1} b_i^{n_i} \right) (1 - \beta_{m-2} - b_{m-1})^{n_m} db_1 \cdots db_{m-1} \\
&= \int_0^1 \int_0^{1-\beta_1} \cdots \int_0^{1-\beta_{m-2}} \int_0^1 \left(\prod_{i=1}^{m-2} b_i^{n_i} \right) \\
&\qquad \times x^{n_{m-1}}(1 - \beta_{m-2})^{1+n_{m-1}}(1 - \beta_{m-2})^{n_m}(1-x)^{n_m} db_1 \cdots db_{m-2} dx \\
&= \int_0^1 \int_0^{1-\beta_1} \cdots \int_0^{1-\beta_{m-2}} \left(\prod_{i=1}^{m-2} b_i^{n_i} \right) \\
&\qquad \times (1 - \beta_{m-2})^{1+n_{m-1}+n_m} \left(\int_0^1 x^{n_{m-1}}(1-x)^{n_m} dx \right) db_1 \cdots db_{m-2} \\
&= I(n_{m-1}, n_m) \cdot K_{m-1}(1, n_1, n_2, \ldots, n_{m-2}, 1 + n_{m-1} + n_m) \\
&= \frac{n_{m-1}! n_m!}{(1 + n_{m-1} + n_m)!} \cdot \frac{n_1! n_2! \cdots n_{m-2}!(1 + n_{m-1} + n_m)!}{(m - 1 + n_1 + n_2 + \cdots + n_m)!} \\
&= \frac{n_1! n_2! \cdots n_m!}{(m - 1 + n_1 + n_2 + \cdots + n_m)!}.
\end{aligned}
$$

∎

Proof of Lemma 14.6. In order to calculate the integral, we first express it in terms of ordinary multiple (iterated) integrals. For $i = 1, 2, \ldots, m$, set $n_i = n\nu(J_n)_i$. It is not difficult to see that

$$\int_{\mathcal{B}} \prod_{i=1}^{n} b_{j_i} d\mu(\mathbf{b}) = \frac{K_m(1, n_1, n_2, \ldots, n_m)}{K_m(1, 0, 0, \ldots, 0)}.$$

(Recall that $K_m(\cdot)$ is given by equation (H.3).) Note that we must normalize and divide by $K_m(1, 0, \ldots, 0)$ since μ is *probability* (uniform) measure. Hence, based on Lemmas H.1 and H.3,

$$\int_{\mathcal{B}} \prod_{i=1}^{n} b_{j_i} d\mu(\mathbf{b}) = \frac{n_1! n_2! \cdots n_m! (m-1)!}{(m-1+n_1+n_2+\cdots+n_m)!}.$$

∎

Bibliography

[1] D. Achlioptas, M. Chrobak, and J. Noga. Competitive analysis of randomized paging algorithms. In *Proceedings of the 4th European Symposium on Algorithms*, LNCS 1136, pp. 419–430. Springer-Verlag, 1996.

[2] A. V. Aho, J. E. Hopcroft, and J. D. Ullman. *Data Structures and Algorithms*. Reading, Mass.: Addison-Wesley, 1983.

[3] S. al-Binali. The competititve analysis of risk taking with application to online trading. In *Proceedings of the 38th Annual Symposium on Foundations of Computer Science*, pp. 336–344, 1997.

[4] S. Albers. Improved randomized on-line algorithms for the list update problem. In *Proceedings of the 6th Annual ACM-SIAM Symposium on Discrete Algorithms*, pp. 412–419, 1995.

[5] S. Albers. Better bounds for on-line scheduling. In *Proceedings of the 29th Annual ACM Symposium on Theory of Computing*, pp. 130–139, 1997.

[6] S. Albers and M. Mitzenmacher, Average case analyses of list update algorithms, with applications to data compression. *Proceedings of the 23rd International Colloquium on Automata, Languages and Programming (ICALP)*. Springer Lecture Notes in Computer Science, vol. 1099, pp. 514–525, 1996.

[7] S. Albers and M. Mitzenmacher. Revisiting the counter algorithms for list update. *Information Processing Letters*, 64(2):155–160, 1997.

[8] S. Albers, B. von Stengel, and R. Werchner. A combined BIT and TIMESTAMP algorithm for the list update problem. *Information Processing Letters*, 56:135–139, 1995.

[9] S. Albers and J. Westbrook. A survey of self-organizing data structures. In *Dagstuhl Proceedings*, 1996. To be published in Springer-Verlag LNCS Lecture Notes.

[10] M. Allais. Le comportement de l'homme rationnel devant le risque, critique des postulats et axiomes de l'école americaine. *Econometrica*, 21:503–546, 1953.

[11] B. Allen and I. Munro. Self-organizing binary search trees. *Journal of the ACM*, 25:526–535, October 1978.

[12] N. Alon, R. M. Karp, D. Peleg, and D. West. A graph-theoretic game, and its application to the k-server problem. *SIAM Journal of Computing*, 24:78–100, 1995.

[13] E. J. Anderson, P. Nash, and R. R. Weber. A counterexample to a conjecture in optimal list ordering. *Journal of Applied Probability*, 19(9):730–732, 1982.

[14] G. E. Andrews. *The Theory of Partitions*, Encyclopedia of Mathematics and its Applications, vol. 2. Addison-Wesley, 1976.

[15] F. J. Anscombe and R. J. Aumann. A definition of subjective probabilities. *The Annals of Mathematical Statistics*, 23:396–407, 1952.

[16] K. J. Arrow. Alternative approaches to the theory of choice in risk-taking situations. *Econometrica*, 19:404–437, 1951.

[17] K. J. Arrow. *Essays in the Theory of Risk-Bearing*. Chicago: Markham, 1971.

[18] K. J. Arrow and L. Hurewicz. An optimality criterion for decision-making under ignorance. In C. F. Carter and J. L. Ford, editors, *Uncertainty and Expectations in Economics*, pp. 1–11. Oxford: Basil Blackwell, 1972.

[19] J. Aspnes, Y. Azar, A. Fiat, S. Plotkin, and O. Waarts. On-line routing of virtual circuits with applications to load balancing and machine scheduling. *Journal of the ACM*, 44(3):486–504, 1997.

[20] P. Auer, N. Cesa-Bianchi, Y. Freund, and R. E. Schapire. Gambling in a rigged casino: The adversarial multi-armed bandit problem. In *Proceedings of the 36th Annual Symposium on Foundations of Computer Science*, pp. 322–331, 1995.

[21] R. J. Aumann. Mixed and behavior strategies in infinite extensive games. In M. Dresher, L. S. Shapley, and A. W. Tucker, editors, *Advances in Game Theory*, vol. 1, pp. 627–650. Princeton, N.J.: Princeton University Press, 1964.

[22] R. J. Aumann, S. Hart, and M. Perry. The absent-minded driver. *Games and Economic Behavior*, 20:102–116, 1997.

[23] B. Awerbuch, Y. Azar, A. Fiat, and T. Leighton. Making commitments in the face of uncertainty: How to pick a winner almost every time. In *Proceedings of the 28th Annual ACM Symposium on Theory of Computing*, pp. 519–530, 1996.

[24] B. Awerbuch, Y. Azar, A. Fiat, S. Leonardi, and A. Rosén. On-line competitive algorithms for call admission in optical networks. In *Proceedings of the 4th Annual European Symposium on Algorithms (ESA)*, LNCS 1136, pp. 431–444. Springer-Verlag, 1996.

[25] B. Awerbuch, Y. Azar, E. F. Grove, M. Kao, P. Krishnan, and J. S. Vitter. Load balancing in the L_p norm. In *Proceedings of the 36th Annual Symposium on Foundations of Computer Science*, pp. 383–391, 1995.

[26] B. Awerbuch, Y. Azar, and S. Plotkin. Throughput-competitive on-line routing. In *Proceedings of the 34th Annual Symposium on Foundations of Computer Science*, pp. 32–40, 1993.

[27] B. Awerbuch, Y. Azar, S. Plotkin, and O. Waarts. Competitive routing of virtual circuits with unknown duration. In *Proceedings of the 5th Annual ACM-SIAM Symposium on Discrete Algorithms*, pp. 321–327, 1994.

[28] B. Awerbuch, Y. Bartal, A. Fiat, and A. Rosén. Competitive non-preemptive call control. In *Proceedings of the 5th Annual ACM-SIAM Symposium on Discrete Algorithms*, pp. 312–320, 1994.

[29] B. Awerbuch, R. Gawlick, F. T. Leighton, and R. Rabani. On-line admission control and circuit routing for high performance computing and communication. In *Proceedings of the 35th IEEE Annual Symposium on Foundations of Computer Science*, 1994.

[30] B. Awerbuch and D. Peleg. Sparse partitions. In *Proceedings of the 31st Annual Symposium on Foundations of Computer Science*, pp. 503–513, 1990.

[31] Y. Azar. On-line load balancing. Presented at 1996 Dagstuhl Meeting on Online Algorithms. To be published in Springer-Verlag LNCS Lecture Notes.

[32] Y. Azar, A. Z. Broder, and A. Karlin. On-line load balancing. *Theoretical Computer Science*, 130(1):73–84, 1994.

[33] Y. Azar and L. Epstein. On-line load balancing of temporary tasks on identical machines. In *5th Israeli Symposium on Theory of Computing and Systems*, pp. 119–125, 1997.

[34] Y. Azar, B. Kalyanasundaram, S. Plotkin, K. Pruhs, and O. Waarts. On-line load balancing of temporary tasks. *Journal of Algorithms*, 22(1):93–110, 1997.

[35] Y. Azar, J. Naor, and R. Rom. The competitiveness of on-line assignments. *Journal of Algorithms*, 18(2):221–237, 1995.

[36] R. Bachrach and R. El-Yaniv. Online list accessing algorithms and their applications: Recent empirical evidence. In *Proceedings of the 8th Annual ACM-SIAM Symposium on Discrete Algorithms*, pp. 53–62, 1997.

[37] A. Bar-Noy, R. Canetti, S. Kutten, Y. Mansour, and B. Schieber. Bandwidth allocation with preemption. In *Proceedings of the 27th Annual ACM Symposium on Theory of Computing*, pp. 616–625, 1995.

[38]   A. Bar-Noy and B. Schieber. Personal communication, 1991.

[39]   Y. Bartal. Personal communication, 1997.

[40]   Y. Bartal. Personal communication, 1997.

[41]   Y. Bartal. A fast memoryless 2-server algorithm in Euclidean spaces, 1994. Unpublished manuscript.

[42]   Y. Bartal. On the k-server conjecture: Simplification of Koutsoupias–Papadimitriou proof, 1996. Unpublished manuscript.

[43]   Y. Bartal. Probabilistic approximation of metric spaces and its algorithmic applications. In *Proceedings of the 37th Annual Symposium on Foundations of Computer Science*, pp. 184–193, 1996.

[44]   Y. Bartal, A. Blum, C. Burch, and A. Tomkins. A polylog(n)-competitive algorithm for metrical task systems. In *Proceedings of the 29th Annual ACM Symposium on Theory of Computing*, pp. 711–719, 1997.

[45]   Y. Bartal, A. Fiat, H. Karloff, and R. Vohra. New algorithms for an ancient scheduling problem. *Journal of Computer and System Sciences*, 51(3):359–366, 1995.

[46]   Y. Bartal, A. Fiat, and S. Leonardi. Lower bounds for on-line graph problems with application to on-line circuit and optical routing. In *Proceedings of the 28th Annual ACM Symposium on Theory of Computing*, pp. 531–540, 1996.

[47]   Y. Bartal and E. Grove. The harmonic k-server algorithm is competitive, 1994. Unpublished manuscript.

[48]   Y. Bartal, H. Karloff, and Y. Rabani. A new lower bound for m-machine scheduling. *Information Processing Letters*, 50:113–116, 1994.

[49]   Y. Bartal and S. Leonardi. On-line routing in all-optical networks. *Proceedings of the 24th International Colloqium on Automata, Languages and Programming*, LNCS 1256, Springer-Verlag, 1997.

[50]   P. Beame, A. Borodin, P. Raghavan, W. L. Ruzzo, and M. Tompa. Time-space tradeoffs for undirected graph connectivity. In *Proceedings of the 31st Annual Symposium on Foundations of Computer Science*, pp. 429–438, 1990.

[51]   L. A. Belady. A study of replacement algorithms for virtual storage computers. *IBM Systems Journal*, 5:78–101, 1966.

[52]   L. A. Belady, R. A. Nelson, and G. S. Shedler. An anomaly in space-time characteristics of certain programs running in a paging machine. *Communications of the ACM*, 12(6):349–353, June 1969.

[53]   R. Bellman. *Dynamic Programming*. Princeton, N.J.: Princeton University Press, 1957.

[54]   S. Ben-David and A. Borodin. A new performance measure for online algorithms. *Algorithmica*, 11:73–91, 1994.

[55]   S. Ben-David, A. Borodin, R. M. Karp, G. Tardos, and A. Wigderson. On the power of randomization in on-line algorithms. In *Proceedings of the 22nd Annual ACM Symposium on Theory of Computing*, pp. 379–386, May 1990. (Journal version [56].)

[56]   S. Ben-David, A. Borodin, R. M. Karp, G. Tardos, and A. Wigderson. On the power of randomization in on-line algorithms. *Algorithmica*, 11:2–14, 1994. (Conference version [55].)

[57]   M. Ben-Or. Lower bounds for algebraic computation trees. In *Proceedings of the 15th Annual ACM Symposium on Theory of Computing*, pp. 80–86, 1983.

[58]   J. L. Bentley and C. McGeoch. Amortized analysis of self-organizing sequential search heuristics. *Communications of the ACM*, 28(4):404–411, 1985.

[59]   J. L. Bentley, D. D. Sleator, R. E. Tarjan, and V. K. Wei. A locally adaptive data compression scheme. *Communications of the ACM*, 29(4):320–330, 1986.

[60]   P. Berman, M. Charikar, and M. Karpinski. On-line load balancing for related machines. *7th Workshop on Algorithms and Data Structures*, LNCS 1272, pp. 116–125. Springer, 1997.

[61]   P. Berman, H. Karloff, and G. Tardos. A competitive 3-server algorithm. In *Proceedings of the 1st ACM-SIAM Symposium on Discrete Algorithms*, pp. 280–290, 1990.

[62] M. Bern, D. H. Greene, A. Raghunathan, and M. Sudan. On-line algorithm for locating check-points. *Algorithmica*, 11(1):33–52, 1994.

[63] D. Bernoulli. Specimen theoriae novae de mensura sortis. *Commenarii Acasemia Scientiarum Imperialis Petropolitanae*, 5:175–192, 1738.

[64] D. Bernoulli. Exposition of a new theory on the measurement of risk. *Econometrica*, 22, 1954. (Translation of the 1738 version [63].)

[65] D. J. Bertsimas and R. Vohra. Linear programming relaxations, approximation algorithms and randomization: A unified view of covering problems. Technical Report Working Paper OR 285-94, MIT Sloan School, Cambridge, 1994.

[66] L. Bic and A. C. Shaw. *The Logical Design of Operating Systems*. Englewood Cliffs, N.J.: Prentice-Hall, 1988.

[67] N. Biggs. *Algebraic Graph Theory*. 2d ed. Cambridge University Press, 1993.

[68] J. R. Bitner. Heuristics that dynamically alter data structures to reduce their access time. Technical Report UIUCDCS-R-76-818, University of Illinois, July 1976. (Ph.D. dissertation.)

[69] J. R. Bitner. Heuristics that dynamically organize data structures. *SIAM Journal on Computing*, 8(1):82–110, February 1979.

[70] D. Blackwell. An analog of the minimax theorem for vector payoffs. *Pacific Journal of Mathematics*, 6:1–8, 1956.

[71] A. Blum and C. Burch. On-line learning and the metrical task system problem. In *Tenth Annual Conference on Computational Learning Theory*, 1997.

[72] A. Blum, M. Furst, and A. Tomkins. What to do with your free time: Algorithms for infrequent requests and randomized weighted caching, July 1996. Unpublished manuscript.

[73] A. Blum and A. Kalai. Universal portfolios with and without transaction costs. In *Tenth Annual Conference on Computational Learning Theory*, 1997.

[74] A. Blum and A. Kalai. Universal portfolios with and without transaction costs. Unpublished extended version of [73], 1997.

[75] A. Blum, H. Karloff, Y. Rabani, and M. Saks. A decomposition theorem and bounds for randomized server problems. In *Proceedings of the 33rd Annual IEEE Symposium on Foundations of Computer Science*, pp. 197–207, 1992.

[76] A. Blum, P. Raghavan, and B. Schieber. Navigating in unfamiliar geometric terrain. *SIAM Journal on Computing*, 26:110–137, 1997.

[77] Z. Bodie, A. Kane, and A. J. Marcus. *Investments*. Richard D. Irwin, 1993.

[78] B. Bollobaś. *Graph Theory, An Intructory Course*. 3d printing. Springer-Verlag, 1990.

[79] A. Borodin and R. El-Yaniv. On randomization in online computation. In *Proceedings of the IEEE Conference on Computational Complexity*, pp. 226–238, June 1997.

[80] A. Borodin, S. Irani, P. Raghavan, and B. Schieber. Competitive paging with locality of reference. *Journal of Computer and System Sciences*, 50(2):244–258, 1995.

[81] A. Borodin, N. Linial, and M. Saks. An optimal online algorithm for metrical task systems. In *Proceedings of the 19th Annual ACM Symposium on Theory of Computing*, pp. 373–382, 1987. (Journal version [82].)

[82] A. Borodin, N. Linial, and M. Saks. An optimal online algorithm for metrical task systems. *Journal of the ACM*, 39:745–763, 1992. (Conference version [81].)

[83] J. Bourgain. On Lipschitz embedding of finite metric spaces in Hilbert space. *Israel Journal of Mathematics*, 52:46–52, 1985.

[84] E. Briys and H. Louberge. On the theory of rational insurance purchasing: A note. *Journal of Finance*, 40(2):577–581, 1985.

[85] D. J. Brown. A lower bound for on-line one-dimensional bin packing algorithms. Technical Report R-864, Coordinated Sci. Lab., University of Illinois, Urbana, 1979.

[86] W. R. Burley. Traversing layered graphs using the work function algorithm. Technical Report CS93-319, Department of Computer Science and Engineering, University of California, San Diego, La Jolla, 1993.

[87] M. Burrows and D. J. Wheeler. A block-sorting lossless data compression algorithm. Technical Report 124, Digital System Research Center, 1994.

[88] P. J. Burville and J. F. C. Kingman. On a model for storage and search. *Journal of Applied Probability*, 10, 3:697–701, September 1973.

[89] A. R. Calderbank, E. G. Coffman, Jr., and L. Flatto. Sequencing problems in two-server systems. *Mathematics of Operations Research*, 10(4):585–598, 1985.

[90] R. Canetti and S. Irani. Bounding the power of preemption in randomized scheduling. In *Proceedings of the 27th Annual ACM Symposium on Theory of Computing*, pp. 606–615, 1995.

[91] A. K. Chandra, P. Raghavan, W. L. Ruzzo, R. Smolensky, and P. Tiwari. The electrical resistance of a graph captures its commute and cover times. In *Proceedings of the 21st Annual ACM Symposium on Theory of Computing*, 1989.

[92] P. Chassaing. Optimality of move-to-front for self-organizing data structures with locality of reference. *Annals of Applied Probability*, 3(4):1219–1240, 1939.

[93] A. Chateauneuf. On the use of capacities in modeling uncertainty aversion and risk aversion. *Journal of Mathematical Economics*, 20:343–369, 1991.

[94] B. Chen, A. van Vliet, and G. J. Woeginger. Lower bounds for randomized online scheduling. *Information Processing Letters*, 51(5):219–222, September 1994.

[95] B. Chen, A. van Vliet, and G. J. Woeginger. New lower and upper bounds for on-line scheduling. *Operations Research Letters*, 16:221–230, 1994.

[96] H. Chernoff. Rational selection of decision functions. *Econometrica*, 22:422–443, 1954.

[97] A. Chou. Optimal trading strategies vs. a statistical adversary. Master's thesis, Massachusetts Institute of Technology, Cambridge, Mass., 1994.

[98] A. Chou, J. R. Cooperstock, R. El-Yaniv, M. Klugerman, and T. Leighton. The statistical adversary allows optimal money-making trading strategies. In *Proceedings of the 6th Annual ACM-SIAM Symposium on Discrete Algorithms*, 1995.

[99] A. Chou, A. Shrivastava, and R. Sidney. On the power of magnitude. Unpublished manuscript, May 1995.

[100] M. Chrobak, H. Karloff, T. Payne, and S. Vishwanathan. New results on server problems. *SIAM Journal on Discrete Mathematics*, 4(2):172–181, May 1991.

[101] M. Chrobak and L. Larmore. A new approach to the server problem. *SIAM Journal on Discrete Mathematics*, 4(3):323–328, 1991.

[102] M. Chrobak and L. Larmore. The server problem and on-line games. In *On-Line Algorithms, Proceedings of a DIMACS Workshop*. Vol. 7 of *DIMACS Series in Discrete Mathematics and Computer Science*, pp. 11–64. American Mathematical Society, New York, 1991.

[103] M. Chrobak and L. L. Larmore. An optimal on-line algorithm for *k*-servers on trees. *SIAM Journal on Computing*, 20(1):144–148, February 1991.

[104] M. Chrobak and L. L. Larmore. A note on the server problem and a benevolent adversary. *Information Processing Letters*, 38:173–175, May 1991.

[105] M. Chrobak and L. L. Larmore. On fast algorithms for two servers. *Journal of Algorithms*, 12:607–614, 1991.

[106] M. Chrobak and L. L. Larmore. Generosity helps, or an 11-competitive algorithm for three servers. *Algorithmica*, 16:234–263, 1994.

[107] M. Chrobak, L. L. Larmore, N. Reingold, and J. Westbrook. Page migration algorithms using work functions. In *Proceedings of the 4th Annual International Symposium on Algorithms and Computation*, Hong Kong, December 1993, p. 93.

[108] M. Chrobak and J. Noga. LRU is better than FIFO. In *Proceedings of the 9th Annual ACM-SIAM Symposium on Discrete Algorithms*, pp. 78–81, January, 1998. Accepted for publication in *Algorithmica*.

[109] F. R. K. Chung, D. J. Hajela, and P. D. Seymour. Self-organizing sequential search and Hilbert's inequalities. In *Proceedings of the 17th Annual ACM Symposium on Theory of Computing*, pp. 217–223, 1985.

[110] K. L. Chung. *A Course in Probability Theory.* New York: Academic Press, 1974.

[111] V. Chvátal. A greedy heuristic for the set covering problem. *Mathematics of Operations Research*, 4:233–235, 1979.

[112] E. G. Coffman and P. J. Denning. *Operating Systems Theory.* Englewood Cliffs, N.J.: Prentice-Hall, 1973.

[113] E. G. Coffman Jr., M. R. Garey, and D. S. Johnson. Approximation algorithms for bin packing: a survey. In D. S. Hochbaum, editor, *Approximation Algorithms for N P-Hard Problems*, pp. 46–93. Boston: PWS Publishing, 1996.

[114] D. Coppersmith, P. Doyle, P. Raghavan, and M. Snir. Random walks on weighted graphs, and application to on-line algorithms. In *Proceedings of the 22nd Annual ACM Symposium on Theory of Computing*, pp. 369–378, 1990.

[115] D. Coppersmith, P. G. Doyle, P. Raghavan, and M. Snir. Random walks on weighted graphs, and applications to on-line algorithms. *Journal of the ACM*, 40:421–453, 1993.

[116] T. H. Cormen, C. E. Leiserson, and R. L. Rivest. *Introduction to Algorithms.* Cambridge, Mass.: MIT Press, 1990.

[117] G. Cornuejols, M. Fisher, and G. Nemhauser. Location of bank accounts to optimize float. *Management Science*, 23:789–810, 1977.

[118] R. Courant and F. John. *Introduction to Calculus and Analysis.* Springer-Verlag, 1989.

[119] T. M. Cover. Universal portfolios. *Mathematical Finance*, 1(1):1–29, January 1991.

[120] T. M. Cover and D. H. Gluss. Empirical Bayes stock market portfolios. *Advances in Applied Mathematics*, 7:170–181, 1986.

[121] T. M. Cover and E. Ordentlich. Universal portfolios with side information. *IEEE Transactions on Information Theory*, March 1996.

[122] T. M. Cover and J. A. Thomas. *Elements of Information Theory.* New York: Wiley, 1991.

[123] J. Cox and M. Rubinstein. *Options Markets.* Englewood Cliffs, N.J.: Prentice-Hall, 1985.

[124] G. Cramer. Letter to Nikolaus Bernoulli, published in [63].

[125] H. Cramér. On the mathematical theory of risk. *Försäkringsaktiebolaget Skandia*, 2:7–84, 1930.

[126] B. de Finetti. La prévision: ses lois logiques, ses sources subjectives. *Annales de l'Institut Henri Poincaré*, 7:1–68, 1937.

[127] B. de Finetti. Recent suggestions for the reconciliation of theories of probability. In *Proceedings of the Second (1950) Berkeley Symposium on Mathematical Statistics and Probability*, 1951.

[128] M. H. DeGroot. *Optimal Statistical Decisions.* New York: McGraw-Hill, 1970.

[129] X. Deng and S. Mahajan. The cost of derandomization: computability or competitiveness. *SIAM Journal of Computing*, 26(3):786–802, 1991.

[130] P. J. Denning. Virtual memory. *ACM Computing Surveys*, 2(3):153–189, 1970.

[131] P. J. Denning and S. C. Schwartz. Properties of the working-set model. *Communications of the ACM*, 15(3):191–198, 1972.

[132] C. Derman. *Finite State Markov Decision Processes.* Academic Press, 1970.

[133] E. D. Domar and R. A. Musgrave. Proportional income taxation and risk-taking. *The Quarterly Journal of Economics*, 58:388–422, 1944.

[134] P. G. Doyle and J. L. Snell. *Random Walks and Electrical Networks.* Washington, D.C.: The Mathematical Association of America, 1984.

[135] S. E. Dreyfus. *Dynamic Programming and the Calculus of Variations.* Academic Press, 1965.

[136] J. H. Dreze. *Essays on Economic Decisions under Uncertainty.* Cambridge: Cambridge University Press 1987.

[137] S. J. Eggers and R. H. Katz. Evaluating the performance of four cache coherency protocols. In *Proceedings of the 16th Annual International Symposium on Computer Architecture*, pp. 2–15, 1989.

[138] R. El-Yaniv. On the decision theoretic foundations of competitive analysis. Unpublished manuscript.

[139] R. El-Yaniv. There are infinitely many competitive-optimal online list accessing algorithms, 1997. Unpublished manuscript.

[140] R. El-Yaniv, A. Fiat, R. M. Karp, and G. Turpin. Competitive analysis of financial games. In *Proceedings of the 33rd Annual Symposium on Foundations of Computer Science*, pp. 327–333, 1992.

[141] R. El-Yaniv, R. Kaniel, and N. Linial. Competitive optimal online leasing. Unpublished manuscript, 1997.

[142] R. El-Yaniv and J. Kleinberg. Geometric two-server algorithms. *Information Processing Letters*, 53:355–358, 1995.

[143] D. Ellsberg. Risk, ambiguity and the savage axioms. *The Quarterly Journal of Economics*, 75:643–669, 1961.

[144] J. Encarnación. On decisions under uncertainty. *The Economic Journal*, 75:442–444, 1965.

[145] L. G. Epstein and M. Le Breton. Dynamically consistent beliefs must be Bayesian. *Journal of Economic Theory*, 61:1–22, 1993.

[146] U. Faigle, W. Kern, and György Turán. On the performance of on-line algorithms for partition problems. *Acta Cybernetica*, 9:107–119, 1989.

[147] A. Feldman. On-line call admission for high-speed network. Technical Report CMU-CS-95-201, Carnegie Mellon University, Pittsburgh, 1995.

[148] W. Feller. *An Introduction to Probability Theory and Its Applications*, vol. I. New York: Wiley, 1968.

[149] E. Feuerstein. *On-line Paging of Structured Data and Multi-threaded Paging*. Ph.D. dissertation, Università Degli Studi Di Roma "La Sapienza," Rome, 1995.

[150] R. P. Feynman, R. B. Leighton, and M. Sands. *The Feynman Lectures on Physics*, vol. I. Reading, Mass.: Addison-Wesley, 1975.

[151] A. Fiat and A. Karlin. Randomized and multifinger paging with locality of reference. In *Proceedings of the 27th Annual ACM Symposium on Theory of Computing*, pp. 626–634, 1995.

[152] A. Fiat, R. M. Karp, M. Luby, L. A. McGeoch, D. D. Sleator, and N. E. Young. Competitive paging algorithms. Technical Report CMU-CS-88-196, Carnegie Mellon University, Pittsburgh, 1988. (Journal version [153].)

[153] A. Fiat, R. M. Karp, M. Luby, L. A. McGeoch, D. D. Sleator, and N. E. Young. On competitive algorithms paging algorithms. *Journal of Algorithms*, 12:685–699, 1991. (Technical report version [152].)

[154] A. Fiat, Y. Rabani, and Y. Ravid. Competitive k-server algorithms. In *Proceedings of the 31st Annual Symposium on Foundations of Computer Science*, pp. 454–463, 1990.

[155] A. Fiat, Y. Rabani, Y. Ravid, and B. Schieber. A deterministic $O(k^3)$-competitive k-server algorithm for the circle. *Algorithmica*, 11:572–578, June 1994.

[156] A. Fiat and Z. Rosen. Experimental studies of access graph based heuristics: beating the LRU standard? In *Proceedings of the 8th Annual ACM-SIAM Symposium on Discrete Algorithms*, 1997.

[157] P. C. Fishburn. A mixture-set axiomatization of conditional subjective expected utility. *Econometrica*, 41:1–25, 1973.

[158] P. C. Fishburn. Utility and subjective probability. In R. J. Aumann and S. Hart, editors, *Handbook of Game Theory*, vol. 2, pp. 1397–1435. Elsevier, 1994.

[159] I. Fisher. *The Nature of Capital and Income*. London: Augustus M. Kelley Publishers, 1956.

[160] P. A. Franaszek and T. J. Wagner. Some distribution-free aspects of paging performance. *Journal of the ACM*, 21(1):31–39, January 1974.

[161] S. French. *Decision Theory: An Introduction to the Mathematics of Rationality*. Ellis Horwood Limited and Halsted Press, 1986.

[162] J. Friedman and N. Linial. On convex body chasing. *Discrete and Computational Geometry*, 9:293–321, 1993.

[163] G. Galambos and G. J. Woeginger. An on-line scheduling heuristic with better worst case ratio than Graham's list scheduling. *SIAM Journal on Computing*, 22:349–355, 1993.

[164] J. A. Garay and I. S. Gopal. Call preemption in communication networks. *Proc. INFOCOM '92*, 44:1043–1050, 1992.

[165] J. A. Garay, I. S. Gopal, S. Kutten, Y. Mansour, and M. Yung. Efficient on-line call control algorithms. *Journal of Algorithms*, 23:180–194, 1997.

[166] T. Garefalakis. A family of randomized algorithms for list accessing. Master's thesis, Department of Computer Science, University of Toronto, January 1997.

[167] M. Garey, R. Graham, and J. Ullman. Worst-case analysis of memory allocation algorithms. In *Proceedings of the 4th Annual ACM Symposium on Theory of Computing*, 1972.

[168] M. R. Garey and D. S. Johnson. *Computers and Intractability*. New York, W. H. Freeman, 1979.

[169] R. Gawlick, A. Kamath, S. Plotkin, and K. G. Ramakrishnan. Routing and admission control in general topology networks. Technical report #1548, Dept. of Computer Science, Stanford University, Stanford, Calif., 1995.

[170] I. Gilboa. Expected utility theory with purely subjective non-additive probabilities. *Journal of Mathematical Economics*, 16:65–88, 1989.

[171] I. Gilboa and D. Schmeidler. Maxmin expected utility with non-unique prior. *Journal of Mathematical Economics*, 18:141–155, 1989.

[172] M. X. Goemans. *Advanced Algorithms, Lecture Notes*. Cambridge, Mass.: MIT Laboratory for Computer Science, 1993.

[173] G. H. Gonnet, J. I. Munro, and H. Suwanda. Towards self-organizing linear search. In *Proceedings of the 20th Annual Symposium on Foundations of Computer Science*, 1979.

[174] G. H. Gonnet, J. I. Munro, and H. Suwanda. Exegesis of self-organizing linear search. *SIAM Journal on Computing*, 10:613–637, 1982.

[175] R. L. Graham. Bounds for certain multiprocessor anomalies. *Bell System Technical Journal*, 45:1563–1581, 1966.

[176] G. R. Grimmett and D. R. Stirzaker. *Probability and Random Processes*. 2d ed. Oxford Science Publications, 1995.

[177] D. Grinberg, S. Rajagopalan, R. Venkatesan, and V. K. Wei. Splay trees for data compression. In *Proceedings of the 6th Annual ACM-SIAM Symposium on Discrete Algorithms*, 1995.

[178] E. Grove. The harmonic online k-server algorithm is competitive. In *Proceedings of the 23rd Annual ACM Symposium on Theory of Computing*, pp. 260–266, May 1991.

[179] E. Grove. The harmonic online k-server algorithm is competitive, 1992. Unpublished manuscript.

[180] L. A. Hall. Approximation algorithms for scheduling. In D. S. Hochbaum, editor, *Approximation Algorithms for NP-Hard Problems*, pp. 1–45. Boston: PWS Publishing, 1997.

[181] P. R. Halmos. *Measure Theory*. Springer-Verlag, 1970.

[182] S. Hart. Games in extensive and strategic forms. In R. J. Aumann and S. Hart, editors, *Handbook of Game Theory*, vol. 1, chap. 2, pp. 19–40. Elsevier, 1992.

[183] S. Hart and A. Mas-Collel. A simple adaptive procedure leading to correlated equilibrium. Center for Rationality DP-126, Hebrew University, January 1997.

[184] F. Haussmann. Probability of survival as an investment criterion. *Management Science*, 15:33–48, 1968.

[185] D. P. Helmbold, R. E. Schapire, Y. Singer, and M. K. Warmuth. On-line portfolio selection using multiplicative updates. In *Machine Learning: Proceedings of the 13th International Conference*, pp. 243–251, 1996.

[186] W. J. Hendricks. An account of self-organizing systems. *SIAM Journal on Computing*, 5, 4:715–723, December 1976.

[187] J. L. Hennessy and D. A. Patterson. *Computer Architecture: A Quantitative Approach*. 2d ed. Morgan-Kaufmann, 1995.

[188] J. H. Hester and D. S. Hirschberg. Self-organizing linear search. *ACM Computing Surveys*, 17(3):295–312, 1985.

[189] M. Hofri. Should the two-headed disk be greedy? *Information Processing Letters*, 16:83–86, 1983.

[190] J. Hull. *Options, Futures, and Other Derivative Securities*. Englewood Cliffs, N.J.: Prentice-Hall, 1993.

[191] L. Hurewicz. Optimality criteria for decision making under ignorance. Cowles Commission Discussion Paper, Statistics, No. 370, (Mimeo) 1951.

[192] L. Hurewicz. Some specification problems and applications to econometric models. *Econometrica*, 19:343–344, 1951. (Abstract.)

[193] L. Hurewicz, H. Wallman, and W. Hurewicz. *Dimension Theory*. Princeton, N.J.: Princeton University Press, 1948.

[194] S. Irani. Coloring inductive graphs on-line. In *Proceedings of the 31st Annual Symposium on Foundations of Computer Science*, pp. 470–479, 1990.

[195] S. Irani. Two results on the list update problem. *Information Processing Letters*, 38(6):301–306, June 1991.

[196] S. Irani. Corrected version of the split algorithm for the list update problem. Technical Report Technical Report 96-53, ICS Department, University of California, Irvine, 1996. (Corrected version of the SPLIT algorithm appearing in [195, 199].)

[197] S. Irani. Page replacement with multi-size pages and applications to web caching. In *Proceedings of the 29th Annual ACM Symposium on Theory of Computing*, pp. 701–710, 1997.

[198] S. Irani, A. Karlin, and S. Phillips. Strongly competitive algorithms for paging with locality of reference. *SIAM Journal on Computing*, 25(3):477–497, 1996.

[199] S. Irani, N. Reingold, J. Westbrook, and D. D. Sleator. Randomized competitive algorithms for the list update problem. In *Proceedings of the 2nd ACM-SIAM Symposium on Discrete Algorithms*, pp. 251–260, 1991.

[200] S. Irani and R. Rubinfeld. A competitive 2-server algorithm. *Information Processing Letters*, 39:85–91, 1991.

[201] S. Irani and S. S. Seiden. Randomized algorithms for metrical task systems. In *Proceedings of the 4th Workshop on Algorithms and Data Structures*, LNCS 955, pp. 159–170. Springer-Verlag, August 1995.

[202] S. Irani and S. S. Seiden. Randomized algorithms for metrical task systems. Unpublished manuscript, October 1996. (Revised version of [201].)

[203] J. R. Isbell. Finitary games. In M. Dresher, A. W. Tucker, and P. Wolfe, editors, *Contributions to the Theory of Games*, vol. III, pp. 79–96. Princeton, N.J.: Princeton University Press, 1957.

[204] F. Jamshidian. Asymptotically optimal portfolios. *Mathematical Finance*, 2(2):131–150, 1992.

[205] D. S. Johnson. *Near-Optimal Bin Packing Algorithms*. Ph.D. dissertation, Massachusetts Institute of Technology, Cambridge, 1973.

[206] D. S. Johnson. Fast algorithms for bin packing. *Journal of Computer and System Sciences*, 8:272–314, 1974.

[207] D. S. Johnson, A. Demers, J. D. Ullman, M. R. Garey, and R. L. Graham. Worst-case performance bounds for simple one-dimensional packing algorithms. *SIAM Journal on Computing*, 3: 299–325, 1974.

[208] D. Kahneman and A. Tversky. Prospect theory: An analysis of decision under risk. *Econometrica*, 47:263–291, 1979.

[209] R. Karger, S. Phillips, and E. Torng. A better algorithm for an ancient scheduling problem. *Journal of Algorithms*, 20:400–430, 1996.

[210] A. R. Karlin, M. S. Manasse, L. A. McGeoch, and S. Owicki. Competitive randomized algorithms for non-uniform problems. In *Proceedings of the 1st ACM-SIAM Symposium on Discrete Algorithms*, pp. 301–309, 1990.

[211] A. R. Karlin, S. J. Phillips, and P. Raghavan. Markov paging. In *Proceedings of the 33rd Annual IEEE Symposium on Foundations of Computer Science*, pp. 208–217, 1992.

[212] A. R. Karlin, M. S. Manasse, L. Rudolph, and D. D. Sleator. Competitive snoopy caching. *Algorithmica*, 3(1):70–119, 1988.

[213] H. Karloff. Personal communication with Y. Ravid, 1994.

[214] H. Karloff, Y. Rabani, and Y. Ravid. Lower bounds for randomized k-server and motion-planning algorithms. In *Proceedings of the 23rd Annual ACM Symposium on Theory of Computing*, pp. 278–288, 1991.

[215] E. Karni. Subjective expected utility theory with state-dependent preferences. *Journal of Economic Theory*, 60:428–438, 1993.

[216] E. Karni and D. Schmeidler. Utility theory with uncertainty. In W. Hildenbrand and H. Sonnenschein, editors, *Handbook of Mathematical Economics*, vol. IV, pp. 1763–1831. Amsterdam: North-Holland, 1991.

[217] R. M. Karp. A $2k$-competitive algorithm for the circle, August 1989. Unpublished manuscript.

[218] R. M. Karp, U. Vazirani, and V. Vazirani. An optimal algorithm for on-line bipartite matching. In *Proceedings of the 22nd Annual ACM Symposium on Theory of Computing*, pp. 352–258, 1990.

[219] R. L. Keeney and H. Raiffa. *Decisions with Multiple Objectives: Preferences and Value Tradeoffs*. New York: Wiley, 1976.

[220] J. G. Kemeny, J. L. Snell, and A. W. Knapp. *Denumerable Markov Chains*. Van Nostrand, 1966.

[221] H. A. Kierstead. An effective version of Dilworth's theorem. *Transactions of the American Mathematical Society*, 268:63–77, 1981.

[222] H. A. Kierstead. The linearity of First-Fit for coloring interval graphs. *SIAM Journal on Discrete Mathematics*, 1:526–530, 1988.

[223] H. A. Kierstead and Jun Qin. First-Fit and interval graphs. In preparation.

[224] H. A. Kierstead and W. T. Trotter. An extremal problem in recursive combinatorics. *Congressus Numerantium*, 33:143–153, 1981.

[225] J. Kleinberg. A lower bound for two-server balancing algorithms. *Information Processing Letters*, 52(1):39–43, October 1994.

[226] J. Kleinberg and M. Sudan. Personal communication, July 1995.

[227] J. Kleinberg and E. Tardos. Disjoint paths in densely embedded graphs. In *Proceedings of the 36th Annual Symposium on Foundations of Computer Science*, pp. 531–540, 1995.

[228] D. E. Knuth. *The Art of Computer Programming*, vol. 1. Reading, Mass.: Addison-Wesley, 1973.

[229] E. Koutsoupias. *On-Line Algorithms and the k-Server Conjecture*. Ph.D. dissertation, Department of Computer Science and Engineering, University of California, San Diego, 1994.

[230] E. Koutsoupias. Personal communication, 1997.

[231] E. Koutsoupias and C. Papadimitriou. Beyond competitive analysis. In *Proceedings of the 35th Annual IEEE Symposium on Foundations of Computer Science*, pp. 394–400, 1994.

[232] E. Koutsoupias and C. Papadimitriou. On the k-server conjecture. *Journal of the ACM*, 42(5): 971–983, September 1995.

[233] E. Koutsoupias and C. Papadimitriou. The 2-evader problem. *Information Processing Letters*, 57(5):249–252, March 1996.

[234] D. M. Kreps. *Notes on the Theory of Choice*. Westview Press, 1988.

[235] D. J. Kuck and D. H. Lawrie. The use and performance of memory hierarchies. Technical Report 363, Dept. of Computer Science, University of Illinois, Urbana, December 1969.

[236] H. W. Kuhn. Extensive games and the problem of information. In H. W. Kuhn and A. W. Tucker, editors, *Contributions to the Theory of Games*, vol. II, pp. 193–216. Princeton, N.J.: Princeton University Press, 1953.

[237] K. Lam, Y. Leung, and K. Siu, Self-organizing files with dependent accesses. *Journal of Applied Probability*, 21:343–359, 1984.

[238] S. Lang. *Real and Functional Analysis*. Springer-Verlag, 1993.

[239] E. L. Lawler, J. K. Lenstra, Alexander H. G. Rinnooy Kan, and David B. Shmoys. Sequencing and scheduling: Algorithms and complexity. In S. C. Graves, A. H. G. Rinnooy Kan, and P. Zipkin, editors, *The Handbooks of Operations Research and Management Science. Vol. IV, Logistics of Production and Inventory*, pp. 445–522. Amsterdam: North-Holland, 1993.

[240] S. Leonardi, A. Marchetti-Spaccamela, A. Presciutti, and A. Rosén. On-line randomized call control revisited. In *ACM-SIAM Symposium on Discrete Algorithms*, pp. 323–332, January, 1998.

[241] L. Levin. Personal communication, July 1994.

[242] H. R. Lewis and L. Denenberg. *Data Structures & Their Algorithms*. Harper Collins Publishers, 1991.

[243] F. Liang. A lower bound for bin packing. *Information Processing Letters*, 10:76–79, 1980.

[244] N. Linial, E. London, and Y. Rabinovich. The geometry of graphs and some of its algorithmic applications. *Combinatorica*, 15:215–245, 1995.

[245] N. Linial and M. Saks. Decomposing graphs into regions of small diameter. In *Proceedings of the 2nd ACM-SIAM Symposium on Discrete Algorithms*, pp. 320–330, 1991.

[246] R. Lipton and A. Tomkins. Online interval scheduling. In *Proceedings of the 5th Annual ACM-SIAM Symposium on Discrete Algorithms*, 1994.

[247] I. H. Loomis. On a theorem of von Neumann. In *Proceedings of the National Academy of Sciences, U.S.A.*, 32, pp. 213–215, 1946.

[248] L. Lovász. On the ratio of optimal integral and fractional covers. *Discrete Mathematics*, 13: 383–390, 1975.

[249] M. Luby. A simplie parallel algorithm for the maximal independent set problem. *SIAM Journal on Computing*, 15:1036–1053, 1986.

[250] F. Luccio and A. Pedrotti. A parallel list update problem. *Information Processing Letters*, 52:277–284, 1994.

[251] R. D. Luce and H. Raiffa. *Games and Decisions*. New York: Wiley, 1957.

[252] C. Lund, S. Phillips, and N. Reingold. IP-paging and distributional paging. In *Proceedings of the 35th Annual IEEE Symposium on Foundations of Computer Science*, pp. 424–434, 1994.

[253] M. J. Machina. Choice under uncertainty: Problems solved and unsolved. *Economic Perspectives*, 1(1):121–154, 1987.

[254] M. J. Machina and D. Schmeidler. A more robust definition of subjective probability. *Econometrica*, 60(4):745–780, 1992.

[255] M. S. Manasse, L. A. McGeoch, and D. D. Sleator. Competitive algorithms for on-line problems. In *Proceedings of the 20th Annual ACM Symposium on Theory of Computing*, pp. 322–333, May 1988. (Journal version [256].)

[256] M. S. Manasse, L. A. McGeoch, and D. D. Sleator. Competitive algorithms for server problems. *Journal of Algorithms*, 11:208–230, 1990. (Conference version [255].)

[257] H. Markowitz. Porfolio selection. *Journal of Finance*, 7(1):77–91, 1952.

[258] H. Markowitz. The utility of wealth. *Journal of Political Economy*, 60:151–158, 1952.

[259] H. Markowitz. *Portfolio Selection. Efficient Diversification of Investments*. 2d ed. Blackwell Publishers, 1970.

[260] J. McCabe. On serial files with relocatable records. *Operations Research*, 13:609–618, July 1965.

[261] C. McGeoch. Analyzing algorithms by simulation: Variance reduction techniques and simulation speedups. *ACM Computing Surveys*, 24(2):195–212, 1992.

[262] L. A. McGeoch. *Algorithms for Two Graph Problems: Computing Maximum-Genus Imbeddings and the Two-Server Problem*. Ph.D. dissertation, Carnegie Mellon University, Pittsburgh, 1987.

[263] L. A. McGeoch and D. D. Sleator. A strongly competitive randomized paging algorithm. *Algorithmica*, 6:816–825, 1991.

[264] J. Milnor. Games against nature. In R. M. Thrall, C. H. Coombs, and R. L. Davis, editors, *Decision Processes*, pp. 49–60. New York: Wiley, and London: Chapman & Hall, 1954.

[265] R. B. Myerson. *Game Theory: Analysis of Conflict*. Cambridge, Mass.: Harvard University Press, 1991.

[266] H. H. Nachtkamp. *Der kurzfristige optimale Angebotspreis der Unternehmen bei Vollkostenkalkulation und unsicheren Nachfrageerwartungen*. Tübingen, 1969.

[267] J. F. Nash. Equilibrium points in *n*-person games. In *Proceedings of the National Academy of Sciences, U.S.A.*, 36, pp. 48–49, 1950.

[268] J. Niehans. Zur Preisbildung bei ungewissen Erwartungen. *Schweizerische Zeitschrift für Volkswirtschaft und Statistik*, 84(5):433–456, 1948.

[269] E. Ordentlich. *Universal Investment and Universal Data Compression*. Ph.D. dissertation, Stanford University, Stanford, Calif., 1996.

[270] E. Ordentlich and T. M. Cover. On-line portfolio selection. In *COLT 96*, 1996. Journal version accepted for publication in *Mathematics of Operations Research* under the title *The cost of achieving the best portfolio in hindsight*.

[271] G. Owen. *Game Theory*. 2d ed. Academic Press, 1982.

[272] C. Papadimitriou and M. Yannakakis. Linear programming without the matrix. In *Proceedings of the 25th Annual ACM Symposium on Theory of Computing*, pp. 121–129, 1993.

[273] J. L. Peterson and A. Silberschatz. *Operating System Concepts*. Reading, Mass.: Addison-Wesley, 1985.

[274] S. Phillips and J. Westbrook. Online load balancing and network flow. In *Proceedings of the 25th Annual ACM Symposium on Theory of Computing*, pp. 402–411, 1993. To appear in *Algorithmica*.

[275] M. Piccione and A. Rubinstein. On the interpretation of decision problems with imperfect recall, August 1994. Working Paper No. 24-94, The Sackler Institute for Economic Studies, Tel Aviv University, Tel Aviv.

[276] S. Plotkin, D. Shmoys, and É. Tardos. Fast approximation algorithms for fractional packing and covering problems. In *Proceedings of the 32nd Annual IEEE Symposium on Foundations of Computer Science*, pp. 495–504, 1991.

[277] S. Ponzio. The combinatorics of computing the resistive inverse, January 1997. Manuscript submitted for publication.

[278] C. K. Poon. *On the Complexity of the st-Connectivity Problem*. Ph.D. dissertation, University of Toronto, Toronto, 1996.

[279] J. W. Pratt. Risk aversion in the small and in the large. *Econometrica*, 32:122–136, 1964.

[280] Y. Rabinovich. Personal communication, November 1996.

[281] P. Raghavan. Personal communication.

[282] P. Raghavan. Probabilistic construction of deterministic algorithms. *Journal of Computer and System Sciences*, 37:130–143, 1988.

[283] P. Raghavan. A statistical adversary for on-line algorithms. DIMACS *Series in Discrete Mathematics and Theoretical Computer Science*, 7:79–83, 1992.

[284] P. Raghavan and M. Snir. Memory versus randomization in on-line algorithms. In *Proceedings of the 16th ICALP*. Vol. 372 of Lecture Notes in Computer Science, pp. 687–703, 1989. (Revised version available as IBM Research Report RC15840, June 1990.)

[285] P. Raghavan and C. D. Thompson. Randomized rounding: A technique for provably good algorithms and algorithmic proofs. *Combinatorica*, 7:365–374, 1987.

[286] T. E. S. Raghavan. Zero-sum two-person games. In R. J. Aumann and S. Hart, editors, *Handbook of Game Theory*, vol. 2, chap. 20, pp. 735–759. Elsevier, 1994.

[287] P. Ramanan, D. Brown, C. Lee, and D. Lee. On-line bin packing in linear time. *Journal of Algorithms*, 10:305–326, 1989.

[288] F. P. Ramsey. Truth and probability (1931). In R. B. Braithwaite, editor, *The Foundations of Mathematics and Other Logical Essays*, 1964.

[289] N. Reingold and J. Westbrook. Randomized algorithms for the list update problem. Technical Report YALEU/DcS/TR-804, Yale University, New Haven, Conn., June 1990.

[290] N. Reingold and J. Westbrook. Optimum off-line algorithms for the list update and paging rules. Technical Report YALEU/DcS/TR-805, Yale University, New Haven, Conn., August 1990.

[291] N. Reingold, J. Westbrook, and D. Sleator. Randomized competitive algorithms for the list update problem. *Algorithmica*, 11:15–32, 1994.

[292] M. B. Richey. Improved bounds for harmonic-based bin packing algorithms. *Discrete Applied Mathematics*, 34:203–227, 1991.

[293] M. Ricklin, June 1994. Personal communication via Y. Rabani.

[294] R. Rivest. On self-organizing sequential search heuristics. *Communications of the ACM*, 19, 2:63–67, February 1976.

[295] S. M. Ross. *Applied Probability Models with Optimization Applications*. San Francisco: Holden-Day, 1970.

[296] A. D. Roy. Safety first and the holding of assets. *Econometrica*, 20:431–449, 1952.

[297] L. Rudolph. As described in a Hebrew University lecture, May 1986.

[298] M. Saks and X. Tetali. Personal communication with M. Saks, September 1994.

[299] P. A. Samuelson. The fundamental approximation theorem of portfolio analysis in terms of means, variances, and higher moments. *Review of Economic Studies*, 37, 1970.

[300] L. J. Savage. The theory of statistical decision. *Journal of the American Statistical Association*, 46:55–67, 1951.

[301] L. J. Savage. *The Foundations of Statistics*. New York: Wiley, 1954.

[302] D. Schmeidler. Integral representation without additivity. *Proceedings of the American Mathematical Society*, 97(2), 1986.

[303] D. Schmeidler. Subjective probability and expected utility without additivity. *Econometrica*, 57:571–587, 1989.

[304] F. Schulz and E. Schömer. Self-organizing data structures with dependent accesses. In *Proceedings of the 23rd International Colloquium on Automata, Languages, and Programming*, LNCS 1099, pp. 526–537, 1996.

[305] D. A. Seale and A. Rapoport. Decision making under strict uncertainty: An experimental test of competitive criteria. *Organizational Behavior and Human Decision Processes*, 64(1):65–75, 1995.

[306] S. S. Seiden. Unfair problems and randomized algorithms for metrical task systems, 1996. Unpublished manuscript.

[307] J. Sgall. On-line scheduling on parallel machines. Technical Report Technical Report CMU-CS-94-144, Carnegie-Mellon University, Pittsburgh, 1994. (Ph.D. dissertation.)

[308] J. Sgall. Online scheduling. In *Dagstuhl Proceedings*, 1996. To be published in Springer-Verlag LNCS Lecture Notes.

[309] G. L. S. Shackle. *Expectation in Economics*. 2d ed. Cambridge, 1952.

[310] F. Shahrokhi and D. Matula. The maximum concurrent flow problem. *Journal of the ACM*, 37:318–334, 1990.

[311] W. F. Sharpe. Mutual fund performance. *Journal of Business*, January 1966.

[312] G. S. Shedler and C. Tung. Locality in page reference strings. *SIAM Journal on Computing*, 1:218–241, 1972.

[313] J. E. Shemer and S. C. Gupta. On the design of Bayesian storage allocation algorithms for paging and segmentation. *IEEE Transactions on Computers*, C-18:644–651, 1969.

[314] A. G. Shilling. Market timing: Better than a buy-and-hold strategy. *Financial Analysts Journal*, pp. 46–50, March–April 1992.

[315] D. B. Shmoys, J. Wein, and D. P. Williamson. Scheduling parallel machines on-line. In *Proceedings of the 32nd Annual IEEE Symposium on Foundations of Computer Science*, 1991.

[316] H. W. Sinn. *Economic Decisions Under Uncertainty*. Amsterdam: North-Holland, 1983.

[317] R. L. Sites and A. Agarwal. Multiprocessor cache analysis using ATUM. In *Proceedings of the 15th IEEE International Symposium on Computer Architecture* (Honolulu), pp. 186–195, 1988.

[318] D. D. Sleator and R. E. Tarjan. Amortized efficiency of list update and paging rules. *Communications of the ACM*, 28(2):202–208, 1985.

[319] D. D. Sleator and R. E. Tarjan. Self-adjusting binary search trees. *Journal of the ACM*, 32: 652–686, 1985.

[320] D. R. Smart. *Fixed Point Theorems*. Cambridge University Press, 1974.

[321] J. R. Spirn. *Program Behavior: Models and Measurements*. New York: Elsevier, 1977.

[322] K. Stange. *Angewandte Statistik*. Vol. 1, *Eindimensionale Probleme*. Berlin, Heidelberg, New York: Springer-Verlag, 1970.

[323] M. K. Starr. *Product Design and Decision Theory*. Englewood Cliffs, N.J.: Prentice-Hall, 1962.

[324] M. K. Starr. A discussion of some normative criteria for decision-making under uncertainty. *Industrial Management Review*, 8:71–78, 1966.

[325] R. E. Tarjan. Amortized computational complexity. *SIAM Journal on Algebraic and Discrete Methods*, 6(2):306–318, April 1985.

[326] B. Teia. A lower bound for randomized list update algorithms. *Information Processing Letters*, 47:5–9, 1993.

[327] J. Tobin. Liquidity preference as behavior towards risk. *Review of Economic Studies*, 67, 1958.

[328] E. Torng. A unified analysis of paging and caching. *Algorithmica*, 20:175–200, 1998.

[329] G. Turpin. Recent work on the k-server problem. Master's thesis, Department of Computer Science, University of Toronto, September, 1989

[330] J. Ullman. The performance of a memory allocation algorithm. Technical Report 100, Department of Electrical Engineering, Princeton University, Princeton, N.J., 1971.

[331] A. van Vliet. On the asymptotic worst case behavior of harmonic fit. *Journal of Algorithms*, 20:113–136, 1996.

[332] J. von Neumann. Zur Theorie der Gesellschaftsspiele. *Mathematische Annalen*, 100:295–320, 1928.

[333] J. von Neumann and O. Morgenstern. *Theory of Games and Economic Behavior*. Princeton, N.J.: Princeton University Press, 1944.

[334] A. Wald. *Statistical Decision Functions*. New York: Wiley, 1950.

[335] I. Wegener. *The Complexity of Boolean Functions*. Stuttgart and New York: Wiley-Teubner, 1987.

[336] A. C. Williams. Attitudes towards speculative risks as an indicator of attitudes towards pure risks. *Journal of Risk and Indurance*, 33:577–586, 1966.

[337] J. H. Williamson. *Lebesgue Intergration*. New York: Holt, Rinehart and Winston, 1962.

[338] M. E. Yaari. *On the Role of "Dutch Books" in the Theory of Choice Under Risk*, 1985. 1985 Nancy L. Schwatz Memorial Lecture.

[339] M. E. Yaari. The dual theory of choice under risk. *Econometrica*, 55:95–115, 1987.

[340] A. C. Yao. Probabilistic computations: Towards a unified measure of complexity. In *Proceedings of the 18th Annual Symposium on Foundations of Computer Science*, 1977.

[341] A. C. Yao. New algorithms for bin packing. *Journal of the ACM*, 27:207–227, 1980.

[342] N. E Young. *Competitive Paging and Dual-Guided On-Line Weighted Caching and Matching Algorithms*. Ph.D. dissertation. Department of Computer Science, Princeton University, Princeton, N.J., October 1991.

[343] N. E. Young. On-line caching as cache size varies. In *Proceedings of the 2nd ACM-SIAM Symposium on Discrete Algorithms*, pp. 241–250, 1991.

[344] N. E. Young. The k-server dual and loose competitiveness for paging. *Algorithmica*, 11(6): 525–541, 1994.

[345] N. E. Young. Bounding the diffuse adversary. In *Proceeding of the 9th Annual ACM-SIAM Symposium on Discrete Algorithms*, pp. 420–425, January 1998.

[346] N. E. Young. On-line file caching. In *Proceeding of the 9th Annual ACM-SIAM Symposium on Discrete Algorithms*, pp. 82–86, January 1998.

Index

Bold page entries designate pages on which the term is defined.